Petrarch and Boccaccio

Mimesis

―
Romanische Literaturen der Welt

Herausgegeben von
Ottmar Ette

Band 61

Petrarch and Boccaccio

The Unity of Knowledge in the Pre-modern World

Edited by
Igor Candido

DE GRUYTER

An electronic version of this book is freely available, thanks to the support of libraries working with Knowledge Unlatched. KU is a collaborative initiative designed to make high quality books Open Access. More information about the initiative and links to the Open Access version can be found at www.knowledgeunlatched.org. The Open Access book is available at www.degruyter.com.

ISBN 978-3-11-068491-9
e-ISBN (PDF) 978-3-11-041930-6
e-ISBN (EPUB) 978-3-11-041958-0
ISSN 0178-7489

This work is licensed under the Creative Commons Attribution NonCommercial-NoDerivatives 4.0 license. For more information, see http://creativecommons.org/licenses/by-nc-nd/4.0/.

Library of Congress Cataloging-in-Publication Data
A CIP catalog record for this book has been applied for at the Library of Congress.

Bibliographic information published by the Deutsche Nationalbibliothek
The Deutsche Nationalbibliothek lists this publication in the Deutsche Nationalbibliografie; detailed bibliographic data are available on the Internet at http://dnb.dnb.de.

© 2019 Igor Candido, published by Walter de Gruyter GmbH, Berlin/Boston
This volume is text- and page-identical with the hardback published in 2018.
Typesetting: Konvertus, Haarlem
Printing and binding: CPI books GmbH, Leck
♾ Printed on acid-free paper
Printed in Germany

www.degruyter.com

Dedicated to Ronald Witt (1932–2017)

Contents

Acknowledgments —— IX

Igor Candido
Introduction —— 1

H. Wayne Storey
The Formation of Knowledge and Petrarch's Books —— 15

Karl Enenkel
Sacra solitudo. Petrarch's authorship and the *locus sacer* —— 52

Ronald Witt
Petrarch, Creator of the Christian Humanist —— 65

Christopher Celenza
Petrarch and the History of Philosophy —— 78

Joachim Küpper
The Secret Life of Classical and Arabic Medical Texts in Petrarch's *Canzoniere* —— 91

Manuele Gragnolati and Francesca Southerden
From Paradox to Exclusivity: Dante and Petrarch's Lyrical Eschatologies —— 129

Igor Candido
Dante, Petrarch, and Boccaccio on Religious Conversion —— 153

Gerhard Regn
The *Incipit* of the *Decameron*: Textual Margins as an Index of Epochal Change —— 176

Andreas Kablitz
The *Proemio* of the *Decameron*. Boccaccio's Hidden Dialogue with Scholasticism —— 194

Francesco Ciabattoni
Boccaccio's Novel Hecuba: Beritola between Ovid and Dante —— 209

Marco Petoletti
Boccaccio, the Classics and the Latin Middle Ages —— 226

Paolo Cherchi
The Inventors of Things in Boccaccio's *De genealogia deorum gentilium* —— 244

Giuseppe Mazzotta
Boccaccio's Critique of Petrarch —— 270

Giorgio Ficara
The Perfect Woman in Boccaccio and Petrarch —— 286

Renzo Bragantini
Petrarch, Boccaccio, and the Space of Vernacular Literature —— 313

Giulio Ferroni
Between Petrarch and Boccaccio: Strategies of the End —— 340

Contributors —— 367

Index of Manuscripts —— 373

Index Nominum —— 375

Acknowledgments

The idea of this volume was born from my research at the Freie Universität Berlin as a fellow of the Alexander von Humboldt Foundation, and took further shape in the form of a conference held at the Freie in June of 2014, entitled *The Unity of Knowledge in the Pre-modern World: Petrarch and Boccaccio between the Middle Ages and the Early Renaissance*. From this first fruitful meeting with the scholars convened in Berlin, the project developed much more fully, giving life to a contribution to the studies of Petrarch and Boccaccio which, with due regard to its diverse critical voices, can be considered organic.

Here I would like to thank: the Alexander von Humboldt Foundation for the generous financial support provided for the conference; the Dahlem Humanities Center, in the person of Joachim Küpper, the Italienzentrum der FUB, in the persons of Bernhard Huss and Sabine Greiner, for financial and intellectual support; the Italian ambassador to Berlin, H. E. Elio Menzione, who honored us with his hospitality at the embassy and with his presence at the opening of the conference; Eef Overgaauw, Director of the manuscripts division of the Staatsbibliothek zu Berlin, and Giuliano Staccioli for organizing the splendid exhibition of Petrarchan and Boccaccian manuscripts in the Berlin library.

I am grateful to Bridget Pupillo, a friend and colleague from the years of my doctorate at Johns Hopkins University in Baltimore, who translated several of the contributions into English and provided many attentive editorial suggestions.

A heartfelt thank you goes to the publisher Walter De Gruyter in the person of Ulrike Krauss, Christine Henschel and Gabrielle Cornefert, for having faith in this publication and for having seen it through all of its many stages with great professionalism and patience; thanks as well to Ottmar Ette for having welcomed it into the series *Mimesis*.

This volume is dedicated to the memory of a great humanist, Ronald Witt, who delivered his final public presentation in Berlin and who left us last March. After our meeting on the occasion of the Berlin conference, he was a great source of inspiration for me, both in my studies and in life itself. I like to recall his emotion at seeing, one last time, the autograph of Petrarch's *De ignorantia* preserved at the Staatsbibliothek. It was his own way of saying farewell to that old friend.

Igor Candido
Introduction

The second volume of Ernst Cassirer's *Das Erkenntnisproblem in der Philosophie und Wissenschaft der neuren Zeit* (1922) opens with an analysis of the Cartesian problem of the unity of knowledge. For the French philosopher, all the sciences together constitute a single system of human knowledge which does not change, however diverse might be the specific subjects to which it is applied. The argument completely transforms the relationship between the unity and multiplicity of knowledge. This change occurs primarily with respect to natural philosophy, in relation to which Descartes affirms that it would be folly to speculate on the mysteries of nature and on the influence of the celestial spheres over the terrestrial world, on the virtues of the plants, on the movement of the stars and the transformation of metals, without ever having reflected deeply on the correct use of the mind and on the universal concept of knowledge itself: indeed, all other matters are to be considered not in and of themselves, but for that express purpose (*Regulae* I and VIII).[1] In very similar terms, approximately three hundred years prior, Petrarch directed his satire against four Averroist doctors and their natural philosophy in the *De ipsius et multorum ignorantia*: "What use is it, I ask, to know the nature of beasts and birds and fish and snakes, and to ignore or neglect our human nature, the purpose of our birth, or whence we come whither we are bound?"[2] The conceptual affinity is surprising, just as it is fascinating to imagine Descartes as reader not only of Cicero and Augustine but also of the famous Petrarchan invective. In any case, the possible connection certainly did not escape Cassirer, editor along with Paul O. Kristeller and John H. Randall, Jr. of the famous volume *The Renaissance Philosophy of Man* (1948), in which he records the *De ignorantia* among the fundamental philosophical texts of the new era.[3]

But even more important than the individual passage in itself is the fact of its insertion into a cohesive corpus of texts which reveal the striking modernity of Petrarch's thought. According to a great historian of Humanism, Hans Baron, Petrarch was a sort of Moses figure straddling the Middle Ages and the

---

1 See Ernst Cassirer: *Das Erkenntnisproblem in der Philosophie und Wissenschaft der neuren Zeit*. Berlin: Verlag Bruno Cassirer 1922³. Erster Band: p. 442–443.
2 Francesco Petrarca: *Invectives*. Edited and Translated by David Marsh. Cambridge, Mass.: Harvard University Press 2003 (The I Tatti Renaissance Library, 11), p. 239.
3 Francesco Petrarca: *On His Own Ignorance and That of Many Others*. In: Ernst Cassirer/ Paul O. Kristeller et al.: *The Renaissance Philosophy of Man*. Chicago and London: The University of Chicago Press 1956, p. 47–133.

Renaissance, able to catch sight of the new Promised Land but unable to set foot in it.[4] Baron's greatest student, Ronald Witt, among the contributors to this volume, instead viewed Petrarch as a third-generation humanist, active after the first pioneering wave of Paduan Humanism which included Lovato dei Lovati and Albertino Mussato, a humanist whose historical role was that of steering the movement toward Christianity from its secular origins through an ideal synthesis of pagan Classicism and new Christian culture.[5] A historical role defined also by spiritual exigencies – whether real or hypothetical matters little – beginning from the refusal to take part in a cultural world with which Petrarch did not wish to identify himself, as testified in the famous letter *Posteritati*, leading to his own internal crisis and his attempt to give unity and coherence to the sparse fragments of the soul, as suggested by the title of the *Canzoniere* itself, *Rerum vulgarium fragmenta,* and the conclusion of the *Secretum*, which represents the most refined analysis and the most carefully conceived theorization of the crisis transcribed within the poetic collection.

The same argument must be made today for Giovanni Boccaccio, though an important and primarily Italian critical tradition has viewed Boccaccio almost exclusively as a medieval author. Even Erasmus, however – as Ugo Foscolo (*Epoche* IV) reminds us – praised the Latin of the Certaldese as less barbarous, in his mind, than that of Petrarch himself. And if Petrarch – continues Foscolo – earned the gratitude of all Europe as the first restorer of classical literature, to Boccaccio is due at least half of this same praise.[6] With Boccaccio, for the first time in the neo-Latin world, the two great cultures of classical antiquity are experienced and relived in their ideal unity (Vittore Branca).[7] They reveal his interest for mythography and mythopoesis and the resulting fecund intuition for a recuperation of Greek culture, which is at the basis of the successive Ficinian and Florentince Renaissance in the broadest sense. But the proud declaration of pioneering recovery, according to the *Genealogia deorum gentilium* (XIV, 7), is in reality the culmination of a cultural process begun in the first years of Boccaccio's education in Naples and which would shape fundamental milestones in his vernacular writing such as the *Filocolo*, the *Filostrato* and the *Teseida*, the *Fiammetta* and the *Decameron*. Of these, the *Decameron* not only embraces wholeheartedly

---

[4] See Hans Baron: *Moot Problems of Renaissance Interpretation: An Answer to Wallace K. Ferguson.* In: *Journal of the History of Ideas* 19 (1958), p. 26–34.
[5] See Ronald Witt: *"In the Footsteps of the Ancients": The Origins of Humanism from Lovato to Bruni.* Leiden: Brill 2000 (Studies in Medieval and Reformation Thought, 74), p. 230–291.
[6] See Ugo Foscolo: *Saggi di letteratura italiana. Parte prima: Epoche della lingua italiana.* Edited by Cesare Foligno. Florence: Le Monnier 1958, p. 184.
[7] See Vittore Branca: *Giovanni Boccaccio. Profilo biografico.* Florence: Sansoni 1977, p. 117.

the classical world but uses it to provide a new representation of reality, able to offer a vision of a world complex in its multiplicity but reduced to unity by the very project of collecting all of reality and recreating it in narrative form within a volume inspired by the Book of the Universe.

If the historical periodizations and readings are different, if diverse are the theoretical, critical or philological approaches that aided the study of Petrarch's and Boccaccio's literary production and culture, central, nonetheless, remains the yet unanswered question of which cultural role the two great *trecentisti* held between the great encyclopedic model of Dante and the idea, already modern, of a new synthesis inside the many-faceted culture within the era of Renaissance humanism. Pioneers in this field of study are Giuseppe Billanovich and Giuseppe Velli, whose respective works have become the benchmark.[8] To the groundbreaking works by these founding fathers we may now add the series *Arezzo e Certaldo* published by Antenore, which dedicates monographic volumes of a comparative bent to the two authors and which describes from diverse hermeneutic perspectives their historical and intellectual relationship: the *grande nodo* (Velli); that is, the most fortunate meeting in all of the Italian literary tradition (Branca).[9] At any rate, the manner by which Petrarch and Boccaccio devised a new point of access to the unity of classical and medieval knowledge by creating an intellectual paradigm markedly different from that of Dante and leading toward a sort of modern consciousness, that which is in many ways already our consciousness, was still to be considered in both its broadest strokes and its most specific nuances, according to interdependent relationships, whether they be historical, philosophical or philological, hermeneutical, critical, or in light of the material culture of the time.

Still unexplored is a theme that flows as an undercurrent beneath many pages of this volume – that of Petrarch's and Boccaccio's influence on the European conscience. What contributions have Petrarch and Boccaccio provided to the formation of the European identity? It scarcely need be remembered that the years in which Petrarch and Boccaccio were active saw the Italian language and its literature become dominant in the European panorama, affirming themselves as direct descendents of the Latin tradition in the context of Romance literatures. So it would remain at least until the end of the sixteenth century, thanks to the cultural identity which was formed above all upon the models offered by Dante,

---

8 See in particular Giuseppe Billanovich: *Petrarca Letterato. I: Lo scrittoio del Petrarca*. Rome: Edizioni di Storia e letteratura 1995² (Storia e letteratura, 16); Giuseppe Velli: *Petrarca e Boccaccio: Tradizione-memoria-scrittura*. Padua: Antenore 1995² (Studi sul Petrarca, 7).
9 See Vittore Branca: *Boccaccio medievale e nuovi studi sul "Decameron"*. Florence: Sansoni 1996, p. 165.

Petrarch and Boccaccio, through the cultural filter of humanism and then of the High Renaissance. This identity of Italian literary civilization has a vocation that is all the more strongly European even while more weakly national (Carlo Ossola).[10] In this way we can better understand Jacob Burckhardt's claim that the Italian humanists, in rediscovering classical antiquity, laid the groundwork for the creation of the modern individual and were therefore to be considered "the first born among the sons of modern Europe."[11] And if the Italian humanists were truly such, then coming just before them, the founding fathers of the modern European spirit who turned their gaze toward antiquity with a perspective not only assimilative, as in the case of Dante, but historical and philological, were precisely Petrarch and Boccaccio. Their intellectual production thus came to constitute the most solid knot in the premodern world to tie the Greco-Roman spirit to the Christian in a new and fertile synthesis, so as to spread their own influence rapidly throughout the various European nations, explored, above all by Petrarch, in the search for manuscripts, texts and witnesses containing traces of their beloved classical *auctores*.

What are the characteristics of this synthesis? It is a question stemming from the history of ideas which has fascinated me for years and which acted as the inspiration for this volume. It became immediately apparent that an undertaking such as this would be far too onerous for the intellectual powers of a single author, and it discouraged the notion of launching an organic research effort on the influence of these authors through the study of the reception of their works. I was persuaded that what was required, instead, was to confront the critical problem according to a perspective that is synchronic and unified in itself, capable of being proven through the attempt to grasp the truly revolutionary aspects of the culture of these two great *trecentisti*, along with – and perhaps even more so – their own heightened awareness of the elements of absolute novelty and clear rupture with respect to their own recent past. In order to attempt a more profound comprehension of this intricate knot of cultural history which inextricably links the Middle Ages with the Renaissance, it was therefore necessary to create a dialogue between experts from diverse and complementary disciplinary fields, who could observe the historical and literary facts independently from the forced relationships existing within a pre-established canon.

---

10 See Carlo Ossola: *Europa, Europa...* In: Carlo Ossola (ed.): *Europa, miti d'identità*. Venice: Marsilio 2001 (Presente storico, 12), p. XI.
11 Jacob Burckhardt: *Die Kultur der Renaissance in Italien: Ein Versuch*. Edited by Horst Günther. Frankfurt am Main: Deutscher Klassiker Verlag 1989; English translation: *The Civilization of the Renaissance in Italy*. Translated by Samuel C. G. Middlemore with an Introduction by Peter Burke London: Penguin 1960, p. 98.

The arrangement of the essays collected in the volume attempts, as far as possible, to follow the intellectual and artistic development of the two authors through a reflection on the works in their chronological order and following that particular rhythm which, from the beginning in both cases, alternates seamlessly between the production in Latin and in the vernacular. In Petrarch the former precedes the latter, while in Boccaccio the opposite occurs. The distinction between these two moments is nevertheless one of convenience and does not reflect, as the close ties between the works of one author and the other show, a true subdivision into different phases of activity: that of the humanist intellectual on the one hand and the poet or narrator on the other.

The opening essay (Chapter 1) introduces us to Petrarch's writing desk and library. H. Wayne Storey investigates the macro- and micro-contexts of the relationships among the forms in which knowledge is developed in books that Petrarch owned and that he produced. "For Petrarch not only was the design of the book a reflection of the edition's intellectual structure, it was also an integral part of its systems of meaning, from the clarity of its script to the unified organization of its knowledge in the text and its apparatus and glosses." (p. 17) From this broader perspective, the study analyses Petrarch's most important manuscripts (such as his own 'Virgilio Ambrosiano' [today: Milano Biblioteca Ambrosiana MS A 79 inf. Sala Prefetto 10/27], the rhetorical miscellany Cologny Bodmer 146, the *opera omnia* of Horace contained and glossed in Laurenziano 34.1, and the partial holograph of Petrarch's own *Rerum vulgarium fragmenta* in Vaticano Latino 3195), considering the multiple layers of textuality and manuscript production that define and connect intellectual and rhetorical-poetic traditions. In this sophisticated *accessus ad auctorem*, Storey elucidates the new principles that guided Petrarch in the search for, the arrangement, study and annotation of his favourite books and in the establishment of his own library, guiding principles that are useful to keep in mind while reading successive essays and that, in general, help to orient us within the interpretation of the Petrarchan text.

Three essays follow which consider Petrarch's Latin production and the influence that it had respectively on his contemporaries, on the evolution of the humanist movement, and on the history of premodern philosophy. Karl Enenkel's paper (Chapter 2) deals with Petrarch's constructions of the place of writing as a *locus sacer*, especially in the *De vita solitaria*, while providing an analysis of the different features of the sacred place, their symbolical meaning, and the literary traditions on which Petrarch drew. The paper explains the ways in which the construction of the *locus sacer* is connected with the special style of authorship Petrarch had in mind and wished to present to his contemporaries. Place is the only element truly able to legitimate Petrarch's authority by guaranteeing, through his readers, the novelty of the invention and the capacity, on the part of the writer, to realize his highest creative potential. The choice of a solitary life is therefore explained as a distance, both physical and metaphorical, from the common public, beginning from the moment that Petrarch, like Horace before him, addresses himself to a few carefully selected readers able to appreciate his writing and his lifestyle, which go hand in hand. With this work Petrarch inaugurates a new kind of writer, not tethered to a physical location, and especially not to the *studiolo*, as prescribed by tradition, but free to meditate in communion with nature from which he or she receives inspiration.

The *De vita solitaria* is revealing of one of Petrarch's great achievements according to Ronald Witt (Chapter 3): the Christianization of the humanist movement, which for two generations had thrived in a secular, communal context. Not only did he endeavour to synthesize the study of pagan letters with Christian writings, but using his own life to dramatize his ideas, he envisaged the Christian scholar as celibate and pursuing scholarship in solitude either by himself or together with a small group of like-minded men. The *De ignorantia* is the work in which Petrarch discusses, with the greatest breadth and depth, the problem of the relationship between pagan and Christian education, arguing in favor of Christian love over pagan knowledge. In its Christianized form, Petrarch's version of humanism had an international appeal in the fourteenth century.

Christopher Celenza's paper (Chapter 4) explores Petrarch's conception of and place within the history of philosophy by focusing on notions that have traditionally stood outside the canonical history of philosophy but that fit Petrarch's case well. These include: philosophy as self-scrutiny; philosophy as the creation of a persona; philosophy and exemplarity; and philosophy as dialogue. These notions form Petrarch's idea of philosophy and lie at the center of his polemic treatise *De ignorantia*. By providing a reading of the invective which sets the work in its (ancient and Christian) philosophical context, Celenza shows how Petrarch sets the tone for much of the humanist world to come, when Aristotle is under discussion.

Concluding the first part of the volume are two studies dedicated to Petrarchan vernacular poetry which examine its relation with antecedents of the Dantean model. The objective of Joachim Küpper's contribution (Chapter 5) is to rethink in part the classic assumption of criticism who wishes to find at the heart of the *Rerum vulgarium fragmenta* a Christianized version of platonic love mediated by the poetic experience of the *Vita nova*. If the figure of the *donna* as angel changes in Petrarch, and her beatific function is reduced, still quite present is the process of spiritualizing the woman and the hypothesis of a final conversion of love from the terrestrial realm to the heavens, as the *canzone alla Vergine* at the conclusion of the work makes clear. But in order to understand the true innovation with respect to the model, which was first initiated by Dante, the scholar proposes "to consider the love concept inherent in the *Canzoniere* as being modeled, at least to a certain extent, after the theory of love developed within the medical discourse of that age, which became known under the name of *hereos*. Its origins are in part Aristotelian, Galenic and Arabic, and the common denominator of these conceptual sources is what I would schematically term an 'anthropological materialism.'"

By focusing on the concept of the resurrection of the body and on the relationship between corporeality and language, Manuele Gragnolati and Francesca Southerden (Chapter 6) explore differences within the eschatological imagination in Dante's *Paradiso* and Petrarch's *Triumphus Eternitatis*, as well as their different modes of textuality and the linguistic concepts informing them. Their paper, in particular, shows a shift from Dante's paradoxical way of maintaining the incompatibility of the divine and the lyric while combining them, to Petrarch's uniquely lyrical eschatology, where the Christian doctrine is adapted to an erotic fantasy that ends up replacing it. "The collective experience of heaven consequently has no place except to validate the supremacy of Laura's image in relation to Petrarch's gaze and to the resurrected landscape of his heart, whose affective current is carried by memory into the furthest reaches of Petrarch's eschatological imagination [...]." (p. 147) This is the very change of relationship which Petrarch establishes with poetic language, and the analysis proposed here is taken up once again in the conclusion of the volume, which tackles the central question of what is the ideological space of vernacular literature in the production of Petrarch and Boccaccio.

My own essay (Chapter 7) serves as a hinge between the two preceding chapters and the two following, and within the volume it acts as a transition between the first part, dedicated primarily to Petrarch, and the second to Boccaccio. In keeping with the two preceding papers, my contribution focuses on Petrarch's and Boccaccio's contrastive readings of Dante's *Comedy*, exploring a consistent set of theological and aesthetic concepts, among which Dante's ideation and representation of Christian conversion. Close attention is paid in particular to the conclusions of Petrarch's *Secretum* and Boccaccio's tale of Ser Cepparello (*Dec.* I, 1), two texts that bear witness to a radical intellectual progression towards the new era of Italian Renaissance humanism. The theme of Francesco's conversion is read in light of the conclusion of the *Canzoniere*, of the affirmations of the *Secretum*, and of the final verses of the *Triumphi*, loci within the Petrarchan macrotext that stand not in contradiction with one another, but instead describe a carefully crafted countersong with respect to the typology of medieval conversion and, more specifically, to the Dantean paradigm of the poem's journey read as a poetics of conversion (John Freccero).[12] In close continuity with the two successive

---

[12] See John Freccero: *Dante: The Poetics of Conversion*. Edited by Rachel Jacoff. Cambridge, Mass.: Harvard University Press 1986.

chapters, the reading of the first Decameronian novella as the suspension of judgment concerning the ultimate truths and theological metaphysics in general is completed with those of Gerhard Regn and Andreas Kablitz.

According to Regn (Chapter 8), the incipit of the *Decameron* is, contrary to medieval practices of textual variance, authorized by the author himself and transmits the elementary message of Boccaccio's book of *novelle*: the paratextual formula points to the work's dimension as a parody of the book of Genesis; it announces its counterfactual relationship to the *Comedy*, especially by abrogating Dante's alliance of numerical order and metaphysical significance for the benefit of a contingency compensated by the sophistication of its storytelling. This implies a reassessment of courtly erotic literature; that is, differently from Dante's work, it is free of ethical blemish. The aesthetics of late medieval aristocratic culture is an instrument of self-empowerment for a tentatively postmedieval world, in which merchants and peers walk side by side: Galeotto, who symbolizes literature, is no longer a dubious pimp as he was in Dante, but acts once again as a noble benefactor for the distressed – this is why Boccaccio restores his old title, which Dante had stripped from him: "il libro chiamato *Decameron* cognominato prencipe Galeotto." [the book called Decameron, otherwise Prince Galeotto]

Kablitz, as well (Chapter 9), focuses primarily on the *Proemio* which, far from being a purely scholarly rhetorical exercise, establishes the very foundation of the *Decameron*'s intellectual profile, and in particular inaugurates its dialogue with scholastic philosophy. The importance of this philosophical framework cannot be underestimated as the *Decameron*'s modernity – the author argues – resides within this framework more than in its narrative structures, so that such conceptual conclusions drawn from scholastic anthropology constitute a real turning point in the development of Western thought. To my knowledge, this is the first interpretation of Boccaccio's narrative masterpiece through the lens of medieval scholasticism set in the context of its historical continuity into the premodern cultural world. The surprisingly strict relationship between literature and philosophy is beautifully expressed in the paper's conclusion: "If the poetics of the *Decameron* defines literature as a substitute for rational control of life-threatening emotions, it describes it as well as a means of satisfaction of sensual desires. The secret dialogue of the *Decameron* with scholastic philosophy and theology does not only reveal the highly explosive implications of Thomas Aquinas' reinterpretation of traditional Christian dogma, it also brings about a concept of literature which responds to this redefinition of human nature." (p. 207)

At the center of the following section is the study of the sources and principal Latin works through which Petrarch and Boccaccio interweave their own (pre)humanistic dialogue with beloved classical authors. In his essay Francesco

Ciabattoni (Chapter 10) analyzes how Boccaccio's intertextual sources for *Decameron* II, 5 and II, 6 – namely Apuleius, Dante and Ovid – create and displace, within the reader, expectations about the tragic ending of the tales. Moving from Giuseppe Velli's notion of literary memory, he then incorporates the results of recent philological research to assess the role of literary models in Boccaccio's compositional strategy; a strategy on which the paper sheds new light by refining our understanding of the writer's complex rhetorical use of parody: "Boccaccio's narrative strategy evokes literary classics in the readers' memory, only to take sudden, displacing turns and avert the expected conclusion. Just as importantly, the responsiveness and interplay among the youths of the *brigata* constitute what Picone calls *mondo commentato* and provide a first layer of hermeneutical and intratextual considerations, while at the same time livening the brigata's overarching tale and making the reading more pleasurable." (p. 223)

After having described the divergent behaviours of Petrarch and Boccaccio in regards to authors of the Latin tradition, the former being more selective while the latter more inclusive, the contribution of Marco Petoletti (Chapter 11) presents the fundamental role Boccaccio played in the transmission of certain texts from classical antiquity and the Latin Middle Ages, with particular attention to the manuscripts within his own library. It takes into consideration, more specifically, the two autograph *zibaldoni*, the one being membranaceous (Florence, Biblioteca Laurenziana, Plut. 29.8 + 33.31) and the other chartaceous (Florence, Biblioteca Nazionale Centrale, Banco rari 50), where Boccaccio, over a period of years, copied numerous works whose fortune was often quite limited (one thinks, for instance, of the case of the *Priapea* and other medieval Latin texts, of which the Boccaccian *zibaldoni* are strategic witnesses). The attentive exploration of the texts which Boccaccio copied, studied and utilized is then further enriched by a successful deciphering of the inscription accompanying the portrait of Homer in the Toledan Dante (Archivo y Biblioteca Capitulares, Zelada 104 6), an inscription that until now has remained illegible. Within the inscription Greek and Latin coexist in a strategic synthesis, as in the famous passage from the *Genealogia* (XIV, 7), in which Boccaccio claims for himself the reconstituted linguistic and cultural unity of Greco-Roman antiquity. For the early chronology of the first text contained in the two *zibaldoni* and no less so for methodological reasons (indeed, those same reasons noted with regards to the contribution by Storey), this study should in fact open the volume's section dedicated to Boccaccio. We preferred, instead, to place it in an intermediary position between the papers on the *Decameron* and those on the later Latin works in order to clarify the problem of the classical and medieval sources within the former, and to open the discussion on the latter. This decision enables us to demonstrate the continuity of the author's inspiration and the artificiality of a distinction between the culture of Boccaccio as narrator in the vernacular and of Boccaccio as erudite scholar who writes in Latin. Likewise, giving priority to the narrative art as a sign of Boccaccio's modernity does not equate to undervaluing the presence in the *Decameron* of classical authors and of the texts copied in the two *zibaldoni*, which are concealed but nevertheless present therein, while they will be plain to see in the erudite Latin works, and above all in the *Genealogia*.

In the first of the two contributions dedicated to the mythographical treatise, Paolo Cherchi (Chapter 12) offers us a new definition of the work and a new reading perspective that takes into account the complexity of a literary and doctrinal design that was wholly ambitious and has never been attempted since. "In order to characterize the *Genealogie* we might define it as a study, indeed a true epos of the art of interpretation, of the exegetical and hermeneutical labours and travails of many generations through the myths, an attempt to understand whether they are pure fantasy, how and when they were formed, what truths they hide, which language they use, and how they are related to history." (p. 248) Alternating with general discussion is the precise vantage point from which Cherchi regards the work and the multifaceted meanings of its myths: the study of the heurematic literary tradition to which Boccaccio, after many centuries of silence, provides a new and original stimulus. These inventors, for Boccaccio, offer a confirmation of the "veracity" of "mythological language": in effect, the inventors die but their creative inventions remain as testimony to their existence. He studies the ideas that have contributed to the progress of human civilization, and inserts their "inventors" into the context of a "genealogy," which renders them "historical". Boccaccio's method was at the source of Renaissance heurematic literature and was vital until the new mode of understanding inventions was profoundly modified by Bacon.

Giuseppe Mazzotta (Chapter 13) studies the intellectual rapport that Boccaccio interweaves with Petrarch during the years that follow their first meeting in 1350: from their initial mutual admiration and Boccaccio's adherence to the Petrarchan cultural project, their relationship is then characterized by a large degree of caution (see also Bragantini's essay) and tends toward a distancing on the part of the younger friend, above all in his writing of the *Genealogia*. For this reason, the paper is largely concerned with this particular text, conceived as a massive encyclopedia of the origins and history of ancient myths. The author carries out this task from two interrelated perspectives. The first is political, namely the political motives of the king in patronizing the work as a strategy of self-legitimation. The second is specifically cultural: with this work Boccaccio articulates his sense of the dangers and difficulties hovering over a modern project that would seek to achieve a unity of knowledge. The second purpose is not Boccaccio's way of indulging in some abstract, merely rhetorical or humanistic exercise. Quite to the contrary: Mazzotta argues that the *Genealogia*, which features Petrarch as Boccaccio's privileged interlocutor, is meant by Boccaccio as a way of targeting and creating a critical distance from Petrarch's own powerful intellectual project of re-thinking culture for his times and for modernity.

Mazzotta's contribution ushers in the conclusory section of the volume, which extends its comparative gaze to the long-standing fidelity of the two authors to the vernacular language. The final three studies ideologically circumscribe that which Renzo Bragantini defines, with an appropriated formula, as "the space of vernacular literature," of which he proposes an analytical reading beginning with the *Canzoniere* and the *Decameron*, both of which would occupy the two authors up to the final days of their lives. Through a close reading of the epistolary exchanges between Petrarch and Boccaccio, spanning from 1350 to June 1374, just a month before Petrarch's death, Bragantini's paper (Chapter 15) aims to discuss and reconsider recent views of the intellectual relationships between the two great protagonists of the third quarter of the fourteenth century. Challenging the view that presents Boccaccio as totally subjugated to Petrarch, the paper reveals their intellectual relationship to be far more complex and intricate. Whilst Boccaccio undoubtedly perceived the aura of intellectual appeal which Petrarch emanated, he nevertheless preserved his own high intellectual profile, which can be attributed only partially to Petrarch's influence. Even if Boccaccio's attempt to reconcile Petrarch's lesson with that of Dante turned out to be only a partial success, he nevertheless contributed to the foundation of the myth of the Trecento's "three crowns." Last but not least, if Boccaccio agreed with Petrarch's substantial scepticism concerning coeval readership, he faced this problem not only from a different perspective, but also from a divergent position regarding the philosophy of love.

This philosophy is at the heart of Giorgio Ficara's contribution (Chapter 15), which offers us what is, in my opinion, the most subtle analysis of the psychology of love as it is represented by Boccaccio and Petrarch. One will note here the inversion of the typical order of names, thus alluding to a departure from the commonplace view of the *magister-discipulus* relationship; instead the essay maintains the notion, already introduced by Branca and with new arguments by Bragantini, of a circulation of ideas rather than the unidirectional flow of Petrarchan influence.[13] From the rupture of the silence that consecrated the Provençal *dame* emerges the impetus of the woman to speak: the *donna* who is transformed into lover and who expresses the full legitimacy of her desire is the first symptom of the prevalence of natural reality over antiquated abstraction and

---

[13] See Branca: *Boccaccio medievale*, p. 300–332.

leads to some of the most revolutionary pages of the *Decameron*. In this direction, the hypertrophic interior monologue of the first female narrator of Italian literature, the elegiac Fiammetta, is an emblematic culmination not only of Boccaccio's narrative research, but of the prehistory of the novelistic genre as such. A Fiammetta who is closer to Francesco *agens* of the *Canzoniere* than to Laura herself (indeed, the two depictions are often confused), a feminine figure so evanescent as to appear as a sort of return to the typology of the Provençal *donna*. However, the author separates Laura from this characterization almost programmatically by the faithfulness of her presence in the mind of the beloved, as told in the *Canzoniere* which is the history or intimate diary of a passion that never dies.

With Petrarch and Boccaccio we cannot overlook, finally, the dialectic meeting of History and microhistory. The tragic date of 1348 is inscribed within the *Canzoniere* and the *Decameron* in a very different, even oppositional way. Moving from this observation, Giulio Ferroni's paper (Chapter 16) follows the forms and structures that Petrarch and Boccaccio used to probe the meaning of an ending through a problematic interlacing between the conclusion of writing and the anxiety brought about by the conclusion of life. In Petrarch this link appears quite differently in the writing of the *Familiares* and in that of the *Canzoniere*, from the moment that the poetic account, whose true title given by the author as *Rerum vulgarium fragmenta*, alluding to its incompleteness, declares that writing cannot possibly terminate prior to the conclusion of life. But it is precisely this incompleteness within the soul, with the subsequent contradiction of its oscillating states, that constitutes the greatness of Petrarch's poetry, thus presenting an alternative and certainly more modern response to that quintessentially theological offering from Dante. Yet another alternative to Petrarch, and once again different with respect to the Dantean model, is the way in which the fateful date of 1348 is inscribed on the soil of the Decameronian world; that is, as a sign of the deadly Plague now brought to life in a literary work and in the author's larger project to bring order back to the world. As such, the project presupposes that the representation of the multiplicity of reality is reduced to unity in the form of the Book of the Universe. The same can be said for the self-proclaimed fragmentariness of Petrarch's writing of the *Canzoniere*, which the author attempts to remedy through the process of selecting and organizing the poems therein.

Both of the respective solutions offered by Petrarch and Boccaccio to the dialectic between multiplicity and unity of knowledge in their two vernacular masterworks allude to the creation of a Book of the World for the new era, a literary undertaking that will never abandon them. For this reason, their solutions can be viewed as trail markers for a philosophical journey that will begin its ripening with Humanism, to be formulated most fully by Descartes.

Igor Candido
Arts Building, Trinity College Dublin,
July, 2017

Bibliography

Primary Literature

Petrarca, Francesco: *On His Own Ignorance and That of Many Others*. In: Ernst Cassirer/ Paul O. Kristeller et al.: *The Renaissance Philosophy of Man*. Chicago and London: The University of Chicago Press 1956, p. 47–133.

Petrarca, Francesco: *Invectives*. Edited and Translated by David Marsh. Cambridge, Mass.: Harvard University Press 2003 (The I Tatti Renaissance Library, 11).

Secondary Literature

Monographs and Anthologies

Billanovich, Giuseppe: *Petrarca Letterato. I: Lo scrittoio del Petrarca*. Rome: Edizioni di Storia e letteratura 1995² (Storia e letteratura, 16).

Branca, Vittore: *Branca: Giovanni Boccaccio. Profilo biografico*. Florence: Sansoni 1977.

Branca, Vittore: *Boccaccio medievale e nuovi studi sul "Decameron"*. Florence: Sansoni 1996.

Burckhardt, Jacob: *Die Kultur der Renaissance in Italien: Ein Versuch*. Edited by Horst Günther. Frankfurt am Main: Deutscher Klassiker Verlag 1989; English translation: *The Civilization of the Renaissance in Italy*. Translated by S. C. G. Middlemore with an Introduction by Peter Burke. London: Penguin 1960.

Cassirer, Ernst: *Das Erkenntnisproblem in der Philosophie und Wissenschaft der neuren Zeit*. 3 vols. Berlin: Verlag Bruno Cassirer 1922³.

Foscolo, Ugo: *Saggi di letteratura italiana. Parte prima, Epoche della lingua italiana*. Edited by Cesare Foligno. Florence: Le Monnier 1958.

Freccero, John: *Dante: The Poetics of Conversion*. Edited by Rachel Jacoff. Cambridge, Mass.: Harvard University Press 1986.

Velli, Giuseppe: *Petrarca e Boccaccio: Tradizione-memoria-scrittura*. Padua: Antenore 1995² (Studi sul Petrarca, 7).

Articles and Papers

Baron, Hans: *Moot Problems of Renaissance Interpretation: An Answer to Wallace K. Ferguson*. In: *Journal of the History of Ideas* 19 (1958), p. 26–34.
Ossola, Carlo: *Europa, Europa…* In: Carlo Ossola (ed.): *Europa, miti d'identità*. Venice: Marsilio 2001 (Presente storico, 12).

H. Wayne Storey
The Formation of Knowledge and Petrarch's Books

With the development of the fields of the history of the book, codicology and material philology in the last 50 years, since the publication of Leon Gilissen's *Prolégomènes à la codicologie: recherches sur la construction des cahiers et la mise en page des manuscrits médiévaux*, we have begun to recover the complex cultural and intellectual relationships inherent in the production of the medieval and early humanist book.[1] It was, as we know, a process that both demanded extraordinary planning and allowed unique flexibility in the layering of texts that would constitute the intellectual canvas of often multiple hands and collaborators.[2] Every aspect of the preparation of the book's page, fascicle, and ultimate unity

---

[1] Parts of Gilissen's seminal study date back to 1969 (Leon Gilissen: Un élément codicologique trop peu exploité: la réglure. In: *Scriptorium* 23 [1969], p. 150–162) and 1972 (Leon Gilissen: La composition des cahiers, le pliage du parchemin et l'imposition. In: *Scriptorium* 26 [1972], p. 3–33). Essential to Gilissen's work are his precise demonstrations ("vérification archéologique" [p. 44–122]) of the formulae of construction of the medieval fascicle according both to aesthetic and mathematical principles that are undeniably confirmed by physical features of the parchment in any number of medieval manuscripts, as well as his analyses of the precise geometric formulae at the heart of the layout, or mise en page, of the medieval *charta* (or page). See especially his "Conclusions": Leon Gilissen: *Prolégomènes à la codicologie: recherches sur la construction des cahiers et la mise en page des manuscrits médiévaux*. Gand [Ghent]: Éditions Scientifiques Story – Scientia 1977, p. 238–244.

[2] The stratification of this collaboration was not only among diverse hands of craftsmen but also temporal, extending at times over even decades of preparation, revision and "modernization" (especially of images and illustrations). See, for example, Carmélia Opsomer: Le Scribe, l'enlumineur et le commanditaire: Àpropos des *Tacuina sanitatis* illustrés. In: Herrad Spillingas (ed.): *La collaboration dans la production de l'écrit médiéval: Actes du XIIIe Colloque du Comité international de paléographie latine (Weingarten, 22–25 september 2000)*. Paris: École nationale des Chartes 2003, p. 183–192; and Francesca Santoni: Copisti-editores di manoscritti giuridici: 1. Il codice Vaticano latino 1406 del *Digestum Vetus* e l'edizione del testo fra copisti e glossatori. In: Herrad Spillingas (ed.): *La collaboration dans la production de l'écrit médiéval*, p. 231–249; Gabriella Pomaro demonstrates the importance and philological implications of the dating of these collaborations, in this case between copyist and illustrator, in her critique of the preparation of MS Cortona 88 (a *Commedia* from the 1370s and not, in Petrocchi's *stemma codicum*, from the 1340s). See Gabriella Pomaro: I testi e il Testo. In: Vincenzo Placella/Sebastiano Martelli (eds.): *I moderni ausili all'Ecdotica: Atti del Convegno Internazionale di studi (Fisciano – Vietri sul Mare – Napoli, 27–31 ottobre 1990)*. Napoli: Edizioni scientifiche Italiane 1994, p. 193–213 (especially p. 194–197); and Dante Alighieri: *La Commedia secondo l'antica vulgata*. Edited by Giorgio Petrocchi. 4 vols. Milano: Mondadori 1966–1967 (Edizion nazionale delle opere di D.A., 7),

among its parts, from its mise en page and script to the composition of its gatherings linked it in the intellectual processes of those who produced the book and those who read it to traditions as diverse as the mercantile culture responsible for vernacular anthologies that would be essential to the early Italian lyric (such as Vatican Latino 3793 and Escorial e.III.23) or the erudition of highly glossed legal and theological texts (such as Vatican Latino 1411, Vatican Urbinate latino 161 and Cesena Biblioteca Malatestiana MS s.IV.2).[3] These and similar systems of preparation signaled cultural ties to location and professions that in themselves defined ways of thinking and the mechanics of knowledge that reflected philosophical orientation. The use of the 'littera bononiensis' identified the mechanisms and influence of Scholastic legal thought defined by the glossators and professors of law at the University of Bologna. The two-column mise en page of tenth- and eleventh-century books, that contained text and gloss in two distinct scripts, ultimately produced a two-column layout in thirteenth- and fourteenth-century Italian manuscripts in gothic and chancery hands that contained texts as diverse as Boccaccio's *Decameron*, Dante's *Commedia*, Petrarch's and Guittone d'Arezzo's letters.[4]

Vol. 1: Introduzione. For a study of the relationship between the compiler and the copyists of the sole, datable fourteenth-century copy of the *Convivio* (MS Biblioteca Nazionale Centrale II.III.47, ca. 1361), see Beatrice Arduini: Assigning the 'Pieces' of Dante's *Convivio*: the Compiler's Notes in the Earliest Extant Copy. In: *Textual Cultures: Texts, Contexts, Interpretation* 3, 2 (2008), p. 17–29.
3 On the influence of these formulaic and highly glossed works produced in Bologna on Petrarch, see John Ahern: Good-bye, Bologna: Johannes Andreae and *Familiares* IV 15 and 16. In Teodolinda Barolini/Wayne Storey (eds.): *Petrarch and the Textual Origins of Interpretation*. Leiden – Boston: Brill 2007, p. 185–204.
4 As we see in the case of the *Decameron* copied by the Benedictine monk "Nicolaus" in 1396 (Firenze, Biblioteca Nazionale Centrale MS Banco rari 37, *olim* II.I.23), the long predominance of gothic script even late into the fourteenth century is witnessed in distinct scribal and cultural contexts. At the same time and in the same general geographical area but in a different cultural environment, we find the progressive semi-gothic script – proposed as a scribal reform of illegible gothic script by Petrarch – used for the transcription of the so-called 'historia Griseldis,' Petrarch's commentary and translation of Boccaccio's *Decameron* X 10 in *Seniles* XVII 3–4, together with a copy of Burley's *De vita et moribus philosophorum*, in MS Bloomington, Lilly Library Poole 26. These two scripts are distinguishable from the cursive chancery hands that were favored for fourteenth-century copies of the *Commedia*, proposed by Savino as a 'virtual autograph' and even for what is, according to Folena and others, probably a late fourteenth-century copy of Guittone's letters and poetry, Ms. Firenze, Riccardiano 2533. It is noteworthy that each of these scribal styles defines intellectual and moral associations between works and the readers for whom each was used. See Gianfranco Folena: Ueberlieferungsgeschicte der altitalienischen Literatur. In: *Geschichte der Textüberlieferung der antiken und mittelalterlichen Literatur* 2 (1964), p. 319–538; Giancarlo Savino: L'autografo virtuale della *Commedia*. In: *"Per correr*

To say that Petrarch was attentive to the meaning of the association among script, mise en page, and intellectual tradition would be an understatement. In both his *Familiares* and his *Seniles*, Petrarch complains about the divisions of labor in the production of modern books, a practice that – in Petrarch's view – damaged the essential unity of the intellectual's command in the preparation of a text.[5] For Petrarch not only was the design of the book a reflection of the edition's intellectual structure, it was also an integral part of its systems of meaning, from the clarity of its script to the unified organization of its knowledge in the text and its apparatus and glosses. It is, as Armando Petrucci has pointed out, Petrarch's preference for the simplicity and clarity of form that drove him to admire copies of the tenth and eleventh centuries in minuscule Caroline hands and to detest the often calligraphic and illegible minuscule forms of Gothic scripts overburdened by abbreviations and compendia, and tied to Scholastic thought.[6] Recalling the gift copy of his *De vita solitaria* to Philippe de Cabassoles, in *Senilis* VI 5 (written in Venice 6 June 1366), Petrarch describes the tribulations of finding a copyist whose simple but elegant and practical writing style stood in direct contrast to the then current writing habits of copyists who "pride themselves on small, cramped lettering that baffles the eye; by heaping and cramming everything together, [...][their writing] confuses the spacing and piles up the letters, as

---

miglior acque...". Bilanci e prospettive degli studi danteschi alle soglie del nuovo millennio. 2 vols. Rome: Salerno Editrice 2001, II, p. 1099–1110. For the question of the role of the 'historia Griseldis' in the interpretation of *Decameron* X, 10 and the witness Poole 26 at the Lilly Library, see Wayne Storey: The Contexts and Histories of the Tale of Gualtieri and Griselda (*Dec.* X 10). Forthcoming in: Michael Papio (ed.): *Lectura Boccaccii: The Tenth Day*. Toronto: University of Toronto Press 2017.

5 See, for example, *Familiaris* XVIII 5 to his brother Gherardo about a copy of Augustine's *Confessions*.

6 Armando Petrucci: *La scrittura del Petrarca*. Città del Vaticano: Biblioteca Apostolica Vaticana 1967, p. 66. One of the clearest expressions of the positive features of Petrarch's ideal script is found in his *Familiaris* XXIII 19, written to Giovanni Boccaccio. The letter announces the nearing to completion of his *Letters on Familiar Matters* (*Rerum familiarium libri*) in the hand of his young assistant, believed by most to be Giovanni Malpaghini, which Petrarch describes as the antithesis of "that pompous and fancy lettering so typical of contemporary scribes [...] as though it were destined for something other than reading." Rather the young scribe's hand is "in neat and clear lettering, affecting more than just the eyes and lacking [...] nothing in orthography and nothing at all in grammatical skill" (from Francesco Petrarca: *Letters on Familiar Matters. Rerum familiarium libri XVII–XXIV*. Trans. by Aldo Bernardo. Baltimore-London: The Johns Hopkins University Press 1985, p. 301; see Francesco Petrarca: *Le familiari*. Ed. by Vittorio Rossi. Firenze: Sansoni 1933–1942 [*Edizione nazionale delle opere di F. P.*, 13], IV, p. 203–207 (p. 205). On the critical question of the identity of Petrarch's copyist, with implications for the partial holography of the *Rerum vulgarium fragmenta*, MS Vatican Library Latino 3195, see Monica Berté: Giovanni Malpaghini copista di Petrarca? In: *Cultura neolatina* 75, 1–2 (2015), p. 205–216.

though they were riding on top of one another, so that the scribe himself could scarcely read them, were he to return a little later, while the patron who commissioned the book would really purchase not so much a book, as blindness because of the book".[7] The paragraph's initial rhetorical play on the general 'artlessness' (*iners*) and 'faithlessness' (*perfidia*) of copyists of Petrarch's day is instilled in the opening attack of *Senilis* VI 5, 6: "Accessit ad causas more scriptorum perfida semper inertia inersque perfidia".[8] Combined with youth's slavishness to fashion, the illegible script against which Petrarch rails also conveys copyists' lack of knowledge and understanding of the very texts they have themselves transcribed. His description of the negative aesthetic and practical dimensions of his day's gothic handwriting amounts to a programmatic condemnation of the very style of writing that forms most of the manuscripts and documents of the late Middle Ages. In this condemnation we find especially Petrarch's rejection of medieval formulae of learning instilled in and identified with the very formation of illegible gothic scripts.[9] At the same time, Petrarch's adoration for the earlier and more legible Caroline minuscule of the tenth- and eleventh-century books he sought out leads us to his 'effective aesthetics of knowledge'. This aesthetics of script and book production constitutes the core of Petrarch's notion of a renewed understandability of the page in the transmission of knowledge, a page that invites study and, as we shall see, intervention and collaboration through emendation

---

[7] Francesco Petrarca: *Letters of Old Age. Rerum senilium libri I–XVIII*. Trans. by Aldo Bernardo and Saul Levin et al. Vol. 1: Books I–IX. Baltimore – London: The Johns Hopkins University Press 1992, p. 198. See Pétrarque: *Lettres de la vieillesse: Rerum senilium, édition critique*. Ed. by Elvira Nota. 5 vols. Paris: Les Belles Lettres 2003 (Classiques de l'Humanisme, 21), II, p. 226 (*Sen.* VI 5, §§ 6–7), in which he explains that the copy he is sending has been completed by a presumably older religious whose simple handwriting is especially adept to their age: "Litera non tam anxie exculta quam nostre atque omni etati, nisi fallor, ydonea". Petrarch's initial play on the general 'artlessness' (*iners*) and 'faithlessness' (*perfidia*) of copyists is instilled in the opening attack of *Senilis* VI 5, 6: "Accessit ad causas more scriptorum perfida semper inertia inersque perfidia". Combined with the fadishness of youth, the illegible script against which Petrarch rails also conveys the copyists' lack of knowledge and understanding of their own texts: "[...] acervans omnia et coartans atque hinc spatio, hinc literarum super literas velut equitantium aggestione confundens que scriptor ipse, brevi post tempore rediens, vix legat, emptor vero non tam librum quam precio cecitatem emat" (Pétrarque: *Lettres de la vieillesse, Rerum senilium IV–VII*. Vol. 2, p. 227: *Sen.* VI 5, § 7).
[8] "Another reason for the delay has been the ever deceitful laziness and lazy deceitfulness of the scribes" (Petrarca: *Letters of Old Age*, p. 198).
[9] For an overview of Petrarch's systematic reform of gothic script in its relationship to legibility and knowledge, see H. Wayne Storey: *Transcription and Visual Poetics in the Early Italian Lyric*. New York – London: Garland Press 1993, p. 201–224; and Armando Petrucci's chapter on Petrarch's aesthetic and graphological ideals in *Scrittura del Petrarca*, p. 58–70.

and glosses. Already a significant influence in his reading in the 1330s, the clarity of the Caroline minuscule had by the 1340s became an essential feature of the 'scriptura notularis' in which Petrarch learned and collaborated in the margins of his ancient manuscripts in 'littera antiqua', through which "Petrarch sought a visual harmony in the composition of the manuscript charta among text, commentary and support".[10]

It is, however, in his letter to the Florentine Lapo Castiglionchio, now *Familiaris* XVIII 12, addressed 'Ad Iacobum Florentinum', that we find the essence of the relationship among learning, reading and writing that fed Petrarch's philosophy of knowledge. In his description of his own copying of an unknown work of Cicero's from Lapo's library ('opus rarissimum' [4]) Petrarch clarifies the seamless unity of these three activities. His letter explains the delay of four years in the return of Lapo's Cicero precisely because of the shortage of intelligent scribes.[11] Unable to part with Lapo's volume without having a copy of his own, and unable to turn – as was his habit – to a trusted copyist, literally 'per scriptorum ignaviam' [3] Petrarch is compelled to pick up his own "worn down and battered pen" ('exesum atque attritum calamum' [3]).[12] The process that Petrarch describes as his own "custom" (*mos*) is not, however, simply the act of copying, but rather a triple act of engagement that fuses the physical and the intellectual: memory and the pen are unified. The possibility that one activity will diminish the other is held in check by the reciprocity of the movement of the eyes that propel the pen and the pen that paces the eyes. Even what should be contrasting participles, 'frenante' and 'urgente', now act in unison:

> Nichil legi nisi dum scribo. [...] procedenti vero per singulos passus, tantum dulcedinis occursabat tantoque trahebar impetu ut legens simul ac scribens laborem unum senserim, quod tam velociter ut optabam calamus non ibat, quem verebar oculis anteire, ne si legissem scribendi ardor ille tepesceret. Sic *igitur calamo frenante oculum atque oculo calamum urgente provehebar*, ut non tantum opere delectatus sim, sed inter scribendum multa didicerim memorieque mandaverim. Quo enim tardior est scriptura quam lectio, eo altius imprimitur heretque tenacius.[13]

---

10 Storey: *Transcription and Visual Poetics*, p. 205.
11 Arnaldo Foresti dates *Fam.* XVIII 11 and 12 to 14 November 1355. For the history of Petrarch's correspondence with the Florentine Lapo and the loan of his copy of Cicero, see Arnaldo Foresti: Le lettere a Lapo da Castiglionchio e il suo libro ciceroniano. In his: *Aneddoti della vita di Francesco Petrarca*. Brescia: Vannini 1928, p. 229–237 (esp. 235–236).
12 In the same letter, Petrarch describes, in fact, the act of copying as an activity that is not properly his: 'non mei negotii' (*Fam.* XVIII 12, 6), a phrase that will become pivotal in the letter.
13 Petrarca: *Le familiari*, XII, p. 296: *Fam.* XVIII 12, § 4–5.

[I read none of the text before I began writing. [...] as I reached particular passages, I experienced such great pleasure and was drawn with such force that, reading and writing at the same time, I became aware [that] my pen did not move as rapidly as I wished it to. I feared that my pen would outstrip my eyes, that my compulsion to write would lessen because of my reading. Thus did I proceed, with my pen checking my eyes and my eyes propelling the pen; and not only did I find a delight in my toil, but I learned a great deal in the act of writing and I committed much to memory. Since writing is slower than reading, it impresses more deeply and clings more tenaciously in the memory.][14]

While seemingly a letter of excuses for a borrowed volume long overdue, the letter to Lapo Castiglionchio crystalizes Petrarch's philosophy of knowledge as the constructive pleasure of intellectual toil ("ut non dicam tedio animi [...] sed labore manuum victus" [I would not say that my spirit got tired but I was defeated by the effort of my hand], *Fam.* XVIII 12, § 6). Physical fatigue is inextricable from learning, reading and copying, just as the author of his exemplar, Cicero, demonstrates in his own copying of the orations of others.

The manuscripts that transmit the patrimony of early Italian and Old Occitan literature supply us many of the formulae that Petrarch would have inherited. Large anthologies and even smaller volumes were often constructed according to divisions by poets and by literary genres. This construction was facilitated by copyists' use of booklets that contained mostly homogeneous content – by poet or genre or even theme – that could then be combined with other similar booklets.[15] In fact the vernacular traditions of early Italy were founded on a system of assembling books by virtually free-standing quires, or fascicle booklets. The thirteenth-century anthology MS Vaticano Latino 3793 is a collection of mostly single quires that usually conclude a 'content unit' at the end of most fascicles.[16] If it were not for the overarching historical and critical program with which MS Latino 3793 – an anthology of early Italian poetry – is organized, these single quires could easily have been placed anywhere in the manuscript without disrupting the reading of any of the texts that make up the single quires. The same

---

[14] Translation from Francesco Petrarca: *Letters on Familiar Matters. Rerum familiarium libri XVII–XXIV*, p. 63–64.

[15] Fundamental to this discussion of the material construction of anthologies, miscellanies, and composition manuscripts is Pamela Robinson: The "Booklet": a Self-Contained Unit in Composite Manuscripts. In: *Codicologia* 3 (1980): p. 46–69.

[16] See Roberto Antonelli: Canzoniere Vaticano Latino 3793. In: Alberto Asor Rosa (ed.): *Letteratura italiana, le opere, 1: Dalle origini al Cinquecento*. Torino: Einaudi 1982, p. 27–44. On the material constructions of the early Italian lyric tradition, see Furio Brugnolo: Libro d'autore e forma-canzoniere: Implicazioni grafico-visive nell'originale dei *Rerum vulgarium fragmenta*. In: Gino Belloni/Furio Brugnolo et al.: *Rerum vulgarium fragmenta. Codice Vat. Lat. 3195. Commentario all'edizione in fac-simile*. Roma – Padova: Antenore 2004, p. 105–129 (esp. 105–119).

could be said for the early transmission of the *Vita Nova*, for example, contained in two symptomatic early- and mid-fourteenth-century manuscripts, respectively MSS Laurenziano Martelli 12 and Magliabechiano Classe VI 143, precisely in two quires of five bifolia each (two quinternions).[17] This 'booklet-structure' served as well for numerous anthologies and even manuals of Old Occitan lyric, *vidas*, and *razos* produced in Italy. Of particular note is the early fourteenth-century manual with lyric repertory, *vidas*, and glossaries, MS Laurenziano 41.42, arranged from distinct fascicles to produce a virtual primer of the language, the poets' lives and their poetry.[18] This notion ultimately of a more rapid execution and diffusion of individual works both as independent booklets and within larger anthologies reveals a cultural orientation to the assembly of texts and knowledge itself in direct contrast to many of the models that Petrarch seems to have chosen for his own books.[19]

---

17 On the structure of MS Magliabechiano Classe VI 143 and its implications, see H. Wayne Storey: Di libello in libro: problemi materiali nella poetica di Monte Andrea e Dante. In: Furio Brugnolo/Gianfelice Peron (eds.): *Da Guido Guinizzelli a Dante. Nuove prospettive sulla lirica del Duecento*. Padova: Poligrafo 2004, p. 285–288. For the construction of the booklet fascicles in MS Laurenziano Martelli 12, see Arrigo Castellani: Sul codice Laurenziano Martelliano 12. In: Leonella Coglievina/Domenico De Robertis (eds.): *Sotto il segno di Dante. Scritti in onore di Francesco Mazzoni*. Firenze: Le Lettere 1998, pp. 85–97; and Sandro Bertelli: Nota sul canzoniere provenzale P e sul Martelli 12. In: *Medioevo e Rinascimento* 18, n.s. 16 (2004), p. 369–375.
18 For a discussion of the organization of MS Laurenziano 41.42 according to the function of its fascicle-units, see H. Wayne Storey: Method, History, and Theory in Material Philology. In: Marc van der Poel (ed.): *Neo-Latin Philology, Old Tradition, New Approaches. Proceedings of a Conference held at the Radboud University, Nijmegen, 26–27 October 2010*. Leuven: Leuven University Press 2014 (Supplementa of Humanistica Lovaniensia, 35), p. 32–39. On the links between MSS Laurenziano Martelli 12 and Laurenziano 41.42 in the assignment and dating of the hands to Pietro Berzoli da Gubbio, see again Bertelli: Nota sul canzoniere provenzale.
19 Essential for an orientation to questions of the books that Petrarch actually owned are: Pierre de Nolhac: Les livres de Pétrarque aprés sa mort. In his: *Pétrarque et l'humanisme*. 2 vols. Paris: Libraire Honoré Champion 1907, I, p. 87–122; and Élisabeth Pellegrin: Nouveaux manuscrits annotés par Pétrarque à la Bibliothèque nationale de Paris. In: *Scriptorium* 5, 2 (1951), p. 265–278. Ancillary to these studies is the fundamental study of BnF Paris MS latin 2201, Berthold Louis Ullman: Petrarch's Favorite Books. In his: *Studies in the Italian Renaissance*, 2nd ed. Rome: Edizioni di Storia e Letteratura 1973, p. 113–133. For a more philosophical-literary orientation, see Michelangelo Picone: Dentro la biblioteca di Petrarca. In: Maurice Brock/Francesco Furlan et al. (eds.): *La Bibliothèque de Pétrarque: Livres et auteurs autour d'un humaniste. Actes du IIe Congrès international sciences et arts, philologie et politique à la Renaissance 27–29 novembre 2003*. Turnhout: Brepols 2011, p. 21–34; see also Ugo Dotti: Le due "biblioteche" di Francesco Petrarca. In: Maurice Brock/Francesco Furlan et al. (eds.): *La Bibliothèque de Pétrarque*, p. 131–141, which, however, examines simply the contrasts between Petrarch's books of classical learning and those of

At the intellectual center of manuscripts that were precious to Petrarch and that supplied him with valuable prototypes, his own 'Virgilio Ambrosiano' (today: Milano Biblioteca Ambrosiana MS A 79 inf. Sala Prefetto 10/27 [olim A 49 inf 1]) stands as one of his 'modern' books that played a central role as the site where he noted the deaths of Laura and others, and where he studied, conjectured, and emended his Virgil and Virgil's canonical commentator Servius.[20] This very personal and textual site devoted to Virgil and Statius also taught him about the unifying intellectual force of a book constructed not of smaller, independent booklets but of integrated pieces of a whole context, of a cultural view in which the intricacy of material unity bears out the broader perspective of a classical intellect's world view and his influence on and relationships to other sources of knowledge. Petrarch's Virgil exerted a lasting influence on his notions of the unity of *mise en page*, *mise en livre*, and the effective transmission of knowledge in the strata of conversations among the text, the commentary and glosses, and future users of the book. Prepared upon a commission from his father – the "Petrus Parentis Florentinus" intuited by Giovanni Mercati as Petracco di Parenzo – well before 1326, the manuscript exhibits the tenets of a harmony of the page and the fascicle within the context of a vast editorial project that lasted

---

the church fathers. But for our purposes in this essay, Nolhac's occasionally overlooked study Pétrarque bibliophile in his *Pétrarque et l'humanisme*, I, p. 13–85, examines the materials, the passions, and early historical development of "sa collection" (p. 36) and of the practical aesthetics of the book, the "habitudes de Pétrarque" (p. 41), that will guide his own book production in later years.

20 For the extensive bibliography on this pivotal book in Petrarch's development as a codicologist and an historian, see Marco Petoletti's introduction to the manuscript: "Petrus parentis florentinus, qui hoc modo volumen hoc instituit": Il codice, in Marco Baglio/ Antonietta Nebuloni Testa/Marco Petoletti (eds): *Le postille del Virgilio Ambrosiano*, Roma-Padova: Antenore 2006, p. 6–29; Marco Ballarini/ Giuseppe Frasso/ Carla Maria Monti (eds.): *Francesco Petrarca. Manoscritti e libri a stampa della Biblioteca Ambrosiana*. Milano: Scheiwiller 2004. Since the manuscript itself can no longer be consulted, either directly or in digital or photographic reproductions, the 1930 facsimile is still the best representation of the codex. See Francisci Petrarcae: *Vergilianus Codex, ad Publii Vergilii Maronis diem natalem Bis Millesimum Celebrandum Quam Simillime Expressus Atque in Lucem Editus Ivvantibus Bibliotheca Ambrosiana et Regia in Insubribus Academia*. Mediolani (Milan): Hoeplianis 1930. Still indispensable are: Giuseppe Billanovich: Dalle prime alle ultime letture del Petrarca. In: *Petrarca ad Arquà. Atti del Convegno degli studi nel VI centenario (1370–1374) Arquà Petrarca, 6–8 novembre 1970*, ed. by Giuseppe Billanovich and Giuseppe Frasso. Padova: Antenore 1975, p. 13–50. Giuseppe Billanovich: Il Virgilio del giovane Petrarca. In: *Lectures médiévales de Virgile. Actes du colloque de Rome (25–28 octobre 1982)*. Rome: École Française de Rome 1985, p. 49–64. Finally, of note are the insights of the director of the Biblioteca Ambrosiana who prepared the facsimile edition: Giovanni Gabiati: *Il libro che il Petrarca ebbe più caro*. Milano: U. Allegretti di Campi 1957.

all of Petrarch's life.[21] It is the work of a single hand and is – in the expanse of its first 232 chartae – devoted primarily to the works of a single author, in a gothic book hand, together with Servius's commentary on the *Aeneid*. However, certainly part of its original program would have included Statius's unfinished epic *Achilleid* and four of Horace's *Odes*. It is, nonetheless, the unified assembly of these works that would have offered Petrarch a unique material model. Composed entirely of quinions, 26 of them complete with a partial 27th, it is noteworthy that no work concludes at the end of a gathering until we reach c. 250, the close of Horace's *Odes*, suggesting that the entire book was carefully planned out so as not to divide its contents materially by fascicles. These will be the texts to which Petrarch will turn throughout his life to study, annotate, and remember, to integrate and – at times – contrast his observations and knowledge with that of Servius's standard commentary of the *Aeneid*. There is nothing sterile or Scholastic in Petrarch's reengagement of these works. Rather we often find the maturation of reflections on passages and works, which develop over years and through different texts. Such is the case most certainly with his marginal gloss of *Georgics* IV 545, "inferias Orphei Lethaea papavera mittes" [you will make funereal offerings of Lethaean poppies to Orpheus], on c. 51v, when Petrarch recalls Ovid's explanation in the *Remedia Amoris* (vv. 550–553) of "Lethaeus Amor, qui pectora sanat" [Lethaeus Love, which heals the souls]: "*Nil melius amanti quam amoris et curarum oblivisci, ideo papaver sompniferum et obliviosum sacrificari precipitur Orpheo; hinc est ille Amor Letheus in templo Erycis, cuius meminit Ovidius in libro de remediis*" [Nothing is better to the lover than forgetting about love and worries, and for that reason it is advised to offer the soporific and amnesiac poppy to Orpheus; hence that Lethaean Love in the temple of Eryx, which Ovid mentioned in the book *De Remediis*]. While the original verse in the *Georgics* sites the effects of the poppy offered to Orpheus that brings sleep and forgetting, Ovid's verses in the *Remedia* focus solely on the Lethaean forgetting of love's vows: "Illic et iuvenes votis oblivia poscunt" [There, young men ask for oblivion through their vows] (553). Nowhere in the *Remedia* is there a single

---

21 The entire inscription is "Petrus Parente Florentinus qui hoc modo volumen instituit" [Petrus Parente Florentinus who thus prepared the volume]. Billanovich (Il Virgilio, 52) formulated one set of explanations for the dates and provenance of the manuscript's production in which Petrarch himself would have had a hand, while Michele Feo proposed a much earlier date of preparation (end of the thirteenth century) for which Petrarch's father would have been responsible and, as in Billanovich's reconstruction, the project would have been executed by an Italian copyist. However, the most cogent discussion of the manuscript's preparation comes from Petoletti: Il codice, in which he proposes a southern French provenance of copyist and commission after Petracco's exile and the transfer of his family to Avignon. See also Giovanni Mercati: *Opere minori*. 5 vols. Città del Vaticano: Biblioteca Apostolica Vaticana 1937 (Studi e testi, 80), IV, p. 422–429.

poppy; instead Petrarch links the two passages on Lethaean oblivion through the "narcotic effect of the poppy" recalled in Virgil's *Aeneid* IV 486, when the witch Massyla – the custodian of the temple of the Hesperides – saves the sacred branches "spargens umida mella soporiferumque papaver" [sprinkling moist honey and soporific poppy].[22] Many years later, Petrarch returns to the remedy of the poppy for forgetting suffering and loss in his long *Senilis* X 4, sent in 1368 to console Donato Albanzani over the death of his son ("Ad Donatum Apenningigenam grammaticum, consolatoria super illius filii suique simul nepotis immaturo obitu").[23] The episode is significant in its lesson. The toil of Petrarch's marginal observations has now found a new context and a new twist. Petrarch prefaces his new development of this classical crossroad of citations by professing his preference, for his friend and himself, for forgetful happiness over "mournful recollection": "mallem ego michi et tibi, mallem iocundam oblivionem quam memoriam luctuosam"[24] [I would prefer, for me and you, I would prefer pleasant oblivion to mournful recollection]. The letter's very next line incorporates first the utility of *oblivio* as an aid to lovers (*Remedia*) and then the poets' consecration of the "soporific and [...] amnesiac poppy". The linkage between the poppy and Orpheus is so strong, especially thanks to Virgil's description in the *Georgics*, that editors have frequently preferred that Petrarch make the same association. But here he surprises us, if we trust Lachmannian stemmatics, by substituting the oblivion of the dream state, Morpheus, in combination with the Lethaean poppy:

> Et est, hercle, oblivio, ut aiunt, amantibus utilis, unde apud poetas somniferum ac perinde obliviosum papaver sacrificatur Morpheo et Letheo sua sunt sacra Cupidini.[25] [And by Hercules, this oblivion is useful to lovers, as they say, and according to the poet, they sacrifice soporific and amnesiac poppy to Morpheus and his sacrifices are Lethaean to desire.]

Aldo Bernardo and Marco Baglio presume that Petrarch has simply made an error by writing "Morpheo" when he must have meant "Orpheo".[26] Certainly this would

---

22 On the tradition of the poppy in Vergil's *Georgics* and its classical tradition, see Gary B. Miles: *Virgil's Georgics: a New Interpretation*. Berkeley: University of California Press 1980, p. 285–287. All quotations from the *Aeneid* are from P. Virgilio Marone: *L'Eneide*, edited by Rosa Calzecchi Onesti. Torino: Einaudi 1967.
23 See Marco Baglio: Le postille di Petrarca al Virgilio. In: Marco Ballarini/Giuseppe Frasso et al. (eds.): *Francesco Petrarca. Manoscritti e libri a stampa della Biblioteca Ambrosiana*. Milano: Scheiwiller 2004, p. 29–39 (esp. p. 32).
24 Petrarch's letter is cited from Pétrarque: *Lettres de la vieillesse: Rerum senilium, édition critique*. Ed. by Elvira Nota. Vol. 3. Paris: Les Belles Lettres 2004, p. 305, § 48.
25 The citation is from ibid.
26 See Petrarch: *Letters of Old Age. Rerum senilium libri I–XVIII*, p. 390; and Baglio: Le postille di Petrarca al Virgilio, p. 32.

be a reasonable correction in light of his previous development of the motif. But perhaps Petrarch's reapplication of readings and expansion of knowledge leads us in a different direction: toward a more complex understanding of forgetting that moves, after years of study and reflection, toward the metaphor of Morpheus's dream state.

Petrarch often supplies glosses as well that bring the history of his sources into the present day in a kind of dialogue with the future, unknown reader of his marginalia. While he engages Virgil directly, Petrarch seems at times to establish a trajectory between Servius's commentary and the present as a means of documenting the continuity of history. When at the beginning of *Aeneid* XI, when Servius comments on the triumphal arch as a reflection on Aeneas's desire to create a tribute to Mars out of Mezentius's arms ("ingentem quercum decisis undique ramis / constituit tumulo fulgentiaque induit arma, / Mezenti ducis exuvias, tibi magne tropaeum / bellipotens" [XI 5–8] [he cut off all around the branches of a huge oak / he set it on a tumulus and hung from it the shining armor, / spoils of war from their leader Mezentius, as a trophy to you / great and powerful in war]), Petrarch draws the tradition into his own day by commenting on his own experience in Rome: "Mos arcuum triumphalium, quibus Roma nunc etiam plena est".[27] In some places, Petrarch's glosses mix sources and personal experience in complex combinations and over long stretches of time. In Book I of the *Aeneid*, Neptune calms the stormy waters created by Juno's wrath for Aeneas (v. 131). Petrarch's annotation points to Apuleius's *Metamorphoses* V 9, 84 and corrects it by reminding his reader of the true dominance of a Christian God in controlling the seas, heavens and the land: "'Ventis ipsis imperat' ut ait Apuleius [...]; quod verius non de puella ut ibi vel de maris de aut hic, sed de celi terreque et maris domino dicitur" ['The winds obeyed her commands,' said Apuleius (...); but truthfully I am not talking about the girl there or that god of the sea, but of the Lord of heaven and earth and sea].[28] As Caterina Tristano has noted, the passage "Ventis imperat" is repeated in the margin by Petrarch in his own copy of Apuleius's *Metamorphoses*, MS Vaticano Latino 2193, c. 56v.[29] Many years later, in 1362, Petrarch wishes his friend Paolo de Bernardo di Venezia a safe journey by sea in *Senilis* X 3, drawing upon his previous engagement of Virgil and Apuleius

---

27 MS Milano, Ambrosiano A 79 inf. Sala Prefetto 10/27 (Olim A 49 inf 1), c. 204r ["The custom of the triumphal arches, of which Rome even in our own day is full"]; see also Marco Petoletti: Le postille del Petrarca a Servio. In Marco Ballarini/Giuseppe Frasso et al. (eds.): *Manoscritti e libri a stampa della Biblioteca Ambrosiana*. Milano: Scheiwiller 2004, p. 43–50.
28 MS Milano, Ambrosiano A 79 inf. Sala Prefetto 10/27 (Olim A 49 inf 1), c. 57r.
29 Caterina Tristano: Le postille del Petrarca nel ms. Vat. lat. 2193 (Apuleio, Frontino, Vegezio, Palladio). In: *Italia medioevale e umanistica* 17 (1974), p. 435, note 939.

and reiterating that it is not Neptune but Christ who is the sole ruler of the sea, the land and the heavens: "maris et terre celique regnator Cristus omnipotens" [Christ almighty ruling over the sea, the earth and heaven].³⁰ It is noteworthy that the letter concludes with a passage from Statius's *Achilleid* that Petrarch would have recalled from the very same manuscript (Ambrosiano A 79 inf. Sala Prefetto 10/27): "what Achilles' wife said in Statius: 'Go safely and come back true to us'" (*Achilleid* IV [I] 942).³¹ It is possible that we are at a personal commonplace for Petrarch, who dreaded the dangers of sea voyages.³² But even stronger – I believe – is the nexus of text, faith, and knowledge to which Petrarch often turned. For the passage in Statius bids Achilles not only a safe return but also recalls that Thetis – remembered not only as Achilles' mother but also one of the deities of the sea – did not fear in vain. Petrarch returns obliquely to the question of who is the true god of the seas:

> i cautus, nec vana thetim timuisse memento,
> i felix nosterque redi! nimis improba posco³³
>
> [And go about carefully, Thetis was not afraid for nothing,
> Go safely and come back true to us! I am asking for too many things]

For Petrarch the gloss or, perhaps more accurately, the space of the gloss represents a place of exchange and of learning in a dialogue between the past and the future. This transmission of knowledge is instilled in the larger site of the text and gloss of the *Aeneid*. Petrarch's annotations are themselves a building site that is intimate, reserved for himself and for the intimates who will inherit his library, his Virgil, his Apuleius, for those who will consult the margins.³⁴

---

30 See Pétrarque: *Lettres de la vieillesse: Rerum senilium VIII–XI*, vol. 3, p. 305, § 48. For the passage from *Senilis* X, 3, see Ibid., p. 275, § 2.
31 "i felix nosterque redi! nimis improba posco" (v. 942). We should note that Petrarch's *Achilleid* in his precious Virgil manuscript was divided into five books, according to the medieval tradition. After the incipit on c. 234r ("Magnanimum eacidem formidatamque tonanti"), Book II begins on c. 236v ("At tetis undisonis per noctem irrupibus astans" [v. 198]), Book III starts on c. 239r ("Interea meritos ultrix europa dolores" [v. 397]), Book IV begins on c. 242v ("Iamque per egeos ibat laercia fluctus" [v. 675]), and Book V's incipit ("Exuit impilcitum ten<e>bris humentibus orbem") marks the first verse of Book II of the classical form of the *Achilleid*. See Paul M Clogan (ed): *The Medieval Achilleid of Statius*. Leiden: Brill 1968, esp. p. 1–9.
32 See Marco Baglio: Le postille di Petrarca al Virgilio, p. 38.
33 See *Vergilianus Codex*, c. 246v (*Achilleid* IV 941–942).
34 On the nature of the late medieval gloss script and Petrarch's relationship to the hand, see Armando Petrucci: *La scrittura del Petrarca*. Città del Vaticano: Biblioteca Apostolica Vaticana 1967, p. 31–42.

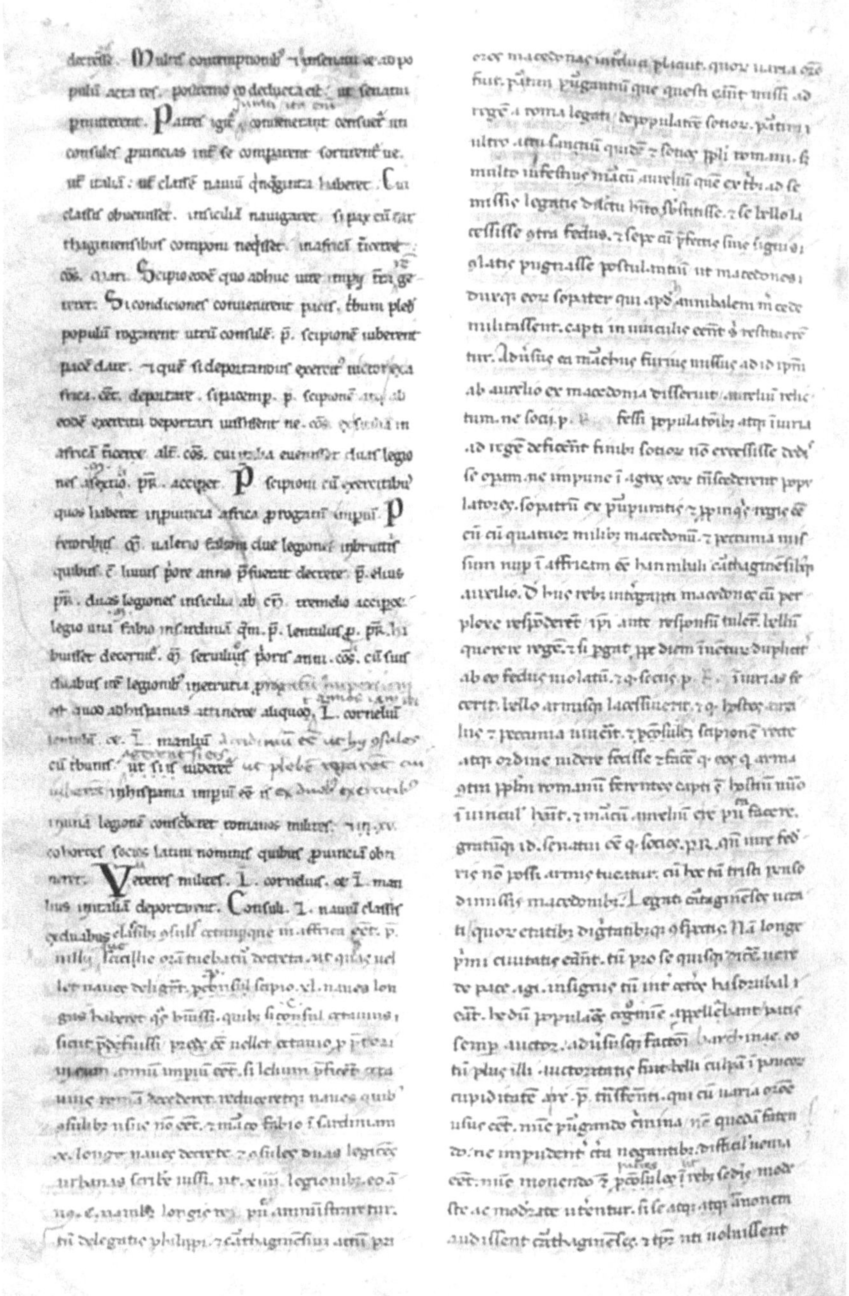

Plate 1: London, British Library, Harley 2493, c. 219v; published with the kind permission of the British Library

This nexus between the intimacy of textual space and learning, especially its unique transmission in Petrarch's manuscripts, certainly is most concentrated in his Virgil. But, as we remember, the manuscript was – by Petrarch's own account – out of his possession from 1326 until 1338. These are, as Armando Petrucci reminds us, essential years – especially 1337–1343 – in the development of Petrarch's studies as well as of his consistent gloss script.[35] In even earlier years, 1325 to 1328, the young scholar will acquire a copy of Augustine's *De civitate Dei* (today MS Padova, Biblioteca universitaria 1490). They are as well the years in which he will prepare what Petrucci calls the first critical edition of Livy's *Ab Urbe condita*: MS London, British Museum Harley 2493 (see Plate 1).[36]

Already in both annotations and texts of these two manuscripts, especially in his gloss on c. 219v (Plate 1), we see the elegance of Petrarch's lighter gothic hand as well as his control of the text's presentation in the coordination of three other contemporary copyists charged with executing Petrarch's edition.[37]

Only in 1962 was the young Petrarch's ownership of a late tenth-century Italian manuscript in a Caroline hand documented in the possession of the Swiss bibliophile Martin Bodmer (today Cologny, Bodmer Library MS 146 [see Plate 2]).[38] It would seem that the codex held a particular fascination for Petrarch both at the time of its original acquisition, sometime around 1330, and again later in his life.

Today a fragment, the MS carries a clear note of its young owner as well as evidence of the young scholar's interest in Cicero's *Partitiones oratoriae*, which Petrarch marks on c. 35r as comprising 15 chartae (Plate 2). Even in the first four chartae that remain of the work in the Bodmer manuscript, we find Petrarch annotating and "marking up" his copy of the text, to whose title he has added "sub dialogo" ("Marcij tulij ciceronis de partitiones [...] re rhetorice sub dialogo incipient" [Begins Marcus Tullius Cicero's dialogue On Oratorical Partitions]) and accordingly added the letters 'C' and 'M' to indicate the changes in voice in the dialogue between Cicero and his son Marcus. But for Petrarch the lesson of the Bodmer codex was far more complex than simply being a copy of one of Cicero's

---

35 See Ibid., p. 38–42.
36 For MS Padova, Biblioteca universitaria 1490, see Giuseppe Billanovich: Il Petrarca e i retori latini minori. In: *Italia medioevale e umanistica* 5 (1962), p. 103–164; for Petrarch's edition of Livy's *Ab Urbe condita* in MS London, British Museum Harley 2493, see Petrucci: *La scrittura del Petrarca*, p. 22–24 and 119, n9: where Petrucci notes that MS Harley 2493 "[è] scritto dal Petrarca anteriormente al 1330."
37 See Giuseppe Billanovich: Petrarch and the Textual Tradition of Livy. In: *Journal of the Warburg and Courtauld Institutes* 14 (1951), p. 203–205.
38 For the discovery of Petrarch's marginalia and an early discussion of the Bodmer codex, see Giuseppe Billanovich: Il Petrarca e i retori latini minori. In: *Italia medioevale e umanistica* 5 (1962), p. 103–164.

Plate 2: Cologny, Fondation Martin Bodmer, Cod. Bodmer 146, c. 35r. Manuscript with rhetorical works, owned by Petrarch; published with the kind permission of the Bodmer Library

minor works on oratorical skills. It is, in fact, the material regularity of this book that gathers together four works by four authors on the theme of rhetorical skills that presented itself as a unique model for a genre that would eventually have greater significance to Petrarch: the unified miscellany.

Produced by a single, late tenth-century copyist on at least six regular quaternions (up to c. 48) on chartae of 36 ruled lines in two columns, the codex would have provided a unique formula of clarity and consistency in the ordering of texts by four different authors on the same topic. The following table is helpful in visualizing the material construction of the miscellany:

Cologny, Bodmer Library MS 146

- 36 ruled lines / 5 Quaternions [A–F; the 6th conjectured]:
- A: 1–8; B: 9–16; C: 17–24; D: 25–32; E: [33a] 34 [34a]–38 [40]; F: [41–48] +
- Fortunatianus, *Ars rhetorica* cc. 1–23r
- Augustinus Hipponensis, *Principia rhetorices*, 23r–29v
- Iulius Severianus, *Precepta artis rhetorice*, 29v–35r
- M. Tullius Ciceronis, *Partitiones oratoriae*, 35r–38v.

Among Petrarch's prized codices devoted to single authorities, such as Virgil, Horace, and Apuleius, the tenth-century Bodmer 146 must have struck him as a unique material site. As Petrucci has suggested, its Caroline script will have a growing influence on Petrarch's development of a clear, almost semigothic gloss hand that would abandon the models of Scholastic glossators.[39] But perhaps even more significant is the construction of the Bodmer manuscript, that will supply him with key material elements for structuring his own *Fragmenta*. The style of Petrarch's glosses in his eleventh-century copy of Augustine's *Enarrationes in Psalmos* (Paris, BnF lat. 1994), copied in an elegant Italian Caroline hand and acquired by Petrarch in 1337, match his annotations in Bodmer 146, especially in Fortunatianus's *Ars rhetorica* (see Plate 3).

By most accounts, in April 1338, Petrarch began to devote time to his recovered Virgil. The intense work of Petrarch's study and glossing reveals a fully formed hand that imitates the clarity and lightness of the Caroline hands in his miscellany on rhetoric (Bodmer 146) and Augustine's *Enarrationes*. To understand the significance of this development, we can compare Petrarch's use in the same period, 1337–1339, of a gothic chancery – or semi-cursive – hand to transcribe drafts of lyric poems in the vernacular that will ultimately find their way into the *Fragmenta*. The regular and posed hand of Petrarch's *scriptura notularis* in this period reflects the scholar's engagement in a process of learning that

---

39 Petrucci: *La scrittura di Francesco Petrarca*, p. 27.

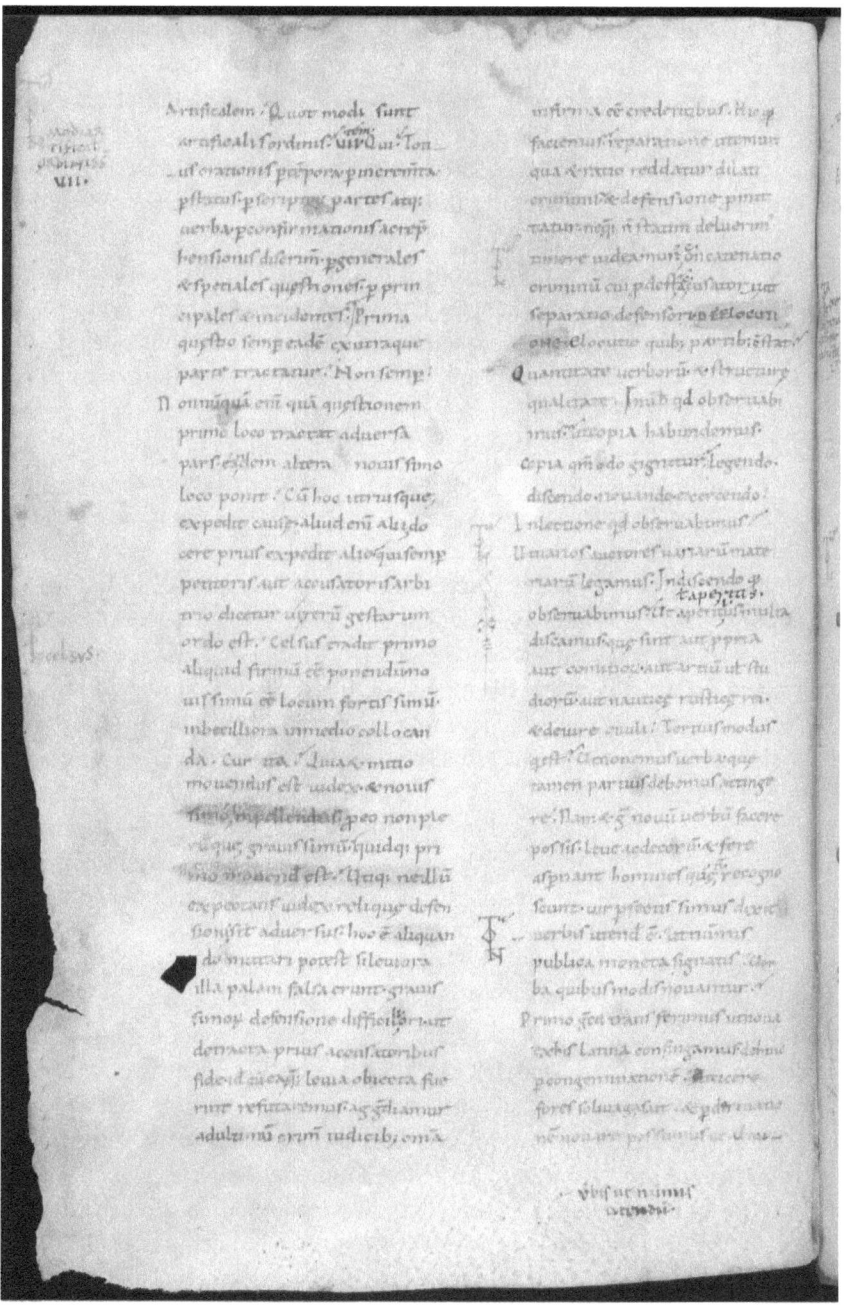

Plate 3: Cologny, Fondation Martin Bodmer, Cod. Bodmer 146, c. 18v. Manuscript with rhetorical works, owned by Petrarch; published with the kind permission of the Bodmer Library

required a stable notational style. Around the same time, the variation evident in the earliest entries of his draft copies in MS Vaticano Latino 3196 – a manuscript to which we shall return later – reveals the experimental nature of his poetic works in the vernacular. As the margins of Latino 3196 demonstrate, Petrarch's writing is here destined for emendation and for subsequent transcription in a fair hand elsewhere, "in alia papiro". It is the script that Petrarch will use to communicate with other scholars in the margins of his copies of classical and patristic authorities that has undergone the most urgent reform away from the dense gothic minuscule of his Scholastic predecessors and toward what would become an elegant semigothic adopted, as Lilly Poole 26 demonstrates, in the last decades of the fourteenth century. While we possess precious few copies of Petrarch's vernacular hand, the witnesses we do have suggest a slower process in adapting the features of his beloved Caroline script, confirming – I would conjecture – Petrarch's attitude toward what he called his little trifles, *nugellae*, in the vernacular ("Nugellas meas vulgares") in his letter of 1373 to Pandolfo Malatesta (*Sen.* XIII 11) as something more than a rhetoric stance.[40]

With the acquisition of his prized eleventh-century Horace in Genova in November of 1347 (today MS Laurenziano 34.1 [see Plate 4, a detail of c. 26v]), Petrarch secures for his own study and references in the glosses of numerous other manuscripts – including his prized Virgil – a codex that offered him not only an authoritative Caroline model in quaternions of an edition of Horace's *opera omnia* but also a site which will collect the widest chronological variety of annotated entries over the years of his ownership, allowing us to chart the often microscopic changes in Petrarch's gloss style. Well beyond a collection of variations in script, Petrarch's possibly oldest manuscript offers us details on the material construction of the transmission of knowledge that influenced Petrarch's own notions of book making.

Central to this manuscript's construction are: 1) an intricate system of strata of glosses that no longer relies on a two-column presentation but on clearly divided spaces of textual function laid out in regularly ruled 29-line chartae for the main text and 52 lines for the glosses in the wide external margins; and 2) the unifying dynamic of the single copyist responsible for the transcription of 140 chartae, recto and verso, in 18 gatherings, or 16 quaternions (or gatherings of eight chartae) plus a single quinion (Fascicle III) and a final bifolium (or 2 chartae) added to complete the second book of Horace's *Satires* (cc. 139–140 of 104r–140v) at the end of the codex. Examining the structure of the gatherings presented in the table below, we see that Horace's six works never

---

40 See Pétrarque: *Lettres de la vieillesse: Rerum senilium XII–XV*, p. 177, § 3.

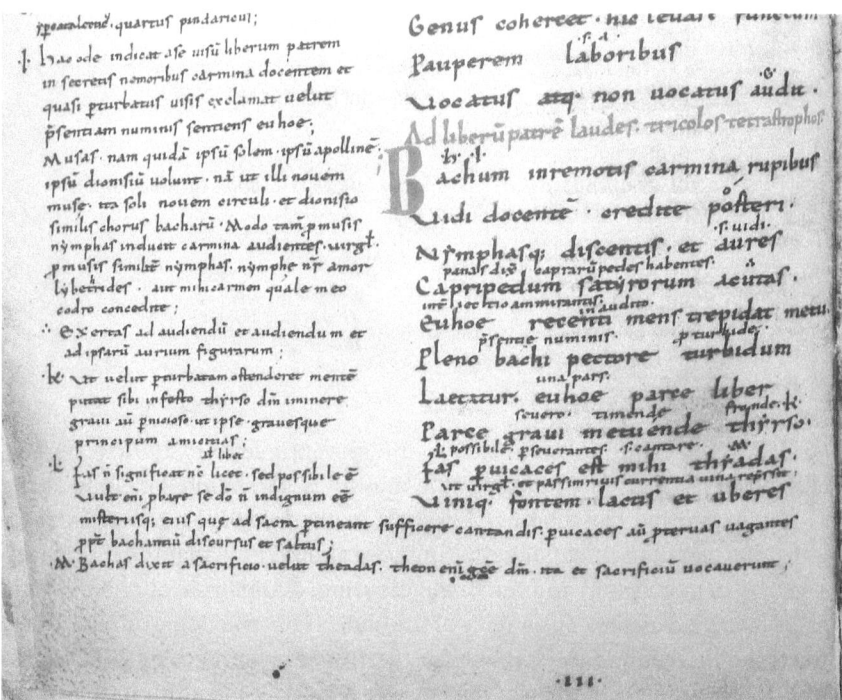

Plate 4: Firenze, Biblioteca Laurenziana, Pluteo 34.1, c. 26v (detail); published with the kind permission of the Biblioteca Laurenziana

conclude at the material end of a quaternion: the *Odes* (cc. 1v–56r [end of Fascicle VII is at c. 58]), the *Ars Poetica* (cc. 56r–64v [end of Fascicle VIII is at c. 66]), the *Epodes* (cc. 65r–76v), the *Carmen Saeculare* (cc. 76v–78r [quaternion X finishes with c. 82]), and the *Epistles* (cc. 78r–104r [Fascicle XIII, a quaternion, ends on c. 106]). Only the *Satires*, the final work in the manuscript, closes the 18th and final gathering, a bifolium (cc. 139–140) added to the final quaternion so that the copyist can complete the final satire:

Fascicle	I: 1–4|5–8;	*Odes* (incipit)
	II: 9–12|13–16;	
	III: 17–21|22–26;	
	IV: 27–30|31–34;	
	V. 35–38|39–42;	
	VI: 43–46|47–50;	
	VII: 51–54|55–58;	*Odes* (explicit) – *Ars Poetica* (incipit): 56r
	VIII: 59–62|63–66;	*Ars Poetica* (explicit): 64v; *Epodes* (incipit): 65r

IX: 67–70|71–74;
X: 75–78|79–82;   *Epodes* (explicit): 76v; *Carmen* (explicit): 78r;
                  Epistles (incipit): 78r
XI: 83–86|87–90;
XII: 91–94|95–98;
XIII: 99–102|103–106;   *Epistles* (explicit) – *Satires* (incipit): 104r
XIV: 107–110|111–114;
XV: 115–118|119–122;
XVI: 123–126|127–130;
XVII: 131–134|135–138;
XVIII: 139–140.   Satires (explicit): 140

Like Petrarch's 'Virgilio Ambrosiano', his eleventh-century Horace scrupulously observes the same unifying rule that no work should conclude at the end of a gathering. Considering Gilissen's methodological norm of examining the placement of irregular gatherings, we should note that the third fascicle, cc. 17–26 (a quinion) and the final gathering, a folded sheet or a bifolium (cc. 139–140), break the consistency of the book's construction in quaternions. In fact, the insertion of the quinion, or the 10-charta gathering (=III), avoids the aesthetic problem of three of the book's six works concluding at the end of a fascicle: the *Odes* at Fascicle VII, the *Ars poetica* at the end of Fascicle VIII, and the *Epistles* at the close of Fascicle XIII. The copyist's simple alteration in the size of the third gathering in the middle of the *Odes* can have little other function besides that of creating a more unified book. Long before the less precise method of constructing manuscripts by confining whole works to individual gatherings and then suturing those gatherings to make miscellanies, we find a model of the integrated edition of a single author carefully constructed across many gatherings, a large edition that would have been complete only through the ordering and sewing together of its dependently component parts.

Some might argue that Petrarch would not have counted chartae and stitchings in the middle of gatherings (signaled in our list by "|") as Gilissen taught us. However, as we see in the examples of cc. 26v (Plate 5), 34v (Plate 6) and 114v (Plate 7), the original copyist of Laurenziano 34.1 has accommodated future readers, and most certainly the observant Petrarch, by inserting a Roman numeral at the bottom of the final verso of each gathering to guarantee the book's sequence of quires when they are sewn together.

The gathering number is always in the same ink and Caroline hand as Horace's central text. While the copyist would have meant it as a tool for guaranteeing the

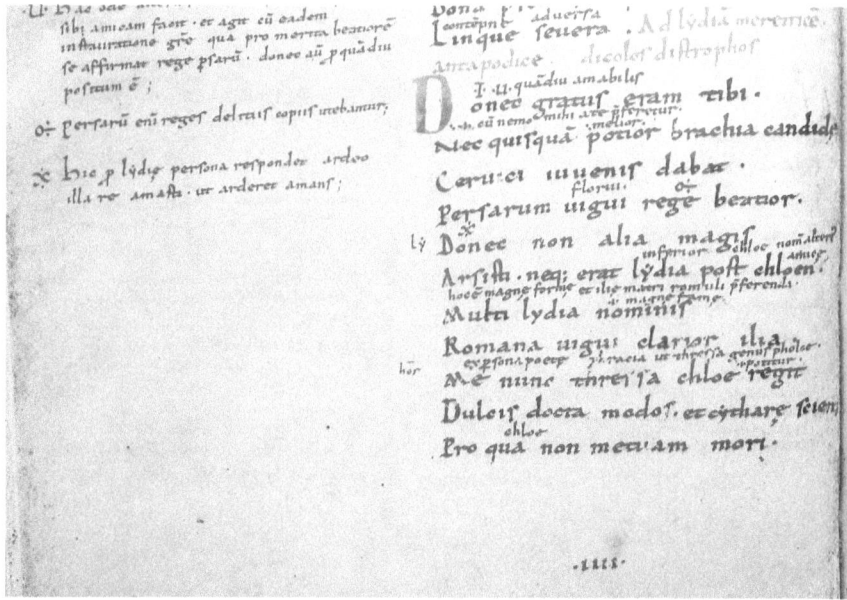

Plate 5: Firenze, Biblioteca Laurenziana, Pluteo 34.1, c. 34v (detail; end of Fascicle IV); published with the kind permission of the Biblioteca Laurenziana

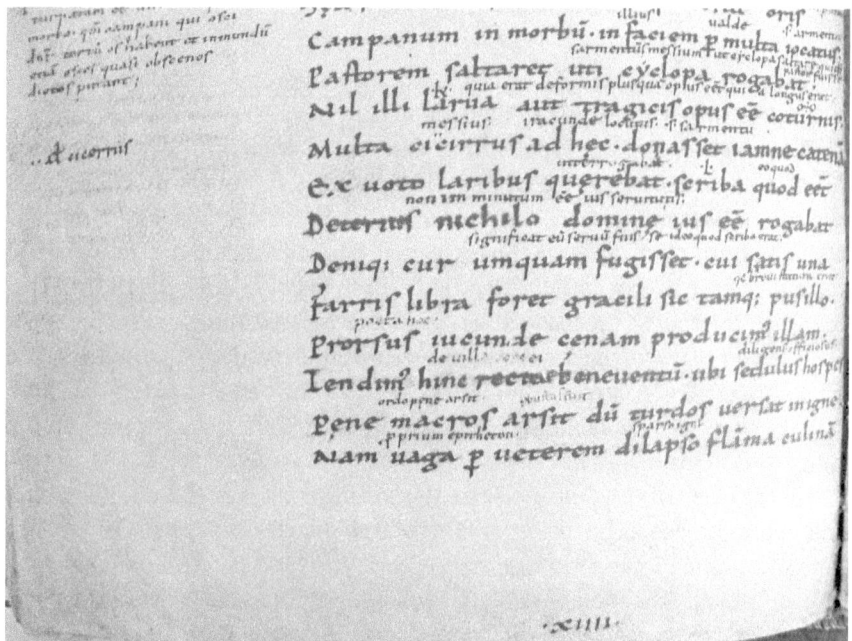

Plate 6: Firenze, Biblioteca Laurenziana, Pluteo 34.1, c. 114v (detail; end of Fascicle XIV); published with the kind permission of the Biblioteca Laurenziana

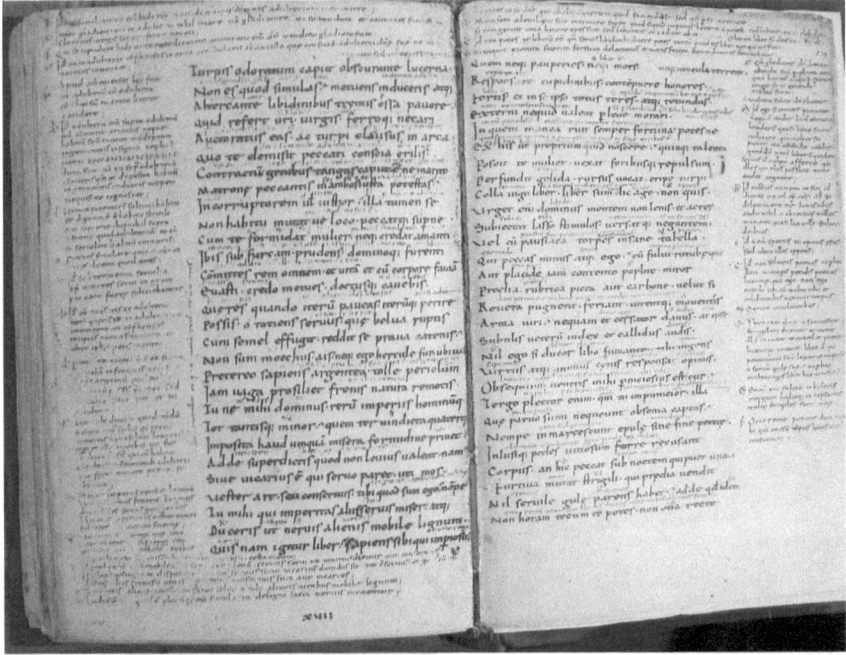

Plate 7: Firenze, Biblioteca Laurenziana, Pluteo 34.1, cc. 138v–139r; published with the kind permission of the Biblioteca Laurenziana

proper order of quires for binding, Petrarch would surely have utilized the numerals to check the completeness of the ancient copy's quires.

The careful planning of the quires and the insertion of irregular fascicles will be techniques that Petrarch himself will utilize in the construction of his own copy of *Rerum vulgarium fragmenta*. To that end, in fact, the final, irregular bifolium added by the copyist of Laurenziano 34.1 to complete the second satire would also have been a particularly useful lesson to Petrarch. At the close of Fascicle XVII, the copyist must add at least two chartae – or a single sheet of parchment, folded in two to make a bifolium – to conclude the second satire. From the last charta (138) of Fascicle XVII onto the recto of the first charta (139) of Quire XVIII, he continues the same mise en page of 29 ruled transcriptional lines for the main text (the gloss lines have expanded to 62).

On the verso of c. 139 he increases the writing canvas to 31 lines. But on the final charta he has at his disposal (c. 140; see Plate 8), the copyist of Laurenziano 34.1 has to fill the recto and verso with 35 and then 36 transcriptional lines to keep from adding another bifolium, which would have left at least three full sides of the two leaves, or three modern pages, completely blank at the close of the codex.

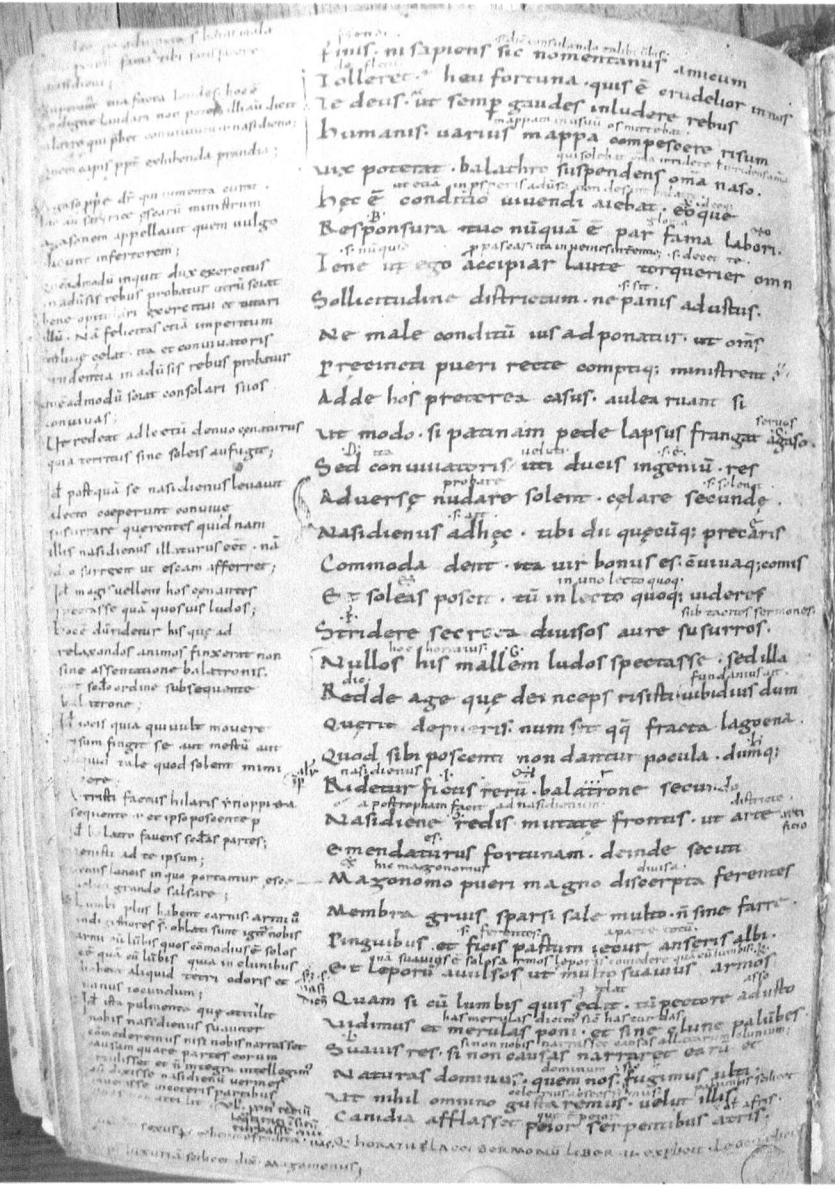

Plate 8: Firenze, Biblioteca Laurenziana, Pluteo 34.1, c. 140v; published with the kind permission of the Biblioteca Laurenziana

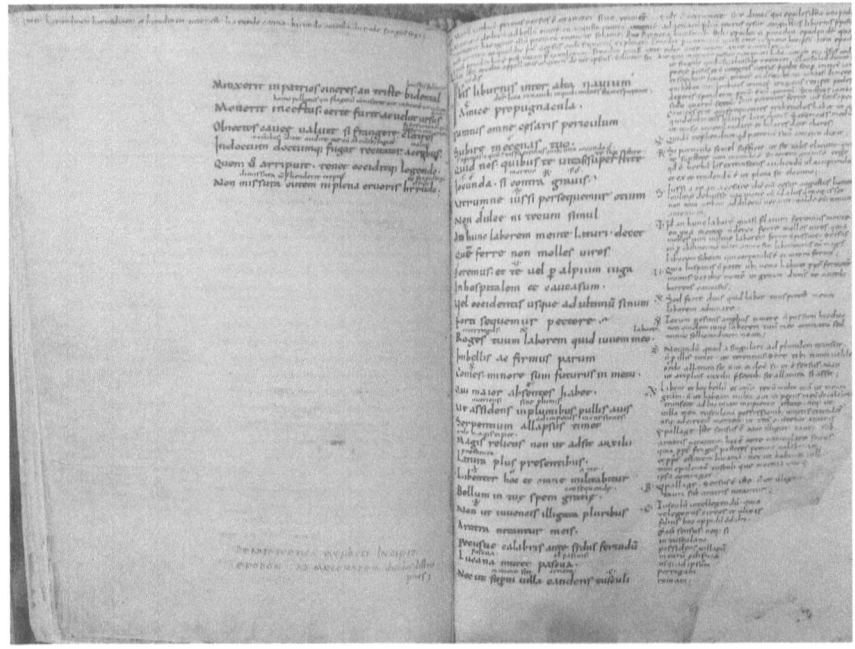

Plate 9: Firenze, Biblioteca Laurenziana, Pluteo 34.1, c. 64v–65r; published with the kind permission of the Biblioteca Laurenziana

The original copyist elects to break the system that he has maintained, the 29-line canvas, for over 138 chartae rather than conclude his work with blank parchment. This is a noteworthy decision. It safeguards the integrity of the book's unity as an integral edition of Horace's *opera*. But it also provides Petrarch with an additional, curious model. For blank space in this manuscript and in medieval manuscripts in general announce divisions between works, or incompletion and poor planning by the copyist or compiler.[41] Only once before has blank space been used in Laurenziano 34.1 to indicate the conclusion of one of Horace's works (see Plate 9). The empty space of c. 64v in MS Laurenziano 34.1 visually announces the pause between the end of Horace's canonical *Ars poetica* and the incipit of the first of his *Epodes* on c. 65r (note the added rubric "*De arte poetica explicit Incipit Epodon ad mecenatem* [...]").

This medieval tradition of spacing between works within the construction of a manuscript would have been a commonly accepted practice by Petrarch's day. And, in fact, those manuscripts of the *Fragmenta* that Petrarch either

---

[41] For example, numerous manuscripts of Dante's *Commedia* contain a blank recto or verso of a charta to signal the division between canticles.

prepared or oversaw, or that can reasonably be assumed to derive from an early generation of manuscripts that he approved, all demonstrate a division between what we might call a Part I and a Part II that Petrarch utilized in his own final service copy of the work (Vaticano Latino 3195).[42] By tradition, the blank space between Parts I and II in Vaticano Latino 3195 should have been confined to the verso of c. 52. But as we know, the blank space between *Rvf* 263 ("Arbor victoriosa triumphale") on c. 49r and *Rvf* 264 ("I' vo pensando") on c. 53r extends over six sides of ruled parchment (cc. 49v–52r) and one unruled side (c. 52v). Petrarch's extensive experience with the preparation and structure of books like the Laurentian Horace (34.1) as well as the construction of early copies of the *Rerum vulgarium fragmenta* suggest that the extensive blank space at the close of Part I in Vaticano Latino 3195 is an anomaly and potentially a space intended for additional poems that would have filled the six ruled sides of cc. 49v–52r. While the outer folded sheet of this binion, cc. 49|52, accommodated *Rvf* 260–263 and the requisite blank side (c. 52v) before the beginning of Part II on c. 53r, the internal folded sheet that is ruled but blank – the bifolium cc. 50|51 – is completely without function in the bound manuscript.[43] The anomaly was certainly noted by two subsequent manuscripts (New Haven, Beinecke M 706 and Vaticano Reginense Latino 1110) as a way of authenticating their own copies and identifying their antegraphs as copies authorized by Petrarch.[44]

The unique state of those unfinished chartae hardly reveals a Petrarch who ignores the structural standards of his time, especially in light of other decisions regarding the spatial organization of what would become one of the most influential manuscripts of early Italian literature (Vaticano Latino 3195). As I have demonstrated elsewhere, the technique of adding bifolia and binions to expand the spatial potential of a work in-progress is nowhere more evident than in the

---

42 Even Boccaccio's transcription of the earlier *Fragmentorum liber* (ca. 1362) in MS Vaticano Chigiano L v 176 makes this division clear, leaving c. 72v blank after the transcription of Part I's final "Passa la nave mia colma d'oblio" (*Fl* 174 [*Rvf* 189]), followed by 28 blank transcriptional lines on c. 72r, before the transcription of "Io vo pensando, et nel pensier m'assale" (*Fl* 175 [*Rvf* 264], vv. 1–83) on c. 73r.

43 We should recall that the fascicles of Vaticano Latino 3195 were unbound and the manuscript still *in fieri* at the time of Petrarch's death in 1374. For a complete view of the fascicles in MS Vaticano Latino 3195, see the "Petrarchive Visual Index (Arranged by Fascicles)" at: http://petrarchive.org.

44 Between Part I and Part II both Beinecke M 706 (whose antegraph is datable to 1393) and Reginense latino 1110 (a mid-fifteenth century copy) note the "four blank chartae" of their exemplars: "Que sequuntur post mortem domine Lauree scripta sunt. Ita enim *proprio codice domini Francisci annotatum est*, et *carte quatuor pretermisse vacue*" (Reginense 1110, c. 107v [my italics]).

second sections of both Part I and of Part II.⁴⁵ Petrarch's knowledge of book assembly is integral to the process of what we could call the "formation of the work's poetic knowledge". This intricate process was founded on the iron-clad repetition of visual-poetic structures that define the 'poetic page', and the component parts of the structures in which that 'page' builds its lyric and intellectual case: the folded sheet (bifolium), the gathering (from the binion [two folded sheets] to the quaternion [four folded sheets]), and the unified book. We know the original project of the *Fragmenta* at the time that Petrarch began what would become Vaticano Latino 3195 contained materially six quaternions (today's cc. 1–8 [I], 9–16 [II], 17–24 [III], 25–32 [IV], 33–40 [V], 53–60 [VI, but today's VII]) and a binion (today's cc. 61–62 and 71–72), all carefully calculated by Petrarch and his copyist to accommodate the contents of the work as it was conceived in 1367. In that plan, Petrarch applied the visual aesthetic of the integrated gatherings, making sure that the first three quaternions were bridged or linked by a canzone.⁴⁶

Like all author-copyists, Petrarch knew the material tools of his trade and how to use them. As the collection began to grow beyond the material limits of its original plan, Petrarch drew upon the experience of manuscripts such as Laurenziano 34.1 to expand the material support eventually by another quaternion (today's cc. 41–48) and three additional binions (today's cc. 49–52, 63–66, and 67–70). Just as the copyist of Laurenziano 34.1 added the bifolium to complete Horace's second satire, Petrarch himself inserted first two binions (cc. 63–66

---

45 One of the first things that must strike us about the material construction of Vaticano Latino 3195 is Petrarch's decision to use the form he found in his tenth- and eleventh-century MSS: quaternions, rather than the far more popular quinion, in which his early fourteenth-century Virgil had been constructed. For an overview of the materials of Vaticano Latino 3195, see H. Wayne Storey: The Legacy of Petrarch's Chartae. In: Ernesto Livorni/Jelena Todorović (eds.): *The Legacies of Petrarch*. Tempe, Arizona: Medieval and Renaissance Texts and Studies, forthcoming. See also H. Wayne Storey: All'interno della poetica grafico-visiva di Petrarca. In: Gino Belloni/Furio Brugnolo et al. (eds.): *Rerum vulgarium fragmenta. Codice Vat. Lat. 3195. Commentario all'edizione in fac-simile*. Roma-Padova: Antenore 2004, p. 131–171 (esp. pp. 143–148 and 160–165). Today the fascicles of Vaticano Latino 3195 are: cc. 1–8 (I), 9–16 (II), 17–24 (III), 25–32 (IV), 33–40 (V), 41–48 (VI), 49–52 (VII), 53–60 (VIII), 61–62|71–72 (IX), 63–66 (X), and 67–70 (XI). For further details see the Pet*archive* at: http://petrarchive.org ("Visual Index [Arranged by Fascicles]").
46 The canzoni are "Sì è debile il filo a cui s'attene" (*Rvf* 37): cc. 8v–9v; "Gentil mia donna i' veggio" (*Rvf* 72): cc. 16v–17r; and "Una donna più bella assai che 'l sole" (*Rvf* 119): cc. 24v–25v. The properties of the manuscript's 31-line-per-page canvas and the single page's "four sonnet principle" mark the passage from the last sonnet on c. 32v, the end of Fascicle IV, "Ponmi ove 'l sole occide i fiori e l'erba" (*Rvf* 145), to the beginning of Fascicle V on c. 33r, the sonnet "O d'ardente vertute ornata e calda" (*Rvf* 146). The overall plan for the "first project", transcribed mostly by Malpaghini and completed by Petrarch before it was sent to a rubricator in Milano in 1368, is described by H. Wayne Storey: La politica e l'antigrafo del FRAGMENTORUM LIBER (Chigiano L V 176). *Heliotropia* 12–13 (2015–2016), p. 305–330.

and then 67–70) inside the original binion of cc. 61–62 | 71–72, knowing all along that the final entry in the original plan, "Vergine bella" (*Rvf* 366), would always be the last poem of the work. Certainly one of the most fundamental lessons in the construction of the integrated book that Petrarch might have taken from his early Caroline manuscripts is also most revealing about his methods for structuring and revising books and their systems for communicating knowledge: his late manipulation of the *Fragmenta* through the opening of the work through the insertion of the final binions of the project, Fascicle VII = cc. 49–52, and Fascicle XI = cc. 67–70. As Stefano Zamponi has shown, the last four sonnets of Part I (*Rvf* 260–263) on c. 49r of the binion represent potentially – together with the added binion of cc. 67–70 – the final addendum to the *Fragmenta*; the sonnet "Cercato ò sempre solitaria vita" (*Rvf* 259) in what was the empty space of c. 48v was the last entry in the added fascicle (VI, cc. 41–48) that Petrarch had begun in 1368 in order to expand his original project for Part I eventually with an additional 60 poems (2 canzoni, 3 sestine and 55 sonnets).[47] The expansion offered by the binion's four chartae (or eight pages) in Part I would have allowed Petrarch to include numerous compositions between the allegorical "arbor [...] triumphale" of *Rvf* 263 and the contrastive, even warring, "pensieri" of *Rvf* 264, the beginning of Part II. The metaphor of Laura's "bel tesoro" (*Rvf* 263, 13) could have opened additional reflections on beauty, just as we see in the definitive turn of sonnets 260–263 on c. 49r in tone and topic toward ancient virtues of glory (*Rvf* 260, 12), fame (*Rvf* 261, 1), and infinite beauty instilled in moral refinement (*Rvf* 261, 12; *Rvf* 262, 2; *Rvf* 263, 12). The final entry in Fascicle VI of "Cercato ò sempre solitaria vita" (*Rvf* 259) and Petrarch's recall of Laura in the moral mud of Avignon (vv. 9–11) linked to his own adversarial fortune prepares us – as Petrarch will so often do in the *Fragmenta* – materially and thematically for the shift that he is undertaking in the added and ruled binion, ready for a new set of lyrics that might well have filled the next three chartae recto and verso (or six pages).

---

47 See Stefano Zamponi: Il libro del *Canzoniere*: modelli, strutture, funzioni. In: Gino Belloni/ Furio Brugnolo et al. (eds.): *Rerum vulgarium fragmenta. Codice Vat. Lat. 3195. Commentario all'edizione in fac-simile*. Roma-Padova, Antenore 2004, p. 38. Zamponi dates Petrarch's work on the end of Fascicle VI and Fascicles VII and XI to the last year and a half of Petrarch's life (Il libro del *Canzoniere*, p. 36). The expansion of the original plan begins already in Fascicle V (=cc. 33–40) with Petrarch's transcription of "Non pur quell'una bella ignuda mano" (*Rvf* 200) on c. 39v, when he abandons the idea of using guide-letters for an eventual rubricator – as he has in cc. 1–39v up to *Rvf* 199 ("O bella man, che mi destringi 'l core") – and uses simple initials at the beginning of each poem from *Rvf* 200 to *Rvf* 259 and, on c. 49r in the added binion, *Rvf* 260–263. The final total of the expansion of Part I in Fascicles V (cc. 39v–40v), VI (cc. 41–48) and VII (c. 49r) is: 64 poems: 2 canzoni (*Rvf* 206 and 207), 3 sestine (*Rvf* 214, 237 and 239) and 59 sonnets (*Rvf* 200–205, 208–213, 215–236, 238, 240–263).

When he prepared the second binion of cc. 67–70 in a service copy, he first had to fit the poems he intended to add within the material limits of the binion's four chartae. With few erasures present and the clarity of the hand and ink noticeable between the previous binion (X, cc. 63–66), it would seem that Petrarch had started by preparing a clean copy of the 23 poems he would eventually add (21 sonnets and 2 canzoni). As he had done in previous addenda in a service-copy form, Petrarch still maintains the intricate transcriptions of his visual poetics for sonnets in Fascicle XI.[48] However he must alter his transcriptional style at first slightly, adding a thirty-second line to his normally 31-line canvas to fit the 71 verses of "Quando il soave mio fido conforto" (*Rvf* 355 [revised as *Rvf* 359]) onto a single side, the recto, of c. 69. But it is the much longer "Quel' antiquo mio dolce empio signore" (*Rvf* 356 [revised 360]) that will force Petrarch to alter his transcriptional style in order to avoid adding yet additional material support to his book. As I have demonstrated, the transcription of the 157 verses of "Quel' antiquo mio dolce empio signore" on cc. 69v–70r should have occupied three sides of two chartae rather than a little over a side and a half of parchment as it now does.[49] To fit the canzone into the binion Petrarch had to forego the strict visual poetics of the canzone's prosodic sister, "Una donna più bella assai che 'l sole" (*Rvf* 119, cc. 24v–25v]) to keep from having to insert an additional bifolium (a folded sheet or two chartae), that would have meant that the book would have had a blank charta (recto and verso) among its final pages. Here in a service copy Petrarch is forced to abandon his signature layout, virtually restored in the edited form of the canzone in the Petrarchive, for a 'service version' that crammed three verses – often hendecasyllables – onto the same transcriptional line.[50]

As an intellectual and an impassioned and prolific writer-scribe, a *grafomane*, Petrarch was for most of his life a master of the gloss. But when it came to producing

---

48 Petrarch's process of organizing materially the *Fragmenta* was founded on three essential principles. The first is that Petrarch conceived of an ideal 'canvas' of 31 transcriptional lines for every charta. An essential dynamic that reinforces and is defined by that 31-line canvas is the repeated structure of two fundamental designs for the charta as a material unit as well as for the second and third principles: the placement of four sonnets per charta using seven transcriptional lines of two verses per line with a dividing line between each sonnet; and the coupling of the sestina, the only genre to be read vertically in Petrarch's system of visual poetics, with a single sonnet on a single charta. These two organizing principles account for just over 40% of the manuscript's material space of 172 sides of chartae, or pages. See H. Wayne Storey/ John Walsh/ Isabella Magni: Glossary: Visual Poetics; Sonnet; and Transcriptional Canvas. In: *Petrarchive*: http://petrarchive.org for a description of Petrarch's visual poetics applied to the sonnet. For the principles governing the other genres of the *Fragmenta*, see Storey: All'interno della poetica grafico-visiva di Petrarca, p. 152–165.
49 See Storey: All'interno della poetica grafico-visiva di Petrarca, p. 161–163.
50 For the form that Petrarch's "Quel' antiquo mio dolce empio signore" would have taken in a fair copy, see the Petrarchive (http://petrarchive.org), c. 69v.

the 'published' fair copy of one of his own works, the assignment usually went to one of his trusted copyists who could be counted on for consistency throughout the copy. For Petrarch – as well as for most medieval readers – the consistency of a single copyist across an entire manuscript lent an additional sense of unity to the book that was difficult to attain with two or more scribes, even when subsequent copyists attempted to imitate the hand of their predecessor. Once Petrarch's primary copyist abandons the project of the *Fragmenta*, clearly visible at cc. 38v and 62r in Vaticano Latino 3195, Petrarch himself will attempt to complete sections of Fascicles V and IX in a fair hand before the manuscript was sent to Milano in 1368 for rubrication.[51] Even after the manuscript's return from the rubricator, Petrarch struggles to maintain his principle of consistency of hands in the preparation of the fair copy. His most famous attempt is the recycling the rounded section of the rubricated gothic D of "Donna mi vene spesso ne la mente" on c. 26r to produce, over the erasure of the rest of the ballata, the madrigal "Or vedi, Amor".[52]

In spite of Petrarch's efforts, a glance at any of the chartae of Fascicle VI (cc. 41–48) or IX (cc. 61–62/71–72) tells us that the character of the fascicles has changed from 'fair copy' to 'service copy'. Even on a charta that has undergone what is normally the final phase of manuscript production (the addition of rubrication and colored initials) such as 39r, we see the multiple strata of erasures and experimentation that mark many of the clearly service-copy sections of the manuscript. From the entire palimpsest of "L'aura gentil, che rasserena i poggi" (*Rvf* 194) to the multiple layers of erasures and rewritings in "L'aura serena che fra verdi fronde" (*Rvf* 196) and "L'aura celeste che 'n quel verde lauro" (*Rvf* 197) we see Petrarch returning to erase, emend and revise in a hand designed to communicate more to a copyist who will then prepare a clean, fair copy of the work than to a reader who would have to study carefully Petrarch's text (see Plate 10).

---

51 See especially cc. 38v–39v and c. 62r-v in Vaticano Latino 3195. On c. 38v, only "Una candida cerva sopra l'erba" (*Rvf* 190) is in the hand of the primary copyist. The sonnets from "Sì come eterna vita è veder Dio" (*Rvf* 191; c. 38v) to "O bella man, che mi destringi 'l core" (*Rvf* 199; c. 39v) are in Petrarch's hand. On c. 62r, "Tranquillo porto avea mostrato amore" and "Al cader d'una pianta che si svelse" (*Rvf* 317 and 318) are in the primary copyist's hand, while "I dì miei più leggier' che nesun cervo", "Sento l'aura mia anticha e i dolci colli" (*Rvf* 319 and 320) are in Petrarch's hand, as is "È questo 'l nido in che la mia fenice" (*Rvf* 321) on c. 69v. All are rubricated. However, the variation in *ductus*, ink and even the pen used for transcription, even in the short space from "Di dì in dì vo cangiando il viso e 'l pelo" (*Rvf* 195) on c. 39r to "O bella man" (*Rvf* 199) on c. 39v, demonstrates the inconsistency of Petrarch's more formal, or "fair", hand, that did not match the primary copyist's regular *ductus*.

52 For an analysis of the scribal process and its implications, see H. Wayne Storey: Mobile Texts and Local Options: Geography and Editing. In: *Textual Cultures: Texts, Contexts, Interpretation* 8, 1 (2013), p. 10–20.

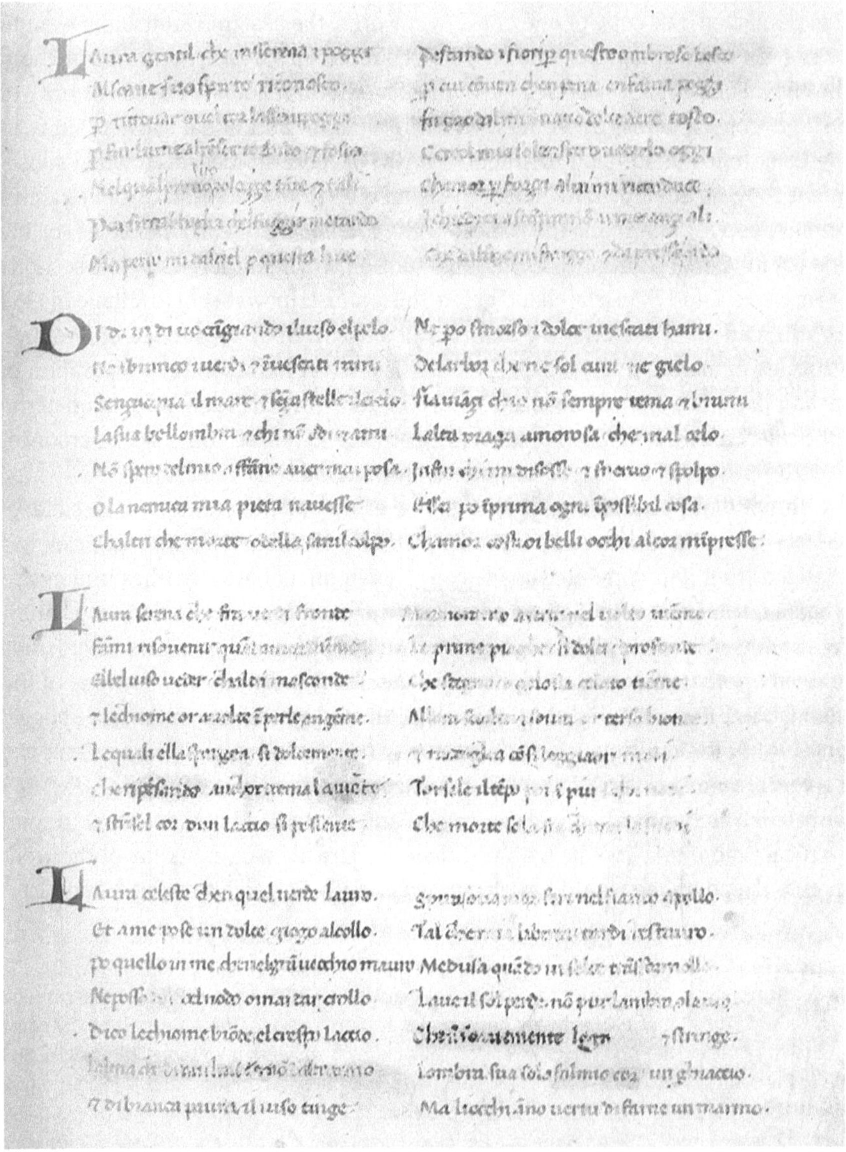

Plate 10: Vatican City, Biblioteca Apostolica, Latino 3195, c. 39r; published with the kind permission of the Biblioteca Apostolica Vaticana

On c. 39r we are virtually at the same level of multiple interventions by the poet as we see in heavily reworked versions of poems in Petrarch's earlier autograph manuscript of draft copies of poems with numerous cross-outs and emendations (Vaticano Latino 3196). Most revealing perhaps is the case of *Rvf* 197,

"L'aura celeste che 'n quel verde lauro", originally drafted as "L'aura amorosa in quel bel verde lauro" at the bottom of c. 2r of Vaticano Latino 3196 (see Plate 11). A careful examination of the poem's extensive experimentation and revision in Latino 3196 and the accompanying notation "tr*anscriptus per me*" (transcribed by me) suggest that Petrarch might have decoded his complex marginalia and final wishes for the poem and transferred it to c. 39r (Plate 10).[53]

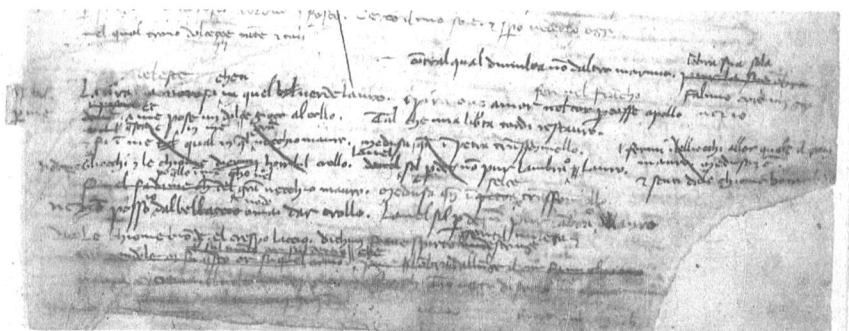

Plate 11: Vatican City, Biblioteca Apostolica, Latino 3196, c. 2r (detail); published with the kind permission of the Biblioteca Apostolica Vaticana

But, in fact, there are still at least two phases of revision that will take place between what we could call a final form suggested by Latino 3196 and the last version that Petrarch leaves us on c. 39r of Latino 3195. Even in the drafts of Latino 3196 Petrarch considers two relatively different versions of the second quartina, especially vv. 5 and 7.

The first version of Latino 3195, what should be a clean copy for rubrication, shows additional alterations, such as in the opening of vv. 7 and 9 ("Pò quello in me [...]" and "Ne posso [dal] bel nodo [...]"), not found in the final draft of Latino 3196, but also at least a second round of revisions that includes two major and two smaller but pivotal erasures and emendations respectively in vv. 10 and 11 and in vv. 7 and 12 (see Plate 12). In v. 10 Petrarch adapts part of a later emendation, "lega et stringe", but alters significantly the syntax of vv. 9 and 10, eliminating the "spirto gentil" and intensifying the power of v. 9's "crespo laccio, / Che sì soavemente

---

[53] For a careful reconstruction of Latino 3196's layers of cross-outs, experiments and revisions, see Laura Paolino: *Francesco Petrarca, Il codice degli abbozzi. Edizione e storia del manoscritto Vaticano latino 3196*. Milano-Napoli: Ricciardi 2000, p. 188–189. Now published online in digital form by the Vatican Library, Latino 3196 can be best examined by consulting the Vatican Library site. For c. 2r of Latino 3196, see: http://digi.vatlib.it/view/MSS_Vat.lat.3196/0011/ (consulted March 24, 2016).

lega et stringe / L'alma, che d'umiltate [...]"; the erasure of the entire v. 11 clarifies the object of the two verbs in a powerful enjambment. Notably, the erasure in v. 7 after "Ne posso" destabilizes the parchment and the reading "dal", and eliminates the ascender of the 'b' of "bel".[54]

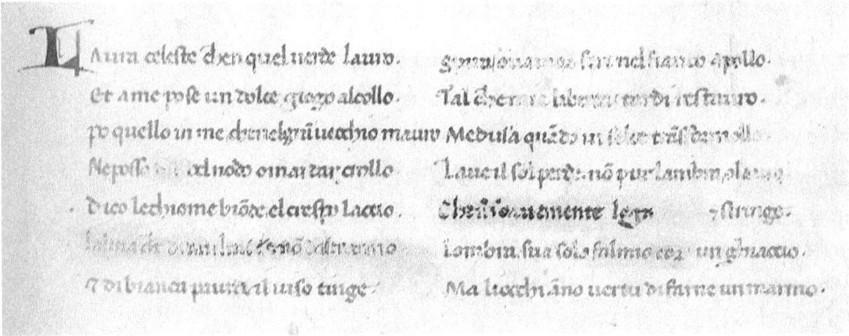

Plate 12: Vatican City, Biblioteca Apostolica, Latino 3195, c. 39r (detail); published with the kind permission of the Biblioteca Apostolica Vaticana

These microscopic details bear witness to a state of Petrarch's Latino 3195 that we can only call, even in this section that has been rubricated, a service copy that abandons the consistent aesthetics – Petrarch's and his contemporaries' – of the fair copy. While many medieval fair copies demonstrate scribal interventions to correct errors, seldom do we find a manuscript such as Vaticano Latino 3195 that has become a site of authorial experimentation on so many levels: from the reordering of compositions and extensive erasures and revisions to the material expansion of the macrotext itself through the addition of quaternions and binions. It is a unique site that draws upon Petrarch's extensive and attentive experience with earlier Latin codices, such as Bodmer 146 and his Laurentian Horace (34.1), and that model book that supplied him his knowledge of Virgil and Statius, Ambrosiano A 79 inf. Sala Prefetto 10/27, and became one of the precious sites of his own memory, both intellectual and personal, in which he recorded not only his observations on key passages of both Virgil and his commentator Servius, but also where he recorded the dates of the deaths of his most beloved friends and, as we know, of Laura.

---

[54] While Modigliani reads "dal" over an erasure, but my own examination of the erasure suggests that "dal" is, like the 'b' of "bel", partially – and mistakenly – erased. See Ettore Modigliani: *Il canzoniere di Francisco Petrarca riprodotto letteralmente dal Cod. Vat. Lat. 3195, con tre fotoincisioni*. Roma: Società Filologica Romana 1904, *ad loc.* (c. 39r).

Bibliography

Primary literature

Manuscripts and Early Printed Sources

Bloomington (Indiana)	Lilly Library	Poole 26
Cesena	Biblioteca Malatestiana	Ms. s.IV.2
Cologny (Geneva)	Bodmer Library	MS 146
El Escorial (Madrid)	Real Biblioteca del Monastero de san Lorenzo	e.III.23
Firenze	Biblioteca Laurenziana	Martelli 12
		Pluteo 34.1
	Biblioteca nazionale centrale	Banco rari 37, *olim* II.I.23
		Fondo principale II iii 47
		Magliabechiano Cl. VI 143
	Biblioteca Riccardiana	2533
London	British Library	Harley 2493
Milano	Biblioteca Ambrosiana	A 79 inf. Sala Prefetto 10/27 (*Olim* A 49 inf. 1)
Padova	Biblioteca Universitaria	1490
Paris	Bibliothèque nationale de France	Lat. 1994
Vatican City,	Biblioteca Apostolica Vaticana	Chigiano L v 176
		Latino 1411
		Latino 2193
		Latino 3195
		Latino 3196
		Latino 3793
		Urbinate latino 161

Texts

Alighieri, Dante: *La Commedia secondo l'antica vulgata*. Edited by Giorgio Petrocchi. 4 vols. Milano: Mondadori 1966–1967 (Edizione nazionale delle opere di D.A., 7).
Francisci Petrarcae: *Vergilianus Codex, ad Publii Vergilii Maronis diem natalem Bis Millesimum Celebrandum Quam Simillime Expressus Atque in Lucem Editus Ivvantibus Bibliotheca Ambrosiana et Regia in Insubribus Academia*. Mediolani (Milano): Hoeplianis 1930.
Francesco Petrarca: *Le familiari*. Ed. by Vittorio Rossi/ Umberto Bosco. Vols. 1–4. Firenze: Sansoni 1933–1942 (*Edizione nazionale delle opere di F. P.*, 10–13).
Francesco Petrarca: *Letters on Familiar Matters. Rerum familiarium libri XVII–XXIV*. Trans. by Aldo Bernardo. 3 vols. Baltimore-London: The Johns Hopkins University Press 1985.
Francesco Petrarca: *Letters of Old Age. Rerum senilium libri I–XVIII*, 2 vols. Trans. by Aldo Bernardo/ Saul Levin et al. Baltimore-London: The Johns Hopkins University Press 1992.
Francesco Petrarca: *Rerum vulgarium fragmenta: Facsimile del codice autografo Vaticano Latino 3195*. Edited by Gino Belloni/ Furio Brugnolo/ H. Wayne Storey/ Stefano Zamponi. Padova-Roma: Antenore 2003–2004 (Itinera Erudita, 5).
Pétrarque: *Lettres de la vieillesse: Rerum senilium, édition critique*. Ed. by Elvira Nota. 5 vols. Paris: Les Belles Lettres 2002–2013.
Statius: *Achilleid*. Ed. with introd., apparatus criticus, and notes by Oswald Ashton Wentworth. Cambridge: Cambridge University Press 1954.

Secondary Literature

Monographs and Anthologies

Baglio, Marco/ Antonietta Nebuloni Testa/ Marco Petoletti: *Le postille del Virgilio Ambrosiano*. 2 vols. Roma-Padova: Antenore 2006.
Ballarini, Marco/ Giuseppe Frasso/ Carla Maria Monti (eds.): *Francesco Petrarca. Manoscritti e libri a stampa della Biblioteca Ambrosiana*. Milano: Scheiwiller 2004.
Clogan, Paul M. (ed.): *The Medieval Achilleid of Statius*. Leiden: Brill 1968.
Galbiati, Giovanni: *Il libro che il Petrarca ebbe più caro*. Milano: U. Allegretti di Campi, 1957.
Gilissen, Léon: *Prolégomènes à la codicologie. Recherches sur la construction des cahiers et la mise en page des manuscrits médiévaux*. Gand [Ghent]: Éditions Scientifiques Story-Scientia 1977.
Miles, Gary B.: *Virgil's Georgics: a New Interpretation*. Berkeley: University of California Press 1980.
Modigliani, Ettore: *Il canzoniere di Francisco Petrarca riprodotto letteralmente dal Cod. Vat. Lat. 3195, con tre fotoincisioni*. Roma: Società Filologica Romana 1904.
Nolhac, Pierre de: *Pétrarque et l'humanisme*. 2 vols. Paris: Libraire Honoré Champion 1907.
Paolino, Laura: *Francesco Petrarca, Il codice degli abbozzi. Edizione e storia del manoscritto Vaticano latino 3196*. Milano-Napoli: Ricciardi 2000.
Petrucci, Armando: *La scrittura del Petrarca*. Città del Vaticano: Biblioteca Apostolica Vaticana 1967.

Rostagno, Enrico: *L'Orazio Laurenziano già di Francesco Petrarca.* Roma: Libreria dello Stato 1933.

Storey, H. Wayne: *Transcription and Visual Poetics in the Early Italian Lyric.* New York-London: Garland 1993.

Articles and Papers

Ahern, John/Good-bye, Bologna: Johannes Andreae and *Familiares* IV 15 and 16. In: Teodolinda Barolini/Wayne Storey (eds.): *Petrarch and the Textual Origins of Interpretation.* Leiden-Boston: Brill 2007, p. 185–204.

Antonelli, Roberto: Canzoniere Vaticano Latino 3793. In: Alberto Asor Rosa (ed.): *Letteratura italiana, le opere, 1: Dalle origini al Cinquecento.* Torino: Einaudi 1982, p. 27–44.

Arduini, Beatrice: Assigning the 'Pieces' of Dante's *Convivio*: the Compiler's Notes in the Earliest Extant Copy. In: *Textual Cultures: Texts, Contexts, Interpretation* 3, 2 (2008), p. 17–29.

Baglio, Marco: Le postille di Petrarca al Virgilio. In: Marco Ballarini/Giuseppe Frasso et al. (eds.): *Francesco Petrarca. Manoscritti e libri a stampa della Biblioteca Ambrosiana.* Milano: Scheiwiller 2004, p. 29–39.

Berté, Monica: Giovanni Malpaghini copista di Petrarca? In: *Cultura neolatina* 75, 1–2 (2015), p. 205–216.

Bertelli, Sandro: Nota sul canzoniere provenzale P e sul Martelli 12. In: *Medioevo e Rinascimento* 18, n.s. 16 (2004), p. 369–375.

Billanovich, Giuseppe: Dalle prime alle ultime letture del Petrarca. In: *Petrarca ad Arquà. Atti del Convegno degli studi nel VI centenario (1370–1374) Arquà Petrarca, 6–8 novembre 1970.* Ed. by Giuseppe Billanovich/ Giuseppe Frasso. Padova: Antenore 1975, p. 13–50.

Billanovich, Giuseppe: Il Petrarca e i retori latini minori. In: *Italia medioevale e umanistica* 5 (1962), p. 103–164.

Billanovich, Giuseppe: Petrarch and the Textual Tradition of Livy. In: *Journal of the Warburg and Courtauld Institutes*, 14 (1951), p. 137–208.

Billanovich, Giuseppe: Il Virgilio del giovane Petrarca. In: *Lectures médiévales de Virgile. Actes du colloque de Rome (25–28 octobre 1982).* Rome: École Française de Rome 1985, p. 49–64.

Bouloux, Nathalie: Pétrarque et les marges des manuscrits géographiques. In: Maurice Brock/ Francesco Furlan et al. (eds.): *La Bibliothèque de Pétrarque: Livres et auteurs autour d'un humaniste. Actes du IIe Congrès international sciences et arts, philologie et politique à la Renaissance 27–29 novembre 2003.* Turnhout: Brepols 2011, p. 61–76.

Brugnolo, Furio: Libro d'autore e forma-canzoniere: Implicazioni grafico-visive nell'originale dei *Rerum vulgarium fragmenta*. In: Gino Belloni/ Furio Brugnolo et al. (eds): *Rerum vulgarium fragmenta. Codice Vat. Lat. 3195. Commentario all'edizione in fac-simile.* Roma-Padova: Antenore 2004, p. 105–29.

Castellani, Arrigo: Sul codice Laurenziano Martelliano 12. In: Leonella Coglievina/ Domenico De Robertis (eds.): *Sotto il segno di Dante. Scritti in onore di Francesco Mazzoni.* Firenze: Le Lettere 1998, p. 85–97.

De Angelis, Violetta: Petrarca, i suoi libri e i commenti medievali ai classici. In: *Acme* 52 (1999), p. 49–82.

De Angelis, Violetta: Petrarca, Stazio, Liegi. In: *Studi petrarcheschi* n.s. 2 (1985), p. 53–84.
De Robertis, Domenico: A quale tradizione appartiene il manoscritto delle rime di Dante letto dal Petrarca? In: *Studi petrarcheschi* n.s. 2 (1985), p. 131–157.
Dotti, Ugo: Le due "biblioteche" di Francesco Petrarca. In: Maurice Brock/ Francesco Furlan et al. (eds.): *La Bibliothèque de Pétrarque: Livres et auteurs autour d'un humaniste. Actes du IIe Congrès international sciences et arts, philologie et politique à la Renaissance 27–29 novembre 2003*. Turnhout: Brepols 2011, p. 131–141.
Fera, Vincenzo: La filologia del Petrarca e i fondamenti della filologia umanistica. In: *Quaderni petrarcheschi* 9-10 (1992–1993), p. 367–391.
Folena, Gianfranco: Üeberlieferungsgeschicte der altitalienischen Literatur. In: *Geschichte der Textüberlieferung der antiken und mittelalterlichen Literatur* 2 (1964), p. 319–538.
Magnaldi, Giuseppina: I codici J (ψ) e il testo delle *Partitiones oratoriae* di Cicerone. In: *Sandalion* 32-33 (2009–2010), p. 57–70.
Mercati, Giovanni: *Opere minori*. 5 vols. Città del Vaticano: Biblioteca Apostolica Vaticana 1937 (Studi e testi, 80).
Opsomer, Carmélia: Le Scribe, l'enlumineur et le commanditaire: Àpropos des *Tacuina sanitatis* illustrés. In: Herrad Spillingas (ed.): *La collaboration dans la production de l'écrit médiéval: Actes du XIIIe Colloque du Comité international de paléographie latine (Weingarten, 22–25 September 2000)*. Paris: École nationale des Chartes 2003, p. 183–92.
Pellegrin, Élisabeth: Nouveaux manuscrits annotés par Pétrarque à la Bibliothèque nationale de Paris. In: *Scriptorium* 5, 2 (1951), p. 265–278.
Pellegrin, Élisabeth: Description of Bodmer 146. http://www.e-codices.unifr.ch/en/list/one/cb/0146 ([1982] consulted 8 June 2014).
Petoletti, Marco: Le postille del Petrarca a Servio. In: Marco Ballarini/Giuseppe Frasso et al. (eds.): *Francesco Petrarca. Manoscritti e libri a stampa della Biblioteca Ambrosiana*. Milano: Scheiwiller 2004, p. 43–50.
Picone, Michelangelo: Dentro la biblioteca di Petrarca. In: Maurice Brock/ Francesco Furlan et al. (eds.). *La Bibliothèque de Pétrarque: Livres et auteurs autour d'un humaniste. Actes du IIe Congrès international sciences et arts, philologie et politique à la Renaissance 27–29 novembre 2003*. Turnhout: Brepols 2011, p. 21–34.
Pomaro, Gabriella: I testi e il Testo. In: Placella, Vincenzo/ Sebastiano Martelli (eds.): *I moderni ausili all'Ecdotica: Atti del Convegno Internazionale di studi (Fisciano- Vietri sul Mare-Napoli, 27–31 ottobre 1990)*. Napoli: Edizioni scientifiche Italiane 1994, p. 193–213.
Ratti, Achille: Ancora del celebre codice manoscritto delle opera di Vergilio già di Francesco Petrarca ed ora della Biblioteca Ambrosiana. In: *Francesco Petrarca e la Lombardia*. Milano: Hoepli 1904, p. 217–242.
Robinson, Pamela: The "Booklet": a Self-Contained Unit in Composite Manuscripts. In: *Codicologia* 3 (1980), p. 46–69.
Santoni, Francesca: Copisti-editores di manoscritti giuridici: 1. Il codice Vaticano latino 1406 del *Digestum Vetus* e l'edizione del testo fra copisti e glossatori. In: Herrad Spillingas (ed.): *La collaboration dans la production de l'écrit médiéval: Actes du XIIIe Colloque du Comité international de paléographie latine (Weingarten, 22–25 September 2000)*. Paris: École nationale des Chartes 2003, p. 23–249.
Savino, Giancarlo: L'autografo virtuale della *Commedia*. In: *"Per correr miglior acque…". Bilanci e prospettive degli studi danteschi alle soglie del nuovo millennio*. 2 vols. Roma: Salerno Editrice 2001, II, p. 1099–1110.

Storey, H. Wayne: All'interno della poetica grafico-visiva di Petrarca. In: Gino Belloni/Furio Brugnolo et al. (eds.): *Rerum vulgarium fragmenta. Codice Vat. Lat. 3195. Commentario all'edizione in fac-simile*. Roma-Padova: Antenore 2004, p. 131–171.

Storey, H. Wayne: Di libello in libro: problemi materiali nella poetica di Monte Andrea e Dante In: Furio Brugnolo/ Gianfelice Peron (eds.): *Da Guido Guinizzelli a Dante. Nuove prospettive sulla lirica del Duecento*. Padova: Poligrafo 2004, p. 271–290.

Storey, H. Wayne: Mobile Texts and Local Options: Geography and Editing. In: *Textual Cultures: Texts, Contexts, Interpretation* 8, 1 (2013), p. 6–20.

Storey, H. Wayne: Method, History, and Theory in Material Philology. In: Marc van der Poel (ed.): *Neo-Latin Philology, Old Tradition, New Approaches. Proceedings of a Conference held at the Radboud University, Nijmegen, 26–27 October 2010* (Supplementa of Humanistica Lovaniensia). Leuven: Leuven University Press 2014, p. 25–47.

Storey, H. Wayne: La politica e l'antigrafo del FRAGMENTORUM LIBER (Chigiano L v 176). In: *Heliotropia* 12–13 (2015–2016), p. 305–330.

Storey, H. Wayne/ John Walsh/ Isabella Magni. *Petrarchive*: http://petrarchive.org ([2013-] consulted 2 January 2016).

Tristano, Caterina: Le postille del Petrarca nel ms. Vat. lat. 2193 (Apuleio, Frontino, Vegezio, Palladio). In: *Italia medioevale e umanistica* 17 (1974), p. 365–468.

Ullman, Berthold Louis: Petrarch's Favorite Books. In his: *Studies in the Italian Renaissance*, 2nd ed. Roma: Edizioni di Storia e Letteratura 1973, p. 113–133.

Zamponi, Stefano. 2004. Il libro del *Canzoniere*: modelli, strutture, funzioni. In: Gino Belloni/ Furio Brugnolo et al. (eds.): *Rerum vulgarium fragmenta. Codice Vat. Lat. 3195. Commentario all'edizione in fac-simile*. Roma-Padova, Antenore 2004, p. 13–72.

Karl Enenkel
Sacra solitudo. Petrarch's authorship and the *locus sacer*

De vita solitaria figures among Petrarch's most important and most influential autobiographical writings;[1] it represents an extended meditation on his life-style that comprises a mixture of a more or less realistic self-definition, the powerful description of an ideal, a highly styled self-image,[2] some strong artistic claims, a grim self-defence as an intellectual, and also a couple of social pretentions. Already from the preface it appears that Petrarch identified himself completely with the life-style that is the topic of the work. The *vita solitaria* is *his* life-style, *he* is the *solitarius*, he knows the topic thoroughly, and by experience, and he claims that he is so much in it that it comes automatically to his mind.[3] If one looks at Petrarch's works one gets the impression that the life-style topic, the *vita solitaria*, functions either as the starting point or as the core business of any meditation

---

[1] For Petrarch as an autobiographical writer cf. Karl Enenkel: *Die Erfindung des Menschen. Die Autobiographik des frühneuzeitlichen Humanismus von Petrarca bis Lipsius*. Berlin-New York: Walter de Gruyter 2008, p. 40–126 (detailed bibliographical annotations and further reading on p. 865–871); for the autobiographical content of *De vita solitaria* see Francesco Petrarca: *De vita solitaria. Buch 1. Kritische Textausgabe und ideengeschichtlicher Kommentar*. Edited by Karl Enenkel. Leiden-New York-Köln-Kopenhagen: Brill 1990, *passim*; and, for the success of *De vita solitaria*, Karl Enenkel: Die monastische Petrarca-Rezeption: zur Autorisierung über den Widmungsempfänger und zu anderen Bedingungen des Erfolgs von *De vita solitaria* in spätmittelalterlichen Klöstern. In: *Neulateinisches Jahrbuch* 14 (2012), p. 27–251. For *De vita solitaria*, cf. also Armando Maggi: You will be my solitude. In: Victoria Kirkham/Armando Maggi (eds.): *Petrarch. A Guide to the Complete Works*. Chicago and London: The University of Chicago Press 2012, p. 179–195; Peter von Moos: Les solitudes de Pétrarque. Liberté intellectuelle et activisme urbain dans la crise du XIVe siècle. In: *Rassegna europea di letteratura italiana* 7 (1996), p. 23–58; Sandra Isetta: Il linguaggio ascetico di Francesco Petrarca nel *De vita solitaria*. In: *Studi umanistici piceni* 23 (2003), p. 75–94; and the English translation of the work by Jacob Zeitlin: *The Life of Solitude by Francis Petrarch*. Urbana, University of Illinois Press 1924.
[2] For its ingredients, cf. Enenkel: *Die Erfindung des Menschen*, p. 137–141. For a much extended version of this contribution cf. Karl A.E. Enenkel: Petrarch's Construction of the Sacred Solitary Place in *De vita solitaria* and Other Writings. With an Appendix: Bucolicum Carmen 1. In: Karl A.E. Enenkel - Christine Göttler (eds.): *Spaces, Places, and Times of Solitude in Late Medieval and Early Modern Europe*. Leiden-Boston: E.J. Brill 2018 (Intersections. Interdisciplinary Studies in Early Modern Culture, 55).
[3] Cf. Petrarca: *De vita solitaria, Buch 1*, p. 176–181 (Die persönliche Erfahrung als Grundlage von *De vita solitaria*); cf. Ibid., I, 1, 4–5: "In hoc autem tractatu magna ex parte solius experientie ducatum habui nec alium ducem querens nec oblatum admissurus liberiore quidem gressu [...] sequor animum meum quam aliena vestigia. [...] A me nunc audies, quod occurrit ex tempore."

∂ Open access. © 2018 Karl Enenkel, published by De Gruyter. [CC BY-NC-ND] This work is licensed under the Creative Commons Attribution-NonCommercial-NoDerivatives 4.0 license.
https://doi.org/10.1515/9783110419306-003

or self-reflection. Take for example his first prose treatise, the *Rerum memorandarum libri*: it is no coincidence that its first chapter deals with the solitary life (*De otio et solitudine*): "Sed michi cuncta versanti cum id solum temporis vixisse videar, quod otiosus et solus vixi, visum est non aliunde quam ab otio et solitudine potissimum ordiri [...]." [Because when thinking thoroughly about my whole life, it seemed to me that I was truly living only when I lived in solitude and when I enjoyed leisure, solitude and leisure seemed to me to be the best starting point.][4] Therefore, the solitary life is for him "the very source of all topics," the "primus dicendorum fons" from which the whole "narration" or subsequent work will flow.[5] The preface of Petrarch's second prose treatise, *De vita solitaria*, starts with a similar argument. When discussing about what kind of topic Petrarch is going to write to his dedicatee, bishop Philippe de Cabassoles, he says: "Quid vero nunc prius ex me speres quam quod et in ore et in corde semper habui et ipse, qui modo sub oculis est, locus hortatur?" – [What would you rather expect of me than the topic I always had in mind and I was always talking about, the topic which the very place suggests I am looking at, just now when I am writing those lines?][6] This time, of course, the solitary life is not only the first part of a meditation, but its main theme. Its initial part, however, is revealing, since it displays a remarkable *ritual*: the ritual of a new intellectual who – when he starts to write – engages in a complex self-assurance and self-reflection;[7] a self-reflection he obviously considered necessary when coming out, so to say, as an author, who longed to be taken serious by his audience.

The last wish, of course, may seem not very spectacular; it is probably the aim of all authors. In Petrarch's case, however, the spectacular thing is the *kind* of ritual he engages in, its ingredients or elements, and the way in which these ingredients function. When he is going to appear as an author, Petrarch always first creates a kind of *sacred space* or *place*; a space and place that will legitimate his authorship; that will safe-guard the power of his *inventio*; and that will persuade his readers to open up their mind for the poet's new and unusual inventions. As he says for example to Philippe de Cabassoles about his authorship: he is always

---

[4] Petrarca: *Rerum memorandarum libri* I, 1, 1. Edited by Giuseppe Billanovich. Florence: Sansoni 1943, p. 3.
[5] Petrarca: *Rerum memorandarum libri* I, 1, 2.
[6] Cf. Petrarca: *De vita solitaria* I, prohemium 8. All translations from Petrarch's *De vita solitaria* are my own.
[7] For the problem of authorship in Neo-Latin literature cf. Karl A.E. Enenkel, *Die Stiftung von Autorschaft in der neulateinischen Literatur (ca. 1350–ca. 1650). Zur autorisierenden und wissensvermittelnden Funktion von Widmungen, Vorworttexten, Autorporträts und Dedikationsbildern*, Leiden-Boston: Brill 2014; for Petrarch esp. p. 32, 48–50, 93, 112, 142, 169–174, 176, 187, 234, 240, 257–258, 265–266, 280–287, 289, 298–301, 303–311, 313, 335, 356, 368, 372, 378, 386–396, 404 etc.

going to present "new things" [res novae] that are "hard to understand" [durasque et rigidas], full of "unusual ideas" [peregrinae sententiae]; ideas that have nothing to do with the mind-set and the opinions of common people, or generally accepted opinions of average intellectuals.[8] I suspect that it is connected with this special type of authorship that Petrarch always constructs a sacred place for the author. In the following paper, I will analyse this construction, and have a closer look at its elements and the way in which they function. I will depart from the treatise *De vita solitaria*, since this work offers a blueprint of Petrarch's authorship.

Now what are the elements of Petrarch's sacred space where his authorship can take place? First, its sacrality seems to have something in common with some ancient sanctuaries. The *locus sacer* of Petrarch's authorship is always located outside cities or towns, crowded and narrow places; places where many people would come together, where one would expect manifold social interaction, and noise. In a sense, Horace's "Odi profanum volgus et arceo" from *Carmina* III, 1 could function as a motto for Petrarch's self-definition as an author. Petrarch claims that his authorship functions only in a place far away from the profane *vulgus* or the town people. Petrarch deliberately writes, as he indicates in the preface of *De vita solitaria*, for a small elite of selected readers, *paucis lectoribus*, another quote from Horace (*Satires* I, 10, 74). Horace indeed functions as one of the main examples for Petrarch's authorship: in the 2nd book of *De vita solitaria* he uses Horace, *Letter* II, 6 as a blueprint, and interprets line 77 as a "universal rule" of authorship: "Scriptorum chorus omnis amat nemus et fugit urbes" [All writers love the woods and flee from the towns.][9] Interestingly, Petrarch takes the line as a "universalis regula," although he must have understood the ironical and satirical tendency of Horace's letter, which is a playful farewell poem as a lyrical poet. Already in his *Epistole metrice*, Petrarch had imitated Horace's line as a golden rule: "Silva placet Musis, urbs est inimica poetis" [The Muses love woods, poets hate towns.][10] In *De vita solitaria*, as yet another form of self-assurance, Petrarch includes this verse too.[11] With this authoritative and exclusive golden rule, Petrarch deauthorizes urban writers. In the 14th century, such a position seems quite remarkable, especially if one takes into account the

---

8 Cf. *De vita solitaria* I, prohemium 2: "[....] posse tibi res meas, pater optime, placere, que ut paucis placeant, laboro, quando, ut vides, sepe res novas tracto durasque et rigidas peregrinasque sententias et ab omnia moderantis vulgi sensibus atque auribus abhorrentes."
9 Francesco Petrarca: *Prose*. Edited by Guido Martellotti. Milano-Napoli: Ricciardi 1955, p. 530.
10 Petrarca: *Epistole metrice* II, 3. In: *Francisci Petrarchae [...] Opera quae extant omnia [...]*. Basel: Henrichus Petri 1554 (Rept. Ridgewood New Jersey: The Gregg Press 1965), p. 1344. Cf. Enenkel: *Die Erfindung des Menschen*, p. 57–58.
11 Petrarca: *Prose*, p. 530.

urbanization of the 12th and 13th centuries, and the important changes in intellectual life that took place in this period: for example the rise of the universities and the canon schools – both situated in towns; and the rise of the urban mendicant orders which participated in education and intellectual life; and, in the 13th and 14th century, of course the rise of vernacular literature.

Petrarch's location of the writer as being outside of towns is a highly ideological statement. He seems to deeply disagree with the whole development of intellectual life from the 12th century up to the middle of the 14th century. It includes a clear stand, inter alia, against scholastic philosophy and theology, Aristotelianism, medicine and physics, jurisprudence, university education in general, lawyers and notaries, teachers of grammar schools, secretaries and other administrators of towns, the mendicant orders, teachers and preachers alike, and vernacular literature. Furthermore, it also included an ideological statement against Avignon as the place of the papal curia. It means that Petrarch, as an author, locates himself deliberately outside of those intellectual mainstream developments. This is remarkable indeed. Furthermore, in Petrarch's works, Avignon appears many times as the negative exemplum par excellence of a town: narrow, extremely crowded, and full of people who came there from all over Europe, very dirty and noisy, and so on. Furthermore, Avignon appears as the symbol of the ongoing moral decay Petrarch ascribed to his times. And, as one can read *ad nauseam* in the *Epistole sine nomine*, Petrarch associated the town Avignon with an elaborate eschatological ideology.[12] This town is the place where the Antichrist will appear, and the eschatological feats will happen.[13] This paper does not allow me to go deeper into this matter, but is necessary to mention it as frame-work for Petrarch's anti-urban position. It indicates that for him the town was the contrary of the sacred place. A place polluted by sinful behaviour and moral decay, a swamp of sins, hell on earth.

Second, Petrarch constructed his sacred space as "free," "liber," in more than one sense.[14] This construction unites juridical, social, ideological, and spiritual

---

12 Cf. Paul Piur: *Petrarcas "Buch ohne Namen" und die päpstliche Kurie*. Halle: M. Niemeyer 1925, passim.
13 Cf. Ibid., p. 6–48; for the concept of the "Antichrist" cf. Gregory C. Jenks: *The Origins and Early Development of the Antichrist Myth*. Berlin: Walter de Gruyter 1991; Gregory C. Jenks: Antichrist., In: *Theologische Realenzyklopädie*. Band 3. Berlin: Walter de Gruyter 1978, p. 20–50; Horst D. Rauh: *Das Bild des Antichrist im Mittelalter. Von Tyconius zum deutschen Symbolismus*. Münster: Aschendorff 1973; Klaus Aichele: *Das Antichristdrama des Mittelalters, der Reformation und Gegenreformation*. Den Haag: Nijhoff 1974; Ulrich Knefelkamp/ Frank Martin (eds): *Der Antichrist. Die Glasmalereien der Marienkirche in Frankfurt (Oder)*. Leipzig: Edition Leipzig, 2008; and Friedrich Baethgen: *Der Engelpapst: Idee und Erscheinung*, Leipzig: Koehler & Amelang 1943.
14 Cf. Petrarca: *De vita solitaria, Buch 1*, p. 249, 297, 354–355, 364, 373, 457, 481, 483, 494–495; for this aspect, see also von Moos: Les solitudes de Pétrarque.

aspects. It was not enough that the *locus sacer* was outside the town: it had to be a *locus liber* in every sense. Petrarch served powerful people, such as Cardinal Giovanni Colonna. If he would have stayed in a villa or castle of one of his lords, Petrarch would not have considered himself "free." The author Petrarch regarded it of the highest importance to be *in his own place*, and in the prefaces of his works, he more than once emphasizes this aspect explicitly. In his autobiography, *Epistola posteritati*, he claims that he did not live in the palaces of his powerful Maecenases, but that it seemed as if they lived in his place.[15] In the preface of *De vita solitaria*, a similar claim occurs, when he focuses attention to the fact that his addressee, Philippe de Cabassoles, who was in fact the Lord of Vaucluse, stayed a fortnight in Petrarch's house.[16] Therefore, it is clear that Petrarch's sacred place cannot be an ordinary monastery which would imply the rule of obedience to the abbot, the rule of *stabilitas loci*, and a carefully structured schedule of the day with prayer, manual labour, meal and sleep. Petrarch's exemplary intellectual, the *solitarius*, prays the hours, but not in a chorus with others, he eats whenever he likes, and he does not engage in any manual labour such as for example the Benedictine rule prescribes. If the author is not completely "liber," he is unable to write, and he will never receive godly inspiration. Rules are profane and kill free invention, the source of true authorship.

According to this view, Petrarch's house in Vaucluse could very well function as a sacred place of authorship, and, in a more practical sense, it certainly served as place of writing. However, in *De vita solitaria*, Petrarch only rarely mentions his house, and he downplays the importance of the *studiolo*, whereas later humanists would celebrate the process of writing as a ritual located in their *studioli*.[17] If one takes into account Petrarch's manner of writing, i. e. to include many quotations from classical authors, it is clear that he must have written his works where he could consult his library. In *De vita solitaria*, however, the intellectual is mostly

---

15 Petrarca: *Epistola posteritati* 8: "Principum ac regum familiaritatibus et nobilium amicitiis usque ad invidiam fortunatus fui. Maximi regum mee etatis et amarunt et coluerunt me. [...] Et ita cum quibusdam fui, ut ipsis quodammodo mecum essent [...]." In: Karl Enenkel/ Betsy de Jong-Crane/ Peter Liebregts (eds.): *Modelling the Individual. Biography and Portrait in the Renaissance. With a Critical Edition of Petrarch's Letter to Posterity*. Amsterdam-Atlanta: Rodopi 1998, p. 260–261.
16 Petrarca: *De vita solitaria* I, prohemium 8; for details of the interpretation cf. Enenkel, *Die Stiftung von Autorschaft in der neulateinischen Literatur (ca. 1350–ca. 1650)*, p. 169–172 (chapter I, 4: Amicitia. Die Inszenierung einer freundschaftlichen Beziehung zwischen Autor und ranghöherem Widmungsempfänger), and Enenkel: Die monastische Petrarca-Rezeption, p. 35–38.
17 Cf. Wolfgang Liebenwein: *Studiolo. Die Entstehung eines Raumtyps und sein Entwicklung bis um 1600*. Berlin: Gebr. Mann 1977 (Frankfurter Forschungen zur Kunst, vol. 6).

active outside the house.[18] The bigger part of his day he seems to walk on the hills and through the woods. It is also there, in this natural environment, where he prays, engages in religious meditation, reads, and writes. This construction of life-style is in a marked difference with the cell of a monk or a hermit, and the monastic rule of *stabilitas loci*. In *De vita solitaria*, it seems that a place inside a house or inside walls implies something profane or ordinary. Walls appear to be a kind of cage for the mind, and bring the high spirit down to earth.

Chapter I, 7 of *De vita solitaria* is especially dedicated to this construction of the sacred place of authorship.[19] Petrarch defends his view against the Roman rhetorician Quintilian of the 1st century AD, who in the 10th book of his *Institutio oratoria* advised intellectuals against composing works outdoors, e. g. on a *locus amoenus*: under a shady tree with birds singing, or in a garden or park.[20] According to Quintilian, writing should take place exclusively in a *studio*. Quintilian's main argument pertains to concentration. Beautiful nature, he says, will only distract the mind. In Petrarch's view, however, exactly the opposite is the case: beautiful nature will optimize the writer's inspiration and power of invention, and walls will only diminish it. Thus, in *De vita solitaria*, the sacred place is always defined as a place outdoors. The process of composing literature is located there. Petrarch's author is a *walking writer*. He takes paper and pen with him, and on a spot that inspires him he will sit down and start to write. Petrarch advises this manner of writing especially for philosophers and poets, among whom he counts himself. They may sit down wherever they experience inspiration, under the open sky, under a rock or under the shade of a large pine tree.[21] They do not need to consult many books: "Non multorum evolutione voluminum est opus."[22] They have read the necessary books before and they keep their content in their minds. When they are inspired and start with their *inventio*, they will "read in their minds, often even write in their minds:" "illis (voluminibus) iam ante perlectis in animo legunt, sepe etiam in animo scribunt."[23] Thus, the sacred place brings forth an inspired, religious, and meditative manner of writing. The sacred place enables an author to "write in his mind;" to concentrate on his "inner view," i. e. speculation, and to reach a high philosophical level of writing.

---

18 This is especially evident in the description of a typical day of the solitarius in *De vita solitaria* I, 2 (cf. also the comment *ad loc.*).
19 Cf. Petrarca: *De vita solitaria*, Buch 1, p. 549–556.
20 Quintilian: *Institutio oratoria* X, 3, 22–25.
21 Petrarca: *De vita solitaria* I, 7, 9: "impetum ingenii sequantur, considant, ubicunque est animus, ubi locus tempusque suaserint aut ubi se stimulis maioribus adigi senserint, seu celo aperto, […] seu solide rupis obtentu, seu patule pinus umbraculo."
22 Ibid.
23 Ibid.

There are certain landscape elements that especially contribute to the sacred character of the place of writing. One of them definitely is a view on the *open sky*. Petrarch does not advise the writer to sit down in a deep dark wood with high, dense trees, or in a small garden, surrounded by high walls or hedges, or in a dark grotto. He required a wide view, and he attributed to it a spiritual and religious function, as a kind of means to gain direct access to God. Petrarch's "open access" to heaven stimulates the "raptus" of the mind, the ecstasy, or inspiration.[24] A maximum of open sky will be provided by mountain tops. *These are, therefore, his sacred places par excellence*. He advises the intellectual to sit down there and to experience the "raptus," I quote: "If one wants to bring forth something more excellent than ordinary people, it is necessary that one is lifted above the ordinary human level: I have experienced that this happens in an easier and more fruitful way in places under the open sky".[25] Although Petrarch mentions literally "montes,"[26] of course, he does not urge the intellectual always first to climb a true mountain top when he wants to write something. In this respect, his argument has certainly a specific autobiographical flavour. Petrarch usually thinks of the rocky hills that surround the valley of Vaucluse like a theatre. They are not very high, only some 150–250 metres above the valley, but all of them offer a tremendous view on the valley and its surroundings. Although Petrarch mostly associates them with "woods" [silvae],[27] they were only scarcely covered with lower pine trees so that it rarely could happen that the walking writer was covered under a roof of trees.

The sacred place of the hilltop is especially fruitful for religious meditation and self-reflection, historical thinking and literary invention. In *De vita solitaria*, Petrarch compares the hilltop with an observation tower [specula], from which one can watch from a distance human life, the "res curasque hominum," oneself, and the universe in transition.[28] To observe the transition of the universe would stimulate the Christian "meditatio mortis;" for Christians this meditation is not a source of depression and despair, but of hope and confidence. Furthermore, from the sacred place of the hilltop the author is able to observe the course of history, of all times and countries: "mittere retro memoriam perque omnia secula perque

---

24 For this type of writers' inspiration, cf. Petrarca: *De vita solitaria*, Buch 1, p. 549–556.
25 Ibid., I, 7, 10: "Nempe supra humanum modum rapiantur oportet, si supra hominem loqui volunt: id sane locis apertissimis expeditius fieri interdum et alacrius animadverti."
26 E. g., ibid., I, 7, 6: "quamvis ego nusquam felicius quam in silvis ac montibus ingenium experiar [...]."
27 As ibid.: "in silvis ac montibus."
28 Ibid., I, 6, 5.

omnes terras animo vagary."[29] Constructed in this way, historical thinking gets a religious and spiritual touch, similar to the communication of the supernatural. Petrarch experiences on the solitary hilltop a kind of historical "raptus," an ecstasy that would enable him to speak directly to the important people of all ages, especially with the classical authors.

The holiness of the hilly and rocky landscape surrounding Vaucluse is reinforced by three other strategies or claims; first by the fact that Petrarch associated his sacred place with the hermitage of the desert fathers, the Egyptian and Syrian *anachoretae*.[30] The desert, "desertum" of the first hermits, of course, may be hilly or rocky too, such as mount Colzim at the Gulf of Suez, where the hermitage of Antonius Abbas (died 356 AD), who figures among the first and most important Eastern monks, was situated.[31] Petrarch, however, was not well acquainted with the geography of the Golf of Suez. It seems more likely that he constructed his desert by identifying it with European landscapes, equipped with hills, mountains, woods, and rivers.

Petrarch made use of the authoritative power of the desert fathers, although there were some marked differences. In the *Vitae patrum* a certain pattern always appears: the life organised as a continuous search for ever extremer forms of solitude, loneliness, and ascesis. The fathers withdrew deeper and deeper into the desert, and the most sacred spot was the least inhabited and civilized spot. Petrarch's solitude was located in a remote valley, but definitely not in a completely uninhabited area outside the civilisation. It belonged to a small village in a small bishopric; and there were always people, shepherds, peasants, servants, and above all, the visitors and friends of the poet. Petrarch constructed his sacred place not as a freaky, uncivilised, and wild spot ("solitudo insolens, ferox, immanis").[32] He would not, as the desert fathers, live in a hut or a cave, sleep on the ground; or walk around in rags or nude. But he would be decently dressed, live in a decent house, sleep in a normal bed, and he would have servants for a decent life-style etc. Petrarch's sacred place would be characterised by the so-called "aurea mediocritas," as advocated by Horace.[33] Petrarch wanted to appear in front of his visitors not as a dirty and miserable freak, but as a pleasant and civilised man.

---

29 Ibid.
30 Petrarca: *Prose*, p. 406 ff.
31 Ibid., p. 414; there, Petrarch regards Antonius as "orientalium atque orientium monachorum princeps."
32 Ibid., I, 7, 20.
33 Ibid.: "Ita plane sentio atque hunc medium inter extrema callem teneo." Cf. Horace: *Carmina* II, 10, 5–8: "Auream quisquis mediocritatem/ diligit, tutus caret obsoleti/ sordibus tecti, caret invidenda/ sobrius aula."

The second strategy is Petrarch's identification of the rocky landscape with the bucolic landscape from Virgil's *Eclogues*. Petrarch constitutes himself on the sacred *Dichterort*, as described by Virgil. This strategy includes certain ritual elements: the poet, under the disguise of a shepherd, shall sit down under a shady tree on a hilltop or under a rock, and he shall start to sing. In this discourse formation, it is certainly the *locus* that triggers poetry. It is revealing to see how Petrarch, in *De vita solitaria*, took over Virgil's authoritative *Lagerungsmotiv*: "Tityre, tu patulae recubans sub tegmine fagi" (the first line of the first *Eclogue*): the poet sits down in *De vita solitaria* "under the shade of a broad pine tree" – "patule pinus umbraculo."[34] Petrarch elaborated this strategy of intertextual nexus especially in his *Bucolicum Carmen*. One of the characters, Silvius, i. e. the man living in the woods, represents the person of the poet. And, not coincidentally, the first eclogue is again a meditation about the live-style, the *vita solitaria*, Petrarch's favourite topic to initiate a work. In the first eclogue, Petrarch discusses the topic with his brother Gherardo, the monk, monachus, called Monicus in the poem.[35] Whereas Monicus stays in a cave, which symbolizes the Carthusian monastery of Montrieu, Silvius is depicted as the *walking writer* who climbs one hilltop after the other. Vaucluse's rocky valley figures in the *Eclogue* as a holy landscape, where one can meet Saints, for example John the Baptist and Mary, but also Christ himself.

The third strategy is well known, and that is why I mention it only briefly. Petrarch who took over the means of authorisation and inspiration of Greek and Roman poets by claiming direct contact with the Muses,[36] identified the rock at

---

34 Ibid., I, 7, 9.
35 Petrarch himself explained the meaning of his allegorical *Bucolicum carmen* I in a prose letter to his brother Gherardo, the dedicatee of the poem; cf. Francesco Petrarca: *Familiarium rerum libri*. Ed. by Vittorio Rossi. Firenze: Sansoni 1935, vol. X, 4 (Edizione nazionale delle opere di F. P., 11), p. 20 ff.: "intentionis autem mee sensus hic est: pastores colloquentes nos sumus; ego Silvius, tu Monicus. Nominum ratio hec est: primi quidem tum quod in silvis res acta est tum propter insitum ab ineunte etate Urbis odium amoremque silvarum, propter quem multi ex nostris in omni sermone sepius me Silvanum quam Franciscum vocant [...]." For the allegorical mode in early Renaissance pastoral poetry cf. Konrad Krauter: *Die Renaissance der Bukolik in der lateinischen Literatur des 14. Jahrhunderts: von Dante bis Petrarca*. Munich: Fink 1983.
36 Cf. Effrosini Spentzou/ Don Fowler (eds.): *Cultivating the Muse. Struggles for Power and Inspiration in Classical Literature*. Oxford: Oxford University Press 2002; Eike Barmeyer: *Die Musen. Ein Beitrag zur Inspirationstheorie*. Munich: Fink 1968; Walter Friedrich Otto: *Die Musen und der göttliche Ursprung des Singens und Sagens*. Düsseldorf: E. Diederichs 1955; Werner Suerbaum: Muse. In: *Enciclopedia Virgiliana*. 6 vols. Roma: Istituto dell'Enciclopedia italiana 1984–1991, III (1987), p. 625–641; Maria Teresa Camilloni: *Le Muse*. Roma: Editori Riuniti 1998; Jean-Luc Nancy: *The Muses*. Trans. by P. Kamuf. Stanford, CA: Stanford University Press 1996; Andrew Barker: The Daughters of Memory. In: *Musica e storia* 2 (1994), p. 171–190; Derek Collins: Hesiod and the Divine Voice of the Muses. In: *Arethusa* 32 (1999), p. 241–262; Athanasios Kambylis, *Die Dichterweihe und ihre Symbolik*. Heidelberg: C. Winter 1965; Godo Lieberg: Die Muse des Properz und seine

the end of the valley of Vaucluse with the mountain of the Muses, the Helicon, where a sanctuary for Apollo and the Muses was situated, and the fountain of the Sorgue with the fountain of the Muses, Hyppocrene.[37] Thus Petrarch constructs his solitary locus, his hermitage, in a learned way as an "all'anticha" sanctuary. This sanctuary functions as a pivotal source for meditation and writing: Petrarch claimed an ongoing, special relationship with Apollo and the Muses, and, differently from the Roman poets, he claimed it as a kind of private property. This is to be taken in a literal sense. He constructed his private garden directly at the fountain. Its main elements were laurel trees, which Petrarch had planted there together with a friend, the poet Guglielmo da Pastrengo.[38] The laurel was of course Apollo's holy tree, but at the same time, it was the trademark of Petrarch the poet, the *poet laureate*. It is clear that Petrarch used the laurel as an important means of authorisation. In the title inscriptions of his works he always calls himself "Franciscus Petrarca poeta laureatus."

It is time now for some concluding remarks. A number of things are remarkable. First the fact that in Petrarch's conception of the contemplative life, the place, the *locus*, played such an important role. This is not the case with medieval treatises on the contemplative or monastic life. Petrarch stressed the importance of the place, and he constructed it as a sacred place, in a complex way, by using a number of different strategies and by drawing on different lines of tradition from antiquity and Christianity. Furthermore, his construction of the sacred place has very strong autobiographical traits. What is the strategy behind this? I think that the main reason behind Petrarch's constructions is his search for authorisation for his new and unusual type of authorship. It is of course still open to discussion how exactly one should define his humanism; however, it is clear that he composed unusual works, with a remarkable content, outside the intellectual mainstream; the revival of antiquity and autobiography were only two of its major topics, which were a bit eccentric in the middle of the 14th century. I suspect that the special character of his works required special attention, if one wanted to legitimize them. That is why Petrarch claimed a special position adorned with sacred elements.

Dichterweihe. In: *Philologus* 107 (1963), p. 116–129; 263–270; Agathe Thornton: Horace's Ode to Calliope (III, 4). In: *Journal of the Australasian Universities Language and Literature Association* 23 (1965), p. 96–102; John F. Miller: Ennius and the Elegists. In: *Illinois Classical Studies* 8 (1983), p. 277–295. For the reception of these concepts, cf. Christoph J. Steppich, *Numine afflatur. Die Inspiration des Dichters im Denken der Renaissance*. Wiesbaden: Harrassowitz 2002 (Gratia, 39).
37 For a more detailed discussion cf. Enenkel, *Die Stiftung von Autorschaft in der neulateinischen Literatur (ca. 1350–ca. 1650)*, p. 387–394 (chap. IV, 1: Autorschaftsstiftung durch antike Gottheiten: Gebet zu den Musen, Bitte um Inspiration, Dichterweihe, Furor poeticus).
38 *Epistole metrice* III, 3; *Poesie minori del Petrarca sul testo latino ora corretto* […]. Edited by D. Rossetti. 3 vols. Milano: Dalla società tipografica de' classici italiani 1829–1834, II, p. 190–192; cf. Enenkel, *Die Erfindung des Menschen*, p. 46–65.

And I think that it contributed to the success of his self-construction that it was connected with visual elements that had a strong symbolical value: a "closed" valley, *Vallis clausa*, separated from the *mundus*; the mountains of contemplation; the fountain of the Apollo and the Muses, the transalpine Helicon, the laurels of the poet laureate, the bucolic landscape etc. And all these elements were deliberately connected with Petrarch's personal life. And another advantage of this self-construction was that it was strong and powerful, but at the same time flexible. It did not require that the poet stayed all the time in Vaucluse, which would have been difficult for him, given his ambitions and obligations. Thus, sometimes, it was enough to desire to be at the *locus sacer*, not actually to be there. The *locus sacer* kept its authorising value, wherever the poet actually was.

Bibliography

Primary Literature

Francisci Petrarchae [...] Opera quae extant omnia [...]. Basileae: Henrichus Petri 1554. Rept. Ridgewood New Jersey: The Gregg Press 1965.
Poesie minori del Petrarca sul testo latina ora corretto [...]. Edited by D. Rossetti. 3 vols. Milano: Dalla società tipografica de' classici italiani 1829–1834.
The Life of Solitude by Francis Petrarch. Ed. and Trans. by J. Zeitlin. Urbana: University of Illinois Press 1924.
Petrarca, Francesco: *Familiarium rerum libri*. Edited by Vittorio Rossi (vols 1–3) and by Vittorio Rossi and Umberto Bosco (vol. 4). Firenze: Sansoni 1933–1942 (Edizione nazionale delle opere di Petrarca, 10–13).
Petrarca, Francesco: *Prose*. Ed. by Guido Martellotti. Milano-Napoli: Ricciardi 1955.
Petrarca, Francesco: *De vita solitaria. Buch 1. Kritische Textausgabe und ideengeschichtlicher Kommentar*. Ed. by Karl Enenkel. Leiden – New York – Köln – Kopenhagen: Brill 1990.
Petrarca, Francesco: *Epistola posteritati*. In: Karl Enenkel/ Betsy de Jong-Crane/ Peter Liebregts (eds.): *Modelling the Individual. Biography and Portrait in the Renaissance. With a Critical Edition of Petrarch's Letter to Posterity*. Amsterdam-Atlanta: Rodopi 1998, p. 260–261.

Secondary Literature

Monographs and Anthologies

Aichele, Klaus: *Das Antichristdrama des Mittelalters, der Reformation und Gegenreformation*. Den Haag: Nijhoff 1974.
Baethgen, Friedrich: *Der Engelpapst: Idee und Erscheinung*. Leipzig: Koehler & Amelang 1943.
Barmeyer, Eike: *Die Musen. Ein Beitrag zur Inspirationstheorie*. Munich: Fink 1968.

Camilloni, Maria Teresa: *Le Muse*. Roma: Editori Riuniti 1998.
Enenkel, Karl A.E.: *Die Erfindung des Menschen. Die Autobiographik des frühneuzeitlichen Humanismus von Petrarca bis Lipsius*. Berlin: Walter De Gruyter 2008.
Enenkel, Karl A.E.: *Die Stiftung von Autorschaft in der neulateinischen Literatur (ca. 1350–ca. 1650). Zur autorisierenden und wissensvermittelnden Funktion von Widmungen, Vorworttexten, Autorporträts und Dedikationsbildern*. Leiden-Boston: Brill 2014.
Jenks, Gregory C.: *The Origins and Early Development of the Antichrist Myth*. Berlin: Walter de Gruyter 1991.
Kambylis, Athanasios: *Die Dichterweihe und ihre Symbolik*. Heidelberg: C. Winter 1965.
Knefelkamp, Ulrich/ Frank Martin (eds): *Der Antichrist. Die Glasmalereien der Marienkirche in Frankfurt (Oder)*. Leipzig: Edition Leipzig 2008.
Krauter, Konrad: *Die Renaissance der Bukolik in der lateinischen Literatur des 14. Jahrhunderts: von Dante bis Petrarca*. Munich: Fink 1983.
Liebenwein, Wolfgang: *"Studiolo". Die Entstehung eines Raumtyps und sein Entwicklung bis um 1600*. Berlin: Gebr. Mann 1977 (Frankfurter Forschungen zur Kunst, 6).
Nancy, Jean-Luc: *The Muses*. Trans. by P. Kamuf. Stanford, CA: Stanford University Press 1996.
Otto, Walter Friedrich: *Die Musen und der göttliche Ursprung des Singens und Sagens*. Düsseldorf: E. Diederichs 1955.
Piur, Paul: *Petrarcas "Buch ohne Namen" und die päpstliche Kurie*. Halle: M. Niemeyer 1925.
Rauh, Horst D.: *Das Bild des Antichrist im Mittelalter. Von Tyconius zum deutschen Symbolismus*. Münster: Aschendorff 1973.
Spentzou, Effrosini/ Don Fowler (eds.): *Cultivating the Muse. Struggles for Power and Inspiration in Classical Literature*. Oxford: Oxford University Press 2002.
Steppich, Christoph J: *Numine afflatur. Die Inspiration des Dichters im Denken der Renaissance*. Wiesbaden: Harrassowitz 2002 (Gratia, 39).

Articles and Papers

Barker, Andrew: The Daughters of Memory. In: *Musica e storia* 2 (1994), p. 171–190.
Collins, Derek: Hesiod and the Divine Voice of the Muses. In: *Arethusa* 32 (1999), p. 241–262.
Enenkel, Karl: Die monastische Petrarca-Rezeption: zur Autorisierung über den Widmungsempfänger und zu anderen Bedingungen des Erfolgs von *De vita solitaria* in spätmittelalterlichen Klöstern. In: *Neulateinisches Jahrbuch* 14 (2012), p. 27–251.
Isetta, Sandra: Il linguaggio ascetico di Francesco Petrarca nel *De vita solitaria*. In: *Studi umanistici piceni* 23 (2003), p. 75–94.
Gregory C. Jenks: Antichrist. In: *Theologische Realenzyklopädie*. Band 3. Berlin: Walter de Gruyter, 1978, p. 20–50.
Lieberg, Godo: Die Muse des Properz und seine Dichterweihe. In: *Philologus* 107 (1963), p. 116–129; 263–270.
Maggi, Armando: You will be my solitude. In: Victoria Kirkham/Armando Maggi (eds.): *Petrarch. A Guide to the Complete Works*. Chicago and London: The University of Chicago Press, p. 179–195.
Miller, John F: Ennius and the Elegists. In: *Illinois Classical Studies* 8 (1983), p. 277–295.
Suerbaum, Werner: Muse. In: *Enciclopedia Virgiliana*. 6 vols. Roma: Istituto dell'Enciclopedia italiana, 1984–1991, III (1987), p. 625–641.

Thornton, Agathe: Horace's Ode to Calliope (III, 4). In: *Journal of the Australasian Universities Language and Literature Association* 23 (1965), p. 96–102.
von Moos, Peter: Les solitudes de Pétrarque. Liberté intellectuelle et activisme urbain dans la crise du XIVe siècle. In: *Rassegna europea di letteratura iltaliana* 7 (1996), p. 23–58.

Ronald Witt
Petrarch, Creator of the Christian Humanist

Among Petrarch's greatest achievements was his Christianization of the humanist movement, the integration of ancient pagan learning with Christian literature. In another place I have described the completely secular character of humanism in the two generations prior to Petrarch.[1] Nothing in the surviving work of the Paduan Lovato dei Lovati (1240/41–1309), the first Italian scholar to make a serious effort to imitate the style of ancient authors, indicates that he had any kind of Christian commitment. Similarly Albertino Mussato (1261–1329), the leader of the second generation of Paduan humanists, showed no interest in Christian teachings until the last two years of his life, when a sudden religious conversion led to his condemning ancient writers.[2] Admittedly, the apparent paganism not only of Lovato and Mussato but of others in their circle may reflect only literary posing and not real beliefs. My point is that the first two generations of humanists made no effort to integrate their new approach to ancient Latin literature and history with their Christian society. According to Petrarch writing in the *De otio,* his own teachers had the same secular attitude as did the Paduans and had little respect for the Bible.[3]

At a certain point in his life, perhaps even as late as the early 1340s, Petrarch decided to face up to reconciling his passion for antiquity with his Christian beliefs. Thereafter he undertook to frame his autobiography so as to identify himself as a Christian scholar by showing that the study of the ancients was both compatible and useful for living a Christian life. By emphasizing certain aspects of his autobiography and by invention Petrarch created the image of the Christian humanist that was to influence the course of humanism in his own generation and the generation following. Moreover, although his influence diminished in the fifteenth century, his amalgam of Christianity and pagan wisdom was to prove an enduring aspect of the later humanist movement.

Fundamental to Petrarch's belief in the relevance of pagan literature to Christianity was Augustine's statement in the *Confessions* that his desire to reform his

---

1 See Ronald Witt: "*In the Footsteps of the Ancients.*" *The Origins of Humanism from Lovato to Bruni.* Boston and Leiden: Brill 2000, p. 170–171.
2 For his attitude on the afterlife, see ibid., p. 121.
3 Francesco Petrarca: *De otio religioso.* Edited by G. Rotondi. Città del Vaticano: Biblioteca Apostolica Vaticana, 1958, p. 103: "[...] eos qui psalterium daviticum, qua ulla pregnantior scriptura est, et omnem divine textum pagine non aliter quam aniles fabulas irriderent"; Eng. trans. *On Religious Leisure.* Ed. and trans. by Susan S. Schearer. New York: Italica Press 2002, p. 145.

life had initially come from reading Cicero's *Hortensius*.⁴ The fact that Augustine had used his extensive education in pagan literature in his effort to interpret Scripture and develop Christian doctrine persuaded Petrarch of the value of using pagan works for his own understanding of the Christian faith and Augustine's example legitimized his devotion to the study of ancient literature.

Petrarch never devoted a treatise to defining his views on the relationship between Christian doctrine and pagan literature. However, in a letter to Francesco Nelli in 1358, he states that he intends to devote the rest of his life to reading Christian writings. He continues to love Cicero and Virgil, Plato and Homer, but "now something greater is at stake and I am more concerned with saving of my own soul than with eloquence."⁵ His orators will be Ambrose, Augustine, Jerome, and Gregory while his philosopher is St. Paul. Once doubtful as to whether David was a greater poet than Homer or Virgil, now guided by experience and the light of truth, he has taken David as his poet. Conscious that his words might be interpreted as questioning the value of studying the ancients, he continues:

> Neque ideo tamen quia hos pretulerim, illos abicio, quod se fecisse Ieronimus scribere potiusquam sequenti stilo approbare visus est michi; ego utrosque simul amare posse videor, modo quos in verborum, quos in rerum consilio preferam non ignorem. (§ 8)
>
> [Not that I prefer the one group (i. e. Christian writers) and attach little value to the other (i. e. the pagan authors), as Jerome wrote that he did, even though, as far as I can judge, he did not act upon his words in his later work. I, it appears, can love both sides at the same time, even though, I know very well whom to prefer when it is a question of expression and whom when it is a question of substance.]⁶

Petrarch's *On His Own Ignorance and That of Many Others*, composed in 1367, is his most extensive discussion of the relationship between pagan learning and Christianity. In this work he links the issue of the relationship to that of the importance of the intellect compared with the will, of knowing compared to loving. Angered at the betrayal of four younger men, supposedly his friends, who behind his back had called him a good man but ignorant, Petrarch replied with a multi-layered attack designed to discredit the accusers and the accusation. Accused of

---

4 Petrarca: *De otio religioso*, p. 103; *On Religious Leisure*, p. 146.
5 My Translation. Latin text in: Petrarca: *Rerum fam.* XXII, 10. In: Petrarca: *Le familiari*. Edited by Vittorio Rossi (vols 1–3) and by Vittorio Rossi and Umberto Bosco (vol. 4). Firenze: Sansoni 1933–1942 (Edizione nazionale delle opere di F. P., 10–13), IV, p. 127: "Amavi ego Ciceronem, fateor, et Virgilium amavi [...]. Amavi similiter Platonem ex Grecis atque Homerum [...]. Sed iam michi maius agitur negotium, maiorque salutis quam eloquentie cura est." (§§ 5–6)
6 My translation. Latin text in: Ibid., p. 127–128.

ignorance because he had disagreed with Aristotle on certain issues, Petrarch declares that he prefers to be judged good rather than wise because morality is superior to wisdom and love to truth.

For this reason Latin writers are superior to Aristotle because his moral teachings were ineffective. "He teaches what virtue is, I do not deny that, but his lesson lacks the words that sting and set afire and urge toward love of virtue and hatred of vice, or, at any rate, they do not have enough of such power. He who looks for that will find it in our Latin writers, especially in Cicero and Seneca, and what may be astonishing to hear, in Horace, a poet somewhat rough in style but more pleasing in his maxims."[7] Implicitly Petrarch is attacking the Scholastic curriculum based on Aristotle as less relevant to the needs of society than one centered on humanistic studies.

Petrarch follows this critique by attacking Aristotle's errors such as his belief in the eternity of the world. Among the ancients Plato and Cicero were far superior in their use of natural reason to attain truth about God and the soul. While coming close to the truth, however, the Platonists failed to reach it, and if occasionally Cicero expressed sentiment that can be interpreted as Christian, the learning of the ancients was dwarfed by what we know through Divine Revelation.

As in the letter to Nelli, Petrarch here emphasizes the importance of pagan rhetorical teachings for Christian eloquence, the enormous moral influence that Cicero's writings exerted on Augustine, and his own love of Cicero: "I confess, I admire Cicero as much or even more than all who wrote a line in any nation."[8] Nevertheless, his love of Cicero must be clearly distinguished from his Christian faith.

Like Augustine he believes that had Cicero known Christ and his teachings, he would have become a Christian. Similarly many Platonists, including Augustine himself, were led to Christianity through their study of Plato's writings. Therefore, Petrarch asks, "If this fundament stands, in what way is Ciceronian eloquence

---

7 Petrarca: *De sui ipsius et multorum ignorantia*. In: Petrarca: *Prose*. Edited by G. Martellotti, P.G. Ricci et al. Milano-Napoli: Ricciardi 1955 (La Letteratura italiana. Storia e testi, vol. 7), p. 744–746: "Docet ille, non infitior, quid est virtus; at stimulos ac verborum faces, quibus ad amorem virtutis vitiique odium mens urgetur atque incenditur, lectio illa vel non habet, vel paucissimos habet. Quos qui querit, apud nostros, precipue Ciceronem atque Anneum, inveniet, quod quis mirabitur, apud Flaccum, poetam quidem stilo hispidum, sed sententiis periocundum." The English translation is taken from *On His Own Ignorance and that of Many Others*. Trans. Charles Trinkaus. In: *The Renaissance Philosophy of Man*. Edited by. Ernst E. Cassirer et al. Chicago: The University of Chicago Press 1950, p. 107.
8 Ibid., p. 760: "Ciceronem fateor me mirari inter, imo ante omnes qui scripserunt unquam qualibet in gente." Eng. trans., p. 115.

opposed to Christian dogma?" Nonetheless, Petrarch affirms unambiguously: "[...] any pious Catholic, however, unlearned he may be, will find much more credit with me in this respect [i. e. regarding religious truth] than would Plato or Aristotle."[9]

Petrarch is clear: at its highest reach religious truth attained by ancient philosophers through natural reason fell short of the truth known to every Christian in his own day. Given the caveat "in this respect" meaning "in regard to religion [hac in parte]," Petrarch in no way intends to impugn the value of ancient learning in other areas of knowledge. Nevertheless, the ascription of religious knowledge to the unlearned fits well with his claim to prize love over wisdom and to prefer being called good rather than wise. In this way he effectively contrasts his Christian humility with his Aristotelian opponents' pride in their knowledge. Shocked and angry that the young men would dare to question his learning, Petrarch struggles to maintain this posture of humility, although occasionally we catch glimpses of his real feelings.

To Petrarch's mind this reconciliation of pagan learning with Christian scholarship is best fostered by a scholar living in solitude. The detailed description in the *De vita solitaria* of his residence in the Vaucluse likely comes close to representing the life style of the Christian scholar that he had in mind. Written in 1346 with minor additions made down to 1371, the work constitutes a brief for the contemplative life of the scholar living in solitude as the surest means of achieving spiritual peace and moral purity.[10] While he admits that active men of a saintly nature who guide straying souls to the right path are superior to contemplatives, he insists that their number is few compared to those who claim to preach God's word while themselves leading unclean lives.[11] In any case, he lacks the spiritual strength to actively help other suffering souls. The best he can do is to pray for their salvation. His primary concern is to see that he himself not perish and solitude encourages him to keep his goal in focus.[12]

---

9 Ibid.: "Stante hoc fundamento, quid cristiano dogmati ciceronianum obstet eloquium? [...] Ceterum multo hanc in parte plus fidei apud me habiturus fuerit pius quisque catholicus, quamvis indoctus, quam Plato ipse vel Cicero."
10 The work has been securely dated by Ernest Hatch Wilkins: *Studies in the Life and Works of Petrarch*. Cambridge, Mass.: Harvard University Press 1955, p. 18–21. References to later biographical and historical events were added over time: Berthold L. Ullman: The Composition of Petrarch's "De vita solitaria" and the History of the Vatican Manuscript. In: *Studies in the Italian Renaissance*. Roma: Edizioni di storia e letteratura 1973, p. 135–75. I have used the edition of the work published in Petrarca: *Prose*, p. 286–591. The English translation is taken from Petrarch: *The Life of Solitude*. Edited by Jacob Zeitlin. Urbana, Ill.: University of Illinois Press 1924.
11 Petrarca: *De vita solitaria*, p. 322; Eng. trans., p. 125.
12 Ibid., p. 324; trans. p. 126.

He conceives of the ideal place of solitude in terms of his own experience in the Vaucluse. He stresses the simple diet, rough clothes, and the uninterrupted hours devoted to study and writing interspersed with contemplative walks in the surrounding woodlands abounding in wild animals and fish-filled streams. By contrast with life in Avignon there is no one to deceive, to impress, to court: solitude "has God for sole witness and puts her trust not in the voice of the blind and unreliable multitude but in her own conscience."[13] He is convinced that although the divine presence is everywhere, God listens and converses with us more intimately in solitude. Absent the noise and distractions of the active life, the mind is open to his voice: "and so the human spirit accustoms itself to celestial contemplation, [and] by continuous intercourse acquires confidence in its salvation and from a guest and stranger becomes a member of God's household."[14]

There follows a description of the state of mind that solitude helps the Christian scholar attain that is one of the most beautiful passages of prose in all Petrarch's writings. I will read it at length:

> Stare interim velut in specula, res curasque hominum sub pedibus intuentem, videre omnia teque imprimis cum universitate transire; nec senectutem tacite subrepentem prius molestam pati, quam proximam suspicari, quod omnibus propemodum occupatis accidit; sed eam multo ante prospicere et preparare illi integrum corpus, equum animum. [...] nonnunquam et teipsum, et supra se elevatum animum inferre rebus ethereis, meditari quid illic agitur, et meditatione desiderium inflammare, teque vicissim cohortari, et ardentium quasi verborum faculas calidis admovere precordiis.
>
> [To stand meanwhile as though on a high tower watching the troubled actions of men beneath your feet, to see all things in this world and yourself along with them passing away, not to feel old age as an affliction which has silently stolen upon you before you suspected that it was so close, as generally happens with busy men, but to expect it long in advance and be prepared for it with a sound body and a serene mind; (...) sometimes to rise, with thoughts that are lifted above yourself, to the ethereal regions, to meditate on what goes on there and by meditation to inflame your desire, and in turn to encourage and admonish yourself with a fervent spirit as though with the power of burning words.][15]

Presumably this tranquility of spirit derives from knowledge that one's soul is not in jeopardy.

Without specifying precisely in what way the study of pagan literature enhances this confidence in the soul's afterlife, Petrarch concludes:

---

13 Ibid., p. 338: "Deum unicum testem habet, nec vulgo ceco et mendaci, sed conscientie proprie de se credit." Trans. p. 137.
14 Ibid., p. 352: "Sic humanus animus assuescit celestibus, frequentique colloquio fiduciam salutarem concipit, et ex hospite atque advena fit domesticus Dei." Trans. p. 148.
15 Ibid., p. 356; trans. p. 150.

> Inter hec, ut notiora non sileam, et lectioni dare operam et scripture, et alterum laborem alterno solatio lenire, legere quod scripserunt primi, scribere quod legant ultimi, et beneficii literarum a maioribus accepti, qua in illos non possumus, in posteros saltem gratum ac memorem animum habere [...]; denique modis omnibus amando, memorando, celebrando, si non parem, certe debitam meritis referre gratiam.
>
> [While I am speaking of these, however, let me not pass over the more obvious pleasures: to devote oneself to reading and writing, alternately finding employment and relief in each, to read, what our forerunners have written and to write what later generations may wish to read, to pay to posterity the debt which we cannot pay to the dead for the gift of their writings (...), and finally, by cherishing, remembering, and celebrating their fame in every way, to pay them the homage that is due to their genius even though it is not commensurate with their greatness.][16]

Petrarch is careful to say that the life of solitude does not require isolation from other human beings. Indeed, he argues that solitude is not disturbed by the presence of a like-minded friend but rather enriched by it. True friends find great pleasure in conversing with friends in whom they can "see their own image reflected, from whose lips they hear truth spoken, in whose presence, according to Cicero [De amicitia], they dare to talk of all things as though they were talking with themselves."[17] In 1349 in fact Petrarch was prepared to join with two of his friends, Luca Cristiani and Mainardo Accursio, in seeking a residence somewhere in Italy where they could live in solitude. His design, however, was frustrated when Mainardo was killed by brigands in the Alps.[18] His ideal of the solitary life, consequently, was either that of the single scholar dwelling apart like Jerome or that of a small community of likeminded men on the model of Augustine's community at Cassiciacum.

Generally speaking, the ideal of *docta pietas* modeled on that of the Church Fathers dominated Petrarch's mature work. Closely associated with the portrait of the Christian scholar as it emerges from his writings, as with Augustine, was his own experience. Indeed Petrarch goes beyond Augustine in presenting his ideas as outgrowths of his own spiritual development. A major cause of the wide readership his writings attained was the fact that he embodied *docta pietas* in the drama of his own life. At the same time, much aware of the importance of living according to the principles that he upheld, Petrarch was careful in detailing his experiences to make sure that they fit the image he intended to project.

---

16 Ibid., p. 356–358; trans. p. 150–151.
17 Ibid., p. 376: "in quo se se videant, ex quo verum audiant, cum quo, ut Cicero idem ait, sic omnia loqui audeant ut secum"; trans. p. 164.
18 See Ernest Hatch Wilkins: *Life of Petrarch*. Chicago: The University of Chicago Press 1961, p. 82–84.

Since at least the sixteenth century Petrarch scholars have debated the extent to which Petrarch intentionally misled his readers about his life and his motives for doing so. For example, all agree on the falsity of his claim in the *Letter to Posterity* that his *Africa,* a text left with gaping lacunae at his death, had been finished at Parma when he was thirty four.[19] In contrast, Petrarch's dating of his first sight of Laura on April 6, 1327 and her death the same day on April 6, 1348, both of which he wants to fall on Good Friday although neither do, has generated a volume of controversy.[20]

Beginning after World War II, however, scholars became particularly focused on Petrarch's honesty when suggesting a dating for some of his most important writings. They have generally accepted Giuseppe Billanovich's position published in 1947 that all the letters found in the first book of the *Familiares,* hitherto dated to the 1320s and early 1330s, were in fact composed in 1352 or 1353.[21] At the same time there is some disagreement with Billanovich's contention that the famous letter of Petrarch's ascent of Mount Ventoux, internally suggesting a date of 1336, was actually composed at the same time as the letters of the first book.[22] Other scholars have argued for other chronological deceptions and distortions of details designed to create the autobiography that Petrarch wanted his own generation and especially posterity to accept as his life.[23]

In the following pages I want to discuss briefly instances of re-dating as they relate to Petrarch's claim that he had attained celibacy, an essential aspect of the ideal Christian scholar for him, by the age of 40. Fortunately, we are able to check his statements against what is almost certainly Petrarch's sex diary, a document introduced in the discussion of Petrarch's celibacy by Hans Baron

---

[19] While at Parma in 1341, guest of the De Correggio, he recalls "cum die quodam in montana conscendens forte trans Entiam amnem reginis in finibus silvam que Plana dicitur adiissem, subito loci specie percussus, ad intermissam *Africam* stilum verti, et fervor animi qui sopitus videbatur excitato, scripsi aliquantulum die illo; post continuis diebus quotidie aliquid, donec Parmam rediens et repostam ac tranquillam nactus domum [...], tanto ardore opus illud non magno in tempore ad exitum deduxi, ut ipse quoque nunc stupeam." See Petrarca: *Posteritati.* In: Petrarca: *Prose,* p. 16.

[20] Carlo Carena: *Nella selva del Petrarca.* Bologna: Cappelli 1942, p. 209–245, examines the literature surrounding this question published since the late nineteenth century down to his own treatment. See discussion of Ugo Dotti: *Vita di Petrarca.* Roma-Bari: Laterza 1987, p. 53–58.

[21] See Giuseppe Billanovich: *Petrarca letterato. I. Lo scrittoio del* Petrarca. Roma: Edizioni di storia e letteratura, 1947, p. 48–55.

[22] Ibid., p. 193–198. See for critique Karlheinz Stierle: *La vita e I tempi di Petrarca. Alle origini della moderna coscienza europea.* It. trans. by Gabriella Pelloni. Venezia: Marsilio 2007, p. 307–308.

[23] For examples, see Marco Santagata: *I frammenti dell'anima: Storia e racconto nel "Canzoniere" di Petrarca.* Bologna: Il Mulino 1992, p. 86–101.

in 1985.[24] Published by Pierre de Nolhac, the diary is found in the end papers of a manuscript in Petrarch's library containing the correspondence between Abelard and Héloise (MS. Paris Lat. 2923), Petrarch's sex diary begins on April 21, 1344.[25] Diary entries specify date and time of day. Accord to the diary, he had sex for the next year-and-a half, remained celibate for the next two-and-a-half years during which time he wrote the *De vita solitaria* and the *De otio*. He began sex again in May 1348 and continued into 1349 down to August 2 when the diary stops and presumably with that Petrarch's indulgence in sex. Frequently accompanied by plaintive "Heu," the entries were surely designed to make him ashamed of his weakness of will.

Petrarch's letter to Boccaccio, written in 1366 (*Sen*. VIII, 1) discussing his successful domination of his sexual desire accords with this account of his last sexual contacts. In that letter he tells his friend that he has been free of sexual pleasure since the jubilee of 1350, that is, since the age of forty-six: "Christ, my liberator, knows that I speak the truth [...] He who, when tearfully implored, often gave me his hand [...] and himself held me up."[26] No scholar has challenged the assumption that he remained celibate for the remaining twenty-four years of his life.

What has particularly troubled recent scholars over the last forty years is Petrarch's claim in his *Letter to Posterity*, written between 1372 and 1374 that he had renounced sexual intercourse by 1344, five years earlier than the diary suggests. As he writes: "As I neared forty, while my heat and virility were still strong, I cast off not only the obscene act but even the memory of it, as if I had never seen a woman."[27] Was this merely wishful thinking on the part of an old man wanting credit for having given up sex in the prime of life or do earlier writing of Petrarch lay the groundwork for this claim in old age?

A survey of Petrarch's corpus shows that celibacy and the age of forty were closely associated for him. When the connection occurs in earlier work, however,

---

24 See Hans Baron: *Petrarch's "Secretum". Its Making and its Meaning*. Cambridge, Mass.: Harvard University Press 1985, p. 23–26.

25 See Pierre de Nolhac, Excursus VI: Les mémoriaux intimes de Pétrarque. In his: *Pétrarque et l'humanisme*. Paris: Champion 1892, 2nd ed. 1907, p. 405–411.

26 My translation. Latin text in: Francesco Petrarca: *Rerum senilium libri* VIII, 1. In his: *Res Seniles. Libri V–VIII*. Edited by Silvia Rizzo. Firenze: Le Lettere 2009, p. 288: "Scit me Cristus, liberator meus, verum loqui, qui sepe michi cum lacrimis exoratus flenti ac misero dexteram dedit secumque me sustulit."

27 Petrarca: *Prose*, p. 4: "Mox vero ad quadragesimum etatis annum appropinquans, dum adhuc et caloris satis esset et virium, non solum factum illud obscenum, sed eius memoriam omnem sic abieci, quasi nunquam feminam aspexissem." Eng. trans. James H. Robinson, *Petrarch: The First Modern Scholar and Man of Letters*. New York: C. P. Putnam 1898, p. 62.

the connection between the two is ambiguous and forty could be interpreted either as the age at which he wanted his readers to believe he had become celibate or the age at which he began a serious reform of his sex drive.

It should be said that Petrarch's sex diary for the years 1344–1349 was introduced by Hans Baron into the debate in 1985 that had been initiated nine years before by Francisco Rico in his *Vida u obra de Petrarca. I. Lectura del "Secretum"*, published in 1974. In this work Rico focuses on Petrarch's reference to the *Secretum* having being written sixteen years after first seeing Laura (1327), that is, in 1342–1343. Purporting to document a conversation of Franciscus with Augustinus over a period of three days, the *Secretum* shows its author despairing of his moral weakness and seeking the counsel of Augustinus for a remedy. Among the major sins to which he confesses or to which he is ultimately forced to confess, is lust.[28]

Rico's work effectively demonstrates that the *Secretum* could not have been a product of 1342/43, but rather was first composed in 1347 with subsequent reworkings in 1349 and 1351.[29] Although scholars have debated the extent to which the 1353 edition varied from that of 1347, there is almost universal agreement that Petrarch intentionally predated the work so that it would appear written when he was 39. According to Rico, one of Petrarch's motivations for the deception was to give the impression that he had become celibate by the following year at 40 in 1344. As defenders of Petrarch's honesty have pointed out, however, there is nothing in the work to indicate that Petrarch expected to achieve celibacy in 1344 and that Rico's interpretation is pure speculation. To my thinking 1342–1343 may well have meant the year in which he undertook serious moral reform following the birth of his second child.

The second piece of evidence that Rico uses to underwrite his accusation of deception is Petrarch's most famous letter, that written to Dionigi of San

---

28 *Secretum* in: Petrarca: *Prose*, p. 77–106.
29 While Rico considers the *Secretum* mostly written in 1353, Hans Baron, *Petrarch's "Secretum"* assigns the larger part of the writing to 1347. See Rico's comments on Baron: Ubi puer, ibi senex: Un libro de Hans Baron y el "Secretum" de 1353. In: *Il Petrarca latino e le origini dell'umanesimo. Atti del convegno internazionale, Firenze, 19–22 maggio, 1991*. Firenze: Le Lettere 1996 (*Quaderni petrarcheschi*, 9–10 [1992–1993]), p. 165–237. Petrarch's *I'vo pensando* [RVF 264], in whose opening lines he writes of the intensity of his weeping [lines 1–5], constitutes the poetic analogue of the *Secretum*. In both, the author's pursuit of love and glory are identified as the root causes of his unhappiness. For the date of the work as 1347–1348, see Baron, *Petrarch's "Secretum"*, p. 47–57. The biographical *Inscriptio* of Petrarch written in Boccaccio's Zibaldone Laurenziano (Michele Feo: *Codici latini del Petrarca nelle Biblioteche fiorentine*. Firenze: Le Lettere 1991, p. 343 and 346) refers to a *De vita et moribus domini Francisci Petracchi*, which Boccaccio refers to as a "dyalagum quemdam prosaice." If, as scholars believe, the reference is to the *Secretum*, then Petrarch was already working on the dialogue in 1341. Cf. Marco Ariani: *Petrarca*. Roma: Salerno 1999, p. 114.

Sepolcro describing his ascent together with his brother Gherardo of Mount Ventoux (*Fam.* IV, 1). According to a chronology of his life given in the course of the narrative, the letter appears written in 1336. In describing the climb, Petrarch reports that Gherardo had reached the summit by a difficult but direct approach while he had lost time trying to follow deceptively easier paths. Nonetheless, he looks forward to his own moral reform. As he writes addressing himself: "If perhaps it happened to you that this fleeting life continue for ten years more, and you were to advance toward virtue over that time as much as you have the past two years [...] might you be able to meet death in your fortieth year, while not certain but at least hopeful, and with old age approaching, calmly leave behind the remainder of life?"[30]

Accepting Billanovich's argument that the letter was actually composed in 1352–1353, Rico argues that Petrarch set the ascent in 1336 in order to show that celibacy by the age of forty had been his goal six or seven years prior to the composition of the *Secretum*.[31] It must be said here, however, that Billanovich's redating is based on a series of four assumptions, none of which convinces me. The first is that Dionigi in 1336 was probably at Avignon and there would have been no need of sending him a letter. The fact is we have no idea where he was in 1336. The second, is that Gherardo did not choose the upward path until he joined a monastery in 1343, but Petrarch may well be referring to a religious conversion in his brother, not necessarily entailing vows. The third reason given by Billanovich is that without knowledge of Cicero's correspondence, discovered in 1345, he could not have written a letter in such classicizing style. He does not question, however, the letters in books II and III of the *Familiares*, which are also classicizing. And fourthly, he argues that the two young men could not have taken the climb they did in only one day.[32] I have done the climb from base to summit twice, once in four and once in three hours. Admittedly, the mountain is 13.2 miles from Malaucène, where Petrarch says he spent the night, or 26.4 miles back and forth, but two young men could make the distance with no problem in the long day that Petrarch describes. Consequently, if the letter was actually written in 1336,

---

[30] My translation. Latin text in: Petrarca: *Le familiari*, I, p. 158, § 23: "'Si tibi forte contingeret per alia duo lustra volatilem hanc vitam producere, tantumque pro rata temporis ad virtutem accedere quantum hoc biennio, [...] nonne tunc posses, etsi non certus at saltem sperans, quadragesimo etatis anno mortem oppetere et illud residuum vite in senium abeuntis equa mente negligere?'"

[31] See Francisco Rico: *Vida u obra de Petrarca. I. Lectura del "Secretum"*. Padova: Antenore 1974 (Studi sul Petrarca, 4), p. 73 f., 76, 193, and 473.

[32] Giuseppe Billanovich: Petrarca e il Ventoso. In: *Italia medioevale e umanistica* 9 (1961), p. 389–401. The arguments for the re-dating are found on p. 396–397 and 399.

the hope for celibacy at 40 is significant to the discussion only in the sense that Petrarch at thirty four aspired to celibacy at forty.

A final oblique reference to the fortieth year occurs in Petrarch's letter to his brother Gherardo probably written in 1352. In the letter Petrarch acknowledges the influence of his brother's advice given when Gherardo left to join the monastery in the spring of 1343, nine years earlier: "Have good hope." Petrarch writes, "Know that I have not forgotten the advice that you gave me at your final departure."[33] According to the letter, of the three counsels given him by Gherardo the third had been to become celibate. Now Petrarch reassures his brother: "As for the third matter, contact with women, without which I once thought that I could not live, I now fear it more than death."[34] Inspired by his brother's counsel, the age of forty might well have marked the beginning of his serious dedication to controlling of his sexual appetite.

While there is no question, then, that the connection of celibacy with the age of forty extends to writings preceding the *Letter to Posterity,* none of these other relevant texts claim victory over the flesh by forty. If, as I suspect, the claim in the *Letter to Posterity* to have become celibate at forty is unique in Petrarch's writings, it becomes like the claim to have finished the *Africa* at thirty four, the wishful thinking of an old man.

Many of Petrarch's most important writings were designed to reorient the study of ancient literature and history that he had inherited from the Paduans from a secular to a Christian context. In part he did this by offering to his readers the quasi-monastic ideal of a devout Christian scholar nurtured in solitude, untroubled by the urgings of the flesh, and illustrated by his own life. But he insisted in the *De vita solitaria* that he was not laying down prescriptions for others: "Thus far I have set forth my opinion with the idea that none who read it [...] should think that I have been establishing a rule for their minds. Let them rather examine the truth of the matter in detail and not feel bound to take me or anyone else on faith but only trust the evidence of their own experience."[35]

---

33 *Rerum fam.* X, 5. In: Petrarca: *Le familiari*, II, p. 316–317, § 25: "[...] spem bonam habes, scito me consiliorum que michi supremo dederas digressu, non oblitum."
34 Ibid., p. 317, § 29: "Tertium est quod consortium femine, sine quo interdum extimaveram non posse vivere, morte nunc gravius pertimesco, et quanquam sepe tentationibus turber acerrimis, tamen dum in animum redit quid est femina, omnis tentatio confestim avolat et ego ad libertatem et ad pacem meam redeo."
35 Petrarca: *Prose*, p. 368–370: "Hactenus ea lege disserui quid sentirem, ut nullam ingeniis legem imposuisse me sentiant qui hec legent [...]; singula igitur examinent de veritate rerum, non tam michi vel aliis experientie credituri." Trans., p. 159.

Detached from its communal setting, humanist scholarship in Petrarch's hands became at once Christian and more cosmopolitan. The writings of Coluccio Salutati in the next generation testify to the strains and stresses encountered by a scholar, intimately conversant with Petrarch's writings, who tried to adapt Petrarchan humanism to an Italian communal milieu. Petrarch's version of humanism, however, proved immensely attractive to a predominantly clerical intelligentsia in fourteenth-century northern Europe. The influence of humanism north of the Alps diminished, however, when after Salutati's death in 1406, Italian humanism returned for more than a half century to its former civic path, and with few exceptions, ignored synthesizing Christianity with the study of the ancients. Christian humanism emerged again as a principal concern of Italian humanism only in the second half of the fifteenth-century and once again, as in Petrarch's time, the revival accounts for much of the enormous success of the movement beyond the Alps.

Bibliography

Primary Literature

Petrarch

Le familiari. Edited by Vittorio Rossi (vols 1–3) and by Vittorio Rossi and Umberto Bosco (vol. 4). Firenze: Sansoni 1933–1942 (Edizione nazionale delle opere di Petrarca, 10–13).
De otio religioso di Francesco Petrarca. Ed. by G. Rotondi. Città del Vaticano: Biblioteca apostolica vaticana 1958. Eng. trans. *On Religious Leisure*. Trans. by Susan S. Schearer. New York: Italica Press 2002.
Posteritati. In: Francesco Petrarca: *Prose*. Edited by G. Martellotti, P.G. Ricci et al. Milano-Napoli 1955 (La letteratura italiana. Storia e testi, 7), p. 2–19. Eng. trans. by James H. Robinson: *Petrarch: The First Modern Scholar and Man of Letters*. New York: C.P. Putnam 1898, p. 56–76.
Secretum. In: Petrarca: *Prose*, p. 22–217.
Res Seniles. Libri V–VIII. Edited by Silvia Rizzo. Firenze: Le Lettere 2009.
De sui ipsius et multorum ignorantia. In: Petrarca: *Prose*, p. 710–767. Eng. trans. *On His Own Ignorance and that of Many Others* by Charles Trinkaus. In: *The Renaissance Philosophy of Man*. Edited by Ernst E Cassirer et al. Chicago: The University of Chicago Press 1950, p. 49–133.
De vita solitaria. In: *Prose*, p. 286–591. Eng. trans. *The Life of Solitude*. Edited by Jacob Zeitlin. Urbana, Ill: University of Illinois Press 1924.

Secondary Literature

Monographs and Anthologies

Ariani, Marco: *Petrarca*. Roma: Salerno Editore 1999.
Baron, Hans: *Petrarch's "Secretum". Its Making and its Meaning*. Cambridge, Mass.: Medieval Academy of America 1985.
Billanovich, Giuseppe: *Petrarca letterato. I. Lo scrittoio del Petrarca*. Roma: Edizioni di storia e letteratura 1947.
Carrara, Ernesto: *Nella selva del Petrarca*. Bologna: Cappelli 1942.
Dotti, Ugo: *Vita di Petrarca*. Roma-Bari: Laterza 1987.
Feo, Michele: *Codici latini del Petrarca nelle biblioteche fiorentine*. Firenze: Le Lettere: Cassa di Risparmio 1991.
Nolhac, Pierre de: Excursus VI: Les mémoriaux intimes de Pétrarque: In his: *Pétrarque et l'humanisme*. Paris: H. Champion 1907.
Francisco Rico: *Vida u obra de Petrarca. I. Lectura del "Secretum"*. Padova: Antenore 1974 (Studi sul Petrarca, 4).
Santagata, Marco: *I frammenti dell'anima: Storia e racconto nel "Canzoniere" di Petrarca*. Bologna: Mulino 1992.
Stierle, Karlheinz: *La vita e I tempi di Petrarca. Alle origini della moderna coscienza europea*. It. trans. Gabriella Pelloni. Venezia: Marsilio 2007.
Wilkins, Ernest Hatch: *The Life of Petrarch*. Chicago: University of Chicago Press 1961.
Wilkins, Ernest Hatch: *Studies in the Life and Works of Petrarch*. Cambridge, Mass.: Medieval Academy of America 1955.
Witt, Ronald: *"In the Footsteps of the Ancients". The Origins of Humanism from Lovato to Bruni*. Boston and Leiden: Brill 2000.

Articles and Papers

Billanovich, Giuseppe: Petrarca e il Ventoso. In: *Italia medioevale e umanistica* 9 (1961), p. 389–401.
Rico, Francisco: Ubi puer, ibi senex: Un libro de Hans Baron y el *"Secretum"* de 1353. In: *Il Petrarca latino e le origini dell'umanesimo. Atti del convegno internazionale, Firenze, 19–22 maggio, 1991*. Firenze: Le Lettere 1996 (*Quaderni petrarcheschi*, 9–10 [1992–1993]), p. 165–237.
Ullman, Berthold L: The Composition of Petrarch's "De vita solitaria" and the History of the Vatican Manuscript. In his: *Studies in the Italian Renaissance*. Roma: Edizioni di storia e letteratura 1973.

Christopher Celenza
Petrarch and the History of Philosophy

"I turned my inner eyes within, and from that moment there was no one who heard me speak until we arrived back at the foot of the mountain."[1] This is what Petrarch says he did when, in 1336 in the company of his brother Gherardo, he opened Augustine's *Confessions* to a random passage and found this: "And they go to admire the summits of mountains and the vast billows of the sea and the broadest rivers and the expanses of the ocean and the revolutions of the stars and they overlook themselves." (*Fam.* IV, 1)[2] Happening upon this passage, Petrarch writes, induced him to feel angry with himself for admiring earthly things when he should have been attending to the state of his soul. Is Petrarch doing philosophy here?

When in the 1740s Johann Jakob Brucker wrote, at the outset of his *Historia critica philosophiae*, that, up until his day, people had been using the terms "philosophy" and "philosopher" quite broadly, to refer to literary thinkers, religious thinkers, and others, he was right. For Brucker, that broad use of the term "philosophy" was something that needed to be curtailed, to be stopped. "Philosophy," henceforth, should refer only to the pure exercise of human reason, and become a critical tool. Brucker's work, so admirably open in its premises, set the modern historiography on a path that wound up excluding large parts of the past from view: post-Plotinian later Platonism, for example and, especially, Italian humanist thought from Petrarch through Poliziano.[3] So in writing and thinking about the history of philosophy the most pressing question is: do we want to write the history of philosophy from the perspective of the actors under study, or from a later perspective? I would argue it is more effective to take the actors' categories seriously, which means that, to comprehend Petrarch's place within and conception of the history of philosophy, we need to understand what he considered the

---

[1] "[…] in me ipsum interiores oculos reflexi, et ex illa hora non fuit qui me loquentem audiret donec ad ima pervenimus" See Francesco Petrarca: *Le familiari*. Ed. by Vittorio Rossi (vols 1–3) and by Vittorio Rossi and Umberto Bosco (vol. 4). Firenze: Sansoni 1933–1942 (Edizione nazionale delle opere di F. P., 10–13), I, p. 159. English translation in: Francesco Petrarca: *Letters on Familiar Matters: Rerum familiarium libri*. Translated by Aldo S. Bernardo. 3 vols. Baltimore: Johns Hopkins University Press 1975–1985, I, p. 178.
[2] "Et eunt homines admirari alta montium et ingentes fluctus maris et latissimos lapsus fluminum et occeani ambitumet giros siderum, et relinquunt se ipsos." For both text and translation, see ibid.
[3] See Christopher S. Celenza: What Counted as Philosophy in the Italian Renaissance? The History of Philosophy, the History of Science, and Styles of Life. In: *Critical Inquiry* 39 (2013), p. 367–401.

Open access. © 2018 Christopher Celenza, published by De Gruyter. This work is licensed under the Creative Commons Attribution-NonCommercial-NoDerivatives 4.0 license.
https://doi.org/10.1515/9783110419306-005

enterprise of philosophy to be: the love of and search for wisdom, an enterprise that could take different forms and be expressed in many genres.[4]

There are four interlinked ways of thinking about philosophy that are important when considering Petrarch: Philosophy as self-scrutiny; philosophy as creation of a *persona*; philosophy and exemplarity; and philosophy as dialogue. In what follows I would like to explore these tendencies in Petrarch's work.

We can return to the *Ascent of Mont Ventoux*, cited above, a letter in origin. Petrarch was writing for other readers as well. He carefully collected his letters, preserving the things he wanted to preserve, so that he could leave behind the image of himself that he desired to foster. In this letter, what impressions would a reader receive? First, we see a Petrarch intensely concerned about the state of his own conscience and behavior, scrutinizing himself for lapses and shortfalls, and exhorting himself to improve. One also observes a Petrarch very interested in having others know that he feels this way, that the *persona* he is cultivating is something that, though seemingly solitary, actually needs to be shared to be actualized. I am borrowing this idea of the search for a *persona* from the work of Condren, Gaukroger, and Hunter's *The Philosopher in Early Modern Europe: The Nature of a Contested Identity*. In their introduction, they write that their approach attempts to shift the "focus from philosophical problems to the institutional contexts in which they are delimited, and from the subject of consciousness to the *persona* of the philosopher that is cultivated in such contexts."[5]

Finally on this front, and perhaps most importantly, there is Petrarch the writer, as he makes a point of telling Dionigi – and us – how and where he decided to write down his experiences. Petrarch's *persona* is that of a writer.

Part of cultivating a *persona* had to do with exemplarity. From this perspective, *De viris illustribus* comes to the fore. The key concern present in this work is Petrarch's belief that the study of exemplary lives constituted one of history's most important functions. Petrarch's beloved Livy had himself said, in his own historical masterpiece, that "It is this especially in the study of history that is healthy and profitable: that you observe instances of every kind of conduct, a record clearly displayed from which you may select for yourself and your country what to imitate and from which you may avoid that which is shameful through and through" (Livy, *Ab urbe condita*, *Praefatio* 10).[6] This view of Livy's

---

4 See Christopher S. Celenza: *Petrarch: Everywhere a Wanderer*. London: Reaktion 2017.
5 Cf. Conal Condren/ Stephen Gaukroger/ Ian Hunter (eds.): *The Philosopher in Early Modern Europe: The Nature of a Contested Identity*. Cambridge: Cambridge University Press 2006, p. 7.
6 "Hoc illud est praecipue in cognitione rerum salubre ac frugiferum, omnis te exempli documenta in inlustri posita monumento intueri; inde tibi tuaeque rei publicae quod imitere capias, inde foedum inceptu foedum exitu quod vites."

was one that Petrarch shared as well: history existed to teach virtue and avoid vice by example; history existed, for individuals at least, to help one craft a *persona*.

Elsewhere in the preface he says that he would have gladly written about contemporary great men, but could not, since contemporary princes "contribute material not for history but for satire."[7]

This "historical" sensibility pervaded much if not all of Petrarch's work. Combined with his strong, proto-Romantic sense of personal identity, it served as a means for Petrarch to produce much interesting and – for its day – admired work. Yet there is one more element that needs to be brought into the picture to understand him the round, an element that, again, became part of the genetics of Italian Renaissance thought: a dialogical sensibility. This dialogical sensibility engendered many types of writing, from actual dialogues, to work written in an open-ended way, to treatises written as letters (after a face-to-face meeting and thus continuing the dialogue, as it were), to, finally, adversarial works. In Petrarch's Latin prose works, many of these tendencies were on view.

As Ronald G. Witt, one of the leading modern scholars of the Renaissance, put it, Petrarch can be considered a third-generation humanist who took an already existing movement that privileged the study of the ancient world and the writing of classicizing Latin and re-oriented it toward religion. Indeed, if there was one factor that marked Petrarch's work, it was this profound religious attitude, something that arose in a number of his other works.[8]

One of these was *On the Solitary Life*. The addressee, Philippe de Cabassoles, was an important local cleric who would later rise to become a cardinal. Petrarch early on became a close friend, and cultivated the relationship throughout his life. Yet in contrast to his *On Religious Leisure*, with its stark, restricted message of avoiding temptation, *On the Solitary Life* emerges as a more public work, in which one sees Petrarch weighing the merits of a certain style of life: the solitary life. As far as philosophy and the dialogical sensibility goes, a particular passage comes to mind: "Though I have always diligently sought for the truth, yet I fear the recesses in which it is hidden, or my own preoccupations, or a certain dullness of mind may have sometimes stood in my way, so that often in my search for the thing I may have been bewildered by false lights. Therefore I have treated these matters not in the spirit of one who lays down the law but as a student

---

[7] Cf. Benjamin Kohl: Petrarch's Prefaces to the "De viris illustribus." *History and Theory* 13, 2 (1974), p. 132–144: p. 138.
[8] See Ronald Witt: *"In the Footsteps of the Ancients:" The Origins of Humanism from Lovato to Bruni*. Leiden: Brill 2000 (Studies in Medieval and Reformation thought, 74), p. 230–291. See also Witt's essay in this volume.

and investigator."⁹ Again, we see a central element of this style of searching for wisdom, "philosophy" in its original meaning: not so much the pronouncement of truths already known but rather the stimulation of further conversation, questioning, and investigation.

When Petrarch offered criticisms of his fellow intellectuals, it was usually because they, in his view, seemed too smugly certain of their expertise. In fact, we possess a remarkable series of invectives that Petrarch penned, dating from the middle and end of his career, all written after he had gained a sizeable reputation. All of them share an underlying theme: the need to cultivate modesty in the face of how much there is to know in the world and the consequent obligation to resist the vanities and temptations to boast that come with professional titles. The message is forceful, and Petrarch uses all of the tricks of the rhetorical trade to get it across. Petrarch's invectives can make for difficult reading today. One has the sense of an author who, despite his urging toward modesty, had a tremendous ego and was one of those men who always believed people were watching him, always on the lookout to be offended. But they represent an important showcase for Petrarch's thought.

Take Petrarch's *Invectives against a Physician*: The story behind the episode is indicative of the times in which Petrarch lived. He had visited Pope Clement VI, the fourth in the sequence of Popes at Avignon, to whom Petrarch appealed (unsuccessfully) to bring the papacy back to the city of Rome. Pope Clement was suffering from a fever and Petrarch offered him advice, indirectly, to avoid doctors. The Pope, having heard this advice, wanted Petrarch's direct counsel, which Petrarch sent in the form of a short letter (*Fam.* V, 19). In the letter Petrarch invoked the ancient idea that doctors were little more than "mechanics," meaning tradesmen, and that those doctors especially were to be avoided who discoursed at length: "[…] I shall stop now by saying that you ought to avoid the doctor who is powerful not in his advice but in his eloquence, just as you would avoid a personal attacker, a murderer, or a poisoner."¹⁰ As this letter become known and made the rounds, local doctors, who were just beginning to see themselves as

---

9 "Ad quam licet enim studio semper aspirem, vereor tamen nequando michi vel illius latebre, vel mee cure, vel tarditas quedam obstet ingenii, ut sepe res querens opinionibus implicer. Hec ergo non diffinitor, sed scrutator vestigatorque tractaverim." See Francesco Petrarca: *Prose*. Edited by Guido Martellotti. Milano-Napoli: Ricciardi 1955, p. 588. English translation in: *The Life of Solitude by Francis Petrarch*. Edited and translated by J. Zeitlin. Urbana: University of Illinois Press 1924, p. 315.
10 Petrarca: *Letters on Familiar Matters*, I, p. 279. Latin text in: Petrarca: *Le familiari*, II, p. 45: "[…] ut vero iam desinam, medicum non consilio sed eloquio pollentem velut insidiatorem vite, sicarium aut veneficum vitare debes."

a professional class, took offense, and one decided to take up the pen to defend himself and his profession. It is to this letter, by an author whose name has not been preserved, that Petrarch responds in his *Invective*.

Among other things, Petrarch suggests that one category of analysis be subject to re-examination: that of "philosophy" and, consequently, who counts as a "philosopher." Petrarch quotes the doctor's letter in his own invective: "Let us hear what you say, and how you present yourself: 'I am a physician. [...] Consequently I am a philosopher'".[11] We can infer that the doctor had claimed that his status as a physician meant that he was automatically a "philosopher." For Petrarch here, as for many humanists after him, it was precisely the significance of this title that he wanted to call into question. Petrarch says: "Do you hear this, Pythagoras, who first invented this name?"[12] Petrarch alludes to a story that he would have known through writings of the ancient orator and politician Cicero, who related a tale about the invention of the word philosophy (one that went back to an ancient Greek source Cicero would have known, Heraclides of Pontus).[13] The story told that Pythagoras had been asked by a king what art Pythagoras thought to be his own, what, in other words, was his own special skill. Pythagoras replied that he had no art but that, instead, he considered himself a "philosopher." The king, surprised by a word he had not heard before, asked Pythagoras what he meant. Pythagoras said that life was like a great concourse, where many people could be found. Some were athletes, who contended with each other, others came to buy and sell. But the most distinctive people were those who came simply to observe, who did not seek applause, or money, but who were present instead to look into the nature of things since they were "lovers of wisdom." This story became proverbial in antiquity, late antiquity, and the Middle Ages. For Petrarch and later humanists, going back to the root meaning of the word "philosophy" had a powerful symbolic resonance and was always used in contexts like these, when a thinker, in this case Petrarch, wants to claim the mantle of the authentic pursuer of wisdom.

For Petrarch, in this case, the mistake that the doctor had made was confusing technical expertise for wisdom. This idea had, and still has, a deep background in the history of philosophy, and can be seen in Plato's early "Socratic"

---

[11] Francesco Petrarca: *Invectives*. Edited and translated by David Marsh. Cambridge, Mass.: Harvard University Press 2004 (The I Tatti Renaissance Library, 11), p. 41. Latin text in: Francesco Petrarca: *Opere latine*. Edited by Antonietta Bufano. 2 vols. Torino: UTET 1975, II, p. 854: "Quid autem de te dicas, quem te facias audiamus: 'Sum,' inquis, 'medicus'. [...] 'Consequenter et philosophus.'"
[12] Ibid.: "Audis ista, Pithagoras, qui nomen hoc primus omnium invenisti?"
[13] See Cicero: *Tusc.* V, 3, 8; Diog. Laert. *Proem.*

dialogues, those works in which Socrates draws out of his interlocutors precisely this sort of admission: that their expertise, or technical proficiency, was that and only that, not real knowledge and certainly not wisdom. Petrarch's point, pungently put as it is, is that the doctor in question is a mere mechanic and that his behavior – charging money for his expertise – vindicates this view: "Philosophers spurn money, in case you don't know. You cannot put philosophy up for sale. Who can sell what he does not possess? Even if you did possess philosophy, you could not put it up for sale; rather, philosophy would prohibit you from selling yourself."[14] So far so good: true philosophy cannot be bought and sold. But as Petrarch goes on, we see, yet again, the differences between his day and ours: "How can I believe you are a philosopher, when I know you are a mercenary mechanic? I gladly repeat this term, since I know that no other reproach stings you more. I often call you a mechanic, not by chance but by choice; and I call you a second-rate one, to cause you more pain."[15] Even in the most vehement modern academic disagreements, one does not observe this level of vitriol in published statements. One instance, then, of Petrarch's resentments, can be found in his *Invective against a Physician*: in this category we can place all those times – and there were many – when he believed that someone diminished the sort of work he did, suggesting that it was not reflective of solid, authentic intellectual work. Needless to say, Petrarch did not use those terms ("solid", "authentic"). But that is what is at stake.

Petrarch was willing, for his entire life, to accept the patronage of many different kinds of men in many different political situations – cardinals in the Church, tyrants in northern Italy, and even, for a while, leading citizens in the republic of Venice. Later in the history of Renaissance intellectual life there emerged more concrete political concerns, but Petrarch was, essentially, looking first and foremost to find resources to do what he thought most important: his work.

As to Venice, it was this environment out of which his last major invective grew. It has come down to us with the title *On His Own Ignorance and That of Many Others*, and of his three invectives, it is the most thought provoking and the least sullied by ad hominem language. Moreover, with his attempts in the work to address the proper (as opposed to wrongheaded) shapes of knowledge, his

---

[14] Petrarca: *Invectives*, p. 71–73. Latin text in: Petrarca: *Opere latine*, II, p. 882: "Philosophi enim, si nescis, pecunias spernunt: philosophiam venalem facere non potes. Quis enim vendit quod non habet? Si eam haberes, non tu illam ideo venalem faceres, sed illa te venalem esse non sineret."
[15] Ibid.: "quomodo ego te philosopum credam cum mercenarium mechanicum sciam? Repeto libenter hoc nomen, quia novi quod nullo magis ureris convitio; non casu, sed sciens sepe te mechanicum voco, et, quo gravius doleas, non primum."

satire of scholastic learning, and his consequent charges of irreligion (against his detractors), Petrarch set a template that later Renaissance thinkers would follow.

Petrarch's travels had taken him to Venice by 1362, where he received a rent-free accommodation from the city government, after promising his library to Venice – to the Church of Saint Mark, precisely – in the hopes of creating what he described in a letter to a friend as the beginnings of a *bibliotheca publica*, a "public library." In his proposal to the city, Petrarch wrote that he hoped his gift would inspire the city to add to the collection of books from public funds from time to time and, what is more, that others would be inspired by his example to donate their own book collections "to the aforesaid Church; and thus it may develop into a great and famous library equaling those of antiquity."[16] The city government (which had control over the Church, as state property) wrote back and accepted the "offer made by Master Francesco Petrarca, whose fame today in the whole world is so great that, in the memory of man, there has never been in Christendom any moral philosopher or any poet who can be compared with him."[17] So you could say that Petrarch and Venice got off to a good start.

Petrarch enjoyed his life in Venice, living as he did in his rent-free house and earning income from yet another ecclesiastical benefice he had been awarded. As ever, he developed a circle of learned, wealthy friends. And for a time, their relationship was idyllic: they would meet and discuss intellectual matters large and small and share the usual mix of seriousness and laughter common among friends. But as time went by, the tenor of their discussions changed. They – there were four of them – favored university-based learning and the philosopher Aristotle especially, something that seems to have rankled Petrarch to such an extent that he began to speak out. Petrarch gives us the tenor of how the discussions unfolded. "These men burn and rage with blind ardor all the more fiercely because they themselves are all scholars and great burners of midnight oil."[18] Yet, "learning is an instrument of madness for many, and of pride for nearly everyone, unless, as rarely happens, it meets with a good and cultivated mind."[19] Petrarch then begins to give examples of useless facts that the learned know and, full of pride as they are, vaunt. "This fourth fellow knows about wild beasts, birds, and fish. He knows how many hairs a lion has in its mane, how many feathers a hawk has in its tail, and how many coils an octopus

---

16 Ernest Hatch Wilkins: *Life of Petrarch*. Chicago: University of Chicago Press 1961, p. 185.
17 Ibid., p. 186.
18 Petrarca: *Invectives*, p. 237. Latin text in: Petrarca: *Opere latine*, II, p. 1036: "Eo vero acrius uruntur et ceco estuant incendio, quod et ipsi studiosi omnes et lucubratores magni sunt."
19 Ibid., p. 239. Latin text, p. 1038: "Sunt enim litere multis instrumenta dementie, cuntis fere superbie, nisi, quod rarum, in aliquam bonam et bene institutam animam inciderint."

wraps around a castaway."[20] Petrarch satirizes "natural philosophy" here, which is to say the brand of philosophy dedicated to studying nature in all its aspects.

Whether the facts cited are true or false (and Petrarch is working from known sources), "What use is it, I ask, to know the nature of beasts and birds and fish and snakes, and to ignore or neglect our human nature, the purpose of our birth, or whence we come whither we are bound?"[21] In other words Petrarch is arguing that moral character matters firstly and most importantly and that knowledge of facts is secondary. At some point his friends' constant citation of Aristotle seems to have got the better of him, and he spoke out:

> Hec et talia huiusmodi adversus hos scribas, non mosaica utique nec cristiana, sed aristotelica, ut sibi videntur, in lege doctissimos, cum sepe liberius agerem quam soliti sint audire, idque fortassis incautius, ut qui inter amicos loquens nichil inde periculi providerem, mirari illi primum, post irasci. Et quoniam contra suam heresim ac paternas leges dici ista sentirent, collegerunt et ipsi concilium, non ut me, quem profecto diligunt, sed ut famam meam, quam oderunt, ignorantie crimine condemnarent.

> [I have often made these and similar objections to these scribes, who consider themselves most learned, not in the law of Moses or Christ, but in that of Aristotle. I spoke with greater freedom than they are accustomed to hear, and perhaps with less caution, since I foresaw no danger involved in speaking with friends. At first they were amazed, and then angered, for they felt that my words ran counter to their sect and its ancestral laws. So they formed a council, not to condemn me, whom they love, but to condemn my fame, which they hate, on a charge of ignorance.][22]

Sect. This word – *secta* in Latin – carried with it an important resonance. The Latin word was a direct translation of the Greek 'haeresis' or 'heresy,' a word that derived from the verb *haereo*, which at its root signified cutting, or segmenting, and more generally meant choosing. A *haeresis* signified a 'choice' at its most basic level. In late antiquity, as early Christian leaders struggled to define the boundaries of the Christian religion, it also came to mean the 'wrong choice,' so that the meaning more familiar to us, *heresy*, emerged then. The word could also be used to describe a group of followers of a certain religious or philosophical emphasis. So when Petrarch uses the word here, coupling it with "ancestral laws," he is very subtly including all those resonances, triggering in a reader's

---

20 Ibid.: "Multa ille igitur de beluis deque avibus ac piscibus: quot leo pilos in vertice, quot plumas accipiter in cauda, quot polipus spiris naufragum liget."
21 Ibid. Latin text, p. 1038–1040: "Nam quid, oro, naturas beluarum et volucrum et piscium et serpentum nosse profuerit, et naturam hominum, ad quid nati sumus, unde et quo pergimus, uel nescire uel spernere?"
22 Ibid., p. 239–241. Latin text, p. 1040.

mind the beginnings of the argument he will go on to develop in the treatise: these former friends of his were *uncritical* followers of Aristotle and (something he will later emphasize) possibly irreligious as well.

But what was it, exactly, that set Petrarch off? Why did he feel the need to write a treatise? He tells us early on. His friends, after saying that Petrarch was eloquent in speech and writing but devoid of knowledge, pronounced a verdict on him, to this effect: "I am a good man without learning."[23] The direction of the treatise changes immediately after this statement, and in its dramatic tension the transition can stand not only for Petrarch's main thrust in the treatise but also for the way he re-oriented the humanist movement. Petrarch writes, in a passage that is worth quoting extensively:

> O utinam veri nichil unquam preter hoc unum dixerint aut dicturi sint! Et, o alme salutiferque Iesu, vere literarum omnium et ingenii Deus ac largitor, vere rex glorie ac virtutum domine, te nunc flexis anime genibus supplex oro, ut si michi non amplius vis largiri, hec saltem portio mea sit, ut vir bonus sim; quod, nisi te valde amem pieque colam, esse non possum. Ad hoc enim, non ad literas natus sum; que si sole obvenerint inflant diruuntque, non edificant: fulgida uincula laboriosumque negotium ac sonorum pondus anime.
>
> [Would that this were the only truth they have spoken or will ever speak! O gracious savior Jesus, true God who bestows all learning and intelligence, true King of glory and Lord of virtues, I pray to you as a suppliant on my soul's bended knee. If You choose to grant me nothing else, let it at least be my portion to be a good man. This I cannot be unless I greatly love and devoutly worship You. I was born for this and not for learning. If learning alone is granted us, it puffs up and ruins, and does not edify. It becomes a gleaming shackle of the soul, a wearisome pursuit, and a noisy burden.][24]

It is obvious that Petrarch is using rhetoric here, counter-posing Christianity to learning, in a time when what he wrote could not, effectively, be gainsaid. No one could disagree, in other words, that worshiping god and practicing Christianity should be a priority over against studying Aristotle. But Petrarch's sentiment here represents far more than rhetoric. Instead, it signals a turn toward religion that he introduced into the humanist movement, in which Christianity, the advocacy of personal humility, and a focus on moral philosophy all came together. Biblically oriented readers will have noticed Petrarch's allusion to St. Paul's Letter to the Corinthians 8:1: "Knowledge puffs up, but love edifies." The idea is to focus on personal conduct, stressing that knowledge of facts alone can make a person arrogant and vain.

---

23 Ibid., p. 245 and 249. Latin text, p. 1044 and 1048.
24 Ibid., p. 245. Latin text, p. 1044.

Petrarch sinuously loops back on his own arguments in this treatise, as if repeating things in a slightly different key would reinforce his message. Petrarch tells how the discussions used to go, first recounting his own style in speaking to his friends: "when I speak to my friends, I use a rambling sort of speech"[25] – in other words, I didn't think I constantly had to be "on" when in the company of friends.

Here is what they would do: "they used to propose some Aristotelian problem or some question about animals for discussion." Fair enough. "I would remain silent, or joke, or introduce some other topic. Sometimes I would smile and ask how Aristotle could have known things that obey no reason and cannot be tested experimentally." Their reaction: "they would be amazed and silently angered, and would look at me as a blasphemer for requiring more than that man's authority as proof of a fact."[26]

At this distance and given that we hear only Petrarch's side of the conversation, who can say what the real tenor of the discussion was? Perhaps his friends were earnest young men, interested in discussing the most current scientific problems of the day ... and there sat Petrarch, ridiculing them, as if these issues could not possibly be important. Perhaps they were indeed arrogant, as Petrarch claimed, and believed that Aristotle was the only legitimate authority and that, to learn truly and to understand the works truly, one needed only to explicate Aristotle.

What we can know is this: it is precisely Aristotle's status as an authority that Petrarch wants to bring into relief. Petrarch tells us so: "Now, I believe that Aristotle was a great man and a polymath. But he was still human and could therefore have been ignorant of some things, or even of many things." This message represents one half – the positive half – of Petrarch's approach in this treatise. The other half is not so positive. Petrarch goes on: "I shall go further, if I am allowed by these men who are greater friends of sects [*sects*, again] than of the truth." Petrarch goes on: "by heaven, I believe without a doubt that he was 'quite on the wrong road,' as the phrase has it" –Petrarch alludes to a line from the ancient comic playwright Terence – "not only in minor questions, in which any error is minor and scarcely dangerous, but also in the major questions that concern our

---

25 Ibid., p. 263. Latin text, p. 1060: "Michi autem sermo vaus inter amicos inelaborateque sententie."
26 Ibid., p. 265. Latin text, p. 1062: "Solebant illi vel aristotelicum problema vel de animalibus aliquid in medium iactare. Ego autem vel tacere vel iocari vel ordiri aliud, interdumque subridens querere quonam modo id scire potuisset Aristotiles, cuius et ratio nulla esset et experimentum impossibile. Stupere illi, et taciti subirasci, et blasphemum velut aspicere, cui ad fidem rerum aliud quam viri autoritas quereretur [...]."

ultimate salvation."[27] Again, we see this turning toward Christianity as part of a rhetorical strategy, a tendency that intensifies soon thereafter.

Petrarch widens his critique when he brings a specific work of Aristotle into play: the *Ethics*, or what we know as the *Nicomachean Ethics*, whose primary purpose was a discussion of "happiness" or "flourishing" (the Greek *eudaimonia* and the Latin *felicitas*). Aristotle's questions had been: what constitutes human flourishing? How does one best pursue it? Aristotle's brilliant, methodical approach to what he called the "philosophy of the human" assured him a continuous audience throughout the Middle Ages and Renaissance, from the time in the thirteenth century when his works were rediscovered and translated from Greek into Latin through to the Renaissance and beyond (*EN* 1181b15). By Petrarch's day Aristotle's works had become staples of university curricula.

Here, in this treatise, Petrarch sets the tone for much of the humanist world to come, when Aristotle is under discussion. It is not so much that Aristotle was wrong – it was after all Aristotle himself who had said that *Ethics* was not a subject we study to gain knowledge but rather to become better. Rather, Aristotle's modern followers are the ones to be singled out. Adhering to institutional models, they have, in Petrarch's view, lost the ability to practice philosophy broadly conceived, to practice, that is, that set of interlinked disciplines that fostered the love and pursuit of human wisdom. Petrarch's *persona*, then, is of someone standing outside institutional life, who only from that outsider perspective can offer incisive critique.

At root, Petrarch's method involved a tight linkage between reading and writing and, as importantly, an imagined (but no less powerful) link between reading and life.[28] We can conclude with a passage from Petrarch's *familiare colloquium*, the *Secret*, where Augustine advises Petrarch as follows:

> Comunis legentium mos est, ex quo monstrum illud execrabile, literatorum passim flagitiosissimos errare greges et de arte vivendi, multa licet in scolis disputentur, in actum pauca converti. Tu vero, si suis locis notas certas impresseris, fructum ex lectione percipies.

---

[27] Ibid.: "Ego vero magnum quendam virum ac multiscium Aristotilem, sed fuisse hominem, et idcirco aliqua, imo et multa nescire potuisse arbitror; plus dicam, si per istos liceat non tam veri amicos quam sectarum: credo *hercle*, nec dubito, illum non in rebus tantum parvis, quarum parvus et minime periculosus est error, sed in maximis et spectantibus ad salutis summam aberrasse tota, ut aiunt, via."

[28] As Igor Candido has suggested in his "Legere quod scripserunt primi, scribere quod legant ultimi:" itinerari della lettura (e della scrittura) tra Petrarca e Boccaccio. In: Giovanna Rizzarelli and Cristina Savettieri (eds): *C'è un lettore in questo testo? Rappresentazioni letterarie della lettura in Italia*. Bologna: Il Mulino 2016, p. 43–67 (p. 47–51).

[That's what usually happens with readers, with the dire and damnable consequence that disgraceful groups of well-read people wander round incapable of translating the art of living into action, even if they are good at arguing about it in the schools.][29]

Bibliography

Primary Literature

Petrarca, Francesco: *The Life of Solitude*. Ed. and trans. by J. Zeitlin. Urbana: University of Illinois Press 1924.
Petrarca, Francesco: *Le familiari*. Ed. by Vittorio Rossi (vols 1–3) and Umberto Bosco (vol. 4). Firenze: Sansoni 1933–1942 (Edizione nazionale delle opere di F. P., vols. 10–13).
Petrarca, Francesco: *Prose*. Ed. by Guido Martellotti. Milano-Napoli: Ricciardi 1955.
Petrarca, Francesco: *Opere latine*. Ed. by Antonietta Bufano. 2 vols. Torino: UTET 1975.
Petrarca, Francesco: *Letters on Familiar Matters: Rerum familiarium libri*. Translated by Aldo S. Bernardo. 3 vols. Baltimore: Johns Hopkins University Press 1975–1985.
Petrarca, Francesco: *Invectives*. Ed. and trans. by David Marsh. Cambridge, Mass.: Harvard University Press 2004 (The I Tatti Renaissance Library, 11).
Petrarca, Francesco: *My Secret Book*. Edited and translated by Nicholas Mann. Cambridge, Mass.: Harvard University press 2016 (The I Tatti Renaissance Library, 72).

Secondary Literature

Monographs and Anthologies

Celenza, Christopher S: *Petrarch: Everywhere a Wanderer*. London: Reaktion 2017.
Condren, Conal, Stephen Gaukroger, Ian Hunter (eds.): *The Philosopher in Early Modern Europe: The Nature of a Contested Identity*. Cambridge: Cambridge University Press 2006.
Wilkins, Ernest Hatch: *Life of Petrarch*. Chicago: University of Chicago Press 1961.

Articles and Papers

Candido, Igor: "Legere quod scripserunt primi, scribere quod legant ultimi:" itinerari della lettura (e della scrittura) tra Petrarca e Boccaccio. In: Giovanna Rizzarelli and Cristina

---

[29] Petrarca: *Prose*, p. 122. English translation in: Francesco Petrarca: *My Secret Book*. Edited and translated by Nicholas Mann. Cambridge, Mass.: Harvard University press 2016 (The I Tatti Renaissance Library, 72), p. 135.

Savettieri (eds): *C'è un lettore in questo testo? Rappresentazioni letterarie della lettura in Italia*. Bologna: Il Mulino 2016, p. 43–67.

Celenza, Christopher S: What Counted as Philosophy in the Italian Renaissance? The History of Philosophy, the History of Science, and Styles of Life. In: *Critical Inquiry* 39 (2013), p. 367–401.

Kohl, Benjamin: Petrarch's Prefaces to the "De viris illustribus." *History and Theory* 13, 2 (1974), p. 132–144.

Joachim Küpper
The Secret Life of Classical and Arabic Medical Texts in Petrarch's *Canzoniere*

0

Petrarch's *Canzoniere* is undoubtedly the most influential collection of poems in the Western tradition. Petrarchism – a specific way to write love poems inspired by the Petrarchan model – was, from the late fourteenth century onward, and for a period of more than two and a half centuries, the dominant mode not only in Italy, but also in Spain, France and England. The influence of Petrarchism reached Germany, Scandinavia, Poland, Russia, and even countries like Cyprus; in terms of timespan, the vestiges of the Petrarchan model may be found up to and including the nineteenth century;[1] an experienced reader will have no difficulties detecting direct or mediated traces of schemes, patterns and forms typical of the Petrarchan collection even in love poems published in our times. And due to his enormous impact on Occidental literary history, Petrarch is an author who has been discussed not only by literary scholars, but also by philosophers and historians of ideas, starting with Rousseau and Hegel.

My modest contribution to this most impressive tradition of literary as well as philosophical readings of Petrarch's work will consist in problematizing a sometimes tacit, but in many cases explicit assumption in scholarship thus far; namely, that the semantic core of Petrarch's collection, the concept of love, would be a continuation of Dante's *Vita nova*, hence a Christianized version of the Platonic model. Within this standard reading, it is assumed that the sublimating, that is, the specifically religious implications – meaning the presentation of the *donna* as an angel not only in the metaphorical, but also in the literal sense – have been reduced in Petrarch as compared to Dante. However, the tendency is considered to be preserved: the spiritualizing of the love object, as well as of the feelings she arouses in the lover, including the ending that refers, in both Dante and Petrarch, to the obligatory last station of the Christian *iter mentis*, the renunciation of earthly love and the conversion to spiritual love – in this case, the substitution of Laura by Mary which seems to be expressed in the *Canzone alla Vergine*, the last poem of the collection.

My reading proposes to consider the love concept inherent in the *Canzoniere* as being modeled, at least to a certain extent, after the theory of love developed

---

[1] I am thinking of certain well-known poems (the most prominent being *A une passante*) from Baudelaire's *Les Fleurs du mal*.

within the medical discourse of that age, which became known under the name of *hereos*. Its origins are in part Aristotelian, Galenic and Arabic, and the common denominator of these conceptual sources is what I would schematically term an 'anthropological materialism.'

Within a Christian framework, the human being is conceived of as a microcosm structured in analogy to the macrocosm. Just as the macrocosm is governed by the one and only God, man is governed by that part which is the God-like feature of human beings; namely, reason. According to Christian dogma, and in line with the Platonic tradition, indulging in bodily pleasures signifies a neglect of the specific dignity granted to humans. It is a symptom of animality, labeled *akrasia*[2] by Plato; Christian theology preserves this negative assessment while supplementing it with a metaphysically relevant condemnation: since such action ignores the potential inherent in God-given reason, it is sinful.

Classical (Galenic) and Arabic (Avicennan and Averroist) anthropological materialism, both in turn based on Aristotelianism, postulates, by contrast, that humans are primarily material beings – meaning that their concrete actions are influenced by bodily constellations that may not be strictly controlled by the rational mind of the person concerned; it is a consequence of such an approach to consider actual patterns of behavior as liable to the eventual influence of external action (that is, cures and therapies) applied by medical doctors. From a Christian vantage point, the highly provocative implication of such a conceptualization consists in the fact that wrong ('sinful') behavior would no longer be systematically imputable to humans. Rather, such behavior might be a symptom of bodily dysfunctions that may or may not be treated successfully. The only way to make this approach compatible with Christian views is a rigorously Augustinian interpretation of the dogma: the body's dysfunction and its consequence – sin – would be conceived of as indicating one's place within the *massa damnata*.

1

My argument proper is divided into three parts. The first section offers some preliminary remarks concerning the general background of my reading; it deals with the relation of medical and humanist discourses in texts from the pre-modern period. The second part presents the, as it were, material basis of my argument, namely, the concrete malady discussed under the name of *hereos* in the medical discourse of the

---

[2] Literally translated: 'acting against one's better judgment'.

Middle Ages. Finally, the third section provides some observations concerning the presence of this concept in vernacular poetry, focusing on the Petrarchan *Canzoniere*.

In present times, the medical discourse and the humanist discourse – literature, philosophy and the scholarly discourses concerning literature and philosophy – have reached a state of complete separation on the epistemological as well as on the practical level, divisions reflective of what we often call the "two cultures."[3] At least in continental Europe, it would be hard to find a young medical doctor who also takes an interest in literature or philosophy, and continental intellectuals typically view science as something threatening to the basis of culture and even to life itself. With respect to the division of the "discursive field,"[4] the actual situation differs fundamentally from that of ancient and medieval times. All important classical and medieval philosophers were "natural philosophers" as well; they treated problems that from the seventeenth century onward belonged to the separate field of exact science.

At first sight, this rough sketch may suggest that the relationship between the scientific and the humanist discourses could be described as a continuous process of separation. One can rather observe that in a specific phase of Western history, the affinity, or, should I say, the interpenetration of the respective discourses was even greater than it had been in classical times. The period to which I am referring comprises the twelfth through the fourteenth centuries and is characterized by the Western reception of Greek philosophy, in particular of Aristotelianism.

Aristotle's writings were imparted to the West via the Arabic intermediary. At least in the beginning, the interest the Islamic cultures took in studying the Greek tradition was not genuinely philosophical. Monotheism does not need a philosophy. The reasons for which Arab scholars began to read the classical texts were pragmatic. They were eager to learn from these texts not how to conceive of the world but rather how to handle it. Since one of the major problems human beings face in dealing with the material world is the physical part of their own selves, it is perhaps no surprise that the Arabic reception of Greek knowledge gave prominence to questions of health and hygiene. And it is very probable that at least in the beginning – that is, in the twelfth century – Western interest in the Arabic texts was motivated by the same reason; namely, the desire to deal with problems neglected by the blending of (unorthodox) Judaism and Platonism we call Christianity.[5] The details of this

---

3 See Charles P. Snow: *The Two Cultures and the Scientific Revolution*. New York: Cambridge University Press 1959.
4 In the sense of the Foucauldian term 'champ discursif' (*L'Archéologie du savoir*. Paris: Gallimard 1969, p. 75–84, esp. p. 84).
5 As early as the Middle Ages, there is a partial plurality in the Christian West, which is linked to the fact that scripturally-fixated monotheism is something other than monotheism *tout court*.

process are not relevant to the topic discussed here.⁶ What matters is the fact that what was in later centuries regarded as separate – the philosophical part of Greek learning on the one hand and the scientific, especially the medical part on the other – was considered at this time one integral corpus of texts. This somewhat striking situation was reflected in the organization of teaching. In the universities of Bologna and Padova, but also in Montpellier, the disciplines of the *quadrivium* (arithmetic, geometry, astronomy, music) were taught mainly by professors of medicine.⁷

Monotheisms claim an all-comprising discursive competency. In principle, no truth is predicable which would be situated outside the system. Yet monotheisms conceiving of themselves as based on a scripturally-fixated revelation confront the problem of texts being finite and focused. By necessity, these texts do not treat all problems humans may face on an equal level. In addition, we have to take into account that Christianity, in contrast to Islam, did not militarily subjugate other cultures in the age when its dogma was shaped; it colonized them by way of subversion from within. In order to do that it was forced to strip off the all-too-obvious remains of its particularistic origins; it tried to become universally acceptable by explicitly rejecting almost all ritualistic practices regulating daily life. Dietary rules, hygienic prescriptions – that is, the norms constituting an elementary system of public health within Judaism – were eliminated in the interest of gaining access to a huge variety of different communities. In short: there is no discourse concerning the body's malfunction within Christianity. It is this *lacuna* that was then filled by importing the medical discourses flourishing in the Arabic world, an import that was considered unproblematic, because it carried the brand of Aristotle, who is systematically denoted as *the* 'philosophus' by Thomas; meaning, the one (and only) who, although a pagan, was allowed by the Christian God to develop concepts the verity of which would become fully obvious only after Christ's self-sacrifice. So, what we have in the Middle Ages are not two competing anthropological discourses (one theological, the other medical). We have a discursive field that is compartmentalized, as it were. The main parts of the field are fiercely guarded and rigorously defended: they are exclusive properties of Christian theology and its various *ancillae*, with philosophy in the first place. There are, however, sections of the field to which Christian theology did not lay absolute claim, since it would not have been able to deliver a meaningful discursification of these parts. The medical discourse is perhaps the most important section to be mentioned here; but I would tentatively suggest that we consider other instances of the discursive *lacuna* described above: these may be the discourse on political power, the discourse of the judiciary, the discourse of economics and, at least in part, the discourse on phenomena of the natural world. More or less unnoticed by the theological authorities, these un(re)claimed sections of the field became, over the course of the following centuries, discursive territories occupied by semantic constellations alien to, or in contradiction to, the Christian dogma. It may have been a more or less conscious, in any case an important work done by moral-philosophical texts of minor, almost negligible value – namely, literary texts – to have secretly opened up the main field, the stronghold of theological orthodoxy, for these heterodoxical discourses to make their way upwards, towards serious acceptability.

6 For all relevant details of the entire process, that is, the transmission of Greek and Arabic knowledge to the West, see Paul O. Kristeller: The School of Salerno. Its Development and its Contribution to the History of Learning. In his: *Studies in Renaissance Thought and Letters*. Rome: Edizioni di Storia e Letteratura 1956 (Storia e Letteratura, 54), p. 495–551.

7 See Hastings Rashdall: *The Universities of Europe in the Middle Ages*. Second edition by Frederick M. Powicke and Alfred B. Emden. 3 vols. London: Oxford University Press 1936, I, p. 261 ff.

Petrarch, the author on whom I will focus in the main section of this paper, had been a student of the *artes liberales* in Bologna and Montpellier. However, with respect to his knowledge of contemporary medical discourses, one need not even speculate. He wrote a text titled *Invective contra medicum*, which is much less known than his collection of love poems. A glance at the title alone makes one anticipate a contribution to the genre of satire well known from later times, such as Molière's *Le Malade imaginaire* or the *Sueños* by Quevedo, both of which are exaggerated incriminations of physicians who promise to save lives and nevertheless become, sooner or later, the messengers of imminent death. Paul O. Kristeller has shown, however, that although Petrarch's text is partly anti-medical in a satirical sense, its main concern is philosophical.[8] It is a document of Petrarch's adherence to the *via moderna* in the controversy on nominalism that characterized the fourteenth century. The anonymous addressee of the *Invective* is a professor of medicine[9] who is incriminated, in his pretentions as a philosopher, as an Averroist, one of those who were convinced that the world in its entirety could be explained by a discourse based on logic. The polemics do not concern the genuinely medical dimensions of Averroism.[10] Such an attitude is characteristic not only of Petrarch but of his contemporaries as well, who, notwithstanding the philosophical controversies and the differences concerning religious belief, considered the practical assumptions of Greek and Arabic medicine as a matter of course, because it was able to provide – in contrast to the obscure knowledge of witches and magicians – at least some curative competency.

There is a second aspect involved in my argument that from a modern standpoint may perhaps seem somewhat strange: the speculation that a highly sophisticated poetic discourse may be based on a quite down-to-earth medical discourse. Such an assumption might appear less odd if one takes into consideration the difference between what is meant when we use the term 'soul' in modern times – that is, from the eighteenth and nineteenth centuries onward – and that which it designated in pre-modern times.[11] It may seem provocative to say that the pre-modern anthropological discourse is much more materialist than its modern

---

8 See Paul O. Kristeller: Il Petrarca, l'Umanesimo e la Scolastica. In: *Lettere italiane* 7, 4 (1955), p. 367–387; see also Klaus Bergdolt: *Arzt, Krankheit und Therapie bei Petrarca: Die Kritik an Medizin und Naturwissenschaft im italienischen Frühhumanismus*. Weinheim: VCH Acta humaniora 1992.
9 Supposedly, the person addressed was the private physician of Pope Clement VI.
10 Francesco Petrarca: *Invective contra medicum*. In: *Opere latine*. Edited by Antonietta Bufano. Turin: UTET 1975, p. 818–981; concerning the author's shifting attitudes towards those he criticizes in his treatise see p. 842, 878, 920, and p. 846, 868, 870, 912.
11 Concerning the concept of *psyche* in Aristotle see the substantial article by Massimo Ciavolella: La tradizione dell'*aegritudo amoris* nel *Decameron*. In: *Giornale storico della letteratura italiana* 147 (1970), p. 496–517, especially p. 502–509.

continuation.[12] In the age of positivism and empiricism, what we typically call the soul became a sort of catch-all term for those aspects of human behavior that cannot (or cannot yet) be explained by a somatic approach. The 'psyche' is the instance of difference as such: it is the abysmal, an 'Unheimliches', the site of the illogical, of those aspects of our selves which elude the discourses of 'normal science'. As what we call the 'soul' has been considered the source of our emotions and especially of love since the beginning of the Western tradition, it is evident that in modern times love, and furthermore the problems linked to love, are conceived of as escaping the discourses based on logic and reason. When in present times a physician is asked to intervene in a case of unhappiness caused by an actual or virtual relationship, the underlying assumption consists in perceiving humans as bodies only and all problems traditionally labeled 'love problems' as being purely sexual. In short: in the modern age, there are the alternatives of an anthropological discourse that is exclusively materialist and a discourse that considers what is specifically human – meaning our emotions and in particular 'love' – as transgressing the capacities of regular, logical and scientific discourse.

The medieval and early modern concept of *anima* or *animus*, which derives from Platonic concepts and owes even more to the theorizing of Aristotle, may perhaps be described as a sort of intermediate stage between these two alternatives, which implies that it is much more materialist than the modern concept of 'psyche.' *Anima* is a sort of principle common to all beings, that is, living objects both human and non-human, including plants. It comprises aspects that are purely material. Specifically the human *anima* integrates bodily and non-bodily, immaterial phenomena. The different parts are hierarchically organized (*pars vegetativa*, *pars sensitiva*, *pars rationalis*), but during a human being's lifetime they are inevitably linked to each other. It is for this reason that in pre-modern anthropological discourses the merely 'vegetative' functions of human bodies (for instance sleeping and waking, laughing and crying), the 'sensitive' functions (in other words, perceptions), and the rational functions are conceived of as being involved in a process of permanent mutual exchange.

Such a conceptualization of the human soul had several consequences: there is no distinct concept of 'feelings,' distinct in the sense of structuralist semantics, that is, as differing from reason on the one hand and from vegetative bodily phenomena on the other. 'Emotions' is a term referring to a specific constellation of bodily functions, of perceptions and of rational activities; or, should I say, a name for a specific constellation of reciprocal data processing between the three *partes* operated by the *anima* as a whole. This approach explains the somewhat strange idea that by administering medical or bodily cures one can influence the most intimate of human feelings.

---

12 By which I mean, to be precise, the pre-postmodern anthropological discourse.

Considering the discursive scenario, it is perhaps not altogether astonishing that literary texts of that age, in their fashioning of love and lovers, frequently refer to the prevalent medical discourses. Still somewhat perplexing are the enunciations[13] of a love discourse based on such a concept of the soul. Particularly in the scholarly treatment of the Petrarchan *Canzoniere* these concrete shapings – as I will call them – of the feeling named 'love,' which differ from our modern understanding and even stand in opposition to it, have been assessed as idiosyncratic utterances of a somewhat strange mind. With the intention of problematizing this standard assessment, I will try to demonstrate that the self of the *Canzoniere* may be considered as being modeled – at least to a certain extent – according to the central assumptions of the medical discourse on *hereos* whose main features will be introduced by way of a concise sketch.

2

My presentation of the malady (*morbus*, *egritudo*) is indebted to Mary F. Wack's book *Lovesickness in the Middle Ages*.[14] Out of several dozen treatises, which belonged to the corpus of texts contemporary students of medicine were obliged to study, Wack chooses six examples: the first is part of the *Viaticum peregrinantis* by

---

[13] Concerning the Foucauldian differentiation between *énonciation* and *énoncé*, see *L'Archéologie du savoir*, p. 45–54.

[14] The book bears the subtitle *The* Viaticum *and Its Commentaries* (Philadelphia, PA: University of Pennsylvania Press 1990). Its convenience results mainly from the fact that it gives well-conceived translations of the treatises which are written in a somewhat wooden scholastic Latin. Wack's work is based on a long tradition of scholarly descriptions of *hereos* which begins in the nineteenth century. I quote some particularly instructive publications: Danielle Jacquart: La maladie et le remède d'amour dans quelques écrits médicaux du Moyen âge. In: Danielle Buschinger/ André Crépin (eds.): *Amour, mariage et transgressions au Moyen âge*. Göppingen: Kümmerle 1984 (Göppinger Arbeiten zur Germanistik, 420), p. 93–101; Massimo Ciavolella: Mediaeval Medicine and Arcite's Love Sickness. In: *Florilegium* 1 (1979), p. 222–241; John Livingston Lowes: The Loveres Maladye of Hereos. In: *Modern Philology* 11 (1913/1914), p. 491–546; Otto Bird: The Canzone d'Amore of Cavalcanti According to The Commentary of Dino del Garbo. In: *Medieval Studies* 2 (1940), p. 150–203; Michel Simonin: *Aegritudo amoris* et *res literaria* à la Renaissance: Réflexions préliminaires. In: Jean Céard (ed.): *La Folie et le corps*. Paris: Presses de l'École normale supérieure 1985, p. 83–90; Marie-Paule Duminil: La mélancolie amoureuse dans l'Antiquité. In: Céard (ed.): *La Folie et le corps*, p. 91–110; Daniele Jacquart/Claude Thomasset: L'Amour héroïque à travers le traité d'Arnaud de Villeneuve. In: Céard (ed.): *La Folie et le corps*, p. 143–158; Bruno Nardi: L'Amore e i medici medievali. In: *Studi in onore di Angelo Monteverdi*. 2 vols. Modena: Società tipografica editrice modenese 1959, II, p. 517–542. Wack provides a critical edition based on extant manuscripts of the treatises by Constantinus Africanus, Gerardus Bituricensis, Petrus Hispanus and Bona Fortuna; since Petrus' text

Constantinus Africanus, who initiated the Western reception of Arabic and Greek medical scholarship when he came from North Africa to the monastery of Montecassino and to Salerno in the middle of the eleventh century.[15] The *Viaticum* is based on Galen, on the *Corpus Hippocraticum*, and on additional Arabic empirical knowledge. All the following texts are commentaries on the corresponding chapter of the *Viaticum*. Gerard de Berry (Gerardus Bituricensis) wrote his gloss (*glosule*) at Paris or Salerno at the end of the twelfth century; he was the first to blend Constantinus Africanus' text with the *Canon medicinae* by Avicenna and the *De anima* by Aristotle.[16] Giles/Egidius (Paris or Santarem, Portugal, early thirteenth century) organized his text according to the scholastic pattern of the *quaestio*. Petrus Hispanus, who later became Pope under the name of John XXI, wrote his commentary at Siena in the middle of the thirteenth century; his text is the most influential of all the extant treatises, including those not considered by Wack. Bona Fortuna wrote his tract at Paris or Montpellier in the first half of the fourteenth century. There are a great number of further commentaries from the fourteenth century, which in substance, however, do not differ from or exceed what one can find in the treatises by Petrus Hispanus or Bona Fortuna. The following portrait will be for reasons of convenience a sort of *cento*, a hybridization of the texts to which I am referring.

Hereos[17] is described in all of the texts as being primarily an illness of the mind. According to its location in the brain, the dysfunction associated with the illness is characterized first and foremost as a hypertrophy of the brain's normal operation of thinking, the thoughts being transfixed by the beauty of a beloved person:

---

exists in two diverging redactions, Wack reproduces these separately, under the names of version A and B. The main passages of Arnaldus' very influential treatise are printed by Massimo Ciavolella: *La malattia d'amore dall'Antichità al Medioevo*. Rome: Bulzoni 1976, p. 77–84; the passages of Bernardus Gordonius' *Lilium medicinae* referring to the malady are to be found in Lowes: The Loveres Malady of Hereos, p. 499–502. I will use the following abbreviations for the treatises (the page numbers refer to Wack's print edition as listed above): Constantinus Africanus, *Viaticum peregrinantis* I. 20 = CA; Gerard de Berry, *Glosule super Viaticum* = GB; Giles/Edigius, *Glose super Viaticum* = E; Petrus Hispanus, *Questiones super Viaticum*, Version A = PH A; Petrus Hispanus, *Questiones super Viaticum*, Version B = PH B; Bona Fortuna, *Tractatus super Viaticum* = BF.

15 See again the article by Kristeller referred to in note 6.

16 The theory of the different "faculties" (*virtutes*) of the soul was first introduced by Avicenna (*Canon medicinae*, lib. I, fen. I, doc. 6, cap. 1–6; see p. 23–26 of the print edition Venice 1507). The *Canon medicinae* contains a passage describing love sickness (*De ilisci*, lib. III, fen. 1, tr. 4, c. 24 [p. 191 in the quoted print edition]), which seems to be the first document extant on the disease.

17 The somewhat strange name of the disease is assumed by the specialists to be a contamination of *eros* and *heroicus*. The theoreticians had observed that people belonging to the nobility

> Amor [hereos] est melancolica sollicitudo mentis cum profunditatione cogitacionum in qua figitur mens propter pulchritudinem [...] est mentis insania qua vagatur animus per inania crebris doloribus permiscens gaudia [...] est [...] cogitacionis in eadem [in re amata] assiduitas.[18]

Beginning with Constantinus Africanus, the theoreticians emphasize that the hypertrophy of *cogitatio* goes along with a strong physical desire: "[hereos] est autem magnum desiderium cum nimia concupiscentia et afflictione cogitationum."[19]

With reference to the etiology, the authors of treatises from Gerard de Berry onward[20] agree that the part of the mind affected by the disease is the *virtus estimativa*, the faculty of the soul or mind that must assess whether something or someone is well- or ill-suited to the person concerned:

> Causa ergo huius passionis est error uirtutis estimatiue que induicitur per intentiones sensatas ad apprehendenda accidencia insensata que forte non sunt in persona. Unde credit aliquam esse meliorem et nobiliorem et magis appetendam omnibus aliis. [...] unde si qua sunt sensata non conueniencia occultantur a non sensatis intentionibus anime uehementer infixis.[21]

This faculty is damaged to such an extent that it offers a positive assessment of a specific person even if this person is not at all suited to ("conveniens") the person affected by the illness: "ad personam quam estimatiua iudicat esse conuenientem, licet non sit."[22] The misled appreciation concerns the visible or sensuous aspects (*forma sensata*) of the 'object', and the *forma insensata*, the attitude of the object towards the person affected by *hereos*. A quote from Petrus Hispanus makes it particularly clear that the malady is – to put it in modern terms – a

---

were particularly susceptible to the malady. In the age I am addressing, this caste was no longer 'heroic,' but was rather on its way to becoming a 'leisure class' (which may explain its propensity to catch somewhat lofty diseases) but went on pretending that it was a warriors' caste in order to veil its parasitic status.
18 PH, B, 6–15. "Love is a melancholic worry of the mind with a depression of thought in which the mind is transfixed because of beauty [...] [it] is a sickness of the mind in which the spirit wanders through emptiness, mixing joy with frequent sorrows [...] [it] is [...] a continual [mental] preoccupation with [the beloved]."
19 CA, 3. "[hereos] is a great longing with intense sexual desire and affliction of the thoughts."
20 Note that Gerard's treatise is the first to blend the *Viaticum* with the *Canon medicinae* by Avicenna.
21 GB, 7–15. "The cause, then, of this disease is a malfunction of the estimative faculty, which is misled by sensed intentions into apprehending non-sensed accidents [better: non-perceptible traits] that perhaps are not within the person. Thus it believes a certain woman to be better and more noble and more desirable than all others. [...] Any unfitting sensations are, as a consequence, obscured by the non-sensed [i. e. supposed] intentions deeply fixed in the soul."
22 GB, 21 sq. "[...] to the person whom the estimative [faculty] judges to be fitting, though this may not be so."

syndrome of an overestimation of a woman's physical qualities and a positively-biased assessment of her attitude, resulting in a unilateral fixation: "In amore hereos estimat virtus estimativa aliquam mulierem [...] esse meliorem [this refers to the *forma insensata*] vel pulchriorem [*forma sensata*] omnibus aliis *cum non sit ita* [...]."[23]

The dysfunction of the *virtus estimativa* has consequences for the faculties of the soul that govern the other mental capacities, as well as those that control the bodily parts. The faculty most affected by the *estimativa*'s dysfunction is the *virtus cogitativa*: "et tunc [*virtus estimativa*] inperat virtuti cogitative ut profundet se in formam illius rei. Et sic in amore hereos est profundacio cogitationis."[24] All the theoreticians underline the particular importance of this point.[25] A second consequence of the appreciative faculty's dysfunction consists in the fact that the *virtus imaginativa*, the faculty which synthesizes the mental representations of the outside world, constantly displays the picture of the beloved in the mind of the person affected: "Estimatiua [...] imperat imaginationi ut defixum habeat intuitum in tali persona."[26] In the treatises based not only on the *Viaticum* but also on the *Canon medicinae,* one may find an explanation of this fixation ("figitur")[27] deriving from the assumptions of humoral pathology: the hyperfunction of the *virtus cogitativa* withdraws energy and heat from the *virtus imaginativa* (the site of which is conceived as adjacent to that of the *virtus cogitativa)*, which consequently becomes cold and dry ("frigida," "sicca"). Since what has been 'impressed' or imprinted into a dry substance is more stable than that which has been impressed into a humid substance,[28] the imagination of the person affected is incapable of detaching itself from the "fortis inpressio alicuius dilecte"[29] it has

---

23 PH A, 37–39 (my italics). "In lovesickness, the estimative faculty judges a certain woman [...] to be better or more beautiful than all the rest, even though it might not be so [...]."
24 PH A, 39–41. "[...] and then it orders the cogitative faculty to plunge itself into the form of that thing. And thus in lovesickness there is depressed thought [better: the state of being deeply mired in thought]."
25 "Cum hec infirmitas forciora anime subsequentia habeat, id est cogitationes nimias, [...] in cogitationibus profundatur." (CA, 17–25); "[Ratio passionis] est inordinatio et profundacio cogitationum circa rem quam omnibus aliis prefert." (PH B 89 f.)
26 GB, 15–18. "The estimative [faculty], then, [...] orders the imagination to fix its gaze on such a person."
27 GB, 23.
28 Although there was no systematic practice of autopsy in that age, it was known that the regular state of the brain as compared to other organs is rather humid; I should like to add in this context that women's bodies including their brains were considered to be more humid (softer) than males' bodies. For this reason *hereos* was seen as a malady affecting males primarily (though not exclusively).
29 PH A, 145.

received. I would like to stress that the picture of the beloved which the *virtus imaginativa* cannot cease to represent again and again is not indeed an 'objective' representation of the person concerned, but rather a picture positively biased due to the *virtus estimativa*'s dysfunction. The "extrinsicum apprehensum" is only *believed* to be 'convenient' ("putatur conveniens et amicum")[30] and the "forma sensata," the physique considered by the patient to be more pleasing than anything else, may be that of any woman ("forma alicuius mulieris").[31] The confused imagination then instructs the faculties governing the body to desire the person concerned and to take action in order to obtain her: "et eam mandat virtuti irascibili et concupiscibili, que sunt virtutes motive [...] Et tunc huiusmodi virtutes inperantes inperant virtuti motive que est in nervis ut moveant membra ad prosecucionem illius rei."[32] The mental fixation thus results in a corresponding fixation of the bodily desires: "unde concupiscibilis hoc solum concupiscit."[33]

To my knowledge, only Petrus Hispanus has discussed the question of *causa* for the dysfunction of the *virtus estimativa*. He observes that *hereos* particularly affects youths who have just had their first sexual experience. Since this encounter, precisely because it is the first one, is perceived by them as overwhelming, they yearn for a repetition. Petrus suggests it is this powerful desire for intercourse that damages their *virtus estimativa*, causing them to regard women[34] who are not particularly beautiful as more beautiful than all others, and those who are not willing to concede them their favors as "conveniens," as ready to convene with them: "Unde [...] est primus coitus qui maxime est delectabilis, quare maxime appetunt coitum. [...] defectus estimative qui est maxime in pueris [...] valet ad generationem amoris hereos."[35]

---

30 BF, 33.
31 BF, 33–37.
32 PH, A, 44–46. "And then the imaginative faculty sends it [the image of the beloved] to the irascible and concupiscible faculties, which are faculties [...] [that] control movement. And then these controlling faculties order the faculty of movement, which is in the nerves, to move the limbs in pursuit of that thing."
33 GB, 19.
34 The fixation may be on the first sexual partner. But according to the formulations to be found in the treatises it is much more probable to conceive of a *hereos* patient's sexual biography in quite another way: first sexual experience with an anonymous love object (a prostitute, a peasant girl, a servant); subsequent random non-sexual encounter with a "worthy" love object of equal status (a *donna*) who then becomes the focus of an obsession although there is not the slightest sign of the readiness to reciprocate.
35 PH, A, 173–177. "Thus the first sexual encounter happens to them, which is most pleasurable, wherefore they desire intercourse most greatly. [...] the failure of the estimative [faculty], which is greatest in boys, contributes [...] to the generation of lovesickness [...]."

The second major point discussed in the treatises is symptomatology ("sign[a] que signant egritudinem").[36] Absentmindedness is the primary symptom of permanent preoccupation with the beloved ("si aliquis de aliquo loquatur, uix intelliget");[37] further symptoms are sleeplessness ("uigilia");[38] weeping as soon as the patient thinks of the beloved – and as he constantly thinks of her, this implies nearly constant weeping; weeping even when he is sleeping ("etiam in sompno accidit eis [...] fletus");[39] unmotivated laughter; the sudden change from laughing to crying and vice versa ("de facili ridet et de facili de fletu ad risum mouetur");[40] rapid movement of the eyes ("oculi [...] cito mobiles propter anime cogitationes");[41] deep sighing ("suspiria profunda";[42] "hanelant cum suspirio");[43] permanent sadness for no evident reason ("tristicia sine causa");[44] and, finally, a preference for solitude ("querunt solitudinem").[45] A symptom noted in particular by Bona Fortuna – which should be mentioned in view of Petrarch – is the weeping or singing of patients when they are far removed from human society ("et quando sunt soli tunc flent aut cantant").[46]

I should perhaps mention a point that may already be evident in the term 'tristicia', which is the Latin term for the Greek *melancholia*: all treatises emphasize that *hereos* is an illness akin to melancholy. The theoreticians differ slightly with respect to the exact relationship between the two maladies. Some only hint at the affinity of the symptoms ("est similis melancolie");[47] others consider *hereos* a version of melancholy ("hereos est sollicitudo melancolica cum profundatione cogitationis");[48] and Gerard de Berry identifies *hereos* as a symptom of incipient melancholy ("unde remanet dispositio melancolica"),[49] which implies that in case it remains without treatment it will necessarily lead to fully developed melancholy ("unde si non eriosis succuratur ut cogitatio eorum auferatur et anima leuigetur, in passionem

---

36 BF, 48 f.
37 GB, 32–34.
38 CA, 21 f.
39 BF, 60–62.
40 GB, 38–39.
41 CA, 18 f.
42 PH, B, 34 f.
43 BF, 68.
44 PH, B, 36.
45 BF, 60.
46 BF, 60–61.
47 GB, 2–3.
48 PH, A, 77 f.
49 GB, 27–28.

melancolicam necesse est incidant";[50] "quando non curantur fiunt melancolici vel manici").[51]

The last point I would like to present – that of therapy – will perhaps be the least astonishing aspect since the cures advised by the theoreticians are largely identical with the well-known Ovidian *remedia amoris* which most probably derive from the antique preliminary stages of the discourse on *hereos*. The authors recommend the moderate consumption of wine, conversations with good friends, socializing, frequent baths and a concentration on the problems of everyday life. The most important recommendation seems to be the change of place ("mutatio [...] regionis")[52] with the intention of diverting the *cogitatio* from its fixation:

> Dicendum quod a patria exire competit in amore hereos quia talis exitus facit videre res pulcras et loca amena et in quibus paciens figit suam cogitationem. Et per consequens retrahit ymaginationem suam a sua amasia et facit patientem oblivisci sue amasie, quod maxime competit in cura amoris hereos.[53]

The second of the remedies with maximum efficiency and which also intends to divert the *cogitatio* is therapeutic sexual intercourse: "Ualet etiam consorcium et amplexus puellarum, plurimum concubitus ipsarum, et permutatio diuersarum."[54] There is also one medication in the literal sense that is mentioned again and again: a concoction of herbs that is described through various details and seems to have been considered highly efficient.

3

In this main section of the paper I will treat my topic proper, the life of the classical and Arabic texts I have just presented, not within medical texts of the West where their influence is manifest, but rather within poetic texts where their discursive presence is veiled to the extent that it has remained largely unnoticed in an age in which the concept of lovesickness has become obsolete as far as the

---

50 CA, 28.
51 BF, 29–30.
52 BF, 153.
53 PH A, 189–194. "It must be said that leaving one's country is beneficial in lovesickness, because such travel causes one to see beautiful things and pleasant places, upon which the patient fixes his thought. And consequently he withdraws his imagination from his beloved, and it makes the patient forget his beloved, which is most beneficial in the cure of lovesickness."
54 GB, 53 f. "Also useful is consorting with and embracing girls, sleeping with them repeatedly, and switching between various ones."

medical sphere is concerned. I would like to comment on the presence or, rather, the transparency of the discourse on *hereos* in the Petrarchan *Canzoniere*.[55]

If the underlying hypothesis is correct, I should be able to demonstrate the statistically relevant recurrence in the collection of basic terms and concepts of the discourse on *hereos* and furthermore of characteristic conceptual configurations. I would like to insist on this latter point. Of course one can find isolated aspects presented above – for example, sadness – in any text on love from any period and any cultural community, Western or non-Western. My argument is therefore dependent not only on evidence indicating statistical recurrence but also on the structurality of the phenomena of correspondence. I would like to add a third point that must be considered; namely, the aspect of historicity. The hypothesis of Petrarch's treatment of love as modeled on *hereos* is only viable if the structure that informs his discourse can be shown to differ significantly from corresponding discourses on unhappy love from other backgrounds.

In the following, I will a) present basic concepts of *hereos* and some basic discursive syndromes (concatenations of concepts) to be found in the *Canzoniere* by quoting one or two examples in each case and by referring to additional – albeit not exhaustive – material in the footnotes; b) comment on two longer poems that will allow for consideration of the aspect of structurality; and c) refer to some

---

[55] In almost every poem of the *Canzoniere*, the love of the lyrical self is said to be located in the heart (and not the brain). This might suggest that Petrarch, in the controversy between orthodox Aristotelians and the theoreticians of *hereos* (who are dependent on the Hippocratic concept of man), agrees with the Aristotelians who consider the heart the location of love. However, all passages in Petrarch where the author refers to the heart as the location of love belong to the conventional Allegory of Amor, which Petrarch borrows from the *dolce stil novo*: the God of love shoots his arrows through the eyes of the beloved into the eyes of the lover, where they continue on until they reach the heart, which is wounded. Cf. e. g. *RVF* III ("Era il giorno ch'al sol si scoloraro"), esp. the tercets ("Trovommi Amor del tutto disarmato/ et aperta la via per gli occhi al core, / che di lagrime son fatti uscio et varco:// però al mio parer non li fu honore/ ferir me de saetta in quello stato, / a voi armata non mostrar pur l'arco."); see also *RVF* II. In some poems one may read that the personification of Amor has its seat in the 'soul' (*anima, animus*), which is to be located physiologically in the brain ("Amor, che dentro a l'anima bolliva" [LXVII, v. 5]). In accordance with my interpretation of the meaning of the term 'heart' in the *Canzoniere* see LXXII, vv. 29 sq., which refer to the 'heart' as the seat of the (love-)*cogitatio* ("empiendo d'un pensier alto et soave/ quel core ond'ànno i begli occhi la chiave."). That is to say, the term 'heart' in Petrarch (as with many other terms in the *Canzoniere*) is to be understood as rhetorical, metaphorical, not in the proper sense of the term; or, to put it in other words: the presence of this term in the *Canzoniere* is not pertinent to the problem I will discuss. I should like to add that in a most famous treatise on *hereos* from the University of Montpellier, written by Arnaud de Villeneuve/Arnaldus de Villanova (which Wack does not consider), the heart as the location of *calor innatus* is integrated in the etiology, based on humoral pathology, of *hereos* as I have presented it.

general structures of the collection that could be considered in light of the malady described in the treatises. My remarks on the problem of historicity as well as the discussion of all further problems (for example, of what use my hypothesis may be for a new reading of the *Canzoniere*) will be formulated in a separate section of concluding remarks.

Since the Petrarchan *Canzoniere* first garnered scholarly attention, there is one aspect of the collection that has seriously irritated many commentators, leading them to suggest more or less problematic explanations for the phenomenon (which I will not discuss here):[56] it is indeed conspicuous that in almost every poem, readers encounter a term that would be extremely unusual in modern love lyric. Moreover, we find this term located in exactly those passages where, in modern contexts, we would find the term "feelings" or one of its synonyms. Petrarch, however, uses a word that, according to the organization of the semantic field with which we are familiar, stands in opposition to 'feelings', namely 'thinking': 'pensare', or 'pensieri', the vernacular terms for 'cogitare', 'cogitatio'.[57] As a first step of my argument, I would propose that the extremely high frequency at which this term appears in the text be considered in connection with the discourse on *hereos*. As mentioned, the treatises consider the *profundatio cogitationis* or, to put it precisely, the lover's constant and exclusive thinking of the beloved as the main symptom of the malady; in Petrarch's words: "[...] e'l pensier mio,/ ch'è sol di lei, sí ch'altra non v'à parte."[58] Considered from the perspective presented here, the frequency of the activity of 'pensare' (this is my first remark with respect to the aspect of historicity) in Petrarch would thus not necessarily imply a de-sexualized, intellectualized or a Platonizing concept of love.

---

56 Within the German-speaking academy there has been a particularly fierce controversy concerning this feature of Petrarch's *écriture* (Karlheinz Stierle: *Petrarcas Landschaften. Zur Geschichte ästhetischer Landschaftserfahrung*. Krefeld: Scherpe Verlag 1979; Bernhard König: Petrarcas Landschaften. Philologische Bemerkungen zu einer neuen Deutung. In: *Romanische Forschungen* 92 [1980], p. 251–282). My reading differs from Stierle's as well as from König's interpretation of Petrarch's insistence on *cogitare*.
57 "D'amorosi penseri [...]" (X, v. 12); "[...] i be' pensier' celati" (XI, v. 5); "Da lei ti vèn l'amoroso pensero" (XIII, v. 9); "l'anima [...]/[...] con molto pensiero indi si svelle." (XVII, vv. 13–14); "miro pensoso le crudeli stelle" (XXII, v. 15); "Da me son fatti i miei pensier' diversi" (XXIX, v. 36); "Allor saranno i miei pensieri a riva/ che foglia verde non si trovi in lauro" (XXX, vv. 7–8); "Dentro pur foco, et for candida neve,/ sol con questi pensier' [...]" (XXX, vv. 31–32); "I' dico a' miei pensier' [...]" (XXXII, v. 5); "del pensiero amoroso che m'atterra." (XXXVI, v. 2); "Allor mi strinsi a l'ombra d'un bel faggio,/ tutto pensoso; [...]" (LIV, vv. 7–8); "Vaghi pensier' che cosí passo passo/ scorto m'avete a ragionar tant'alto,/ [...]" (LXX, vv. 21 sq.); "L'amoroso pensero/ ch'alberga dentro [...]" (LXXI, vv. 91–92); "[...] un sol dolce penser l'anima appaga" (LXXV, v. 6); "Amor, con cui pensier mai non amezzo" (LXXIX, v. 5); "Cosí potess'io ben chiudere in versi/ i miei pensier' [...]" (XCV, vv. 1-2)
58 LXI, vv. 13 sq.

The second point I would like to mention concerns a concatenation of terms that I have characterized above as belonging to the basic syndromes of *hereos*. For a modern reader, one of the most striking features of the *Canzoniere* is the concomitance of weeping or crying, and a strong physical desire, as, e. g., in *RVF* LXI, vv. 9–11: "Benedette le voci [...]/ e i sospiri, et le lagrime, e'l desio". It is a peculiarity of Petrarch's discourse to permanently insist on the lover's weeping ("lagrime"),[59] on his suffering ("la doglia mia"),[60] on exhaustion ("lasso";[61] "[il] corpo stancho ch'a gran pena porto"),[62] on lamenting ("lagnarsi," "lamentar"),[63] on the "affann[i]"[64] – a disposition that advances to the point of permanent weeping, which continues day and night.[65] This feature alone is quite unusual, considered from a modern standpoint; but what is even more irritating is the frequently overlooked, or rather unrealized fact – unrealized because it seems to not fit the semantic feature of weeping or lamenting – that the lyrical self expresses

---

59 "[...] gli occhi [...]/ che di lagrime son fatti uscio et varco: [...]" (III, vv. 10–11); "[...] anzi che sian venute/ l'ore del pianto, [...]" (XIV, vv. 11–12); "et gli occhi in terra lagrimando abasso./ Talor m'assale in mezzo a' tristi pianti" (XV, vv. 8–9); "Piovonmi amare lagrime dal viso" (XVII, v. 1); "che le lagrime mie si spargan sole." (XVIII, v. 14); "però con gli occhi lagrimosi e'nfermi" (XIX, v. 12); "poi quand'io veggio fiammeggiar le stelle/ vo lagrimando [...]" (XXII, vv. 11–12); "come costei ch'i'piango a l'ombra e al sole;" (XXII, v. 21); "Lagrima anchor non mi bagnava il petto/ né rompea il sonno [...]" (XXIII, vv. 27–28); "piansi molt'anni il mio sfrenato ardire" (XXIII, v. 143); "Amor piangeva, et io con lui talvolta" (XXV, v. 1); "Lagrime dunque che dagli occhi versi" (XXIX, v. 29); "sempre piangendo andrò per ogni riva" (XXX, v. 33); "per gli occhi che di sempre pianger vaghi/ [...]/ Et io son un di quei che'l pianger giova; et par ben ch'io m'ingegni/ che di lagrime pregni/ sien gli occhi miei [...]/ Et per pianger anchor con piú diletto" (XXXVII, vv. 63–97); "et par che dica: Or ti consuma et piagni." (XXXVIII, v. 8); "Però i dí miei fien lagrimosi et manchi" (XLVI, v. 5); "Per lagrime ch'i' spargo a mille a mille,/ [...]/ Qual foco non avrian già spento et morto/ l'onde che gli occhi tristi versan sempre? (LV, v. 7 and v. 11–12); "Ma, lasso, [...]/ anzi piango al sereno et a la pioggia" (LXVI, vv. 19–20); "[...] il fin de' miei pianti" (LXXII, v. 72); "Lagrime omai dagli occhi uscir non ponno" (LXXXIII, v.9); "Occhi, piangete [...]" (LXXXIV, v. 1); "quel dolce loco, ove piangendo torno" (LXXXV, v. 3); "[...] onde conven ch'eterne/ lagrime per la piaga il cor trabocchi." (LXXXVII, vv. 7–8); "forse non avrai sempre il viso asciutto: / ch'i' mi pasco di lagrime [...]" (XCIII, vv. 13–14); "fanno le luci mie di pianger vaghe." (C, v. 14).
60 LXXI, v. 6; see also CLV, v. 7; CCXXIII, v. 14; CCLV, v. 3.
61 The word 'lasso' is so extremely frequent that I consider it sufficient to refer to the corresponding (eighty) entries in Kenneth McKenzie: *Concordanza delle rime di Francesco Petrarca*. Oxford: Clarendon Press 1969 (examples: XIV, v. 1; XV, v. 4).
62 XV, v. 1 sq.; "veggio a molto languir poca mercede" (CI, v. 5); see also CLXXIV, v. 12; CCXXIV, v. 2; CCXLIV, v. 7.
63 XXXVIII, v. 5 and LXXXIV, v. 4; see also CCV, v. 5; CCCXI, v. 7; CXXXII, v. 6.
64 LXXII, v. 15; see also XII, v. 2; LXI, v. 5; LXII, v. 12.
65 The concept of permanent weeping is to be found in its most explicit version in the first quatrain of CCXVI ("Tutto 'l dí piango; et poi la notte, quando/ prendon riposo i miseri mortali, / trovomi in pianto, et raddopiarsi i mali: / cosí spendo 'l mio tempo lagrimando.").

at the same time a strong sexual desire: "cieco" or "possente" or "fermo" or "vago desir"; "ardente" or "caldo desio"; "bram[a]"; "amorosa" or "fera" or even "vil voglia"; "voglia ardente"; "infiammate voglie"; "fero ardore"; "sfrenato ardire."[66]

Modern ignorance of *hereos* has led not only to the neglect of the massive physical implications of the feelings expressed by the lyrical self of the collection; it has also led to a characterization of the lover presented by Petrarch as unmanly, effeminate, and even somewhat ridiculous.[67] Indeed, in modern love discourses, 'tears' and 'physical desire' are – to put it in terms of structuralist semantics – distributed complementarily; where one may find item A, one will not find item B, and vice versa. And if the two terms appear together, this would be in most cases the utterance of a female person.

I will draw some provisional and still highly hypothetical conclusions from the preceding remarks: one need not judge the semantic substratum of the *Canzoniere* as a point of Petrarch's poetic discourse which should be benignly neglected because it seems somewhat embarrassing from a modern perspective. One should perhaps be more cautious to affiliate the love concept found in the *Canzoniere* with Platonic love. Finally, one should keep in mind that according to the contemporary discourse, the story of an unhappy love that informs the poems of the collection is to be considered an articulation of 'normal discourse,' implying that it is not informative or does not bear a specific meaning as such. The *Canzoniere* is not the story of an absolutely exceptional or highly idiosyncratic love put into verse; if we want to continue speaking of emerging subjectivity with reference to Petrarch's collection, we will have to find this subjectivity elsewhere; meaning, not in the semantic substratum of the emotions expressed in the collection.

I will now proceed to comment more in detail on two poems in order to substantiate my above suggestions. The first poem is *RVF* CXXIX, the famous *canzone* "Di pensier in pensier." I will skip some verses and will focus on those that are particularly pertinent to my argument:[68]

---

66 LVI, v. 1; CLXI, v. 3; XXII, v. 24; CLXXVIII, v. 6; see also XXIII, v. 147; LVII, v. 2; LXXIII, v. 78; CXLVII, v. 11; CLXXXI, v. 14. As to "desio" see XXXVII, v. 50; VI, v. 1; XVIII, vv. 10 and 13; LXXIII, v. 17; LXXIX, v. 4; CXIII, v. 8; CXXVII, v. 52; XLVII, vv. 5 and 14; XLVIII, v. 12; LXXI, v. 18; LXXXV, v. 13; XCV, v. 11; XCVI, v. 3; CCXXXVI, v. 5; CCXL, v. 14. For "brama" see CXVI, v. 5; see also LXXI, v. 5; CLXVIII, v. 4; CCVII, v. 34. As to "voglia" see CCLXX, v. 66; XXIII, v. 3; XLVIII, v. 8; CLIV, v. 14; CCXC, v. 13; LXXIII, v. 2; CXXXII, v. 5; XXXVII, v. 94; CCCLI, vv. 3–4; CLXXIII, v. 10; LIII, v. 69; LXXIII, v. 2. For "ardore" see CLXI, v. 2; see also CLXXV, vv. 7 and 12; CXCIV, v. 14; CCIII, vv. 1 and 9; XXIII, v. 143; CXL, v. 8.
67 This line of interpretation is accentuated perhaps most heavily in Hugo Friedrich: *Epoche della lirica italiana*. Milan: Mursia 1974, p. 158; see also p. 139, 144, 146.
68 All quotes from the Petrarchan *Canzoniere* are from the edition by Gianfranco Contini, Turin: Einaudi 1964; the translations are drawn from the bilingual edition: *Petrarch's Songbook. Rerum vulgarium fragmenta*. Translated by James Wyatt Cook. Binghampton, NY: Medieval & Renaissance Texts & Studies 1995 (I have made slight emendations).

Di pensier in pensier, di monte in monte mi guida Amor [...]	From thought to thought, from mount to mount, Love leads me on [...]
[...]	[...]
Se 'n solitaria piaggia, rivo o fonte,	If by a lonely heath or shore or fount
se 'n fra duo poggi siede ombrosa valle,	Or if between two lofty hills there lies
ivi s'acqueta l'alma sbigottita;	A shadowed vale, there my soul terrified
et come Amor l'envita,	Grows calm; as Love invites
or ride, or piange [...]	It laughs, now weeps [...]
[...]	[...]
onde a la vista huom di tal vita experto	Thus seeing it, one expert in such life
diria: "Questo arde, et di suo stato è incerto".	Would say, "Uncertain of his state, he burns."
Per alti monti et per selve aspre trovo	Amidst high mountains and in rugged woods
qualche riposo: ogni habitato loco	I find some peace; each spot that's tenanted
è nemico mortal degli occhi miei.	Of my eyes is a deadly enemy.
A ciascun passo nasce un penser novo	At every stride springs up a fresh thought of
de la mia donna [...]	My lady [...]
[...]	[...]
Ove porge ombra un pino alto od un colle	Where some tall pine tree or a hill gives shade
talor m'arresto, et pur nel primo sasso	Sometimes I pause and, on the very first
disegno co la mente il suo bel viso.	Stone with my mind trace her fair countenance.
Poi ch'a me torno, trovo il petto molle	Then, coming to myself, I feel my breast
de la pietate; et alor dico: "Ahi lasso,	Wet through with pity; then I say: "Ah, woe!
dove se' giunto! et onde se' diviso!"	Where have you come? From what are you cut off?"
Ma mentre tener fiso	But while I can hold firm
posso al primo pensier la mente vaga,	On that first thought my straying intellect,
et mirar lei, et oblïar me stesso,	Can gaze upon her and forget myself,
sento Amor sí da presso,	so near is Love, I feel
che del suo proprio error l'alma s'appaga[.]	the soul with its own error is content.
[...]	[...]
I' l'ò piú volte (or chi fia che mi 'l creda?)	Alive I've seen her many times (now who
ne l'acqua chiara et sopra l'erba verde	Is there to credit me?), in water clear
veduto viva, [...]	And on green grass, [...]
[...]	[...]
Poi quando il vero sgombra	When truth sweeps sweet illusion out, there I
quel dolce error, pur lí medesmo assido	Sit down, cold through, dead stone on living stone,
me freddo, pietra morta in pietra viva,	
in guisa d'uom che pensi et pianga et scriva.	Shaped like a man who thinks and weeps and writes.

(vv. 1–52)

Aside from some not uninteresting but – at least with respect to this *canzone* – less crucial aspects of etiology,[69] I would like to emphasize the following aspects: firstly the motif of *profundacio cogitationis*, which constitutes the semantic isotopy of the poem and is characterized explicitly, not so much as permanent thoughtfulness, but as a permanent or even obsessive preoccupation of the lover's activity of *cogitare* with the person of Laura (vv. 17–18: "A ciascun passo nasce un penser novo / de la mia donna [...]"). Then there is a sort of secondary isotopy for this *canzone* which is one of the strangest features of the Petrarchan discourse and a syndrome rarely found in other texts. I am referring to the lyrical self's tendency to see his beloved wherever he looks even when she is not actually present,[70] a feature perhaps most evident in vv. 28–29: "[...] et pur nel primo sasso / disegno co la mente il suo bel viso." What is expressed in these lines is that the mind ("la mente") designs a picture of Laura – which must consequently be understood as an imaginary picture – in or on a contingent object of the surrounding world ("nel primo sasso"). Let me reiterate that the regular task of the *virtus imaginativa* is to synthesize the data realized by the senses in order to convey an adequate picture of the world to the mind. What happens in the process described in the poem is, rather, that the *imaginativa* of the perceiving person is fixated on a certain picture to the extent that it constantly blends the sensory perceptions with what is already firmly impressed or imprinted on the mind. What is more: this interior picture is the dominant component, so that the self 'really' sees, or believes it sees Laura in places where she is not in fact present: "I' l'ò piú volte [...] / ne l'acqua chiara et sopra l'erba verde / veduto viva [...]." (vv. 40–42). The corresponding operation of the mind is evaluated by the self as an "error [del] l'alma"; the reason

---

69 I refer to v. 8 (the continuous change from laughing to crying and vice versa); to vv. 30–32 and to v. 52 (the thematizing of permanent lamenting and weeping); to v. 55, which I did not quote here (the concomitant thematizing of "desiderio intenso"), and finally to the symptom "querunt solitudinem" which is the theme of the *canzone*.
70 I would like to stress the importance of genre for the more or less far-reaching consequences of this feature. In several of Boccaccio's novellas one can easily detect the 'secret life' of the *hereos* treatises (II, 8; IV, 8; X, 7; V, 9; II, 10; IV, 5). Within a third person-narrative, however, these vestiges take on a quite different shape. As to the fixation of the *virtus imaginativa*, e. g., one may read in II, 8, 40: "sì forte s'innamorò, che più avanti di lei non vedeva." Within the *Canzoniere*, in contrast, the *results* of such a subjectivized view are thematized and exhibited to the reader at length. It is only by way of this device that the feature I will below apostrophize as 'perspectivism' is able to emerge. I would like to add that the second prominent text to which I shall refer in this context – Cervantes' *Quijote* – has its characters articulate their views to a large extent in direct, first-person speech (in accordance with its author's comprehensive (ethical and poetological) Aristotelianism, the Stagirite recommending the 'mimetic' mode not only for drama, but also – whenever it is possible or plausible – for epic texts).

for not attempting to overcome it lies in the fact that the mind perceives the result of its own dysfunction as pleasurable: "che del suo proprio error l'alma s'appaga." (v. 37) And when, finally, the 'real' reality destroys the "dolce error," the lover changes from 'normal' to 'abnormal'; he becomes cold ("freddo") and is petrified ("pietra morta in pietra viva," v. 51). From the standpoint of humoral pathology, these two states are symptoms of melancholy, which in turn is the result of long-lasting lovesickness.

The most important point for my general argument is, however, that the *canzone* seems to evidence the two main aspects of *hereos* to be found in the treatises: namely, the fixation of the *virtus cogitativa* and the ensuing dysfunction of the *virtus imaginativa*. What has up until now, and particularly with reference to this *canzone*, been interpreted as idiosyncratic, or even as an expression of a decidedly subjective attitude of the lyrical self towards the world, seems rather to correspond to a wide-spread form of behavior. This enables not everyone, but the 'experts' to state the problem of the person concerned: ardent love without fulfillment ("onde a la vista huom di tal vita experto / diria: Questo arde, et di suo stato è incerto." vv. 12–13).

The second poem I would like to address is the *canzone* "Quel'antiquo mio dolce empio signore" (CCCLX), which is a text from the last section of the *Canzoniere* that analyzes the self's suffering in retrospect. The analysis is construed as an *altercatio*, a dispute between a person referring to himself as 'I' and a personification of love, 'Amor'. The 'I' laments his past whereas 'Amor' emphasizes the positive aspects of the love story; the dispute takes place before "la reina che la parte divina / tien di nostra natura e 'n cima sede," (vv. 2–4), meaning, before the rational part of the mind. The dialogue must be understood, therefore, as a versified *psychomachia*; that is, as a dispute within the person's mind. 'Reason' here does not refer to an abstract concept but rather to the *pars rationalis* of the self; the person lamenting named 'I' is the suffering part of the self, while the person named 'Amor' is a reference to the God of love on the literal level, whereas it refers on the allegorical level to the loving component of the self.[71] In anticipation of my analysis I would like to stress that at the end of the poem, the *pars rationalis* evades the judgment it is asked to pronounce; that is, whether the position of the lamenting or of the loving component of the self is correct: "Nobile donna, tua sententia attendo. / Ella allor sorridendo: / Piacemi aver vostre questioni udite, / ma piú tempo bisogna a tanta lite." (vv. 154–157) The rational part of the self is not able to

---

[71] This constellation is evidenced by v. 75, in which Reason – that is, the *pars rationalis* – is addressed with the words: "Giudica tu, che me conosci et lui."

The Secret Life of Classical and Arabic Medical Texts in Petrarch's *Canzoniere* — 111

pass judgment, which means that it is involved as well; its normal function – in this case, the appreciation or evaluation of objects perceived, including their constellation – is damaged or blocked.

The most interesting aspects of the *canzone* are in fact the descriptions of the self's state from two different perspectives and the analytical implications of these descriptions. I shall limit my quotes once again to passages that are particularly pertinent to the points discussed here:

[...]	[...]
ivi [dinanzi a la reina, *i.e.* the reason]	There holds court [the queen, *i. e.* reason]
[...]	[...]
mi rappresento carco di dolore,	I represent myself, weighed down with pain,
[...]	[...]
e' ncomincio: "Madonna, il manco piede	Thus I begin: "My lady, my left foot,
giovenetto pos'io nel costui regno,	In tender youth I set within his realm.
ond'altro ch'ira et sdegno	From this naught have I known
non ebbi mai; et tanti et sí diversi	But anger and disdain; there I've endured
tormenti ivi soffersi,	So many torments cruel
ch'alfine vinta fu quell'infinita	That finally my patience infinite
mia patïentia, e 'n odio ebbi la vita.	Was overcome, and life grew odious.
Cosí 'l mio tempo infin qui trapassato	So up till now my time here has been spent in
è in fiamma e 'n pene: et quante utili honeste	fire and grief: what useful paths and chaste,
vie sprezzai, quante feste,	how many joys I scorned
per servir questo lusinghier crudele!	In serving this deceiver harsh and cruel!
[...]	[...]
O poco mèl, molto aloè con fele!	But little honey, aloes much with gall!
[...]	[...]
Questi [Amor] m'à fatto men amare Dio	This one [Love] caused me, less than I
ch'i' non deveva, et men curar me stesso:	ought, to love My God, and to myself
per una donna ò messo	to pay less heed; And for a lady's sake
egualmente in non cale ogni pensero.	Each care I have neglected equally.
Di ciò m'è stato consiglier sol esso,	To that end, only he has counselled me,
sempr'aguzzando il giovenil desio	While ever honing on an evil stone
a l'empia cote [...]	My youthful passion; [...]
[...]	[...]
Misero, a che quel chiaro ingegno altero,	Poor wretch! For what was bright and lofty wit
et l'altre doti a me date dal cielo?	And other talents given me by heaven?
ché vo cangiando 'l pelo,	Although my hair is changing
né cangiar posso l'ostinata voglia:	I cannot force my stubborn will [desire] to change.
cosí in tutto mi spoglia	In every way he steals

di libertà questo crudel ch'i' accuso,	My freedom, this cruel one that I accuse;
ch'amaro viver m'à vòlto in dolce uso.	To sweet use he has turned my bitter life!
Cercar m'à fatto deserti paesi	He's driven me to seek out desert lands,
[...]	[...]
dure genti et costumi,	Harsh people and harsh ways,
[...]	[...]
né costui [Amor] né quell'altra mia nemica	Not for one instant did he [Love] leave me
ch'i' fuggia, mi lasciavan sol un punto;	free, No more will she, that other foe I fly.
[...]	[...]
Poi che suo fui non ebbi hora tranquilla,	Since I was his, I've had no tranquil hour,
né costui [Amor] né quell'altra mia nemica	Nor do I hope to have; and sleep my nights
sbandiro, et più non ponno	Have exiled; no more can
per herbe o per incanti a sé ritrarlo.	They recover it with herbs or spells.
Per inganni et per forza è fatto donno	Deceit and force have made him ruler of
sovra miei spirti; et non sonò poi squilla,	My spirits; when I stay within some town,
ov'io sia, in qual che villa,	There rings no midnight bell
ch'i' non l'udisse. [...]	That I hear not. [...]
[...]	[...]
Quinci nascon le lagrime e i martiri,	In it are born the tears and sufferings,
le parole e i sospiri,	The words and sighs, that have
di ch'io mi vo stancando, et forse altrui.	Exhausted me, and others too perhaps.
Giudica tu [Ragione], che me conosci et lui".	Pass judgment [Reason], you who know both him and me."
[The speaker of the following verses is Amor; that is, the loving part of the self]	
"Ei sa che 'l grande Atride et l'alto Achille,	"he knows that I let great Atrides, Achilles high,
[...]	[...]
lasciai cader in vil amor d'ancille:	sink low in passion for a slave;
et a costui di mille	Yet for this man I picked
donne electe, excellenti, n'elessi una,	One from a thousand ladies choice and rare,
qual non si vedrà mai sotto la luna,	whose like will not be seen beneath the
[...]	moon [...]
Questi fur con costui li 'nganni mei.	And such were my deceptions with this
Questo fu il fel [...]	man. This was the gall[72] [...]
[...]	[...]
Et per dir a l'extremo il gran servigio,	To mention last my greatest help to him,
da mille acti inhonesti l'ò ritratto,	I've saved him from a thousand unchaste
ché mai per alcun pacto	acts, for in no circumstance

---

72 The translation quoted has "my gall" which may be misleading, since it is in fact not only about a metaphorical gall, but also an excess of the body fluid in its very literal and thus trans-personal sense.

a lui piacer non poteo cosa vile:	Could he be pleased by an unworthy thing –
giovene schivo et vergognoso in acto et in penser, poi che fatto era huom ligio	A bashful youth, and timid in his deeds And thoughts – then he became her liegeman true;
di lei ch'alto vestigio li'mpresse al core, et fecel suo simíle.	With her high image graven Upon his heart, and in her likeness formed,
[...] Mai nocturno fantasma d'error non fu sí pien com'ei ver' noi: [...] Di ciò il superbo si lamenta et pente."	[...] Ne'er nighttime spectre was As full of error as he is towards us! [...] For that this proud one wails and has regrets!"

(vv. 5–135)

This *canzone* differs from the first one I presented in so far as it does not focus on one or two major symptoms of *hereos* but gives a nearly complete catalogue of the etiology, the symptomatology and even the curative aspects. I shall not delve into all of the details; I will rather point out some of the most salient references in the verses quoted above.

In vv. 9 ff. ("Madonna, il manco piede [...]"), the 'I' presents a description of the development of his state which corresponds to what may be found in the medical treatises. He was affected at the age of adolescence ("giovenetto"). The result is suffering ("tormenti") since the fixation is unilateral ("altro ch'ira et sdegno non ebbi mai"). The affective fixation, which, as we learn in vv. 41–42, is resistant to therapy ("ché vo cangiando 'l pelo, né cangiar posso l'ostinata voglia"), finally leads to a general abomination ("odio") of life, which is the typical result of *hereos* that remains uncured; namely, melancholy. In v. 24, we find the manifestation of this latter disease according to humoral pathology: an excess of gall ("molto aloè con fele"), which we encounter once again in v. 106 ("questo fu il fel").

As far as the resistance to therapy is concerned, the text provides an amount of additional information. The cure of a concoction of herbs propagated by the experts of Petrarch's time apparently proved ineffective, as did the popular magic practices ("et piú non ponno / per herbe o per incanti a sé ritrarlo." vv. 63–64). Also ineffective were the remedies of *mutatio regionis* ("Cercar m'à fatto deserti paesi / [...] né costui né quell'altra mia nemica ch'i' fuggia, mi lasciavan sol un punto"; v. 46 and vv. 54–55) and the strategies of diversion by useful occupations as well as by pleasurable social activities ("et quante utili honeste / vie sprezzai, quante feste"; vv. 17–18). Finally, 'Amor' conveys that the remedy of therapeutic intercourse praised by the medical authorities was not applicable in this case because of the intensity of the fixation ("da mille acti inhonesti l'ò ritratto, / ché mai per alcun pacto / a lui piacer non poteo cosa vile"; vv. 122–124).

As far as the non-bodily dimension of the illness is concerned, I would like to direct attention to the complete lack of regard for the problems of the *souci de soi* ("Questi m'à fatto [...] / men curar me stesso," vv. 31–32). Next, I would like to emphasize the explanation for the state of permanent "profundacio cogitationum" (vv. 33–34): as *causa* the 'I' names the "giovenil desio" (v. 36), this having been misdirected ("aguzzando [...] / a l'empia cote [...]") by a "consiglio" ("consiglier," v. 35) – that is, an act of the *virtus estimativa* – which was biased by "questi," meaning by 'Amor' or love. The damage to the *estimativa* goes so far as to completely block the normal function of the *virtus volitiva* (vulgo: *liberum arbitrium*; "cosí in tutto mi spoglia / di libertà questo crudel ch'i' accuso," vv. 43–44), and, what is even worse, it reaches a point at which the entire rational part seems useless to the self ("a che quel chiaro ingegno altero, / et l'altre doti a me date dal cielo?" vv. 39–40).

Particularly conspicuous in the justification pronounced by 'Amor' (meaning: by the loving part of the self) is the boundless overestimation of the beloved's qualities, an error that is – according to the treatises – so typical of those suffering from *hereos*. The idea of this overestimation being based on a loss of reality is foregrounded by the mode of the praise: "[...] una, / qual non si vedrà mai sotto la luna" (vv. 98–99). Laura – says the loving part of the self – is not only more beautiful than any other woman of her age; she is not only more beautiful than any other woman who has ever lived on earth; but rather, she is more beautiful than all the women who will ever exist in the sublunary worlds. In light of this complete irreality – in the very logical sense – of the loving self's appreciation of Laura, we should perhaps read the "inganni" to which 'Amor' refers in v. 105 with ironic intention as the proper verdict on his past actions.

I would like to conclude my commentary on this *canzone* with some short remarks on vv. 126–132, where it seems that the Petrarchan discourse is transparent to the underlying concept of *hereos* almost like the superior layer of a palimpsest. In these verses, 'Amor' describes how the self turned into a "huom ligio / di lei" (that is, of Laura): a lover. He says that a "vestigio" of Laura has been impressed or imprinted ("li 'mpresse al core," vv. 126–128) on the lover's heart. I would suggest these verses be read according to the concept of the impression ("imprimitur") of the beloved's picture on the lover's mind described in the treatises as an act whose consequence is a lasting fixation.[73] In particular, I would like to draw attention to what in particular is impressed on the mind of this lover, which qualifies as an "alto vestigio"; meaning, not as a picture in the sense of photographic representation but as a 'trace' produced by the person concerned. So, what is imprinted on the self's heart or mind is a metonymy of Laura, a complex of characteristics that are contiguous to what she really is, and furthermore an "*alto vestigio,*" a complex that gives prominence to the positive aspects. It is from this metonymy that the loving self extrapolates the image of the person with whom he is obsessed since he is not obsessed with the "vestigio," but with the image of the person. The effect of this fixation was: "et fecel suo simîle" (v. 128). Laura – says 'Amor' (in proper terms, the self-deceiving part of the 'I') – has made him similar to herself. This may be read as an allusion to a specific problem expounded in the treatises; namely, that the person suffering from *hereos* subjectively believes that there is a relationship of reciprocal accordance or *convenientia* between the person desired and the patient. The chronological arrangement of the steps described in the verses above evidences that the relationship of convenience (in the etymological sense of the term: *convenire*) does not exist between the lover and the real person of the beloved but between the lover and the image of the beloved impressed or imprinted on his mind, which is based on the extrapolation of a positively biased metonymy. The loving part of the self articulates this diagnosis but is nevertheless incapable of mentally realizing it, though he should have inferred it from the permanent indifference of the person concerned towards him. And it is for this reason that the polemically-intended qualification of the 'I' as being stuck in a "nocturno fantasma / d'error" (vv. 131–132) exactly hits the mark.

As a last point in my remarks with reference to the texts of the Petrarchan collection, I will present a most provisional re-interpretation of some general structures in light of what I have discussed so far.

What is perhaps the most conspicuous feature of *hereos* we find in the *Canzoniere* is the dysfunction of the *virtus imaginativa* with respect to its normal task:

---

[73] The last aspect on which I commented with reference to poem CCCLX, which is particularly important to my hypothesis, is perhaps best evidenced in *RVF* L, vv. 63–68: "Misero me, che volli/ quando primier sí fiso/ gli tenni nel bel viso/ per iscolpirlo imaginando in parte/ onde mai né per forza né per arte/ mosso sarà [...]" (L, vv. 63–68). The first intense look at the beloved causes her face, mediated by an act of the *imaginativa* ("imaginando") – that is, not the face as such, but the face as re-synthesized by the lover's imagination – to be from then on as though sculpted ("iscolpirlo") in a "parte" (Latin: *pars*) of the lover. Her face is set in a material that is hard and dry and can neither be removed by force nor by 'arte' (and *ars* in this age does not refer only to modern 'art' or to a general concept of know-how in the sense of Greek 'techne,' but also to the disciplines included in the university curriculum, including medicine).

the synthesizing of data of the surrounding world, which are mediated by sense perceptions. The feature is not only present in the *canzone* analyzed above, it is a characteristic of the entire collection and it is actualized by the device of explicitly contrasting the subjective, hallucinatory perceptions with their objective counterparts: the loving self is said to consistently see Laura in objects only vaguely or metonymically related to her and which sometimes have no evident relationship to her at all: "e 'l suo parlare, e' l bel viso, et le chiome / mi piacquen sí ch'i' l'ò dinanzi agli occhi,/ ed avrò sempre, ov'io sia, in poggio o 'n riva." (vv. 4–6)[74]

---

74 See also XCVI, vv. 5–8: "Ma 'l bel viso leggiadro che depinto/ porto nel petto, et veggio ove ch'io miri,/ mi sforza; onde ne' primi empii martiri/ pur son contra mia voglia risospinto." See also CCLXIV, vv. 102–108, where the activity of the *virtus imaginativa*, which is misguided by the 'piacere' and which itself also misguides, is apostrophized ("Et questo ad alta voce ancho richiama/ la ragione svïata dietro ai sensi;/ ma perch'ell'oda, et pensi/ tornare, il mal costume oltre la spigne,/ et agli occhi depigne/ quella che sol per farmi morir nacque,/ perch'a me troppo, et a se stessa, piacque."); see also CVII, vv. 5–11: "Fuggir vorrei: ma gli amorosi rai,/ che dí et notte ne la mente stanno,/ risplendon sí, ch'al quintodecimo anno/ m'abbaglian piú che 'l primo giorno assai;// et l'imagine lor son sí cosparte/ che volver non mi posso, ov'io non veggia/ o quella o simil indi accesa luce."; also CXVI, vv. 5–14: "[...] et ò sí avezza/ la mente a contemplar sola costei,/ ch'altro non vede, et ciò che non è lei/ già per antica usanza odia et disprezza.// In una valle chiusa d'ogni'ntorno,/ ch'è refrigerio de' sospir' miei lassi,/ giunsi sol cum Amor, pensoso et tardo.// Ivi non donne, ma fontane et sassi,/ et l'imagine trovo di quel giorno/ che'l pensier mio figura, ovunque io sguardo."; CXXV, vv. 66–74: "Ovunque gli occhi volgo/ trovo un dolce sereno/ pensando: Qui percosse il vago lume./ Qualunque herba o fior colgo/ credo che nel terreno/ aggia radice, ov'ella ebbe in costume/ gir fra le piagge e'l fiume,/ et talor farsi un seggio/ fresco, fiorito et verde." The metonymic nexus between the flowers that the speaker picks and those between which Laura moves is purely subjective ("credo che nel terreno/ aggia radice, [...]"), the objective status of which is called into question through the generic qualification of the plants alone ("Qualunque herba o fior colgo [...]"). See also CLVIII, vv. 1–4 ("Ove ch'i' posi gli occhi lassi o giri/ per quetar la vaghezza che gli spinge,/ trovo chi bella donna ivi depinge/ per far sempre mai verdi i miei desiri."); CLXXVI, vv. 5–8: "et vo cantando (o penser' miei non saggi!)/ lei che'l ciel non poria lontana farme,/ ch'i' l'ò negli occhi, et veder seco parme/ donne et donzelle, et sono abeti et faggi." See also CXXVII, vv. 71–98: "Se mai candide rose con vermiglie/ in vasel d'oro vider gli occhi miei/ allor allor da vergine man colte,/ veder pensaro il viso di colei/ [...]/ Ma pur che l'òra un poco/ fior' bianchi et gialli per le piagge mova,/ torna a la mente il loco/ e'l primo dí ch'i' vidi a l'aura sparsi/ i capei d'oro, ond'io sí súbito arsi./ [...]/ perch'agli occhi miei lassi/ sempre è presente, ond'io tutto mi struggo./ Et cosí meco stassi,/ ch'altra non veggio mai, né veder bramo,/ né'l nome d'altra ne' sospir' miei chiamo." See also CXLIII, vv. 1–10: "Quand'io v'odo parlar sí dolcemente/ com'Amor proprio a' suoi seguaci instilla,/ [...]/ Trovo la bella donna allor presente/ ovunque mi fu mai dolce o tranquilla/ [...]/ Le chiome a l'aura sparse, et lei conversa/ indietro veggio; [...]".

A second manifestation of this basic structure consists in the fact that after Laura's death, the 'I' continues to speak about his encounters with her in quite the same way as when she was alive,[75] although in these later cases he qualifies the encounters as hallucinations produced by his mind.[76] And if one pays attention to

---

[75] The hope uttered at the end of CCLXX ("Morte m'à sciolto, Amor, d'ogni tua legge:/ quella che fu mia donna al ciel è gita,/ lasciando trista et libera mia vita." [vv. 106–108]) will be proven as having been illusionary. Already in CCLXXIII, we read: "Anima sconsolata, che pur vai/ giungendo legne al foco ove tu ardi?" (vv. 3–4) In CCLXXVII, it is said in v. 10 that Laura is dead ("è sotterra"), but the first nine verses of the poem present a situation that does not differ from the scenarios of the poems 'in vita' ("S'Amor novo consiglio non n'apporta,/ per forza converrà che 'l viver cange:/ tanta paura et duol l'alma trista ange,/ che 'l desir vive, et la speranza è morta;// onde si sbigottisce et si sconforta/ mia vita in tutto, et notte et giorno piange,/ stanca senza governo in mar che frange,/ e 'n dubbia via senza fidata scorta.// Imaginata guida la conduce,/ ché la vera è sotterra [...]"). The difference is that in the poems of the last part of the collection, the imaginary situation is not in opposition to a factual situation, but supplements (in the Derridean sense of 'supplément') a possibly factual situation of the past that is no longer possible. See also the first quatrain of CCCXLII: "Del cibo onde 'l signor mio sempre abonda,/ lagrime et doglia, il cor lasso nudrisco,/ et spesso tremo et spesso impallidisco,/ pensando a la sua piaga aspra et profonda." The most evident proof of the incapacity to distinguish between imagination and reality is perhaps *RVF*, CCCXXXVI. The lyrical self believes, for a while, that Laura is still alive because of her imaginary presence in his mind ('mente'), where she will 'dwell forever,' as he says; but finally the self has to remind him that Laura, in fact, is no longer among the living ("Tornami a mente, anzi v'è dentro, quella/ ch'indi per Lethe esser non pò sbandita,/ qual io la vidi in su l'età fiorita,/ tutta accesa de' raggi di sua stella.// Sí nel mio primo occorso honesta et bella/ veggiola, in sé raccolta, et sí romita,/ ch'i' grido: 'Ell'è ben dessa; anchor è in vita',/ e 'n don le cheggio sua dolce favella.// Talor risponde, et talor non fa motto./ I' come huom ch'erra, et poi piú dritto estima,/ dico a la mente mia: 'Tu se' 'ngannata.// Sai che 'n mille trecento quarantotto,/ il dí sesto d'aprile, in l'ora prima,/ del corpo uscío quell'anima beata.'").

[76] "Se lamentar augelli, o verdi fronde/ mover soavemente a l'aura estiva,/ o roco mormorar di lucide onde/ s'ode d'una fiorita et fresca riva,// là 'v'io seggia d'amor pensoso et scriva,/ lei che 'l cielo ne mostrò, terra n'asconde,/ veggio, et odo, et intendo ch'anchor viva/ di sí lontano a' sospir' miei risponde.// 'Deh, perché inanzi 'l tempo ti consume?/ – mi dice con pietate – a che pur versi/ degli occhi tristi un doloroso fiume?// Di me non pianger tu, ché' miei dí fersi/ morendo eterni, et ne l'interno lume,/ quando mostrai de chiuder, gli occhi apersi." (CCLXXIX); "Quante fiate, al mio dolce ricetto/ fuggendo altrui et, s'esser pò, me stesso,/ vo con gli occhi bagnando l'erba e 'l petto,/ rompendo co' sospir' l'aere da presso!// Quante fïate sol, pien di sospetto,/ per luoghi ombrosi et foschi mi son messo,/ cercando col penser l'alto diletto/ che Morte à tolto, ond'io la chiamo spesso!// Or in forma di nimpha o d'altra diva/ che del piú chiaro fondo di Sorga esca,/ et pongasi a sedere in su la riva;// or l'ò veduto su per l'erba fresca/ calcare i fior' com'una donna viva,/ mostrando in vista che di me le 'ncresca." (CCLXXXI); "Se quell'aura soave de' sospiri/ ch'i' odo di colei che qui fu mia/ donna, or è in cielo, et anchor par qui sia,/ et viva, et senta, et vada, et ami, et spiri,// ritrar potessi, or che caldi desiri/ movrei parlando! [...]" (CCLXXXVI, vv. 1–6); see also CCLXXXII, CCLXXXIII, CCXCI and CCI.

the far-reaching parallels between the encounters "in vita" and those "in morte di madonna Laura," one might perhaps even question the status of those poems "in vita," in which the self describes Laura as showing a positive attitude towards him (looking, greeting, smiling).⁷⁷ When, after death, her existence cannot be

---

77 In this context, it must be taken into account, however, that the division of the cycle into poems 'in vita di madonna Laura' and 'in morte di madonna Laura' is not Petrarch's, and that the poems on the whole are not in chronological order (see for example CCXI, which deals with the *innamoramento* and the following CXXII, where we read in the second tercet that the speaker's sufferings have been going on for twenty years). Nevertheless, there are poems in which it is clear that she is already dead, and others in which she is not dead, but still alive and which, notwithstanding this difference, describe Laura's attitude in an almost identical way. Cf. e. g. the poem 'in vita' LXIII, in which the lyrical self thanks Laura for having greeted him. This poem should be compared with the poems 'in morte', such as CCCXLVI, vv. 9–12, CCCXLII, vv. 5–11, CCCXLI, vv. 10–14, CCCLVI, vv. 9–14, CCCLIX, vv. 67–71, and CCCV, vv. 1–8. On the other hand, it must also be related to the (immediately following) poem LXIV, where we read that Laura avoids greeting him. Another one of those poems that might suggest that Laura's *amicicia* only exists in the lyrical self's mind is CLV, where the 'I' says: "Piangea madonna"; but adds: "Quel dolce pianto mi depinse Amore,/ anzi scolpío, et que' detti soavi/ mi scrisse entro un diamante in mezzo 'l core" (v. 5 and vv. 9–11); see also the quatrains of CLVI, where it is insinuated that Laura's tears are not real, but rather imaginary or that they originate from a biasing of the self's memory by his wishes ("I' vidi in terra angelici costumi/ et celesti bellezze al mondo sole, tal che di rimembrar mi giova et dole,/ ché quant'io miro par sogni, ombre et fumi;/ et vidi lagrimar que' duo bei lumi,/ ch'àn fatto mille volte invidia al sole;/ et udí' sospirando dir parole/ che farian gire i monti et stare i fiumi."). The impression that Laura's entire 'existence' as presented in the cycle is, to a large extent, imaginary, is furthermore reinforced by all those poems in which the lyrical self has visionary encounters, explicitly characterized as such, with the beloved woman when she is still alive; cf. e. g. CXI: "La donna che 'l mio cor nel viso porta,/ là dove sol fra bei pensier' d'amore/ sedea, m'apparve; et io per farle honore/ mossi con fronte reverente et smorta.// Tosto che del mio stato fussi accorta,/ a me si volse in sí novo colore/ ch'avrebbe a Giove nel maggior furore/ tolto l'arme di mano, et l'ira morta.// I' mi riscossi; et ella oltra, parlando,/ passò, che la parola i' non soffersi,/ né'l dolce sfavillar degli occhi suoi.// Or mi ritrovo pien di sí diversi/ piaceri, in quel saluto ripensando,/ che duol non sento, né sentí' ma' poi." See also CXXVI, vv. 40–63: "Da' be' rami scendea/ (dolce ne la memoria)/ una pioggia di fior' sovra l'suo grembo;/ et ella si sedea/ humile in tanta gloria,/ coverta già de l'amoroso nembo./ [...]/ Quante volte diss'io/ allor pien di spavento:/ Costei per fermo nacque in paradiso./ [...]/ e' l volto e le parole e' l dolce riso/ m'aveano, et sí diviso/ da l'imagine vera,/ ch'i' dicea sospirando:/ Qui come venn'io, o quando?;/ credendo esser in ciel, non là dov'era."; CXXVII, vv. 71–98 (quoted in n. 74); CXLIII, vv. 1–10 (quoted in n. 74). The etiology, so to speak, of this loss of reality is perhaps best expressed in LXXIII, vv. 24–26: "sí possente è 'l voler che mi trasporta;/ et la ragione è morta,/ che tenea 'l freno, et contrastar nol pote."; of the same tenor CXLI, vv. 7–11, with an additional hint at the damage of the *estimativa* ('chi discerne'): "[...] che 'l fren de la ragion Amor non prezza,/ e chi discerne è vinto da chi vòle.// E veggio ben quant'elli a schivo m'ànno,/ e so ch'i' ne morrò veracemente,/ ché mia vertú non pò contra l'affanno"; see also CCXL, vv. 5–7: "I' nol posso negar, donna, et nol nego,/ che la ragion, ch'ogni bona alma affrena,/ non sia dal voler vinta"; see also "[...] ad or ad ora a me stesso m'involo/ pur lei cercando che fuggir devria" (CLXIX, vv. 3–4); "[...] per lo gran desire/ di riveder cui non veder fu 'l meglio." (CCCXII, vv. 13–14).

other than imaginary, this purely hallucinatory Laura speaks to him, is full of pity towards him, sits down on his bed, addresses him as "fedel caro mio" (CCCXLI, 12), begins to sigh and even to weep when she sees him.[78] If one considers on the other hand the many poems "in vita," in which Laura demonstrates her "sdegno" – that is, her unwillingness to consider the self a potential suitor[79] – one might come to the conclusion that at least parts of the whole story as narrated in the *Canzoniere*, in particular the many "positive" (in vita) encounters between the self and Laura, may be the chronicle of a person who suffers from what one might call a loss of reality with respect to another person.[80] The unilateral fixation has reached not only the point of permanent preoccupation with the beloved but also of ascribing acts of *amicicia* to her that may only exist in the lover's deranged *virtus estimativa*.[81]

---

78 "Ella, contenta aver cangiato albergo,/ si paragona pur coi piú perfecti,/ et parte ad or ad or si volge a tergo,// mirando s'io la seguo, et par ch'aspecti" (CCCXLVI, vv. 9–12); "Ma chi né prima simil né seconda/ ebbe al suo tempo, al lecto in ch'io languisco/ vien tal ch'a pena a rimirar l'ardisco,/ et pietosa s'asside in su la sponda.// Con quella man che tanto desïai,/ m'asciuga li occhi, et col suo dir m'apporta/ dolcezza ch'uom mortal non sentí mai." (CCCXLII, vv. 5–11); "co la sua vista, over co le parole,/ intellecte da noi soli ambedui:// 'Fedel mio caro, assai di te mi dole,/ ma pur per nostro ben dura ti fui',/ dice, et cos' altre d'arrestare il sole." (CCCXLI, vv. 10–14); "Ella si tace, et di pietà depinta/ fiso mira pur me; parte sospira,/ et di lagrime honeste il viso adorna:// onde l'anima mia dal dolor vinta,/ mentre piangendo allor seco s'adira,/ sciolta dal sonno a se stessa ritorna." (CCCLVI, vv. 9–14); "I' piango; et ella il volto/ co le sue man m'asciuga, et poi sospira/ dolcemente, et s'adira/ con parole che i sassi romper ponno:/ et dopo questo si parte ella, e'l sonno." (CCCLIX, vv. 67–71); "Anima bella da quel nodo sciolta/ che piú bel mai non seppe ordir Natura,/ pon' dal ciel mente a la mia vita oscura,/ da sí lieti pensieri a pianger volta.// La falsa opinion dal cor s'è tolta,/ che mi fece alcun tempo acerba et dura/ tua dolce vista: omai tutta secura,/ volgi a me gli occhi, e i miei sospiri ascolta." (CCCV, vv. 1–8).
79 Cf. e. g. XLIV, vv. 13–14: "né lagrima però discese anchora/ da' be' vostr'occhi, ma disdegno et ira."; see also CCIII, esp. v. 9 and vv. 12–14; CCXXXIX, vv. 10–12. The difference between these passages and the corresponding aspects in Provençal and *dolce stil novo* texts consists in the fact that the lyrical self of the *Canzoniere* not only implores the *donna* for 'pity,' but he firmly believes he has succeeded in making her change her attitude to that of a loving *donna*. This absolute misreading of the *donna*'s reactions is seldom found in the pre-Petrarchan love lyric.
80 In CCCXXXV, the lyrical self 'sees' Laura, who is already dead, but he sees her in 'pictures,' 'imaginations,' which he says 'cannot be false' ("mirandola in imagini non false," v. 3). What he 'sees' is Laura appearing like the angels ("a li spirti celesti in vista eguale," v. 4). This perception, however, is based on a picture of Laura that is avertedly imagined so that the text itself (i. e. the *Canzoniere* as a whole) seems to imply that the beauty of Laura 'in vita,' as described by the lyrical self, is not so much a fact as a reflection of her image in the self's mind.
81 In addition to the material expounded above, I provide a randomized catalogue of a few minor aspects pertaining to my argument. On the level of symptomatology we find, of course,

4

I should like to conclude with some remarks in a more general tenor. If one accepts the thesis that the lyrical self of the *Canzoniere* is fashioned according to the contemporary medical concept of *hereos*, this implies that there is not much that we

---

constant sighing ("Voi ch'ascoltate in rime sparse il suono/ di quei sospiri [...]" [I, vv. 1–2]; "Quando io movo i sospiri a chiamar voi" [V, v. 1]; "[...] un vento angoscioso di sospiri" [XVII, v. 2]; "non ò mai triegua di sospir' [...]" [XXII, v. 10]; "[...] et quasi in ogni valle/ rimbombi il suon de' miei gravi sospiri" [XXIII, vv. 12–13]; "per lei sospira l'alma, [...]" [XXIX, v. 34]; "[...] oggi à sett'anni/ che sospirando vo di riva in riva/ la notte e 'l giorno, al caldo ed a la neve." [XXX, vv. 28–30]; "et come spesso indarno si sospira." [XXXII, v. 14]; "piú folta schiera di sospiri accoglia!" [XXXVII, v. 68]; "et voi sí pronti a darmi angoscia et duolo,/ sospiri [...]" [XLIX, vv. 12 sq.]; "[...] però ch'ò sospirato sí gran tempo/ [...]" [LXX, v. 12]; "[...] quell'accesa voglia/ che m'à sforzato a sospirar mai sempre,/ [...]" [LXXIII, vv. 2sq.]; "[...] per fuggir de sospir' [...]" [LXXIV; v. 4]; "[...] et or con gran fatica/ [...]/ in libertà ritorno sospirando." [LXXVI, vv. 6–8]; "di sospir' molti mi sgombrava il petto" [LXXVIII, v. 5]; "Onde piú volte sospirando indietro/ dissi [...]" [LXXXIX, vv. 9–10]; "Io son [...] sí vinto,/ [...] de la lunga guerra de' sospiri" [XCVI, vv. 1–2]), weeping even when the lover is sleeping ("spesso dal somno lagrimando desta" [VIII, v. 4]; "[...] mia speme [...]/ giunse nel cor, non per l'usata via/ che 'l sonno tenea chiusa, e 'l dolor molle" [XXXIII, vv. 9–11]; "Lagrime triste, et voi tutte le notti/ m'accompagnate, [...]" [XLIX, vv. 9–10]; "perché dí et notte gli occhi miei son molli?" [L, v. 62]), the unmotivated vacillation ("vaneggiar") between laughing and weeping ("[...] quella speranza/ che ne fe' vaneggiar sí lungamente,/ e 'l riso e 'l pianto, [...]" [XXXII, vv. 9–11]; "che l'extremo del riso assaglia il pianto" [LXXI, v. 88]; "De' passati miei danni piango et rido" [CV, v. 76]; "Pascomi di dolor, piangendo rido" [CXXXIV, v. 12]; "Simil fortuna stampa/ mia vita, che morir poria ridendo" [CXXXV, vv. 80–81]; "[...] e' l cor si lagna/ [...] e' n vista asciutta et lieta,/ piange [...]" [CL, vv. 9–11]; "Questa humil fera [...]/ in riso e 'n pianto [...]/ mi rota [...]" [CLII, vv. 1–4]), rapid eye movement ("Gli occhi invaghiro allor sí de' lor guai," XCVII, v. 5), the desire for solitude ("Solo et pensoso i più deserti campi/ vo mesurando a passi tardi et lenti,/ et gli occhi porto per fuggire intenti/ ove vestigio human l'arena stampi." [XXXV, vv. 1–4]; see also CCXXXVII, v. 25: "Le città son nemiche, amici i boschi"; CCLIX, vv. 1–3: "Cercato ò sempre solitaria vita/ (le rive il sanno, et le campagne e i boschi)/ per fuggir questi ingegni sordi et loschi"; see also CCLXXXVIII, *passim*; CCXCII, v. 4.), the insistence on adolescence as the onset of the suffering ("Questa mia donna mi menò molt'anni/ pien di vaghezza giovenile ardendo," CXIX, vv. 16–17; see also CCVII, v. 13, and *passim*), a suffering that persists, in its two dimensions, as a violent physical desire and as an endless, weeping lamentation, for decades ("[...] [il] mio primo giovenile errore/ quand'era in parte altr'uom da quel ch'i' sono" [I, vv. 3–4]; "ch'i' son già pur crescendo in questa voglia/ ben presso al decim' anno,/ né poss'indovinar chi me ne scioglia." [L, vv. 54–55]; "Quel foco ch'i' pensai che fosse spento/ dal freddo tempo et da l'età men fresca,/ fiamma et martír ne l'anima rinfresca." [LV, vv. 1–3]); in CCCLXIV the duration of the sufferings is enumerated exactly: "Tennemi Amor anni ventuno ardendo,/ [...]/ poi che madonna e'l mio cor seco inseme/ saliro al ciel, dieci altri anni piangendo." (vv. 1–4); see also the additional hint at the fact that the "fera voglia," which later on became the cause of his misfortune, was already virulent in him at a time when Amor (love) had not visited him ("Nel dolce tempo de la prima etade,/ che nascer vide et anchor quasi in herba/ la fera voglia che per mio mal crebbe,/ perché cantando il duol si disacerba,/ canteró com'io vissi in libertade,/

might consider "individual" about the story narrated in the collection. Nevertheless, it is not beside the point to consider it a document of the rise of subjectivity at

---

mentre Amor nel mio albergo a sdegno s'ebbe." [XXIII, vv. 1–6]). Of the same tenor XC, v. 1 ("Erano i capei d'oro a l'aura sparsi"), where the lyrical self says that he bore the 'tinder' of love already in his bosom when he met Laura, so that it was not at all 'miraculous' that he at once began to 'burn' with desire ("i' che l'ésca amorosa al petto avea,/ qual meraviglia se di súbito arsi?" vv. 7–8; in this context I would like to mention once again the sexual etiology of *hereos*: the illness is preceded by a first, purely physical encounter with a random female partner who need not be identical with the *donna*); the impossibility of overcoming his physical desire ("[...] travïato è 'l folle mi' desio/ [...]/ né mi vale spronarlo, o dargli volta," VI, vv. 1–7); the praising of the beloved as more beautiful than any other woman ("[...] quanto ciascuna è men bella di lei," XIII, v. 3; "Non fur già mai veduti sí begli occhi/ o ne la nostra etade o ne' prim'anni," XXX, vv. 19–20; "Amor e 'l ver fur meco a dir che quelle/ ch'i' vidi, eran bellezze al mondo sole,/ mai non vedute piú sotto le stelle," CLVIII, vv. 9–11). In this context, the self sometimes makes explicit that his appreciation of Laura differs from the *communis opinio*, but that he does not regard this divergence as his problem, but instead as the problem of the rest of the world, thereby foregrounding the manic dimension of his feelings: "Parrà forse ad alcun che 'n lodar quella/ ch'i' adoro in terra, errante sia 'l mio stile,/ faccendo lei sovr'ogni altra gentile,/ santa, saggia, leggiadra, honesta et bella.// A me par il contrario [...]/ [...]/ et chi no 'l crede, venga egli a vedella;// sí dirà ben: Quello ove questi aspira/ è cosa da stancare Athene [..]/ [...]/// Lingua mortale al suo stato divino/ giunger non pote: [...]" (CCXLVII, vv. 1–13). See also CCXLVIII, vv. 3–4, the incrimination of those who do not realize that Laura is the 'only one to be qualified as the sun' as being 'blind': "ch'è sola un sol, non pur a li occhi mei,/ ma al mondo cieco [...]"; in other poems we do not find this direct opposition between the self's view and the *communis opinio*, but it is frequently made explicit that Laura is the most beautiful woman *for the lyrical self* ("tal che null'altra fia mai che mi piaccia," XX, v. 4; "Et se di lui fors'altra donna spera,/ vive in speranza debile et fallace," XXI, vv. 5–6). – Finally, I would like to mention the lack of interest not only in any other woman ("[...] Anima [i. e. of the lyrical self] [...]/ pocho prezando quel ch'ogni huom desia;" XIII, vv. 7–11; "Gli occhi [...]/ [...] ànno a schifo ogni opera mortale:/ [...]/ Amor in altra parte non mi sprona,/ né i pie' sanno altra via, né le man come/ lodar si possa in carte altra persona." XCVII, vv. 5–14), but in any other sort of 'diletti' in favor of his constant obsession with the beloved ("tutti gli altri diletti/ di questa vita ò per minori assai,/ et tutte altre bellezze indietro vanno." LXXIII, vv. 64–66). Even the point that the 'desio,' which originates in the damaged *imaginativa*, finally communicates its orders to the *membra* – to the limbs of the body – is to be found here ("et che' pie' miei non son fiaccati et lassi/ a seguir l'orme vostre in ogni parte/ perdendo inutilmente tanti passi;" LXXIV, vv. 9–11), and the corresponding context evidences that the weakness, the lassitude expressed *passim* in the *Canzoniere* ("oimè, lasso") is not to be interpreted as a physical, bodily weakness, but as psychic exhaustion and indifference that constitute – along with the hypertrophy of cogitation – the main symptom of melancholy (the aspect of *aboulia* for example in CXVIII: "Rimansi a dietro il sestodecimo anno/ de' miei sospiri, [...]/ [...] Or qui son, lasso, et voglio esser altrove;/ et vorrei piú volere, et piú non voglio;/ et per piú non poter fo quant'io posso;// et d'antichi desir' lagrime nove/ provan com'io son pur quel ch'i' mi soglio,/ né per mille rivolte anchor son mosso." vv. 1–2 and vv. 9–14). The weariness of life and the indifference towards death, or, rather, towards the death of the soul is to be found, e. g., in CXLI, v. 14: "et cieca al suo morir l'alma consente." As to metaphorical references to *acedia* in the sense of melancholy see CLIII, v. 10 ("che 'l nostro stato è inquïeto et fosco"); a reference based

the end of the Middle Ages.[82] Even from an archaeological or historicist standpoint, such an interpretation is justified, considering the relationship of the Petrarchan discourse to the theological discourse, a point I do not discuss in this paper.[83] As regards the love story proper, one should, on the contrary, consider this line of interpretation a hermeneutic potentiality. Its being actualized originates in the complete shift of basic anthropological concepts over the centuries which separate Petrarch from us; that is to say, it is contingent on the course (intellectual) history has taken. But, it cannot be derived from the Petrarchan text as a structure. Designing in one's mind ("disegno co la mente il suo bel viso," CXXIX, 29) a picture of the world that differs from the commonsensical view would have to be qualified from a modern standpoint as subjective, or at least as potentially subjective. From the standpoint of Petrarch's time, it would have to be qualified as pathological. What creates the legitimacy to implement a dimension of subjectivity[84] into the love story presented in the *Canzoniere* is the fact that the self or the author makes his pathological status productive: by taking literally the description of the patients

---

on humoral pathology in CCXVI; v. 5 ("In tristo humor vo li occhi consumando"). On the level of therapy, besides the aspects already mentioned – the most important of these being the remedy of *mutatio regionis* ("le man bianche sottili,/ et le braccia gentili,/ [...]/ mi celan questi luoghi alpestri et feri;" XXXVII, vv. 98–104; "fuggia le tue mani, et per camino,/ agitandom' i vènti e 'l ciel et l'onde,/ m'andava sconosciuto et pellegrino:" LXIX, vv. 9–11; "O poggi, o valli, o fiumi, o selve, o campi, o testimon' de la mia grave vita,/ quante volte m'udiste chiamar morte!" LXXI, vv. 37–39) – we find intimations of therapeutical intercourse ("cosí, lasso, talor vo cerchand'io,/ donna, quanto è possibile, in altrui/ la disïata vostra forma vera." XVI, vv. 12–14). But since all these therapies prove ineffective, the lyrical self degenerates over the course of the years into a fully developed state of melancholy, into *tristitia*, even *acedia*, perpetual contemplation of his own death, and even the wish to die ("Questa speranza mi sostenne un tempo:/ or vien mancando, et troppo in lei m'attempo. [...]/ Ogni loco m'atrista ov'io non veggio/ quei begli occhi soavi/ che portaron le chiavi/ de' miei dolci pensier', mentre a Dio piacque;/ et perché'l duro exilio più m'aggravi,/ s'io dormo o vado o seggio,/ altro già mai non cheggio,/ et ciò ch'i' vidi dopo lor mi spiacque," XXXVII, vv. 15–40; "tal ch'io non penso udir cosa già mai/ che mi conforte ad altro ch'a trar guai." XXXVII, vv. 95–96). Already in LXXIX we read: "ché la morte s'appressa, e 'l viver fugge." (v. 14; of the same tenor the following poems: LXXX, esp. v. 4 and vv. 23–24, LXXXI, esp. v. 14, and LXXXII, esp v. 5).

82 As is well-known this reading of the *Canzoniere* was first introduced by Rousseau and continued by Hegel; without mentioning Petrarch, Wack qualifies the introduction of *hereos* as "an important contribution to medieval subjectivity" (Wack: *Lovesickness in the Middle Ages*, p. 59).
83 See my Philology and Theology in Petrarch. In: *MLN* 122, 1 (2007), p. 133–147. See also *Mundus imago Laurae*. Il sonetto petrarchesco *Per mezz'i boschi* e la 'modernità' del *Canzoniere*. In: *MLN* 126, 1 (2011), p. 1–28. In this latter publication I attempt to give a theological interpretation of the self's subjectivized view of the surrounding world. As with every text of the high canon, the *Canzoniere* is extremely complex. It allows for different interpretations of the self's state as "alma disvïata" (CCCLV, v. 7).
84 Which means to be aware that this is an act of projection and not an archaeological reading.

in the treatises, "flent aut cantant," and by then interpreting the "cantare" in the humanist, classical, Virgilian sense, he converts a pathological view into a poetic discourse. Poetry and literature are considered, from Aristotle to Yuri M. Lotman,[85] as a discourse that refers to something particular but communicates the universal or something of general relevance. So, one could be tempted to formulate that Petrarch introduces in his *Canzoniere* the concept that a subjective look at the world may be of general pertinence. He introduces the concept later labeled "perspectivism"; but it is highly improbable that he was aware of this innovation.

As a second point of these concluding remarks, I will address the question of historicity. I would propose that there are in the history of Western thought three models for conceptualizing humans' most intimate feelings: the Platonic model, the model of courtly love, and *hereos*. It will not be necessary to emphasize that the three models have much in common and that these generalities cover the love discourses of other cultures, too, as there are aspects one may call anthropological constants grounded in our belonging to one species. Instead, I will foreground the differences, while trying to characterize the three models by way of ideal types; as to concrete textual manifestations, there will be in many cases partial hybridization.

I will not say anything further about *hereos*. Readers may be astonished by my rather strict dissociation of *hereos* and courtly love.[86] Notwithstanding certain features they share, I would posit that the concept of courtly love[87] is somewhat different. It is a social ritual. This means that it is a code which implies that it is a form of communication, an exchange of signals, the meaning of which is not liable to subjective interpretation. There may be diverging aspirations and desires, but there is no basic hiatus between the "real" behavior of the *donna* and the "reading" of this behavior on her suitor's part. Understanding courtly love as a ritual means, thirdly, that the love story is a *mise en scène*. The feelings exhibited by the persons involved are certainly not superficial only, but they are less "profound" than the love associated with *hereos*.

Deepness, trustworthiness, non-ritual, non-codified status, giving prominence to the lover's personal, subjective view of things – all these features situate *hereos* much closer to the love concept of Romanticism than to courtly love. I would nevertheless maintain that identifying *hereos* with romantic love might be

---

85 *Poetics* 1451a–b; Yuri M. Lotman: *The Structure of the Artistic Text*. Ann Arbor: University of Michigan Press 1977, p. 211.
86 Mary Wack, in contrast, refers to the canon of courtly literature as another example of the presence of *hereos* in literary texts.
87 Concerning the description of courtly love, there is still no better publication than Georges Duby's short book, *Que sait-on de l'amour en France au XII*ᵉ *siècle?* Oxford: Clarendon Press 1983.

problematic. The romantic concept seems to me one version of the basic model of Platonic love among the many we have had in the course of Western history. Platonic love does not deny the sensuous dimensions; but, it is characterized by dissociating the sensuous and the spiritual, at least in terms of normative processes (from the pleasure excited by viewing bodily beauty to the pleasure originating in the completely immaterial beauty of pure ideas), and by an evaluative judgment implied in this temporalization.[88] Physical beauty and all bodily aspects of love are ultimately assessed as less dignified.

It is perhaps not necessary to expound why Western culture, at least up until the end of high modernism, has preferred the Platonic model and not the courtly one, let alone that of *hereos*. The traditional ideology (in the sense of world model) of Western civilization is Christian. As Hegel claims in his *Lectures on the Philosophy of History,* this implies a tendency towards interiorization and subjectivity that was in the end unfavorable to ritualized concepts of behavior. With regard to body and mind or soul, it favors dissociation and ensuing hierarchization. These were unfavorable conditions for the establishment of a love discourse like *hereos*, which was not autochthonous. Nevertheless, it is this ideologically marginalized concept that was the basis for some of the texts about love which the Western tradition holds in highest esteem, from Petrarch's *Canzoniere* to Cervantes' *Quijote*, which gives a parodistic version of the theme. And it may be that the prestige of these texts is linked – at least to a certain extent – to the fact that they impart a concept of love that the official ideology of Western culture is (or, rather, was) hardly able to articulate: the knowledge that what we call love is ultimately corporeal, material; but that our somewhat objectionable and irrational bodily needs may bring forth our most refined feelings, the most intense psychic sufferings, and perhaps may even lead to such basic innovations in our conceptualizing of the world as perspectivism, the rise of which we can observe in the two texts to which I have just referred.

As a codicil to these concluding remarks, I would like to add a few words with reference to the broader conceptual frame of this paper as indicated by its title. The reception of ideologically exotic texts (from classical pagan or from Muslim cultures) never posed a serious problem within the rising Occidental civilization, as long as those texts focused primarily on parts of the discursive field that held the status of *lacunae* within the theological discourse of Christianity. Mathematics, pre-concepts of natural science, logic – all these topics were eagerly received by a West whose Holy Book and whose patristic interpretive

---

[88] See *Symposion* 210a ff.

tradition did not care about these sections of the field. Things became less irenic as soon as a heterogeneous material had potential repercussions on a section that was considered a stronghold of religious orthodoxy: namely, moral philosophy. Regarding *hereos*, the problem involved is linked to the concept of free will (*liberum arbitrium*). If sinful behavior (actual or imaginary *luxuria*) is the consequence of a corporeal dysfunction, it is hardly to be categorized as imputable. The only solution to the problem to be found within the limits of Christian theology is a strictly interpreted Augustinian concept of predestination,[89] which became acceptable in parts of the early modern West only after three hundred years of a fierce ideological battle and after thirty years of a most bloody struggle in the literal sense. For the period I have been discussing, the solution was proscription. The famous anti-Averroist decree of 1277 promulgated by the Bishop of Paris, Étienne Tempier, condemned as n. 136 of 219 incriminated positions the following: "Quod homo agens ex passione coacte agit."[90] ("that a human being who acts under the impact of passion acts compulsively"). From this time onward, the life of the treatises I presented was a secret one, as far as the non-disciplinary discourses are concerned. It is one of the most salient elements of Occidental culture, however, to have from the very beginning[91] tolerated texts that are by definition bound to convey something 'general' underneath a surface apparently recounting only 'particular' events or facts. Thus, the fictionalized

---

[89] To avoid misunderstanding I would like to stress that within Augustinian theology the sins committed under the imperative of a 'negative' predestination, are, of course, imputable. The paradox of *servum arbitrium* and guilt, however, has erosive implications for the believers' loyalty. It is not without reason that the Church which postulates to be the "common" one rejects the concept of unwilling sinful behavior even today. As to Petrarch, I should like to stress that in terms of theology he is a strict Augustinianist (thereto see my Das Schweigen der Veritas. Zur Kontingenz von Pluralisierungsprozessen in der Frührenaissance (Überlegungen zum *Secretum*). In: *Poetica* 23 [1991], p. 425–475). From such a standpoint, a *persona* as presented in the *Canzoniere* – mired in sin, conscious of being mired in sin, but unable to do anything about it – would be perfectly coherent.

[90] *Opiniones ducentae undeviginti Sigeri de Brabantia, Boetii de Dacia aliorumque a Stephano episcopo Parisiensi de consilio doctorum sacrae scripturae condemnatae*; a modern print is available in *Chartularium universitatis parisiensis*. Edited by Henri Denifle. 4 vols. Paris: Université de Paris 1891–1899, I, p. 543–558.

[91] The situation is in fact a bit more complex than stated above. Also in the West the theoreticians of literature (Dante and Petrarch, in the first place) had to fight astutely in order to preserve and expand the discursive margins for texts such as the ones they wrote (see my Zu einigen Aspekten der Dichtungstheorie in der Frührenaissance. In: Andreas Kablitz/ Gerhard Regn (eds.): *Renaissance – Episteme und Agon. Für Klaus W. Hempfer anlässlich seines 60. Geburtstags*, Heidelberg: Winter 2006 [Neues Forum für allgemeine und vergleichende Literaturwissenschaft, 33], p. 47–71). But one must put this controversial discussion in perspective. It is to be assessed in

life of a non-repentant sinner[92] was able to become the discursive instrument to secretly vehiculate the idea of love-as-nothing-but-corporeal to a period in which anthropological materialism became once again a widely accepted view. The fact that, to date, this 'secret' has remained largely undetected testifies to the impression that not only amateur reading, but also humanistic scholarship is much more committed to its 'horizon of expectations'[93] than to the actual structures of the text.

Bibliography

Primary Literature

Chartularium universitatis parisiensis. Edited by Henri Denifle. 4 vols. Paris: Université de Paris 1891–1899.
Petrarca, Francesco: *Canzoniere*. Edited by Gianfranco Contini. Turin: Einaudi 1964.
Petrarca, Francesco: *Invective contra medicum*. In his: *Opere latine*. Edited by Antonietta Bufano. Turin: UTET 1975.
Petrarca, Francesco: *Petrarch's Songbook. Rerum vulgarium fragmenta*. Translated by James Wyatt Cook. Binghamton, New York: Medieval & Renaissance Texts & Studies 1995.

---

comparison to cultures which until recently (or even: throughout the present day) were (are) not ready to concede such discursive licenses. All this can hardly be claimed as a specific 'merit' of Western culture (let alone of its present-day heirs); it is a feature produced by different theological frames: in this case, by the difference between written language as God's own language on the one hand, and written language as a post-Babylonian phenomenon; that is, an instrument which is (morally and linguistically) corrupt anyway.

92 In accordance with a broad stream of scholarship, I have questioned the seriousness of the attitude expressed in the last three pieces of the *Canzoniere*. My argument is, however, not based on any assumptions concerning the author's state of mind or his biography; it refers to the formulations of which he makes use in these poems, which seem to destabilize the explicitly-articulated repentance (see my Palinodia e polisemia nella canzone alla Vergine del Canzoniere (con alcune brevi considerazioni sulle condizioni della differenza tra arte classica ed arte moderna). In: Klaus W. Hempfer/ Gerhard Regn (eds.): *Letture petrarchesche*. Florence: Le Lettere 2004 [Quaderni petrarcheschi, 14], p. 147–190).

93 Concerning this category, introduced by reader-response criticism (*Rezeptionsästhetik*), see Hans Robert Jauss: *Literaturgeschichte als Provokation*. Konstanz: Unversitätsverlag 1967 (Konstanzer Universitätsreden. 3). It needs to be stressed that my reading of the *Canzoniere* as expounded above is a consequence of mere contingency, in the literal sense of the term. During a medievalists' conference at Stanford in the early nineties of the last century, I overheard two colleagues talking about a recent publication on lovesickness. I then took a look at Wack's book, and while teaching a graduate course on Italian poetry one or two semesters later, I began to reflect according to the lines detailed in this essay.

Secondary Literature

Monographs and Anthologies

Bergdolt, Klaus: *Arzt, Krankheit und Therapie bei Petrarca: Die Kritik an Medizin und Naturwissenschaft im italienischen Frühhumanismus*. Weinheim: VCH Acta humaniora 1992.
Céard, Jean (ed.), *La Folie et le corps*. Paris: Presses de l'École normale supérieure 1985.
Ciavolella, Massimo: *La malattia d'amore dall'Antichità al Medioevo*. Rome: Bulzoni 1976.
Duby, Georges: *Que sait-on de l'amour en France au XIIe siècle?* Oxford: Clarendon Press 1983.
Foucault, Michel: *L'Archéologie du savoir*. Paris: Gallimard 1969.
Friedrich, Hugo: *Epoche della lirica italiana*. Milan: Mursia 1974.
Jauss, Hans Robert: *Literaturgeschichte als Provokation*. Konstanz: Unversitätsverlag 1967 (Konstanzer Universitätsreden, 3).
Kristeller, Paul O: *Studies in Renaissance Thought and Letters*. Rome: Edizioni di Storia e Letteratura 1956 (Storia e Letteratura, 54).
Lotman, Yuri M: *The Structure of the Artistic Text*. Ann Arbor: University of Michigan Press 1977.
McKenzie, Kenneth: *Concordanza delle rime di Francesco Petrarca*. Oxford: Clarendon Press 1969.
Rashdall, Hastings: *The Universities of Europe in the Middle Ages*. Second edition by Frederick M. Powicke and Alfred B. Emden. 3 vols. London: Oxford University Press 1936.
Snow, Charles P: *The Two Cultures and the Scientific Revolution*. New York: Cambridge University Press 1959.
Stierle, Karlheinz: *Petrarcas Landschaften. Zur Geschichte ästhetischer Landschaftserfahrung*. Krefeld: Scherpe Verlag 1979.
Wack, Mary Frances: *Lovesickness in the Middle Ages: the* Viaticum *and its Commentaries*. Philadelphia: University of Pennsylvania Press 1990.

Articles and Papers

Bird, Otto: The Canzone d'Amore of Cavalcanti According to The Commentary of Dino del Garbo. In: *Medieval Studies* 2 (1940), p. 150–203.
Ciavolella, Massimo: La tradizione dell'*aegritudo amoris* nel *Decameron*. In: *Giornale storico della letteratura italiana* 147 (1970), p. 496–517.
Ciavolella, Massimo: Mediaeval Medicine and Arcite's Love Sickness. In: *Florilegium* 1 (1979), p. 222–241.
Duminil, Marie-Paule: La mélancolie amoureuse dans l'Antiquité. In: Jean Céard (ed.): *La Folie et le corps*. Paris: Presses de l'École normale supérieure 1985, p. 91–110.
Jacquart, Danielle: La maladie et le remède d'amour dans quelques écrits médicaux du Moyen âge. In: Danielle Buschinger/ André Crépin (eds.): *Amour, mariage et transgressions au Moyen âge*. Göppingen: Kümmerle 1984 (Göppinger Arbeiten zur Germanistik, 420), p. 93–101.
Jacquart, Danielle/Thomasset, Claude: L'Amour héroique à travers le traité d'Arnaud de Villeneuve. In: Jean Céard (ed.): *La Folie et le corps*. Paris: Presses de l'École normale supérieure 1985, p. 143–158.

König, Bernhard: Petrarcas Landschaften. Philologische Bemerkungen zu einer neuen Deutung. In: *Romanische Forschungen* 92 (1980), p. 251–282.

Kristeller, Paul O.: Il Petrarca, l'Umanesimo e la Scolastica. In: *Lettere italiane* 7, 4 (1955), p. 367–387.

Küpper, Joachim: Das Schweigen der Veritas. Zur Kontingenz von Pluralisierungsprozessen in der Frührenaissance (Überlegungen zum *Secretum*). In: *Poetica* 23 (1991), p. 425–475.

Küpper, Joachim: Palinodia e polisemia nella canzone alla Vergine del Canzoniere (con alcune brevi considerazioni sulle condizioni della differenza tra arte classica ed arte moderna). In: Klaus W. Hempfer/ Gerhard Regn (eds.): *Letture petrarchesche*. Florence: Le Lettere 2004 (Quaderni petrarcheschi, 14), p. 147–190.

Küpper, Joachim: Zu einigen Aspekten der Dichtungstheorie in der Frührenaissance. In: Andreas Kablitz/ Gerhard Regn (eds.): *Renaissance – Episteme und Agon. Für Klaus W. Hempfer anlässlich seines 60. Geburtstags*. Heidelberg: Winter 2006 (Neues Forum für allgemeine und vergleichende Literaturwissenschaft, 33), p. 47–71.

Küpper, Joachim: Philology and Theology in Petrarch. In: *MLN* 122, 1 (2007), p. 133–147.

Küpper, Joachim: Mundus imago Laurae. Il sonetto petrarchesco *Per mezz'i boschi* e la 'modernità' del *Canzoniere*. In: *MLN* 126, 1 (2011), p. 1–28.

Lowes, John Livingston: The Loveres Maladye of Hereos. In: *Modern Philology* 11 (1913–1914), p. 491–546.

Nardi, Bruno: L'Amore e i medici medievali. In: *Studi in onore di Angelo Monteverdi*. 2 vols. Modena: Società tipografica editrice modenese 1959, II, p. 517–542.

Simonin, Michel: *Aegritudo amoris* et *res literaria* à la Renaissance: Réflexions préliminaires. In: Jean Céard (ed.): *La Folie et le corps*. Paris: Presses de l'École normale supérieure 1985, p. 83–90.

Manuele Gragnolati and Francesca Southerden
From Paradox to Exclusivity: Dante and Petrarch's Lyrical Eschatologies

This essay brings Petrarch and Dante's poetry into dialogue in order to highlight some crucial tensions that have to do with the continuing presence of a fundamentally lyric component within the framework of Christian paradise. 'Lyric', in our analysis, stands for an aspect of identity bound up with the relation to the beloved and to a desire contained in the body and expressed in the longing for it. Our focus is on the different modes of textuality at play in Dante's *Paradiso* and Petrarch's *Triumphus Eternitatis* and the ways they express the "form of desire" informing each poet's work and especially his eschatological imagination.[1] Our approach draws on Manuele Gragnolati's reading of Dante's *Paradiso* in *Amor che move: linguaggio del corpo e forma del desiderio in Dante, Pasolini e Morante* (2013) and extends some of the questions raised there to Petrarch's *Triumphus Eternitatis*. In particular, we aim to examine the relationship between language and corporeality as explored in the concept of the resurrection of the body, which carries a relational sense of identity bound up with the individual's memory, desires, and history and both complicates and opens up an understanding of poetry and eschatology.

Our point of departure are the shores of Dante's Purgatory, where the pilgrim encounters a shade who has also just arrived at the realm of purgation: the shade of Casella, an old friend from the times of youth when Dante had not yet been exiled from Florence. This episode re-writes the Virgilian motif of the failed embrace between a living and a dead person: the pilgrim and the shade of the old friend try to embrace each other but they cannot because – as the poet laments – shades in the otherworld are "vane", empty (*Purg*. II, 79).[2] Indeed, as the figure of Statius explains in *Purgatorio* XXV, shades in Dante's afterlife have an aerial body that gives them an appearance – "aspetto" – but no substantiality: "Ohi ombre vane, fuor che ne l'aspetto! / tre volte dietro a lei le mani avvinsi, / e tante mi tornai con esse al petto" [Oh empty shades, except in seeming! / Three times I clasped my hands behind him / only to find them clasped to my own chest]

---

[1] On the notion of the "form of desire", see Manuele Gragnolati's recent study: *Amor che move: Linguaggio del corpo e forma del desiderio in Dante, Pasolini e Morante*. Milan: Il Saggiatore 2013.
[2] On the motif of the failed embrace, see: Manuele Gragnolati: Nostalgia in Heaven: Embraces, Affection and Identity in the *Commedia*. In: John C. Barnes/Jennifer Petrie (eds.): *Dante and the Human Body: Eight Essays*. Dublin: Four Courts Press 2007, p. 117–37.

Open access. © 2018 Manuele Gragnolati and Francesca Southerden, published by De Gruyter. This work is licensed under the Creative Commons Attribution-NonCommercial-NoDerivatives 4.0 license.
https://doi.org/10.1515/9783110419306-007

(*Purg.*, II, 79–81).³ What is important to note is that both friends, who have just arrived in Purgatory, are still entrapped by their earthly desires. Casella tells Dante that although he is now a soul deprived of his mortal body, he continues to love his friend in the same way that he did on earth: "Così com'io t'amai / nel *mortal corpo*, così t'amo sciolta" ["Even as I loved you in *my mortal flesh*," he said, / "so do I love you freed from it"] (*Purg.* II, 89–90). And Dante also shows nostalgia for the past and asks his friend to sing in the same way he used to sing in their youth. Casella performs Dante's canzone *Amor che nella mente mi ragiona* in such a way that everybody remains enchanted by its sweetness, "'*Amor che ne la mente mi ragiona*' / cominciò elli allor sì dolcemente, / che la dolcezza ancor dentro mi suona" ["Love that converses with me in my mind," / he then began, so sweetly / that the sweetness sounds within me still] (*Purg.* II, 112–14).⁴

As is well known, the rest of the episode shows that the mutual affection which the two friends still feel for each other is wrong and that attachment to the mortal body, affection for friends and beloved, and nostalgia for the past must change in Purgatory.⁵ Indeed, the moral structure of Dante's Purgatory prescribes that the souls learn to detach themselves from anything transient and re-direct all their desires towards God. According to what Teodolinda Barolini calls Dante's Augustinian paradigm of desire, attachments to one's earthly body and nostalgia for the earthly affections symbolized by it are considered as distractions that the purging soul must abandon if it wants to attain the complete love for God that is necessary to reach Heaven.⁶

---

3 See in particular Statius's description of the formation of the aerial body in *Purg.* XXV, 85–108, and Manuele Gragnolati's discussion of it in: *Experiencing the Afterlife: Body and Soul in Dante and Medieval Culture*. Notre Dame, IN: University of Notre Dame Press 2005, p. 67–77. Quotations from the *Commedia* are from Dante Alighieri: *La "Commedia" secondo l'antica vulgata*. Edited by Giorgio Petrocchi. 2nd rev. edn. 4 vols. Florence: Le Lettere 1994 (Edizione Nazionale delle opere di D. A., 7). English translations come from: Dante Alighieri: *The Divine Comedy*. Translated by Robert Hollander and Jean Hollander. 3 vols. New York: Doubleday 2000–2007.
4 *Amor che nella mente mi ragiona* is one of Dante's *Rime*, included in Book III of *Convivio*, where it heralds the transfer of Dante's affection from Beatrice to Lady Philosophy. On the importance of this auto-citation in the *Commedia*, see Teodolinda Barolini: *Dante's Poets: Textuality and Truth in the 'Comedy'*. Princeton: Princeton University Press 1984, p. 31–40.
5 For readings of this episode, see for example, Charles Singleton: *Dante Studies 1. 'Commedia': Elements of Structure*. Cambridge, MA: Harvard University Press 1957, p. 23–29; Robert Hollander: *Purgatorio* II: Cato's Rebuke and Dante's *Scoglio*. In: *Italica* 52, 3 (Autumn, 1975), p. 348–63; and John Freccero: Casella's Song: *Purgatorio* II, 112. In his: *Dante: The Poetics of Conversion*. Edited by Rachel Jacoff. Cambridge, MA: Harvard University Press 1986, p. 186–194.
6 In Chapter 5 of Teodolinda Barolini: *The Undivine 'Comedy': Detheologizing Dante*. Princeton, NJ: Princeton University Press 1992, p. 99–121, especially p. 103–108.

A similar point is also made by Beatrice in her scolding of the pilgrim in the garden of Eden, when, pointing to her beautiful limbs now scattered on earth and reduced to ashes – her "belle membra [...] / che so' 'n terra sparte" (*Purg.* XXXI, 50–51) –, she explains that it is precisely when her body died that the pilgrim should have loved her most because this would have meant loving her soul, the immortal part of her that will never fail him. Actually, he should love her more now that she is a shade than when she was in her fleshly body on earth: albeit beautiful, the earthly body is mortal, and one should neither love it as though it were not doomed to die nor, as the pilgrim did after Beatrice's death, replace it with some other mortal good that distracts from fully directing one's love to God:

> Mai non t'appresentò natura o arte
> piacere, quanto *le bella membra* in ch'io
> rinchiusa fui, e *che so' 'n terra sparte*,
>   e se *'l sommo piacer* sì ti fallio
> per la mia morte, qual *cosa mortale*
> dovea poi trarre te nel suo disio?
>   Ben ti dovevi, per lo primo strale
> de le cose fallaci, levar suso
> di retro a me che *non era più tale*. (*Purg.* XXXI, 49–57)

> [Never did art or nature set before you beauty
> as great as in *the lovely members* that enclosed me,
> now *scattered and reduced to dust.*
>   And if the *highest beauty* failed you
> in my death, what *mortal thing*
> should then have drawn you to desire it?
>   Indeed, at the very first arrow
> of deceitful things, you should have risen up
> and followed me *who was no longer of them.*]

Beatrice's words not only confirm that one should not love earthly goods too much, but also that there is something problematic in the mortal, fleshly body that is related to an intimate desire for others that must be overcome. Flesh would not seem to be required in the eschatological panorama of the *Commedia*, where by releasing a body of air, the souls are able to acquire the corporeality that is necessary for the full experience of the afterlife and the full expression of the self. As the *Inferno* and *Purgatorio* place emphasis on the intensity of the souls' pain, so the *Paradiso* is full of passages indicating that in Heaven the fleshless souls have access to the beatific vision, which satisfies all their desires and grants them perfect bliss:

> Lume è là sù che visibile face
> lo creatore a quella creatura
> che solo in lui vedere ha la sua pace. (*Par.* XXX, 100–02)[7]

> [There is a light above that makes the Creator
> visible to every creature
> that finds its only peace in seeing Him.]

Purgatory can therefore be considered as the experience, at once painful and productive, that allows the soul to transform personal and individual love into *caritas*, that is, the absolute and unconditional love for God which is also gratuitous love for one's neighbour and implies the possibility to open oneself to others and free oneself from sin's monomania and self-obsession.[8]

Several interesting studies have shown that this condition achieved and manifested by the souls in heaven corresponds to a state of merging with God that opens up the self and radically changes it. Thus, for instance, Lino Pertile and Steven Botterill have indicated that Beatrice must also eventually leave and be replaced by St Bernard before the pilgrim can reach the ultimate union with God and the Universe;[9] and Robin Kirkpatrick has spoken of a "spirit of dispossession" that characterizes the condition of being in Heaven, while Christian Moevs indicates that the redirection of desire from mortal to immortal goods can be understood as a "spontaneous crucifixion of the self" and that "love is selflessness, and self is lovelessness."[10]

There is something fascinating about the loss of self that uniting with God implies in Dante's concept of heaven and in the kind of subjectivity that this loss entails. But if an important component of the heavenly state imagined by Dante is

---

[7] On the fullness of the separated souls' experience in Hell and Heaven, see Gragnolati: *Experiencing the Afterlife*, p. 77–87, and his: *Amor che move*, p. 69–90.

[8] On the notion of productive pain in the *Purgatorio*, see Manuele Gragnolati: Gluttony and the Anthropology of Pain in Dante's *Inferno* and *Purgatorio*. In: Rachel Fulton/Bruce W. Holsinger (eds.): *History in the Comic Mode: Medieval Communities and the Matter of Person*. New York: Columbia University Press 2007, p. 238–250; and Gragnolati: *Experiencing the Afterlife*, p. 89–137. On sin in Hell as "obsessive monomania", see Peter Hawkins: *Dante: A Brief History*. London: Blackwell 2006, p. 40.

[9] Lino Pertile: *La punta del disio: Semantica del desiderio nella 'Commedia'*. Fiesole: Cadmo 2005, especially p. 235–246: Dimenticare Beatrice; Steven Botterill: *Dante and the Mystical Tradition: Bernard of Clairvaux in the "Commedia."* Cambridge: Cambridge University Press 1994, p. 64–86, where he speaks of Dante's "process of [...] detachment from Beatrice" as realized through Bernard's replacement of her as guide (p. 85).

[10] See Robin Kirkpatrick: Polemics of Praise: Theology as Text, Narrative and Rhetoric in Dante's *Commedia*. In: Vittorio Montemaggi/Matthew Treherne (eds): *Dante's 'Commedia': Theology as Poetry*. Notre Dame: University of Notre Dame Press 2010, p. 14–35: p. 23; and Christian Moevs: *The Metaphysics of Dante's 'Comedy'*. New York: Oxford University Press 2005, p. 89–90.

constituted by this transformation and shattering of the self, nonetheless it is also necessary to complicate this idea by acknowledging that there is actually something about their past that the souls in heaven continue to be attached to and that cannot be tamed, disciplined, or fully abandoned – an identity, that is, that goes in the opposite direction of transformation. Central to this dimension is the celebration of the resurrection of the flesh that takes place in *Paradiso* XIV, a moment in the *Commedia* in which Dante conveys with sublime intensity the nostalgia for one's own mortal body and the intimate affections that it represents. The first passage that contributes to an appreciation of what is at stake for Dante is Solomon's celebration of the resurrection of the body at the end of time as the event which will allow for an increase of the souls' beatific vision and subsequent happiness:

> "Come la carne glorïosa e santa
> fia rivestita, la nostra persona
> più grata fia *per esser tutta quanta*:
>   per che *s'accrescerà ciò che ne dona
> di gratüito lume il sommo bene*
> lume ch'a lui veder ne condiziona;
>   onde la visïon *crescer* convene,
> *crescer* l'ardor che di quella s'accende,
> *crescer* lo raggio che da esso vene". (*Par.* XIV, 43–51).
>
> [When we put on again our flesh,
> glorified and holy, then our persons
> will be more pleasing *for being all complete*,
>   so that *the light, granted to us freely
> by the Highest Good, shall increase,*
> the light that makes us fit to see Him.
>   From that light, vision must *increase*
> and love *increase* what vision kindles,
> and radiance *increase*, which comes from love.]

The second passage in the same canto expresses the souls' joyful reaction at Solomon's celebration of the resurrection of the flesh:

> "Tanto mi parver sùbiti e accorti
> e l'uno e l'altro coro a dicer "Amme!",
> che ben mostrar *disio d'i corpi morti*:
>   forse non pur per lor, ma *per le mamme,
> per li padri e per li altri che fuor cari*
> anzi che fosser sempiterne fiamme" (*Par.* XIV, 61–66).
>
> [So quick and eager seemed to me both choirs
> to say their *Amen* that they clearly showed

> their desire for their dead bodies,
>   not perhaps for themselves alone, *but for their mothers,*
> *for their fathers, and for others whom they loved*
> before they all became eternal flames.]

The joy with which the souls react at the prospect of reuniting with their fleshly body – that mortal body which has remained on earth and is now a corpse –, reveals the intensity of their nostalgia for it ("disio d'i corpi morti").[11] Unlike many other passages of the *Paradiso* that stress the souls' current happiness, here Dante's poem emphasizes the intensity with which they long for reuniting with their bodies, when they will be happier. In particular, the rhyme words "amme" / "mamme" / "fiamme'" express that after the recovery of what are now dead bodies, the separated souls – which in heaven have become splendid lights, enflamed by their beatitude and love for God – will become again veritable individuals with their own singularity, made of relations and memory.

What is important to note is that the souls' desire for their dead body is connected not only with the increase of their vision of God, but also with their personal attachments and is the passionate "expression of their desire to love fully in heaven what they loved on earth"[12] – that is, the souls' "disio d'i corpi morti" seems to contradict the Augustinian paradigm of detachment which, as we have seen, characterizes the process of Purgatory as selflessness and dispossession. Moreover it appears that the relational sense expressed by the souls' desire for their resurrected body is somewhat of a novelty with respect to contemporary theologians, who focused mainly on the exclusive relation of the individual to God and were less interested in the idea that personal and individual attachments continue in heaven among the blessed.[13] The connection Dante makes in *Paradiso* XIV

---

[11] On the motif of the resurrection of the body in the *Commedia*, see Gragnolati: *Experiencing the Afterlife*, p. 139–178, and his: *Amor che move*, p. 104–110 and p. 149–161, both with ample bibliography. See also Anna Maria Chiavacci Leonardi: "Le bianche stole": il tema della resurrezione nel *Paradiso*. In: Giovanni Barblan (ed.): *Dante e la Bibbia. Atti del Convegno Internazionale promosso da "Biblia": Firenze, 26–27–28 settembre 1986*. Florence: Olschki 1988, p. 249–271; and Caroline Walker Bynum: Faith Imagining the Self: Somatomorphic Soul and Resurrection Body in Dante's *Divine Comedy*. In: Sang Huyn Lee/Wayne Proudfoot et al. (eds.): *Faithful Imagining: Essays in Honor of Richard R. Neibuhr*. Atlanta: Scholars Press 1995, p. 81–104.
[12] Barolini, *The Undivine 'Comedy'*, p. 138.
[13] See Colleen McDannell and Bernhard Lang: *Heaven: A History*. New Haven: Yale University Press 1998, p. 90 ff. For example, Bernard of Clairvaux does not permit any notion of interaction between the saints in his concept of Heaven, notwithstanding his praise of friendship on earth. On Bernard in particular, see Anna Harrison: Community among the Saints in Heaven in Bernard of Clairvaux's *Sermons for the Feast of All Saints*. In: Caroline Walker Bynum/Paul Freedman (eds.): *Last Things: Death and Apocalypse in the Middle Ages*. Philadelphia: University of Pennsylvania Press 2000, p. 191–204.

between the body's materiality and fleshliness, memory and individuality, is striking and these features emerge as fundamental parts of the experience of heaven in his conception, and consequently of his anthropology. As such, there arises a tension in the *Commedia* between the state of heaven as a dissolution of the self and the blessed souls' "disio d'i corpi morti", which arguably includes not only the desire to embrace Casella at the end of time but also to recuperate Beatrice.[14]

Such a tension culminates in the last cantos of the *Paradiso* (XXX–XXXIII) with Dante's staging of a highly original eschatological situation. Here, in the Empyrean, Dante-pilgrim's desire to see the blessed with their resurrected bodies as they will be at the Last Judgment is fully realized as the poet subverts traditional eschatological temporalities and anticipates the scene of resurrection before the end of time.[15] As such Dante unites the two eschatological emphases structuring his "sacrato poema" [sacred poem] (*Par.* XXIII, 62) – that is to say the immediacy and intensity of the soul's experience straight after it has separated from the earthly body *and* the fully material, relational and corporeal sense of identity that will only come back with the resurrection of the body.[16] Most importantly, this integration happens not only at a thematic and eschatological level but also poetically. In a very complex way, the final cantos of the poem harness a "jumping" textuality (one that, as Barolini states, is "non-discursive, non-linear, de-chronologized and affective") and a form of poetic language that both embrace the vernacular in all its fluidity and range of expression and replicate the resurrection of the body textually, *within* language.[17]

---

14 On this point, see Gragnolati: *Amor che move*, especially Chapter 5: "Forse non pur per loro, ma per le mamme": La nostalgia del *Paradiso* e gli abbracci della *Commedia*, p. 91–110, and Chapter 7: Forme del desiderio, p. 139–161.

15 Dante makes this claim explicit in *Paradiso* XXX, 43–45, when he writes: "Qui vederai l'una e l'altra milizia / di paradiso, e l'una *in quelli aspetti / che tu vedrai a l'ultima giustizia*" [Here you shall see both soldieries of Paradise, / one of them in just such form / as you shall see it at the final judgment].

16 See Chapter 4 of Gragnolati: *Experiencing the Afterlife* for a detailed discussion, p. 139–178.

17 See Barolini: *The Undivine 'Comedy'*, Chapter 10: The Sacred Poem is Forced to Jump: Closure and the Poetics of Enjambment, p. 218–256: p. 221. Her notion of a "jumping" textuality as fundamentally lyric rather than narrative in nature derives from her analysis of the terzina from *Paradiso* XXIII, 61–63, in which Dante acknowledges that he must leap over the moment of ecstatic, lyrical, mystical vision he cannot describe and rejoin his path further up: "e così, figurando il paradiso, / *convien saltar* lo sacrato poema / come chi trova suo cammin reciso" [And so, in representing Paradise, / the sacred poem must make its leap across, / as does a man who finds his path cut off]. On the poetic language of the high *Paradiso* as incorporating a Kristevan dimension of semiotic affect which recuperates the fluid and maternal component of the vernacular, see Gary P. Cestaro: *Dante and the Grammar of the Nursing Body*. Notre Dame: University of Notre Dame Press 2003, especially p. 135–166; and Gragnolati, *Amor che move*, p. 149–161.

If therefore, as indicated above, the heavenly state can be interpreted as the dissolution of one's identity into the movement of God's cosmic order and his love ("l'amor che move il sole e l'altre stelle" [The Love that moves the sun and all the other stars], *Par*. XXXIII, 145), paradoxically it also continues to express an individuality accepted in its relational singularity that persists in the body and the desire for it. Perhaps most importantly, we can say that Dante's collapse of eschatology in the final cantos of the *Paradiso* actually replicates the pleasure of losing oneself, of merging with God, and finding oneself again through the memory of the body, associated at once with Beatrice, the vernacular, and the lyric.[18] It constitutes a paradoxical fullness of textuality, which replicates in turn the paradoxical fullness of a desire experienced as glory, a state of eschatological plenitude in which, to quote Caroline Walker Bynum, "Desire is *now*."[19] As such, the textuality of the high *Paradiso* also succeeds in recuperating the corporeal dimension that the poem associates with memory, desire and relationality, none of which is wholly subsumable into the God pole yet remain a fundamental component of identity in beatitude.

Bearing in mind Dante's performance and embrace of paradox as the very essence of desire in the *Paradiso*, it is appropriate now to turn to Petrarch's *Triumphi* and to a consideration of the kind of eschatology and textuality they embody, especially when read relationally with Dante's *Commedia* and Petrarch's own *Rerum vulgarium fragmenta*. The *Triumphi*, likely composed between 1352–1374, are written in the form of a vision and in *terza rima* – the meter Dante invented for his *Commedia* – and as such explicitly invite a comparison with Dante's magnum opus. They narrate a triumphal procession of six allegorical figures, each of which is defeated in turn by a greater victor – Love, Chastity (represented by Laura, Petrarch's beloved), Death, Fame, and Time – until Eternity triumphs over them all. As in the *Commedia* with respect to the *Vita nova*, in the *Triumphi* the love poetry of the *Rerum vulgarium fragmenta* opens up to a moral and eschatological dimension that culminates with paradise. In turn, the epic

---

18 For example, these elements come together in *Paradiso* XXX, 70–75, in the affective and eroticized language Beatrice employs to describe the transformation of the pilgrim's desire in the moment he drinks from the river of light: "'L'alto disio che mo t'infiamma e urge, / d'aver notizia di ciò che tu vei, / tanto mi piace più quanto più turge; / ma di quest' acqua convien che tu bei / prima che tanta sete in te si sazi': / così mi disse il sol de li occhi miei" ["The deep desire that now inflames and prods you / to understand at last all that you see / pleases me the more the more it surges / But you must drink first of these waters / before your great thirst may be satisfied." / Thus the sun of my eyes spoke to me]. They are, however, a notably constant feature of the last cantos of the poem describing the beatific vision.
19 Caroline Walker Bynum: *The Resurrection of the Body in Western Christianity, 200–1330*. New York: Columbia University Press 1995, p. 339. Italics in the original.

framework of the *Triumphi* (modelled on the classical epic as much as Dante's vernacular one), and the movement generated by the *terza rima* itself, instigate a "vertical" drive largely absent from the *rime sparse* of the *Rerum vulgarium fragmenta*.[20]

In particular, it is important to explore the notion of desire conveyed by the *Triumphi*'s finale, which offers a depiction of heaven that goes against the development of some key theological assumptions about the afterlife in the late Middle Ages, specifically regarding the beatific vision and Dante's own eschatology in the *Commedia*. As earlier discussed, the eschatological focus had shifted during this period from a concern with the event of the Last Judgment, and the resurrection of the body at the end of time, towards the experience of the separated soul in the time between death and the resurrection. This development concluded with the 1336 promulgation of the papal bull *Benedictus Deus*, which officially declared that in heaven a separated soul enjoys ultimate beatitude and does not need its body in order to have access to full vision of God. This edict was passed in Avignon, the place where Petrarch lived and worked in and around the papal curia, and it is not surprising that, as Maria Cecilia Bertolani has shown, he knew well contemporary theological debates on the beatific vision.[21] In c.1336, Petrarch even wrote a letter to Benedict XII in which he acknowledged the Pontiff's view that the resurrection of the body is not necessary for the blessed souls' glory and that they are granted the beatific vision straight after physical death.[22] Yet the *Triumphi* imagine quite a different eschatology, not only focused on the resurrection of the body, but also conveying the rather profane potential of resurrection as a recovery of the beloved's body. Instead of redirecting desire from a mortal lady to an immortal God, the *Triumphi* seem to justify the poet-lover's

---

[20] On the poetics of the *Triumphi*, and the nature of Petrarch's vernacular project in that work, see at least, Zygmunt G. Barański: "To hail in triumph Caesar or poet": Petrarch's *Triumphi*. In: Albert Russell Ascoli / Unn Falkeid (eds): *The Cambridge Companion to Petrarch*. Cambridge: Cambridge University Press 2015, p. 74–86; Fabio Finotti: The Poem of Memory: Petrarch's *Triumphi*. In: Victoria Kirkham/Armando Maggi (eds.): *Petrarch: A Critical Guide to the Complete Works*. Chicago and London: The University of Chicago Press 2009, p. 63–83; Marco Ariani: I *Triumphi*. In his: *Petrarca*. Rome: Salerno 1999, p. 286–310; and Marguerite R. Waller: Negative Stylistics: A Reading of Petrarch's *Trionfi*. In her: *Petrarch's Poetics and Literary History*. Amherst: The University of Massachusetts Press 1980, p. 107–132. On the notion of a "vertical" drive in the *Triumphi*, see Finotti: The Poem of Memory, p. 63.
[21] For example those put forward by Robert of Anjou, Benedict XII, and Durand of St Pourçain. See the first two chapters of Maria Cecilia Bertolani's: *Petrarca e la visione dell'eterno*. Bologna: Il Mulino 2005, p. 1–126; and Bynum's discussion of "the controversy over the beatific vision" in: *The Resurrection of the Body*, p. 283–91.
[22] The letter in question is *Epistola* I, 5, analysed by Bertolani in: *Petrarca e la visione dell'eterno*, p. 99–126.

desire for his lady by imagining that the resurrection of her body will cure it of the imperfections that had made it problematic on earth. They almost entirely ignore Dante's focus on the separated soul's experience after physical death and exclude almost all mention of the *visio Dei*, suggesting instead that ultimate happiness lies neither in the beatific vision nor in the recovery of one's own body, but in the contemplation of Laura's resurrected body, made impassable (to time) and incorruptible (to death).

As earlier discussed, Dante went to great lengths to enable his souls to have full experience of either bliss or pain immediately after death, inventing the theory of the *ombra*, whereby a soul unfolds a body of air in the afterlife, which allows it to have shape and to express all sensitive faculties. At the same time, as we have seen in *Paradiso* XIV, Dante's accordance with the recent eschatological interest for the experience of the separated soul does not prevent him from also stressing the increase in beatitude that will coincide with the return of the resurrection body at the end of time. Yet, with the "disio d'i' corpi morti", Dante makes this eschatological emphasis entirely his own in emphasizing the kind of relationality it embodies. It is a relationality expressed not only in the joyous intensification of the *visio Dei* that ensues from the soul's becoming even more open and pleasing to God, as He gives even more of Himself ("per che s'accrescerà *ciò che ne dona / di gratüito lume il sommo bene*", [so that the light, granted to us freely / by the Highest Good, shall increase], *Par.* XIV, 46–47), but also in the desire to embrace one's loved ones and reactivate the memory and affective identity carried by the body as a locus of desire in all its specificity and relationality, and for Dante bound up both with the resurgence of a lyric form of textuality and with the vernacular. In the *Triumphi*, by contrast, Petrarch's relationality is made more exclusive in narrowing to focus on Petrarch and Laura alone in their poetic (and eschatological) singularity. As such, the beatific experience of the *Triumphi* is not located in the gratuitous giving of the self to God or even to others (or Him to you), but in a carefully choreographed vision of the triumph of the beloved, which actually puts that vision outside of any known eschatological parameters in the strictest sense.

As in Petrarch's *Secretum*, turning to God is a moral issue (the desire to seek refuge from sin, to find a way out of the *cor inquietum*), and what seems to be lacking is the most profound and intense desire of the soul, from the moment it exists, to reunite with its Maker that was for instance expressed by Dante in *Convivio* IV and beautifully reiterated by Beatrice in *Par.* VII, 142–44: "Ma vostra vita sanza mezzo spira / la somma beninanza, *e la innamora / di sé sì che poi sempre la disira*" [But supreme goodness breathes life in you, / unmediated, *and He so enamors your soul / of Himself that it desires Him forever after*].²³ While Dante's concept of the love uniting creature and Creator culminates in the *Paradiso* with the soul's desire to merge with the divinity up to and including the dissolution of the ego, Petrarch cannot really contemplate such a surrender and establishes instead a different eschatology, a lyric fantasy whereby all of heaven is subsumed to Laura's restoration in her corporeal wholeness, as *eros* triumphs over *caritas* and the blessed, and even God Himself, make way for her final apotheosis.

As though to underscore the radical departure Petrarch will ultimately make, both from the dominant eschatological position of his time and Dante's, the *Triumphus Eternitatis* begins by implying that Petrarch's poetic subject, still shaken and dispersed by the vicissitudes of desire, time, and history staged in the earlier Triumphs, is on the point of conversion and preparing to move into God:

> Da poi che sotto 'l ciel cosa non vidi
> stabile e ferma, tutto sbigottito
> *mi volsi a me*, e dissi: "In che ti fidi?"
> Risposi: "Nel Signor, che mai fallito
> non à promessa a chi si fida in lui.
> [...] Tarde non fur mai gratie divine;
> in quelle spero che 'n me anchor faranno
> alte operatïoni e pellegrine".
> Così detto e risposto. Or, se non stanno
> queste cose che 'l ciel volge e governa,
> dopo molto voltar, *che fine avranno*?
> Questo pensava; e mentre più *s'interna*
> la mente mia, veder mi parve un mondo
> novo, in etate immobile ed eterna,
> e 'l sole e tutto 'l ciel disfar a tondo
> con le sue stelle, anchor la terra e 'l mare,
> e rifarne un più bello e più giocondo.
> Qual meraviglia ebb'io, quando ristare
> vidi *in un punto* quel che mai non stette,
> ma discorrendo suol tutto cangiare!
> E le tre parti sue vidi ristrecte

---

23 See *Convivio* IV.12 and, as counterpoint, Petrarch's *Secretum* I, 15, 1 in which Augustinus, as he laments Franciscus's blindness in matters of desire and especially his entrapment in the blind prison of the body, accuses him of having forgotten his divine origins and neglected his Creator, allowing his soul to be alienated by the *cupiditas* resulting from the unchecked indulgence of the passions, "Audi ergo. Animam quidem tuam, sicut celitus bene institutam esse non negaverim, sic ex contagio corporis huius, ubi circumsepta est, multum a primeva nobiltate sua degenerasse ne dubites; nec degenerasse duntaxat, sed longo iam tractu temporis obtorpuisse, facta velut proprie originis ac superni Conditoris immemorem". In Francesco Petrarca: *Secretum*. Edited by Ugo Dotti. Rome: Archivio Guido Izzi 1993.

ad una sola, e quella una esser ferma
sì che, come solea, più non s'affrette;
   e quasi in terra d'erbe ignuda ed herma,
né 'fia', né 'fu', né 'mai', né 'inanzi' o "indietro",
ch'umana vita fanno varia e 'nferma!
   Passa il penser sì come sole in vetro,
anzi più assai, però che nulla il tene.
O, qual *gratia* mi fia, se mai l'impetro,
   ch'i'veggia ivi presente *il sommo bene*,
non alcun mal, che solo il tempo mesce
e con lui si diparte e con lui vène. (*TE*, 1–5; 13–39)[24]

[When I had seen that nothing under heaven
Is firm and stable, in dismay *I turned
To my heart*, and asked: "Wherein has thou thy trust?"
   "In the Lord", the answer came, "Who keepeth ever
His covenant with one who trusts in Him.
[...] Divine mercies never come too late:
In them I hope, that they may work in me
A transformation deep and excellent."
   'Twas thus my heart made answer. If all things
That are beneath the heavens are to fail,
How, after many circlings, *will they end*?
   So ran my thought; and as I *pondered it
More and more deeply*, I at last beheld
A world made new and changeless and eternal.
   I saw the sun, the heavens, and the stars
And land and sea unmade, and made again
More beauteous and more joyous than before.
   Greatly I marveled, seeing time itself
Come to an end, that ne'er before had ceased,
But had been wont its course to change all things.
   Past, present, future: these I saw combined
In a single term, and that unchangeable:
No swiftness now, as there had been before.
   As on an empty plan, I now could see

---

24 Quotations from Petrarch's *Triumphi* come from: Francesco Petrarca: *Trionfi, Rime estravaganti, Codice degli abbozzi*. Edited by Vinicio Pacca and Laura Paolino. Milan: Mondadori 1996. English translations are from: *The Triumphs of Petrarch*. Translated by Ernest Hatch Wilkins. Chicago and London: The University of Chicago Press 1962. Subsequent quotations from the *Triumphus Eternitatis* will be given using the short form *TE*, followed by the line numbers. Any quotations from the *Rerum vulgarium fragmenta* [*RVF*] come from: Francesco Petrarca: *Canzoniere*. Edited by Marco Santagata. Rev. edn. Milan: Mondadori 2004. Any translations come from: *Petrarch's Lyric Poems: The 'Rime Sparse' and Other Lyrics*. Edited and translated by Robert M. Durling. Cambridge, MA: Harvard University Press 1976.

No "shall be" or "has been," "ne'er" or "before"
Or "after," filling life with doubtfulness.
   Thought passes as a ray of the sun through glass –
More swiftly still, for there is nought to impede.
What *grace*, if I am worthy, shall be mine,
   If I may there behold *the Highest Good*,
And none of the harm that is poured out by Time,
And comes with Time, and disappears with Time!]

This passage includes many references to Dante's *Paradiso* and a few of its features are especially significant for understanding Petrarch's eschatological and apocalyptic imagination, the initial suggestion of orthodoxy, and the hints at the deviation to come. Firstly, and most importantly, while the *Triumphus Eternitatis* begins where the *Triumphus Temporis* had ended,[25] with the 'I' caught in the onslaught of time, it quickly moves towards the point of stability and fixity that Petrarch claims to find in God as the absolutely non-contingent presence at the centre of the universe (vv. 4–6), but ultimately aligns with the Apocalyptic perspective of the 'new heaven and new earth' (Apoc. 21) that emerge only at the end of time, at the Last Judgment. The question posed in lines 16–18, "Or, se non stanno / queste cose che 'l ciel volge e governa, dopo molto voltar, che *fine* avranno" marks the transition to considering 'last things', and is the moment when Petrarch's emphasis on resurrection surfaces, here already played almost exclusively in terms of vision and the visionary ("vidi"; "veggio"; "veggio"; "veder mi parve"; "vidi"; "vidi"; "veggia"), carried through the length of the *Triumphus Eternitatis* in the recurring (Dantean) phrase "vedrassi" (*TE*, 93; 106; 115) – referred to the revelation of God's providential plan for humankind at the end of time, including the final Judgment of the righteous and the wicked.[26] Yet Petrarch's reading and appropriation of Apocalypse is partial and restrictive: while he emphasizes the importance of revelation and the unprecedented power of the vision of the 'new world' to subsume the old, he underplays the theocentric, sustaining and titanic presence of God as "Alpha and Omega" (Apoc. 1), as Source and destination of all created being, as well as the final

---

25 See *Triumphus Temporis*, 142–45, "Tutto vince e ritoglie il Tempo avaro; / chiamasi Fama, ed è morir secondo, / né più che contra'l primo è alcun riparo. / Così il Tempo triunfa i nomi e'l mondo" [Time in his avarice steals so much away: / Men call it Fame;'tis but a second death, / And both alike are strong beyond defense. / Thus doth Time triumph over the world and Fame].
26 The crucial intertext from Dante's *Paradiso* is *Par*. XIX, 115–141, where, in the Heaven of Justice, the Eagle utters forth the names of the corrupt Christian rulers as they shall be written in the Book of Judgment. The nine *terzine*, three of which begin "Lì si vedrà" [There they shall see], and three "Vedrassi" [The text will show] form, with the last three beginning "E" [And], the acrostic "LVE" [plague].

victory of the Lamb (since Christ's glorious Triumph will be replaced by Laura's lyric apotheosis).

Petrarch's rewriting of Dante is arguably even more radical, and according to Christian Moevs, can be taken as evidence not only of Petrarch's resistance to metaphysics, but also a doubt about the very ontological foundations of the soul and its relationship to its Maker. Able to join with God only through a superhuman effort of the will (a "macho" act, in the *Secretum*) that would quell all other desires, the Petrarchan subject does not possess that innate desire propelling it to reunite with its Source and the ground of all being (as articulated in *Par.* VII, and indeed through the length of the *Commedia*) but rather has to strive even just to seek God among the things of the world.[27] As a result, in the *Triumphus Eternitatis*, Petrarch's eternity results as:

> a strange affair: it is not a transcendence of time and flux, but rather it is time and flux frozen, fixed, stopped. It is not a beatific vision of the divine light, of pure being or consciousness as the ontological foundation of the world; it is rather a dream that the fleeting world itself could be made a "cosa [...] stabile e ferma" [...]: in short, a spatiotemporal world that is non-contingent, stable, unchanging, permanently new, whole, dependable and gathered together.[28]

Petrarch's eternity is consequently without end and, insofar as time is suspended, timeless too. But it is definitively not the *totum simul* of Dante's *Paradiso*, where, as Barolini has shown, the poet actually aims to recreate textually the experience of "ontological simultaneity": eternity not as mere duration, but God's "plenitude of presence in a never-fading instant".[29]

Petrarch's recasting of the Dantean "punto", the verb "s'interna" and the phrase "sommo bene", are all revealing of this eschatological *scarto*. All drawn from *Paradiso* XXXIII, where they have a deeply metaphysical and mystical valence, they turn on the identity of the human soul with God and, in the case of the "punto", on the divine mind (the Empyrean, "[che] non è in loco e non s'impola" [is not in space and does not turn on poles], *Par.* XXII, 67) in which all creation finds its place and where Dante, having penetrated into the very mystery of the Incarnation, will ultimately gaze upon an image of "la nostra effige" [our likeness] painted in the second Person of the Trinity (*Par.* XXXIII, 130–32). To this we might also add the "gratia" of line 36 of Petrarch's *Triumphus Eternitatis*, which

---

[27] See Christian Moevs: Subjectivity and Conversion in Dante and Petrarch. In: Zygmunt G. Barański/Theodore J. Cachey Jr. (eds.): *Petrarch and Dante: Anti-Dantism, Metaphysics, Tradition*. Notre Dame: University of Notre Dame Press 2009, p. 226–259 (p. 242; p. 246).
[28] Moevs: Subjectivity and Conversion, p. 234.
[29] Barolini: *The Undivine 'Comedy'*, p. 168.

is likely not the ecstatic flowing of love and grace from God to the blessed soul, but rather the dispensation that would allow for Petrarch's vision of eternity to take place, and for the 'I' to transcend time and death and be reunited with Laura.

Moreover, unlike the progression that defines all of the *Commedia*, in these opening lines of the *Triumphus Eternitatis*, we find at most a pseudo-progression: a simulated movement toward what we think might be the *visio Dei* but which will end not with God but with Laura (as though He might be an intermediary to reach *her*). All in all, Petrarch radically alters Dante's mystical terminology since his self-absorption will ultimately be lyric and not mystical, not an opening up or turning oneself inside out to merge with the other but a closing in or down to focus exclusively on one individual in all her (lyric) specificity. The "sommo bene" (*TE*, 37), which recalls the passage of *Paradiso* XIV quoted above, as well as Beatrice's "sommo piacer" (*Purg.* XXXI, 52), referred to her earthly body now scattered in earth, consequently results as retroactively ambiguous. It could be God, but given how the *Triumphus Eternitatis* evolves it is more likely to be a no longer synecdochic symbol of Laura in her fully embodied glory and perfection at the resurrection.[30]

The thing that seems to hold Petrarch's vision of eternity together is not divine love, then, but rather the indissolubility of the ego, which resists surrendering itself into God because, as Moevs indicates, it has become detached from the principle that would make that an attractive or certain possibility.[31] While he argues that, as such, the ego, "cannot come to know the world as itself, and cannot give up itself without ceasing to exist entirely", our interpretation considers that ego also as a fundamentally lyric entity in Petrarch, and opens up to a more positive way of viewing that "locus of thought and desire". The latter may be, in Moevs's words, "evanescent" but it still carries an impassable affective and erotic drive bound to the corporeal dimension of an individual made unique by its personal affective history.[32]

To speak of 'lyric' in relation to our two authors is precisely to emphasize the corporeal, intersubjective, and relational aspect of their poetic eschatologies. In Dante's case, we call 'lyric' that undisciplinable, affective component bound up with the body as a locus of desire, memory and relationality; with the past; and

---

30 On the synecdochic representation of Laura in the *Rerum vulgarium fragmenta*, see for example, Giuseppe Mazzotta: *The Worlds of Petrarch*. Durham, NC: Duke University Press 1993, p. 9–10 and p. 78–79; Cesare Segre: Les isotopies de Laure. In: Herman Perret/Hans-George Ruprecht (eds.): *Exigences et perspectives de la sémiotique: recueil d'hommages pour Algirdas Julien Greimas*. 2 vols. Amsterdam; Philadelphia: J Benjamins 1985, II, p. 811–826; and John Freccero: The Fig Tree and the Laurel: Petrarch's Poetics. In: *Diacritics* 5, 1 (Spring, 1975), p. 34–40.
31 Moevs: Subjectivity and Conversion, p. 245.
32 See Moevs: Subjectivity and Conversion, p. 227.

ultimately with Beatrice. In Dante, this lyric dimension, not entirely subsumable into the more mystical, self-dissolutory merging with God, is precisely what the text of the *Commedia* shows there is a resistance to relinquishing, and therefore keeps in paradoxical tension right to the end of the poem. In Petrarch's *Triumphus Eternitatis*, by contrast, the lyric pole is that which takes over, becomes the only thing that matters, to the exclusion of everything else (especially: the experience of *caritas* and the radical openness of the self to the Other through ecstatic union and the *visio Dei*, as well as a more broadly inter-subjective dimension beyond Laura and Petrarch themselves). In other words, 'lyric' implies a specific relationality but the way Dante and Petrarch treat and integrate that relationality into their vision of heaven is very different.

Unsurprisingly, Petrarch's lyric eschatology fully unfolds itself in the moment when Laura herself appears in the text of the *Triumphus Eternitatis*, where there is also a resurgence of the lyric mode in all its specificity and – in Petrarch's case – exclusivity:

> O felici quelle anime che 'n via
> sono o *seranno* di venire al fine
> di ch'io ragiono, *quandunque e' si sia*.
>   E tra l'altre leggiadre e pellegrine
> beatissima lei, che morte occise
> assai di qua dal natural confine!
>   *Parranno allor* l'angeliche divise
> e l'oneste parole e i penser casti
> che nel cor giovenil natura mise.
>   Tanti volti, che Morte e 'l Tempo à guasti,
> torneranno al suo più fiorito stato;
> e vedrassi ove, Amor, tu mi legasti,
>   ond'io a dito ne sarò mostrato:
> "Ecco chi pianse sempre, e nel suo pianto
> sovra 'l riso d'ogni altro fu beato!"
>   E quella di ch'anchor piangendo canto
> avrà gran meraviglia di se stessa,
> vedendosi fra tutte dar il vanto.
> [...]
>   E 'l Tempo, a disfar tutto così presto,
> e Morte, in sua ragion cotanto avara,
> morti inseme seranno a quella e questo.
>   E quei che Fama meritaron chiara,
> che 'l Tempo spense, e i be' visi leggiadri
> che 'mpallidir fe' 'l Tempo e Morte amara,
>   l'oblivïon, *gli aspetti oscuri e adri*,
> *più che mai bei tornando*, lasceranno
> a Morte impetüosa, a' giorni ladri.

Ne l'età più fiorita e verde avranno
con immortal bellezza eterna fama.
Ma innanzi a tutte ch'a rifarsi vanno
   è quella che piangendo il mondo chiama
con la mia lingua e con la stancha penna:
ma 'l ciel pur di vederla intera brama.
A riva un fiume che nasce in Gebenna,
Amor mi die' per lei sì lunga guerra,
che la memoria ancora il cor accenna.
   Felice sasso che 'l bel viso serra!
Che, poi che avrà preso il suo bel velo,
se fu beato chi la vide in terra,
   or che fia dunque a rivederla in cielo? (*TE*, 82–99; 125–145)

[Blessèd those souls that now are on the way,
Or will be soon, to reach the final goal,
Whereof I speak, *whenever it may be*;
   And among all the rare and beauteous ones,
Most blessèd she, who long before she came
To the bound that nature sets was slain by death.
   Then will be manifest the angelic modes,
The honorable words, and the chaste thoughts
That nature set within her youthful heart.
   The countenances hurt by death and time
Will now appear in perfect flowering,
The bond wherewith Love bound me will be seen.
   And pointing toward me will be some who say:
"He ever wept, and yet amid his tears
Was blest above the joys of other men."
   And she of whom, still weeping, I sing,
Will find it very wonderful that she
Should have the highest praise among them all.
(...)
   Time, ever ready to destroy all things,
And Death, so greedy in her evil power,
One and the other, shall together die.
   And those who merited illustrious fame
That Time had quenched, and *countenances fair
Made pale and wan* by Time and bitter Death,
   Becoming still more beauteous than before
Will leave to raging Death and thieving Time
Oblivion, and aspects dark and sad.
   In the full flower of youth they shall possess
Immortal beauty and eternal fame.
Before them all, who go to be made anew,
   Is she for whom the world is weeping still,
Calling her with my tongue and weary pen,

> *But heaven too desires her, body and soul.*
>   *Beside a stream that rises in the Alps*
> *Love gave to me for her a war so long*
> *My heart still bears the memory thereof.*
>   *Happy the stone that covers her fair face!*
> *And now that she her beauty hath resumed,*
> *If he was blest who saw her here on earth,*
>   *What then will it be to see her again in heaven!*]

Again, Petrarch's text makes clear that we are in an apocalyptic perspective, emphatically looking forward to the end of time, when the resurrection of the body will take place: "sono o *seranno*", "paranno *allor*", "*torneranno*", "*vedrassi* [...]". Yet, as he interpolates the god of Love (*Amor* is a lyric figure representing eros and not the Christian God here) and even himself into that vision as a kind of celebrity (vv. 93–96), Petrarch's eschatological vision takes a decisive turn toward the phantasmatic. There is absolutely no reference to the increase in beatific vision, to Dante's "ardore" or his "gratüito lume", but only to the hypostatized "*immortal* bellezza e *eterna* fama" which in turn conflate three poles together: the lyric ("bellezza"), Christian ("immortal", "eternal", again "bellezza"), and classical ("fama"). Petrarch's emphasis is not on selfless giving (Dante's "dona"), or receiving (in the return of love from creature to Creator) but rather on the self-centred and self-centring forces of beauty and fame redeemed from Time's grasp.

Thus while we do remain within a Christian framework, and in the shadow of the Apocalypse, there is no reference to Christ, the Trinity, or to God, but the staging of an eschatological fantasy, which culminates with the vision of Laura alone. The final question mark of the poem suspends, as much as it extends, the text into the fourth dimension. As a result, notwithstanding its vertical drive and final burst of lyric energy, the *Triumphus Eternitatis* ends on a kind of stasis, just as the projected vision of Laura in her corporeal wholeness retains a sense of distance and detachment consonant with the still unrealized status of the question or wish formulated in the closing lines. With the mention of her "bel velo", Petrarch stresses Laura's resurrected beauty as well as the material continuity connecting her resurrected flesh to the "mortal veil" whose loss and decay was so lamented in the second part of the *Rerum vulgarium fragmenta*.[33] Yet she remains an object of beauty to be contemplated, rather than the subject of an embrace that (in Dante's case) truly allowed for the inter-subjective experience of affective union through the medium of the body in all its specific, relational extensions.

---

33 See, for example, *RVF* 268, "Che debb'io far?" and *RVF* 302, "Levòmmi il mio pensier", which has interesting parallels with the last sonnet of Dante's *Vita Nuova*, "Oltre la spera che più larga gira" (XLI).

Laura's body is perhaps, as is so frequently the case in the *Rerum vulgarium fragmenta*, fetishized by poetry more than it is embodied into it, though this is the closest Petrarch gets – and it is further than ever before – to making it (textually) present. Nonetheless, in emphatically delaying the experience of fullness until the body will return at the end of time, Petrarch endows his language with a kind of spectrality that is actually in tension with the eschatological emphasis on resurrection on which he bases the entire *Triumphus Eternitatis*.

We remember that in the final cantos of Dante's *Paradiso*, with the collapse of eschatology into poetry there is a resurrection of a lyric textuality, whereby the pilgrim actually experiences the resurrection and the poem replicates it in the text. Everything is simultaneously present in a form of relationality which also preserves and extends desire and memory into the eschatological present of the resurrection itself. In the *Triumphus Eternitatis*, by contrast, Petrarch does not experience (eschatological) fullness because it is projected into a still undetermined future (cf. "*quandunque sia*"), and what may be missing is precisely the felt affect so materially present in the *Paradiso*'s lyric textuality. For Petrarch, the moment can be imagined, and the subject can gain a kind of satisfaction from the fantasy, but it cannot be experienced or expressed except between the lines, and at the very margins of the text.

Petrarch, in the end, does away completely with the collective, non-subjective, 'universal' part of the heavenly experience, which Dante posits in the *visio Dei* and the experience of selfless love and loving selflessness. As a result, Petrarch's "disio d'i'corpi morti" is something else as well: focused on the single body of the beloved, and not even on the lover's body, it is still paradigmatic of Petrarch's eschatology but paradigmatic of an obsessive, almost tyrannical 'monomania bi-soggettiva' (the term is ours) focused on Petrarch and Laura alone. Making eternity itself a mere extension and deification of a quintessentially lyric fantasy, the poet can state without irony that all of heaven desires, with almost cupidinous force (the word Petrarch uses is "brama"), to look upon Laura's body in its restored corporeal wholeness and to celebrate her immortal beauty and eternal fame ("dar il vanto").

The collective experience of heaven consequently has no place except to validate the supremacy of Laura's image in relation to Petrarch's gaze and to the resurrected landscape of his heart, whose affective current is carried by memory into the furthest reaches of Petrarch's eschatological imagination ("A riva [...] rivederla in cielo?"), where as noted earlier it remains only describable in part, and certainly intensified more than actually transformed.[34]

---

[34] And note the strong echo of the sweetness of Casella's *amoroso canto*, "che la dolcezza ancor dentro mi suona" (*Purg.* II, 114), cited earlier, as well as Petrarch's potential rewriting

As the memory of the lyric past floods back, the prospect of entering a celestial Jerusalem (if it ever existed) is completely supplanted by the vision of a new and timeless Vaucluse transposed into this paradise at the end of time. It leads us back all the way to the "chiuso loco" with which the *Triumphus Cupidinis* opened, as the scene of both the writing subject's dream and his subjection to love, here both redeemed and valorized in light of the final vision of Laura's resurrected body.[35] In this vision of eternity, God cannot but be absent: within the confines of Petrarch's redeemed lyric universe of the *Triumphi*, where Laura is restored – however conditionally – to presence, if she has taken God's place, He is relegated to hers in a stunning reversal of the substitution of Laura by the Virgin Mary in *RVF* 366.

At the same time, the experience of desire and language also changes. Whereas with the textual 'fireworks' Dante stages at the end of the *Paradiso*, the pilgrim's own desire and will ("disio" and "*velle*") are brought into a perfect cosmological circulation with "l'amor che move il sole e l'altre stelle" (*Par.* XXXIII, 142–45), at the end of the *Triumphus Eternitatis* it feels paradoxically like the movement of desire is absent or at least held in a kind of suspended animation. Perhaps this is because Petrarch, in doing away with the paradox that had sustained his earlier lyric production, also removes some of the tension as well, making his language less dazzling or bright and more subdued, to create a different kind of textuality, both with respect to Dante's *Commedia* and Petrarch's own *Rerum vulgarium fragmenta*.

Dante's *Paradiso* is sustained by presence, to the extent that even where, as in *Paradiso* XIV, the body is felt as absent, the lack of it can still be celebrated as joyous. In Petrarch, by contrast, what is absent really *isn't* there: in the *Rerum vulgarium fragmenta*, Laura dissolves even when she comes back and the lack of her *mortal corpo* remains irreducible even in the face of its promised return at the

---

of *Par.* XXXIII, 61–63: "cotal son io, ché quasi tutta cessa / mia visïone, *e ancor mi distilla / nel core il dolce che nacque da essa*" [such am I, my vision almost faded from my mind / *while in my heart there still endures / the sweetness that was born of it*], referring in Dante's text to the visio Dei.

35 Cf. *Triumphus Cupidinis* I, 8, and Marco Ariani's intertextual reading of the two moments of the work in Francesco Petrarca: *Triumphi*. Edited by Marco Ariani. Milan: Mursia 1988, p. 384: "è dunque il corpo glorioso di Madonna che fa rifiorire la landa desolata del tempo annientato: il *topos* del *plazer* primaverile, corroso all'inizio del poema, ritorna, alla fine, in un cerchio perfettamente concluso, radicalmente riavvalorato." [thus it is the glorified body of the Lady that causes the desolate moor of annihilated time to reflower: the topos of the springtime *plazer*, corroded at the start of the poem, returns, at the end, in a perfectly completed circle, radically reaffirmed]. Translation is ours.

end of time.³⁶ In the *Triumphi*, Petrarch's wish – mediated through Laura's body – is realized (and consolidated by the repetition of the "bel velo" in *TE*, 143) but realized precisely still as a wish projected forward to an indeterminate future. Everything is put off until the resurrection, because it cannot stand before, to the point at which we may even end up further from God than we were in the *Rerum vulgarium fragmenta*. Nonetheless we might yet suggest that the delay or deferral in desire's ultimate fulfilment, and the quite radical gesture of supplanting God with Laura while still contemplating her from a distance, is still a form of pleasure for Petrarch, if a masochistic one. In this form of desire, fore-pleasure counts as much as end-pleasure and the subject seeks to remain in that state as long as possible since it too can be – paradoxically – satisfying.³⁷

Yet it is not only Petrarch's concept of love and desire that so radically alters his eschatological anthropology with respect to Dante's, but also Petrarch's relationship to language. The ending of the *Triumphus Eternitatis*, which constitutes in effect Petrarch's last word on his vernacular production, raises the questions of what the vernacular itself might be for Petrarch, in distinction to Dante. Certainly, it does not appear to be the affective, maternal, even abject, "wild corporeality of natural language" that we find in the *Commedia* (as Elena Lombardi has recently defined it); but something more constructed or codified.³⁸ Petrarch's *volgare* is

---

36 See e. g. *RVF* 302, "Levòmmi il mio pensier", especially lines 10–11: "te solo aspetto et quel che tanto amasti / e là giuso è rimaso, il mio bel velo" [I only wait for you and for that which you loved so much and which remained down there, my lovely veil]; and *RVF* 362, 3–4, "esser mi par ch'àn ivi il suo tesoro / lasciando in terra lo squarciato velo" [it seems to me I am almost one of those who there possess their treasure, leaving on earth their rent veils]. On the notion of absence in the *Triumphi* as connected to Laura, see Santagata's comment in his Introduzione that: "Il finale [del *Triumphus Eternitatis*], diviso tra rievocazione storica e speranza ultraterrena, è in una certa misura inattesa. In fondo, il lettore aveva dimenticato Laura e l'amore per lei. E proprio questo è il punto dolente del suo personaggio. Non la saltuaria presenza, ma il fatto che quando esso è assente lo è per vero. [...] Ripeto, Laura non è Beatrice." [The ending [of *Triumphus Eternitatis*], suspended between the re-evocation of history and otherworldly hope, is to some extent unexpected. Deep down, the reader had forgotten about Laura and the poet's love for her. Indeed this is the sore spot of her character. Not her only occasional presence, but the fact that when she is absent, she is absent for real. [...] I repeat, Laura is not Beatrice]. In: Petrarca, *Trionfi*, p. XIII–LII (p. XLVIII–XLIX). Translation is ours.
37 Our reading of masochistic desire in these terms derives from Leo Bersani's thesis in: *The Freudian Body: Psychoanalysis and Art*. New York: Columbia University Press 1986. See especially his reading of Freud's *Three Essays on the Theory of Sexuality*, in Chapter 3: Sexuality and Aesthetics, p. 29–50.
38 See Elena Lombardi: Plurilingualism *sub specie aeternitatis* and the Strategies of a Minority Author. In Sara Fortuna/Manuele Gragnolati et al. (eds.): *Dante's Plurilingualism: Authority, Knowledge, Subjectivity*. London: Legenda 2010, p. 133–147: p. 136; and Erich Auerbach: *Sermo humilis*: The Christian Form of the Sublime. In his: *Literary Language and Its Public in Late Latin Antiquity and in the Middle Ages*. Translated by Ralph Manheim. London: Routledge and Kegan Paul 1965, p. 25–66.

assimilated less through the inter-subjective relationality that Dante ultimately posits in the image of the infant suckling at the mother's breast, so prominent in the high *Paradiso*, than from a return to the preceding lyric tradition that celebrated the very absence Petrarch internalizes, and that one still feels in the *Triumphi*'s uniquely erotic and lyric vision of eternity.[39]

Bibliography

Primary Literature

Alighieri, Dante: *The Divine Comedy*. Translated by Robert Hollander and Jean Hollander. 3 vols. New York: Doubleday 2000–2007.
Alighieri, Dante: *'La Commedia' secondo l'antica vulgata*. Edited by Giorgio Petrocchi. 2nd rev. edn. 4 vols. Florence: Le Lettere 1994 (Edizione Nazionale delle opere di D. A., 7).
Petrarca, Francesco: *Canzoniere*. Edited by Marco Santagata. Rev. edn. Milan: Mondadori 2004.
Petrarca, Francesco: *Trionfi, Rime estravaganti, Codice degli abbozzi*. Edited by Vinicio Pacca and Laura Paolino. Milan: Mondadori 1996.
Petrarca, Francesco: *Secretum*. Edited by Ugo Dotti. Rome: Archivio Guido Izzi 1993.
Petrarca, Francesco: *Triumphi*. Edited by Marco Ariani. Milan: Mursia 1988.
Petrarca, Francesco: *Petrarch's Lyric Poems: The 'Rime Sparse' and Other Lyrics*. Edited and translated by Robert M. Durling. Cambridge, MA: Harvard University Press 1976.
Petrarca, Francesco: *The Triumphs of Petrarch*. Translated by Ernest Hatch Wilkins. Chicago and London: The University of Chicago Press 1962.

Secondary Literature

Monographs and Anthologies

Ariani, Marco: *Petrarca*. Rome: Salerno 1999.
Auerbach, Erich: *Literary Language and Its Public in Late Latin Antiquity and in the Middle Ages*. Translated by Ralph Manheim. London: Routledge and Kegan Paul 1965.

---

[39] On Petrarch's conception of the *volgare*, especially as rooted in his reading of the Occitan and early Italian lyric traditions, see Marco Santagata, Introduzione. In Petrarca, *Canzoniere*, p. XIX–CII; and Marco Ariani: La lingua poetica del Petrarca volgare. In his: *Petrarca*, p. 311–335. Moevs similarly acknowledges Petrarch's return to a prior (lyric) position when he notes that, "With the last vernacular lines he wrote, Petrarch [...] wiped out the entire philosophizing and mysticizing history of the Italian lyric that culminates with Dante, everything between the Sicilians and himself; or at least he has wiped out the *Commedia*, and brought us back to the last poem of *Vita Nova*, 'Oltre la spera che più larga gira'". In: Subjectivity and Conversion, p. 237–238.

Barolini, Teodolinda: *The Undivine 'Comedy': Detheologizing Dante*. Princeton, NJ: Princeton University Press 1992.
Barolini, Teodolinda: *Dante's Poets: Textuality and Truth in the 'Comedy'*. Princeton: Princeton University Press 1984.
Bersani, Leo: *The Freudian Body: Psychoanalysis and Art*. New York: Columbia University Press 1986.
Bertolani, Maria Cecilia: *Petrarca e la visione dell'eterno*. Bologna: Il Mulino 2005.
Botterill, Steven: *Dante and the Mystical Tradition: Bernard of Clairvaux in the* 'Commedia'. Cambridge: Cambridge University Press 1994.
Bynum, Caroline Walker: *The Resurrection of the Body in Western Christianity, 200–1330*. New York: Columbia University Press 1995.
Cestaro, Gary P: *Dante and the Grammar of the Nursing Body*. Notre Dame: University of Notre Dame Press 2003.
Gragnolati, Manuele: *Amor che move: Linguaggio del corpo e forma del desiderio in Dante, Pasolini e Morante*. Milan: Il Saggiatore 2013.
Gragnolati, Manuele: *Experiencing the Afterlife: Body and Soul in Dante and Medieval Culture*. Notre Dame, IN: University of Notre Dame Press 2005.
Hawkins, Peter: *Dante: A Brief History*. London: Blackwell 2006.
Mazzotta, Giuseppe: *The Worlds of Petrarch*. Durham, NC: Duke University Press 1993.
McDannell, Colleen/Bernhard Lang: *Heaven: A History*. New Haven: Yale University Press 1998.
Moevs, Christian: *The Metaphysics of Dante's 'Comedy'*. New York: Oxford University Press 2005.
Pertile, Lino: *La punta del disio: Semantica del desiderio nella 'Commedia'*. Fiesole: Cadmo 2005.
Waller, Marguerite R: *Petrarch's Poetics and Literary History*. Amherst: The University of Massachusetts Press 1980.

Articles and Papers

Barański, Zygmunt G: "To hail in triumph Caesar or poet": Petrarch's *Triumphi*. In: Albert Russell Ascoli/U. Falkeid (eds): *The Cambridge Companion to Petrarch*. Cambridge: Cambridge University Press 2015, p. 74–86.
Bynum, Caroline Walker: Faith Imagining the Self: Somatomorphic Soul and Resurrection Body in Dante's *Divine Comedy*. In: Sang Huyn Lee/Wayne Proudfoot et al. (eds.): *Faithful Imagining: Essays in Honor of Richard R. Neibuhr*. Atlanta: Scholars Press 1995, p. 81–104.
Chiavacci Leonardi, Anna Maria: "Le bianche stole": il tema della resurrezione nel *Paradiso*. In: Giovanni Barblan (ed.): *Dante e la Bibbia. Atti del Convegno Internazionale promosso da "Biblia": Firenze, 26–27–28 settembre 1986*. Florence: Olschki 1988, p. 249–271.
Finotti, Fabio: The Poem of Memory: Petrarch's *Triumphi*. In: Victoria Kirkham/Armando Maggi (eds.): *Petrarch: A Critical Guide to the Complete Works*. Chicago and London: The University of Chicago Press 2009, p. 63–83.
Freccero, John: Casella's Song: *Purgatorio* II, 112. In his: *Dante: The Poetics of Conversion*. Edited by Rachel Jacoff. Cambridge, MA: Harvard University Press 1986, p. 186–194.
Freccero, John: The Fig Tree and the Laurel: Petrarch's Poetics. In: *Diacritics* 5, 1 (Spring, 1975), p. 34–40.

Gragnolati, Manuele: Nostalgia in Heaven: Embraces, Affection and Identity in the *Commedia*. In: John C. Barnes/Jennifer Petrie (eds.): *Dante and the Human Body: Eight Essays*. Dublin: Four Courts Press 2007, p. 117–137.

Gragnolati, Manuele: Gluttony and the Anthropology of Pain in Dante's *Inferno* and *Purgatorio*. In: Rachel Fulton/Bruce W. Holsinger (eds.): *History in the Comic Mode: Medieval Communities and the Matter of Person*. New York: Columbia University Press 2007, p. 238–250.

Harrison, Anna: Community among the Saints in Heaven in Bernard of Clairvaux's *Sermons for the Feast of All Saints*. In: Caroline Walker Bynum/Paul Freedman (eds.): *Last Things: Death and Apocalypse in the Middle Ages*. Philadelphia: University of Pennsylvania Press 2000, p. 191–204.

Hollander, Robert: *Purgatorio* II: Cato's Rebuke and Dante's *Scoglio*. In: *Italica* 52, 3 (Autumn, 1975), p. 348–363.

Kirkpatrick, Robin: Polemics of Praise: Theology as Text, Narrative and Rhetoric in Dante's *Commedia*. In: Vittorio Montemaggi/Matthew Treherne (eds): *Dante's 'Commedia': Theology as Poetry*. Notre Dame: University of Notre Dame Press 2010, p. 14–35.

Lombardi, Elena: Plurilingualism *sub specie aeternitatis* and the Strategies of a Minority Author. In Sara Fortuna/Manuele Gragnolati et al. (eds.): *Dante's Plurilingualism: Authority, Knowledge, Subjectivity*. London: Legenda 2010, p. 133–147.

Moevs, Christian: Subjectivity and Conversion in Dante and Petrarch. In: Zygmunt G. Barański/Theodore J. Cachey Jr. (eds.): *Petrarch and Dante: Anti-Dantism, Metaphysics, Tradition*. Notre Dame: University of Notre Dame Press 2009, p. 226–259.

Segre, Cesare: Les isotopies de Laure. In: Herman Perret/Hans-George Ruprecht (eds.): *Exigences et perspectives de la sémiotique: recueil d'hommages pour Algirdas Julien Greimas*. 2 vols. Amsterdam; Philadelphia: J Benjamins 1985, II, p. 811–826.

Igor Candido
Dante, Petrarch, and Boccaccio on Religious Conversion

The investigation into the cultural transition between the Middle Ages and the early Renaissance from a literary perspective, or more broadly from that pertaining to the history of ideas, has generally moved back in time. Once focused on Petrarch, often considered to be the father of Italian Renaissance Humanism, more recently it has shifted, thanks to the work of Ronald Witt, onto the earlier generations of Lovato dei Lovati and Albertino Mussato, contemporaries respectively of Dante's father and Dante himself.[1] Whatever our understanding of what Italian humanism was, and when and how it began, it would probably be very difficult, if not impossible, to establish a concrete, universally acknowledged canon of fourteenth-century authors and texts that foreshadow or in some way already belong to the new intellectual milieu of the fifteenth century. This is why I will focus my attention only on Petrarch and Boccaccio and their contrastive readings of Dante's *Comedy*. In my paper I will explore a consistent set of theological and aesthetic concepts, foremost among them the medieval (and especially Dante's) idea and representation of Christian conversion in Augustinian terms. The two main poles around which my investigation revolves are the conclusions respectively of Petrarch's *Secretum* and Boccaccio's tale of Ser Ciappelletto (*Dec.* I, 1), two texts that bear witness to the radical intellectual turn towards the new era of Italian Renaissance humanism. With the lone exception of Francesco De Sanctis, critics have surprisingly devoted scant attention to the revolutionary meaning these two texts have as signposts – signposts which lead the way to an insightful understanding of the historical transition between the Middle Ages and the early Renaissance.

In Petrarch's *Secretum* the arguments used by Augustinus, the Christian figure of the father-confessor, are aimed at convincing Franciscus that he must radically change his life. This means in particular that he must rethink the complex of ethical values with which he has so far identified himself, as well as the cultural values by which his literature is oriented. The very conclusion of the dialogue, however, implies that Franciscus is unwilling to curb his desire and undergo the final *mutatio animi*, or in other words that he will undergo no lasting religious conversion after the preliminary steps of *confessio* and

---

[1] See in particular Ronald Witt: *"In the Footsteps of the Ancients": The Origins of Humanism from Lovato to Bruni*. Leiden: Brill 2000 (Studies in Medieval and Reformation Thought, 74).

contritio. What is more, Augustinus himself reaches a surprising conclusion, sanctioning the impossibility of Franciscus's religious conversion: "We are," Petrarch has him concede, "back where we started our argument: you describe your will as weakness. But so be it, since it cannot be otherwise. I pray to God and beg Him to accompany you on your way, and to grant that your errant footsteps will nonetheless lead you to a place of safety."[2] In fact, as Marco Santagata has convincingly argued, the *Secretum*, set in 1343 but most likely begun in 1347, is meant only to foreshadow the final *mutatio animi* that will take place some years later in Petrarch's life.[3] It is interesting to note that in 1347 Petrarch began writing the *De otio religioso,* whose second book contains a passage that sets the parallel between the uncertain condition of Augustine before his conversion and that of Petrarch, a passage which the dialogue *de secreto conflictu* turns into narrative fiction.[4] Thus, the characters of Augustinus and Franciscus, who together form another split alter ego of Petrarch,[5] do not hesitate to recognize within the existential parable of Franciscus signs of the one recounted in the *Confessions*. From this point of view, then, Franciscus's reluctance closely reflects Augustine's own lingering unwillingness to surrender himself to God in the *Confessions*.

> F. How often have I told you that I could do no more? A. And how often have I replied that in truth you didn't want to? But I am not surprised to see you entangled in the very same complications that once tormented me when I was contemplating setting off on the path of a new life. [...] From that moment onward, since I wanted it, I could do it instantly, and so was transformed happily, and remarkably quickly, into another Augustine, whose unfold-

---

2 Francesco Petrarca: *My Secret Book*. Edited and translated by Nicholas Mann. Cambridge, Mass.: Harvard University Press 2016 (The I Tatti Renaissance Library, 72), p. 257. Latin text in: Francesco Petrarca: *Opere latine*. Edited by Antonietta Bufano. 2 vols. Torino: UTET 1975, I, p. 258: "In antiquam litem relabimur, voluntatem impotentiam vocas. Sed sic eat, quando aliter esse non potest, supplexque Deum oro ut euntem comitetur, gressusque licet vagos, in tutum iubeat pervenire."
3 See Marco Santagata: *I frammenti dell'anima: Storia e racconto nel "Canzoniere" di Petrarca*. Bologna: Il Mulino 1992, p. 56–75. On the *Secretum*'s dates of composition, see Francisco Rico: *Vida u obra de Petrarca. I. Lectura del "Secretum"*. Padova: Antenore 1974; Id.: *"Sospir trilustre". Le date dell'amore e il primo "Canzoniere"*. In: *Critica del testo* 6 (2003), p. 31–48.
4 "Inter fluctuationes meas, quas si percurrere cepero et michi confessionum liber ingens ordiendus erit, Augustini Confessionum liber obvius fuit." (Petrarca: *Opere latine*, I, p. 802). Francisco Rico explained how the inspiration of both the *Secretum* and *De otio* refers to the same period of interest in Augustine and his *De vera religione*, to be placed around 1347. See Rico: *Vida u obra de Petrarca*, p. 113–117.
5 See also David Marsh: The Burning Question: Crisis and Cosmology in the "Secret". In: *Petrarch: A Critical Guide to the Complete Works*. Edited by Victoria Kirkham and Armando Maggi. Chicago: University of Chicago Press 2009, p. 211–218 (p. 212).

ing story you know, unless I'm mistaken, from my *Confessions*. [...] F. [...] I do recognize some trace of your unrest amid my own troubles. The result is that every time that I read your *Confessions*, torn as I am between two conflicting emotions of hope and fear, I weep with joy at the impression that what I am reading is not the story of someone else's wanderings, but of my own.⁶

This process of self-identification with Augustine's religious experience in Books I and II of the *Secretum* is another clear sign that the dialogue is ultimately supposed to lead to a conversion. Furthermore, Petrarch parallels Dante's referring to Augustine's experience in the *Convivio*, which Dante does to legitimate speaking about himself in that context,⁷ and thus we can infer that Franciscus's moral and religious experience too is indeed representative – and it certainly is, but in a very different way from Dante's. This is perhaps another reason why this extraordinarily modern dramatization of a moral conflict lies at the center of a work which only pretends to remain secret, or in other words is not aimed at contemporary readers but rather at posterity.

If we now consider *Secretum*'s Book III, which was probably completed around 1353, we will immediately perceive Franciscus's change of attitude and behaviour towards his ideal father-confessor and mentor. The interlocutors now take two very different positions which at the very end, as we already know, will remain irreconcilable. The two chains, love and glory (*amor et gloria*), that according to Augustinus are hindering Franciscus's soul are interpreted by Franciscus himself not as chains but – far from it – as wonderful object of his love, *speciosissimae curae*. The metaphor of the two chains obviously refers to Petrarch's tight bonds with Laura and literature, the latter to be identified with both amorous lyric poetry and the two *opera magna* to which Petrarch had entrusted his future

---

6 Petrarca: *My Secret Book*, p. 27. Latin text in: Petrarca: *Opere latine*, I, p. 66–69: "F. Quotiens dixi me ulterius nequivisse? A. Quotiensque respondi, imo verius noluisse? Nec tamen admiror te in his nunc ambagibus obvolutum in quibus olim ego ipse iactatus, dum novam vite viam carpere meditarer. [...] Itaque postquam plene volui, ilicet et potui, miraque et felicissima celeritate transformatus sum in alterum Augustinum, cuius historie seriem, ni fallor, ex Confessionibus meis nosti. [...] F. [...] inter procellas meas fluctuationis tue vestigium recognosco. Ex quo fit ut, quotiens Confessionum tuarum libros lego, inter duos contrarios affectus, spem videlicet et metum, letis non sine lacrimis interdum legere me arbitrer non alienam sed propriam mee peregrinationis historiam."
7 See Dante Alighieri: *Convivio*. Edited by Franca Brambilla Ageno. 2 vols. Firenze: Le Lettere 1995 (Edizione nazionale delle opere di Dante Alighieri, 3), II, to. 2, p. 11: "L'altra [*scil*. necessaria cagione] è quando, per ragionare di sé, grandissima utilitade ne segue altrui per via di dottrina; e questa ragione mosse Agustino nelle sue Confessioni a parlare di sé, ché per lo processo della sua vita, lo quale fu di meno buono in buono, e di buono in migliore, e di migliore in ottimo, ne diede essemplo e dottrina, la quale per altro sì vero testimonio ricevere non si potea."

fame, the *De viris illustribus* and the *Africa*. But it is Laura, in the end, who is the unintentional prime mover of all of Franciscus's passions. And whatever the nature of his attachment and how sublime his relationship with her really was, Augustinus points out, she has turned him away from divine love as he has worshipped the creature rather than the Creator, the shortest path to sin. And, he concludes, if all the things created have to be loved for the love for the Creator, Franciscus, on the contrary, loved God not for Himself, but for being the creator of a human being, Laura.

This is a key passage for the interpretation of Book III and of the *Secretum* as a whole. As far as I know, the best scholarly contribution for understanding the meaning of this passage, and then, *e contrario*, for discovering the modernity of the entire dialogue, is to be found, surprisingly enough, not in an essay on Petrarch's *Secretum*, but in Charles Singleton's reading of the Casella episode in the *Purgatory*. In Canto 2, Dante and Virgil have just reached the shore of the mountain-island of Purgatory when they hear a group of souls singing a Psalm of the Exodus, *In exitu Israel de Aegypto*. This is a first sign declaring they are pilgrims, as are Virgil and Dante, who have just arrived in the new, otherworldly realm. As Singleton notes, this detail is essential for understanding the meaning of the episode that now develops. Suddenly, out of the group of souls comes one who makes as to embrace Dante: he is Casella, an old friend of his and a Florentine musician, and Dante asks his friend to console him with a song of love as he used to in the past.

> "Amor che nella mente mi ragiona"
> cominciò elli allor sì dolcemente,
> che la dolcezza ancor dentro mi suona.
>   Lo mio maestro e io e quella gente
> ch'eran con lui parevan sì contenti,
> come a nessun toccasse altro la mente.
>   Noi eravam tutti fissi e attenti
> a le sue note; ed ecco il veglio onesto
> gridando: "Che è ciò, spiriti lenti?
>   qual negligenza, qual stare è questo?
> Correte al monte a spogliarvi lo scoglio
> ch'esser non lascia a voi Dio manifesto."
>   Come quando, cogliendo biado o loglio,
> li colombi adunati a la pastura,
> queti, sanza mostrar l'usato orgoglio,
>   se cosa appare ond'elli abbian paura,
> subitamente lasciano star l'esca,
> perch'assaliti son da maggior cura;
>   così vid'io quella masnada fresca
> lasciar lo canto, e fuggir ver' la costa,

> com'om che va, né sa dove rïesca;
> né la nostra partita fu men tosta. (*Purg.* II, 112–133)

> ["Love that converses with me in my mind,"
> he then began, so sweetly
> that the sweetness sounds within me still.
> My master and I and all those standing
> near Casella seemed untroubled,
> as if we had no other care.
> We were spellbound, listening to his notes,
> when that venerable old man appeared and cried:
> "What is this, laggard spirits?
> What carelessness, what delay is this?
> Hurry to the mountain and there shed the slough
> that lets not God be known to you."
> As when doves, gathered at their feeding,
> pecking here and there at wheat or tares,
> without their usual display of pride –
> should something suddenly make them afraid –
> will all at once forget their food
> because they are assailed by greater care,
> thus I saw these new arrivals, their song cut short,
> flee toward the mountain's slope
> like those who take an unfamiliar road.
> And we, with no less haste, departed.]

It is now worth quoting Singleton's commentary at length:

> Taken literally, as simply an incident in Purgatory, there is nothing especially surprising in Cato's coming to scatter these 'tardy' souls and send them on their proper way. They are here of course to purge themselves, to become ready to rise to the final beatitude [...]. But if what happens there is seen to reflect what might happen in our life's journey, then evidently a new aspect of meaning enters in. [...] By what right then does old Cato come up (in this life) with his cry that this is wrong? And how is it that the conscience of all will thereupon acknowledge that Cato is right? The answer is readily at hand, of course, when we have remembered (and Cato's cry reminds us) that in this life it is our proper condition as Christians to be as pilgrims. And our thought turns to that distinction which Augustine had made between using and enjoying things.

And then follows a quotation from Augustine's *De doctrina christiana*:

> For to enjoy a thing is to rest with satisfaction in it for its own sake. To use, on the other hand, is to employ whatever means are at one's disposal to obtain what one desires, if it is a proper object of desire; for an unlawful use ought rather to be called an abuse. Suppose, then, we were wanderers in a strange country, and could not live happily away from our fatherland, and that we felt wretched in our wanderings, and wishing to put an end to our misery, determined to return home. [...] But the beauty of the country through which we

pass, and the very pleasure of the motion, charm our hearts, and turning these things which we ought to use into objects of enjoyment, we become unwilling to hasten the end of our journey, and becoming engrossed in a factitious delight, our thoughts are diverted from that home whose delights would make us truly happy. Such is a picture of our condition in this life of mortality. We have wandered far from God; and if we wish to return to our Father's home, this world must be used, not enjoyed, so that the invisible things of God may be clearly seen, being understood by the things that are made (Romans I, 20) – that is, that by means of what is material and temporary we may lay hold upon that which is spiritual and eternal. (I, 4)[8]

If Petrarch's ultimate source is indeed Augustine (see also *Doctr.* I, 12),[9] the episode of Casella singing to quiet the soul's desires could offer him an insightful explanation of the tight bond of love and literature in the *Secretum* and, more importantly, could trigger his reaction against Dante's choice to assign aesthetic pleasure a subordinate role with respect to doctrine. Seen in this light, the interpretation of the episode can also account for why and how some of Petrarch's works, considered through the contrastive views of medieval doctrine and pre-modern aesthetics, are an intended deviation from the path to conversion.

David Marsh has recently drawn attention to the presence of the *Comedy*'s three canticles within the three books of the *Secretum*, respectively. Particularly insightful is the idea that "in book 2, when Augustinus examines Franciscus's conscience, we retrace the steps of Dante's gradual ascent-through-confession in the *Purgatorio*."[10] The structure of *Purg.* XXXI alone is revealing of the threefold path of confession (ll. 1–42), contrition (ll. 43–90), and conversion (ll. 91–105)

---

8 See Charles S. Singleton: *Dante Studies 1: Elements of Structures.* Cambridge, Mass: Harvard University Press 1958, p. 23–25. Latin text in: Sant'Agostino: *L'Istruzione cristiana.* Edited by Manlio Simonetti. Milano: Mondadori 2006³, p. 22: "Frui est enim amore inhaerere alicui rei propter seipsam. Uti autem, quod in usum venerit ad id quod amas obtinendum referre, si tamen amandum est. Nam usus illicitus abusus potius vel abusio nominanda est. Quomodo ergo, si essemus peregrini, qui beate vivere nisi in patria non possemus, eaque peregrinatione utique miseri et miseriam finire cupientes, in patriam redire vellemus, opus esset vel terrestribus vel marinis vehiculis, quibus utendum esset ut ad patriam, qua fruendum erat, pervenire valeremus; quod si amoenitates itineris et ipsa gestatio vehiculorum nos delectaret, conversi ad fruendum his quibus uti debuimus, nollemus cito viam finire et perversa suavitate implicati alienaremur a patria, cuius suavitas faceret beatos: sic in huius mortalitatis vita peregrinantes a Domino, si redire in patriam volumus, ubi beati esse possimus, utendum est hoc mundo, non fruendum, ut invisibilia Dei, per ea quae facta sunt, intellecta conspiciantur (Rom 1, 20), hoc est, ut de corporalibus temporalibusque rebus aeterna et spiritalia capiamus." (I, 4).
9 "Sed quoniam cupiditate fruendi pro ipso creatore creatura homines configurati huic mundo et mundi nomine congruentissime vocati, non eam [sapientiam] cognoverunt [...]." (I, 12; see ibid, p. 32).
10 Marsh: The Burning Question, p. 216.

which the Christian (Dante as a figure of everyman) must take.[11] Petrarch must have paid close attention to this canto, as we can see that it focuses on some of the key concepts later deployed in the *Secretum*.

> "O tu che se' di là dal fiume sacro,"
> volgendo suo parlare a me per punta,
> che pur per taglio m'era paruto acro,
>   ricominciò, seguendo sanza cunta,
> "dì, dì se questo è vero: a tanta accusa
> tua confession convien esser congiunta". (*Purg.* XXXI, 1–6)

> ["O you on the far side of the sacred stream,"
> turning the point of her words on me
> that had seemed sharp enough when I felt their edge,
>   she then went on without a pause: "Say it,
> say if this is true. To such an accusation
> your confession must be joined."][12]

Purg. XXXI does not only exemplify a doctrinal tenet that lies at the center of the poem, but also confirms an important aspect of Dante's poetics, which Guglielmo Gorni explains quite beautifully: Dante tends toward a dialectic dramatization of his own and everyman's process of redemption and spiritual emancipation; not only in purgatorial examples but in all of his poetry, the state of grace is measured as the distance from the negative point of departure.[13] In a similar vein, if remorse is one of the most certain sources of the sacred poem's inspiration, Étienne Gilson points out that, as a poem and as an act, the *Comedy* is a work of penitence. "Like every true act of penitence, Dante's was also the remedy which saved him; not only his expiation, but his redemption. To make expiation, he had to awaken in the fallen man the poet whom his friend Cavalcanti strove to recall to life, but in vain, for only Beatrice could do so."[14] But even if she could do so, it was not an easy task. "Beatrice has had to insist in order to make herself understood and, what is more, the only decisive argument capable of breaking

---

11 See the canto outline in Dante Alighieri: *Purgatorio*. Translated by Robert Hollander and Jean Hollander. New York: Doubleday 2004, p. 689–691. Hollander, surprisingly enough, does not mention the final moment of Dante's baptism which allegorizes the final moment of the Christian conversion.
12 For the text of the *Comedy*, see Dante Alighieri: *La "Commedia" secondo l'antica vulgata*. Edited by Giorgio Petrocchi. 2nd rev. edn. 4 vols. Firenze: Le Lettere 1994 (Edizione Nazionale delle opere di Dante, 7). English translation in: Dante Alighieri: *Purgatorio*, p. 693. All translations are drawn from this edition, which also includes *Inferno* (2002) and *Paradiso* (2007).
13 See Guglielmo Gorni: *Il nodo della lingua e il verbo d'amore*. Firenze: Olschki 1981, p. 13.
14 Gilson: *Dante and Philosophy*. Translated by David Moore. New York: Harper and Row 1963, p. 66.

down his resistance has been furnished not by the heaven of Beatrice but by the hell of Virgil."[15]

Later in canto XXXI, the very use of "catene" [chains] (l. 25) which, according to Beatrice, impeded Dante from loving the eternal and only Good, is unlikely to be a mere verbal coincidence and calls the interpreter's attention to the same situation dramatized in the *Secretum*. But if the situation is undoubtedly the same, as the narratological construction aims to explain the same doctrine in both texts, the conclusion of the two debates concerning conversion, respectively between Beatrice and Dante and between Augustinus and Franciscus, is exactly the opposite. To understand it, it is necessary to reread ll. 22–36 which Petrarch will imitate as a way to ground his distanced perspective:

> Ond'ella a me: "Per entro i mie' disiri,
> che ti menavano ad amar lo bene
> di là dal qual non è a che s'aspiri,
>   quai fossi attraversati o quai catene
> trovasti, per che del passare innanzi
> dovessiti così spogliar la spene?
>   E quali agevolezze o quali avanzi
> ne la fronte de li altri si mostraro,
> per che dovessi lor passeggiare anzi?"
>   Dopo la tratta d'un sospiro amaro,
> a pena ebbi la voce che rispuose,
> e le labbra a fatica la formaro.
>   Piangendo dissi: "Le presenti cose
> col falso lor piacer volser miei passi
> tosto che 'l vostro viso si nascose." (*Purg.* XXXI, 22–36)
>
> [At that she said to me: "In your desire for me
> that guided you to love that good
> beyond which there is nothing left to long for,
>   what ditches or what chains did you encounter
> across your path to make you cast aside
> all hope of going forward?
>   And what profit or advantage showed
> in the face of other things so that you felt
> you must parade yourself before them?"
>   After heaving a bitter sigh
> I hardly had the voice to give the answer
> my lips were laboring to shape.
>   In tears, I said: "Things set in front of me,

---

15 Ibid., p. 68 and *Purg.* XXX, 136–141: "Tanto giù cadde, che tutti argomenti / a la salute sua eran giù corti, / fuor che mostrarli le perdute genti. / Per questo visitai l'uscio d'i morti / e a colui che l'ha qua sù condotto, / li preghi miei, piangendo, furon porti."

with their false delights, turned back my steps
the moment that Your countenance was hidden."]

The first observation we can make is that Beatrice plays here the twofold role of Dante's beloved and confessor, and this indeed happens for a reason: from the early *Vita nova* to (almost all of) the *Comedy*, she is for Dante the true mediator between God and man. According to the character of Augustinus, as we have seen, this is no longer the case of Laura who has, on the contrary, kept Franciscus from directing himself and his desires toward God, an argument which probably accounts for Petrarch's choice of sharing Beatrice's attributes between the figures of Laura (beloved) and Augustinus (confessor). This argument, nonetheless, does not put an end to the debate on Petrarch's conversion, nor does the conclusion of the *Canzoniere*, which dramatizes the poet's inner conflict as not completely solved.[16] For this reason, I see no contrast – as some interpreters believe – between *RVF* CCCLXVI and the lines which seal the *Triumphus Eternitatis* (and the work as a whole) reaffirming Laura's secular beatific power and the (possible) future beatitude of contemplating her in the afterlife.[17] Petrarch's aim was different. As Christian Moevs insightfully pointed out, "with the last vernacular lines he wrote, Petrarch has wiped out the entire philosophizing and mysticizing history of the Italian lyric that culminates in Dante, everything between the Sicilians and himself; or at least, he has wiped out the *Commedia*, and brought us back to the last poem of the *Vita nova*, *Oltre la spera che più larga gira*, in which Dante's sigh ascends to contemplate his lady in heaven."[18] Or maybe – we can add – he has not wiped out the entire *Comedy*, but only its conclusion which in fact, by switching focus from Beatrice to the Virgin, betrays the original project (if such was really the project) as it is outlined at the end of the *Vita nova*. So Petrarch's defining the Virgin as "vera beatrice" (*RVF* CCCLXVI, 52) could allude to his choice of distancing himself from Dante's stilnovistic poetics which entirely revolved around the beatific role of Beatrice. In any case, it is clear at this point that in the *Secretum* Augustinus implicitly recommends that Franciscus imitate Dante's theological (and literary) example of conversion, which Petrarch only pretends to

---

16 But see Paolo Cherchi: *Verso la chiusura. Saggio sul "Canzoniere" di Petrarca*. Bologna: Il Mulino 2008, for a new thought-provoking interpretation which sees Petrarch's *mutatio vitae* as final attained.
17 "felice sasso che 'l bel viso serra!/ che, poi ch'avrà ripreso il suo bel velo,/ se fu beato chi la vide in terra,/ or che fia dunque a rivederla in cielo!" (ll. 142–145) See Francesco Petrarca: *Triumphi*. Edited by Marco Ariani. Milano: Mursia 1988, p. 409–450. Santagata (*I frammenti*, p. 341) rightly points out that the end of the *Canzoniere* excludes Laura. It is true nonetheless that she is still present as the stumbling block on the way of conversion.
18 Christian Moevs: Subjectivity and Conversion in Dante and Petrarch. In: Zygmunt Barański/ Theodore J. Cachey, Jr. (eds): *Petrarch and Dante. Anti-Dantism, Metaphysics, Tradition*. Notre Dame, Ind.: University of Notre Dame Press 2009, p. 237–238.

do by addressing the Virgin in CCCLXVI. This is, in fact, nothing more than a dramatization of the last attempt of conversion, which results in a new failure with no other alternative than reverting to Laura in the *Triumphus Eternitatis*.

That Petrarch's prayer to the Virgin is in fact unable to bring about the desired spiritual freedom which prepares the supplicant for conversion is witnessed by the proemial sonnet of the *Canzoniere*, *Voi ch' ascoltate in rime sparse il suono*, a tormented balance of the poet's never-abandoned secular love for Laura. What is indeed interesting – and to my knowledge still unnoticed – is that *Voi c'ascoltate* is most likely an intended answer to Beatrice's lesson on spiritual constancy which follows Dante's confession in *Purg.* XXXI, 34–36:

> Ed ella: "Se tacessi o se negassi
> ciò che confessi, non fora men nota
> la colpa tua: da tal giudice sassi!
>   Ma quando scoppia de la propria gota
> l'accusa del peccato, in nostra corte
> rivolge sé contra 'l taglio la rota.
>   Tuttavia, perché mo vergogna porte
> del tuo errore, e perché altra volta,
> udendo le serene, sie più forte,
>   pon giù il seme del piangere e ascolta:
> sì udirai come in contraria parte
> mover dovieti mia carne sepolta.
>   Mai non t'appresentò natura o arte
> piacer, quanto le belle membra in ch'io
> rinchiusa fui, e che so' 'n terra sparte;
>   e se 'l sommo piacer sì ti fallio
> per la mia morte, qual cosa mortale
> dovea poi trarre te nel suo disio?
>   Ben ti dovevi, per lo primo strale
> de le cose fallaci, levar suso
> di retro a me che non era più tale. [...]" (*Purg.* XXXI, 37–57)

> ["Had you stayed silent or denied what you confess,"
> she said, "your fault could not be any less apparent
> since it is known to such a Judge.
>   But when a man's own blushing cheek reveals
> the condemnation of his sin, in our high court
> the grindstone dulls the sharp edge of the sword.
>   Nonetheless, so that you now may bear
> the shame of your shameful straying and the next time
> that you hear the Sirens' call be stronger,
>   stop sowing tears and listen.
> Then you shall hear just how my buried flesh
> should have directed you to quite a different place.

> Never did art or nature set before you beauty
> as great as in the lovely members that enclosed me,
> now scattered and reduced to dust.
> And if the highest beauty failed you
> in my death, what mortal thing
> should then have drawn you to desire it?
> Indeed, at the very first arrow
> of deceitful things, you should have risen up
> and followed me who was no longer of them. (...)]"

The situation dramatized in the two texts is doctrinally the same – the confession of a penitent soul who in the end is meant to convert himself – but different is the way in which this situation develops in Dante and Petrarch. Beatrice's warning clarifies that forgiveness requires confession ("Ma quando scoppia de la propria gota / l'accusa del peccato [...]." [But when a man's own blushing cheek reveals / the condemnation of his sin (...)], ll. 40–42), as well as repentance or shame for one's mistake ("[...] perché mo vergogna porte / del tuo errore" [(...) so that you now may bear / the shame of your straying (...)], ll. 43–44). In a similar way, in the first quartina of *Voi ch'ascoltate* Petrarch addresses the intended readers of the *rime sparse*, those who have experience of love, in order that he may earn their forgiveness for his "giovanil errore" [youthful error]. A closer analysis, however, can reveal Petrarch's imitative distance from the model.[19] Dante's mistake was not his love for Beatrice and was not made in his youth, when Beatrice could lead him to moral perfection and put him on the path to divine truth. His spiritual fall occurred later, around the age of thirty-five, which instead, according to the Bible (e. g.: Is. 38, 10), was the proper time for conversion. The spiritual reading of Dante's life is clear: after his fall, through Beatrice divine grace grants him the privilege to see the "state of the souls after death" (*Ep.* XIII), the knowledge of which is the only means to redeem his soul. Quite differently, *Voi ch'ascoltate* bears witness to the *impasse* of a man who, while writing, is still only "in parte altr'uom" [in part another man] (l. 4). In the *Secretum*, likewise, Franciscus feels shame, pain, and repentance for his condition, but cannot do anything else, so that Augustinus can rebuke him for being unable to change.[20]

---

[19] 'Imitative distance' is Robert Hollander's apt definition of Boccaccio's relationship with Dante, which can be extended to Petrarch's as well. See Robert Hollander: *Boccaccio's Dante: Imitative Distance (Decameron I, 1 and VI, 10)*. In: *Studi sul Boccaccio* 13 (1981–1982), p. 169–198.
[20] "Fr. Pudet, piget et penitet, sed ultra non valeo. [...] Aug. Pudeat ergo, pudeat animum nunquam mutari, cum corpus mutetur assidue." (Petrarca: *Opere latine*, I, p. 226–227). Cf. also Petrarch's *De ignorantia*: "Sed propter infirmitates ac sarcinas vite mortalis, quas nedum ferre, sed enumerare difficile est, non possum, fateor, ut vellem, sic inferiores partes anime, in quibus est irascibilis et concupiscibilis appetitus, attollere, quin adhuc terris inhereant." (Petrarca: *Opere latine*, II, p. 1120).

Later in *Purg.* XXXI, Beatrice asks Dante to stop weeping and listen ("pon giù il seme del piangere e ascolta," l. 46) to her moral teaching so that he will never happen to fall again. This image as well is overturned in Petrarch. Since the first encounter with Laura, the poet's life has experienced falls and resurrections, and his confession has indulged so much in weeping that it has become the metaphor of the *Canzoniere*'s tormented lyric poetry.[21] Interestingly enough, the hendiadys of the "[...] vario stile in ch'io piango e ragiono" [the varied style in which I weep and speak] (l. 5) reflects the condition of Dante's infernal sinners such as Francesca ("dirò come colui che piange e dice." [I shall tell as one who weeps in telling], *Inf.* V, 126) or Ugolino ("parlare e lagrimar vedrai insieme." [then you will see me speak and weep together], *Inf.* XXXIII, 9),[22] which is ultimately Petrarch's own sinful condition. The reuse of another stileme of *Purg.* XXXI, "le belle membra [...] / [...] 'n terra sparte." (ll. 50–51), echoed respectively in *RVF* CXXVI, 2; CCC, 7 ("le belle membra") and CXXXVII, 9 ("in terra sparsi"), helps clarify how Petrarch also aimed to contrast the theology of Beatrice's dead body. The *imago mortis* of "le belle membra in ch'io / rinchiusa fui, e che so' 'n terra sparte," in its Christian Platonic fashion, does not need any explanation as a medieval reflection on the deceptive attraction of physical beauty. As we know from the *Secretum*, Franciscus has loved the creature, Laura, more than her Creator "as the most beautiful thing that He had ever created," ignoring that "physical beauty is the lowest form of beauty."[23] But it is again the *Triumpus Eternitatis*, the "ultimus cantus" in any possible sense,[24] which marks a different vision of Laura among the blessed. Marco Ariani has called attention to Lodovico Castelvetro's interpretation of the text as a definitive response to

---

21 See also Augustinus in the *Secretum*: "Forma [di Laura] quidem tibi visa est tam blanda, tam dulcis, ut in te omnem ex nativis virtutum seminibus proventuram segetem ardentissimi desiderii estibus et assiduo lacrimarum imbre vastaverit."; "Quid autem insanius quam, non contentum presenti illius vultus effigie, unde hec cunta tibi provenerant, aliam fictam illustris artificis ingenio quesivisse, quam tecum ubique circunferens haberes materiam semper immortalium lacrimarum? Veritus ne fortassis arescerent, irritamenta earum omnia vigilantissime cogitasti, negligenter incuriosus in reliquis." (ibid., I, p. 184 and 198).
22 See Francesco Petrarca: *Canzoniere*. Edited by Marco Santagata. Milano: Mondadori 1997², comm. *ad loc.*, p. 9.
23 Petrarca: *My Secret Book*, p. 169. Latin text in Petrarca: *Opere latine*, I, p. 186: "[...] Creatorem non qua decuit amasti, sed miratus artificem fuisti quasi nichil ex omnibus formosius creasset, cum tamen ultima pulcritudinum sit forma corporea."
24 See Petrarch's gloss in the Vat. Lat. 3196: "1374, dominico ante cenam. 15 Januarii, ultimus cantus." In: Angelo Romanò: *Il codice degli abbozzi (Vat. Lat. 3196) di Francesco Petrarca*. Roma: G. Bardi 1955, p. 282 and 284. See also Francesco Petrarca: *Il codice degli abbozzi: Edizione e storia del manoscritto Vaticano latino 3196*. Edited by Laura Paolino. Milano-Napoli: Ricciardi 2000, p. 136–137.

Augustinus's accusations in *Secretum* III (Franciscus's desire for Laura's body and eternal glory) and implicitly, as we already noted, to Dante.[25] By relying on the Pauline tenet of the resurrection of the body, Petrarch could finally focus his vision on the unity of Laura's body and soul as well as on the permanence of glory beyond time.[26]

The comparison with Dante's purgatorial cantos (II and XXXI) helps us discern and understand Petrarch's contrastive reading of the poem as well as, ultimately, his astounding modernity.[27] It is, therefore, not surprising that the same inner conflict dramatized in the "secret" dialogue surfaces in other texts which are milestones of Petrarch's ideal autobiographical construction, such as the *Fam.* IV, 1 to Dionigi da Borgo San Sepolcro (1351–1353), *RVF* CCCLX, which mirrors the *Secretum* and may be contemporary to it, and the prayer to the Virgin which seals the *Canzoniere* (*RVF* CCCLXVI).[28] Written "not yet being in port," the former bears witness to an Augustinian "very insistent and uncertain battle for control of my [Petrarch's] two selves."[29] The latter two once again dramatize the poet's inner conflict between the spiritual and the temporal as still unresolved or in fact, no matter the endless attempts, unresolvable. They outline the narrative boundaries of a last attempt of conversion, *in extremis*, to be told

---

25 "Vuole adunque il Petrarca per lo triomfo dell'eternità significare l'appagamento dell'uno e dell'altro suo desiderio, che tanto lo molestavano, ciò è dell'amore di Laura e della vaghezza di fama, perciò che per l'eternità cessano le principali cagioni nocive alle cose desiderate, cioè il guastamento delle bellezze di Laura che fu per morte, e il guastamento della fama, che viene per tempo, li quali per l'eternità mancano." See Petrarca: *Triumphi*, p. 382.
26 See ibid.
27 On Petrarch's modernity in explicit constrast to Dante's world vision, see also Karlheinz Stierle: *La vita e i tempi di Petrarca: alle origini della moderna coscienza europea*. Translated by Gabriella Pelloni. Venezia: Marsilio 2007, p. 39.
28 See also Ugo Dotti's remarks in: Francesco Petrarca: *Epistole*. Edited by Ugo Dotti. Torino: UTET 1978, p. 15–16. On Petrarch's very productive 1350s and contemporary (re)reading of Dante's *Comedy*, see Enrico Santangelo: Petrarch Reading Dante: The Ascent of Mont Ventoux (*Familiares* 4. 1). In: Martin L. McLaughlin/ Letizia Panizza/ Peter Hainsworth (eds): *Petrarch in Britain: Interpreters, Imitators, and Translators over 700 Years*. Oxford: Oxford University Press 2007 (Proceedings of the British Academy, 146), p. 95–111 (p. 98). As to *RVF* CCCLX and the *Secretum*, see Moevs: Subjectivity, p. 226–259. On the dates of *RVF* CCCLX and CCCCLXVI, see Petrarca: *Canzoniere*. Ed. Santagata, p. 1366–1367 and 1401.
29 Latin text in: Francesco Petrarca: *Le familiari*. Edited by Vittorio Rossi (vols 1–3) and by Vittorio Rossi and Umberto Bosco (vol. 4). Firenze: Sansoni 1933–1942 (Edizione nazionale delle opere di Petrarca, 10–13), I, p. 157–158: "nondum enim in portu [...] inter quas [voluntates] iandudum in campis cogitationum mearum de utriusque hominis imperio laboriosissima et anceps etiam nunc pugna." (§§ 19–22) Translation in: Francesco Petrarca: *Letters on Familiar Matters: Rerum familiarium libri*. Translated by Aldo S. Bernardo. 3 vols. Baltimore: The Johns Hopkins University Press 1975–1985, I, p. 176–177.

in the last six poems.[30] In particular, the final canzone fails to meet the expectations which the previous sonnet of repentance has raised by invoking divine help (*RVF* CCCLXV, 5–11).[31] If the metaphor of the ship going through the stormy sea of passions recalls the memory of Augustine's pre-conversion past, here as well throughout Petrarch's *oeuvre*,[32] the spiritual condition of man afraid of his near death, who finally invokes the Virgin's help, is only that of a "cor contrito humile" [a contrite and humble heart] (*RVF* CCCLXVI, 120), whereas he shows no clear sign of an imminent conversion. In this way, as Joachim Küpper pointed out, the formal ascensional movement from sonnet to canzone contrasts with the ontological descent from God to Mary: that is, from the actual source of grace to the creature as its mediator. This corresponds to a palinody of the previous cycle of sonnets wherein the genuine remorse for one's past life is the necessary (Dantean) condition of reconciliation with God (*RVF* CCCLXIII–CCCLXV).[33] Petrarch's focusing on the Virgin as creature and mediator – it must be added – foreshadows his final return to Laura in the *Triumphi*, so that she remains the actual stumbling block on the way to conversion.

The theological distance from Dante could not be greater. In *Par.* XXXIII, rightly considered the palimpsest of *RVF* CCCLXVI, Beatrice the theologian has finally yielded her role as guide and mediator to Saint Bernard the mystic, who acts as mediator to a second mediator, the Virgin, who in turn leads the pilgrim to the true and only Mediator between man and God; that is, Christ.[34] At the end of the sacred poem it is the mystical *via brevis*, and not the theological *via longa*,

---

30 For the notion of an *in extremis* conversion, see Santagata: *I frammenti*, p. 335–340.
31 "Tu che vedi i miei mali indegni et empi, / Re del cielo invisibile immortale, /soccorri a l'alma disvïata e frale, / e 'l suo defecto di Tua gratia adempi: / sí che, s'io vissi in guerra et in tempesta, /mora in pace et in porto; et se la stanza/ fu vana, almen sia la partita honesta." Francesco Petrarca: *Canzoniere*. Edited by Gianfranco Contini. Torino: Einaudi 1975⁶, p. 454. All quotations from the *Canzoniere* are drawn from this edition; all translations from *Petrarch's Lyric Poems. The "Rime sparse" and Other Lyrics*. Translated and Edited by Robert Durling. Cambridge, Mass.: Harvard University Press 1976.
32 Here: "Vergine chiara et stabile in eterno, / di questo tempestoso mare stella, / d'ogni fedel nocchier fidata guida, / pon' mente in che terribile procella/ i' mi ritrovo sol, senza governo, / et ò già vicin l'ultime strida." (ll. 66–71).
33 See Joachim Küpper: Palinodia e polisemia nella Canzone alla Vergine (con alcune brevi considerazioni sulle condizioni della differenza tra arte classica ed arte moderna). In: *Quaderni petrarcheschi* 14 (2004), p. 147–190 (p. 149–150).
34 "Opus est enim mediatore ad Mediatorem istum, nec alter nobis utilior quam Maria." See *Dominica infra octavam Assumptionis B. V. Mariae sermo*. In: *Sancti Bernardi Opera omnia. Sermones II*. Romae: Editiones cistercenses 1968, p. 263. See also Vincenzo Pernicone: Il canto 32 del "Paradiso". Torino: Società Editrice internazionale 1965 (Lectura Dantis Romana, n.s.), p. 6–7. For the notion of Christ as unique mediator, see August. *De civ. D.* IX, 15.

that allows Dante to have the supreme vision of God, a doctrinal construction which is allegorized in Beatrice's disappearance.[35] More importantly, Bernard's association with the Virgin makes his spiritual condition become such that no other creature could ever reach it, not even Beatrice. This is why the doctrinal trajectory of the *Comedy* as a whole coincides with Dante's poetic journey to Beatrice (his original project?) only to a certain well established point. Beatrice's final absence must not have escaped Petrarch, whose character of Laura, on the contrary, in both the *Canzoniere* and the *Triumphi*, as well as explicitly in the *Secretum*, rightly belongs to modernity in that she can hold sway over the poet's mind until the very end.[36] In order to do so, Laura must yield her role of divine mediator and in the *Secretum*, in fact, Petrarch concludes the discussion on the role of Laura as mediator with Franciscus's admission that she did what she could before abandoning him.[37] Transformed into allegory, Beatrice can disappear once she has led Dante to his final vision; Laura, having in fact no doctrinal function in Petrarch's fiction, remains at the center of the poet's thoughts until the end. Petrarch, as poet and intellectual, lays no claim to an exemplary (Augustinian / Dantean) conversion allowed to him alone through an angelic lady and by divine grace: the exemplarity of his experience lies instead in the choice of providing the first subjective account of a secular life that is common and unique at the same time.

In an essay entitled *The Vistas in Retrospect* Singleton has epitomized the intellectual trajectory spanning from the Middle Ages to the Renaissance in the key opposition, again drawn from Augustine's *Confessions*, between Dante's unquiet and Boccaccio's quiet hearts. Boccaccio's quiet heart, the critic explains, is a possible translation of the French *nonchalance du salut*, a label Blaise Pascal had used to characterize the spirit of Michel de Montaigne's *Essais*.[38] Before Singleton, Francesco De Sanctis had divided up the Middle Ages into two long time periods, the centuries of Dante, the Duecento and Trecento on the one hand, and those spanning from Boccaccio to the Cinquecento on the other, in which scheme Petrarch was considered the transition between Dante and Boccaccio (*Storia*

---

35 That theology must finally yield way to mysticism is the interpretation of the end of the poem provided by Étienne Gilson and is still today one of the most fascinating. See Étienne Gilson: *Dante and Philosophy*, p. 48.
36 See also Ficara and Regn in this volume.
37 "F. Fecit hoc illa quantum potuit. [...] postremo, cum lorifragum ac precipitem videret deserere maluit quam sequi." (Petrarca: *Opere latine*, I, p. 192–194).
38 See Charles S. Singleton: The Vitas in Retrospect. In: *Modern Language Notes* 81, 1 (1966), p. 55–80.

della lett. it. XI, 17).[39] In principle, I think that De Sanctis and Singleton were right in tracing a sharp dividing line between Dante's and Boccaccio's worlds, inasmuch as the metaphor of the pilgrim's unquiet heart is, in Augustinian terms, the base of the entire symbolic structure of medieval thought. But this metaphor cannot of course account for all the differences. Boccaccio was in fact far from being uninterested in religious questions, as the first three tales of the *Decameron* clearly demonstrate.[40] As we shall see by examining the tale of Ser Ciappelletto (*Dec.* I,1), Boccaccio conceived of the worldly perspective as the only one open to human investigation, and thus that is the one he chose for his work.[41] I propose therefore to replace Pascal's concept of *nonchalance du salut* with that of *epoché* (suspension of assent), a product of ancient Stoicism. In this vein, a study of the term *epoché* from the standpoint of historical semantics, spanning from antiquity to Descartes and then up to Husserl,[42] would prove to be helpful to conceptualize the religious distance between Dante and Boccaccio.

The tale of ser Cepparello holds the first place in the *Decameron*, and in many respects it plays a programmatic role in the work's general framework. As the tale's rubric reads, "Ser Ciappelletto cheats a holy friar by a false confession, and dies; and, having lived as a very bad man, is, on his death, reputed a saint, and called San Ciappelletto." Boccaccio's entire narrative is a parody of the rite of confession and carefully prepares Panfilo's final meditation on the otherworldly destiny of Ser Ciappelletto and its doctrinal consequences.[43]

> Così adunque visse e morì ser Cepparello da Prato e santo divenne come avete udito. Il quale negar non voglio esser possibile lui esser beato nella presenza di Dio, per ciò che, come che la sua vita fosse scellerata e malvagia, egli poté in su lo stremo aver sì fatta contrizione, che per avventura Idio ebbe misericordia di lui e nel suo regno il ricevette: ma per ciò che questo n'è occulto, secondo quello che ne può apparire ragiono, e dico costui più tosto

---

39 See Francesco De Sanctis: *Storia della letteratura italiana*. Edited by Niccolò Gallo. With an Introduction by Giorgio Ficara. Torino: Einaudi-Gallimard 1996, p. 377. See also my *Il "cor inquietum" di Dante e il "cor quietum" di Boccaccio nella "Storia" di Francesco de Sanctis*. In: *Lettere italiane* 67, 2 (2015), p. 225–249.
40 See Carlo Ossola: Boccaccio riprodotto al millimetro. In: *Il Sole 24 ore* (17 March 2013), p. 40; Ilaria Tufano: Boccaccio e la letteratura religiosa: la Prima e la Seconda Giornata del "Decameron". In: *Critica del Testo* 16, 3 (2013), p. 185–207.
41 See also Francesco Bruni: *Boccaccio. L'invenzione della letteratura mezzana*. Bologna: Il Mulino 1990, p. 260.
42 See Giovanni Fornero: Epoché. In: Nicola Abbagnano: *Dizionario di Filosofia*. Edited by Giovanni Fornero. Torino: UTET 1998³, p. 378–379.
43 See Carlo Delcorno: *Exemplum e letteratura. Tra Medioevo e Rinascimento*. Bologna: Il Mulino 1989, p. 269–276; Id.: Ironia/parodia. In: Renzo Bragantini /Pier Massimo Forni (eds): *Lessico critico decameroniano*. Torino: Bollati Boringhieri 1995, p. 162–191 (p. 179–180).

dovere essere nelle mani del diavolo in perdizione che in Paradiso. E se così è, grandissima si può la benignità di Dio cognoscere verso noi, la quale non al nostro errore ma alla purità della fé riguardando, così faccendo noi nostro mezzano un suo nemico, amico credendolo, ci essaudisce, come se a uno veramente santo per mezzano della sua grazia ricorressimo. E per ciò, acciò che noi per la sua grazia nelle presenti avversità e in questa compagnia così lieta siamo sani e salvi servati, lodando il suo nome nel quale cominciata l'abbiamo, Lui in reverenza avendo, ne' nostri bisogni gli ci raccomanderemo sicurissimi d'essere uditi. – E qui si tacque. (I, 1, §§ 89–92)

[So lived, so died Ser Cepperello da Prato, and came to be reputed a saint, as you have heard. Nor would I deny that it is possible that he is of the number of the blessed in the presence of God, seeing that, though his life was evil and depraved, yet he might in his last moments have made so complete an act of contrition that perchance God had mercy on him and received him into His kingdom. But, as this is hidden from us, I speak according to that which appears, and I say that he ought rather to be in the hands of the devil in hell than in Paradise. Which, if so it be, is a manifest token of the superabundance of the goodness of God to usward, inasmuch as He regards not our error but the sincerity of our faith, and hearkens unto us when, mistaking one who is at enmity with Him for a friend, we have recourse to him, as to one holy indeed, as our intercessor for His grace. Wherefore, that we of this gay company may by His grace be preserved safe and sound throughout this time of adversity, commend we ourselves in our need to Him, whose name we began by invoking, with lauds and reverent devotion and good confidence that we shall be heard. And so he was silent.]⁴⁴

After the rubric has determined the narrative core of the confession (certainly a false confession, but nonetheless a confession), Panfilo's conclusion introduces – in the same ironic spirit – the term 'contrition,' the second step on the path to conversion. This is done, I believe, according to a conscious rhetorical strategy whose aim is to flesh out the possibility of Ser Ciappelletto's salvation in the reader's mind. To the Christian faithful, this possibility is in fact open to the very end, even for "il piggiore uomo forse che mai nascesse" [the worst man that ever was born] (§ 15), ser Ciappelletto himself, as Panfilo notes at the beginning of his speech: "Nor would I deny that it is possible that he is of the number of the blessed in the presence of God, seeing that, though his life was evil and depraved, yet he might in his last moments have made so complete an act of contrition that perchance God had mercy on him and received him into His kingdom." Panfilo's following parenthetic clause, "ma per ciò che questo n'è occulto" [as this is hidden from us], echoing what he says at the beginning about God, "al quale niuna cosa è occulta" [to whom nothing is hidden], is revealing: the truth is that we are unable to know anything about Ser Ciappelletto's destiny, about anyone's destiny after death. That is to say, in the terms of Dante's Letter to Cangrande

---

44 For text and translation, see respectively: Giovanni Boccaccio: *Decameron*. Edited by Vittore Branca. Torino: Einaudi 1980; *The Decameron of Giovanni Boccaccio Faithfully Translated by James M. Rigg*. 2 vols. London: The Navarre Society 1932 (quotation: vol. I, p. 32–33).

della Scala, that the condition of souls after death, the "status animarum post mortem," is totally concealed from human minds. The parallel with the Letter to Cangrande is indeed striking and it calls into question the doctrinal foundations of Dante's vision itself.[45] This is confirmed by a close reading of Panfilo's conclusion in the light of the cantos devoted to Guido and Buonconte da Montefeltro (respectively *Inf.* XXVII and *Purg.* V), as well as that featuring King Manfredi (*Purg.* III).

> "Francesco venne poi, com' io fu' morto,
> per me; ma un d'i neri cherubini
> li disse: 'Non portar; non mi far torto.
>   Venir se ne dee giù tra' miei meschini
> perché diede'l consiglio frodolente,
> dal quale in qua stato li sono a' crini;
>   ch'assolver non si può chi non si pente,
> né pentere e volere insieme puossi
> per la contradizion che nol consente.'
>   Oh me dolente! come mi riscossi
> quando mi prese dicendomi: 'Forse
> tu non pensavi ch'io löico fossi!'
>   A Minòs mi portò; e quelli attorse
> otto volte la coda al dosso duro;
> e poi che per gran rabbia la si morse,
>   disse: 'Questi è d'i rei del foco furo';
> per ch'io là dove vedi son perduto,
> e sì vestito, andando, mi rancuro."
>   Quand' elli ebbe 'l suo dir così compiuto,
> la fiamma dolorando si partio,
> torcendo e dibattendo 'l corno aguto. (*Inf.* XXVII, 112–132)

> ["The moment I was dead, Francis came for me.
> But one of the dark Cherubim cried out:
> 'No, wrong me not by bearing that one off.
>   He must come down to serve among my minions
> because he gave that fraudulent advice.
> From then till now I've dogged his footsteps.
>   One may not be absolved without repentance,
> nor repent and wish to sin concurrently –
> a simple contradiction not allowed.'
>   Oh, wretch that I am, how I shuddered
> when he seized me and said: 'Perhaps
> you didn't reckon I'd be versed in logic.'

---

[45] See also Kurt Flasch: *Poesia dopo la peste. Saggio sul "Decameron"*. Bari: Laterza 1995 (Quadrante, 77), p. 6.

> He carried me to Minos, who coiled his tail
> eight times around his scaly back
> and, having gnawed it in his awful rage,
> said: 'Here comes a sinner for the thieving fire.'
> And so, just as you see me, I am damned,
> cloaked as I am. And as I go, I grieve."
> Once he had brought his words to this conclusion,
> the weeping flame departed,
> twisting and tossing its pointed horn.]

In his commentary on the tale of Ser Ciappelletto, Vittore Branca has rightly pointed out the intertextual references to the abovementioned cantos of the *Comedy*. But if the assimilation of Ser Ciappelletto and Guido da Montefeltro to a similar damnation (since one may not be absolved without repentance) is implicitly suggested by Panfilo's words, as the most likely outcome according to human understanding, it is not confirmed by Boccaccio, as we have seen. The author instead asks the reader to suspend judgment, as it is impossible for humans ever to penetrate God's mind.[46] Moreover, the possibility that Ser Ciappelletto "might in his last moments have made so complete an act of contrition that perchance God had mercy on him" must be applied not only to the destiny of Manfredi, as Branca does, but in the first instance to that of Buonconte da Montefeltro. Buonconte also turned to God in the last moments of his life ("nel nome di Maria fini', e quivi / caddi, e rimase la mia carne sola" [I ended on the name of Mary and there I fell/and only my flesh remained], *Purg.* V, 101–102) and his example proves to be more consistent than that of Manfredi, as he is the son of Guido da Montefeltro, who suffered Buonconte's opposite fate. In fact, as Anna Maria Chiavacci Leonardi notes, Dante has designed *Inf.* XXVII and *Purg.* V as a pair of mirrored cantos dramatizing the opposite judgments that result from different individual choices, that is from contrasting exercises of free will, in a given situation.[47]

On a closer analysis, we can see that the Manfredi episode plays another role in Boccaccio's tale, helping the author dive more deeply into the question at stake. First of all, we should note that, in the words of one of his Florentine hosts, Ser Ciappelletto's crimes "son tanti e sí orribili" [such and so horrible have

---

46 On Boccaccio's suspension of assent in opposition to Dante, see also Mario Baratto: *Realtà e stile nel "Decameron"*. Roma: Editori Riuniti 1984, p. 52–54; Bruni: *Boccaccio*, p. 270; Lucia Battaglia Ricci: *Boccaccio*. Roma: Salerno 2000, p. 173; Ead: *Scrivere un libro di novelle. Giovanni Boccaccio autore, lettore, editore*. Ravenna: Longo 2013 (Memoria del Tempo, 39), p. 140. See also Attilio Bettinzoli: Recensione a Francesco Bruni: *Boccaccio. L'invenzione della letteratura mezzana*. In: *Studi sul Boccaccio* 19 (1990), p. 278.
47 See Dante Alighieri: *La Divina Commedia. Inferno*. Edited by Anna M. Chiavacci Leonardi. Milano: Mondadori 2005, p. 800; *Purgatorio*. Ibid., V, 85 and comm. *ad loc.*

been], which echoes Manfredi's confession, "orribil furon li peccati miei" [horrible were my sins], he says. Like Manfredi, Branca rightly notes, ser Cepparello will have no Christian funeral nor burial, but the import is probably greater than that. Manfredi is expressing here the canto's key concept, namely the infinite mercy of God. Let us read the tercets in their entirety: "Orribili furon li peccati miei; / ma la bontà infinita ha sì gran braccia, / che prende ciò che si rivolge a lei." [Horrible were my sins, / but Infinite Goodness with wide-open arms / receives whoever turns to it] (*Purg.* III, 121–123). It is not a coincidence, then, that earlier in the same canto Virgil condemns the pride of human intellect and in this context, incidentally, we should also consider *Par.* XIII, 139–142.[48] This probably means that Boccaccio uses Manfredi's words to allude once again to the fact that we can have no knowledge of Ser Ciappelletto's condition after death. In this way, the reader is finally led back to what Panfilo had said in his introduction to the tale, that what the story will serve to make apparent is the judgment of man, not the judgment of God.

If we fail to notice all this, we will not be able to understand Boccaccio's suspension of assent in Panfilo's speech, which amounts to a rejection of Dante's claim to an unerring vision of divine justice in action, or, in other words, of the possibility that such justice can be represented in a work of art.[49] Boccaccio's standpoint here aims to call into question Dante's religious and cultural right to construct his poem, to use Singleton's famous sentence, as a fiction "that (it) is not a fiction."[50] That Boccaccio's perspective is far from being – we could say – metaphysical emerges once and for all in the preface of the sixth book of the *De casibus*, where we read he will devote his writing to *res humanae*, human things, since his natural limitations do not permit him other topics like the works and the glory of God, the secrets of nature, and the right of fortune.[51] Furthermore, in his intellectual dialogue with Dante, Boccaccio aims to suggest a philosophical (namely ethical) alternative to the theological vision and judgment dramatized in the *Comedy*, and this very use of Dante against Dante's own position reflects the very original nature of Boccaccio's modern art. By tracing a clear dividing line between Dante's religiously-oriented cultural world and his own, he was the first able to stand outside the textual mirror game, as Teodolinda Barolini aptly called

---

[48] "Matto è chi spera che nostra ragione / possa trascorrer la infinita via / che tiene una sustanza in tre persone. / State contenti, umana gente, al *quia*; / ché, se potuto aveste veder tutto, / mestier non era parturir Maria." (*Purg.* III, 34–39) "Non creda Monna Berta e Ser Martino/ per vedere un furare, altro offerere/ vederli dentro al consiglio divino." (*Par.* XIII, 139–142).
[49] See also Flasch: *Poesia dopo la peste*, p. 6.
[50] Singleton: *Dante Studies 1*, p. 62.
[51] On this see also Carlo Ossola: Boccaccio anima laica. In: *Il Sole 24 ore* (29 Jan. 2012), p. 33.

it, which Dante had skilfully built around his readers with the simplest rhetorical construction of a fiction which never declares itself to be a fiction.⁵²

Bibliography

Primary Literature

Sant'Agostino: *L'Istruzione cristiana*. Edited by Manlio Simonetti. Milano: Mondadori 2006³.
Alighieri, Dante: *La "Commedia" secondo l'antica vulgata*. Edited by Giorgio Petrocchi. 2nd rev. edn. 4 vols. Firenze: Le Lettere 1994 (Edizione Nazionale delle opere di Dante, 7).
Alighieri, Dante: *Purgatorio*. Translated by Robert Hollander and Jean Hollander. New York: Doubleday 2004.
Alighieri, Dante: *La Divina Commedia. Inferno*. Edited by Anna Maria Chiavacci Leonardi. Milano: Mondadori 2005.
Alighieri, Dante: *La Divina Commedia. Purgatorio*. Ed. by Anna Maria Chiavacci Leonardi. Milano: Mondadori 2005.
Sancti Bernardi Opera omnia. Sermones II. Romae: Editiones cistercenses 1968.
Boccaccio, Giovanni: *The Decameron of Giovanni Boccaccio Faithfully Translated by James M. Rigg*. 2 vols. London: The Navarre Society 1936.
Boccaccio, Giovanni: *Decameron*. Edited by Vittore Branca. Torino: Einaudi 1980.
Petrarca, Francesco: *Le familiari*. Edited by Vittorio Rossi (vols 1–3) and by Vittorio Rossi and Umberto Bosco (vol. 4). Firenze: Sansoni 1933–1942 (Edizione nazionale delle opere di Petrarca, 10–13).
Petrarca, Francesco: *Canzoniere*. Edited by Gianfranco Contini. Torino: Einaudi 1975⁶.
Petrarca, Francesco: *Opere latine*. Edited by Antonietta Bufano. 2 vols. Torino: UTET 1975.
Petrarch's Lyric Poems. The "Rime sparse" and Other Lyrics. Translated and Edited by Robert Durling. Cambridge, Mass.: Harvard University Press 1976.
Petrarca, Francesco: *Epistole*. Edited by Ugo Dotti. Torino: UTET 1978.
Petrarca, Francesco: *Letters on Familiar Matters: Rerum familiarium libri*. Translated by Aldo S. Bernardo. 3 vols. Baltimore: Johns Hopkins University Press 1975–1985.
Petrarca, Francesco: *Triumphi*. Edited by Marco Ariani. Milano: Mursia 1988.
Petrarca, Francesco: *Canzoniere*. Edited by Marco Santagata. Milano: Mondadori 1997².
Petrarca, Francesco: *Il codice degli abbozzi: Edizione e storia del manoscritto Vaticano latino 3196*. Edited by Laura Paolino. Milano-Napoli: Ricciardi 2000.
Petrarca, Francesco: *My Secret Book*. Edited and translated by Nicholas Mann. Cambridge, Mass.: Harvard University Press 2016 (The I Tatti Renaissance Library, 72).

---

52 For Barolini's definition, see her: *The Undivine Comedy: Detheologizing Dante*. Princeton, NJ.: Princeton University Press 1992, p. 16, 35 and 94.

Secondary Literature

Monographs and Anthologies

Baratto, Mario: *Realtà e stile nel "Decameron"*. Roma: Editori Riuniti 1984.
Barolini, Teodolinda: *The Undivine Comedy: Detheologizing Dante*. Princeton, NJ.: Princeton University Press 1992.
Battaglia Ricci, Lucia: *Boccaccio*. Roma: Salerno 2000.
Battaglia Ricci, Lucia: *Scrivere un libro di novelle. Giovanni Boccaccio autore, lettore, editore*. Ravenna: Longo 2013 (Memoria del Tempo, 39).
Bruni, Francesco: *Boccaccio. L'invenzione della letteratura mezzana*. Bologna: Il Mulino 1990.
Cherchi, Paolo: *Verso la chiusura. Saggio sul "Canzoniere" di Petrarca*. Bologna: Il Mulino 2008.
De Sanctis, Francesco: *Storia della letteratura italiana*. Edited by Niccolò Gallo. With an Introduction by Giorgio Ficara. Torino: Einaudi-Gallimard 1996.
Flasch, Kurt: *Poesia dopo la peste. Saggio sul "Decameron"*. Bari: Laterza 1995 (Quadrante, 77).
Gilson, Étienne: *Dante and Philosophy*. Translated by David Moore. New York: Harper and Row 1963.
Gorni, Guglielmo: *Il nodo della lingua e il verbo d'amore*. Firenze: Olschki 1981.
Pernicone, Vincenzo: *Il canto 32 del "Paradiso"*. Torino: Società Editrice internazionale 1965 (Lectura Dantis Romana, n.s.).
Rico, Francisco: *Vida u obra de Petrarca I. Lectura del "Secretum"*. Padova: Antenore 1974.
Romanò, Angelo: *Il codice degli abbozzi (Vat. Lat. 3196) di Francesco Petrarca*. Roma: G. Bardi 1955.
Santagata, Marco: *I frammenti dell'anima: Storia e racconto nel "Canzoniere" di Petrarca*. Bologna: Il Mulino 1992.
Singleton, Charles S: *Dante Studies 1: Elements of Structures*. Cambridge, Mass: Harvard University Press 1958.
Stierle, Karlheinz: *La vita e i tempi di Petrarca: alle origini della moderna coscienza europea*. Translated by Gabriella Pelloni. Venezia: Marsilio 2007.
Witt, Ronald: *In the Footsteps of the Ancients: The Origins of Humanism from Lovato to Bruni*. Leiden: Brill 2000 (Studies in Medieval and Reformation Thought, 74).

Articles and Papers

Bettinzoli, Attilio: Recensione a Francesco Bruni: *Boccaccio. L'invenzione della letteratura mezzana*. In: *Studi sul Boccaccio* 19 (1990), p. 273–278.
Candido, Igor: Il "cor inquietum" di Dante e il "cor quietum" di Boccaccio nella "Storia" di Francesco de Sanctis. In: *Lettere italiane* 67, 2 (2015), p. 225–249.
Delcorno, Carlo: *Exemplum e letteratura. Tra Medioevo e Rinascimento*. Bologna: Il Mulino 1989.
Delcorno, Carlo: Ironia/parodia. In: Renzo Bragantini/Pier Massimo Forni (eds): *Lessico critico decameroniano*. Torino: Bollati Boringhieri 1995, p. 162–191.

Fornero, Giovanni: Epoché. In: Nicola Abbagnano: *Dizionario di Filosofia*. Edited by Giovanni Fornero. Torino: UTET 1998³, p. 378–379.
Hollander, Robert: Boccaccio's Dante: Imitative Distance (*Decameron* I, 1 and VI, 10). In: *Studi sul Boccaccio* 13 (1981–1982), p. 169–198.
Küpper, Joachim: Palinodia e polisemia nella Canzone alla Vergine (con alcune brevi considerazioni sulle condizioni della differenza tra arte classica ed arte moderna). In: *Quaderni petrarcheschi* 14 (2004), p. 147–190.
Marsh, David: The Burning Question: Crisis and Cosmology in the Secret. In: *Petrarch: A Critical Guide to the Complete Works*. Ed. by Victoria Kirkham and Armando Maggi. Chicago: University of Chicago Press 2009, p. 211–218.
Moevs, Christian: Subjectivity and Conversion in Dante and Petrarch. In: Zygmunt Barański/ Theodore J. Cachey, Jr. (eds): *Petrarch and Dante. Anti-Dantism, Metaphysics, Tradition*. Notre Dame, Indiana: University of Notre Dame Press 2009, p. 226–259.
Ossola, Carlo: Boccaccio anima laica. In: *Il Sole 24 ore* (29 Jan. 2012), p. 33.
Ossola, Carlo: Boccaccio riprodotto al millimetro. In: *Il Sole 24 ore* (17 March 2013), p. 40.
Rico, Francisco: "Sospir trilustre". Le date dell'amore e il primo "Canzoniere". In: *Critica del testo* 6 (2003), p. 31–48.
Santangelo, Enrico: Petrarch Reading Dante: The Ascent of Mont Ventoux (Familiares 4. 1). In: Martin L. McLaughlin/ Letizia Panizza/ Peter Hainsworth (eds): *Petrarch in Britain: Interpreters, Imitators, and Translators over 700 Years*. Oxford: Oxford University Press 2007 (Proceedings of the British Academy, 146), p. 95–111.
Singleton, Charles S: The Vistas in Retrospect. In: *Modern Language Notes* 81, 1 (1966), p. 55–80.
Tufano, Ilaria: Boccaccio e la letteratura religiosa: la Prima e la Seconda Giornata del "Decameron". In: *Critica del Testo* 16, 3 (2013), p. 185–207.

Gerhard Regn
The *Incipit* of the *Decameron*: Textual Margins as an Index of Epochal Change

The paratextual complex, having first become central thanks to structuralism,[1] has acquired new importance in the setting of contemporary currents of poststructuralist literary criticism. From the perspective of New Historicism,[2] paratexts are espoused as true indicators of a new way of understanding the literary text. New perspectives on literature can be obtained – so goes the hypothesis – only by abandoning the idea of unity and coherency within the literary text (structured around a central theme) in order to direct attention instead to its open, incomplete, resistant, peripheral and marginal dimensions.[3] Marginality itself is thus transformed into a poetological concept, whose potential seems able to reveal itself in a particularly marked manner, thanks to the study of the textual margins.

It is without doubt that the poststructuralist approach has provided stimulating results in the study of literature, and especially that of the medieval and premodern eras. However, unlike its staunchest supporters, I do not think it is possible to generalize this approach by rendering it a universal method, applicable in every context. Indeed, this methodology becomes particularly ineffective where authors have given their works a clear conceptual structure, in which unifying criteria such as composition, coherency and unity play a fundamental role. This is particularly true for investigations into paratexts.

Boccaccio's *Decameron* is one of these cases, and furthermore a case of great historic potential. In Boccaccio's work the possibilities inherent within postmedieval storytelling are exemplarily visible: evident in the calculated game that contributes to the creation of narrative coherency is the path toward a modelization

---

[1] As we know, the investigation of the paratextual complex has received renewed and, from there forward, systematic interest thanks to Genette's volume on this argument. See Gérard Genette: *Seuils*. Paris: Editions du Seuil 1987.
[2] On New Historicism see Harold Aram Veeser: *The New Historicism Reader*. New York and London: Routledge 1994.
[3] Regarding the textual theory of New Historicism see Greenblatt's programmatic statement, which notes in particular the aspect of textual margins: "I propose [...] to look less at the presumed center of the literary domain than at its borders, to try to track what can only be glimpsed, as it were, at the margins of the text. The cost of the shift in attention will be the satisfying illusion of a 'whole reading.'" Stephen Greenblatt: *Shakespearian Negotiations. The Circulation of Social Energy in Renaissance England*. Berkeley and Los Angeles: University of California Press 1988, p. 4.

∂ Open access. © 2018 Gerhard Regn, published by De Gruyter. This work is licensed under the Creative Commons Attribution-NonCommercial-NoDerivatives 4.0 license.
https://doi.org/10.1515/9783110419306-009

of reality typical of the early modern era, which takes into account that which is incalculable; that is, the contingency of the world,[4] precisely through the instruments of compositional calculation.[5] The most effective key for accessing this compositional structure can be found in the very margins of the Certaldese's text: it is the rubric of the *incipit* which contains the *titulus* of the work.

In the *Decameron*, the opening words of the text do not in fact have the task of attracting the reader's attention to the marginal; rather, they have the function of opening a breach toward the center, and therefore toward the work in its totality which, as we know, is not a simple anthology of *novelle* without structure but a carefully constructed book. This thesis, however, is plausible only if the rubric of the *incipit*, which I maintain to be a programmatic reference to the work as a whole, can be traced directly to the author: he would have been quite concerned that his work, going against the practices of the medieval *varietas*,[6] would have a stable textual *facies*. While cases of marked textual variation are attested for the *Decameron* as well, even within Boccaccio's direct circle, Boccaccio himself (just

---

4 For Boccaccio, contingency has vast theological and philosophical resonances: the concept implies that the legibility of the 'book' of divine creation, as guaranteed by scholastic thought, begins to fail; instead of revealing itself as the indubious product of the *potentia ordinata*, the world presents itself as a kind of radical contingency that mirrors the omnipotence of a God no longer rationally knowable. The consequence of this situation is the increasing self-affirmation of human reason. For this widely studied notion, see above all Hans Blumenberg: *Säkularisierung und Selbstbehauptung*. 2 Auflage. Frankfurt am Main: Suhrkamp 1983.
5 As we can see, unlike that of Branca's *Boccaccio medievale* (Firenze: Sansoni 1981), my argument derives from the hypothesis of a Boccaccio who, even if closely tied to the culture of the Middle Ages, opens up new conceptual horizons with his *Centonovelle*. I will limit myself to highlighting the development of an autonomous rationality unfettered from religious norms, which stimulates mankind to orient itself, using its own resources, in a world experienced in large part as contingent (see also note 4). This concept is realized in the decision of the *brigata* to replace God's space (the church of Santa Maria Novella) with human space (the 'palace' outside of Florence; see X *Intr.* 3). The *Decameron* does not 'stand alongside' the *Commedia* – as Branca would like it to do – by completing it as a "'commedia dell'uomo' rappresentata attraverso i paradigmi canonici alla visione cristiana e scolastica della vita" ['human comedy' depicted through paradigms canonical to the Christian and scholastic vision of life; p. 29]. Rather, it is postitioned most decidedly after Dante's "poema sacro" (*Par.* XV, 1): the 'after' here is not merely a temporal indicator but signifies a true epochal turning point.
6 On the concept of the variant as a constitutive factor of medieval textuality, see Bernard Cerquiglini: *Eloge de la variante: Histoire critique de la philologie*. Paris: Editions du Seuil 1989; Marina Brownlee/Kevin Brownlee et al.: *The New Medievalism*. Baltimore: Johns Hopkins University Press 1991; Jacqueline Cerquiglini-Toulet: Conceiving the Text in the Middle Ages. In: R. Howard Bloch/Alison Calhoun et al. (eds.): *Rethinking the New Medievalism*. Baltimore: Johns Hopkins University Press 2014, p. 151–161; Stephen G. Nichols: *From Parchment to Cyberspace. Medieval Literature in the Digital Age*. New York: Peter Lang 2016, p. 107–142.

like Petrarch) moves within a conceptual panorama that views the author as sovereign of his own text: it therefore becomes fundamental for this type of author to ensure that the transmission of his work occurs in a way most faithful to the original textual *facies*. This is particularly true for those parts of the text – such as the paratexts – most subject to alterations according to the medieval conception of variation and therefore most often redacted by the copyist and not stemming from the author himself. Therefore, I will attempt to show firstly that the *incipit* of the *Decameron* is authored by Boccaccio, in order to demonstrate how this marginal portion of the text serves to underscore quite markedly the *intentio auctoris*, with the aim of controlling the reception of the work right from the start.

1 The Tradition of the Text

According to the critical edition published by Vittore Branca, the rubric of the *Decameron*'s *incipit* is worded as such:

> Comincia il libro chiamato *Decameron* cognominato prencipe Galeotto, nel quale si contengono cento novelle in diece dí dette da sette donne e da tre giovani uomini. (*Proemio* 1)

> [Beginneth here the book called Decameron, otherwise Prince Galeotto, wherein are contained one hundred novels told in ten days by seven ladies and three young men.][7]

The Branca edition is based primarily on an autograph codex of the *Decameron* now held at the Staatsbibliothek in Berlin: the renowned *Hamilton 90*. This manuscript presents a serious hitch with respect to this study: the beginning of the work, up to a part of the introduction of the narrative frame, is not in fact an autograph of Boccaccio, but a later addition in a different hand.[8] Notwithstanding

---

[7] Giovanni Boccaccio: *Decameron*. Edizione critica secondo l'autografo hamiltoniano per cura di Vittore Branca, Firenze: Presso l'Accademia della Crusca 1976. It is quoted here from the edition prepared by Branca for the Nuova Universale Einaudi: Giovanni Boccaccio: *Decameron*. Edited by Vittore Branca. Torino: Einaudi 2004¹⁴. All English translations taken, with minor alterations, from Giovanni Boccaccio: *The Decameron of Giovanni Boccaccio Faithfully Translated by James M. Rigg*. 2 vols. London: The Navarre Society 1903.

[8] See Vittore Branca: *Tradizione delle opere di Giovanni Boccaccio*. Vol. 2: *Un secondo elenco di manoscritti e studi sul testo del "Decameron" con due appendici*. Roma: Edizioni di Storia e Letteratura 1991, p. 215. For a list of the most important studies dedicated to the Berlin codex, see Marco Cursi: *Il Decameron: scritture, scriventi, lettori. Storia di un testo*. Roma: Viella 2007, p. 163–164. Even though the conclusory formula of the text, which is attributable to Boccaccio's own hand, contains both title and subtitle – that is, 'Decameron' and 'prince Galeotto' – it makes no mention of the narrators, their gender or their number.

this difficulty, it is possible to consider the above-cited *incipit* as authorial: it is allowed in the first place by the stemmatic reconstruction of the rather complex textual tradition (we know of at least sixty codices dating to the fourteenth and fifteenth centuries).[9] It is also allowed by a direct witness, the codex *Parigino It. 482*, now in the Bibliothèque Nationale of Paris. As Branca has demonstrated, this manuscript, most certainly completed before 1359, contains the copy of a redaction of the *Decameron* that precedes the one dated to the 1370s and transcribed from the *Hamilton* codex. The copyist was, as the codex itself indicates, Giovanni d'Agnolo Capponi, descendent of an important family of Florentine merchants with close ties to Boccaccio.[10] But what is more, even if the eighteen well-known illustrations in pen and bistre[11] which Ciardi Duprè attributed to the hand of Boccaccio himself[12] were not – as Battaglia Ricci has recently claimed[13] – ascribable to the Certaldese, the codex's close proximity to Boccaccio remains without doubt. Marco Cursi's extremely detailed paleographic investigations corroborate Branca's hypothesis that the *Parigino It. 482* was written with all probability at Boccaccio's desk and therefore under his very eyes.[14] The codex created by Capponi is not only "la più antica testimonianza del *Decameron* a noi nota [e] tratta direttamente da un autografo di Boccaccio ormai perduto" [the oldest witness of the *Decameron* known to us and taken directly from an autograph by Boccaccio now lost],[15] but is also closest to the author of the *Centonovelle* – and

---

9 For the textual tradition see Cursi: *Il Decameron*, p. 31–36.
10 This proximity is not only of a spatial nature (Boccaccio and the Capponi lived in the same neighborhood, Santo Stefano), but above all of a social one: "I Capponi erano una nota famiglia di lanaioli, legata nell'arte di Calimala con i Bardi e quindi con i Boccacci, loro collaboratori; inoltre, come il Boccaccio, erano consiglieri per le opere d'arte e i lavori edilizi della Compagnia di Or San Michele" [The Capponi were a renowned family of wool merchants, connected through the Calimala guild to the Bardi family and therefore to the Boccacci, their associates; furthermore, just like Boccaccio, they were advisors for the art commissions and building projects of the Compagnia di Or San Michele.], Cursi: *Il Decameron*, p. 32, n. 100. For further information on the biography of Giovanni Capponi see ibid.
11 For the illustrated *Decameron* see Giovanni Boccaccio: *Decameron con le illustrazioni dell'autore e di grandi artisti fra Tre e Quattrocento*. Edited by Vittore Branca. Firenze: Le Lettere 1999.
12 Maria Grazia Ciardi Dupré dal Pogetto: Corpus dei disegni e cod. Parigino It. 482. In: Maria Grazia Ciardi Duprè/Vittore Branca: Boccaccio visualizzato dal Boccaccio. *Studi sul Boccaccio* 22 (1994), p. 197–225. The drawings play a decisive role in the dating of the codex.
13 See Lucia Battaglia Ricci: *Scrivere un libro di novelle: Giovanni Boccaccio autore, lettore, editore*. Ravenna: Longo Editore 2013, p. 62–96.
14 See Cursi: *Il Decameron*, p. 33, where he argues – albeit with some amount of caution – in favor of Branca's hypothesis that the *Parigino It. 482* was "prodotto all'interno del suo [i. e. Boccaccio] scrittoio" [produced at his writing desk.]
15 Lucia Battaglia Ricci: *Scrivere un libro di novelle*, p. 60. This opinion is correct, if one considers complete versions of the *Decameron*; if one also includes the fragmentary witnesses, the prize

not only in a spatial sense, given that the copyist attempts to respect his antigraph even "al limite dell'imitazione grafica" [to the point of graphic imitation.][16] All of this confers to the text transcribed in Capponi's manuscript an authority similar to that of an actual authorial redaction. The most decisive point for us is that the *Decameron* of the *Parigino It. 482* contains an *incipit* substantially identical to that of Branca's critical edition,[17] and to which we can therefore attribute with the highest probability an authorial status.

2 The Parody of Creation

'Prencipe Galeotto' is the work's second name, and therefore its subtitle; its actual name is 'Decameron.' The latter is a neologism constructed analogously to forms like 'Hexaemeron' and, as noted, means 'in ten days.' Unlike its subtitle, the principal title does not speak to the content of this collection of *novelle*. Instead, it refers exclusively to the temporal aspect of their production.

It is useful to remember this point, because it is this lack of description which permits us to better interpret a textual detail of the Introduction to the Fourth Day, likewise a part of the complex paratextual structure of the *Centonovelle* which would otherwise be difficult to understand. Here, in the third paragraph, the author notes how his "novelette [...] in fiorentin volgare e in prosa" [little stories [...] in the vulgar Florentine, and in prose; IV *Intr.* 3] are a work "senza titulo" [without title; IV *Intr.* 3]: one can comprehend this affirmation, both unique and in apparent contrast to the *incipit*, by considering more closely the possible implications of the expression. Coming to our aid is Boccaccio's commentary to Dante's *Commedia*. Here, in fact, it becomes clear that the expression "sine titulo" is utilized for those works that do not have a cohesive subject matter, as occurs in the majority of collected poems or in anthologies of *novelle* with widely varied content.[18] Thus they are macrotexts made up of microtexts, each different from the others and legible individually: in this sense Petrarch's *Rerum vulgarium*

---

for oldest goes to the so-called *frammento magliabechiano* (which contains the *novella* IX 10 and the conclusions of days I–IX). For the problems with dating the codices in question, see Cursi: *Il Decameron*, p. 21–36.

16 Cursi: *Il Decameron*, p. 33.
17 In the *Hamilton 90* the rubric of the *incipit* ends with "Proemio," therefore introducing generically the author's preface; in *Parigino It. 482* we instead read: "Proemio di Giovanni Boccaccio autore;" see Cursi: *Il Decameron*, p. 218.
18 Referring to Ovid, Boccaccio declares: "Appresso, ne compose uno [*scil.* libro], partito in tre, il quale alcun chiamano *Liber amorum*, altri il chiamano *Sine titulo*: e può l'un titolo e l'altro avere,

fragmenta would be considered a work without title. When inserted into this tradition, 'Decameron' becomes merely a formal denomination; or rather, it is an improper title, so to speak, which gives no information on the content of the stories narrated within. Nevertheless, it possesses a strong sense of intertextual reference.

The reference in question is, quite obviously, to the biblical *Genesis*, and therefore to the creation of the world in six days by the hand of God; or better, to the enormous quantity of commentaries on *Genesis* circulating in the Middle Ages, the most celebrated of which was the *Hexameron* of Ambrose. With its title the *Decameron* refers to the story of creation, and does so by making use of the possibilities that parody, in the medieval sense of the term, can offer.[19] Boccaccio's parody does not allow itself to be reduced to a mere comic counterpoint which, with the intention of amusing its public, would seek to ridicule its serious hypotexts. It instead attempts to create a new vision of the world which goes beyond the limits marked by medieval religious thought. By imitating the work of God, Boccaccio wishes to demonstrate the possibilities of human creation,[20] above all in a specific context such as that of the chaos caused by the plague of 1348. An extremely formal sign of the serious setting for this Boccaccian parody is the fact that for his *Centonovelle* our author has adopted – through the complex and hierarchically organized system of dividing the text

---

per ciò che d'alcuna altra cosa non parla che di suoi innamoramenti [...]; e puossi dire similemente *Sine titulo*, per ciò che d'alcuna materia continuata, dalla quale si possa intitolare, favella, ma alquanti versi d'una e alquanti d'un'altra, e così possiam dire di pezi, dicendo, procede." [Later he composed a book, divided into three parts, which some call *Liber amorum*, others call it *Sine titulo*: and it can have either title, because it speaks of nothing other than his many enamorments; (...) and one could also call it *Sine titulo*, because it does not talk about a continuous subject matter, by which it can be titled, but rather some verses on one thing and some on another, and thus we can say its telling proceeds piecemeal]. The passage, which Branca cites without bibliographic information in his commentary on the *Decameron* edited for Nuova Universale Einaudi (p. 460, n.1), can be found in Lezione 13 on Canto IV, esp. litt., § 119. See Giovanni Boccaccio: *Tutte le opere di Giovanni Boccaccio*. Edited by Vittore Branca. Vol. 7/8: *Esposizioni sopra la "Commedia"*. Edited by Giorgio Padoan: Milano: Mondadori 1965, p. 200.
19 For the parodical dimension of the *Decameron* see Luciano Rossi: Ironia e parodia nel "Decameron:" Da Ciappelletto a Griselda. In: *La novella italiana. Atti del Convegno di Caprarola (19–24. 9. 1988)*. Roma: Salerno Editrice 1988 (Biblioteca di Filologia e critica, 3), p. 385–398, with reference to the links between the *Decameron* and the Ambrosian model.
20 In this sense Rossi also speaks of the "'re-creation' of the world;" see Luciano Rossi: Il paratesto decameroniano: Cimento d'armonia e d'invenzione. In: *Introduzione al "Decameron"*. Edited by Michelangelo Picone / Margherita Mesirca. Firenze: Franco Cesati Editore 2004 (Lectura Boccaccii Turicensis), p. 35–54: p. 37.

and of the capital headings – the precise style of the erudite treatise which would be read by "fruitori esperti dei libri universitari" [expert users of university textbooks].[21] The subtle reference to the treatise form serves to imbue the *Decameron* with a status above that of literature for pure entertainment. Its principal function, however, is the establishment of the parodical structure as such, the basis of which, as noted above, is the relationship that Boccaccio institutes between his book of *novelle* and the *Hexameron* with its various commentaries by medieval scholars. Regarding the specific case of the system of division and capital headings, the parodic façade is very subtle, almost hidden. Most of the time, however, the parodical traits are clearly visible and easy to locate. Divine creation occurs through the *logos*, through the word: in the biblical *Genesis* 'to speak' and 'to create' are considered two sides of the same coin.[22] Similarly the words, and more precisely the words of the *novelle*, are the instrument with which the narrators of the "lieta brigata" (I *Intr.* 103) recreate the world: a world quite contrary to that of chaotic Florence devastated by the plague. Their author, obviously, is not God, but instead are the human beings (predominantly women) who create an existential space well suited to them by means of cultured and sociable conversation.

Divine creation takes place over six days, to which is added a seventh day of repose for the creator. Our parody of *Genesis* also recognizes the principle of the rest day, but it is striking in that its repose does not coincide with the day of our Lord. Sunday is a day of storytelling, as if it were just like any other weekday and not a day of rest: a day of work, therefore, in the creation of our *Decameron-Genesis*, in which one continues to weave the fabric of order that the narration creates. Nevertheless, even the *brigata* has its day of repose from the efforts of narration-creation. One could therefore object that the lack of Sunday observance has no strong argumentative value, seeing that in one way or another – with the rest day on Friday – compensation is offered for the lack of respect for Sunday, and not the least in consideration of the fact that the explanation given for the choice of Friday as the day of pause is of a religious nature: Friday is the day of the crucifixion and is reserved for prayer "a onor di Dio" [in honor of God; II *Concl.* 5] and not for storytelling. The religious argument, however, has a rather supplementary character, given that the primary motivation for resting regards

---

[21] See Lucia Battaglia Ricci: Edizioni d'autore, copie di lavoro, interventi di autoesegesi: testimonianze trecentesche. In: Guido Baldassarri (ed.): *Di mano propria. Gli autografi dei letterati italiani*. Roma: Salerno 2010, p. 123–157: p. 139, with reference to the pertinent studies of Patrizia Rafti, Teresa Nocita, and Francesca Malagnini.

[22] One should recall, alongside the prologue of the *Gospel of John*, the seriality of the "*dixit*" which *Genesis* uses to signify the creational act of God.

the particular victuals to be consumed on this day of abstinence;[23] but above all – and it is this that renders the religious motivation even less clear – the Friday pause is mirrored uniquely when the narrations are likewise interrupted for the entire next day, Saturday. The motivations, here, are predominantly worldly in nature:[24] Saturday is not only another day of abstinence, but is above all dedicated to "wellness," and therefore to care for the physical body. Thus the repetition of the day of repose also serves to accentuate the element of parody.

The very duration of the creation as a whole is therefore doubled: in the *Decameron* the narrators tell stories for a total period of two weeks,[25] in contrast to the single week narrated in *Genesis*. In the time span of creation – a span that, as Dioneo makes clear in the conclusion of the last day, theoretically could have been further elongated[26] – the divine *ordo* of creation is dissolved and an entirely human structure takes its place. The ten days of storytelling, of which the *incipit* speaks, are therefore not an expression of divine perfection, as the number could lead one to believe, but should be understood in parodical terms.

3 Contingency and Order

But how does one arrive, within the logic of the literary fiction, at the number ten, which in the *mare magnum* of medieval numerology can easily be traced to perfection, and above all divine perfection? By which paths? The response to this question is: by happenstance. And it is happenstance that pushes the parodical game even further along.

---

[23] Therefore: if one does not eat well, neither can one work/narrate. Formal signs of this supplementary character are the *dispositio* and the syntax: the reference to the passion of Christ is introduced only after the thematization of food to be consumed, and moreover with a "senza che" that underscores the secondary value of the adopted religious argument: "senza che il venerdì, avendo riguardo che in esso Colui che per la nostra vita morì sostenne passione, è degno di riverenza" [to say nothing of the reverence in which Friday is meet to be held, seeing that'twas on that day that He who died for us bore His passion; II *Concl.* 5].

[24] In this case as well, the religious theme – the "reverenza della Vergine" [reverence of the Virgin; II *Concl.* 6] is of a supplementary nature.

[25] The storytelling begins on Wednesday and ends two Tuesdays later; see I *Intr.* 40 e X *Concl.* 3: at the end of the tenth day Dioneo announces their departure on the following day with reference to the two weeks they passed in holiday: "domani saranno quindici dí […] uscimmo di Firenze" [Now, to-morrow, as you know,'twill be fifteen days since (...) we took our departure from Florence.]

[26] The decision (which Dioneo decreed in his role as king) to end the storytelling is due not to necessity, but rather to simple convenience: continuing might lead to boredom; see X *Concl.* 6.

Seven young ladies (the number is mentioned in the *incipit*) meet on a Tuesday of the year 1348, after Mass in the church of Santa Maria Novella. They meet *either* because they are friends *or* because they are related *or* only as neighbors.[27] The paratactic structure formed by the repetition of the conjunction "either/or" functions as an indicator of a potentially serial casualness by which the group comes together, and which is confirmed by the arrival of three young men who will complete the *lieta brigata*: while the ladies are discussing the option of escaping a Florence infested with plague, suddenly – and with no explanation provided by the author – three young men (this number is specified in the *incipit* as well), of an equal social status to that of the women, enter the church, and after some indecision the ladies finally choose them as suitable companions for their endeavor. Here as well the syntax underscores the casual aspect of the happenings and does so through the adverbial locution "e ecco" [and see here] which connotes an unforeseen, or even unforeseeable moment: "Mentre tralle donne erano così fatti ragionamenti, e ecco entrar nella chiesa tre giovani [...]" [While the ladies were thus conversing, see here there came into the church three young men (...); I *Intr.* 78].

Governing the formation of the *lieta brigata*, therefore, is this principle of casualness which, as noted, will also play a primary role in the world of the narrative tales. Seven and three make ten. Boccaccio chooses to work with numbers that have a connotation of perfection and sacredness in the medieval symbolic order, but as we have seen, he does so in such a way that this metaphysical dimension can be identified primarily as the pure product of chance. However, it is a chance that men can use to their advantage and for their own purposes. And this is exactly what the narrators of the *lieta brigata* do: moving from the number ten, established quite casually, they then realize a numerical order that is consistent, clear and harmonious in and of itself – ten days for ten *novelle* and likewise ten storytellers. But it is not only the fictitious figures who, from this casual beginning, come to constitute a numerically coherent and well-structured order. The author himself does the same when he subdivides ten days into three plus seven, numbers already given in relation to the men (three) and the women (seven) – here I obviously refer to the structural caesura marked by the second proemio after the third day, a caesura that sheds light once again on the process of repetition linked to parodical intention.

Albeit casual within the narrative fiction, the numbers three, seven and ten become the basis of an order that signifies perfection. This order, however, no longer has religious meaning, but is essentially of an aesthetic nature, and owes its

---

[27] "Si ritrovarono sette giovani donne tutte l'una a l'altra o per amistà o per vicinanza o per parentado congiunte" [There were found seven young ladies (...) all were connected either by blood or at least as friends or neighbours; I *Intr.* 49].

raison d'être to a human decision: the decision to have a numerology with strong metaphysical implications become a mere element of the free play of *póiesis*. This shift becomes clear if one considers another detail of the *Decameron's* structure.

In what is a true repetition of the beginning – the *Introduction* to the Fourth Day – the author once again takes the floor in order to illustrate his poetics. Presented in this context is the wonderful story of the *donne-papere*: farmer Filippo Balducci tries to protect his son, just come of age, from the power of feminine beauty, and in the end is defeated heartily (and to the reader's great delight) in his attempt to oppose the course of nature. The author rightly defines this anecdote as a "novella" (IV *Intr.* 30), and of little worth are Neuschäfer's strident efforts to demonstrate that it is not, in fact, a novella, but rather a traditional *exemplum*:[28] in other words, another story, encased in one of the *Decameron's* proems. How should we interpret this fact? Boccaccio wishes to create movement within the established numerology linked to the perfect numbers three, seven, ten, and one hundred, thus causing them to waver a bit. If in fact we consider the Introduction to the Fourth Day as an integral part of the work, the total number of *novelle* in the *Decameron* becomes one hundred and one, and the narrators eleven. This complex composition allows Boccaccio to instill doubt within the reader that the total of one hundred *novelle* and ten narrators is perhaps not quite so objective, immutable, or metaphysical, but that possible alternatives to this rigid and defined structure might exist.[29] One could even say that at the level of human creation, the author of the *Decameron* acts like the omnipotent God of late scholasticism:[30] he makes clear that the order he has established is the product of an absolute free will which could also have made very different choices.

The narrative order is therefore a human creation: the nucleus of the structured space within which the members of the *brigata* recount for one another their hundred *novelle*. The *brigata* makes use of an imposing villa – the text even speaks of a "palagio" [palace; X *Intr.* 3] – to create an actual court dedicated to

---

28 See Hans-Jörg Neuschäfer: *Boccaccio und der Beginn der Novelle. Strukturen der Kurzerzählung zwischen Mittelalter und Neuzeit*. München: Wilhelm Fink Verlag 1969, p. 56–58.
29 For Rossi, Boccaccio's use of numbers constitutive of Decameronian architecture would allow him to re-evaluate, at the expense of the Christian Middle Ages, the Pythagorean numerology and with it the proto-humanistic "componente pagana o politeista della filosofia classica" [pagan or polytheistic component of classical philosophy]; Luciano Rossi: Il paratesto, p. 36. Rossi rightly emphasizes the aesthetic aspect inherent in Boccaccio's choice, overestimating however the metaphysical dimension ascribable to it.
30 See Joachim Küpper: Affichierte "Exemplarität", tatsächliche A-Systematik. Boccaccios "Decameron" und die Episteme der Renaissance. In: Klaus W. Hempfer (ed.): *Renaissance. Diskursstrukturen und epistemologische Voraussetzungen*. Stuttgart: Franz Steiner Verlag 1993, p. 84–87.

the narration, with a king, an entourage of courtiers and all the figures necessary to courtly life such as the seneschal, the treasurer, the butler, the cooks, etc.[31] The members of the *brigata* thus simulate a courtly-aristocratic world, free from the obligations of a mercantile existence and devoted completely to the pleasures of culture and conversation. The narrative space created by the characters of the narrative frame has *per se* the status of fiction: fiction that creates a point of connection for other fictions, coming before and after, each with a different hierarchical status. In the narrative frame Boccaccio invents a story (first level) within which the characters, the fictitious members of the *brigata*, construct an invented world (second level), which in its turn has as its singular purpose the narrative production of other fictional worlds, those of the narrated *novelle* (third level). The fiction's potential is thus pushed to its extreme.

Particularly important for our argument are the aristocratic semantics of the world inhabited by the characters of the *brigata*. They reveal a normative function for the often stylistically "low" narrative of the *novelle* – and in particular for their frequently comic, repeatedly saucy, and occasionally even vulgar aspects.[32] In the Introduction to the Fourth Day the author speaks explicitly of the "istilo umilissimo e rimesso" [as homely and simple a style as may be; IV *Intr.* 3] of the *novelle* narrated by the *brigata*: they are thus described as narrations quite separate from the world of those who tell them. This is also true of the style. The narration of the frame makes use of a methodically formal register, very different from that of the majority of the *novelle*. It is thus the simulation of an aristocratic custom of dabbling in the "informal" with gusto, because that which amuses belongs to another world. It is precisely this ostentatious diversity of the aesthetics of informality that reveals a more peculiar function, that of provoking laughter, of lightening the burden of social and religious norms and of the many difficulties that belong indissolubly to life: in the *Decameron*, the most dramatic manifestation of these burdens is the plague. But the real world cannot be substituted in a lasting way by fiction. Once the narrative programme reaches its end, the space created as a function of the story loses its *raison d'être*: after the tenth *novella* of the Tenth Day, Dioneo decrees that the narrations must come to an end. The *lieta brigata* must dissolve and its members must return, from the artificial and well-ordered world of the idyllic "palagio" (X *Intr.* 3), to chaotic and plague-ridden Florence. We have no word of their eventual fate. In this sense the *Decameron* has an open ending, an expression of skepticism that takes into account the power of Fortune, which is nothing more than an allegory

---

[31] See I *Intr.* 98–101.
[32] As we know, the informal register, while dominant, does not hold exclusive sway in the *Decameron*, where we also find touching and even tragic *novelle*.

for contingency.³³ Despite the underlying skepticism about the fate of the world, the work affirms that art is an undeniable instrument for living well. To better clarify the multifaceted function that Boccaccio attributes to art in the *Decameron* we must return to the *incipit*, this time with Dante's *Commedia* in mind.

4 The *Decameron* and the *Commedia*

The reference to Dante is evident even at the numerological level: the one hundred *novelle* correspond to the one hundred cantos of the *Commedia*. The formal link that Boccaccio institutes between his book and the *Commedia* is itself of a parodical nature. The formal structure of Dante's "poema sacro" (*Par.* IV, 1) is a sign of the divine order represented within; that of the *Decameron*, as we have seen, is distinctly human. However, there is much more here than a rudimentary consideration of the numerical relationships between the two compositional structures. To delve deeper we must return once again to our *incipit* and in particular to the motif of Prince Galehaut.

It is to be expected that the first of the Parigino codex's eighteen illustrations depicts the opening lines of the text. Unexpected, and therefore highly informative, is the fact that this first drawing refers not to the work's title, but to its subtitle, here placed in sharp relief. The first drawing represents, in diptych form, two couples on horseback who make their way toward the center in which stands a copse of trees. The now widely held interpretation views the couple to the right, formed by two lovers in an embrace, as Lancelot and Guinevere (the queen bears a crown in accordance with her social rank), while the couple to the left is meant to depict Galehaut accompanied by the Lady of Malehaut.³⁴ Readers of the

---

33 For the fundamental differences between the medieval concept of Fortune and that of Boccaccio, see Andreas Kablitz: Zur Fortuna-Konzeption in Boccaccios "Decameron". In: *Italienische Studien* 12 (1990), p. 7–25.

34 See Lucia Battaglia Ricci: *Scrivere un libro di novelle*, p. 80–81: "La coppia di innamorati a destra [...] è l'ennesima rappresentazione di Lancilotto e Ginevra. Contro una tradizione critica che tende a vedere raffigurati nell'altra coppia Tristano e Isotta, Daniela Delcorno Branca ha suggerito che si tratti piuttosto di Galeotto e della dama di Malehaut, anche perché la dama è priva di corona. [...] questa è, come anche a me pare, la lettura corretta." [The two lovers at the right (...) are one of countless representations of Lancelot and Guinevere. Going against the critical tradition that tends to view the other couple as Tristan and Iseult, Daniela Delcorno Branca has suggested that it instead depicts Galehaut and the Lady of Malehaut, in particular because this lady has no crown. (...) this is, in my view as well, the correct reading.] Delcorno Branca's interpretation can be found in: Daniela Delcorno Branca: "Cognominato prencipe Galeotto". Il sottotitolo illustrato del Parigino It. 482. In: *Studi sul Boccaccio* 23 (1995), p. 79–88.

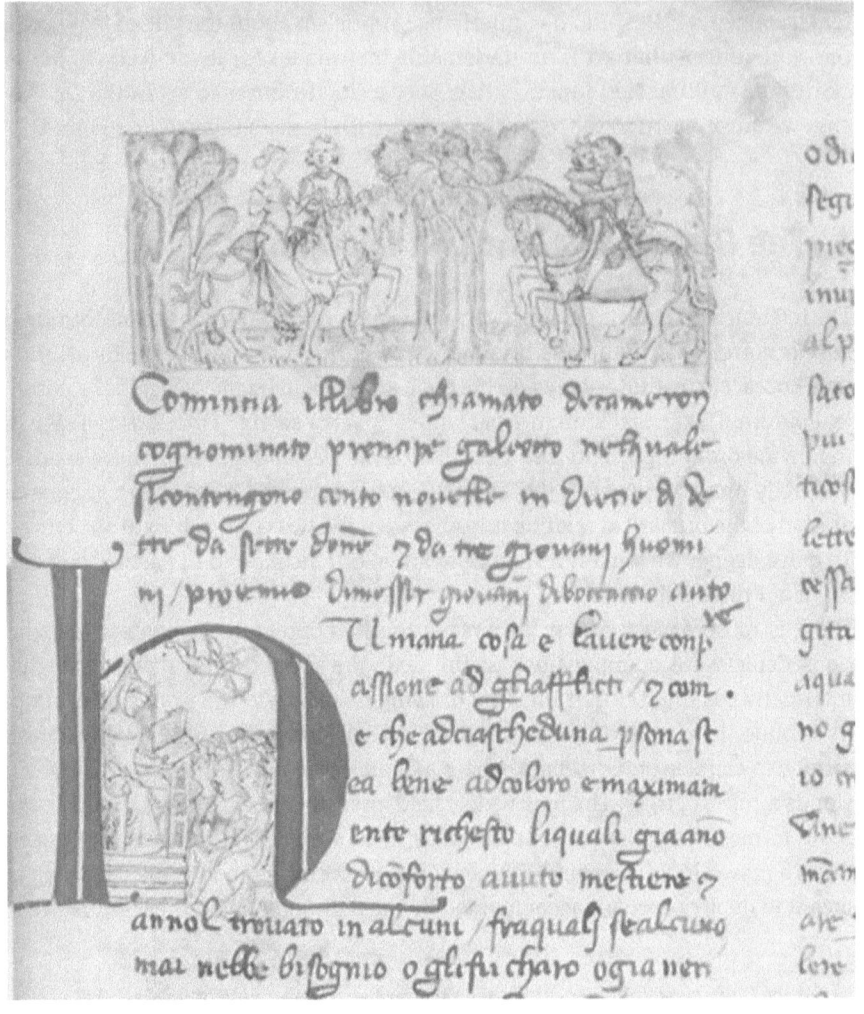

Plate 1: Paris, Bibl. Nationale de France, Cod. Par. It. 482, f. 5r.

Decameron in Boccaccio's age would most certainly have known the *Commedia* as well and therefore would also have been quite familiar with the episode of Paolo and Francesca. The episode is so widely known that a summary of the salient facts would be superfluous. I would like instead to underscore certain aspects of the celebrated passage which permit us to identify the elements of Dantean parody present in Boccaccio's text. The damnation of the lovers, punished for their adultery, is not caused by love itself, but by the pleasureable reading ("'Noi leggiavamo un giorno per diletto'" [One day, to pass the time in pleasure, we read];

Inf. V, 127)³⁵ of a great story of courtly love, so powerful as to break down all barriers of self control and Christian morals. Dante thematizes the motif of reading four times in just a handful of verses: "leggiavamo" [we were reading], "lettura" [the reading], "leggemmo" [we had read], and once again "leggemmo".³⁶ The emphasis falls on the act of reading in its physical, corporeal dimension. It is their eyes, the true *causa amoris* in a courtly sense, which lead Paolo and Francesca to fall in love: "'Per più fiate li occhi ci sospinse / quella lettura'" [More than once that reading made our eyes meet; *Inf.* V, 130–1].³⁷

On the book read by the lovers and on its author – the parties truly guilty of the adultery – Dante expresses a clear moral judgment; they are considered panderers: "Galeotto fu il libro e chi lo scrisse." [A Galeotto was the book and he that wrote it; *Inf.* V, 137]. In calling his *Decameron* "Galeotto," with the same metonymy as Dante, Boccaccio not only eliminates every negative connotation from the expression but turns the original meaning on its head. One can perceive this reversal through a small stylistic clue: the insertion of the aristocratic title 'prencipe,' which is absent in the *Commedia*. Indeed, the "Galeotto" of *Inferno* V becomes "Prince Galehaut" in Boccaccio's work. Galeotto, in the *Decameron*, is not a panderer heralding moral corruption: on the contrary, he is described as a benefactor, his role considered to be a positive one both in Prose Lancelot³⁸ and in the sphere of aristocratic and courtly culture, and restored to him once again by Boccaccio after the brief Dantean interlude. In the medieval tradition, the reason Galehaut enabled the physical union of Lancelot and Guinevere was due to compassion for his *ami*,³⁹ a man consumed by passion for Queen Guinevere to the point of flirting with self destruction. Galehaut, who in the French romance bears the title of Prince,⁴⁰ is the symbol of a humanity based on affection, which

---

35 English translations of the *Commedia* are taken from Dante Alighieri: *Inferno*. Translated by Robert Hollander and Jean Hollander. New York: Doubleday 2000.
36 *Inf.* V 127, 131, 133, 138.
37 Paolo and Francesca therefore imitate not an actual but rather a narrated act; see Peter Strohschneider: *Höfische Textgeschichten. Über Selbstentwürfe vormoderner Literatur*. Heidelberg: Winter 2014, p. 218–231.
38 On Prose Lancelot (which in its turn quotes abundantly from Chrétien de Troyes's *Il Chevalier de la Charrette*) as Dante's hypotext, see Thomas Klinkert: Zum Status von Intertextualität im Mittelalter: Tristan, Lancelot, Francesca da Rimini. In: *Deutsches Dante-Jahrbuch* 81 (2006), p. 27–70: p. 60; on the details of Dante's reading see Daniela Delcorno Branca: Dante and the Roman de Lancelot. In: Norris J. Lacy (ed.): *Text and Intertext in Medieval Arthurian Literature*. New York and London: Garland 1996, p. 133–145.
39 This motif returns at the beginning of the proem where Boccaccio presents the *Centonovelle* as an expression of the author's compassion for those in need: "umana cosa è aver compassione degli afflitti" ['tis humane to have compassion on the afflicted; *Proem* 2].
40 See Delcorno Branca: Dante and the Roman de Lancelot, p. 141.

is intentionally placed above the norms of "official" ethical standards enforced at the court of King Arthur. It is precisely this aspect that Boccaccio has in mind. Clearly we are quite far from the Dantean ethic that distinguishes between objective norms and subjective perception. Even Dante the pilgrim shows compassion for the lovers, but the subjective passion of Pilgrim Dante cannot change the narrator's attitude. The objectivity of divine justice never comes into doubt: the chain of divine law for Dante supersedes the pity that the character feels for the heartbreaking consequences of the verdict of divine Judgment.[41]

I will now conclude with a brief return to our *Incipit*, and this time in relation to the proem.

5 *Incipit* and *Proem*

"Umana cosa è avere compassione degli afflitti" ['Tis humane to have compassion on the afflicted; *Proem* 2]: from these words one might assume that Boccaccio wishes to begin his work in a genuinely Christian way, but it is not the case. His compassion, unlike that of Dante, stems from a secular anthropology not bound to Christian morals. For this reason he strongly emphasizes the human dimension of the problem in question.[42] His model is, as mentioned previously, the commiseration with which Galehaut, oblivious to the 'official' ethics of the world in which he lives, lends aid to his friend who is afflicted by adulterous love. In the *Decameron* the author directs his compassion toward those "vaghe donne" [gentle ladies; *Proem* 9] in love, house-bound and in need of a *remedium melancholiae* in the form of the *Decameron* itself,[43] thanks to its amusing stories. Its usefulness to the women in love,[44] which the *Proem*'s author does not neglect to

---

[41] For the relationship between human commiseration and the validity of divine judgment, see Gerhard Regn: Zeitsemantiken des Jenseits in Dantes "Commedia". In: Susannes Köbele/Coralie Rippl (eds.): *Gleichzeitigkeit. Narrative Synchronisierungsmodelle in der Literatur des Mittelalters und der Frühen Neuzeit*. Würzburg: Königshausen & Neumann 2015, p. 110–120.

[42] The beginning of the proem can be interpreted as a parody of the Pauline principle, that everything should be done in the Lord's name (Colossians 3:17). As we can see, Boccaccio substitutes this divine principle with its human counterpart. On this aspect see the contribution by Andreas Kablitz in this volume.

[43] The causes of melancholy are described in *Proem* 10–12, with particular emphasis given to love (obviously not of the conjugal sort) which must be kept hidden, and to the conditions of a sedentary life, cloistered and controlled by persons who hold a position of authority (fathers, mothers, brothers, and husbands).

[44] In speaking of the "utile consiglio" [useful counsel] that the female readers "potranno pigliare, in quanto potranno conoscere quello che sia da fuggire e che sia similmente da seguitare"

mention among the work's aims, is made secondary, while in the foreground is the Epicurean "diletto" [pleasure; *Proem* 14] which gives comfort and relieves the pressure of the norms that rule the life of a society governed by Christian morals.

The *Proem* has the same meaning for both the public to which it is addressed and for the members of the *brigata* who listen to the *novelle*. The stories told remain forever tied to the context in which they were narrated, and this is characterized by aristocratic refinement. Throughout the narrative frame, aristocratic elegance is blended with the world of a prevalently bourgeois public, as is confirmed by the tradition's history. The so-called *frammento magliabechiano*, which is counted among the oldest witnesses of the *Decameron*, focuses primarily on the narrative frame.[45] This is a codex prepared at the Neapolitan court of Anjou for an aristocratic public. Its aesthetic ideals are most apparent in the frame itself, where the formulation of a subtle narrative structure combines with the representation of a simulated life at court. But that which was so pleasing to the Anjovin court was at the same time an expression of the "ambizioni aristocratiche della ricca borghesia fiorentina" [aristocratic ambitions of the wealthy Florentine bourgeoisie.][46] In other words, the largely humble and 'informal' narration of Boccaccio's *novelle* passes through the filter of French aristocratic culture. For this reason it makes even more sense that Boccaccio, in giving a second name to his *Decameron*, would restore the original aristocratic title from the original French romance, which Dante refused to recognize: "Prince Galehaut."

Bibliography

Primary Literature

Alighieri, Dante: *Inferno*. Trans. by Robert Hollander and Jean Hollander. New York: Doubleday 2000.
Boccaccio, Giovanni: *Tutte le opere di Giovanni Boccaccio*. Edited by Vittore Branca. Vol. 7/8: *Esposizioni sopra la "Commedia"*. Edited by Giorgio Padoan: Milano: Mondadori 1965.
Boccaccio, Giovanni: *Decameron*. Edizione critica secondo l'autografo hamiltoniano per cura di Vittore Branca. Firenze: Presso l'Accademia della Crusca 1976.

[may derive, in that they may learn what to shun, and likewise what to pursue; *Proem* 14], the author refuses to restrict the meaning of "useful" to that of the ethical dimension, thus including his own interpretation in a more pragmatic sense.
45 See Marco Cursi: *Il Decameron*, p. 21–31.
46 Antonio Lanza: *La letteratura tardogotica. Arte e poesia a Firenze e Siena nell'autunno del Medioevo*. Anzio: De Ubeis 1994, p. 354.

Boccaccio, Giovanni: *Decameron con le illustrazioni dell'autore e di grandi artisti fra Tre e Quattrocento*. Edited by Vittore Branca. Firenze: Le Lettere 1999.
Boccaccio, Giovanni: *Decameron*. Ed. by Vittore Branca. Torino: Einaudi 2004[14].
Boccaccio, Giovanni: *The Decameron of Giovanni Boccaccio Faithfully Translated by James M. Rigg*. 2 vols. London: The Navarre Society 1903.

Secondary Literature

Monographs and Anthologies

Battaglia Ricci, Lucia: *Scrivere un libro di novelle: Giovanni Boccaccio autore, lettore, editore*. Ravenna: Longo Editore 2013.
Blumenberg, Hans: *Säkularisierung und Selbstbehauptung*. 2 Auflage. Frankfurt am Main: Suhrkamp 1983.
Branca, Vittore: *Boccaccio medievale*. Firenze: Sansoni 1981.
Branca, Vittore: *Tradizione delle opere di Giovanni Boccaccio*. Vol. 2: *Un secondo elenco di manoscritti e studi sul testo del "Decameron" con due appendici*. Roma: Edizioni di Storia e Letteratura 1991.
Brownlee, Marina /Kevin Brownlee et al.: *The New Medievalism*. Baltimore: Johns Hopkins University Press 1991.
Cerquiglini, Bernard: *Eloge de la variante: Histoire critique de la philologie*. Paris: Editions du Seuil 1989.
Cursi, Marco: *Il Decameron: scritture, scriventi, lettori. Storia di un testo*. Roma: Viella 2007.
Genette, Gérard: *Seuils*. Paris: Editions du Seuil 1987.
Greenblatt, Stephen: *Shakespearian Negotiations. The Circulation of Social Energy in Renaissance England*. Berkeley and Los Angeles: University of California Press 1988.
Lanza, Antonio: *La letteratura tardogotica. Arte e poesia a Firenze e Siena nell'autunno del Medioevo*. Anzio: De Ubeis 1994.
Neuschäfer, Hans-Jörg: *Boccaccio und der Beginn der Novelle. Strukturen der Kurzerzählung zwischen Mittelalter und Neuzeit*. München: Wilhelm Fink Verlag 1969.
Nichols, Stephen G: *From Parchment to Cyberspace. Medieval Literature in the Digital Age*. New York: Peter Lang 2016.
Strohschneider, Peter: *Höfische Textgeschichten. Über Selbstentwürfe vormoderner Literatur*. Heidelberg: Winter 2014.
Veeser, Harold Aram: *The New Historicism Reader*. New York and London: Routledge 1994.

Articles and Papers

Battaglia Ricci, Lucia: Edizioni d'autore, copie di lavoro, interventi di autoesegesi: testimonianze trecentesche. In: Guido Baldassarri (ed.): *Di mano propria. Gli autografi dei letterati italiani*. Roma: Salerno 2010, p. 123–157.

Cerquiglini-Toulet, Jacqueline: Conceiving the Text in the Middle Ages. In: R. Howard Bloch/Alison Calhoun et al. (eds.): *Rethinking the New Medievalism*. Baltimore: Johns Hopkins University Press 2014, p. 151–161.

Ciardi Duprè dal Poggetto, Maria Grazia: Corpus dei disegni e cod. Parigino It. 482. In: Maria Grazia Ciadra Dupré/Vittore Branca: Boccaccio visualizzato dal Boccaccio. *Studi sul Boccaccio* 22 (1994), p. 197–225.

Delcorno Branca, Daniela: "Cognominato prencipe Galeotto". Il sottotitolo illustrato del Parigino It. 482. In: *Studi sul Boccaccio* 23 (1995), p. 79–88.

Delcorno Branca, Daniela: Dante and the Roman de Lancelot. In: Norris J. Lacy (ed.): *Text and Intertext in Medieval Arthurian Literature*. New York and London: Garland 1996, p. 133–145.

Küpper, Joachim: Affichierte "Exemplarität", tatsächliche A-Systematik. Boccaccios "Decameron" und die Episteme der Renaissance. In: Klaus W. Hempfer (ed.): *Renaissance. Diskursstrukturen und epistemologische Voraussetzungen*. Stuttgart: Franz Steiner Verlag 1993, p. 84–87.

Kablitz, Andreas: Zur Fortuna-Konzeption in Boccaccios Decameron. In: *Italienische Studien* 12 (1990), p. 7–25.

Klinkert, Thomas: Zum Status von Intertextualität im Mittelalter: Tristan, Lancelot, Francesca da Rimini. In: *Deutsches Dante-Jahrbuch* 81 (2006), p. 27–70.

Regn, Gerhard: Zeitsemantiken des Jenseits in Dantes "Commedia". In: Susannes Köbele/Coralie Rippl (eds.): *Gleichzeitigkeit. Narrative Synchronisierungsmodelle in der Literatur des Mittelalters und der Frühen Neuzeit*. Würzburg: Königshausen & Neumann 2015, p. 110–120.

Rossi, Luciano: Ironia e parodia nel "Decameron": Da Ciappelletto a Griselda. In: *La novella italiana. Atti del Convegno di Caprarola (19–24. 9. 1988)*. Roma: Salerno Editrice 1988 (Biblioteca di Filologia e critica, 3), p. 385–398.

Rossi, Luciano: Il paratesto decameroniano: Cimento d'armonia e d'invenzione. In: *Introduzione al 'Decameron'*. Ed. by Michelangelo Picone/Margherita Mesirca. Firenze: Franco Cesati Editore 2004 (Lectura Boccaccii Turicensis), p. 35–54.

Andreas Kablitz
The *Proemio* of the *Decameron*. Boccaccio's Hidden Dialogue with Scholasticism

Much attention has been paid to the *Introduzione* of the First Day in Boccaccio's *Decameron*. Indeed, this drastic description of the Great Pestilence, of its physiological symptoms and its ruinous social consequences for the urban life in Florence seem to deserve the reader's particular interest. And, yet, this *Introduzione* is not the beginning of the *Decameron*. The text opens with a *Proemio*, a prologue, which has been widely neglected by literary criticism. Some translations even totally omit this *Proemio*. Of course, its content is or, at least, seems to be much less spectacular than the thrilling depiction of a disastrous disease. Nonetheless, as I will try to demonstrate in this paper, the *Proemio*, far from being a purely scholarly rhetorical exercise, establishes the very foundation of the intellectual profile of the *Decameron* and, especially, inaugurates its dialogue with scholastic philosophy. And, though the description of the raging disease might appear more striking, the conceptual conclusions that Boccaccio draws from scholastic anthropology are hardly less remarkable. On closer consideration, they constitute a real turning point in the development of Western thought. It is in this conceptual framework, even more than its narrative structures that the modernity of the *Decameron* comes to light, a subversive theoretical potential that undermines quite radically the idea of a *Boccaccio medievale*.[1]

Note: This article constitutes the first draft of a project I am working on. It aims at the publication of a book *The 'Decameron' and Boccaccio's Dialogue with Scholasticism*.

---

1 This expression, obviously refers to one of the most prominent books of research on the *Decameron*: Vittore Branca: *Boccaccio medievale*. Firenze: Sansoni 1956. This book belongs itself to an ongoing discussion that starts, at the latest, with Francesco de Sanctis' *Storia delle letteratura italiana*, where the modernity of Boccaccio's *Decameron* is emphasized. Branca's book constitutes an explicit counter-project in many regards stressing the adherence of Boccaccio's one hundred tales to the tradition of medieval literature. The many links between the *Decameron* and the narrative world of the Middle Ages Branca succeeds to show are indisputable. Nonetheless, Hans-Jörg Neuschäfer was right to claim that Boccaccio's tales, though widely belonging to a medieval tradition, in the *Decameron* underwent decisive changes that are tantamount to a transgression of medieval concepts (H.-J. N.: *Boccaccio und der Beginn der Novelle: Strukturen der Kurzerzählung auf der Schwelle zwischen Mittelalter und Neuzeit*. München: Wilhelm Fink 1969 [Theorie und Geschichte der Literatur und der schönen Künste, 8]). Without any doubt, Neuschäfer elaborates convincingly the modernity of Boccaccio's *Decameron*, even though he

---

Open access. © 2018 Andreas Kablitz, published by De Gruyter. This work is licensed under the Creative Commons Attribution-NonCommercial-NoDerivatives 4.0 license.
https://doi.org/10.1515/9783110419306-010

At first sight, it might appear quite astonishing that a collection of short stories, generally considered to be rather risqué than intellectually ambitious, should enter into a dialogue with the most prominent and, at the same time, most powerful contemporary discourse of the Trecento – a discourse, in addition, of considerable intellectual complexity. And, yet, it is the implicit debate with scholasticism, which leads us to the central ideological premises of Boccaccio's *Decameron*. His *novelle* react to the frequently latent transformation of traditional dogma in scholastic theology by further developing its consequences. In the dogmatic text itself these consequences tend to remain implicit or even unrecognized. Such reluctance or even blindness is all the more understandable as they dangerously threaten the integrity of the Christian dogma. Yet, the licences of poetic discourse seem to allow for an investigation into the tacit implications of scholastic thought which in the hundred tales of the *Decameron* become more than apparent.

> Umana cosa è aver compassione degli afflitti: e come che a ciascuna persona stea bene, a coloro è massimamente richiesto li quali già hanno di conforto avuto mestiere e hannol trovato in alcuni; fra quali, se alcuno mai n'ebbe bisogno o gli fu caro o già ne ricevette piacere, io sono uno di quegli. (*Proemio* 2)
>
> ['Tis humane to have compassion on the afflicted; and as it shews well in all, so it is especially demanded of those who have had need of comfort and have found it in others: among whom, if any had ever need thereof or found it precious or delectable, I may be numbered.][2]

By this ostentatious appeal to humanity Boccaccio opens his *Proemio*. The following sentence immediately explains the motivation for this stress on compassion. But, at first, this urgent appeal to human solidarity itself merits our attention. Why does Boccacio insist so intensively on humanity? An answer to this question might become possible by taking into account a remarkable difference between the beginning of Boccaccio's *Proemio*, that is to say, the very beginning of the

---

might somehow exaggerate its innovative character. Therefore, two more recent studies emphasised the rather transitional character of the *Decameron* between medieval and Renaissance forms of narrative (Joachim Küpper: Affichierte Exemplarität, tatsächliche A-Systematik. Boccaccios *Decameron* und die Episteme der Renaissance. In: Klaus W. Hempfer (ed.): *Renaissance. Diskursstrukturen und epistemologische Voraussetzungen. Literatur-Philosophie-Bildende Kunst.* Stuttgart: Steiner 1993 [Text und Kontext, 10], p. 47–93; Andreas Kablitz: Boccaccios *Decameron* zwischen Archaik und Modernität. Überlegungen zur achten Novelle des zehnten Tages. In: Andreas Kablitz/Ulrich Schulz-Buschhaus (eds.): *Literarhistorische Begegnungen.* Festschrift zum 60. Geburtstag von Bernhard König. Tübingen: Narr 1993, p. 149–185).
2 The texts from the *Decameron* and their respective translations are drawn from Giovanni Boccaccio: *Decameron*. Edited by Vittore Branca. Turin: Einaudi 1980; *The Decameron of Giovanni Boccaccio Faithfully Translated by James M. Rigg*. 2 vols. London: The Navarre Society 1932.

whole *Decameron*, and the opening lines of the first *novella*. Panfilo, its narrator, explicitly states that whatever you begin, you should begin do in the name of God:

> – Convenevole cosa è, carissime donne, che ciascheduna cosa la quale l'uomo fa, dallo ammirabile e santo nome di Colui, il quale di tutte fu facitore, le dea principio. (I, 1, 2)
>
> [A seemly thing it is, dearest ladies, that whatever we do, it be begun in the holy and awful name of Him who was the maker of all.]

Panfilo's pious words are more than a devout gesture, as he refers to a famous word of Saint Paul. In his *Epistle to the Colossians* the Apostle to the Gentiles recommends, rather demands to begin everything in the name of God:

> omne quodcumque facitis in verbo aut in opere omnia in nomine Domini Iesu gratias agentes Deo et Patri per ipsum. (Col. 3, 17)
>
> [And whatsoever ye do in word or deed, do all in the name of the Lord Jesus, giving thanks to God and the Father by him.]

It is significant that the author of the *Decameron* himself apparently, not to say ostentatiously differs from St. Paul's recommendation, which on the other hand is recalled by his first narrator. And this difference is all the more striking as, syntactically, Boccaccio's first sentence in the *Proemio* and Panfilo's first sentence in his novella I, 1 show an unmistakable parallelism: *Umana cosa è – Convenevole cosa è*. But this comparison also demonstrates the loss of relevance of St. Paul's principle that already Panfilo's formulation reveals. Paul's categorical request in the wording of his novella becomes a pleasant, conventional custom: *convenevole cosa è*. On the other hand, it is the human thing, *umana cosa*, which gains normative force. Panfilo only apparently argues in favour of St. Paul's request to begin everything in the name of God. For the first time, we encounter a rhetorical device that is characteristic for the entire *Decameron*. Boccaccio frequently refers to dogmatic principles, the validity of which he seems to reaffirm. Yet on closer consideration this reaffirmation proves a hidden rejection. In this way the appeal to human solidarity within the *Proemio* stands in opposition to a beginning in the name of God.

Unavoidably, this substitution leads to the question if there is any connection between both positions. Does it make sense to replace the invocation of God by a claim for the *compassione degli afflitti*? At least a hint to an answer might be offered by the fact that Boccaccio even suggests something like a caring society of the mournful who have the obligation to support each other. Somehow he outlines the idea of humanity as a kind of insurance company, as a mutually-supportive group which provides protection against risks. And especially those who benefited from the help of others have the duty to support those who need help. Gratitude appears to be no longer a mutual obligation between single persons. Thankfulness, rather, becomes an obligation towards the society of mankind. But why does mankind need solidarity to such a high degree? An answer will be found in Boccaccio's description of his own personal case, as he presents himself as someone who more than anyone else is obliged to be grateful:

> Per ciò che, dalla mia prima giovinezza infino a questo tempo oltre modo essendo acceso stato d'altissimo e nobile amore, forse più assai che alla mia bassa condizione non parrebbe, narrandolo, si richiedesse, quantunque appo coloro che discreti erano e alla cui notizia pervenne io ne fossi lodato e da molto più reputato, nondimeno mi fu egli di grandissima fatica a sofferire, certo non per crudeltà della donna amata, ma per soverchio fuoco nella mente concetto da poco regolato appetito: il quale, per ciò che a niuno convenevole termine mi lasciava un tempo stare, più di noia che bisogno non m'era spesse volte sentir mi facea. Nella qual noia tanto rifrigerio già mi porsero i piacevoli ragionamenti d'alcuno amico le sue laudevoli consolazioni, che io porto fermissima opinione per quelle essere avvenuto che io non sia morto. (*Proemio* 3–4)

> [Seeing that from my early youth even to the present I was beyond measure aflame with a most aspiring and noble love more perhaps than, were I to enlarge upon it, would seem to accord with my lowly condition. Whereby, among people of discernment to whose knowledge it had come, I had much praise and high esteem, but nevertheless extreme discomfort and suffering, not indeed by reason of cruelty on the part of the beloved lady, but through superabundant ardour engendered in the soul by ill-bridled desire; the which, as it allowed me no reasonable period of quiescence, frequently occasioned me an inordinate distress. In which distress so much relief was afforded me by the delectable discourse of a friend and his commendable consolations, that I entertain a very solid conviction that to them I owe it that I am not dead.]

Telling stories as a strategy for survival: This might, at first sight, appear to be nothing else but a hyperbolic exaggeration, a quite dubious strategy of enhancing the value of poetic discourse. But the sentence immediately following in the text of the *Proemio* does not allow for any other interpretation of Boccaccio's assertion than taking it seriously as a theoretical concept:

> Ma sì come a Colui piacque il quale, essendo Egli infinito, diede per legge incommutabile a tutte le cose mondane aver fine, il mio amore, oltre a ogn'altro fervente e il quale niuna forza di proponimento o di consiglio o di vergogna evidente, o pericolo che seguir ne potesse, aveva potuto né rompere né piegare, per sè medesimo in processo di tempo si diminuì in guisa, che sol di sè nella mente m'ha al presente lasciato quel piacere che egli è usato di porgere a chi troppo non si mette né suoi più cupi pelaghi navigando; per che, dove faticoso esser solea, ogni affanno togliendo via, dilettevole il sento esser rimaso. (*Proemio* 5)

[But, as it pleased Him, who, being infinite, has assigned by immutable law an end to all things mundane, my love, beyond all other fervent, and neither to be broken nor bent by any force of determination, or counsel of prudence, or fear of manifest shame or ensuing danger, did nevertheless in course of time abate of its own accord, in such wise that it has now left nought of itself in my mind but that pleasure which it is wont to afford to him who does not adventure too far out in navigating its deep seas; so that, whereas it was used to be grievous, now, all discomfort being done away, I find that which remains to be delightful.]

In this description, erotic desire appears in all its force. It is, more than anything else, the powerlessness of reason, the loss of any rational control over love which causes the insuperable strength of the erotic affect. The specific character of this love follows, not least, from its end: In spite of its intensity, it unexpectedly ends without any discernable reason. The portrait of such a history of love, within the realm of 14th century Italian literature, has an easily definable model: It is the *Canzoniere* of Petrarch. Petrarch's lyric poetry serves as an example for Boccaccio's emotional autobiography. But, in telling his own past, Boccaccio not only refers to the work of his friend and rival Francesco Petrarca, he also refers to a specific theoretical discourse. The term *appetito, poco regolato appetito* serves as a key signalling the reference to scholastic psychology. Indeed, *appetitus* is the technical term used, for instance, by Thomas Aquinas to name the basic stimulus of all human behaviour.

The specific complex nature of man includes three different types of *appetitus*. The *appetitus naturalis* controls the vegetative part of human life. Man shares the *appetitus sensitivus* with all animals, whereas his *appetitus rationalis* or Will constitutes the privilege of the *animal rationale*. In scholastic theology, as well as in previous Christian thought, the categorical loss of control by reason over the *appetitus sensitivus* is the typical consequence of the original sin. As especially St. Augustine has argued, the insurmountable weakness of the Will is the most specific symptom of the nature of Fallen Mankind. Therefore, Boccaccio's description of his invincible incapacity to control his love could appear to be nothing else than a quite traditional description of his involvement in original sin. Yet, as we shall see, his self-portrait rather undermines the traditional concept of original sin. And, this subversion of the traditional dogma is due to the latent changes that the dogma itself has undergone in scholastic theology.

The major difference between the traditional Christian anthropology, mainly defined by St. Augustine, and Thomas Aquinas' concept of Man lies in the fact, that Thomas requires the necessity of God's grace for human action already under the conditions of the *status naturae*, whereas Augustine claims its necessity only for the Fallen World. This difference brings about an important change in the concept of *original sin*.

Thomas Aquinas' most detailed discussion of original sin is to be found in his *Quaestiones disputatae de malo*. Of central importance for his understanding of this concept was the notion of *iustitia originalis*. The very name of this concept reveals that it was conceived as a counterpart to *peccatum originale*:

> Est autem considerandum quod primo homini in sua institutione datum fuerat divinitus quoddam supernaturale donum, scilicet originalis iustitia, per quam ratio subdebatur Deo, et inferiores vires rationi, et corpus animae. Hoc autem donum non fuerat datum primo homini ut singulari personae tantum, sed ut cuidam principio totius humanae naturae, ut scilicet ab eo per originem derivaretur in posteros.[3]

> [Now we must observe that to man, at his creation, was given by God a certain supernatural gift, id est the original justice, by which reason is subdued to God, the inferior powers to reason and the body to the soul. This gift, however, was not given the first man as to a singular person, but as a kind of principle of human nature, in order to transmit it to his descendants.][4]

It is important to note that Thomas explicitly calls the *iustitia originalis* a supernatural gift: *supernaturale donum*. He also meticulously avoids the term 'creation' talking instead of *institutio*. This reluctance to use this term obviously is due to the fact that Man is given the *originalis iustitia* in addition to the human nature created by God. Thomas expressedly makes a distinction between the nature of Man and the *originalis iustitia* given in addition to his nature by God's generosity:

> Ad undecimum dicendum, quod originalis iustitia fuit superaddita primo homini ex liberalitate divina; sed quod huic animae non detur a Deo, non est ex parte eius, sed ex parte humanae naturae, in qua invenitur contrarium prohibens.[5]

> [The original justice was super-added to the nature of the first man by God's generosity: But, whatever is not given to this soul by God, does not belong to him, but to human nature, where some resistance can be found.]

In these sentences the *iustitia originalis* obviously does not belong to the *humana natura*. If God was obliged to give Man a supernatural gift in addition to his human nature, the reason for this donation is to be found in an undeniable defect of the *humana natura*:

---

[3] *Sancti Thomae de Aquino Opera Omnia Iussu Leonis XIII P.M. edita*. Tomus XXIII *Quaestiones disputates de malo*, Cura et studium fratrum predicatorum. Roma/ Paris: J. Vrin 1982. Ivi q. 4, art. 1, co. All Thomistic quotes are translated by the author.

[4] The present and all the following passages from the works of Thomas Aquinas have been translated by the author of this article.

[5] Ibid., q. 4, a. 1, ad 11.

> Creatura ergo rationalis in hoc praeeminet omni creaturae, quod capax est summi boni per divinam visionem et fruitionem, licet ad hoc consequendum naturae propriae principia non sufficiant, sed ad hoc indigeat auxilio divinae gratiae. Sed circa hoc considerandum est, quod [..] necessarium fuit homini aliud supernaturale auxilium, ratione suae compositionis. Est enim homo compositus ex anima et corpore, et ex natura intellectuali et sensibili; quae quodammodo si suae naturae relinquantur, intellectum aggravant et impediunt, ne libere ad summum fastigium contemplationis pervenire possit. Hoc autem auxilium fuit originalis iustitia, per quam mens hominis si subderetur Deo, ei subderentur totaliter inferiores vires et ipsum corpus, neque ratio impediretur quo minus posset in Deum tendere.[6]
>
> [The rational creature is superior to all other creatures inasmuch as it is capable of the vision and fruition of God, although his own forces are not sufficient and divine support is necessary. But we have to take into account that Man needed another supernatural support also because of his composite nature. For he is composed of body and soul, of an intellectual and a sensitive nature. If they are left to themselves they hinder the intellect so that we cannot reach without obstacles the perfection of contemplation. This support was the original justice by which human mind was made subordinate to God, and his inferior forces and his body were totally made subordinate to his mind, and his reason was no longer hindered to direct itself towards God.]

These lines are central for a correct understanding of the implicit transformation that the traditional dogma undergoes in Thomas Aquinas' theology of original sin. It is the complexity of human nature, the very fact of its being composed by different types of nature, a *natura vegetabilis*, a *natura sensitiva* and a *natura rationalis*, that makes necessary a *divine auxilium* to help reason impose its superiority over all other human forces. Without any supernatural help reason obviously lacks power. The perhaps most important consequence of this theological analysis lies in the fact that, this way, human nature itself becomes defective. Such basic inherent flaw of human nature is particularly important for the explanation of the consequences of original sin. For, in Thomas Aquinas' view, it is nothing else than a loss of the *iustitia originalis*. And, as a result of this loss, human nature is left to itself:

> Sed quia per peccatum primi parentis, ut infra dicetur, natura est sibi relicta, subtracto supernaturali dono quod homini divinitus erat collatum.[7]
>
> [But because human nature, by the sin of the first parents, is left to itself, as will be said later on, for the supernatural gift which had be given to man by God was taken away from him.]

If, as a result of original sin, human nature is left to itself, the status of Fallen Man still is a *status naturae*. It is in this very consequence, that the implicit, but highly

---

[6] Ibid., q. 5, a. 1, co.
[7] Thomas de Aquino: *Summa theologica*, traduzione e commento a cura dei Domenicani Italiani, testo dell'edizione Leonina. Bologna 1984. Here I–II, q. 17, a. 9, ad 3, p. 357.

momentous change of traditional concepts of moral theology becomes apparent. It is no longer possible to identify the nature of Fallen Man as a *status naturae lapsae*, as Augustine did. The most important change of traditional concepts of original sin in Thomas Aquinas' theology is constituted by a naturalisation of Fallen Man. Even under these conditions, the status of Man is natural, for human nature itself is defective. It only lacks the *supernaturale donum* that the Creator had generously given to Man in addition to his natural properties.

But why – this question seems to be unavoidable – does Thomas transform so decisively both the traditional concept of original sin and, at the same time, certain elementary features of a Christian anthropology? This question appears all the more necessary as it includes some essential threat to the very integrity of Christian dogma. But why does Thomas incur the risk of a, as will be seen, quite subversive change of traditional dogma? The answer to this question might be found in his scrupulous analysis of the cause of Man's Fall:

> Ad undecimum dicendum quod originalis iustitia fuit superaddita primo homini ex liberalitate divina. Set quod huic animae non detur a Deo, non est ex parte eius, sed ex parte humane nature, in qua invenitur contrarium prohibens.[8]

> [The original justice was super-added to the nature of the first man by God's generosity: But, whatever is not given to this soul by God, does not belong to him, but to human nature, where some resistance can be found.]

On closer consideration, these words prove remarkably hazardous, as they tend to hide the divine origin of man's nature (*humanae naturae*). However, according to Christian belief, Man's natural equipment, too, is, as well as any graceful gift to the creatures, necessarily due to the Creator himself: *Credo in unum Deum, Patrem omnipotentem, factorem caeli et terra, visibilium omnium et invisibilium* [I believe in one God, the Father Almighty, Maker of heaven and earth, of all things visible and invisible]: There is no exception to that principle. On the other hand, Thomas' tacit contradiction with one basic assumption of Christian dogma, according to which everything that exists originated from the Almighty, reveals all the more clearly the specific interest underlying Thomas' precarious argument. It looks as if, at any cost, he had to find a means to deny or, at the very least, to hide God's responsibility for Adam's sin, even at the prize of other incongruence. The rationalization of Christian dogma by scholastic philosophy, obviously, makes this problem a central issue: How could it happen that God's most noble creature on earth failed so substantially and so quickly? The traditional, mainly Augustinian answer, centred on the reprehensible action of a rebellious

---

8 Thomas de Aquino: *Quaestiones disputatae de malo*, q. 4, a. 1, ad 11.

creature in God's perfect Creation, does no longer suffice to guarantee the integrity of the omnipotent and omnibenevolent Creator. This is why Thomas attempts to identify an autonomous area of nature, given exclusively into the responsibility of Man, in order to get the chance to play off Adam's ingratitude for a gift full of grace against the deficiencies of his natural equipment. As helpful as that argument might appear, at first sight, it affects the very base of God's uniqueness and omnipotence. The solution it offers to the intricate problem it is intended to resolve, therefore, proves quite precarious. Accordingly, Thomas' transformation of the *status naturae lapsae* into the natural equipment of Man produces a number of quite remarkable consequences that will seriously menace the integrity of Christian belief. It is these side effects that come to light in the Italian literature of the 14th century as Boccaccio's *Decameron* can paradigmatically demonstrate.[9]

Scholastic theology itself seems to shrink from the consequences that can be drawn from this transformation of traditional dogma. On the contrary, Boccaccio's *Decameron* reflects the implications of this change in a very radical way. They become, paradigmatically, clear in his tacit rejection of the traditional explication for Man's death. As the Christian dogma unmistakably states, human mortality constitutes a punishment, it is punishment for Man's resistance to God's commandments in the Garden of Eden. But no trace of the traditional argument is to be found in the *Deameron*. We already mentioned the respective passage of its *Proemio*: "Ma sì come a Colui piacque il quale, essendo Egli infinito, diede per legge incommutabile a tutte le cose mondane aver fine." [But, as it pleased Him, who, being infinite, has assigned by immutable law an end to all things mundane] As he pleased: The finitude of human life and all earthly things seems to be not more than a caprice of the Creator who, being himself infinite, liked his creatures to be finite. The Creator's whim demonstrates, at the same time, his immense power. The difference between infinity and mortality establishes God's unconditioned superiority. No longer punishment for sin has to motivate Man's death, but his mortality is part of the very order of creation. But not only the traditional explanation of Man's mortality is put into doubt. Boccaccio's description of the Creator also puts into question any possibility of salvation. If Boccaccio states that God decided that finitude should be the *legge incommutabile*, the invariable law of man, one might ask, if this invariability does not exclude, from the very beginning, all salvation and guarantee of eternal life.

---

[9] The consequences of this change, though in a different way, appear as well in Petrarch's *Canzoniere*. Cf. Andreas Kablitz: Petrarch and the Senses. Petrarch's Anthropology of Love and the Scholastic Transformation of Christian Ethics; which will be printed in: Gaia Gubbini (ed.): *Body and Spirit in the Middle Ages: Literature, Philosphy, Medicine*. Berlin/New York: Walter De Gruyter 2017.

Reason's loss of control over emotions, over the *appetitus sensitivus*, was the most significant symptom of the *status naturae lapsae* of Fallen Man. In Boccaccio's world, where the weakness of Will is no longer a pure consequence of original sin, but a natural part of *conditio humana*, the loss of rational control constitutes no longer only a threat of eternal punishment, it is a danger for physical life. In this world human society has to become a caring society where everyone has the obligation to support everyone, because everybody might become dependent on somebody else's help. Therefore Man, and no longer God, becomes the source of moral duty: "Umana cosa è aver compassione degli afflitti." ['Tis humane to have compassion on the afflicted] The idea of mankind as a sort of insurance company that requires mutual protection, as the guarantee of a graceful God who takes care of his creatures is lost.

It is under these conditions that the life saving function of telling stories gains its plausibility. Because Boccaccio was unable to control his fervent love he was about to die if *piacevoli ragionamenti*, if pleasant stories had not kept him alive. In this argument the very nucleus of Boccaccio's poetics becomes clear. Literature replaces reason. Reason's incapacity to overcome emotion requires a substitution. And this substitution is delivered in form of stories, of *piacevoli ragionamenti*. Literature becomes a guarantee for survival in a world where the weakness of Man's reason is an integral part of his nature. Of course, a decisive difference persists between the performance of reason and the function of literature. Reason was able to *control* the emotion, its duty was to dominate the *appetitus sensitivus*. On the contrary, literature is unable to gain such control over emotions. Literature is no more than a diversion. But this diversion, nonetheless, allows for survival.

If literature is substantially diversion, Boccaccio's preference for a female audience is more than conclusive.

> E quantunque il mio sostentamento, o conforto che vogliam dire, possa essere e sia à bisognosi assai poco, nondimeno parmi quello doversi più tosto porgere dove il bisogno apparisce maggiore, sì perché più utilità vi farà e si ancora perché più vi fia caro avuto. E chi negherà questo, quantunque egli si sia, non molto più alle vaghe donne che agli uomini convenirsi donare? Esse dentro à dilicati petti, temendo e vergognando, tengono l'amorose fiamme nascose, le quali quanto più di forza abbian che le palesi coloro il sanno che l'hanno provate: e oltre a ciò, ristrette dà voleri, dà piaceri, dà comandamenti de' padri, delle madri, de' fratelli e de' mariti, il più del tempo nel piccolo circuito delle loro camere racchiuse dimorano e quasi oziose sedendosi, volendo e non volendo in una medesima ora, seco rivolgendo diversi pensieri, li quali non è possibile che sempre sieno allegri. E se per quegli alcuna malinconia, mossa da focoso disio, sopravviene nelle lor menti, in quelle conviene che con grave noia si dimori, se da nuovi ragionamenti non è rimossa: senza che elle sono molto men forti che gli uomini a sostenere; il che degli innamorati uomini non avviene, sì come noi possiamo apertamente vedere. (*Proemio*, 8–11)

[And though my support or comfort, so to say, may be of little avail to the needy, nevertheless it seems to me meet to offer it most readily where the need is most apparent, because it will there be most serviceable and also most kindly received. Who will deny, that it should be given, for all that it may be worth, to gentle ladies much rather than to men? Within their soft bosoms, betwixt fear and shame, they harbour secret fires of love, and how much of strength concealment adds to those fires, they know who have proved it. Moreover, restrained by the will, the caprice, the commandment of fathers, mothers, brothers, and husbands, confined most part of their time within the narrow compass of their chambers, they live, so to say, a life of vacant ease, and, yearning and renouncing in the same moment, meditate divers matters which cannot all be cheerful. If thereby a melancholy bred of amorous desire make entrance into their minds, it is like to tarry there to their sore distress, unless it be dispelled by a change of ideas. Besides which they have much less power to support such a weight than men. For, when men are enamoured, their case is very different, as we may readily perceive.]

On the contrary, men seem have more or less infinite opportunities of diversion at their disposal:

Essi, se alcuna malinconia o gravezza di pensieri gli affligge, hanno molti modi da alleggiare o da passar quello, per ciò che a loro, volendo essi, non manca l'andare a torno, udire e veder molte cose, uccellare, cacciare, pescare, cavalcare, giucare o mercatare: de' quali modi ciascuno ha forza di trarre, o in tutto o in parte, l'animo a sé e dal noioso pensiero rimuoverlo almeno per alcuno spazio di tempo, appresso il quale, con un modo o con un altro, o consolazion sopraviene o diventa la noia minore. (*Proemio*, 12)

[They, if they are afflicted by a melancholy and heaviness of mood, have many ways of relief and diversion; they may go where they will, may hear and see many things, may hawk, hunt, fish, ride, play or traffic. By which means all are able to compose their minds, either in whole or in part, and repair the ravage wrought by the dumpish mood, at least for some space of time; and shortly after, by one way or another, either solace ensues, or the dumps become less grievous.]

From a modern point of view, it might appear quite astonishing, that *mercatare*, that commerce can have the same function as literature. But their functional equality mirrors a remarkably different concept of art. There is no sharp distinction, no substantial difference between art and pragmatic life, between *Ernst* and *Spiel*, to quote Friedrich Schiller.[10] Boccaccio's *Decameron* is not, as frequently claimed, one of the many origins of modern aesthetics that have been identified more or less everywhere. Its aesthetical concept remains, obviously, that of an undeniably premodern area. There is no claim for any basic autonomy of art. However, considered in its *longue durée* consequences, the changes that the

---

10 See Friedrich Schiller: *Über die ästhetische Erziehung des Menschen in einer Reihe von Briefen.* Edited by Klaus L. Berghahn. Stuttgart: Reclam 2008.

traditional dogma undergoes in Thomas Aquinas' rationalisation of Christian dogma will, ultimately, bring about a conception of art where literature is no longer mimesis or remedy, but the construction of an alternative world imagined by nobody else than man himself.

The lack of diversion in a world where life is always life-threatening makes a female audience Boccaccio's favourite addressee of the *Decameron*. In this sense, his poetics presents the author as solicitous about women and their natural destiny. But not only women are beneficiaries of his care, he himself is too. Two reasons have to motivate Boccaccio's preference for a female audience. Women are more in need of diversion and women know to appreciate his work much more: "sí perché piú utilità vi farà e si ancora perché piú vi fia caro avuto" [because it will there be most serviceable and also most kindly received] (§ 8). As far as the first argument is concerned, the women will be the beneficiaries, as far as the second argument is concerned, Boccaccio himself will be. His *Decameron* also proves a quest for women's favour.

Taking a closer look at one of the passages we have already read, we even are able to discover more precisely the kind of favour Boccaccio is looking for: "Esse dentro à dilicati petti, temendo e vergognando, tengono l'amorose fiamme nascose" [Within their soft bosoms, betwixt fear and shame, they harbour secret fires of love] (§ 10). The *dilicati petti* are primarily in this context a metonymy for the women's emotional sensibility. But, at the same time, this formulation refers to a quite corporal phenomenon, to their tempting breast. Boccaccio's quest for women's favour, for literary prestige, is as well a quest for erotic generosity.

From here it becomes clear, why his depressing depiction of his life-threatening erotic desire, nonetheless, paradoxically left a quite pleasant memory: "[...] nella mente m'ha al presente lasciato quel piacere che egli è usato di porgere a chi troppo non si mette né suoi più cupi pelaghi navigando; per che, dove faticoso esser solea, ogni affanno togliendo via, dilettevole il sento esser rimaso." [it has now left nought of itself in my mind but that pleasure which it is wont to afford to him who does not adventure too far out in navigating its deep seas; so that, whereas it was used to be grievous, now, all discomfort being done away, I find that which remains to be delightful] (§ 5). Though love might become a threat to live as reason proves incapable of controlling its excesses, erotic affect remains, nonetheless, a source of potential pleasure. From here, it also becomes clear why the title of the *Decameron*, at first sight, has a thoroughly confusing subtitle:

> Comincia il libro chiamato Decameron cognominato prencipe Galeotto, nel quale si contengono cento novelle in diece dí dette da sette donne e da tre giovani uomini. (*Proemio*, 1)

> Beginneth here the book called Decameron, otherwise Prince Galeotto, wherein are contained one hundred novels told in ten days by seven ladies and three young men.

Who is *Prencipe Galeotto* and why does the book bear his name? The decisive name is to be found in the commentary of Branca's edition.[11] He points to verse 137 of the fifth canto of Dante's *Inferno*. "Galeotto fu'l libro e chi lo scrisse." [A Galeotto was the book and he that wrote it][12] This verse refers to the story of Paolo and Francesca, who, seduced by the novel of Lancelot, abandon themselves to their erotic desire. Galeotto is the matchmaker between Lancilotto and Ginevra, and for Paolo and Francesco he is replaced by the novel that tells the story of these lovers. Therefore, the *Decameron* as well claims for matchmaking.

This, also, is a consequence of the scholastic naturalisation of Fallen Man. In his world, in a world where human nature is left to itself, the *appetitus sensitivus*, although uncontrolled by reason, becomes a natural desire beyond moral restrictions. And if, nonetheless, the same desire has a dangerous potential, his destructive effects no longer follow from the original sin, but form the original defect of Man's natural equipment.

The *Proemio* of Boccacio's *Decameron* investigates into the deep ambivalence of erotic desire whose ambiguity will, to a large extent, characterize its hundred stories. Because the *appetitus sensitivus* is no longer controlled by reason, it has a destructive potential that may become life-threatening. But erotic desire, at the same time, gains the status of a natural drive, for the lack of rational control is part of human nature. And despite its potentially destructive effects, as a natural drive, erotic desire also constitutes a pleasant drive. The poetics of the *Decameron*, which is outlined in its *Proemio*, programmatically mediates between both aspects of the *appetitus sensitivus*. On the one hand, it is a remedy against its dangerous potential by means of diversion. But, on the other hand, the *Decameron* serves as a means of satisfaction of erotic desire. The text presents itself, contemporarily, as a potential contribution to the struggle for surviving in a life-threating nature, as well as an instrument of gaining success in the perpetual quest of female favour.

Boccaccio has been considered to be an apostle of hedonism, preaching in his *Decameron* the gospel of sensual pleasure. But the same Boccaccio, in his *novelle*, appears as well as a narrator of deeply melancholic stories that uncompromisingly depict the great misery of Man. As our analysis of the *Proemio* has demonstrated, both aspects of human life are interdependent in his anthropology. And, Boccaccio's insight into their interdependence is due to the conclusions

---

11 Boccaccio: *Decameron*, p. 3.
12 Dante Alighieri: *La Divina Commedia. Inferno*. Edited by Maria Chiavacci Leonardi. Milano: Mondadori 1991. Here *Inf.* V, 137 (p. 165). Translation in: Dante Alighieri: *Purgatorio*. A Verse Translation by Jean Hollander and Robert Hollander. Introduction and Notes by Robert Hollander. New York: Anchor Books 2002, ad loc.

he draws from the tacit implications of scholastic theology, of Thomas Aquinas' reinterpretation of original sin.

The naturalisation of the status of Fallen Man involves the naturalness of the highly destructive potential of his emotions, of his *appetitus sensitivus*, as well as it implies the naturalness of sensual pleasure. It is this fundamental ambivalence of human life, which determines the basic characteristics of Boccaccio's poetics. If the poetics of the *Decameron* defines literature as a substitute for rational control of life-threatening emotions, it describes it as well as a means of satisfaction of sensual desires. The secret dialogue of the *Decameron* with scholastic philosophy and theology does not only reveal the highly explosive implications of Thomas Aquinas' reinterpretation of traditional Christian dogma, it also brings about a concept of literature which responds to this redefinition of human nature.

Bibliography

Primary Literature

Alighieri, Dante: *La Divina Commedia. Inferno*. Edited by Maria Chiavacci Leonardi. Milano: Mondadori 1991.
Alighieri, Dante: *Inferno*. A Verse Translation by Jean Hollander and Robert Hollander. Introduction and Notes by Robert Hollander. New York: Anchor Books 2002.
Boccaccio, Giovanni: *The Decameron of Giovanni Boccaccio Faithfully Translated by James M. Rigg*. 2 vols. London: The Navarre Society 1932.
Boccaccio, Giovanni: *Decameron*. Edited by Vittore Branca. Turin: Einaudi 1980.
Sancti Thomae de Aquino Opera Omnia Iussu Leonis XIII P.M. edita. Tomus XXIII *Quaestiones disputates de malo, Cura et studium fratrum predicatorum*. Roma/ Paris: J. Vrin 1982.
Schiller, Friedrich: *Über die ästhetische Erziehung des Menschen in einer Reihe von Briefen*. Edited by Klaus L. Berghahn. Stuttgart: Reclam 2008.

Secondary Literature

Monographs and Anthologies

Branca, Vittore: *Boccaccio medievale*. Firenze: Sansoni 1956.
Kablitz, Andreas/Ulrich Schulz-Buschhaus (eds.): *Literarhistorische Begegnungen. Festschrift zum 60. Geburtstag von Bernhard König*. Tübingen: Narr 1993.
Neuschäfer, Hans-Jörg: *Boccaccio und der Beginn der Novelle: Strukturen der Kurzerzählung auf der Schwelle zwischen Mittelalter und Neuzeit*. München: Wilhelm Fink 1969 (Theorie und Geschichte der Literatur und der schönen Künste, 8).

Articles and Papers

Kablitz, Andreas: Petrarch and the Senses. Petrarch's Anthropology of Love and the Scholastic Transformation of Christian Ethics. In: Gaia Gubbini (ed.): *Body and Spirit in the Middle Ages: Literature, Philosphy, Medicine*. Berlin/New York: Walter De Gruyter 2017.

Küpper, Joachim: Affichierte Exemplarität, tatsächliche A-Systematik. Boccaccios *Decameron* und die Episteme der Renaissance. In: Klaus W. Hempfer (ed.): *Renaissance. Diskursstrukturen und epistemologische Voraussetzungen. Literatur-Philosophie-Bildende Kunst*. Stuttgart: Steiner 1993 (Text und Kontext, 10), p. 47–93.

Francesco Ciabattoni
Boccaccio's Novel Hecuba: Beritola between Ovid and Dante

Giuseppe Velli's 1991 essay on the presence of Seneca in the *Decameron* broke ground that was later profitably trodden by several scholars who wished to emphasize the humanistic component of Boccaccio's writing. In recent years, the identifications of Boccaccio's autograph copies of texts by Martial, Ovid, Paul the Deacon and Apuleius have confirmed the Certaldese's openness to classical authors. Indeed, paleographical research carried out by Maurizio Fiorilla, Marco Cursi, Marco Petoletti, Laura Pani, Igor Candido and others have shown clearly that the *Decameron* cannot be correctly understood outside of a framework of intertextual relationships with the classical tradition.

Velli's study on the form and function of the reminiscence of classical texts in the *Decameron* helps us realize that Boccaccio's invention and writing is not a self-sufficient fact. Instead, it lives in relation or tension with the "other"; that is, the writer's mental library, his classical memory.[1] For example, Velli showed that the following introductory speech of Pampinea to her tale of Cisti the baker has its origin in Seneca's *Moral Letters to Lucilius*, whose n. 44 begins with the dyad nature / fortune employed by the senior woman of the *brigata*.[2]

> Belle donne, io non so da me medesima vedere che piú in questo si pecchi, o la natura apparecchiando a una nobile anima un vil corpo, o la fortuna apparecchiando a un corpo dotato d'anima nobile vil mestiero, sí come in Cisti nostro cittadino e in molti ancora abbiamo potuto vedere avvenire; il qual Cisti, d'altissimo animo fornito, la fortuna fece fornaio. E certo io maladicerei e la natura parimente e la fortuna, se io non conoscessi la natura esser discretissima e la fortuna aver mille occhi, come che gli sciocchi lei cieca figurino. Le quali

---

[1] "L'invenzione, la scrittura del Decameron [...] non è fatto autosufficiente: vive, per contro, nella relazione o tensione con altro: quell'"altro' che è la biblioteca mentale dello scrittore, la sua memoria culta." Cf. Giuseppe Velli: Memoria. In: Renzo Bragantini/Pier Massimo Forni (eds.): *Lessico critico decameroniano*. Torino: Bollati Boringhieri 1995, p. 224. See also Velli's *Petrarca e Boccaccio: Tradizione, memoria, scrittura*. Padova: Antenore 1979 (Studi petrarcheschi, 7).

[2] Panfilo will reconnect to this theme in his tale for Day Six: "Carissime donne, egli avviene spesso che, sí come la *fortuna* sotto vili arti alcuna volta grandissimi tesori di vertú nasconde, come poco avanti per Pampinea fu mostrato, cosí ancora sotto turpissime forme d'uomini si truovano maravigliosi ingegni dalla natura essere stati riposti." (*Dec.* II 5, § 3) [Dearest ladies, if Fortune, as Pampinea has shewn us, does sometimes hide treasures most rich of native worth in the obscurity of base occupations, so in like manner 'tis not seldom found that Nature has enshrined prodigies of wit in the most ignoble of human forms]. Trans. J.M. Rigg (*The Decameron of Giovanni Boccaccio*. Edited by J. M. Rigg with an introduction. 2 vols, London: A. H. Bullen 1903).

io avviso che, sí come molto avvedute, fanno quello che i mortali spesse volte fanno, li quali, incerti de' futuri casi, per le loro oportunità le loro piú care cose ne' piú vili luoghi delle lor case, sí come meno sospetti, sepelliscono, e quindi ne' maggior bisogni le traggono, avendole il vil luogo piú sicuramente servate che la bella camera non avrebbe. E cosí le due ministre del mondo spesso le lor cose piú care nascondono sotto l'ombra dell'arti reputate piú vili, acciò che di quelle alle necessità traendole piú chiaro appaia il loro splendore. Il che quanto in poca cosa Cisti fornaio il dichiarasse, gli occhi dello 'ntelletto rimettendo a messer Geri Spina, il quale la novella di madonna Oretta contata, che sua moglie fu, m'ha tornata nella memoria, mi piace in una novelletta assai piccola dimostrarvi. (*Dec.* VI 2, §§ 3–7)

[Fair ladies, I cannot myself determine whether Nature or Fortune be the more at fault, the one in furnishing a noble soul with a vile body, or the other in allotting a base occupation to a body endowed with a noble soul, whereof we may have seen an example, among others, in our fellow-citizen, Cisti; whom, furnished though he was with a most lofty soul, Fortune made a baker. And verily I should curse Nature and Fortune alike, did I not know that Nature is most discreet, and that Fortune, albeit the foolish imagine her blind, has a thousand eyes. For'tis, I suppose, that, being wise above a little, they do as mortals ofttimes do, who, being uncertain as to their future, provide against contingencies by burying their most precious treasures in the basest places in their houses, as being the least likely to be suspected; whence, in the hour of their greatest need, they bring them forth, the base place having kept them more safe than the dainty chamber would have done. And so these two arbitresses of the world not seldom hide their most precious commodities in the obscurity of the crafts that are reputed most base, that thence being brought to light they may shine with a brighter splendour. Whereof how in a trifling matter Cisti, the baker, gave proof, restoring the eyes of the mind to Messer Geri Spina, whom the story of his wife, Madonna Oretta, has brought to my recollection, I am minded to shew you in a narrative which shall be of the briefest.]

While Boccaccio had copied fragments of *Letters to Lucilius* in the Zibaldone Magliabechiano, under the rubric "De nobilitate generis,"[3] the following incipit of Seneca's letter 44, that most directly resonates with Pampinea's words, is not among the Senecan sections that Boccaccio copied into the Zibaldone:

Iterum tu mihi te pusillum facis et dicis malignius tecum egisse naturam prius, deinde fortunam, cum possis eximere te vulgo et ad felicitatem hominum maximam emergere.[4]

[You are again insisting to me that you are a nobody and saying that nature in the first place, and fortune in the second, have treated you too scurvily, and this in spite of the fact that you have it in your power to separate yourself from the crowd and rise to the highest human happiness!]

---

3 Cf. Velli: Seneca, p. 325.
4 Lucius Annaeus Seneca: *Ad Lucilium epistulae morales*. With an English Translation by Richard Gummere. 3 vols. New York: Putnam 1917–1925 (Loeb Classical Library, 75–77), I, p. 286.

One excellent example of how the memory of the classics combines with the author's invention is Panfilo's introduction to his tale of Alatiel, which incorporates themes from Juvenal's *Satire* IV x (of which it constitutes a thematic summary, or *abbreviatio*). Such themes include excessive beauty that leads to perdition, wealth attracting thieves and the unreasonable prayers that men address to the gods, which are then fulfilled to the ruin of those who had uttered them. Velli shows Panfilo's textual debts to Juvenal, including a reflection on Fortune:[5]

> Malagevolmente, piacevoli donne, si può da noi conoscer quello che per noi si faccia, per ciò che, sí come assai volte s'è potuto vedere, molti estimando se essi ricchi divinissero senza sollecitudine e sicuri poter vivere, quello non solamente con prieghi a Dio adomandarono ma sollecitamente, non recusando alcuna fatica o pericolo, d'acquistarle cercarono; e, come che loro venisse fatto, trovarono chi per vaghezza di cosí ampia eredità gli uccise, li quali, avanti che arrichiti fossero, amavan la vita loro. Altri di basso stato per mille pericolose battaglie, per mezzo il sangue de' fratelli e degli amici loro saliti all'altezza de' regni, in quegli somma felicità esser credendo, senza le infinite sollecitudini e paure di che piena la videro e sentirono, cognobbero, non senza la morte loro, che nell'oro alle mense reali si beveva il veleno. Molti furono che la forza corporale e la bellezza e certi gli ornamenti con appetito ardentissimo disiderarono, né prima d'aver mal disiderato s'avidero, che essi quelle cose loro di morte essere o di dolorosa vita cagione. E acciò che io partitamente di tutti gli umani disiderii non parli, affermo niuno poterne essere con pieno avvedimento, sí come sicuro da fortunosi casi, che da' viventi si possa eleggere: per che, se dirittamente operar volessimo, a *quello prendere e possedere ci dovremmo disporre che Colui ci donasse, il quale solo ciò che ci fa bisogno conosce e puolci dare.* (*Dec.* II 7, §§ 3–6)

(Hardly, gracious ladies, is it given to us to know that which makes for our good; insomuch that, as has been observable in a multitude of instances, many, deeming that the acquisition of great riches would ensure them an easy and tranquil existence, have not only besought them of God in prayer, but have sought them with such ardour that they have spared no pains and shrunk from no danger in the quest, and have attained their end only to lose, at the hands of some one covetous of their vast inheritance, a life with which before the days of their prosperity they were well content. Others, whose course, perilous with a thousand battles, stained with the blood of their brothers and their friends, has raised them from base to regal estate, have found in place of the felicity they expected an infinity of cares and fears, and have proved by experience that a chalice may be poisoned, though it be of gold, and set on the table of a king. Many have most ardently desired beauty and strength and other advantages of person, and have only been taught their error by the death or dolorous life which these very advantages entailed upon them. And so, not to instance each particular human desire, I say, in sum, that there is none of them that men may indulge in full confidence as exempt from the chances and changes of fortune; wherefore, if we would act rightly, we ought to school ourselves to take and *be content with that which He gives us, who alone knows and can afford us that of which we have need.*)

---

5 Cf. Velli: Memoria, p. 246.

This long preamble expounds, *per abbreviationem*, Juvenal's themes in the tenth satire of the fourth book, with a final emphasis on "fortunosi casi" and the necessity of being content with whatever God sends our way. Such an invitation to prudence ensures continuity with the discourse of Fortune initiated by Filomena in Day 2. Panfilo's encouragement to seize the opportunities sent by God is textually linked to Juvenal: "Permittes ipsis expendere numinibus *quid / conveniat nobis rebusque sit utile nostris; / nam pro iucundis aptissima quaeque dabunt di*" (*Sat.* IV x 347–349) [Entrust thy fortune to the Powers above; / *Leave them to manage for thee, and to grant / What their unerring wisdom sees thee want*, my emphasis.] A collection of Juvenal's satires is found in the ms. Laurenziano 34.39, identified as the item in banco II, liber sextus, which Antonia Mazza includes among those certainly belonging to Giovanni Boccaccio.[6]

When we see through Boccaccio's intertextual fabric, we discover that Panfilo's connection between God and an unreliable Fortune filters from Juvenal's satire. But Boccaccio's selection and re-elaboration of previous texts is not limited to the classics of Latin verse and prose. For example, Andreuccio's descent into the well as he tries to wash his filth away is vaguely reminiscent of the fourth branch of the fabliau *Le Roman de Renart*, in which Renart the fox tricks Ysengrin the wolf into jumping into a well.[7] Renart, who had foolishly fallen in, promises Ysengrin that he will gain heaven and beatitude by sitting in the bucket (a ploy that *Dec.* III 4 also reminisces in Frate Puccio's naïveté). Renart is thus pulled up as the gullible Ysengrin falls into the pit to his disillusion. The first branch of *Le Roman de Renart* also contains an episode titled "Le siège de Malpertuis," in which we unequivocally hear an anticipation of Andreuccio's misadventurous night in Malpertugio, Naples.[8]

---

[6] See Antonia Mazza: L'inventario della 'Parva libraria' di Santo Spirito e la biblioteca del Boccaccio. In: *Italia medioevale e umanistica* 9 (1966), p. 20–21 and 62. It was Oskar Hecker who identified the Laur. 34.39 as the item described in *banco II liber sextus* of the catalogue of the Santo Spirito library. Cf. Oskar Hecker: *Boccaccio-Funde. Stücke aus der bislang verschollenen Bibliothek des Dichters darunter von seiner Handgeschriebenes Fremdes und Eigenes*. Braunschweig: G. Westermann 1902, p. 30.

[7] The early fourteenth-century manuscript BNF, Paris Ms fr.12584, contains an illumination of a wolf being tugged out of a well by an ass on fol. 42r. The entire codex has been scanned and is available at: http://gallica.bnf.fr/ark:/12148/btv1b60004625/f89.image. See Luciano Rossi: L'evoluzione dell'intreccio: Boivin e Andreuccio. In: *Filologia e critica* 1 (1976), p. 5–14. See also Philippe Ménard: Les sources françaises d'un conte de Boccace: *Decameron* IX, 6. In: Simonetta Mazzoni Peruzzi (ed.): *Boccaccio e le letterature romanze tra Medioevo e Rinascimento*. Atti del convegno internazionale Boccaccio e la Francia. Firenze: Alinea 2006, p. 113–134.

[8] In a footnote at the beginning of II 5 Branca also indicates Xenophon of Ephesus's *Antheia and Habrocome* (book III 8) as a source for Andreuccio's theft of the bishop's ring from the tomb. See Giovanni Boccaccio: *Decameron*. 2 vols. Edited by Vittore Branca. Torino: Einaudi 1992, I, p. 176.

Thus, when we look at the watermark of Boccaccio's readings in Day Two, we find two subtexts that deserve special consideration. Tales II 5 and II 6 reveal a series of connections, respectively, to Apuleius's *Metamorphoses* books II and III and Ovid's story of Hecuba (*Metamorphoses* XIII) in part filtered via Dante, *Inferno* XXX.

Boccaccio's relations to Apuleius have been widely investigated, most recently by Igor Candido, especially in reference to three manuscripts in particular.[9] These are the heavily annotated Laurenziano Pluteus 29.2 (also referred to as φ, first half of the thirteenth century, containing Apuleius's *Metamorphoses* and marginal notes and signs now attributed to Zanobi da Strada); Laurenziano 54.32 (Boccaccio's holograph copy of Apuleius's *Metamorphoses*); and Laurenziano 68.2 (containing portions of Apuleius's *Metamorphoses*, plus portions of Tacitus's *Annales* and *Historiae*).[10] Indeed, even the less postillated sections of the Apuleian text may have significantly inspired entire novellas of the *Decameron*.[11] My contrastive reading of the intertextual layers in *Dec.* II 5 and II 6 will also reveal Boccaccio's strategic play with his audience's literary memory. If for Boccaccio's connection with Apuleius we can avail ourselves of a number of surviving manuscripts copied by or belonging to the author of the *Decameron*, the manuscript of

---

9 Igor Candido: *Boccaccio umanista*. Ravenna: Longo 2014, especially p. 21.
10 The matter of attributing the *marginalia* in φ is a thorny one. Billanovich attributed all notes in φ to Zanobi, ruling out Boccaccio, while Emanuele Casamassima restituted some of them to the Certaldese. See Giuseppe Billanovich: Zanobi da Strada tra i tesori di Montecassino. In: *Atti dell'Accademia Nazionale dei Lincei. Rendiconti. Classe di scienze morali, storiche e filologiche* 7 (1996), p. 655; Emanuele Casamassima: Dentro lo scrittoio del Boccaccio: i codici della tradizione. In: Aldo Rossi (ed.): *Il "Decameron": pratiche testuali e interpretative*. Bologna: Cappelli 1982, p. 253–260. That Boccaccio and Zanobi attended the same schools, received the same instruction, and thus learned the same graphic style and sign system further complicates the matter. Most recently Maurizio Fiorilla and Marco Cursi have convincingly argued that most of the annotations are by the hand of Zanobi. Fiorilla, however, reminds us that even if all the marginal notes were by Zanobi, they would still have brought Boccaccio's attention to those *loci* of Apuleius's text: "Va sottolineato però che il confronto filologico tra le postille di φ e le opere del Boccaccio conserva il suo valore anche in caso di annotazioni apposte da Zanobi da Strada, che agiva nel suo stesso ambiente, o da altri lettori. Postille già presenti nel manoscritto potrebbero infatti aver attirato l'attenzione del Certaldese, soprattutto se si pensa alla capacità che avevano le glosse di portare l'occhio su una particolare zona testuale." Maurizio Fiorilla: La lettura apuleiana del Boccaccio e le note ai manoscritti laurenziani 29, 2 e 54, 32. In: *Aevum* 73, 3 (1999), p. 637.
11 I follow Luciano Rossi: I tre gravi accidenti della novella di Andreuccio da Perugia (*Decameron* II 5). In: *Strumenti Critici* 20 (1996), p. 385–400. See also Marylin Migiel: *A Rhetoric of the Decameron*. Toronto: University of Toronto Press 2003, p. 46–51.

Ovid's *Metamorphoses* once in the *Parva libraria* has been lost, but the book was of course among Boccaccio's favorites.[12]

If we compare the scene from the second book of the *Metamorphoses*, in which Lucius ambulates aimlessly in Hypata, Thessaly – a city he is a stranger to and for which he feels a mix of fear and fascination – with Andreuccio's gallivanting in the market of Naples we will find some similarities:

> Sic attonitus, immo vero cruciabili desiderio stupidus, nullo quidem initio vel omnino vestigio cupidinis meae reperto cuncta circumibam tamen. *Dum in luxum nepotalem similis ostiatim singula pererro, repente me nescius forum cupidinis intuli, et ecce mulierem quampiam frequenti stipatam famulitione ibidem gradientem adcelerato vestigio comprehendo; aurum in gemmis et in tunicis, ibi inflexum, hic intextum, matronam profecto confitebatur.* Huius adhaerebat lateri senex iam gravis in annis, qui ut primum me conspexit: "Est," inquit "hercules, est Lucius," et offert osculum et statim incertum quidnam in aurem mulieris obganniit; "*Quin*" *inquit* "*etiam ipse parentem tuam accedis et salutas?*" "Vereor" inquam "*ignotae mihi feminae*" et statim rubore suffusus deiecto capite restiti. At illa optutum in me conversa: "En" inquit "sanctissimae Salvae matris generosa probitas, sed et cetera corporis exsecrabiliter ad [regulam qua diligenter aliquid adfingunt] sim congruentia: inenormis proceritas, suculenta gracilitas, rubor temperatus, flavum et inadfectatum capillitium, oculi caesii quidem, sed vigiles et in aspectu micantes, prorsus aquilini, os quoquoversum floridum, speciosus et immeditatus incessus." Et adiecit: "*Ego te, o Luci, meis istis manibus educavi, quidni? parentis tuae non modo sanguinis, verum alimoniarum etiam socia.* Nam et familia Plutarchi ambae prognatae sumus et eandem nutricem simul bibimus et in nexu germanitatis una coalvimus. Nec aliud nos quam dignitas discernit, quod illa clarissimas ego privatas nuptias fecerimus. Ego sum Byrrhena illa, cuius forte saepicule nomen inter tuos educatores frequentatum retines. *Accede itaque hospitium fiducia, immo vero iam tuum proprium larem.*" (Apuleius: *Metamorphoses* II 2–3)

> [Thus being astonished or rather dismayed and vexed with desire, knowing no certaine place whither I intended to go, *I went from street to street, and at length (as I curiously gazed on every thing) I fortuned unwares to come into the market place, whereas I espied a certaine woman, accompanied with a great many servants, towards whom I drew nigh, and viewed her garments beset with gold and pretious stone, in such sort that she seemed to be some noble matron.* And there was an old man which followed her, who as soon as he espied me, said to himself, Verily this is Lucius, and then he came and embraced me, by and by he went unto his mistresse and whispered in her eare, and came to mee againe saying, *How is it Lucius that you will not salute your deere Cousin and singular friend?* To whom I answered, Sir I dare not be so bold as to take acquaintance of an unknown woman. Howbeit as halfe ashamed I drew towards her, and shee turned her selfe and sayd, Behold how he resembleth the very same grace as his mother Salvia doth, behold his countenance and stature, agreeing thereto in each poynt, behold his comely state, his fine slendernesse, his Vermilion colour, his haire yellow by nature, his gray and quicke eye, like to the Eagle, and his trim and comely gate, which do sufficiently prove him to be the naturall childe of Salvia. And moreover she sayd,

---

[12] See Antonia Mazza: L'inventario della 'Parva libraria', p. 54. The volume is classified as "item in eodem banco settimo liber undecimus."

> O Lucius, I have nourished thee with myne owne proper hand: and why not? For I am not onely of kindred to thy mother by blood, but also by nourice, for wee both descended of the line of Plutarch, lay in one belly, sucked the same paps, and were brought up together in one house. And further there is no other difference betweene us two, but that she is married more honourably than I: I am the same Byrrhena whom you have often heard named among your friends at home: wherfore I pray you to take so much pains as to *come with me to my house, and use it as your owne*. (My emphasis)]

This connection was first noted by Luciano Rossi and Jonathan Usher:[13] Lucius, who hangs around "in luxum nepotalem" and randomly ends up in the market, sets the scene for Andreuccio, who boasts of his bag of florins in the market square, thus raising young Fiordaliso's fraudulent interest. Lucius too is approached by a beautiful and elegant woman, who claims to be like a second mother to him, although Lucius does not recognize her. Byrrhena invites Lucius for dinner, just as Fiordaliso does with Andreuccio, but Byrrhena does not want to deceive her guest. In fact she tries to warn him against the guiles of Milo's wife, a woman versed in the magical arts, whose name "Pamphiles" resonates with the *Decameron*'s character. Pamphiles will indeed be partially responsible for Lucius's metamorphosis into an ass, with the unintentional complicity of Photis, the servant of Milo and Pamphiles with whom Lucius is in love. But let us proceed in an orderly fashion: Lucius accepts Byrrhena's invitation and goes to her house, against Photis' warning that Hypata teems with dangers at night. This foreshadows Andreuccio's nightly mishaps and encounter with the robbers, especially because on his way back, tired and drunk, Lucius will find three thugs trying to break into his house (*Metamorphoses* II.32). Lucius bravely faces and defeats them only to discover that they were not real people but three large goatskins magically animated by Pamphiles (*Metamorphoses* III.9 and III.17). A striking coincidence between Lucius and Andreuccio is cast when a man from Fiordaliso's house insultingly calls Andreuccio, half-naked, robbed and smeared in excrements, a "drunken and tedious *ass*" ["*asino* fastidioso e ebriaco" (*Dec.* II 5, § 53)].

Adding further to the similarities between *Dec.* II 5 and Lucius' misadventures, this passage from Telyphron's interpolated account of his night watch over a corpse resonates with Andreuccio's tale (654n40), as noted by Branca (198) and Usher (89–90): "Ne Deus quidem Delphicus ipse facile discerneret duobus nobis iacentibus quis esset magis mortuus." [Apollo himself could not discern which of us two was the dead corpse.] (*Met.* II 25); "E chi allora veduti gli avesse malagevolmente avrebbe conosciuto chi più si fosse morto, o l'arcivescovo o egli." [Whether of the

---

[13] Luciano Rossi: I tre gravi accidenti; Jonathan Usher: 'Desultorietà' nella novella portante di Madonna Oretta (*Decameron* VI, 1) e altre citazioni apuleiane nel Boccaccio. In: *Studi sul Boccaccio* 29 (2001), p. 67–104. See also Igor Candido: *Boccaccio umanista*, p. 86–89.

twain were the more lifeless, Andreuccio or the Archbishop,'twould have puzzled an observer to determine.] (*Dec.* II 5, § 79) The description of Andreuccio trapped in the tomb with the bishop's corpse is modeled after Telyphron's account of his standing guard over a dead body. Telyphron will not be as lucky as Andreuccio, as night witches will mutilate him, but the most interesting aspect of this Boccaccian borrowing is that next to this passage in φ (fol. 28r) there is no annotation or attention sign. This indicates that the annotated sections are not the only ones we should look to in order to investigate the Certaldese's inspiration from Apuleius.[14]

In Apuleius's text, therefore, we find a series of embryonic situations that Boccaccio develops in *Decameron* II 5, with at least one direct textual borrowing. The way in which Boccaccio develops the Apuleian cues is deliberately displacing: the potentially dangerous situations into which Lucius blunders (for instance, being robbed in an inhospitable and foreign city, as suggested by Photis, and encountering criminals at night) all come to naught in Apuleius's text. Even his brawl with the robbers turns out to be only the result of his drunkenness and some magic illusion. Boccaccio, instead, turns these situations into actual incidents. The unknown woman that lures Andreuccio is indeed a swindler. He does get ripped off and encounters actual criminals in the streets of Naples at night. Only a stroke of luck and his quick reflexes will save him from the horrible fate of being buried alive next to a decomposing body.

But there is an intertextual connection has surprisingly escaped critical attention. If *Decameron* 2.5 materializes the dangers that Apuleius's text merely adumbrated and then thwarted, the following tale – that of Madama Beritola – travels in the opposite direction, evoking the story but diverting the tragedy of Hecuba, as told in Ovid's *Metamorphoses*. Giuseppe Chiecchi noted that Beritola is the only character in the *Decameron* whose function is an emblem of maternity, a category otherwise underrepresented in the collection:[15] even Griselda is not only a mother but also and mostly a wife. While the Trojan queen's tragic end is told with some differences by Virgil,[16] Boccaccio favors Ovid's version with the

---

[14] Filosa shares the same opinion; see Elsa Filosa: Ancora su Seneca (e Giovenale) nel *Decameron*. In: *Giornale storico della letteratura italiana* 175 (1998), p. 210–219.

[15] Giuseppe Chiecchi: *Dante, Boccaccio, l'origine: Sei studi e una introduzione*. Firenze: Leo S. Olschki 2013, p. 161.

[16] Leontius Pilatus had translated Euripides's *Hecuba* into Latin in the 1360s, so after the writing of the *Decameron*; however, Boccaccio's exchanges with the Calabrian translator testify to the Certaldese's continuous interest in the figure of Hecuba. See Agostino Pertusi: *Leonzio Pilato fra Petrarca e Boccaccio*. Venezia-Roma: Istituto per la collaborazione culturale 1964 (Civiltà veneziana. Studi, 16); Antonio Rollo: Leonzio lettore dell'*Ecuba* nella Firenze di Boccaccio. In: *Studi Petrarcheschi* 12–13. Petrarca e il mondo greco. Vol. 2 (2002–2003); David Lummus: Boccaccio's Hellenism and the Foundations of Modernity. In: *Mediaevalia* 33 (2012), p. 101–167.

final metamorphosis, as is proven also by *De casibus virorum illustrium* and *De mulieribus claris*. In both of these Latin works, Boccaccio summarizes Ovid and quickly dismisses the other accounts:

> Non nulli dicunt in servitutem ab hostibus cum reliquis tractam et, ne miseriarum illi particula deesset ulla, vidisse ultimo Cassandram, occiso iam Agamenone, Clitemestre iugulari iussu.
> (*De mulieribus claris* XXXIV 8)

> [Others claim that the enemy took Hecuba into slavery along with the remaining survivors, and that her misery was complete when she saw Cassandra's throat cut at Clytemnestra's order after the murder of Agamemnon.][17]

> Esto sint qui illam in servitutem, cum Cassandra et Andromaca aliisque, a Grecis tractam affirment; et inter eos insanam clausisse diem. (*De casibus virorum illustrium* I 13).

> [Others have reported that she was made a slave by the Greeks with Cassandra and Andromache and others, and, demented, she ended her days among them.][18]

Hecuba, turned from queen of Troy to slave of the Greeks, sees the corpses of her last two living children, Polyssena and Polydorus, and, with them, she loses her mind and identity. She then turns into a blood-thirsty beast that only seeks vengeance and abandons herself to a murderous rage, howling ravenously as she gouges Polymnestor's eyes. Ovid prepares Hecuba's metamorphosis by comparing her to a lioness mad with sorrow for losing her cub, thus preluding her final transformation into a bitch. The scene takes place on the shore of Thrace, where the old queen is about to make a most horrible discovery:

> Dixit et *ad litus* passu processit anili,
> albentes lacerata comas. 'date, Troades, urnam!'
> dixerat infelix, liquidas hauriret ut undas:
> adspicit eiectum Polydori *in litore* corpus
> factaque Threiciis ingentia vulnera telis;
> Troades exclamant, obmutuit illa dolore,
> et pariter vocem lacrimasque introrsus obortas
> devorat ipse dolor, duroque simillima saxo
> torpet et adversa figit modo lumina terra,
> interdum torvos *sustollit ad aethera vultus*,
> *nunc positi spectat vultum, nunc vulnera nati*,

---

[17] Giovanni Boccaccio: *Famous Women*. Edited and Translated by Virginia Brown. Harvard, Mass.: Harvard University Press 2003 (I Tatti Renaissance Library, 1), p. 67.
[18] Giovanni Boccaccio: *The Fates of Illustrious Men*. Translated by Louis Brewer Hall. New York: Frederick Ungar Publishing 1965, p. 32.

> *vulnera praecipue*, seque armat et instruit ira.
> qua simul exarsit, tamquam regina maneret,
> ulcisci statuit poenaeque in imagine tota est,
> utque *furit catulo lactente orbata leaena*
> signaque nacta pedum sequitur, quem non videt, hostem,
> sic Hecabe, postquam cum luctu miscuit iram,
> non oblita animorum, annorum oblita suorum,
> vadit ad artificem dirae, Polymestora, caedis
> conloquiumque petit; (*Met.* XIII 533–547)

[She spoke, and *went to the shore*, with the stumbling steps of an old woman, tearing at her white hair. "Give me an urn, women of Troy!" said the unhappy mother, wanting to draw water from the sea. There, she saw Polydorus's body, thrown *on the beach*, covered with open wounds made by Thracian spears. The Trojan women cried out, but she was dumb with grief. The grief itself obliterated both her powers of speech and the tears welling inside, and she stood unmoving like solid rock, at one moment with her gaze fixed on the ground, the next lifting her face grimly towards the sky. Now *she looked at her dead son's face, now at his wounds, mostly at his wounds*, awakening a growing anger in herself. Then it blazed out, and she, as if she were still a queen, determined on vengeance, her whole mind filled with thoughts of punishment. Hecuba, her grief mixed with anger, forgetting her age, but not forgetting her rage, *like a lioness maddened by the theft of her unweaned cub*, that, though she cannot see her enemy, follows the traces she finds of his footsteps, found her way to the author of the dreadful crime, Polymestor. (*Emphasis added*)]

First deprived of her royal status, the queen of Troy then loses her children and finally her identity. The tragedy culminates in her transformation into a bitch ravenously howling in pain whose crude fate even Juno will pity. Like the Trojan queen, Beritola is about to lose her wits when she sees the ship with her children aboard sail away and leave her on a deserted island. But contrary to what happens for the tale of Andreuccio and Apuleius's text, this tale, *Dec.* II 6, rewrites *in melius* Hecuba's tragic fate. Through textual links and parallel situations, Boccaccio evokes in the reader's mind the memory of the Ovidian story, but the tragic expectations it carries are thwarted by a happy ending, a family reunion, and a wedding. Elsa Filosa, developing an idea of Giuseppe Velli's, has recently shown how this strategy is not new to Boccaccio, specifically with reference to Zinevra (II 9), which constitutes a version with a happy ending of Titus Livius' Lucretia (*Ab urbe condita* I 58), and to the daughter of the King of England (II 3), whose story "corrects" the story of Pope Joan in Boccaccio's *De mulieribus claris*.[19]

---

[19] Cf. Filosa: *Tre Studi*, p. 106, 114. Giuseppe Velli (Memoria, p. 232–234) had originally traced this relationship.

Let us detail these links and similarities. Beritola, also a noblewoman in disgrace, loses her two children on the deserted shores of Ponza. She too undergoes a transformation, though only partial, when she begins to breastfeed two baby goats. She acts, to them, as a mother, whose description resonates with Ovidian echoes: "[...] non essendolesi ancora del nuovo parto rasciutto il *latte del petto*, quegli teneramente prese e al petto gli si pose. Li quali, non rifiutando il servigio, cosí lei *poppavano* come la madre avrebber fatto" [having, by reason of her recent delivery, *milk still within her*, she took them up tenderly, and *set them to her breast*. They, nothing loath, sucked at her teats as if she had been their own dam. *Dec.* II 6, §§ 15–16] As we can see, this image replicates, albeit metaphorically, that of Hecuba/lioness deprived of the cub still suckling at her breast: "[...] utque furit catulo *lactente* orbata laena" (*Met.* XIII 547, above). Even the topographic setting of the events coincides in Boccaccio and Ovid: at the very moment of realization that they have lost their children, both women are standing on the shore. Hecuba advances wearily on the shore ("*ad litus* passu processit anili") when she spots Polydorus's dead body, just like the other, eventually more fortunate, mother:

> Madama Beritola, finito il suo diurno lamento, tornata *al lito per rivedere i figliuoli*, come usata era di fare, niuna persona vi trovò; di che prima si maravigliò e poi, subitamente di quello che avvenuto era sospettando, *gli occhi infra'l mar sospinse* e vide la galea, non molto ancora allungata, dietro tirarsi il legnetto: per la qual cosa ottimamente cognobbe, sí come il marito, aver perduti i figliuoli. E povera e sola e abbandonata, senza saper dove mai alcuno doversene ritrovare, quivi vedendosi, tramortita il marito e' figliuoli chiamando cadde *in su il lito*. (*Dec.* II 6, § 11)

> [When Madam Beritola, her wailing for that day ended, returned, as was her wont, *to the shore to solace herself with the sight of her sons*, she found none there. At first she was lost in wonder, then with a sudden suspicion of the truth *she bent her eyes seaward*, and there saw the galley still at no great distance, towing the ship in her wake. Thus apprehending beyond all manner of doubt that she had lost her sons as well as her husband, and that, alone, desolate and destitute, she might not hope that any of her lost ones would ever be restored to her, she fell down *on the shore* in a swoon with the names of her husband and sons upon her lips.]

The horizontal gaze that Beritola directs toward the sea and the departing ship recalls the analogous and silent vertical movement of the Trojan queen's eyes from the earth to the wounds on Polydorus's body, then to the sky and finally resting on the boy's face:

> [...] adversa figit modo lumina terra,
> interdum torvos *sustollit ad aethera vultus,*
> *nunc positi spectat vultum, nunc vulnera nati,*
> vulnera praecipue [...]. (*Met.* XIII 541–544)

[At one moment with her gaze fixed on the ground, the next *lifting her face* grimly *towards the sky*. Now *she looked at her dead son's face*, now *at his wounds*, mostly at his wounds.]

The sudden realization of having lost everything lies precisely in this hesitation of Hecuba's eyes ("lumina [...] sustollit", which generates Boccaccio's "gli occhi [...] sospinse") on the face and wounds of her son (and we can easily imagine the cultural and emotional associations a Christian reader would make with such an icon) and in Beritola's sighting the ship that, seized by corsairs, sails off tugging away the lifeboat. The Trojan women offer Hecuba moral support on the Thracian shore as they help her get the water with which to wash Polyssena's body,[20] while Beritola, left completely alone, faints because "[q]uivi non era chi con *acqua fredda* o con altro argomento le smarrite forze rivocasse" [None was there to administer *cold water* or aught else that might recall her truant powers; *Dec.* II 6, § 12].

The historical background of *Dec.* II 6 is the war between Hohenstaufen and Anjou over the island of Sicily. Beritola's husband, Arrighetto Capece, regent of the Kingdom of Sicily for defeated King Manfred, loses his status. Consequently, of course, Beritola and their children lose their status too, as had happened to Priam, Hecuba, and their children. But the reference to the fall of the queen of Troy also cannot fail to recall Dante's brief treatment in the opening tercets of *Inferno* 30. Here the impostors – that is, those who took up another identity and concealed their own – are punished:

> E quando la *fortuna* volse in basso
> L'altezza de' Troian che tutto ardiva,
> sì che'nsieme col regno il re fu casso,
>   *Ecuba* trista, misera e cattiva,
> poscia che vide Polissena morta,
> e del suo Polidoro in su la riva
>   del mar si fu la *dolorosa* accorta,
> *forsennata latrò sì come cane;*
> tanto *il dolor le fé la mente torta.* (*Inf.* XXX 13–21)

[And when *Fortune* had subdued the haughty,
all-daring spirit of the Trojans,
so that both king and kingdom were brought low,
Hecuba – wretched, sorrowing, a captive –

---

[20] Hecuba asks for her maids' assistance as she proceeds to fill up an urn for the funeral rite: "[...] ad litus passu processit anili, / albentes lacerata comas. 'Date, Troades, urnam!' / dixerat infelix, liquidas hauriret ut undas" *Met.* XIII 533–535 ['Give me an urn, women of Troy!' said the unhappy mother, wanting to draw water from the sea].

when she saw Polyxena slaughtered and,
grieving woman, when she saw
Polydorus lying dead upon the shore,
went mad and started barking like a dog,
so greatly had her grief deranged her mind.]

The memory of the metamorphosis of Ovid's Hecuba into a bitch prepares Dante's reader for the apparition of the impostors. The queen's loss of identity foreshadows the false identities taken by Gianni Schicchi, Griffolino, and Capocchio. In Boccaccio's tale, loss or concealment of identity also takes up an important role, when Beritola's son Giusfredi must hide his Ghibelline affiliations. The denouement of *Dec.* II 6 suggests that leaving aside one's pride, concealing one's identity and biding one's time are key steps to the successful recovery of a lost aristocratic status, a benefit that was not allowed to the Trojan royals. Giusfredi must necessarily become Giannotto, faithfully playing the part for many years, until the changed political scene allows him to come out of hiding. His reward will be his redemption and wedding with the daughter of Currado Malaspina.

And we would not even need the presence of an important character from Dante's *Purgatory* to link this tale to a Dantean context, because Dante's reference to Hecuba in *Inf.* XXX constitutes another subtext for Boccaccio's figure of Hecuba. An introductory sketch, of which the wretched Athamas is also part (*Met.* IV 512–542), Dante's tercets on Hecuba serve to show contrastively the insufficiency of Ovid's art in describing Hell's bestiality.[21] But it is precisely Dante's powerful visualization of the howling queen turned bitch that inspires Boccaccio's description of his own Hecuba in the *De casibus virorum illustrium*, where a loan translation of "latrò sì come cane" bespeaks the Dantean matrix of the scene: "Qui *dolor* ultimus tanta cum vi effetum pectus invasit, *ut in rabiem illam raperet, latrantemque canum more* per arva consumeret" (*De casibus virorum illustrium* I xiii) [(...) whose exhausted breast was filled with such terrible *pain* that *sorrow sent her into a rage* and she was consumed through the fields *howling like a bitch.*]

In the *De casibus*, Boccaccio models his Hecuba on that of Dante ("il dolor le fé la mente torta" also becomes "ut in rabiem illam raperet") because the queen of Troy was, since Ovid, the epitome of the royal fall in the feminine. The *Inferno* and the *Metamorphoses* thus provide the ideal substrata on which to build the story of Beritola.

---

21 "Ma né di Tebe furie né troiane / si vider mäi in alcun tanto crude, / non punger bestie, nonché membre umane, quant'io vidi in due ombre" *Inf.* XXX 22–24 [But no Theban crazed with rage – / or Trojan – did ever seem as cruel / in rending beasts, much less human parts.]

If, as Zatti observes, *Decameron* Day Two is a triumph of the disguised body, we can see why Boccaccio counts on his readers' poetic memory of both Ovid and Dante to prepare the ground:[22] the Christian poet's account reinforces the readers' expectations of an imminent tragedy, brought about by blind fortune ("quando la *fortuna* volse in basso" *Inf.* XXX 13). But the unfolding of the Decameronian tale thwarts this expectation again, for a benign star shines on Beritola, thus fulfilling the promise of a moral teaching that Emilia had made when introducing her tale:

> Gravi cose e noiose sono i movimenti varii della fortuna, de' quali però che quante volte alcuna cosa si parla, tante è un destare delle nostre menti, le quali leggiermente s'addormentano nelle sue lusinghe, giudico mai rincrescer non dover *l'ascoltare e a' felici e agli sventurati, in quanto li primi rende avvisati e i secondi consola*. (*Dec.* II 6, § 3)
>
> [Grave and grievous are the vicissitudes with which Fortune makes us acquainted, and as discourse of such matter serves to awaken our minds, which are so readily lulled to sleep by her flatteries, I deem it worthy of attentive hearing by all, *whether they enjoy her favour or endure her frown, in that it ministers counsel to the one sort and consolation to the other*.]

The above passage is key in linking the vicissitudes of Beritola to Hecuba, since it recalls an analogous comment by Boccaccio to introduce the misfortunes of the Trojan royals (a family with which our author felt a particular connection if he chose Troiolo, one of Hecuba and Priam's sons, as the protagonist of his *Filostrato*): "Verum, quanto celsius quis extollitur, tanto magis letali casui, dum sibi non cavet, vicinus efficitur: quod quidem in Priamo atque suis Fortuna miserabili declaravit exitu" (*De casibus virorum illustrium* I xiii) [The higher one is lifted in glory, the closer he is brought to a lethal fall, if he does not take precautions: which Fortune showed in Priam and his family with a miserable end.]

Written during a period of some twenty years (1350s–1370s), the *De casibus virorum illustrium* tells the exemplary tragedies of great men (Hecuba shares her husband's destiny). Because Fortune strikes the unprepared more fiercely, the warning Boccaccio issues to Priam and his family ("dum sibi non cavet") bears the same preparatory and consolatory function as Emilia's address at the beginning of her tale of Beritola. Both *felici* and *sventurati* will equally benefit from her tale of apparently adverse Fortune.

The mythologem of Hecuba as the mother-queen falling into utter disgrace stands as an archetype influencing Boccaccio in more than one work. We have

---

[22] See Sergio Zatti: Il mercante sulla ruota: la seconda giornata. In: Michelangelo Picone and Margherita Mesirca (eds.): *Introduzione al "Decameron"*. Firenze: Cesati 2004 (Lectura Boccaccii Turicensis), p. 84.

come full circle: in both *Decameron* II 6 and *De casibus* I xiii, Boccaccio takes a cue from Dante's treatment of Hecuba. In *Decameron* II 6 the evocation of Dante's Hecuba – a preamble to the impostors – prepares the ground for the argument that a temporary change of identity is justifiable and indeed necessary under certain circumstances.

Sergio Zatti emphasizes the romance-like nature of Day 2, dominated by fortune and love rather than ingenuity. Merchants, here, are the privileged male protagonists, while the dispersion (and subsequent reunion) of families is the *motif* of female characters. These figures all move on a canvas of interwoven literary genres: devotional literature (*Dec.* II 1 and II 2 in my opinion, which differs from Zatti's, who sees II 7 as devotional); fabliaux and parodic adventures (II 1 again, II 5 and II 7); epic (II 3 and II 4); and Hellenistic romance (II 6, II 7, II 8, II 9). Boccaccio's narrative strategy evokes literary classics in the readers' memory, only to take sudden, displacing turns and avert the expected conclusion. Just as importantly, the responsiveness and interplay among the youths of the *brigata* constitute what Picone calls *mondo commentato*[23] and provide a first layer of hermeneutical and intratextual considerations, while at the same time livening the brigata's overarching tale and making the reading more pleasurable.

Bibliography

Primary Literature

Alighieri, Dante: *Inferno*. Translated by Robert Hollander and Jean Hollander. New York: Doubleday 2000.
Apuleius, Lucius: *Metamorfosi*. Introduction by Federico Roncoroni. Translated by Nino Marziano. Milano: Garzanti 1998.
Apuleius, Lucius: *The Golden Ass. The Metamorphoses of Lucius Apuleius*. Translated by William Adlington. Auckland: The Floating Press 2009.
Boccaccio, Giovanni: *De casibus virorum illustrium*. Edited by Pier Giorgio Ricci and Vittorio Zaccaria. Milano: Mondadori 1983.
Boccaccio, Giovanni: *The Decameron of Giovanni Boccaccio*. Ed. by J. M. Rigg with an introduction. 2 vols. London: A. H. Bullen 1903.
Boccaccio, Giovanni: *Decameron*. Edited by Vittore Branca. 2 vols. Torino: Einaudi 1992.
Boccaccio, Giovanni: *Famous Women*. Ed. and Trans. by Virginia Brown. Harvard, Mass.: Harvard University Press 2003 (I Tatti Renaissance Library, 1).

---

[23] Cf. Michelangelo Picone: Il macrotesto. In: Michelangelo Picone and Margherita Mesirca (eds.): *Introduzione al "Decameron"*, p. 36.

Juvenal: *The Satires of Decimus Junius Juvenalis*. Translated by John Dryden. Chiswick: Whittingham 1822.
Ovid: *Metamorphosis*. Translated by Anthony S. Kline, available at http://ovid.lib.virginia.edu/trans/Ovhome.htm#askline.
Seneca, Lucius Annaeus: *Ad Lucilium epistulae morales*. With an English Translation by Richard Gummere. 3 vols. New York: Putnam 1917–1925 (Loeb Classical Library, 75–77).

Secondary Literature

Monographs and Anthologies

Albanese, Gabriella/Lucia Battaglia Ricci et al. (eds.): *Favole parabole istorie. Le forme della scrittura novellistica dal Medioevo al Rinascimento*. Atti del Convegno di Pisa, 26–28 ottobre 1998. Roma: Salerno 2000.
Baratto, Mario: *Realtà e stile nel Decameron*. Roma: Editori Riuniti 1996.
Bragantini, Renzo/Forni, Pier Massimo (eds.): *Lessico critico decameroniano*. Torino: Bollati Boringhieri 1995.
Candido, Igor: *Boccaccio umanista. Studi su Boccaccio e Apuleio*. Ravenna: Longo 2014.
Filosa, Elsa: *Tre studi sul De mulieribus claris*. Milano: LED 2012.
Hecker, Oskar: *Boccaccio-Funde. Stücke aus der bislang verschollenen Bibliothek des Dichters darunter von seiner Handgeschriebenes Fremdes und Eigenes*, Braunschweig: G. Westermann 1902.
Marchesi, Simone: *Stratigrafie decameroniane*. Firenze: Olschki 2004.
Mazzoni Peruzzi, Simonetta: *Boccaccio e le letterature romanze tra Medioevo e Rinascimento. Atti del convegno internazionale Boccaccio e la Francia*. Firenze: Alinea 2006.
Migiel, Marylin: *A Rhetoric of the Decameron*. Toronto: University of Toronto Press 2003.
Muscetta, Carlo: *Boccaccio*. Bari: Laterza 1989.
Pertusi, Agostino: *Leonzio Pilato fra Petrarca e Boccaccio*. Venezia-Roma: Istituto per la collaborazione culturale 1964 (Civiltà veneziana. Studi, 16).
Sanguineti White, Laura: *Boccaccio e Apuleio: caratteri differenziali nella struttura narrativa del Decameron*. Bologna: EDIM 1977.
Velli, Giuseppe: *Petrarca e Boccaccio. Tradizione, memoria, scrittura*. Padova: Antenore 1979 (Studi petrarcheschi, 7).

Articles and Papers

Billanovich, Giuseppe: Zanobi da Strada tra i tesori di Montecassino. In: *Atti dell'Accademia Nazionale dei Lincei. Rendiconti. Classe di scienze morali, storiche e filologiche* 7 (1996), p. 653–655.
Candido, Igor: La *fabula* di Amore e Psiche dalle chiose del Laur. 29.2 alle due redazioni delle Genealogie di Boccaccio e ancora in *Dec.* X 10. In: *Studi Sul Boccaccio* 37 (2009), p. 171–196.

Candido, Igor: Apuleio alla fine del "Decameron": la novella di Griselda come riscrittura della *lepida fabula* di Amore e Psiche. In: *Filologia e critica* 32, 1 (2007), p. 3–17.

Casamassima, Emanuele: Dentro lo scrittoio del Boccaccio: i codici della tradizione. In: Aldo Rossi (ed.): *Il "Decameron": pratiche testuali e interpretative*. Bologna: Cappelli 1982, p. 253–260.

Chiecchi, Giuseppe: *Dante, Boccaccio, l'origine: Sei studi e una introduzione*. Firenze: Leo S. Olschki 2013.

Filosa, Elsa/Luisa Flora: Ancora su Seneca (e Giovenale) nel *Decameron*. In: *Giornale storico della letteratura italiana* 175 (1998), p. 210–219.

Fiorilla, Maurizio: La lettura apuleiana del Boccaccio e le note ai manoscritti laurenziani 29, 2 e 54, 32. In: *Aevum* 73, 3 (1999), p. 635–668.

Lummus, David: Boccaccio's Hellenism and the Foundations of Modernity. In: *Mediaevalia* 33 (2012), p. 101–167.

Malato, Enrico: La nascita della novella italiana. In: Gabriella Albanese/Lucia Battaglia Ricci et al. (eds.): *Favole, parabole, istorie. Le forme della scrittura novellistica dal Medioevo al Rinascimento*. Atti del Convegno di Pisa, 26–28 ottobre, 1998. Roma: Salerno 2000, p. 17–29.

Marchesi, Simone: Boccaccio's Vernacular Classicism: Intertextuality and Interdiscoursivity in the *Decameron*. In: *Heliotropia* 7, 1–2 (2010), p. 31–50.

Martinez, Ronald: Apuleian Example and Misogynist Allegory in the Tale of Peronella (*Decameron* VII 2). In: Thomas C. Stillinger/F. Regina Psaki (eds.): *Boccaccio and Feminist Criticism*. *Annali d'Italianistica* 2006 (Studi e testi, 8), p. 201–216.

Mazza, Antonia: L'inventario della 'Parva libraria' di Santo Spirito e la biblioteca del Boccaccio. In: *Italia medoevale e umanistica* 9 (1966), p. 1–76.

Ménard, Philippe: Les sources françaises d'un conte de Boccace: *Decameron* IX 6. In: Simonetta Mazzoni Peruzzi (ed.): *Boccaccio e le letterature romanze tra Medioevo e Rinascimento*. Atti del convegno internazionale Boccaccio e la Francia. Firenze: Alinea 2006, p. 113–134.

Petronio, Giuseppe: Da Apuleio a Boccaccio. In: *Italica. Bollettino annuale dell'universitià di Iassi*, Iași: University of Iași Press 1941.

Picone, Michelangelo: Il macrotesto. In: Michelangelo Picone/ Margherita Mesirca (eds.): *Introduzione al "Decameron"*. Firenze: Cesati 2004 (Lectura Boccaccii Turicensis).

Rollo, Antonio: Leonzio lettore dell'Ecuba nella Firenze di Boccaccio. In: *Studi Petrarcheschi* 12–13. Petrarca e il mondo greco, vol. 2 (2002–2003).

Rossi, Luciano: L'evoluzione dell'intreccio: Boivin e Andreuccio. In: *Filologia e critica* 1 (1976), p. 5–14.

Rossi, Luciano: I tre gravi accidenti della novella di Andreuccio da Perugia (*Decameron*, II 5). In: *Strumenti Critici* 20 (1996) p. 385–400.

Usher, Jonathan: 'Desultorietà' nella novella portante di Madonna Oretta (*Decameron* VI 1) e altre citazioni apuleiane nel Boccaccio. In: *Studi sul Boccaccio* 29 (2001), p. 67–104.

Velli, Giuseppe: Seneca nel *Decameron*. In: *Giornale storico della letteratura italiana* 168 (1991), p. 321–334.

Velli, Giuseppe: Memoria. In: Renzo Bragantini/Pier Massimo Forni (eds.): *Lessico critico decameroniano*. Torino: Bollati Boringhieri 1995, p. 222–248.

Vio, Gianluigi: Chiose e riscritture apuleiane di Giovanni Boccaccio. In: *Studi sul Boccaccio* 20 (1991–1992), p. 139–166.

Zatti, Sergio: Il mercante sulla ruota: la seconda giornata. In: Michelangelo Picone/ Margherita Mesirca (eds.): *Introduzione al Decameron*. Firenze: Cesati 2004 (Lectura Boccaccii Turicensis), p. 79–98.

Marco Petoletti
Boccaccio, the Classics and the Latin Middle Ages

The name of Boccaccio, together with his *praeceptor* Petrarch, appears in the prefaces of many critical editions of Latin classics: in the first century of Italian Humanism the meeting of these two great minds, in person or through their letters, promoted the circulation of texts which were limited until then to the sporadic consultation of a few readers. The manner by which Petrarch and Boccaccio approached Latin literature was quite different, because they had a different education.[1] Petrarch's highly selective judgment contrasts with the curiosity of Boccaccio, attracted by the most obscure works of the classical tradition and generously open to collecting into his own Pantheon the immense literary patrimony of the Middle Ages.[2] Medieval Latin writers were never banished from the canon of *auctoritates*, even after Boccaccio's erudite conversion that developed from his friendship with Petrarch, whom he met in Florence for the first time in 1350 and then visited often in Milan, Padua and Venice. Their methods were different and likewise their results; nevertheless, it is fair to place the names of Boccaccio and Petrarch side by side in the fascinating history of the rediscovery of classical antiquity in the Renaissance. Petrarch is the *sospitator* of Cicero, whose letters to Atticus, to Brutus and to Quintus he discovered in Verona in 1345. We owe to Boccaccio, with the assistance of Zanobi da Strada, the rediscovery of part of Tacitus' *Annales* and *Historiae*. However, Petrarch reserved to Cicero a philological attention that Boccaccio was not able to bestow upon the complicated prose of Tacitus.

There survive a good number of manuscripts, many of them autographs, which belonged to Boccaccio. We have a sort of inventory of his personal library, which was not as rich as that of Petrarch, but nonetheless inhabited by rare texts.[3]

---

[1] Vincenzo Fera: Storia e filologia tra Petrarca e Boccaccio. In: *Quaderni petrarcheschi* 15–16 (2005–2006), p. 369–390.
[2] Michele Feo: Petrarca e Boccaccio: Critica e filologia. In: Paolo Orvieto (ed.): *Storia della letteratura italiana. XI. La critica letteraria dal Due al Novecento*. Roma: Salerno Editrice 2003, p. 103–129, in particular p. 123–124.
[3] Antonia Mazza: L'inventario della 'parva libraria' di Santo Spirito e la biblioteca del Boccaccio. In: *Italia medioevale e umanistica* 9 (1966), p. 1–74; Teresa De Robertis: L'inventario della 'parva libraria' di Santo Spirito. In: Teresa De Robertis/Carla Maria Monti et al. (eds.): *Boccaccio autore e copista*. Firenze: Mandragora 2013, p. 403–409. On Boccaccio's personal books see Maddalena Signorini: Considerazioni preliminari sulla biblioteca di Giovanni Boccaccio. In: *Studi sul Boccaccio* 29 (2011), p. 367–395; Marco Cursi and Maurizio Fiorilla: Giovanni Boccaccio. In: Giuseppina Brunetti/Maurizio Fiorilla et al. (eds.): *Autografi dei letterati italiani*.

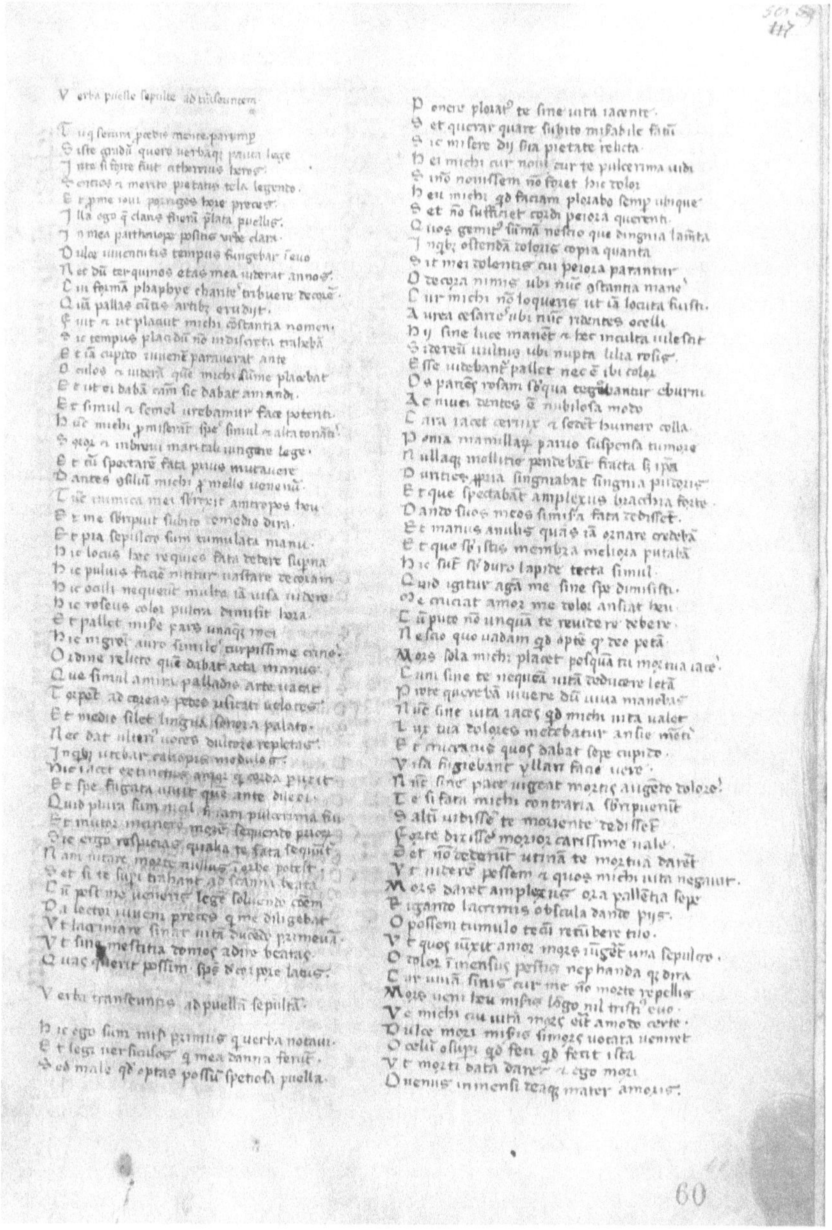

Plate 1: Firenze, Biblioteca Laurenziana, Plut. 29.8, fol. 60r (*Costanza's Elegy*, copied by Boccoccio)

Le Origini e il Trecento. Vol. 1. Roma: Salerno Editrice 2013, p. 43–103; Marco Cursi: *La scrittura e i libri di Giovanni Boccaccio.* Roma: Viella 2013, p. 129–134.

In his will of 28 August 1374 Boccaccio arranged to leave his books to the Augustinian friar Martino da Signa establishing that after the death of Martino the volumes would move to the library of the Florentine convent of Santo Spirito, *ut quilibet de dicto conventu possit legere et studere super dictis libris* ("so that whosoever of this convent might read and study the abovementioned books").[4] In 1451, the volumes of the Augustinian convent were finally inventoried. Thus it became possible, at that time and more recently, to recognize certain books that first belonged to Boccaccio and therefore to the Santo Spirito collection. Others, either missing or yet to be identified, may still reveal their presence on his bookshelf.

It is impossible to trace all the paths of the Latin textual traditions to which Boccaccio had access, but some episodes allow us to establish general guidelines.[5] A starting point could be the Laurentian *zibaldone* and Miscellanea (Plut. 29.8 and 33.31) which, as we now know, originally constituted a single volume, in part assembled by reusing older parchment from a liturgical book in Beneventan script. It would be useful to call these two manuscripts 'Boccaccio's membranaceous *zibaldone*'.[6] With its surprisingly broad collection of ancient, medieval and contemporary texts, which Boccaccio prepared before the meeting with Petrarch in 1350, it is the most significant book of his youth. A whole autograph, it was written since Boccaccio's boyhood until 1348 (a letter to Zanobi da Strada transcribed at fol. 50v belongs to the beginning of this year), in Naples during his formative years, in Florence after his return at the beginning of the 1340s, and later in Romagna. More than 140 texts were entrusted to those pages, from short maxims in prose or verse to more ample works. Ancients and Moderns are welcomed in this membranaceous *zibaldone*, which even included technical treatises by Andalò di Negro, a master of astronomy. Different traditions come together in the apparently disordered tumult of this archive of memory, so different from the other great book of the Trecento, the Ambrosian Virgil of Petrarch.[7] Nevertheless, perhaps it is possible to reconstruct the project or, rather, the distinct projects that explain the genesis of this rhetorical collection. Here Boccaccio wished to include among the modern authors the two stars of his cultural firmament:

---

[4] Laura Regnicoli: *I testamenti di Giovanni Boccaccio*. In: Teresa De Robertis/Carla Maria Monti et al. (eds.): *Boccaccio autore e copista*, p. 387–393, on p. 392.

[5] Marco Petoletti: Il Boccaccio e la tradizione dei testi latini. In: Michaelangiola Marchiaro/Stefano Zamponi (eds.): *Boccaccio letterato. Atti del Convegno internazionale (Firenze-Certaldo, 10–12 ottobre 2013)*. Firenze: Accademia della Crusca 2015, p. 105–121.

[6] For a complete description see Marco Petoletti and Stefano Zamponi: Gli zibaldoni. In: Teresa De Robertis/Carla Maria Monti et al. (eds.): *Boccaccio autore e copista*, p. 289–326, in particular p. 300–313.

[7] Antonietta Nebuloni Testa/Marco Baglio et al. (eds.): *Francesco Petrarca. Le postille del Virgilio Ambrosiano*. 2 vols. Padova-Roma: Antenore 2006.

Dante's bucolic *tenzone* with Giovanni del Virgilio, whose transmission Boccaccio promoted, and three Latin epistles, copied as example of the *ars dictandi*;[8] and Petrarch's works which Boccaccio was able to read at that moment (some poetic epistles and the eclogue *Argus*). The section dedicated to Petrarch opens with an evocative page that shows Boccaccio's devotion not yet supported by direct acquaintance: the memory of the coronation ceremony in Rome, when the laurel wreath was placed upon Petrarch's temples, is fixed in epigraphic writing.[9] In his works in Latin prose and verse, Boccaccio tried to imitate both Dante and Petrarch: the four fictitious epistles of 1339, daringly complicated by a sophisticated lexicon, the obscure *Allegoria mitologica*, and the so-called *Elegy to Constance*, in which he hides the imitation, nearly verbatim, of an ancient epitaph still conserved in Rome and made popular by the epigraphic and poetic anthologies of the humanists. Boccaccio is the first to demonstrate knowledge of this inscription, even if the way he knew it remains obscure.[10] Alongside the elaborate Latin experiments constructed in Naples, he places the exchange of eclogues with master Checco di Meletto of Romagna, anchored to the model of Dante's *tenzone* with Giovanni del Virgilio; the *Faunus*, which marked his moving to an imitation of bucolic Petrarch;[11] and a letter, this one real, sent at the beginning of 1348 to his friend Zanobi da Strada, in which he alludes to the question of Varro, *Varronem quidem nondum habui* ("Also, I have not yet received the Varro"). Therefore, Boccaccio was already engaged in negotiations in order to obtain the old manuscript in Beneventan script, today in the Laurentian Library of Florence (Plut. 51.10), containing the *De lingua Latina*, Cicero's *Pro Cluentio* and the *Rhetorica ad Herennium*, from which he extracted a missing copy sent to Petrarch, as the *Fam.* XVIII.4 of 1355 proves.[12] Notwithstanding this, he abraded the name *Iohannes de Certaldo* from the titles of his creations copied in this book: while he did not condemn to flames and destruction those texts of his youth, elaborated during

---

[8] Marco Petoletti: Boccaccio editore delle egloghe e delle epistole di Dante. In: Luca Azzetta/Andrea Mazzucchi (eds.): *Boccaccio editore e interprete di Dante. Atti del Convegno internazionale (Roma, 28–30 ottobre 2013)*. Roma: Salerno Editrice 2014, p. 159–183.
[9] Jonathan Usher: Monuments More Enduring than Bronze: Boccaccio and Paper Inscriptions. In: *Heliotropia* 4, 1 (2007), p. 1–30.
[10] Boccaccio refers to the epitaph of Claudia Omonea (first century B.C.), now in Rome in the Capitoline Museums (*CIL*, VI/2, nr. 12652). See Roberto Weiss: *La scoperta dell'antichità classica nel Rinascimento*. Padova: Antenore 1989, p. 50; Augusto Campana: *Studi epigrafici ed epigrafia nuova nel Rinascimento umanistico*. Roma: Edizioni di Storia e letteratura 2005, p. 6.
[11] Simona Lorenzini: *La corrispondenza bucolica tra Giovanni Boccaccio e Checco di Meletto Rossi. L'egloga di Giovanni del Virgilio ad Albertino Mussato*. Firenze: Leo S. Olschki 2011.
[12] Silvia Rizzo: Testi classici scoperti dal Boccaccio e donati al Petrarca. In: Michele Feo (ed.): *Codici latini del Petrarca nelle biblioteche fiorentine*. Firenze: Le Lettere 1991, p. 14–16.

his literary apprenticeship, he did flee almost modestly from laying claim *coram populo* to the authorship of these works.[13] The membranaceous *zibaldone* allows us to recognize even the models Boccaccio used. He copied Persius' text with glosses from an eleventh-century MS., now Laur. Plut. 37.19. So modern scholars have the opportunity to verify directly Boccaccio's talent as a scribe. In this case he can be acquitted of the charge against the congenital distraction attributed to him in copying texts.[14] Other classics copied in this book arouse more interest, for example a collection of *carmina* from the *Anthologia Latina*, preceded by the *Culex* and the pseudo-Virgilian *Dirae* (at fols. 17r–38r of the Laur. Plut. 33.31): all those texts derive from a Carolingian compilation. The juxtaposition in the membranaceous *zibaldone* of Ovid's *Ibis* and *Amores* and the *Cosmographia* of Bernard Silvestre allows us to identify another of Boccaccio's sources: in some twelfth- and thirteenth-century MSS from the Norman area we find the very same succession of texts. Therefore, it is highly probable that in this case the Certaldese transcribed from a previously assembled *corpus*, whose origin is traceable to France. Angevin Naples, which Boccaccio loved and where he dwelt between 1327 and 1341, must have placed at his disposition an unimaginable treasure of books, and not limited to those dispensed by the nearby library of Montecassino, often considered the sole source of literary rarities. Among the works copied in the membranaceous *zibaldone* one must certainly mention the most unusual: the *Priapea*, a collection of 86 epigrams whose protagonist is the jocose and impudent keeper of gardens. Boccaccio's transcription is the first one in the history of the transmission of this text and it is most authoritative for the critical edition.[15]

As for the *Priapea*'s transmission, Laur. Plut. 29.8 and 33.31 offer a substantial contribution even on the side of medieval Latin literature: for example, among the three twelfth-century elegiac comedies that Boccaccio transcribed – Vital de Blois' *Geta*, Guillaume de Blois' *Alda* and the *Lidia* attributed to Arnulf of Orléans (all well-known texts to those who have read the *novelle* of the *Decameron*) – the last one had a so poor circulation that only another surviving witness, possibly of English origin and dating back to XIII century, is known. In a similar way, the membranaceous *zibaldone* is the other only surviving MS of some works as well: Berthold of Hohenburg's *Lamentatio* and a Latin translation of a section of the

---

13 Victoria Kirkham: Iohannes de Certaldo: la firma dell'autore. In: Michelangelo Picone/Claude Cazalé Bérard (eds.): *Gli Zibaldoni di Boccaccio. Memoria, scrittura, riscrittura. Atti del seminario internazionale (Firenze-Certaldo, 26–28 aprile 1996)*. Firenze: Cesati 1998, p. 455–468.
14 Felice Ramorino: De duobus Persii codicibus qui inter ceteros Laurentianae bibliothecae servantur. In: *Studi italiani di filologia classica* 12 (1904), p. 229–260; Dorothy M. Robathan: Boccaccio's Accuracy as a Scribe. In: *Speculum* 13 (1938), p. 458–460.
15 Marco Petoletti: *Il Boccaccio e la tradizione dei testi latini*, p. 110–112.

Roman d'Alexandre concerning an episode of the siege of Tyre.[16] The satire in goliardic strophes attributed to Pier della Vigna, "Vehementi nimium commotus dolore" ("Moved by a powerful affliction"), had a slightly widespread circulation. Boccaccio's copy shows significant variants and additions in comparison to the other three known manuscripts.[17] Another short poem, which the title assigns to Thomas Aquinas – "Versus beati Thome de Aquino" ("Verses of the blessed Thomas Aquinas") –, but probably composed in the twelfth century in France, as stylistic analysis suggests, is transmitted in Laur. Plut. 29.8 at fols. 52r–v.[18] This medieval Latin relic is saved only by Boccaccio's transcription.[19]

The thirst for knowledge spurred Boccaccio's mind as well as his pen to collect in his book miscellaneous epigraphic texts without any barriers between ancients and moderns. Thus he transcribed two medieval inscriptions, the first an epitaph for Beltramo Aringheri, called Porrina, who was buried in the Church of Santa Maria Assunta at Casole d'Elsa in a tomb sculpted by Marco Romano. If Boccaccio did not copy this funeral eulogy, it would not have survived to our day.[20] Four lines for the Church of San Miniato in Florence also survive only by way of Boccaccio's transcription.[21] At a much later date, in the 1360s, he copied onto a folio that had remained partially blank a Greek epigraph: it is the epitaph for a dog, found near the church of San Felice a Ema in the suburbs of Florence, which is transmitted exclusively by this copy.[22] This text is a visible witness of Boccaccio's interest in Greek culture. Alongside the great collection of ancient, medieval and modern

---

16 Ibid., p. 113.
17 Antonio Montefusco: Petri de Vinea 'Vehementi nimium commotus dolore': la restituzione del testo tra storia e filologia. In: *La parola del testo* 11, 2 (2007), p. 299–365.
18 Angelo Piacentini: Un carme attribuito a san Tommaso d'Aquino nello Zibaldone membranaceo di Boccaccio. In: *Studi sul Boccaccio* 44 (2016), p. 207–234.
19 Boccaccio's interest in medieval Latin poetry emerges from his autograph transcription of Joseph of Exeter's *Ylias*, a sort of versification of the *Historia destructionis Troiae* by Dares Phrygius, dedicated to Baldwin, archbishop of Canterbury. The MS. Laur. Ashburnham App. 1856, copied around 1355, transmits in its current state the first 387 verses of Joseph of Exeter's poem. See Marco Petoletti: L'*Ylias* di Giuseppe Iscano copiata da Boccaccio. In: Teresa De Robertis/Carla Maria Monti et al. (eds.): *Boccaccio autore e copista*, p. 346–348.
20 Marco Petoletti and Stefano Zamponi: *Gli zibaldoni*, p. 306; Silvia Coazzin: L'epitafio a Porrina trascritto da Giovanni Boccaccio. In: Alessandro Bagnoli (ed.): *Marco Romano e il contesto artistico senese fra la fine del Duecento a gli inizi del Trecento*. Cinisello Balsamo (Milano): Silvana 2010, p. 318–319; Silvia Coazzin: Potere, cultura e committenza artistica. I Porrini di Casole d'Elsa (XIII–XIV secolo). In: *Bullettino Senese di Storia Patria* 117 (2011), p. 34–120, in particular p. 79–94.
21 Marco Petoletti and Stefano Zamponi: *Gli zibaldoni*, p. 309.
22 Ibid., p. 309; Guillermo Galán Vioque: Notes on three Greek epigrams in MS Leiden, Voss. Misc. 13. In: *Aevum* 87 (2013), p. 87–98.

texts copied in his membranaceous miscellany, Boccaccio transcribed on paper another great *zibaldone*, now Florence, Bibl. Nazionale Centrale, Banco rari 50: this is his first autograph to be studied with diligence and passion by Sebastiano Ciampi in the first half of the nineteenth century.[23] In contrast to the membranaceous *zibaldone*, no poetic texts are preserved here, with the exception of a few *versus memoriales* that summarize in hexameters the subject of the first book of Ovid's *Metamorphoses*. If one excludes the actual quires 7–9, corresponding to fols. 79r–120v, in the other part of this huge manuscript Boccaccio copied well-structured excerpts of medieval historical encyclopediae. In fact, the fols. 1r–63r include a history of the emperors from Julius Caesar (at least in its current state: the manuscript lacks its first 19 fols.) to Louis IX of France, combining three different texts: the *Historie* of Riccobaldo of Ferrara, a great chronicle built on well-chosen sources, which Boccaccio retrieved during his first sojourn in Romagna, between Ravenna and Forlì (1346–1348);[24] the more widely circulating *Historiae adversus paganos* of Paulus Orosius, which moreover he copied in part in another MS., Firenze, Bibl. Riccardiana, 627;[25] and, finally, the very popular *Chronicon imperatorum* of the Dominican Martinus Polonus, a compendium of

---

23 Marco Petoletti and Stefano Zamponi: *Gli zibaldoni*, p. 313–326, and bibliography.

24 Teresa Hankey: Riccobaldo of Ferrara, Boccaccio and Domenico di Bandino. In: *Journal of the Warburg and Courtauld Institutes* 21 (1958), p. 208–226; Teresa Hankey: *Riccobaldo of Ferrara: his life, works and influence*. Roma: Istituto Storico Italiano per il Medio Evo 1996 (Fonti per la storia dell'Italia medievale. Subsidia, 2), p. 62–64.

25 The Riccardiano 627, whose first 28 folios belong to the twelfth century, is part of a more complex manuscript that also included the codex London, British Library, Harley 5383, and the Riccardiano 2795, fols. 70–76, identified respectively by Laura Pani and Teresa De Robertis. In its entirety the volume transmits, in addition to Paulus Orosius, the *Additamentum in Eutropii Breviarium* (*Historia Romana* XIII–XVI) and the *Historia Langobardorum* of Paul the Deacon, and the extraordinary letter by Pasquale Romano, *De origine civitatis Aretii* (of which it is the only witness). Boccaccio restored the twelfth-century manuscript in the 1350s, copying the missing part of the *Historiae* of Orosius, the texts of Paul the Deacon and the 'geographical' epistle of Pasquale Romano. See Teresa De Robertis: Restauro di un autografo di Boccaccio (con una nota su Pasquale Romano). In: *Studi sul Boccaccio* 29 (2001), p. 215–227; Laura Pani: "Propriis manibus ipse transcripsit". Il manoscritto London, British Library, Harley 5383. In: *Scrineum* 9 (2012), p. 305–325; Teresa De Robertis: Orosio, Paolo Diacono e Pasquale Romano: un autografo finalmente ricomposto. In: Teresa De Robertis/Carla Maria Monti et al. (eds.): *Boccaccio autore e copista*, p. 343–346; Laura Pani: "Simillima pestis Florentie et quasi per universum orbem": Boccaccio e la 'Historia Langobardorum' di Paolo Diacono. In: Antonio Ferracin/Matteo Venier (eds): *Giovanni Boccaccio: tradizione, interpretazione, fortuna. In ricordo di Vittore Branca*. Udine: Forum 2014, p. 93–131. For the epistle of Pasquale Romano see Pierluigi Licciardello, Una lettera da Bisanzio sulla citta di Arezzo. In: *Notizie di storia. Periodico della Società Storica Aretina* 8 (2006), p. 18–21; Giulio Firpo: Un frammento di itinerario tardoantico in un manoscritto di Boccaccio. In: *Geographia antiqua* 22 (2013), p. 109–124.

political and pontifical history. Polonus' *Chronicon pontificum* is copied at fols. 69v–72v, even if Boccaccio abruptly interrupts the transcription (another hand completes the whole work).²⁶ Beyond these three authors – one from the patristic age, the others medieval – the first section of the chartaceous *zibaldone* collects various excerpts from English chronicles, which deserve in-depth research for a more precise identification. These excerpts highlight Boccaccio's interests and his lively curiosity. Polonus' description of the ancient monuments of imperial Rome (a sort of summary of the *Mirabilia urbis Romae*) is copied by Boccaccio before the *Chronicon pontificum*.

This rather homogeneous bulk of historical texts is followed by a section which apparently present a more confuse appearance. Here many texts are collected: the *sermo* in praise of poetry dictated by Zanobi da Strada, which must not be confused – as it often happened – with the speech *de fama* Zanobi delivered on the occasion of his poetic coronation in 1355 in Pisa, but rather to be identified with the speech Boccaccio praised to his friend in a letter dated January 1348; two of Boccaccio's letters – the *epistle* IX, datable to April 1353, and the *epistle* VIII, as well as one from Petrarch, *Fam.* XVIII 15, dated December 1355, in a folio now in Krakow;²⁷ the very rare *Genealogies* of Paolo da Perugia, a master of mythology warmly praised in the *Genealogia deorum gentilium*; and the mythological *compendium* of Franceschino degli Albizzi and Forese Donati.²⁸

Latin classics are represented by the first 27 chapters of Sallust's *De coniuratione Catilinae* and by some excerpts from Pliny the Elder's *Naturalis historia*, used by Boccaccio in his erudite Latin works and, contrary to common belief, not copied from the famous Par. lat. 6802, which Petrarch bought in 1350.²⁹ Boccaccio also entrusted to the pages of this *zibaldone* the valuable report, transmitted only here, of the discovery of the Canary Islands, which took place only a

---

26 Aldo Maria Costantini: Studi sullo Zibaldone Magliabechiano. IV. La presenza di Martino Polono. In: *Studi sul Boccaccio* 11 (1979), p. 363–370.

27 Vittore Branca: Una carta dispersa dello Zibaldone Magliabechiano. Una Familiare petrarchesca autografa del Boccaccio. In: *Studi sul Boccaccio* 2 (1964), p. 5–14; Giancarlo Savino: Petrarca e Boccaccio deportati in Polonia. In: Michele Feo (ed.): *Codici latini del Petrarca nelle biblioteche fiorentine*. Firenze: Le Lettere 1991, p. 141–145.

28 Attilio Hortis: *Studj sulle opere latine di Giovanni Boccaccio*. Trieste: J. Dase 1879, p. 525–542; Teresa Hankey: Un nuovo codice delle 'Genealogie deorum' di Paolo da Perugia (e tre manualetti contemporanei). In: *Studi sul Boccaccio* 18 (1989), p. 65–121.

29 Marco Petoletti: Boccaccio e Plinio: gli estratti dello Zibaldone Magliabechiano. In: *Studi sul Boccaccio* 41 (2013), p. 257–293; Michael D. Reeve: The text of Boccaccio's excerpts from Pliny's 'Natural History'. In: *Italia medioevale e umanistica* 54 (2013), p. 135–152.

few years earlier.[30] Thus follows a rich miscellany of Senecan maxims, gleaned from the *Epistulae ad Lucilium* and organized by arguments. The enormous orthographic problems prove that Boccaccio copied this section during the first Neapolitan period. Only a part of this Senecan collection survives, because of the losses suffered by the MS.[31] The last part of this book, copied in the second half of the 1350s, as chronological clues disseminated in its pages certify (the date 1356 appears explicitly), is largely indebted to the *Compendium* of the bishop of Pozzuoli Paolino Veneto, a tireless chronicler, and to Hayton's *Flos historiarum terre Orientis*. Boccaccio's thirst for histories and anecdotes led him to Paolino's encyclopedia, based on Vincent of Beauvais' *Speculum historiale*, but so poorly organized and so confused, because of repetitions, distractions and errors, that Boccaccio's hostile judgment expressed in his marginal notes can be justified.[32] All the material copied in fols. 121v–221v, with the exception of some small digressions, derived in fact from Paolino's *Compendium* read by Boccaccio in Par. lat. 4939, where he left a violent note against the bishop, accusing him of adulation towards Pope John XXII, biblically branded with infamy as a *vir sanguinum*.[33] At least for the portraits of the tyrant Ezzelino da Romano and of Muhammad, he also used the *Satyrica historia*, which is a less schematic version of the *Compendium*.[34] The complex form of Paolino's work, in which the historical material

---

30 Manlio Pastore Stocchi: Il 'De Canaria' boccaccesco e un locus deperditus nel 'De insulis' di Domenico Silvestri. In: *Studi sul Boccaccio* 10 (1959), p. 143–156; Giorgio Padoan: Petrarca, Boccaccio e la scoperta delle Canarie. In: *Italia medioevale e umanistica* 7 (1964), p. 263–277; Giovanni Boccaccio: *De Canaria*. Edited by Manlio Pastore Stocchi. In: *Tutte le opere di Giovanni Boccaccio*. Edited by Vittore Branca. Milano: Arnoldo Mondadori 1994, vol. 2, p. 963–986.
31 Aldo Maria Costantini: Studi sullo Zibaldone Magliabechiano. II. Il florilegio senechiano. In: *Studi sul Boccaccio* 8 (1974), p. 79–126.
32 Aldo Maria Costantini: Studi sullo Zibaldone Magliabechiano. III. La polemica con fra Paolino da Venezia. In: *Studi sul Boccaccio* 10 (1977–1978), p. 255–275; Isabelle Heullant-Donat: Boccaccio lecteur de Paolino da Venezia: lectures discursives et critiques. In: Michelangelo Picone/Claude Cazalé Bérard (eds.): *Gli Zibaldoni di Boccaccio: memoria, scrittura, riscrittura: atti del seminario internazionale di Firenze-Certaldo, 26–28 aprile 1996*. Firenze: F. Cesati 1998, p. 37–52. For Paolino see Isabelle Heullant-Donat: Entrer dans l'histoire. Paolino da Venezia et les prologues de ses chroniques universelles. In: *Mélanges de l'École Française de Rome. Moyen Âge* 105 (1993), p. 381–442; Isabelle Heullant-Donat: L'Encyclopedisme sous le pontificat de Jean XXII, entre savoir et propagande. L'exemple de Paolino da Venezia. In: Jacqueline Hamesse (ed.): *La vie culturelle, intellectuelle et scientifique à la cour des papes d'Avignon*. Turnhout: Brepols 2006, p. 255–276; Carla Maria Monti: La Campania nel 'De mappa mundi' di Paolino Veneto. In: *Italia medioevale e umanistica* 54 (2013), p. 285–342.
33 Irene Ceccherini and Carla Maria Monti: Boccaccio lettore del 'Compendium sive Chronologia magna' di Paolino Veneto. In: Teresa De Robertis/Carla Maria Monti et al. (eds.): *Boccaccio autore e copista*, p. 373–376.
34 Roberta Morosini: De Mauhmeth propheta. In: *Studi sul Boccaccio* 40 (2012), p. 273–313.

is organized in chronological order, distinguished by kingdoms and supported by drawings and portraits that help the poor reader to recover the narrative thread, was often reorganized by Boccaccio. He summarizes the topics that the Venetian *laberintator* had distributed throughout his whole encyclopedia into monographic chapters, each devoted to a specific theme. A classic example – but certainly not the only one – is that of the chapter about famous men, in which Boccaccio regrouped according to thematic affinity all of the information that Paolino had distributed in chronological order. Boccaccio explained in a sort of brief *accessus* why he decided to transcribe extracts from a work he discredited: notwithstanding the confusion, the indiscriminate accumulation of news both true and false and the absence of source references, Paolino was in any case the only author who allowed Boccaccio to find otherwise inaccessible information. A writer who, like he himself, was attending to the *De mulieribus claris* and the *De casibus virorum illustrium*, both of which cover a long chronological period from ancient times up to the contemporary era passing through the whole Middle Ages, could not ignore such a great number of histories and anecdotes, despite the effort and inconvenience provoked by Paolino's scholarly unreliability. It is no coincidence that the most uncouth insults, in Latin and in vernacular (the appellative of *bergolo* – 'blabbermouth' – applied to the bishop is all too well known), are addressed to Paolino in connection with those very passages that most interested the curious Boccaccio and which he developed, along with contributions from other sources, in his erudite works. Patience was not his most practiced virtue, and the objective shortcomings of the Venetian dilettante did not favor a quiet discussion in his glosses.[35] With more prudence, but still subtly distancing himself, Boccaccio quotes Paolino in the *Genealogia* (XIV 8, 3) as a *hystoriarum investigator permaximus* – "a great investigator of historical accounts" – (not *historiographus*: after all, as we read in the note on fol. 148r, *imbractator est Venetus et non ystoriografus* – "the Veneto is a hack and not a historian"); thus he does not hide his opinion on the verbosity and lack of authority of this author.

Boccaccio was less severe with regard to Hayton, as he makes clear in the brief introduction to his adaptation of the *Flos historiarum terre Orientis*, a work of the early 14th century which, moreover, was quite popular. However, to remedy the *superfluitas verborum* – "superfluity of words" – and the stylistic improprieties, Boccaccio decided to transcribe Hayton's report of the Eastern lands and nations eliminating the unnecessary elements and improving its form (as he

---

[35] Marco Petoletti and Stefano Zamponi: *Gli zibaldoni*, p. 319–325, with further bibliography.

did regarding Saint Peter Damian's life dictated by Giovanni da Lodi, who was, however, the subject of heavy criticisms in his letter to Petrarch, *epistle* XI).[36]

Boccaccio's *zibaldoni* therefore are concrete proof of the passion that he had for the classics as well as for medieval Latin texts. In a certain sense they reiterate in a very concrete manner the cultural interests that also emerge from other surviving volumes of his personal library and from those, now lost, whose presence on his desk is attested by the fifteenth-century inventory of the *parva libraria* of Santo Spirito. A path yet to be explored is the study of Boccaccio as a reader of "l'antiche storie e le cose moderne" ("ancient histories and modern things"), to have a full comprehension – for example – of his late Latin writings, which are based on extensive reading of many classical and medieval *auctoritates*. The analysis of his library will contribute to understand Boccaccio's approach to the ancient literature.[37]

Two pages of Boccaccio's books are outstanding examples of his cultural breadth and of his love for the Greek world, for the classics and for the moderns, regardless of language. The last folio of the famous Dante today preserved in Toledo (Archivo y Biblioteca Capitulares, Zelada 104 6), in which Boccaccio copied in his own hand the *Trattatello*, the *Vita nuova*, Dante's arguments in

---

[36] Ibid., p. 325. It is worthwhile to read this brief premise, on fol. 223v of the chartaceous *zibaldone*: "*Liber Aythonis domini Curci*. Tempore Clementis V summi pontificis, anno vero ab incarnato verbo MCCCVII°, Ayton ex regulis Armeniorum, vir illustris et Curci dominus, abdicatis rebus transitoriis regique supero obsequium pro viribus prestare dispositus, fratrum beati Augustini habitu sumpto Pictavium venit, ubi iam dicti pontificis iussu gallico sermone de dispositionibus regnorum Asie, Niccolao quodam Falconis scribente, dictavit habunde. Qui tandem Niccolaus ex gallico transtulit in latinum. Verum quoniam et stilus inconptus est et plurima verborum superfluitate lasciviens, superflua resecans, paululum decentius scribere concitus sum, de substantialibus nil obmittens nec illustris viri ordinem mutans in aliquo". ("The book of Hayton, Lord of Corycus. In the time of Pope Clement V, the year 1307 AD, Hayton from the Kingdom of Armenia, illustrious man and ruler of Corycus, abdicated his reign and earthly belongings in order to give himself with all his might in service to a higher power. So, wearing the garb of the friars of the blessed Augustine, he came to Poitiers. Here by order of the Pope he dictated in French language the dispositions of the kingdoms of Asia, which were written down by a certain Nicolaus Falconi. This Nicolaus then translated the work from French to Latin. Because in truth the style is unadorned and tends toward a great amount of superfluous words, I am compelled to rewrite this a bit more gracefully, trimming back the superfluity, neither omitting anything of substance nor changing the order of the illustrious man in any way.") On the life of Saint Peter Damian see Antonietta Bufano: Il rifacimento boccacciano della 'Vita Petri Damiani' di Giovanni di Lodi. In: *Studi sul Boccaccio* 11 (1979), p. 333–362; Susanna Barsella: Boccaccio, Petrarch, and Peter Damian: Two Models of the Humanist Intellectual. In: *Modern Language Notes* 121 (2006), p. 99–113; Agnese Bellieni: Le vite di Petrarca, di san Pier Damiani e di Livio. In: Teresa De Robertis/Carla Maria Monti et al. (eds.): *Boccaccio autore e copista*, p. 215–217, with further bibliography.

[37] Marco Petoletti: *Il Boccaccio e la tradizione dei testi latini*, p. 114–117.

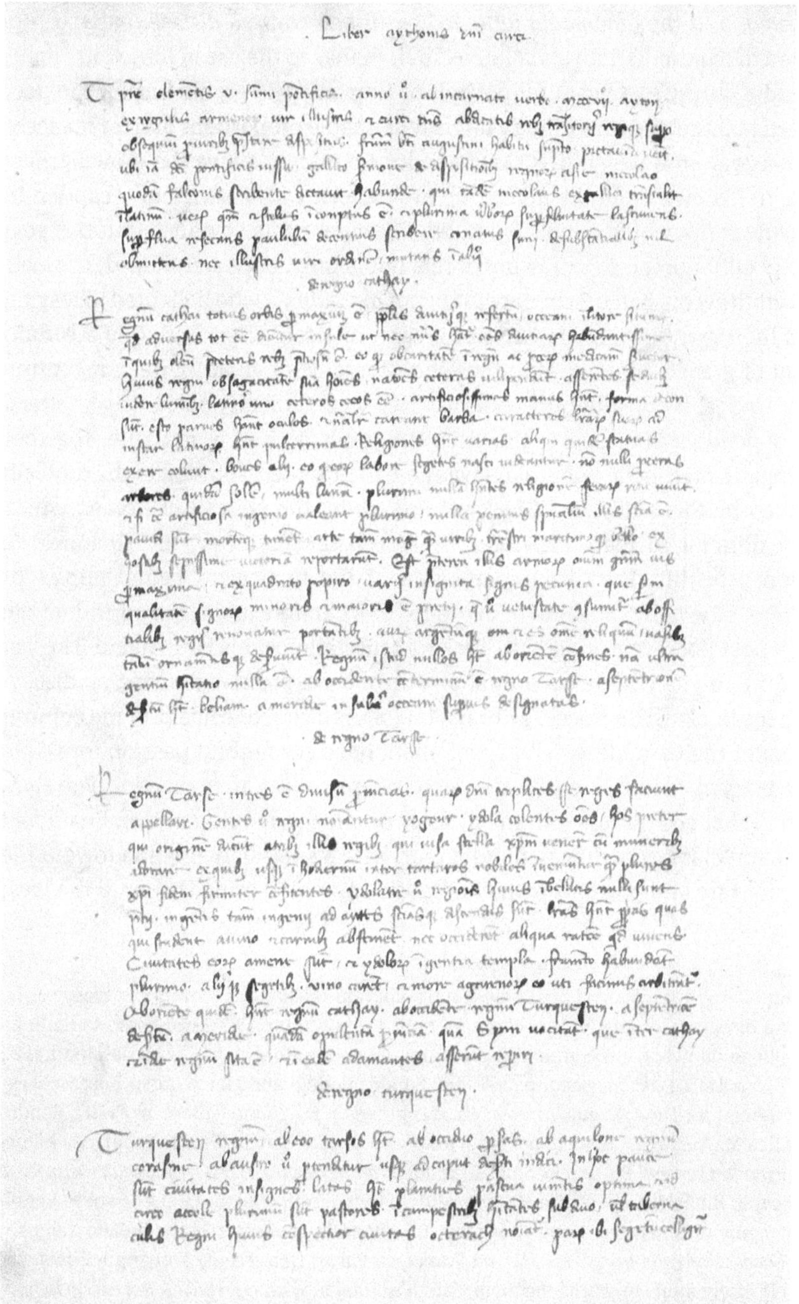

Plate 2: Firenze, Biblioteca Nazionale Centrale, Banchi rari 50, fol. 223v (Hayton's *Flos historiarum terre Orientis*, copied by Boccaccio).

terza rima, and the *Commedia* followed by fifteen *canzoni distese*, has recently revealed to Sandro Bertelli and Marco Cursi, thanks to the use of ultraviolet light, a splendid surprise: a beautiful portrait of Homer.[38] The profile bust of the poet crowned in laurel is extraordinary for its remarkable proportions and for the technical mastery with which it is sketched. In the margin above the drawing Boccaccio, in his own hand, identifies the protagonist with a vernacular caption in majuscule script which quotes *Inf.* x, 88: "Homero poeta sovrano" ("Homer sovereign poet"). Boccaccio's drawing of this noble bust, once scrutinized, compels us to withdraw his name from the number of *amateurs* – who delighted in leaving within their manuscripts drawings of greater or lesser effort and even a certain amount of grace – and add it to the official catalog of great fourteenth-century artists. Under the drawing one can discover with difficulty some Greek letters, a sort of *pendant* in respect to the other 'epigraph' derived from Dante. Together with Stefano Martinelli Tempesta, I was able to propose a solution to the problem presented by this additional Greek caption under the portrait of Homer, which is very difficult to read: "Ηοαννες δε Χερθαλδω π/φ[...]ητ" (or "Ioannes de Certaldo p/f[...]it", the likely completion of the final word being 'p[inx]it'or 'f[inx]it' – "drawn by Giovanni of Certaldo").[39] Therefore under the portrait of the ancient poet Boccaccio wrote the Greek transliteration of his Latin name. The last folio of the Toledan Dante not only shows the most expressive drawing yet discovered in the books of Boccaccio's library, but offers a concrete image of the cultural program of the Certaldese, who never abandoned his faithful passion for Dante which marked his artistic experience so deeply, even after meeting Petrarch, master of that generation and true pioneer on the road to Humanism. Enamored of the Latin classics both major and minor, with a special inclination toward the search for rare and precious texts, Boccaccio aspired to bring Homer to the West

---

38 Sandro Bertelli and Marco Cursi: Novità sull'autografo Toledano di Giovanni Boccaccio. Una data e un disegno sconosciuti. In: *Critica del testo* 15, 1 (2012), p. 287–295; Sandro Bertelli: La prima silloge dantesca: l'autografo Toledano. In: Teresa De Robertis/Carla Maria Monti et al. (eds.): *Boccaccio autore e copista*, p. 266–268; Sandro Bertelli and Marco Cursi: Boccaccio copista di Dante. In: Luca Azzetta/Andrea Mazzucchi (eds.): *Boccaccio editore*, p. 73–111; Sandro Bertelli and Marco Cursi: "Homero poeta sovrano". In: Sandro Bertelli/Davide Cappi (eds.): *Dentro l'officina di Giovanni Boccaccio. Studi sugli autografi in volgare e su Boccaccio dantista*. Città del Vaticano: Biblioteca Apostolica Vaticana 2014 (Studi e testi, 486), p. 131–136; Sandro Bertelli: L'immagine di Omero nel Dante Toledano. In: Michaelangiola Marchiaro/Stefano Zamponi (eds.), *Boccaccio letterato*, p. 171–176; and Francesca Pasut: Una recente scoperta e il rebus di Boccaccio disegnatore. In: Michaelangiola Marchiaro/Stefano Zamponi (eds.), *Boccaccio letterato*, p. 177–188.
39 Stefano Martinelli Tempesta/Marco Petoletti: Il ritratto di Omero e la firma greca di Boccaccio. In: *Italia medioevale e umanistica* 54 (2013), p. 399–409.

with the help of Leontius Pilatus, hoping that the Latin translation of the *Iliad* and *Odyssey* could be the first step in recovering once again Greek culture. In a very important page of the *Genealogia deorum gentilium*, XV 7, defending himself from the criticism of certain detractors ready to attack his choice of introducing quotations in Greek into his Latin work, Boccaccio proudly claims for himself the merit of bringing Homer to the West and affirms that it will not do to search in a little brook what is possible to obtain directly from the source. And, piling it on even thicker, he declares his pity for the Latin world, which had at that point abandoned the study of Greek to such an extent that it was no longer able to recognize the mere letters of that alphabet.

In this folio one can find Dante, not only transcribed by Boccaccio's own hand in the previous pages but directly quoted in the caption to the drawing; Homer, illustrated with care and exceptional technical ability and transfigured into a portrait that evokes the quintessential image of the laureate poet, and Boccaccio himself, biographer of Alighieri with his *Trattatello* committed to the parchments, and explicitly present in his usual signature "Giovanni da Certaldo," where Latin and Greek coexist in strategic synthesis. If the verb *pinxit*, much more difficult to decipher, follows the name of Boccaccio in Greek letters, we have an open statement that he is really the author of the drawing. It is a thrilling page like the one on fol. 88v of the Ambr. C 67 sup. where, disregarding the confines of time, Boccaccio compares a character from the famous *novella* of his *Decameron* (6, 10) to Filomuso, a swindler from antiquity who, as Martial teaches in his epigram (9, 35), was able to procure dinner for himself with his deceiving rhetoric. The marginal note in the vernacular on fol. 88v reads: "Frate Cepolla".[40]

Bibliography

Primary Literature

Giovanni Boccaccio: *De Canaria*. Ed. by Manlio Pastore Stocchi. In: *Tutte le opere di Giovanni Boccaccio*. Edited by Vittore Branca. Milano: Arnoldo Mondadori 1994, vol. 2, p. 963–986.

---

[40] Marco Petoletti: Il Marziale autografo di Giovanni Boccaccio. In: *Italia medioevale e umanistica* 46 (2005), p. 35–55, in particular. p. 44–45; Marco Petoletti: Le postille di Giovanni Boccaccio a Marziale (Milano, Biblioteca Ambrosiana, C 67 sup.). In: *Studi sul Boccaccio* 39 (2006), p. 103–184, in particular p. 114–115 and 162–163.

Secondary Literature

Monographs and Anthologies

Campana, Augusto: *Studi epigrafici ed epigrafia nuova nel Rinascimento umanistico*. Roma: Edizioni di Storia e Letteratura 2005.
Cursi, Marco: *La scrittura e i libri di Giovanni Boccaccio*. Roma: Viella 2013.
Hankey, Teresa: *Riccobaldo of Ferrara: his life, works and influence*. Roma: Istituto Storico Italiano per il Medio Evo 1996 (Fonti per la storia dell'Italia medievale. Subsidia, 2).
Hortis, Attilio: *Studj sulle opere latine di Giovanni Boccaccio*. Trieste: J. Dase 1879.
Lorenzini, Simona: *La corrispondenza bucolica tra Giovanni Boccaccio e Checco di Meletto Rossi. L'egloga di Giovanni del Virgilio ad Albertino Mussato*. Firenze: Leo S. Olschki 2011.
Nebuloni Testa, Antonietta and Marco Baglio et al. (eds.): *Francesco Petrarca. Le postille del Virgilio Ambrosiano*. 2 vols. Padova-Roma: Antenore 2006.

Articles and Papers

Barsella, Susanna: Boccaccio, Petrarch, and Peter Damian: Two Models of the Humanist Intellectual. In: *Modern Language Notes* 121 (2006), p. 99–113.
Bellieni, Agnese: Le vite di Petrarca, di san Pier Damiani e di Livio. In: Teresa De Robertis/Carla Maria Monti et al. (eds.): *Boccaccio autore e copista*. Firenze: Mandragora 2013, p. 215–217.
Bertelli, Sandro and Marco Cursi: Novità sull'autografo Toledano di Giovanni Boccaccio. Una data e un disegno sconosciuti. In: *Critica del testo* 15, 1 (2012), p. 287–295.
Bertelli, Sandro: La prima silloge dantesca: l'autografo Toledano. In: Teresa De Robertis/Carla Maria Monti et al. (eds.): *Boccaccio autore e copista*. Firenze: Mandragora 2013, p. 266–268.
Bertelli, Sandro and Marco Cursi: Boccaccio copista di Dante. In: Luca Azzetta/Andrea Mazzucchi (eds.): *Boccaccio editore e interprete di Dante: Atti del Convegno internazionale di Roma 28–30 ottobre 2013*. Roma: Salerno Editrice 2014, p. 73–111.
Bertelli, Sandro and Marco Cursi: "Homero poeta sovrano". In: Sandro Bertelli/Davide Cappi (eds.): *Dentro l'officina di Giovanni Boccaccio. Studi sugli autografi in volgare e su Boccaccio dantista*. Città del Vaticano: Biblioteca Apostolica Vaticana 2014 (Studi e testi, 486), p. 131–136.
Bertelli, Sandro: L'immagine di Omero nel Dante Toledano. In: Michaelangiola Marchiaro/Stefano Zamponi (eds.), *Boccaccio letterato. Atti del convegno internazionale (Firenze-Certaldo, 10–12 ottobre 2013)*. Firenze: Accademia della Crusca 2015, p. 171–176.
Branca, Vittore: Una carta dispersa dello Zibaldone Magliabechiano. Una Familiare petrarchesca autografa del Boccaccio. In: *Studi sul Boccaccio* 2 (1964), p. 5–14.
Bufano, Antonietta: Il rifacimento boccacciano della 'Vita Petri Damiani' di Giovanni di Lodi. In: *Studi sul Boccaccio* 11 (1979), p. 333–362.
Ceccherini, Irene and Carla Maria Monti: Boccaccio lettore del 'Compendium sive Chronologia magna' di Paolino Veneto. In: Teresa De Robertis/Carla Maria Monti et al. (eds.): *Boccaccio autore e copista*. Firenze: Mandragora 2013, p. 373–376.

Coazzin, Silvia: L'epitafio a Porrina trascritto da Giovanni Boccaccio. In: Alessandro Bagnoli (ed.): *Marco Romano e il contesto artistico senese fra la fine del Duecento a gli inizi del Trecento*. Cinisello Balsamo (Milano): Silvana 2010, p. 318–319.

Coazzin, Silvia: Potere, cultura e committenza artistica. I Porrini di Casole d'Elsa (XIII–XIV secolo). In: *Bullettino Senese di Storia Patria* 117 (2011), p. 34–120.

Costantini, Aldo Maria: Studi sullo Zibaldone Magliabechiano. II. Il florilegio senechiano. In: *Studi sul Boccaccio* 8 (1974), p. 79–126.

Costantini, Aldo Maria: Studi sullo Zibaldone Magliabechiano. III. La polemica con fra Paolino da Venezia. In: *Studi sul Boccaccio* 10 (1977–1978), p. 255–275.

Costantini, Aldo Maria: Studi sullo Zibaldone Magliabechiano. IV. La presenza di Martino Polono. In: *Studi sul Boccaccio* 11 (1979), p. 363–370.

Cursi, Marco and Maurizio Fiorilla: Giovanni Boccaccio. In: Giuseppina Brunetti/Maurizio Fiorilla et al. (eds.): *Autografi dei letterati italiani. Le Origini e il Trecento*. Vol. 1. Roma: Salerno Editrice 2013, p. 43–103.

De Robertis, Teresa: Restauro di un autografo di Boccaccio (con una nota su Pasquale Romano). In: *Studi sul Boccaccio* 29 (2001), p. 215–227.

De Robertis, Teresa: Orosio, Paolo Diacono e Pasquale Romano: un autografo finalmente ricomposto. In: Teresa De Robertis/Carla Maria Monti et al. (eds.): *Boccaccio autore e copista*. Firenze: Mandragora 2013, p. 343–346.

De Robertis, Teresa: L'inventario della 'parva libraria' di Santo Spirito. In: Teresa De Robertis/Carla Maria Monti et al. (eds.): *Boccaccio autore e copista*. Firenze: Mandragora 2013, p. 403–409.

Feo, Michele: Petrarca e Boccaccio: Critica e filologia. In: Paolo Orvieto (ed.): *Storia della letteratura italiana. XI. La critica letteraria dal Due al Novecento*. Roma: Salerno Editrice 2003, p. 103–129.

Fera, Vincenzo: Storia e filologia tra Petrarca e Boccaccio. In: *Quaderni petrarcheschi* 15–16 (2005–2006), p. 369–390.

Firpo, Giulio: Un frammento di itinerario tardoantico in un manoscritto di Boccaccio. In: *Geographia antiqua* 22 (2013), p. 109–124.

Galán Vioque, Guillermo: Notes on three Greek epigrams in MS Leiden, Voss. Misc. 13. In: *Aevum* 87 (2013), p. 87–98.

Hankey, Teresa: Riccobaldo of Ferrara, Boccaccio and Domenico di Bandino. In: *Journal of the Warburg and Courtauld Institutes* 21 (1958), p. 208–226.

Hankey, Teresa: Un nuovo codice delle 'Genealogie deorum' di Paolo da Perugia (e tre manualetti contemporanei). In: *Studi sul Boccaccio* 18 (1989), p. 65–121.

Heullant-Donat, Isabelle: Entrer dans l'histoire. Paolino da Venezia et les prologues de ses chroniques universelles. In: *Mélanges de l'École Française de Rome. Moyen Âge* 105 (1993), p. 381–442.

Heullant-Donat, Isabelle: Boccaccio lecteur de Paolino da Venezia: lectures discursives et critiques. In: Michelangelo Picone/Claude Cazalé Bérard (eds.): *Gli Zibaldoni di Boccaccio: memoria, scrittura, riscrittura: atti del seminario internazionale di Firenze-Certaldo, 26–28 aprile 1996*. Firenze: F. Cesati 1998, p. 37–52.

Heullant-Donat, Isabelle: L'Encyclopedisme sous le pontificat de Jean XXII, entre savoir et propagande. L'exemple de Paolino da Venezia. In: Jacqueline Hamesse (ed.): *La vie culturelle, intellectuelle et scientifique à la cour des papes d'Avignon*. Turnhout: Brepols 2006, p. 255–276.

Kirkham, Victoria: Iohannes de Certaldo: la firma dell'autore. In: Michelangelo Picone/Claude Cazalé Bérard (eds.): *Gli Zibaldoni di Boccaccio. Memoria, scrittura, riscrittura. Atti del seminario internazionale (Firenze-Certaldo, 26–28 aprile 1996)*. Firenze: Cesati 1998, p. 455–468.

Licciardello, Pierluigi: Una lettera da Bisanzio sulla citta di Arezzo. In: *Notizie di storia. Periodico della Società Storica Aretina* 8 (2006), p. 18–21.

Mazza, Antonio: L'inventario della 'parva libraria' di Santo Spirito e la biblioteca del Boccaccio. In: *Italia medioevale e umanistica* 9 (1966), p. 1–74.

Montefusco, Antonio: Petri de Vinea 'Vehementi nimium commotus dolore': la restituzione del testo tra storia e filologia. In: *La parola del testo* 11, 2 (2007), p. 299–365.

Monti, Carla Maria: La Campania nel 'De mappa mundi' di Paolino Veneto. In: *Italia medioevale e umanistica* 54 (2013), p. 285–342.

Morosini, Roberta: De Mauhmeth propheta. In: *Studi sul Boccaccio* 40 (2012), p. 273–313.

Giorgio Padoan: Petrarca, Boccaccio e la scoperta delle Canarie. In: *Italia medioevale e umanistica* 7 (1964), p. 263–277.

Pani, Laura: "Propriis manibus ipse transcripsit". Il manoscritto London, British Library, Harley 5383. In: *Scrineum* 9 (2012), p. 305–325.

Pani, Laura: "Simillima pestis Florentie et quasi per universum orbem": Boccaccio e la 'Historia Langobardorum' di Paolo Diacono. In: Antonio Ferracin/Matteo Venier (eds): *Giovanni Boccaccio: tradizione, interpretazione, fortuna. In ricordo di Vittore Branca*. Udine: Forum 2014, p. 93–131.

Pastore Stocchi, Manlio: Il 'De Canaria' boccaccesco e un locus deperditus nel 'De insulis' di Domenico Silvestri. In: *Studi sul Boccaccio* 10 (1959), p. 143–156.

Pasut, Francesca: Una recente scoperta e il rebus di Boccaccio disegnatore. In: Michaelangiola Marchiaro/Stefano Zamponi (eds.), *Boccaccio letterato. Atti del convegno internazionale (Firenze-Certaldo, 10–12 ottobre 2013)*. Firenze: Accademia della Crusca 2015, p. 177–188.

Petoletti, Marco: Il Marziale autografo di Giovanni Boccaccio. In: *Italia medioevale e umanistica* 46 (2005), p. 35–55.

Petoletti, Marco: Le postille di Giovanni Boccaccio a Marziale (Milano, Biblioteca Ambrosiana, C 67 sup.). In: *Studi sul Boccaccio* 39 (2006), p. 103–184.

Petoletti, Marco: L'*Ylias* di Giuseppe Iscano copiata da Boccaccio. In: Teresa De Robertis/Carla Maria Monti et al. (eds.): *Boccaccio autore e copista*. Firenze: Mandragora 2013, p. 346–348.

Petoletti, Marco and Stefano Zamponi: Gli zibaldoni. In: Teresa De Robertis/Carla Maria Monti et al. (eds.): *Boccaccio autore e copista*. Firenze: Mandragora 2013, p. 289–326.

Petoletti, Marco: Boccaccio e Plinio: gli estratti dello Zibaldone Magliabechiano. In: *Studi sul Boccaccio* 41 (2013), p. 257–293.

Petoletti, Marco: Boccaccio editore delle egloghe e delle epistole di Dante. In: Luca Azzetta/Andrea Mazzucchi (eds.): *Boccaccio editore e interprete di Dante. Atti del Convegno internazionale (Roma, 28–30 ottobre 2013)*. Roma: Salerno Editrice 2014, p. 159–183.

Petoletti, Marco: Il Boccaccio e la tradizione dei testi latini. In: Michaelangiola Marchiaro/Stefano Zamponi (eds.): *Boccaccio letterato. Atti del Convegno internazionale (Firenze-Certaldo, 10–12 ottobre 2013)*. Firenze: Accademia della Crusca 2015, p. 105–121.

Piacentini, Angelo: Un carme attribuito a san Tommaso d'Aquino nello Zibaldone membranaceo di Boccaccio. In: *Studi sul Boccaccio* 44 (2016), p. 207–234.

Ramorino, Felice: De duobus Persii codicibus qui inter ceteros Laurentianae bibliothecae servantur. In: *Studi italiani di filologia classica* 12 (1904), p. 229–260.

Reeve, Michael D: The text of Boccaccio's excerpts from Pliny's 'Natural History'. In: *Italia medioevale e umanistica* 54 (2013), p. 135–152.

Regnicoli, Laura: I testamenti di Giovanni Boccaccio. In: Teresa De Robertis/Carla Maria Monti et al. (eds.): *Boccaccio autore e copista*. Firenze: Mandragora 2013, p. 387–393.

Rizzo, Silvia: Testi classici scoperti dal Boccaccio e donati al Petrarca. In: Michele Feo (ed.): *Codici latini del Petrarca nelle biblioteche fiorentine*. Firenze: Le Lettere 1991, p. 14–16.

Robathan, Dorothy M: Boccaccio's Accuracy as a Scribe. In: *Speculum* 13 (1938), p. 458–460.

Savino, Giancarlo: Petrarca e Boccaccio deportati in Polonia. In: Michele Feo (ed.): *Codici latini del Petrarca nelle biblioteche fiorentine*. Firenze: Le Lettere 1991, p. 141–145.

Signorini, Maddalena: Considerazioni preliminari sulla biblioteca di Giovanni Boccaccio. In: *Studi sul Boccaccio* 29 (2011), p. 367–395.

Usher, Jonathan: Monuments More Enduring than Bronze: Boccaccio and Paper Inscriptions. In: *Heliotropia* 4, 1 (2007), p. 1–30.

Weiss, Roberto: *La scoperta dell'antichità classica nel Rinascimento*. Padova: Antenore 1989.

Paolo Cherchi
The Inventors of Things in Boccaccio's *De genealogia deorum gentilium*

The topic of this paper can be defined as "modest," considering that we will discuss only a small amount of the vast body of Boccaccio's *De genealogia deorum gentilium*, otherwise known simply as the *Genealogie*; it can be defined as "important," given the vital function that material has on the work as a whole; and it can be defined as "fundamental" insofar as the *Genealogie* has contributed greatly to revamping a literary genre. The paper's subject is Boccaccio's "inventor of things," upon which he touches in his *Genealogie*. He did not devote any special section to it, instead discussing the topic in a number of passages of varying length, ranging from one paragraph to entire chapters, scattered throughout the work. Yet taken together these fragments create a discourse that, properly put into context, sheds light on Boccaccio's notion of myth, mythical language, and the relationship between myth and history. By dealing with the subject of the "inventors," Boccaccio brought to light an ancient theme that had been forgotten for many centuries; most importantly to us, he developed the essential notion of "historical truthfulness" in myths, thus touching upon the crucial debate over the nature of myths: are they pure fiction, or do they refer to historical realities under the disguise of fabulous language?

Inventors were so highly esteemed in the classic world that a literary genre was "invented" to celebrate them; "heurematic" literature had origins dating back to the ancient Sophists, according to Plato.[1] In his *Protagoras*, Plato notes the importance of inventors when he touches on the story of Prometheus (320C–344A), the myth that focuses on the man as maker and shaper of things, as the creator of the *techné* that fosters the development of societies, frees man from limitations of the *physis*, and gives a decisive role to the *nomos*, the law.

---

[1] For the scholarship on the heurematic literature see Karl Thraede: Erfinder II. In: *Reallexikon für Antike und Christentum*. Edited by Theodor Klauser/ Ernst Dassmann/ Franz Joseph Dölger. Stuttgart: A. Hiersemann 1950. Vol. 5, coll. 1191–1278; Karl Thraede: *Das Lob des Erfinders: Bemerkungen zur Analyse der Heuremata-Kataloge*. In: *Rheinisches Museum zur Vorgeschichte* 105 (1961), p. 158–186; Brian Capenhaver: *The Historiography of Discovery in the Renaissance: the Sources and Composition of Polydore Vergil's 'De inventoribus rerum'* I–III. In: *Journal of Warburg and Courtauld Institutes* 41 (1978), p. 192–214; Patricia Falguières: *Les inventeurs des choses. Enquêtes sur les arts et naissance d'une science de l'homme dans les cabinets du XVIe siècles*. In: *Histoire de l'art et anthropologie*. Actes de Colloques Musée du quai Branly. In: www.actesbranly.revues.org/94; Catherine Atkinson: *Inventing Inventors in Renaissance Europe: Polydore Vergil's 'De inventoribus'*. Tubingen: Siebeck 2007.

ə Open access. © 2018 Paolo Cherchi, published by De Gruyter. This work is licensed under the Creative Commons Attribution-NonCommercial-NoDerivatives 4.0 license.
https://doi.org/10.1515/9783110419306-013

A considerable contribution to the theme of the significance of inventors came from Herodotus who, viewing things from an historical angle, maintained that many inventions had come to Greece from Egypt and Babylon (2:53), where inventors were held as divinities. This notion pointed the heurematic theme in a theological direction and led to the thinking of gods as benefactors of humanity, especially insofar as they invented all sorts of things useful to mankind.

These ideas were elaborated upon by Euhemerus in a work that has been lost to us. However, ample sections of it were preserved by Lactantius (*Inst.* I; XI; XIII; XIV; etc.) one of the Fathers of the Church. From Euhemerus we have "Euhemerism:" the theory that gods must be seen as creations of the human imagination, which transformed great rulers, legislators, and inventors into superior and eternal beings after their deaths.

There was a third way of seeing the inventors; in this view, they were merely fantastic creations of the human imagination because the inventions themselves were the results of incidental factors. For example, the melting of metals was not the invention of any particular man but rather the result of volcanic activities or of stones or ores burning in some forest fire (we can see this kind of explanation in Lucretius' *De rerum natura*, V. 1241–1268).

These varying opinions led to the three types of theology described by Varro. The first was "natural" theology, which excluded the figures of the inventors because the inventions themselves were the fruit of nature; the second was "mythical" theology, which considered the inventors mythical figures; and the third was the theology of "religious cults," which considered the inventors to be divinized creatures, worthy of religious devotion. This classification by Varro was borrowed by Saint Augustine, and Boccaccio refers to it in the *Genealogie*;[2] it is clear that he was well aware of this tradition.

The ancient world dealt repeatedly with this topic and often produced catalogues of "inventors of things." Confining ourselves to the Latin world, we see Lucretius dwelling on the inventions of things worked out by nature; we have seen the fusion of metals, and we may add now hunting, farming, and other inventions of this kind. Pliny thought the inventors were real people, only some of whom were divinized; for him the inventions were the result of the *techné* or *ars*, and not of chance or Nature. Pliny made a list of over two-hundred inventors, gathering them in a chapter of his *Naturalis historia* (VII 56), a passage that would become

---

[2] Prohemium 1, 18, p. 50. Our references here and henceforth are to *Genealogie deorum gentilium*. Edited by Vittorio Zaccaria. 2 vols. Milan: Mondadori 1998. This edition – which constitutes vol 7 and 8 of *Tutte le opere di Giovanni Boccaccio* edited under the direction of Vittore Branca – contains the Latin text and the translation into Italian.

an indispensable piece of the heurematic literature, referenced and plagiarized endlessly. To the Greek and Latin tradition we must add the Biblical one, headed by Josephus Flavius, who maintained that all inventors of things were present in the books of the Bible, and the pagan inventors did nothing more than carry the knowledge forward; for example, Moses taught the art of music to Orpheus.

With the advent of Christianity the theme experienced a rapid decline as the pagan divinities faded away or were degraded to demonic figures, and the inventions were thought to be gifts of divine providence, sent to provide mankind with the tools to live increasingly well. Mythology, too, saw a remarkable decline to the point of disappearance, since it was considered a dangerous carrier of pagan values. In Fulgentius and Macrobius, mythology is a "typological" interpretation that sees myths as precursors to Christian truths; in this context the inventors are all but forgotten. The brief chapter that St. Isidore devotes to them in his *Origenes* (or *Etymologiae* VII 11) has a purely informative function, a simple entry in his *summa*.

Rumblings of a revival were heard in the so-called "Twelfth Century Renaissance." In that climate of cultural curiosity, ancient mythology did not awaken fears of contaminating the Christian creed; in fact, it aroused so much curiosity that several mythographic collections were produced. These handbooks told the mythical stories and occasionally explained their allegorical meanings, in order to satisfy the needs of readers of ancient texts containing mythological references, chiefly poetry.[3] Among the best-known collections are the so-called *Mythographi vaticani*: three books, each by a different author, each different in the arrangement and wealth of materials, all three helpful for reading and commenting on ancient authors. Boccaccio mentions them often – especially the third, which he attributes to Alberico. In the works of these mythographers the qualification of "inventor" crops up only occasionally in the story of some individuals, and on those few occasions their inventions are recalled merely as part of their memorable deeds.

The first notable consideration of "inventors" occurs in Hugh of Saint Victor's *Didascalicon*, in which all of the arts and disciplines have their inventors. It is easy to understand why the author is interested in pointing out the "inventors"

---

[3] A survey of the Medieval mythographic literature in: Robert Earl Kaske/ Arthur Gross/ Michael W. Twomay (eds.): *Medieval Christian Literary Imagery: A Guide to Interpretation*. Toronto: University of Toronto Press 1998, the chapter 6 "Mythography" p. 104–116. A wealth of data can be found in Jeane Chance's studies on mythography, of which I recommend the last volume published because of its relevancy to our subject: Jean Chance: *Medieval Mythography. Volume 3: The Emergence of Italian Humanism, 1321–1475*. Gainesville: University of Florida Press 2014.

of philosophy, of grammar, of weaving or ironwork, because these disciplines constitute a knowledge which must be transmitted through teaching; thus it is normal to think about their "first teachers," who must also be considered their inventors: they know *per causas*, and nobody can teach something better than its inventor.

About a century later in Italy, in a culture already tinged by proto-humanistic curiosity, the *De viribus illustribus et de originibus* by Guglielmo da Pastrengo appeared.[4] It presents a very long catalogue of "firsts," among which are listed the "inventors." Opening the list is Abel, the "first to offer gifts to God," and Adam, the first man. This gives us a hint that the list follows an alphabetical order. In it we find not only biblical characters but also persons like Cato the Censor, Gorgias the Sophist, Epicurus, a Roman who created a tank to breed eels, and an endless number of people who were the "firsts" at something or otherwise distinguished themselves. One has the impression that Pastrengo is composing a "heuristic" catalogue rather than a "heurematic" one; that is, he has compiled a catalogue useful to writers of histories and encyclopedias.

What's interesting about Pastrengo's work is that it was composed around the same time Boccaccio was composing his *Genealogie*. The proximity highlights the huge difference between the two works: Pastrengo was composing a work of erudition, drawing on classical and biblical sources in the proto-humanistic style, whereas Boccaccio was set to claim the legitimacy of myth both as history and as poetry. In Boccaccio's ambitious and original plan the "inventors" acquired a new and important role.

To begin, we must say that the inventors' theme in the *Genealogie* does not occupy the space one would expect in a work focusing on "origins," as the title implies. In fact it is fair to say that the inventors' presence is disappointingly scarce, especially if we consider the opinion that the *Genealogie* is an euhemeristic work.[5] I find such a reading generally unacceptable, because even though the *Genealogie*

---

4 Guglielmo da Pastrengo: *De viris illustribus et de originibus*. Edited by Guglielmo Bottari. Padova: Antenore 1991.
5 The bibliography on the *Genealogie* is relatively limited compared to other works of Boccaccio. For our purposes we point out some of the most recent studies: Manlio Pastore Stocchi: *Giovanni Boccaccio. La «Genealogia deorum gentilium»: una novità bibliografica*. In: Piero Gibellini (ed.): *Il mito nella letteratura italiana*. Vol. 1, *Dal Medioevo al Rinascimento*. Ed. by Gian Carlo Alessio. Milano: Morcelliana 2005 (Biblioteca morcelliana, 1), p. 229–245; Luigi Canetti: *Boccaccio teologo. Poesia e verità alla fine del Medioevo*. In: *Intersezioni* 31, 2 (2011), p. 179–196; Bodo Guthmüller: *Il mito tra teologia e poetica*. In: *Intersezioni*, 31, 2 (2011), p. 219–230; Jon Solomon, *Gods, Greeks, and Poetry* (Genealogia deorum gentilium). In: Victoria Kirkham/ Michael Sherberger/ Janet Levarie Smarr (eds.): *Boccaccio: A Critical Guide to the Complete Works*. Chicago: University of Chicago Press 2014, p. 235–244; Jon Solomon is in the process of editing the *Genealogy of the*

contains euhemeristic elements, Boccaccio's general way of approaching myths is not based on the "rationalization" that was typical of euhemeristic analysis. What can be euhemeristic in the description of Demagorgon, that primitive divinity utterly invented by Boccaccio, which opens the work? In fact, the *Genealogie* inverts that course: it is not that men are deified because of their extraordinary achievements, as Euhemerus maintained, but rather that the divinities descend to the world of men through the concept of "genealogy" – or, at best, both meet at the intermediate level of a "superior man," who, like Prometheus, steals the power of the gods and bestows it upon mortals. We will come back to this important point.

In order to characterize the *Genealogie* we might define it as a study, indeed a true epos of the art of interpretation, of the exegetical and hermeneutical labors and travails of many generations through the myths, an attempt to understand whether they are pure fantasy, how and when they were formed, what truths they hide, which language they use, and how they are related to history. The *Genealogie* holds an immense legacy of stories that have fascinated generation after generation from the early philosophers on. Hence the most conspicuous aspects of the work. First, the congestion of the ancient sources, or *auctoritates*. Second, the position taken by the author: Boccaccio places his own interpretations of the myths alongside those of the other *auctores*, who only chronologically precede him. He does not impose his own interpretation, nor does he take sides; rather, he simply adds his proposals to the others, and he is far from giving them as definitive. All proposals are more or less acceptable because the interpretation of myth is like that of poetry; these are opinions rather than definitive statements. This is because the language of myth is polysemous – their meanings are inexhaustible, and Boccaccio must have thought future interpreters might come along with new interpretations.

In this sense he was aware that his *Genealogie* was an *opera aperta* ("open work"), able to expand infinitely that exegetical epos of which he was just one bard. If we see the *Genealogie* in this way, then we may understand why Boccaccio added two books to the main corpus of his work, but did not examine any new myths. Books fourteen and fifteen are dedicated to the defense of poetry, one of the earliest and most important in medieval times, just at the threshold of the Humanistic period. Far from being the appendix many critics have seen, these

---

Pagan Gods. Cambridge, Mass.: Harvard University Press 2011 (The I Tatti Renaissance Library, 46) the only volume (bks I–V) that has appeared so far. Special mention deserves the essay of David Lummus: Boccaccio's Poetic Anthropology: Allegories of History in the "Genealogie deorum gentilium libri". In: *Speculum* 1987, 3 (July 2012), p. 724–765: "special" because I was not able to see it in time to use it for this present work, and special because of its quality and originality. It gives me great comfort to see that some of the ideas I present here coincide in some points with Lummus's notion of "historic anthropology."

books are an integral part of the larger work, one that grows organically from the main conception of the *Genealogie*, offering the "aesthetic" key to the thesis that the work advances in a different way.

The accumulation of myths and interpretations makes the work feel like a *summa*, and it is often seen and used as such. It is a plausible characterization, and the presence of the *Genealogie* in the histories of mythographic literature and the pictorial arts – as well as the constant consultation by poets and writers – confirms the *summa* role it has played. Boccaccio himself may have contributed to the view of his work as an attempt to impose order on myth, to classify the intricate legacy of ancient mythologies. He pretends to have undertaken this enormous task at the request of the King of Cyprus, who confesses a strong wish to have a clear picture of the distant and confused world of myth, where kinships are multiple, where histories have many variations, where different names designate the same individual, where discrepancies are only too frequent. But we have learned to be cautious with similar authorial statements, since they often turn out to be a rhetorical device used to explain the birth of a work, and a noble one at that. The lengthy research the *Genealogie* required makes it hard to believe that Boccaccio started planning the work only when the king of Cyprus put forth his request, which, from what we can gather from Boccaccio's indications, must have occurred in 1362 or thereabouts. Since the first edition of the *Genealogie* was ready in 1365, the time span for the composition would have been just three years, too short for a work of such magnitude.

We have clues that Boccaccio was exposed to the idea of a "genealogy of gods" in his Neapolitan days; sketches on this subject were jotted down in his *Zibaldone*. Would it be too daring to say that he began toiling with the idea at the time he closed the *Decameron*, and began dealing then with the problem of how to interpret a tale? In that epilogue – so similar to the two final books of the *Genealogie* – Boccaccio had the surprise of seeing his *novelle* interpreted in ways he did not intend. As the author, he saw interpreters take his tales out of context, extrapolating words and expressions and freely twisting their meanings. It was a lesson in hermeneutics that found its ideal testing ground in ancient mythology.

Myths are stories with no known author, therefore there is no way to go back and settle a dispute among different readings, nor is there any test to distinguish a good interpretation from a bad one except good sense. This holds true when interpreting any text, especially those that are quite distant from us in time, as Petrarch tells us.[6] However, myths present additional difficulties that

---

[6] Petrarch makes this point in his *Seniles* IV 5. In: Pétrarque, *Lettres de la vieillesse. Rerum senilium libri*. Edited by Elvira Nota. 4 vols. Paris: Les Belles Lettres. 2002–2006; our letter is found in vol. II, 2003, p. 73–103.

literary texts in general may not present, and the majority of these difficulties depend on our ignorance of the culture that produced them: what was their context, where and when were they born, who listened to them, and how did they understand them?

Moreover in most cases myths are "unbelievable," utterly fantastic. The task of a mythographer, as Boccaccio sees it, is not to collect myths, but to enlighten their contexts, because only then may we appreciate them not just as beautiful stories but as a chorus of voices from a remote and primordial past, when people spoke a different language and filtered the world through a different mentality. But how can we understand that language and that mentality, since we do not have documents besides the myths themselves? We do it through interpretation and by organizing the mythological material into a system in which one myth explains the nature of another. These interpretations reconstruct a language that was a way of understanding the world, and the resulting linguistic system reconstructs the history in which that language existed.

First, let us examine the interpretations. The process of reconstructing something through its effects is quite unusual, but not inconceivable. It depends upon what we intend to reconstruct. If we want to reconstruct the "fabula," or the plot of a given myth, the problem is fairly simple, and any philologist or comparatist can identify the original tale, its variations, and even the stages through which it traveled and eras in which it appeared. But the problem becomes much harder if we try to reconstruct its meaning. Often this difficulty is dictated by the fantastic nature of the story and its characters; we tend to assume they must have a hidden meaning. The interpretations flourish and multiply, and the "meaning" as a single result vanishes. Boccaccio reports as many interpretations as he is able to find, even adding his own, to prove the only truth that can possibly be found: that myths are told by a language that personifies things and gives them a soul, a language that represents reality in symbolic terms. It is a language very similar to that of poetry, which conveys truth by disguising it in fantastic clothes.

Such a language, so distant from our normal process of denotation, is by nature polysemic. No interpretation is definitive, all are relative; but taken together they are a testimony to the poetical nature of the language of the myth. This is, I believe, the great novelty offered by the *Genealogie*: the rapport between context and interpretation, a virtual circle in which the two feed each other. We should not see this rapport as dialectical, but rather as a relationship in which both elements work simultaneously. As the interpretations multiply, the nature of their object becomes clearer: a semantic field of inexhaustible potential. This is the secret of myths's longevity in the memory of mankind.

The systematic arrangement of this immense collection of stories is the other strategy that helps us understand the nature of myths; this is another of the great innovations offered by the *Genealogie*. One single myth does not offer sufficient elements to apprehend its "nature," the particular way in which it combines language and meaning. A system, on the other hand, can give insight into mythical patterns and, at the same time, provide an overview of the culture in which myths were the only method of explaining the world. Thus interpretation and system work together to make myths understandable.

The system devised by Boccaccio is structured around the notion of "genealogy." The idea of "genealogies of gods" was not an original one: Boccaccio could have drawn it from the *Mythographus Vaticanus II* or from Paolo da Perugia, whom he met in Naples and who authored a dry *Genealogia deorum*.[7] However, no antecedent can explain the complexity of the system built by Boccaccio because the "genealogy" structure carries a meaning and a thesis hitherto unknown. We know that it was a useful tool for organizing the immense amount of mythological materials. However, it was not completely successful since Boccaccio had to find several Jupiters and Junos in order to create "genealogical families" capable of hosting the innumerable characters of the work. He did not make up these family trees; many mythographers provided information about kinships, and in spite of the inevitable gaps and holes he did not hesitate to use them. He could not do without them once he understood what great potential they brought into his plan: the idea of a genealogy developed the notions of society and history, the two bases upon which his grandiose project found its cornerstone. These notions created a chronology resembling that of any society where real men live, procreate, think, and speak.

Of course, when a character in the *Genealogie* offers genealogical data about him or herself, it is limited to indications of the closest relatives (mother, father, children) and not of a complete genealogical tree. Boccaccio reconstructs these familial ties, collecting the data from other mythographers who supposedly had access to oral sources or to documents that are lost to us. The genealogical thread gives an aura of realism to the lives of the characters, locating them in space and time. But it has a further function. All myths are presented as a complete body, which in its wholeness gives the picture of a society with its own language patterns.

We can understand the value of this genealogical grouping if we compare the *Genealogie* with the fragmentary system adopted by previous mythographers or with the large contemporary mythographic collections known as the *Ovidius moralizatus* by Pierre Bersuire, or Bercorius. Clearly, Boccaccio departs from

---

[7] On Paolo da Perugia's model, see Manlio Pastore Stocchi: *La 'Genealogia deorum gentilium': una novità bibliografica*, p. 230–232.

the myth-by-myth analysis adopted by his predecessors and inaugurates an "all myths" panorama, considering a culture as a whole that unifies all myths; within that union one finds the key to reading each individual myth. In other words, the genealogies are maps that offer the coordinates to locate and interpret any single myth, as in the *Decameron*, where the single *novelle* would be devoid of any justification if they did not relate to the "cornice," which not only unifies them all, but also explains each one's role in the work as a whole.

The notion of a genealogy implies the chronology that is the skeleton of history. Although he never states it explicitly, Boccaccio confines the world of myths to the period of the common language found in the myths themselves: a language capable of transforming real events into fabulous stories, a language that mixes realistic and unrealistic elements, that blurs space and time, that personifies abstract concepts and gives physical bodies to natural forces, that records historical information through metaphors, a language in which fantastic elements take the places of logical ones. It is the language of a civilization circumscribed to a remote past, at the origins of time.

Boccaccio marks the beginning of this civilization at the dawn of the world of men – which are not those indicated by the Bible with Adam and Eve – commencing with the disaster of the Tower of Babel, when men, deprived of their "original" language, began to group into nations, cultivate land, and build houses; that is, he begins when civilization began to take shape, when large communities started to embrace common living patterns and share the same beliefs. Boccaccio traces the end of this civilization to the time of the Trojan War.

We must remember that the *Genealogie*'s chronology can occasionally be compared with the *Chronologia* of Eusebius/Hieronimus, the standard medieval chronology wherein biblical events are set down in chronological order, and each one is dated by the year. But in order to put their time into a world perspective, the Biblical chronology is set side by side with the heathen chronology. So, for example, in the *Genealogie* we see that Abraham's days were the same as those in which the Theban wars took place, (Prohemium I 10, p. 50). Boccaccio encloses the civilization of myths within that indefinite space and time, and he does not include any myths of a more recent period. He explicitly refuses to incorporate in his work the myth of the divine births of Alexander the Great and Scipio the African, since they bear no mark of authenticity and are purely encomiastic (*Genealogie* XII 71). With the mention of these two inauthentic myths Boccaccio closes his genealogies; here is a clear sign that the modern age has begun and the old mythical one is over and already remote in time. In general, Boccaccio avoids being precise as far as historical coordinates go, not for lack of documentation but because vagueness helps to create the aura of remoteness and enchantment that surrounds the world of myths.

Identifying a civilization of myths is indispensable for understanding the nature of these marvelous stories; the myths are more intelligible if seen within an epistemic system, a cognitive system, a communication system (David Lummus calls it "poetic anthropology") that narrates its own world through metaphors, fables, and other semantic methods that create the mythical language.

But settling these questions of civilization, language, and chronology is just the beginning of our inquest. Other questions remain, and two of them are crucial: First, how do we know that Boccaccio really envisioned a world with a particular language and epistemic system? Second, how do myths relate to some truth, to some real event?

The first question is foundational, and we can answer it in several ways. Boccaccio says in the prefaces and in the concluding books of the *Genealogie* that myths are like poetry and have a language unlike the usual one based on denotation; the wealth of myths and their anonymity is a clear indication that once upon a time this was the spoken language – a sign of a different mentality.

Another proof of Boccaccio's idea of a separate epistemic system is the use of genealogies of gods rather than ordinary genealogies. The genealogy structures a world and shapes it into a form of history where families are the nuclei of a society. When these genealogies cease to produce any more branches and fruits, then it means that their world is finished and a new world has come to take its place – the mythical world is over and the historical world has begun. The choice of the gods for the genealogy was in part inevitable: mythology has an abundance of gods and their offspring. But this was not the only reason. Mythology is also filled with heroes, supermen fighting the forces of fate and vengeful gods; besides, the mythical world was originally populated by individuals born of gods. The presence of gods in the genealogy makes it clear that mythology belongs to the pagan world, so there is therefore no danger of contaminating the Christian faith. Furthermore, myths could not exist without a superior system of powers to move the world, to make its rivers run and its heavens go in circles. The mythical world's people must be responsible to a superior will: the divine is an indispensable element of the mythical mentality.

The second question is much more difficult. The relationship of myths to truth was a crucial one in the culture of Boccaccio's day, and indeed throughout much of the Middle Ages. Myths are fiction, and fiction is mendacious. So was poetry, which tells lies in the same way that myths do; their language and content are fictional, metaphorical, fantastical. Medieval theologians regarded poetry as dangerous because its seductive language was a deceptive representation of the real world. Boccaccio and the so-called "proto-humanists" led a memorable battle to defend the value of poetry, to redeem it from accusations of deception, to prove its moral value and its truthful depiction of history and of reality in general.

In fact, in the last two books of the *Genealogie*, Boccaccio defends poetry by defending myth. He does not defend any specific myths, however, but rather the fantastic language that is the language of both poetry and myth. In these books the defense is articulated in a sort of theoretical treatise, but there are other defenses to be found in the main body of work. One defense, the most pervasive, is represented by the myths themselves, or at least the major ones.

Our traditional view of the *Genealogie* as a *summa* has caused us to neglect the work as a narrative jewel. Among the hundreds of myths collected in this vast work, a large number of them could be collected as a book of short stories, a book that would be among the best produced in the fourteenth century. Some myths read as beautiful *novelle* or pithy *exempla*, wholly worthy of Boccaccio the great writer. It does not matter that he rewrites well known stories; the way he does so puts him far above mythographers who retell the same myths. We cannot dwell on this neglected aspect of the *Genealogie*, but if scholars chose to analyze it as a literary work, chances are they would enlist it as a new masterpiece.

However the *Genealogie*'s beauty seems to play into the hands of the enemies of poetry, as seductive fiction with no truth to show. It may appear as such, but Boccaccio brings forth a host of respected scholars who attempt to grasp the inner meanings of these beautiful stories, and they cannot be all wrong. Their authority and number carry the weight of the work, for in medieval times the *auctoritas* held the value that scientific proof would possess in modern times. They may disagree on the meanings, but they are convinced that some truth exists within the myths; the languages they read and the ways in which the stories are constructed lead them to believe it must be so. The process of interpreting begins when we do not understand something, and myths and poetry use language and imagery that solicit interpretation. The principal difference may be that myths "spontaneously" create their fantastic language, whereas poetry builds its own language with the purpose of communicating in a highly artful form. The difficulty in finding a meaning or interpretation upon which everyone agrees depends precisely on the polysemic nature of that language.

Boccaccio demonstrates that myths are close to reality in a way that is more direct than the ones just mentioned, and this demonstration is provided by the "inventors of things." So, after a long detour, we come to our main theme, and what we have heretofore seen will now acquire a fuller sense.

When we gather the dates that concern our inventors, perhaps we feel slightly disappointed by the scarcity of our findings; we might expect a richer harvest, considering that the *Genealogie* deals with the founders of large families, and therefore the notion of a "first" is central, as it is in heurematic literature where any inventor is by definition a "first." Here is the list of inventors; they are arranged in the order in which they are found in the work, as indicated by the book and chapter listing. Whenever possible we have added in square brackets the possible source for Boccaccio's data, indicating them as *Myth* for the *Mythographi Vaticani* with their respective number,[8] and as *Pl* for Pliny's *Naturalis historia*, precisely to Bk. XXXVII, ch. 56, as previously mentioned.

I, 4: the Arcadians invented music; I, 12: Tagetis taught haruspicy; II, 2: the first Jupiter (in fact, a certain Lisania) was the first to give laws, civic institutions, and marriage to the Attics; II, 3: Minerva was the inventor of numbers, of spinning, of weaving, and of many other arts; II, 55: Phoenix was the first to give alphabet letters to the Phoenicians; he also invented the vermillion or Phoenician color, called also punic (scarlet); II, 63: Cadmus was the inventor of marble quarries, and he was able to melt gold and other metals; III, 19: Chiron was the first to recognize the virtues of herbs and medications [*Pl* quoted as a source]; III, 25: Tossius invented mud bricks [*Pl*]; IV, 31: Atlas was the inventor of astrology [*Pl*, quoted as a source together with Lactantius and Augustine]; IV, 42: Epimetheus, who was the first to build a mud statue; IV, 44: Prometheus created the human body [*Myth* II]; Apollo was the first to recognize medicinal herbs [*Myth* III]; Orpheus invented the cither [*Myth* II], but the same invention is attributed to Apollo, and some attribute it to Amphion or to Linus; V, 21: Asclepius was the inventor of medicine; V, 23: Arabe revealed medicine to the Babylonians; V, 25: Bacchus or Liberus was the first to plant the grapevine; VII, 23: Phoroneus was the first to sacrifice to Juno [*Pl* and *Myth* II]; VII, 26: Phegoo invented the shrine to the gods and taught primitive men how to divide time by months and years; VII, 35: Daphnis was the first shepherd in the woods; VIII, 2: Mercury invented measurements and weights for the merchants; he was called by the Gauls the inventor of many arts and a guide of routes and travels; VIII, 2: Mercury and Isis taught the alphabet letters [*Myth* III]; the Athenian Buzige found the oxen and the plow [*Pl*]; VIII, 8: Chiron invented surgery [*Pl*, and *Myth* I; according to the latter he invented also the irrigation of orchards]; VIII, 10: Pico found the way to fertilize the fields with animal dung [see his relation to Stercutio/Saturn. According to Pliny he invented the playing ball]; IX, 41: Romulus was the first to divide the year into twelve months; XII, 30: Amphitrio was the first to interpret prodigies and dreams [*Pl*, quoted as the source]; XII, 35: the Achemenides invented the sacrifices to Apollo; XII, 40: Perses was the first to invent arrows [Pl]; XIII, 45: Amphiaraus was the first to invent pyromancy, the art of divining through fire

---

8 The *Mythographi Vaticani* are quoted from the *Scriptores rerum mythicarum latini tres*. Edited by Georg Heinrich Bode. Cellis: Schulz 1834.

(but Boccaccio doubts Pliny's testimony because he recalls having read about the same art from the Chaldeans, as brought to them by Nembrot).

This list elicits some considerations. Leaving aside the reduced number of "inventors" – though it is a feature that begs explanation – we notice that the names are for the most part fairly well known. Boccaccio does not want to surprise us with rare data because his novelty lies somewhere else. It is noteworthy that the dependence on Pliny and on the Vatican mythographers is sporadic and not systematic. We quote these two sources to show that Boccaccio's philology was not limited to the authority of Pliny, the most important source for a Pastrengo, and also to show that mythographers were not particularly interested in inventors. Boccaccio's philology had an unusual range; indeed, it was unique among his contemporaries. Furthermore as we have seen, philology, understood primarily as exegetical tradition, plays a fundamental role in the *Genealogie*.

The inventors are mostly men, though some gods like Bacchus and Minerva keep their title of inventor, as established by long tradition. The inventors are more frequent in the central books, and they are practically absent from the first and last two books: the first is of "cosmogonic" nature, and the human presence is rare (the myth of Pan we will see is "cosmogonic" in nature); the last two books deal with "literary theory."

The "inventors" are distributed throughout the other books, covering a period that extends from the origins of time down to the beginning of historical time. There is no demonstrable sequence in the inventors' history, but it is plausible to infer a sequence from the narrative of the work, which lists music as the earliest invention and arrows as the last invention. This beginning holds a metaphysical aura, while the end evokes an image of war, announcing, as it were, the beginning of the Iron Age that succeeded the golden civilization of myths. Boccaccio focuses on what modern mythographers call "the age of gods and men," an age where gods mixed with humans and mortals were heroes.

The most interesting element in our list is the nature of the inventions themselves. Essentially they consist of music, the wool arts, architecture (the invention of the brick), medicine, writing, the division of time, agriculture, religious cults, and finally weapons for war. It would seem, therefore, that Boccaccio was interested only in the foundational inventions of human civilization, inventions that mark the greatest leaps forward in the history of mankind, wherein mankind moved from the caves and woods into societies capable of building houses, working the fields, and using herbs to cure physical problems. The attention to these culture-changing events explains why Boccaccio remembers only a reduced number of inventors. These inventors disappeared – they likely never existed – but their inventions survived and were still present in Boccaccio's day, as they are in ours. Thus we can assume those myths refer to something real; consequently they are in essence truthful. Myths are not the truths they carry, but the way in which they tell those truths.

To see how these truths grow into a fiction or how a fiction envelops a real event, let us take two myths, the first and last of those gathered in the *Genealogie*. The first, quite long, appears in the first book and takes up the entire chapter 4:

> *De Pane secundo Demogorgonis filio.-* Pana Demogorgonis fuisse filium iam satis supra monstratum est. De quo talem Theodontius recitat fabulam. Dicit enim eum verbis irritasse Cupidinem et inito cum eo certamine superatum, et victoris iussu Syringam nynpham arcadem adamasse, que cum satyros ante lusisset, eius etiam sprevit coniugium. Pan autem cum illam urgente Amore fugiente sequeretur, contigit ut ipsa a Ladone fluvio impedita consisteret et nympharum auxilium precibus imploraret, quarum opere factum est ut in palustres calamos verteretur. Quos cum Pan motu ventorum sensisset, dum invicem colliderentur, esse canoros, tam affectione puelle a se dilecte quam delectatione soni permotus, calamos libens assumpsit, et ex eis septem disparibus factis, fistulam, ut aiunt, compsuit, eaque primus cecinit, ut etiam testari Virgilius: «Pan primus calamos cera coniungere plures Instituit, etc.». Huius preterea poete et alii insignes viri mirabilem descripsere figuram. Nam, ut Rabanus in libro *De origine rerum* ait: «Is ante alia fronti habet infixa cornua in celum tendentia, barbam prolixam et in pectus pendulam, et loco pallii pellem distinctam maculis, quam nebridem vocavere prisci, sic et manu virgam atque septem calamorum fistolam». Preterea inferioribus membris hirsutum atque hispidum dicit, et pedes habere capreos et, ut addit Virgilius, purpuream faciem. Hunc unum et idem cum Silvano arbitrabatur Rabanus, sed diversos esse describit Virgilius dicens: «Venit et agresti capitis Silvanus honore, Florentes ferulas et grandia lilia quassans». Et illico sequitur: «Pan deus Arcadie venit». Et alibi: «Panaque Silvanumque senem nymphasque sororores» etc.
>
> His igitur premissis, ad intrinseca veniendum est. Et quoniam supra Pana naturam naturatam esse dictum est, quid sibi voluerint fingentes eum a Cupidine superatum, facile reor videri potest. Nam quam cito ab ipso Creatore natura producta est, evestigio cepit operari, et suo delectata opere, illud cepit amare, et sic a delectatione irritata amori succubuit. Syringa autem, quam aiunt a Pane dilectam, ut dicebat Leontius, dicitur a syren grece, quod latine sonat deo cantans et sic poterimus dicere Syringam esse celorum seu sperarum melodiam, que, ut Pictagore placuit, ex variis inter se motibus circulorum sperarum conficiebatur, seu conficitur; et per consequens tanquam deo et Nature gratissimum, a natura conficiente diligitur. Seu volumus potius Syringam esse circa nos agentibus super celestibus corporibus Naturae opus tanto organizatum ordine, ut dum in certum et determinatum finem continuo deducitur tractu, non aliter quam faciant rite canentes armoniam facere, quod Deo gratissimum fore credendum est. Cur autem hanc nynpham arcadem fuisse dixerint et in calamos versam, ideo dictum puto quia, ut placet Theodontio Arcades primi fuere, qui, excogitato cantu, emicentes, per calamos longos et breves, spiritum, quattuor vocum invenere discrimina, et demum addidere tria, et ad postremum quod permultos faciebant calamos, in unam contraxere fistulam, foraminibus oriflantis proximis et remotioribus excogitatis. Macrobius vero hoc repertum dicit Pictagore, ad ictus malleorum gravium atque levium. Iosephus vero in libro Antiquitatis Iudaice dicit longe vetustius Iubal inventum fuisse ad tinnitum malleorurm Tubalcayn fratris sui, qui ferrarius faber fuit. Verum quoniam fingentibus verius visum est Arcades invenisse, eo quod illo forsan evo ceteros excderent fistula,

arcadem nynpham fuisse voluere. Syringam autem lusisse satyros et Pana fugientem, atque a Ladone moratam et nynpharum suffragio in calamum versam, circa nostros cantus iudicio meo aliquid bone considerationis abscondit. Hec enim spretis satyris, it est ingeniis rubdibus, fugit Pana, id est hominem natura aptum natum ad musicalia, nec equidem actu fugit, se existimatione cupientis, cui in dilatione videtur cessari quod optat. Hec tunc a Ladone sistitur donec instrumentum ad emictendam meditationem perficitur. Est enim Ladon fluvius in ripa nutriens calamos, in quos versam Syringam aiunt, ex quibus postmodum confectam fistulam novimus; ex quo sumere debemus, uti calamorum radix terre infixa est, sic et meditatio musice artis et compertus exinde cantus tam diu latet in pectore inventoris, donec emictendi prstetur organum, quod ex calamis suffragio humiditatis a radice emissis conficitur, quo confecto , sonus premeditatus emicitur suffragio humiditatis spiritus emicentis. Nam si siccus esset, nulla sonoritatis dulcedo, sed mugitus potius sequeretur, ut vidimus ex igne per fistulas emisso contingere; et sic in calamos versa videtur Syringa, eo quod per calamos resonet. Possibile preterea fuit a compertore fistule calamos ad hoc primo fuisse compertos Ladonem sucus, et sic a Ladone detenta. (I 4, §§ 1–9, pp. 88–92)

[We have already shown that Pan was the son of Demogorgon. Theodontius tells a fable about him. He says that Pan irritated Cupid with words, and he lost a contest that had been started by Cupid; Pan was ordered by the winner to love Syrinx, an Arcadian nymph, who used to play with the satyrs but had rejected Pan's company. Pan, however, urged by love, pursued the fleeting nymph, who came to a halt, impeded by the river Ladon. She implored the aid of the nymphs, who turned her into a swamp of reeds. When Pan noticed that the wind caused those reeds to produce a sound while colliding with one another and made melodious sounds, he was moved both by the love for the girl and by the delight of the sounds. He gathered the reeds and, as it is said, out of them he made a pipe of seven different lengths. He was the first to sing, as Vergil also testifies: "Pan was the first to show how to join several reeds with wax." In addition, poets and other celebrated men described his remarkable figure. As a matter of fact, Rabanus in his *On the Nature of Things* said: "Most remarkable were his upwardly bent horns, set on his forehead, his long beard reaching all the way down to his chest, and instead of a cloak he wore a pelt marked with spots which the ancients called *nebris*, and also as a wand in his hand and the seven-reed pipe." He added that his lower limbs were hairy and shaggy, and his feet were goat-like, and his face, as Vergil added, was purple. Rabanus thought that this was one and the same as Silvanus, but Vergil described them as being different: "And Silvanus came with a rustic honor on his head, shaking flowering fennel plants and tall lilies." It goes on, saying: "Pan, the Arcadian god, came." And elsewhere: "Both Pan and the old Silvanus and their sister nymphs." Given these preliminary facts, we must now move on to the innermost part. Because it was said above that Pan was *natura naturata*, I think that we can easily understand what the ancients meant when they imagined that he was conquered by Cupid. Indeed, as soon as Nature was created, she immediately began to work, and being delighted by her work, she fell in love with it. According to Leontius, Syrinx, whom Pan is said to love, takes her name from the Greek *syren* which means "singing to the gods," so we can say that Syrinx is the melody of the heavens and spheres, which, according to Pythagoras, is generated by the various interrelated motions of the orbits of spheres. Because this motion is so pleasing to God and nature, it is loved by Nature that forms it. Or we could rather say that Syrinx, because of the effect of the bodies circling around us, is a work of Nature organized in such an order that while it is forced to go into a certain and predetermined end, produces harmony not differently from those who sing according to roles. And one has to believe that this was pleasing to God. The reason why we said that this nymph was Arcadian, I think, is due to the fact that – as Theodontius likes to say – Arcadians were the first ones who, once they found a melody, discovered four distinct tones by blowing into pipes long and short, and then added three more; finally they contracted into a single pipe all that was previously done by many reeds, placing newly created holes closer and further from the blower's mouth. Macrobius instead says that this an invention by Pythagoras, obtained through the percussion of heavy and light hummers. Then Josephus in his *Jewish Antiquities* claims that it was an earlier discovery made by Iubal, while hearing the pings of hammers of his brother Tubalcain, who was a blacksmith. Yet, since some more truthful poets believed that the inventors were the Arcadians, perhaps because they excelled in pipe playing, they decided that the nymph was an Arcadian. Concerning Syrinx and her playing with satyrs and running away from the desiring Pan, and being turned into a reed with the approval of the nymphs, in my opinion this hides some useful things regarding our songs. Syrinx, spurning the satyrs, that is, the unruly passions, flees Pan, that is, the man who is by nature fit for music. In reality she flees only in the opinion of he who desires her, but he sees in the delay of reaching her the vanishing of what he ardently desires. She is stopped by Ladon, until she becomes the instrument that produces the sound she has imagined. As a matter of fact Ladon is a river that on its banks grows the reeds into which it is said Syrinx was transformed, and out them was formed the pipe that we know. From this we could deduce that, as the reed's root is fixed into the earth, in the same way the conception of the art of music and the ensuing songs remained hidden in the heart of its inventor until the instrument for emitting it was ready. This emission is done by reeds, which sprung from the roots with the help of moisture, and as the instrument was formed, the sound earlier imagined was released through the humidity of the breath that emits it. If the breath were dry it would come out not a sounding sweetness but a noise similar to that of fire released by a reed. So Syrinx seems to have been transformed into reeds because she produces sound through reeds. Moreover it is possible that the pipe's reeds were found by the inventor for the first time near the Ladon river; and this is why it said that Syrinx was detained by the Ladon.]

Before analyzing this myth, let us transcribe the story of Perses, the last inventor of the *Genealogie*. In fact the last inventor should have been Amphiaraus, but Boccaccio seems to have doubts about his story because the testimony of Pliny is disproved by the Bible; consequently we have not included it in our list – biblical inventors are not taken into account by Boccaccio.

De Perse, Persei filio: Persem filium fuisse Persei in libro Naturali hystorie testatur Plinius, de quo nil aliud comperi, preter quod idem Plinius asserit, eum scilicet primum sagittarum repertorem fuisse, quod forsan apud suos verum est, cum apud alias nationes illas longe antiquiores legerimus. (XII 40, p. 1202)

[Of Perses, Perseus' son: Pliny testifies that Perses was the son of Perseus. I know nothing of him except what Pliny himself says, that is that Perses was the first inventor of the arrows. This is perhaps true according to his people, but we have read that, according to other people, arrows were invented earlier.]

The differences between the two myths are obvious, beginning with the dimensions of the stories and the number of *auctoritates* that dealt with them: Pan's fable is a compilation of different testimonies, whereas Perses's story is found only in one source, and it is a rather unreliable one at that. The major difference, however, is that no story is told about Perses and consequently there can be no interpretation as in other myths; thus it is left to us to understand what justifies the presence of this inventor and his invention among so many other myths in the *Genealogie*.

A few explanations come readily to mind. One may be the position Perses's story has in the work; being placed toward the end makes it a supreme relic of a vanishing world, a borderline story, as it were, between the world of myths and the world of history. Another explanation may simply be that no ancient mythographers or poets known to Boccaccio told any story about Perses, not even Pliny, and Boccaccio never invents a mythological fable because it would go against his own idea of myths as spontaneous creations of a specific age in the history of mankind. Both explanations may be correct, but they are perhaps not necessary. The only certainty we have is that Perses's story is in the *Genealogie*, and the family or linkage structure that organizes the work is sufficient to justify it; with its bareness, Perses's story highlights the function of the "genealogy." In any case, this bare-bones story juxtaposed with that of Pan, so sophisticated, tells us a good deal about the wealth and variety of materials contained in this encyclopedia of sorts.

Boccaccio's analysis of Pan's myth sets up a pattern that he almost always repeats: he begins by presenting the "literature" on the subject, and then he presents his own reading. The literature offers two kinds of information: one, we may say, is iconographic in nature – the pictorial representation of Pan, his "concrete" physical appearance – the other is exegetical insofar as it attempts to explain "allegorically" or symbolically some points of the story. Boccaccio accepts them all because together they prove the vitality of the myth, its capacity to stimulate the imagination and to challenge the ingenuity of the interpreter to find its inner meaning. He does not take a position against or in favor of any of them, but he seems to go alongside them, adding to them without imposing his own thesis.

Yet, in spite of this modest presentation, it is clear that his interpretation, questionable as it may be, is different in its approach. For one thing, it is holistic in the sense that it does not dwell on details as other interpreters do, but instead envisions the whole story in order to understand better its particulars. This approach delves not so much into the meaning of the story but rather into the psychology of the story's maker.

In other words, Boccaccio tries to understand and describe the mechanism by which a certain type of mind sees and understands events or facts, a mind that functions in a cognitive way and may be called pre-logical or fantastical. It is a mind that needs personifications to explain concepts, concrete figures to explain abstract facts. Thus in studying myths the first step is not to look for their meanings, but instead to hunt for a system of communication that bears no resemblance to our "logical" language. It is a language that we can call mythopoetic because it creates fictions, characters, and stories not intending to mean something different but rather to mean exactly what they say. We allegorize myths in order to legitimate them as truthful, but they were not conceived in any allegorical fashion, for they were meant to be "true" stories in their own right. Boccaccio enters into this creative mechanism, which is very similar to the poetic one. This language is born in the same way the pipes and the melodies were: first it was "contemplated" in our souls, and then it burst out in the form of a harmony, a representation of what was inside of us. This is one of the reasons Boccaccio takes the "psychological" approach previously mentioned, shunning rationalistic and euhemeristic explanations.

In this respect, the myth of Pan and Syrinx is particularly instructive; not only is it the first, or one of the first, of the *Genealogie*, but it also deals both with an inventor and an invention. It is also a good example of that "natural theology" described by Varro: a fabulation of a natural phenomenon. The advantages it offers are multiple. First, we can be sure that this myth contains a truth, which we do not have to guess: music exists today, as it must have existed in the mythological civilization. Thus Boccaccio, contrary to other students of myths, can start from a fact and see how it was perceived, rather than starting from the myth and figuring out what it means. That perception coincides perfectly with the myth it creates, because the perceiving does not occur through words or conventional signs, as later cultures would know them, but rather through a process that imagines any object perceived as a living thing that is better understood by knowing what produces it and what it produces.

For example, wind is understood through its maker: behind the wind there must be an agent that causes the air to move and to make a sound. Once an agent is invented a story must go with it, imagining the reason for the action. If one perceives feelings or passions, the same process gives them a face and a story, creating a *fictio* in its original meaning of a "personification." In other words the creators of myths have an animistic conception of the world, a primitive mind that creates religions, superstitions, and magic. In this creative process myths must be understood as a language, a body, and a system of signs rather than the creations of a wild and baseless imagination or, equally wrong, a device used to disguise profound truths. Myths are both: they are an imaginative creation, but they are not "baseless," or devoid of any connection to the real world; they contain some truth, but they were not purposefully created to disguise it.

We must decode this special language, as we must with all ancient languages, especially if they use a different system of representation (hieroglyphics, for example); but we should not assume that the language of myths was "in code" just to enclose some higher meaning; that is, we should not confuse our reading or interpreting process with the creative one. Myths have an immediacy of communication that allegorical fables do not have, and even though they can be read allegorically they are not created by a mind that says one thing in order to mean something else. They are "spontaneous" creations without interference from the intellectual faculties. Myths, like all fables, can be read allegorically; however, the purpose of such a reading is not to bring to light the truth they hide, but instead to see how those truths are transformed into stories, into images. We must justify our interest in myths because of their beauty and not because of the "truthfulness" of their content. We must read them as we read poetry, appreciating their beauty and knowing that they contain a truth. We may disagree on what that truth may be (a good part of the *Genealogie* is devoted to these different interpretations), but this only proves that basic similarity between poetry and myth, insofar as both convey a plurality of meanings due to the nature of their non-logical languages.

To appreciate Boccaccio's new way of looking at mythological fables we can compare his readings of Orpheus and Eurydice's story to that of his contemporary Bercorius. The myth is well known, so it is not necessary to quote the long text from the *Genealogie*. Boccaccio bases his reading on Ovid's version of the myth. Orpheus' persuasive voice means that the character was a great orator; his lyre represents his oratorical skills. The bushes and the plants that he moves with his eloquence indicate the persuasiveness of his speech, which eradicates passions and tames the fiercest beasts. Eurydice culling flowers represents her concupiscence, therefore she runs away from Aristaeus, who represents virtue and courts her. While fleeing she is bitten by a snake, which represents the temptation hidden among temporal things. When Eurydice (concupiscence) falls into Hell, man with his oratory skills demonstrates his appeal of goodness and tries to bring her up to the highest reality. On his way upwards man should not turn back to look at her – that is, at his sexual desire – because if he does so it may mean that he is still tempted by earthly and perishable things.

If we remove the *integumentum* it appears that the story deals with the power of the word over human appetites: abstract notions like oratory skillfulness are personified by the music-like voice of a man, concupiscence is personified by a woman, and liberation is represented by the upward journey. Around these elements the myth builds an enchanting story that is truthful in the sense that it dramatizes real and universal feelings concerning the fascination men have for words and their weakness for sexual passion. Yet this understanding of the story takes nothing away from its beauty – the powerful tale of a singer who stills all passions around him, who causes trees to dance with the spell of his voice, and who finally is won over by the love of lady who embodies grace and physical beauty. If anything, the interpretation makes one appreciate even more the myth's value because it is not "pure" invention but fictionalizes very beautifully a drama that every man lives in his soul. It is a combination also found in great poetry.

And as happens with poetry, Boccaccio's interpretation of Orpheus and Eurydice's myth is not the only possible one. Around the same time Pierre Bersuire, or Bercorius, read the same myth from a totally different perspective. In his *Ovidius moralizatus* Bercorius sees the myth in a Christian key.[9] Orpheus is the son of the Sun as Christ is the son of God; he makes a covenant with Eurydice as God does with the human soul; the snake that bites Eurydice is the devil, and he bites her while she culls flowers, which are the desire of the forbidden fruit; the snake kills her and sends her down to Hell. When Orpheus sees, as Christ did, the soul in Hell he goes in person to rescue her. Christ rescued mankind from the hellish darkness, but Orpheus cannot rescue Eurydice because he contravenes the agreement not to look back to see whether she is following him. Bersuire's interpretation is a "typological" one, namely one that sees in an ancient story as a precursor to a Christian one.[10] Boccaccio would not dispute the plausibility of this kind of interpretation, yet he would miss in it the lack of attention to the beauty of the story and the neglect of the myth's "origin." For Bersuire the truth of the myth lies in its fulfillment outside of the myth itself, in another story, in the same way that the "figural" interpretation of history appreciates events only in light of what they have prefigured, typically a Biblical event and its fulfillment in the world of Revelation.

Boccaccio's approach is just the opposite. He looks *ad intrinseca* at what causes a myth to be born, at the ways it goes about shaping itself into a "complete" form of knowledge, that is, into a story or a character that "narrates" reality. Bercorius looks *ad extrinseca*, verifying the truthfulness of myths on the bases of "revealed" truth, indeed the very word of God. This does not mean that Boccaccio was insensitive to the problem of truth. Quite the contrary. After all, one of the basic premises of the *Genealogie* was that of dispelling the notion that myths are frivolous and mendacious fables. But Boccaccio has in mind a different

---

[9] Bersuire's text can be seen in *Metamorphosis ovidiana moraliter explanata*, wrongly attributed to Thomas Walley, first published Paris: Badius 1509, where Orpheus story is at fols. 58r–59r. This edition is reprinted by Stephen Orgel: New York: Garland 1979.
[10] For a comparative analysis of Orpheus' myth in Boccaccio and in Bersuire, see Bodo Guthmüller: *Il mito tra teologia e poetica*, p. 224–226.

kind of truth: neither that of philosophers nor of theologians, but rather that of poets, a truth that must be unchanging, expressed in a language of its own.

Of course it is very difficult, if not impossible, to "verify" the truthfulness of myths if we understand "truth" to be a faithful retelling of specific "historical" facts. The best proof we can offer is to see myths as poetry, that is, they have coherence as stories at the literary level (*sensus historialis*) and a credible meaning in their content. As for the latter point, experience offers the best testing ground: an interpreter who relies as much as possible on psychological and natural observations has a better chance of being convincing, because his arguments are of a universal nature. Myths, like poetry, transform particulars into universals, and Boccaccio seems to stick as much as possible to these guidelines of interpretation. For those who demand "evidence" of such truthfulness, the mythical "inventors" offer the best evidence with their historically "verifiable" inventions.

Boccaccio was not a heurematologist in the way Pastrengo was, and he would not be seen as such even if we took into account the few additional inventors mentioned in the *De mulieribus*.[11] It was not his intention to be one. Yet the few instances where he happened to touch on the subject are of the highest cultural significance. Boccaccio presented a new way of looking at myths, and in that new way he taught generations to come how "inventors were invented," that is, how a past culture was able to make sense of itself by creating heroes and a universe and telling about them in an imaginative language that later generations called "mythological."

Like many masterpieces, the *Genealogie* had a profound impact but not an immediate one; its innovative weight had to be absorbed. Its first immediate impact is visible in *De laboribus Herculis* (1406) by Coluccio Salutati, who is considered to be a close "student" of Boccaccio's, indeed we know for sure that he owned a copy of *Genealogie*.[12] Like his master, Salutati defended poetry, paying close attention to the exegetical tradition that guaranteed not only the vitality of myths but also their inexhaustible meanings. He saw each of the labors of Hercules as marking the phases of civilization; thus he gave a "cultural" interpretation to the myth, just as Boccaccio had done. The Quattrocento made ample use of ancient mythology in different ways, ranging from the satyr of

---

[11] *De mulieribus claris*. Edited by Vittorio Zaccaria. Milano: Mondadori 1967, chapter 27, §§ 12–13 where we find Carmenta as the inventor of the letters of the alphabet, and chapter 44, § 3, where we find the inventor of spinning.

[12] See Ernest Hatch Wilkins: *The University of Chicago Manuscript of 'De genealogia Deorum Gentilium' of Boccaccio*. Chicago: University of Chicago Press 1927.

Leon Battista Alberti's *Momus* to the dramatic use in Politianus's *Orfeo*; but it did not have the ample resonance it had in the Cinquecento.[13]

The sixteenth century was the most glorious for the triumph of the *Genealogie*. It featured several imitations: *De deis gentium varia et multiplex historia* by Lelio Gregorio Giraldi (1548), the *Immagini colla sposizione degli dei antichi* by Vincenzo Cartari (1556), and the *Mythologiae, sive explicationum fabularum libri X* by Natale Conti (1568). Furthermore, the following century saw Spain's *Teatro de los dioses gentiles* by Baltasar de Victoria (1646), to cite some of the most famous imitations. And when the interest in ancient mythology abated by the end of the seventeenth century, the *Genealogie* survived long into Neoclassical art thanks to iconographic masterworks like the *Iconologia* by Cesare Ripa, published in 1598 and reprinted in many editions up to 1786, a work that looted the *Genealogie* in the Italian translation of Betussi (1547). But of course, it was an imitation of a different nature; limited to single episodes, the iconographic imitation lost the sense of "genealogy" that Renaissance imitators had preserved with some variations.[14]

This genealogical notion was more than a device to organize the luxuriant world of myths. Boccaccio himself was not fully aware of the consequences it would have. The "genealogy" was a physical chain that bound the divinities to men, and it was not always a chain pointing upwards to the gods. In general we assume that ancient divinities were men divinized because of their great deeds, but in Boccaccio this kind of "euhemerism" is not a central thesis of the work, and certainly not when it comes to the "inventors," the "great benefactors" of mankind. In the *Genealogie* inventors are gods as well as men. Not any men, of course, but those that belong to the lineage of the gods. The last "inventor" on our list, Perses, was neither a god nor even a semi-god, but nonetheless he belonged in a lineage of gods, and this was sufficient reason to include him in the *Genealogie*.

This link between gods and men is an important point because it opened the way for the Hermetic traditions, which flourished by the end of the Quattrocento. One of the mythological heroes who became the symbol of that movement was Prometheus, the son of Japetus, a descendent of Titanus. The Prometheus who

---

13 On this aspect, some data in Susanna Gambino Longo: *La fortuna delle 'Genealogie Deorum Gentilium' nel '500 italiano da Marsilio Ficino a Giorgio Vasari'*. In: *Cahiers d'études italiennes* 8 (2008), p. 115–130.

14 It is interesting to notice that when the Inquisitions raised concern about the "pagan" mythology, the works censured were the ones that interpreted the myths in a typological way (Bersuire's is an example), and not the *Genealogie*. The explanation is that Boccaccio never saw the myths as forerunners of a Christian message. Indeed in the *Genealogie* Boccaccio limits his interpretation to the literal and allegorical senses, and almost never uses the moral and anagogic ones.

creates a mud statue of man and gives him a rational soul, the Prometheus who steals fire from the gods and gives it to man, is a hero who embodies the "renaissance man," the maker, the godlike man who builds his own world into which he brings the "creative" powers he takes or inherits from the gods. Boccaccio gave ample space to Prometheus (*Genealogie* IV 44–47), but he did not foresee the symbolic or emblematic value that Prometheus would attain. Boccaccio, however, was aware of the fact that the idea of "genealogy" would ultimately show the presence of the divine in man, it would "transfer" the divine powers into man's ability to create a world in his own likeness, even creating a language in which naming things meant creating them, as in the age of myths when creation was an anthropomorphic process by which the entire universe took on a human face or could be explained in human terms. This "transferring" of the divine to man was an epochal event, even if it was only implied in the *Genealogie*. The man who understood those implications was Coluccio Salutati, whose Hercules got from his divine parents those superhuman powers that he used to civilize the world.

The most influential aspect of Boccaccio's lesson was more explicit, namely that of contextualizing myths, seeing them as part of a culture, "historicizing" them; this, Boccaccio's epoch-making approach, was favored by Petrarch's new understanding of history and culture. The combination of these factors brought the Humanists to emphasize the "dignity of man," a confidence that provided the background for the celebration of man as an "inventor." The heurematic literature received a great impulse from this combination. Some of this literature followed the "archeological" path of the Pastrengo (Marcantonio Sabellico, *De rerum inventoribus*), and some followed the Biblical line (most famously Polydorus Virgilius, *De rerum inventoribus*, 1499), but others can be seen in Boccaccio's line (Giovanni Tortelli, *De orthographia*, [1471] specifically in the article "Horologium", and Guido Ponciroli, *De rerum memorabilium libri duo, quorum prior deperditarum posterior noviter inventarum est* [1599]), who in general examine the "new inventors," that is the inventors of the compass, printing, gunpowder and such, "modern" inventions that were by necessity "inventions in their history." But Boccaccio's lesson was most unquestionably vital to the Renaissance mythographers, who understood that inventors were invented, as Boccaccio had pointed out, and through them (especially Natale Conti) Boccaccio's lesson reached Vico.[15] However, by this time the mythographers were not interested in proving the veracity of myths so much as in confirming Boccaccio's thesis, namely that myths were the language spoken at a time when language was not regulated by a grammar based on logical categories.

---

15 Vico mentions the *Genealogia* in his *Scienza nuova*, paragraph 586 in the edition by Fausto Nicolini, Milano-Napoli: Ricciardi 1953, p. 229.

Bibliography

Primary Literature

Alberti, Leon Battista: *Momo o del principe*. Edited by Rino Consolo. Genova: Costa & Nolan 1996.
Bersuire, Pierre: *Metamorphosis ovidiana moraliter explanata*. Paris: Badius 1509. Rpt. by Stephen Orgel. New York: Garland 1979.
Boccaccio, Giovanni: *De mulieribus claris*. Edited by Vittorio Zaccaria. Milano: Mondadori 1967; vol. X *of Tutte le opere di Giovanni Boccaccio*. Edited by Vittore Branca. Milano: Mondadori 1964–1998.
Boccaccio, Giovanni: *Genealogie deorum gentilium*. Edited by Vittorio Zaccaria. Milano: Mondadori 1998. Vols. VII–VIII *of Tutte le opere di Giovanni Boccaccio*.
Boccaccio, Giovanni: *Genealogy of the Pagan Gods*. Books I–IV. Edited and Translated by Jon Solomon. Cambridge, Mass.: Harvard University Press 2011 (The I Tatti Renaissance Library, 46).
Boccaccio, Giovanni: *Zibaldoni: Edizione diplomatico-interpretativa codificata*. http://rmcisadu.let.uniroma1.it/boccaccio
Cartari, Vincenzo: *Le imagini. Con la spositione de i dei degli antichi*. Venezia: Marcolini 1556.
Conti, Natale: *Mythologiae, sive explicationum fabularum libri decem*. Venezia: Comin da Trino 1568.
Giraldi, Lilio Gregorio: *De deis gentium varia et multiplex historia*. Basilea: Oporinus 1548.
Hugh of Saint Victor: *Didascalicon: A Medieval guide to Arts*. Translated from the Latin with an Introduction and Notes by Jerome Taylor. New York: New York University Press 1961.
Lactantius, Firmianus: *Divinae Institutiones*. Edited by Eberhard Heck/ Antoine Wlosk. Berlin-Boston: Walter de Gruyter 2009.
Lucretius Carus, Titus: *De rerum natura*. With an English Translation by William Henry Denham Rouse. Cambridge, Mass: Harvard University Press 1982 (Loeb Classical Library, 181).
Mythographi Vaticani in *Scriptores rerum mythicarum latini tres*. Ed. Georg Heinrich Bode. Cellis: Schulz 1834.
Panciroli, Guido/ Heinrich Salmuth: *De rerum memorabilium iam olim deperditarum et contra recens atque ingeniose inventarum libri duo*. Ambergae: Typis Fosterianis 1599–1602.
Pastrengo, Guglielmo da: *De viris illustribus et de originibus*. Edited by Guglielmo Bottari. Padova: Antenore 1991.
Pétrarque: *Lettres de la vieillesse. Rerum senilium libri*. Edited by Elvira Nota. 4 vols. Paris: Les Belles Lettres 2002–2006.
Plato: *Protagoras*. Edited by Christopher Charles Winston. Oxford: Clarendon Press 1976.
Pliny the Elder: *Natural History*. With an English Translation by H. Rackham. 10 vols. Cambridge, Mass: Harvard University Press. 1939–1962 (Loeb Classical Library 330, 352–353, 370–371, 392–394, 418–419).
Poliziano, Angelo: *Orfeo*. Ed. by Antonia Tissoni Benvenuti. Padova: Antenore 2000.
Ripa, Cesare: *Iconologia overo descrittione di diverse immagini cavate dall'antichità et di propria inventione*. Roma: Faci 1603.
Sabellico, Marcantonio: *De rerum et artium inventoribus*. (See: Vergilius, Polydorus)
Salutati, Coluccio: *De Laboribus Herculis*. Edited by Berthold L. Ullman. 2 vols. Zurich: Thesaurus Mundi 1951.

Sardi, Alexander: *De rerum inventoribus* (See: Vergilius, Polydorus)
Tortelli, Giovanni: *De orhographia dictionum e graecis tractarum*. Venezia: Jenson 1471.
Vico, Giovan Battista: *Scienza nuova*. Edited by. Fausto Nicolini. Milano-Napoli: Ricciardi 1953.
Victoria, Baltasar de: *Teatro de los dioses de la gentilidad*. Madrid: Imprenta Real 1623–1688.
Vergilius, Polydorus: *De rerum inventoribus libri octo*. Argentorati: Zetzer 1606. (In this edition are found also the works of Alessandro Sardi, p. 13–68, and Marcantonio Sabellico, pp. 69–76, which we mention; they are found, among others, including Pliny, in a separate section, "Scriptores varii" with an independent pagination).

Secondary Literature

Monographs and Anthologies

Atkinson, Catherine: *Inventing Inventors in Renaissance Europe: Polydore Vergil's 'De inventoribus'*. Tübingen: Siebeck 2007.
Canetti, Luigi: *Boccaccio teologo. Poesia e verità alla fine del Medioevo*. In: *Intersezioni* 31, 2 (2011), p. 179–196.
Capenhaver, Brian: *The historiography of discovery in the Renaissance: the sources and composition of Polydore Vergil's* De inventoribus rerum I–III. In: *Journal of Warburg and Courtauld Institutes* 41 (1978), p. 192–214.
Chance, Jean: *Medieval Mythography. Volume 3: The Emergence of Italian Humanism, 1321–1475*. Gainesville: University of Florida Press 2014.
Kaske, Robert Earl/ Arthur Gross/ Michael W. Twomay (eds.): *Medieval Christian Literary Imagery: A Guide to Interpretation*. Toronto: University of Toronto Press 1998.

Articles and Papers

Falguières, Patricia: *Les inventeurs des choses. Enquétes sur les arts et naissance d'une science de l'homme dans les cabinets du XVIe siècles,* in *Histoire de l'art et anthropologie*. Actes de Colloques Musée du quai Branly. In: www.actesbranly. revues.org/94.
Gambino Longo, Susanna: *La fortuna delle Genealogie Deorum Gentilium nel '500 italiano da Marsilio Ficino a Giorgio Vasari*. In: *Cahiers d'études italiennes* 8 (2008), p. 115–130.
Guthmüller, Bodo: *Il mito tra teologia e poetica*. In: *Intersezioni* 31, 2 (2011), p. 219–230.
Lummus, David: *Boccaccio's Poetic Anthropology: Allegories of History in* the Genealogie deorum gentilium libri. In: *Speculum* 1987/3 (July 2012), p. 724–765.
Pastore Stocchi, Manlio: *Giovanni Boccaccio. La 'Genealogia deorum gentilium': una novità bibliografica*. In: Piero Gibellini (ed.): *Il mito nella letteratura italiana*. Vol. 1: *Dal Medioevo al Rinascimento*. Edited by Gian Carlo Alessio. Milano: Morcelliana 2005 (Biblioteca morcelliana, 1), p. 229–245.
Solomon, John: *Gods, Greeks, and Poetry* (Genealogia deorum gentilium). In: Kirkham, Victoria/ Sherberg, Michael/ Janet Levarie Smarr (eds.): *Boccaccio: A Critical Guide to the Complete Works*. Chicago: University of Chicago Press 2014, p. 235–244.

Thraede, Karl: Erfinder II. In: *Reallexikon für Antike und Christentum*. Edited by Theodor Klauser/ Ernst Dassmann/ Franz Joseph Dölger. Stuttgart: A. Hiersemann 1950. Vol. 5, coll. 1191–1278.

Thraede, Karl: *Das Lob des Erfinders: Bemerkungen zur Analyse der Heuremata-Kataloge*. In: *Rheinisches Museum zur Vorgeschichte* 105 (1961), p. 158–186.

Giuseppe Mazzotta
Boccaccio's Critique of Petrarch

Boccaccio's career as a writer began in the shadow of Dante and Petrarch, but Petrarch was Boccaccio's privileged interlocutor till the end of their lives. The two of them freely exchanged flatteries (*Seniles* XVII, 2): Petrarch would call Boccaccio the "Lactantius and Plautus of our time," and Boccaccio would reciprocate calling Petrarch the equal of Virgil and Cicero.

Their intellectual friendship was officially inaugurated with Boccaccio's gift of St. Augustine's *Commentary on the Psalms* (1353) and did not seem to falter when, a short time later, Petrarch disappointed his friend's desire to see him reconciled to the city and turbulent history of Florence. From the *Life of Petrarch* we get a sense of what Boccaccio deeply admired in Petrarch and what made him simultaneously somewhat uneasy: he admired the Florentine compatriot-writer who, even while living abroad, won international acclaim. But he was puzzled by Petrarch's political ties to despots and princes.

This paper will ponder their relation. I will make the case that deep intellectual differences between them emerged in time. They revolved mainly around issues that characterize their respective ideas about the modern age and are crystallized by Petrarch's powerful project of a renewed Western culture. That the two of them steadily engaged in this shared concern is evident from a number of views they held over, say, the "place" of Dante in literary history.

Boccaccio hardly spared reprimanding Petrarch for not acknowledging the role Dante played in that history. Boccaccio was right. Petrarch refused to take part in Boccaccio's "cult of Dante"[1] that led him to write the *Life of Dante* and, eventually, to end his career lecturing on Dante's *Inferno*. Both the reproach and the defense, if taken seriously, and not as questionable psychological symptoms of poetic rivalry toward Dante, highlight Petrarch's conviction that modernity needed a new esthetics, a new way of thinking, and a new style that would look beyond an older view of the sacredness of politics and would be capable of expressing the demands of the times.

Note: This essay appeared in: F. Ciabattoni, E. Filosa and K. Olson (eds.): *Boccaccio 1313-2013. Proceedings of the Second Triennial American Boccaccio Association Conference.* Georgetown University, October 4-6, 2013. Ravenna: Longo editore 2015, p. 29-41. Many thanks to the publisher that granted permission to reprint it the essay with minor changes.

---

1 See Maria Rosa Menocal: *Writing in Dante's Cult of Truth: From Borges to Boccaccio.* Durham: Duke University Press 1991.

The signal was clear: Petrarch thought of himself as the major actor in the drama of modern history, which was marked by momentous historical events such as the crisis of the Avignonese Church, the failure of the sciences – such as medicine – during the Black Plague that had altered his society, the hundred years war between France and England, and the collapse of Cola's effort to establish the Roman Republic. In the middle of this topsy-turvy world, so he felt, it was impossible to formulate a general truth that would encompass the whole world. For the broken, divided reality of history (which Petrarch experienced within his own self) he would provide a new esthetics that was centered on the freedom of the self and would be open to the irreducibly contradictory facets of his experiences.

His project meant bidding farewell to Dante's political fantasies of reviving the Roman Empire or similar universalizing schemes. It entailed the retrieval of a form of religious interiority, such as St. Augustine's, and, along with it, the focus on individualities and cultural elites. Such a project posited the establishment of an autonomous culture, free from ecclesiastical and political institutions, and such that it would safeguard the full weight of Latin classical culture against the encroachments of peddlers of philosophical abstractions by scholastic and neo-Aristotelian philosophers. To realize this grandiose plan, Petrarch sought to co-opt, among others, Boccaccio, as the *Seniles* (V, 2) makes painfully clear to Boccaccio himself.[2]

Did Boccaccio, in turn, ever tear himself out of the tight intimacy and collaboration with Petrarch, out of the sort of alliance both of them were interested in forging? The question admits of no simple answer. Their relation, strained by occasional peeves, became at times problematic and was colored by ambivalences on both sides and by differences that could not but be brought to a head. And yet their polemics were always tinged with genuine affection.

One show of affection is typified by Petrarch's decision to translate into Latin the last novella of the *Decameron*, the story of Gualtieri and Griselda. By translating it, Petrarch wanted the vernacular text by his "dear brother" Boccaccio to reach a larger European audience. There is a flip side to this generous gesture:

---

[2] Francesco Petrarca: *Res seniles: Libri V–VIII*. Edited by Silvia Rizzo. Firenze: Le lettere 2009, p. 36–38, § 30: "Quod autem secundum tertium ve pati nequis, vide ne superbie vere sit. Ut ego etenim te antistem – cui utinam par essem!, ut te precedat ille nostri eloquii dux vulgaris, id ne adeo moleste fers, ab uno vel altero, concive presertim tuo, seu omnino a paucissimis te prieri?" ["Take care lest it really be pride that you cannot endure second or third place, or that I should surpass you when I wish to be your equal, or that the master of our vernacular literature should be preferred to you. Do you bear it so ill to be thus outdone by one or two men, especially fellow citizens, or at most very few?"] Here and elsewhere I quote from F. Petrarch: *Letters of Old Age*. Edited and translated by Aldo S. Bernardo, Saul Levin & Reta A. Bernardo. 2 vols. Baltimore: The Johns Hopkins University Press 1992, I, p. 160.

something is lost in Petrarch's translation, and what is lost is Boccaccio's literalness, the sense of political arbitrariness in his narrative of the private and public despotism of the Prince. With an arbitrariness equal to the despot's, Petrarch de-historicizes and de-politicizes the novella: the vernacular turns into Latin, and the narrative becomes a metaphysical allegory of the soul's surrender to God. Personal affections aside, Boccaccio does finally come to grips with Petrarch's perspective on the shape and direction he wanted to impart to modernity. He goes his way and knows that the road he will take could mean disrupting the principles undergirding his master's intellectual edifice.

The text where Boccaccio presents his own comprehensive grasp and couples together questions about the self, freedom, history, nature, and modernity (which is to be understood as the time of coming to consciousness of and of linking up these four points) is the *Genealogy of the Gentile Gods*.[3] He had started in 1360 and finished in 1374, at a time when he was also giving public lectures on Dante in Florence. In its most general outline, the *Genealogy* arrays the world-history of myth from its dark beginnings in Demogorgon, which literally means the "demon of the earth." Each myth gives the imaginative representation of the quandaries and violence undergirding the human condition. The key to the dark depths of mythology and human existence, Demogorgon turns into the figuration of primal productive, fecund Chaos. The other end of the *Genealogy* features books XIV and XV, which are devoted to a discussion of modern poetry and poets, as well as, to the rational, rhetorical apparatus of literature, namely, the question of allegory in literary narratives. Clearly, a genetic relation is posited between the myth of origins and the event of modernity. In locating classical pagan myths as the vital source of modernity, Boccaccio assigns priority to Chaos and casts it as the matrix and shadow of modern self-conscious rational order. Consistently, he produces a unified narrative, the formal totality of which is made of heterogeneous and dismembered parts.

The central purpose of the *Genealogy* – to see myths as a whole made of parts – is achieved through the account of Boccaccio's own diligent quest into the extant archives of tradition and antiquarian sources, and the quest is figured as a journey across time and space that results in a universal history of myth or mythography. He calls it a "*Genealogy*," a term that revises and adapts the earlier medieval sense of "history." But there is a difference between the two.

---

[3] Giovanni Boccaccio: *Genealogia doerum gentilium*. Edited by Vittorio Zaccaria. In: *Tutte le opere di Giovanni Boccaccio*. Edited by Vittore Branca. Milano: Mondadori 1998. The text has been recently studied in Italy in a volume of essays in *Intersezioni* 2 (2011), *Il mito al tempo dei Mercanti: una proposta* edited by Francesco Citti and Sebastiana Nobili (p. 175–178). See also David Lummus: Boccaccio's Poetic Anthropology: Allegories of History in the *Genealogie deorum gentilium libri*. In: *Speculum* 87 (2012), p. 724–765.

The semantic field of the word "history", to be sure, is broad and it encompasses autobiographies, representations of events, encyclopedic writings etc.

Whether one reads Abelard's *Historia calamitatum,* Vincent of Beauvais's encyclopedic *Speculum historiale* (a history of the world up to 1240), Peter Comestor's *Historia scholastica*, Bede's *Historia anglorum*, or Dante's sense of *istoria* (*Purgatorio* X, 70–73), the semantic arc of this historiographic genre implies a chronology and an inquiry into the documented facts of ancient epochs, that are both believed to be true and organized by a teleology.

Boccaccio goes out of the way to cite Vincent of Beauvais's encyclopedic work. Like Beauvais' deliberate mixture of the encyclopedic and the historical genres in his *Speculum Historiale*, the *Genealogy* features some of its traits and asks to be viewed as a mythic deepening of *historia*: it lacks a precise chronological order, but it comes forth as an imaginative, conjectural rediscovery of oblique byways and crossing paths of cultural traditions distant from one another in the geography of the classical imagination. To this end Boccaccio roams from the authority of Dictys in Crete about the Trojan dynastic lines (*Genealogy* II, xxvi) to Egypt and Greece, all the way to the legendary genealogy of historical figures of Greek and Roman history, such as Alexander and Scipio Africanus. All the myths are linked together in a persistent system of kinship or, to say it in the language of emblems introducing every book of the *Genealogy*, as an organic family tree and a tree of poetic knowledge engendered by the insights of the exegete, Boccaccio himself.

From this standpoint, the *Genealogy of the Gentile Gods* presupposes and belongs to the hybrid genre of medieval encyclopedism. The forerunner was Isidore of Seville's *Etymologies*, a seventh century alphabet of knowledge in which etymology provides access to the world of concepts and things. In the thirteenth century Vincent of Beauvais forcefully rejected Isidore's model for the unity of knowledge in favor of a historical and chronological narrative order. In between, however, European letters witnessed the production of the likes of Rabanus Maurus, Honorius of Autun, Alexander Neckham, and Bartholomew Anglicus, down to Brunetto Latini. Boccaccio, who had practiced the encyclopedic mode in literary works, such as *De casibus*, *De claris mulieribus*, and *De montibus*, reaches in the *Genealogy* for the ultimate foundation of knowledge in mythical consciousness so that he can arrive at his own re-organization of knowledge for modern times.

At roughly the same time, Boccaccio was engaged in his encyclopedic *Genealogy*, a significant event happened. Although Petrarch had compiled earlier in his career an encyclopedic-historical text, *Rerum memorandarum libri*, he wrote a text, *On His Own Ignorance,* that unleashed a searing attack against the phenomenon of encyclopedias. He dismissed the genre as a mindless classification of fossils and arbitrary ordering of knowledge.

In this tract, signed off in Padua on January 13, 1368, he relates a strange encounter with four young neo-Aristotelians (or Averroists) who had made the fateful error of accusing Petrarch – who thought of himself as a classic – of being out of fashion and of lacking a rigorous knowledge of modern philosophy or scholasticism. Petrarch's defense branches out in different directions. He rebuffs his visitors with the Socratic argument that true knowledge coincides with ignorance – mindful of the ethical edge of the claim. He turns his attention to the Socratic conception of the examined life, the self as the only object worthy of examination, in the persuasion that the self can reveal and shape the world. Finally, he dismisses out of hand precisely Vincent of Beauvais's encyclopedia, which is based on the premise that in a rigorous empirical study of nature and the new knowledge made available by Arab science (medicine, above all), lay the foundation of a valid knowledge.

To Petrarch, scientific knowledge and naturalism amount to a trivial, empty description of natural reality and of the external architectonics of knowledge. With ruthless sarcasm, he caricatures Vincent of Beauvais's own brand of naturalism. Vincent, he says, "[...] knows how many hairs a lion has in its mane, [...] that elephants mate from behind, and are pregnant for two years; [...] that a hunter can trick a tiger with a mirror [...], that moles are blind, tat bees are deaf."[4]

The overt satire encompasses the chaotic, undisciplined catalogue of mere legends, fanciful fossils of lore, commonplace observations of natural phenomena and, above all, the principle of a possible objective order subtending the tabulations of knowledge. To this abstract structure Petrarch juxtaposes a different model of education: the autobiographical account of his own apprenticeship from the liberal arts to ethics and theology. The process of education is represented through the classical *topos* of a journey through stages leading to the citadel of the philosophical life. He identifies these intellectual stages as the real geographical places of his early youth: Montpellier, Avignon, Bologna etc. on the basis of the belief that genuine knowledge is rooted in the depth of living and is woven in the texture of one's own experience.

On *His Own Ignorance*, in reality, draws and recapitulates the main lines of Petrarch's cultural project. This project is centered on his own individual self. Thus, he writes an *apologia* for his own intellectual and moral claims. His personal superiority – so he overtly states – rests on the foundations of the Latin tradition, on the masters of introspective self-analysis such as Augustine, Boethius, Bonaventure, Bernard of Clairvaux, the Victorines (Hugh and Richard),

---

[4] Francesco Petrarca: *On His Own Ignorance*. In his: *Invectives*. Edited and translated by David Marsh. Cambridge, Mass: Harvard University Press 2003 (The I Tatti Renaissance Library, 11), p. 239, § 17. Latin text in ibid., p. 238, § 17: "Multa ille igitur de beluis deque avibus ac piscibus: quot leo pilos in vertice, [...] ut aversi coeunt elephantes biennioque uterum tument, [...] ut venator speculo tigrem ludit [...]; ut ceci talpe, surde apes."

etc. Petrarch identifies true wisdom with the interiority of religious faith over and against Aristotle's rationalism. As a consequence of his belief in the centrality of rhetoric, poetry, and theology in the scheme of knowledge, he posits the equation between poetry and theology. The point is really driven home in the letter he sent to Boccaccio's disciple, Benvenuto da Imola (*Seniles* XV, 2) in 1373. In an open polemic with Augustine (who had dismissed as a pagan confusion the purported similarity between poetry and theology), Petrarch insists on the valorization of the Roman rhetorical tradition (Cicero, Quintilian).

At first glance, Petrarch's project of a humanistic culture, with its allegiance to the theology of Augustine's "way of the heart," has its point of departure in the *now* of everyday life, in the daily exploration of one's moods to be conducted through the lenses of the ethical, historical, and rhetorical funds of classical and patristic wisdom – Cicero, Seneca, Boethius, Ambrose, Augustine, etc.

Plainly enough, Boccaccio agrees with much of Petrarch's vision. The *Decameron*, for instance, manifestly takes as its point of departure the *now* of the political, historical catastrophe of 1348. Yet he reconceives the configuration of Petrarch's project and subjects it to a sharp critique. What exactly separates their parallel lines of inquiry and where do they lead?

I have claimed that Petrarch is both the interlocutor and the polemical target of Boccaccio's own understanding of his work. The *Genealogy of the Gentile Gods* is framed by two explicit references to Petrarch. The first occurs in the *Proem* to book I. In point of fact, these introductory pages are addressed to Hugh, king of Jerusalem and Cyprus, and the address makes visible the political overtone of the *Genealogy*. We can extrapolate the king's intent in commissioning this huge bibliographical undertaking: he expected nothing less than the proof of kings' descent from gods – as Aeneas and Augustus do from Venus. This belief survived, so Boccaccio relates, till the time the Greek state came into being.

It is within this context that Boccaccio mentions for the first time Petrarch by name. He simply tells the king that the work he expects of him could best be done by "the famous Francesco Petrarch." The detail cannot make us infer even the hint of a difference in moral-political orientation between the two of them. To the contrary, Boccaccio goes on acknowledging his discipleship to Petrarch by listing a number of qualities edging toward the hyperbolic: he is gifted with a *celesti ingenio* (a divine intelligence), a strong memory, admirable eloquence, and an intimate familiarity with history and philosophy. (*Proem* I, 21)[5]

---

[5] "Homo quippe est celesti ingenio preditus et perenni memoria, ac etiam facundia admirabili, cui familiarissime quarumcunque gentium hystorie sunt, sensus fabularum notissimi, et breviter quicquid phylosophie sacro iacet in gremio, manifestum est." See Giovanni Boccaccio: *Genealogy of the Pagan Gods: Books I–IV*. Edited and translated by Jon Solomon. Cambridge: Harvard University Press 2011 (The I Tatti Renaissance Library, 46), vol. I, p. 10–11.

Donnino da Parma, the king's emissary and secretary, responds that he has not been fortunate to meet this extraordinary man, whose *fame* has reached the sky. What may be a simple touch of elegant diplomatic rhetoric to praise a great man who did not get the job, brings to the surface an issue central to the *Genealogy* and to Petrarch: fame, which crystallizes the will of the self to transcend time and its ruptures.

The other explicit reference to Petrarch comes off like an intellectual portrait of the man, whose love of freedom goes hand in hand with his being enamored with political power. Just as Dante was bound by great friendship to Frederick of Sicily and to Cangrande della Scala, so did Petrarch – Boccaccio writes – cultivate close ties with kings and popes alike, from John king of France to Popes Clement VI and Innocent VI. Above all, Petrarch is praised for his ability in teaching a king (XIV, xxii, 5) and for reversing the hierarchy of power between king and poet. He is specifically credited with brilliant insights into the "arcane meanings" of Virgil's poetry which he unveiled to the king of Naples (a confidence made to Boccaccio by Petrarch). Nor was his knowledge valuable only to ingratiate that powerful king. Boccaccio praises Petrarch for treating sacred theology in a poem such as *Bucolicum Carmen*, much as Dante himself had done (XIV, xxii, 8). In short, he enshrines Petrarch as a classic worthy of standing shoulder to shoulder with Dante. The last time Petrarch's name appears (XV, vi, 11) Boccaccio circles back to the beginning and expresses the hope his "teacher" will read the *Genealogy* and correct its likely errors.

We are watching through these gracious acknowledgements the staging of a dialogue *manqué* between a self-styled modest Boccaccio and Petrarch as the absent protagonist. The theatrical sketch lets us glimpse what Boccaccio does not actually say but he is steadily implying: the problematic question of Petrarch's own standpoint on the world and its history. He casts Petrarch as one who occupies a higher point of view than Boccaccio does, and from that high standpoint he can embrace with seeming ease, thanks to his formidable memory, all epochs of history and all perspectives.

In *De remediis utriusque fortune* Petrarch memorably writes "we are never whole, never just one, but at odds with ourselves, self-destructing. [...] torn between wholly unstable states of mind, wavering without any let up, from the beginning to its very end, the life of man."[6] But he steps back from this sort of

---

[6] My translation. Latin text in Pétrarque: *Les remédes aux deux Fortunes. De remediis utriusque fortunae*. 2 vols. Grenoble: Editions Jérôme Millon 2002 (Atopia), I, p. 550: "[...] nusquam totus, nusquam unus secum ipse dissentiens, se discerpens. [...] sine ulla requie ab ingress usque ad exitum fluctuat vita mortalis." English edition: *Petrarch's Remedies for Fortune Fair and Foul: A Modern English Translation of the* De remediis utriusque fortune. With a Commentary by Conrad H. Rawski. 5 vols. Bloomington: Indiana University Press 1991.

self-consciousness that shapes his lyrical self-representation through the myths of Echo and Narcissus in the *Canzoniere*. In *On His Own Ignorance* he looks from a high and solitary altitude at his own time and at the young people who, in telling him of his untimeliness, embody the images of modern life and its likely future values. Confronted with them, the figure Petrarch cuts is that of a classic, as Boccaccio hints, perched above the flow of time-bound events and retiring into himself to a life of cloistered and yet free self-reflection.

In reality, Petrarch is never simply the detached spectator of life's drama. He is its protagonist who affirms the values of the universe his work has called into existence. *On His Own Ignorance* comes through exactly as the breviary of a man who fights, who engages in invectives, refuses the fashion of the day and asserts the perennial significance of the intellectual / moral tradition he has forged.

Petrarch's mythology of the self that Boccaccio deftly brings out is based on a number of attributes that need recapitulation. Boccaccio places him on a pedestal of authority, for his fame allows him to hold the world as if it lay at his feet. He teaches kings and would counsel popes. By linking Petrarch with Dante (for whom theology was the real homeland), Boccaccio may well believe that Petrarch sees theology as the horizon of history and of all knowledge. In fact, both Boccaccio and Petrarch subscribe to the identification of poetry with theology and both agree that theology is the "poetry of God" (cf. XIV, xviii).

This portrait of Petrarch goes beyond the rhetoric of innocent praise. Through it Boccaccio reaches down to the cause of their rift and brings the very origin of the crisis of contemporary thought back to the heart of Petrarch's project: the question of subjectivity. What Petrarch saw as a remedy – the self, and more precisely the standpoint of the self in history – Boccaccio considers a flawed perspective. A thematic double focus – the self and history, the self in history – sustains the narrative movement of the *Genealogy of the Gentile Gods*, and I turn to it.

Boccaccio dramatizes the sense of his own self in strikingly non-Petrarchan terms. In the Proem to book I, which gets going by highlighting the origin of Boccaccio's own text, he describes the difficult circumstances of his undertaking. He stages his own self from two distinct angles. The first is political, and it concerns the relation between knowledge and power, between himself as the author of the text and King Hugh, who pays for the job and whose authority he acknowledges. Boccaccio's initial exchange with the king's courtier, Donnino da Parma, as well as a series of addresses to the king punctuating the *Genealogy*, cast an ambiguous light on the hierarchical relation between them. Boccaccio is no Lactantius (an intellectual who became the advisor of Constantine), as Petrarch with some malice had called him. The king's sovereignty is countered by Boccaccio's doubts as the teacher of the king. Unlike Petrarch with King Robert, Boccaccio does not teach his king the arcane secrets of power. Aware of the underlying, possible manipulation of the evidence dug up by the research, Boccaccio engages in a display of skepticism (in the form of authorial modesty) about the scientific validity of his work-in-progress. The modesty carefully and yet flatly denies the possibility of establishing, out of ancient forgeries and documentary gaps, the legitimacy of the king's royal / divine origin. The disavowal is an exercise in freedom.

The second angle on the representation of the self confirms and yet it is ostensibly kept separate from the first. Boccaccio, as the author who is researching his topic, stages himself as a sailor navigating uncharted seas in rough weather. He cannot master the world of myth, and his journey of discovery of treasures troves in unknown lands may end in shipwreck as he goes from one harbor to another. One example out of many will suffice: "the sky darkened with clouds, the splendor of the sunlight disappeared, the air trembling in the wind [...] I began to fear that everything had turned to primal chaos [...] thus, not without horror, do I leave behind the shores of the Ocean to direct the prow of my little boat [...]" (VIII, *Proem* 1–5).[7]

The point of his navigational rhetoric for the act of writing – a literary topos that prominently figures in literary history (Homer, Virgil, Dante etc.) for the philosophical quest – is that Boccaccio is literally at sea, that is, he understands the specifically political danger inherent in his literary adventure. That book VIII describes Saturn and his fall from Heaven by an act of usurpation unveils the nature of the fear he feels at the gathering of a storm. The metaphor of his sailing over stormy waters, moreover, conveys his awareness that he cannot turn the sea's shapelessness into a scientific chart of a universal, true historiography. He can only concoct a genealogy of the imagination. The dubious availability of empirical evidence makes him re-enact the work of the old physician Aesculapius: like Aesculapius, he has to dig into graves and bring the ghosts of the past back to life, that is, arrange the ancient myths into a system of relations conveying an intelligible moral sense. At the same time, the figure of Theodontius, who may never have existed, is ironically treated as Boccaccio's main privileged source of the history of myths.

At stake in this representation of self is Boccaccio's willed limitation of the authority of his own voice: it lacks any solid ground of certainty and admits to his fear of never reaching the firm land of knowledge. Thus, the text he has produced amounts to the sum total of ancient and recent hypotheses about the dark

---

[7] "Offuscari nebulis celum, et solis preclarum deficere iubar, turbari ventis aera [...] ceptum est. Ego autem [...] timere cepi, ne in antiquum chaos omnia verterentur [...]. [...] Non ergo absque horrore quodam Occeani litora prolemque relinquo [...] directurus fragilis navigii proram [...]." My translation.

and lost origins of cosmos and of their mythical imagination (Ovid, Varro, Augustine, Hyginus, Chalcydius, Barlaam, Leontius etc.). This rhetorical procedure highlights Boccaccio's sense of his place in the story he tells. His divergence from Petrarch's sense of an omniscient, sovereign voice that transcends and controls the universe of discourse in *On His Own Ignorance* is plain. Unlike Petrarch, Boccaccio adopts a strategy that demands that he move beyond the partition of self and others; he can, thus, try to reach for a place from which a different, alternative model of culture can be envisioned.

The many textual echoes, citations, and authors' names interlocking throughout the *Genealogy* can remind the reader of the multiple narrators and shifting perspectives deployed in the *Decameron*. They chiefly reflect Boccaccio's sense of both what it takes to reach a panoramic vision and of the stumbling block in his way toward untangling the weave of contradictory, fragmentary evidence and shifting identities. From this standpoint, the strategy recalls the productivity and the shadow of Chaos, Demogorgon, from whom all myths stem and who hovers over the confusing, frequent re-appearance in time of the same mythical names, such as Jupiter.

We are approaching the leading thought of the *Genealogy of the Gentile Gods*. Demogorgon, the first pagan god, is a shapeless chthonic entity that lives hidden in the womb of the earth accompanied by Chaos and Eternity. This mythical, poetic trinity reflects and paradoxically epitomizes the enigma of origins: the reality of contradictory hypotheses about the beginning of the cosmos put forth by the early philosophers / theologians of Greece (Thales, Anaximander etc.). The founding role assigned to Demogorgon points to a second critical difference between Boccaccio and Petrarch: their respective visions of history, within which they ponder the question of subject.

The ultimate foundation of Petrarch's imaginative world lies, as stated earlier, in his subjectivity and in the rational will of the self. So does Boccaccio assess his thinking: he stresses that Petrarch, agreeing with Leontius, believed that poetry originated with the Greeks (XIV, viii). Poetry began, that is, not in the shadowy depths of the pre-rational mythical age of Demogorgon, but in the philosophical, enlightened time of Greek rationality. Barlaam's teaching of Greek, I suspect, had its own unacknowledged impact on Petrarch, and this suspicion flows from Boccaccio's suggestion that his friend's cultural paradigm is modeled on and is narrowly circumscribed within the orbit of the Greek tradition.[8] To be sure, classical

---

[8] Lummus has argued about Boccaccio's openness to the Greeks. His point is well taken, but it has to be seen in the light of the charge that Petrarch misunderstands the Greek model. See David Lummus: Boccaccio's Hellenism and the Foundations of Modernity. In: *Mediaevalia* 33 (2012), p. 101–167.

myths – Narcissus, Echo, Apollo, Diana, Venus etc. – span Petrarch's poetry, but the hallmark of his poetic imagination lies in the lucid, self-conscious analysis of the contingency of daily moods. In this sense, Petrarch shuns the profundity and passion of the mythological age and drives a wedge between it and the rationality of allegory. Boccaccio, on the contrary, erases the drastic juxtaposition between antiquity and modernity, myth and poetry, and theology and poetry. He retrieves the untamed, primordial Chaos, such as the tragic history of Thebes, Troy, the Plague etc. – and views them as recurrent phenomena of the Chaos steadily threatening all fictions of order. The fictions aim at relieving suffering, but they also remind us of the inevitability of coming face to face with the Chaos lurking behind appearances.

Most of Boccaccio's works begin with the evocation of the shadows Chaos casts on historical experiences, and then he proceeds to weigh the possible virtues – rationality, prudence, moderation, chastity, *eutrapelia* – capable of neutralizing the hold Chaos has on the world. To give a few random examples, let me mention the Black Plague in the *Decameron* – when nature seemed to go mad – behind the decision of the young women and men to escape the city and reach a pastoral landscape on the hills of Fiesole. The *Elegy of Madonna Fiammetta* internalizes the images of Chaos as it portrays the tortured, delirious psyche of Fiammetta under the impact of her love disappointment. In the *Filostrato*, as the city of Troy edges near destruction, Troilo's love for Criseida has Boccaccio reach into the darkest corners of his mind (as he had done with the labyrinthine puzzle of Fiammetta's). For both characters Boccaccio adopts a Petrarchan language. Troilo – like Chaucer's Troilus – gives vent to his grief by quoting one of Petrarch's sonnets (*S'amor non è, che dunque è quel ch'io sento? RVF* 132). Fiammetta's melancholy over the absence of her lover resembles the solipsism of the Petrarchists *avant-la-lettre*.

Boccaccio's notion of the persistent recurrence of Chaos in history and in the individual mind, that which pushes human beings into the obsessiveness of destructive passions, is rooted in a definable ideology of nature, of the links between nature and history. It is a vision at odds with a rational view of history as a plot one can control and shape. The question he obliquely raises and must be answered is whether or not he thinks culture must be explained in terms of nature, though not in a regressive-positivistic manner. Boccaccio's figuration of Demogorgon, I would suggest, derives from the tradition of Naturalism that was developed in the twelfth century at the school of Chartres and found its imaginative extension into texts such as Brunetto Latini's *Tesoretto*, the *Roman de la Rose*'s ideas of nature, and into debates about nature and law.

Brilliant figures such as Chalcydius, Guillaume de Conches, Bernard Silvester, Alain de Lille and Thierry of Chartres were engaged in the difficult project of harmonizing the Platonic cosmology of the *Timaeus* with the account of Creation in Genesis. Boccaccio, I would further suggest, patterned his *Genealogy* on one text that he knew well and encapsulates this tradition: the *Cosmographia* of Bernard Silvester.

The poem is extant thanks to Boccaccio who copied it down and preserved it. At any rate, the poem is divided into two components, the *Megacosm* and the *Microcosm*. In its cosmological and man-centered components, the *Cosmographia* features the Christian moral tradition on the role of Nature as the protagonist of Creation. In other texts, beginning with Boethius's *The Consolation of Philosophy*, Nature is variously identified with the law of Nature and with Reason; she is called the procreative *Mater generationis* or *Vicaria-Dei* (the agent of God). Bernard defines it as the "womb of life," as a cosmic power that begs Divine Providence to shape Silva according to esthetic principles of beauty and order. The prayer amounts to a radical shift in the understanding of Plato's *hyle*: Silva is "[...] an intractable, formless chaos, a hostile coalescence, the motley appearance of being, and a mass discordant with itself" who holds "the first beginning of things in their ancient state of confusion."[9]

Boccaccio registers the divergences between Petrarch's and his own idea of nature. For instance, in *Genealogy* XIV, x, which argues that poets spin out hidden truths under the veil of their fables, Boccaccio discusses some pastoral poetry of Nature. He singles out Petrarch's *Bucolicum Carmen*, Virgil's *Bucolics*, and his own *Buccolicum Carmen*, as he calls it to distinguish it from Petrarch's poem. Petrarch's eclogues have little or no representation of nature, and in this sense they offer a mutilated version of Vergil's *Bucolics*, and, above all, a flight from ethical naturalism (4–6). The twelve poems comprising Petrarch's pastoral make up an autobiographical narrative of how the self achieves its liberty and they end in eclogue XII with the poet plunged into the world of history exemplified by the mighty war between France and England. To it, Boccaccio juxtaposes his own poem of nature as well as Virgil's *Georgics* and *The Aeneid*. For him, as for Vergil, nature is fashioned into history. But Boccaccio's complex figuration of Nature goes beyond the polemics with Petrarch and it involves the theories debated at the School of Chartres.

For the physicists at Chartres, for Bernard as well as his disciples Alain de Lille's *De planctu naturae* and for their epigone Brunetto Latini's *Tesoretto,* Nature

---

[9] Bernard Sylvester: *Cosmographia*. Translated by Winthrop Wetherbee. New York: Columbia University Press 1973, p. 67; Bernardus Silvestris: *Cosmographia*. Edited with Introduction and Notes by Peter Dronke. Leiden: Brill 1978, p. 7, vv. 1–19: "[...] cum Silva teneret /Sub veteri confusa globo primordia rerum, / [...] Silva rigens, informe chaos, concretio pugnax / Discolor Usie vulutus, sibi dissona [...]."

provides the moral standards for reforming man and for re-founding a livable political society. The optimistic view predominant at Chartres, the belief in the goodness of Nature's laws and of sex in repairing death's devastation are certainly attenuated by Jean de Meun's ironic view of the distance separating Nature from the pleasures of Venus.[10] Furthermore, the anthropomorphism of Nature's allegorical personification presupposes the principle of the intelligibility and rationality of Nature and affirms the continuity between Nature and the human world.

Thanks to Brunetto Latini, these debates filter into the Italian literary landscape. At the beginning of the *Inferno* Dante adopts the Platonic "hyle" (Bernard's *Silva*) and calls it "*Selva*" (I, 2) to lay the basis for the pilgrim's spiritual disorder he will eventually transcend. In the *Decameron* to the chaos of the Plague Boccaccio contrasts the play of utopia ruled by laws of reason in an artifice of nature, known as the *locus amoenus*, while in the novella of Tancredi and Ghismunda (*Decameron* IV, I) the relation between nature and law – the very principle of natural law – is drawn in a tragic light.

The *Genealogy*, on the other hand, focuses on something prior to the fragile fabric of Nature: the ambivalence of Chaos disguises its formless excess under a variety of masks and proliferates into myriad myths scattered all over the face of the earth. By showing how from Chaos, as from a matrix, derives a no less chaotic view of history, politics, society, and laws, Boccaccio rejects as too simple the Chartrians' benevolent view of Nature.

The point is made in the Proem to book I. It evokes Eternity, Demogorgon's companion, unknowable and inaccessible to the human mind. Everything that reaches its gate – so Boccaccio writes – does so by re-joining the kingdom of Nature, to whom he refers in the lexicon of *natura naturans* (creating Nature) and *natura naturata* (created Nature), which derives from John Scotus Erigena (*De divisione naturae* II, 2). But this theological language for Nature as a creative force and the sum of created things is quickly bracketed. By the scholastic rhetoric (which Petrarch claimed he abhorred) it is as if Boccaccio wants to dispel the suspicion that he posits the idea of the eternity of Nature and that he reduces it to the condition of an eternal immanence. At the same time, by the scholastic lexicon he does not impose – as the Neo-Platonists do – the myth of harmony reconciling the representation of Chaos and the biblical story of Creation. Myth and theology, in short, stand as two parallel representations running independently of each other, but joining together at the end of time. They are

---

[10] See Hugh White: *Nature, Sex, and Goodness in Medieval Tradition*. Oxford: Oxford University Press 2000, especially p. 110–113.

linked by a relation – a word implying differences and convergences – such as one finds in poetry and theology.

After evoking Eternity and Nature, Boccaccio turns to the phantasmagoria of the natural sequence of created beings. From the Earth – the eighth of the nine daughters of Demogorgon – are born five children, among whom is *Fama*, love, death (Erebus), and time. It is difficult to resist recalling the ordered, progressive, hierarchical ascent of Petrarch's *Trionfi* (love, time, fame, death, and Eternity), which Boccaccio dismantles. The neat rank ordering is displaced, and with it, Petrarch's luminous self-consciousness plunges into the opacity of the mythology of Demogorgon who transcends all order and all individualities.

Fama, moreover, is the other name of Clio, the muse of history. In the wake of the *Aeneid* (IV, 17 ff.) and the *Metamorphoses* (XII, 39 ff.), we gather that *Fama*, from *fari*, to speak, is bound to malicious rumor, slander, reputation and opinion and she stands for the ever ambiguous, shifty and contradictory language of history.

Against the background of *Fama*, the history of the self that longs to attain a stable, posthumous existence is seen more skeptically than in any of Boccaccio's representations. Discussing Narcissus and Echo (*Genealogy* VII, lviii–lix) – two crucial figures of Petrarch's self in the *Canzoniere* – Narcissus is identified as the son of a river: like water, he flows inexorably away. Echo, who only fragments and repeats words she has heard, fades like her own sounds in the wind. Of her Boccaccio writes, "Famam ego intelligo," (VII, lix, 3) and he adds that she describes those who die as if they never lived. As pure sound, Echo, thus, joins the noises of history, and neither she nor Narcissus will ever triumph over it.

So this final chapter ends on two figures of self and history who are indistinguishable from each other. They are the figures that turned Boccaccio in search of a way, his way beyond Petrarch's theories. Petrarch, no doubt, appears to Boccaccio as the one great thinker of his time who has taken seriously the question of agency in history and who has affirmed the will of the self as the power of the individual consciousness to confront and shape the world in which he is situated.

But Boccaccio also reminds Petrarch, whom he imagines as his reader, of the two critical issues of his own project. One is that history, as Petrarch saw it, must be construed as the sum total of perspectival experiences held together by one's subjective consciousness. The other concerns the limitations of the self in time: the representation of a faltering author undercuts the noblest dreams of re-inventing history. Boccaccio reminds us of the need to envision the future from the standpoint of the memory of the foggy, shaky origins of human culture especially when he seeks to open up a new, unexplored way into the knowledge of myth.

In response to Petrarch's contention that Fortune and the mutability of time must be confronted by the virtues harbored within oneself (the ethical virtues, the intellectual virtues, and God's gifts), Boccaccio etches a theory that surpasses Petrarch's. He had turned to prose, the prose of the *Decameron*, based on an idea of alterity and had introduced the model of a style capable of representing the complicity between seemingly unrelated themes, such as, for instance, sexuality and theology (see on this the previous chapter). Above all, the recurring, impending reality of Chaos leads him to produce an art which is both inscribed within and capable of provisionally holding at bay the sovereignty of Chaos. The work of art, its virtues of prudence and rigor, coincides with and makes available the power of language to open up the ambiguities of history and the self.

Language was the remedy Madonna Fiammetta found to get her out of her madness. It was the *brigata*'s logotherapy (la *curacion de la palabra* as Laín Entralgo called it)[11] that sheltered them from the plague, and it is language that annuls Echo's very existence. The virtues of poetic language hidden at the heart of every myth lie in their meaning, which both contains and exceeds their literal sense.

The excess precedes the economy of the literal determination of every statement, the way Chaos precedes order, and it coincides with the very idea of "Genealogy," which both posits the uncontainable energy of Demogorgon and entails the generosity of myths, their multiplicity and their process of steady regeneration. In grasping the priority of Chaos or excess, forever transgressive and forever going beyond the boundaries of the literal, Boccaccio uncovered a new perspective on poetic language as a relation of bodies and passions that are grounded in myths.

One last question is in order: which one of the two ways, Petrarch's and Boccaccio's, is preferable to the other? The answer can only be genealogical: each depends on and presupposes the other, and both together draw the double face of Humanism, that is to say either face reflected in a mirror. Petrarch, who founds a "world of words" not without a political scheme underlying it, leads to Machiavelli. Boccaccio's *Genealogy of the Gentile Gods* reads like the preamble to Vico's *New Science*.

---

[11] See Pedro Laín Entralgo: *La curación de la palabra en la antigüedad clásica*. Madrid: Revista de Occidente 1958.

Bibliography

Primary Literature

Bernard Sylvester: *Cosmographia*. Trans. by Winthrop Wetherbee. New York: Columbia University Press 1973.
Bernardus Silvestris: *Cosmographia*. Edited with Introduction and Notes by Peter Dronke. Leiden: Brill 1978.
Giovanni Boccaccio, Giovanni: *Genealogia deorum gentilium*. Edited by Vittorio Zaccaria. In: *Tutte le opere di Giovanni Boccaccio*. Edited by Vittore Branca. Vol. 7/8. Milano: Mondadori 1998.
Giovanni Boccaccio: *Genealogy of the Pagan Gods: Books I–IV*. Edited and translated by Jon Solomon. Cambridge: Harvard University Press 2011.
Francesco Petrarca: *Petrarch's Remedies for Fortune Fair and Foul: A Modern English Translation of the 'De remediis utriusque fortune'*. With a Commentary by Conrad H. Rawski. Bloomington: Indiana University Press 1991.
Francesco Petrarca: *Letters of Old Age*. Edited and translated by Aldo S. Bernardo, Saul Levin & Reta A. Bernardo. 2 vols. Baltimore: The Johns Hopkins University Press 1992.
Pétrarque: *Les remédes aux deux Fortunes. De remediis utriusque fortunae*. 2 volumes. Grenoble: Editions Jérôme Millon 2002 (Atopia).
Francesco Petrarca: *On His Own Ignorance*. In his: *Invectives*. Edited and translated by David Marsh. Cambridge, Mass: Harvard University Press 2003 (The I Tatti Renaissance Library, 11).
Francesco Petrarca: *Res seniles: Libri V–VIII*. Edited by Silvia Rizzo. Firenze: Le lettere 2009.

Secondary Literature

Monographs and Anthologies

Citti, Francesco and Sebastiana Nobili (eds.): *Il mito al tempo dei mercanti: una proposta*. In: *Intersezioni* 31, 2 (2011), p. 175–178.
Laín Entralgo, Pedro: *La curación de la palabra en la antigüedad clásica*. Madrid: Revista de Occidente 1958.
Menocal, Maria Rosa: *Writing in Dante's Cult of Truth: From Borges to Boccaccio*. Durham: Duke University Press 1991.
White, Hugh: *Nature, Sex, and Goodness in Medieval Trans*. Oxford: Oxford University Press 2000.

Articles and Papers

Lummus, David: Boccaccio's Poetic Anthropology: Allegories of History in the *Genealogie deorum gentilium libri*. In: *Speculum* 87 (2012), p. 724–765.
Lummus, David: Boccaccio's Hellenism and the Foundations of Modernity. In: *Mediaevalia* 33 (2012), p. 101–167.

Giorgio Ficara
The Perfect Woman in Boccaccio and Petrarch

Every form, every poem falls apart when separated from its ideas and, conversely, 'idea,' in one of its primitive acceptations, means precisely form and poem. Let us now read the youthful verses of a writer who, with his conception of humanity and nature, would change the very institutions of writing:

> Intorn' ad una fonte, in un pratello
> di verdi erbette pieno e di bei fiori,
> sedean tre angiolette, i loro amori
> forse narrando, ed a ciascuna 'l bello
>   viso adombrava un verde ramicello
> ch'i capei d'or cingea, al qual di fuori
> e dentro insieme i dua vaghi colori
> avvolgea un suave venticello.
>   E dopo alquanto l'una alle due disse
> (com'io udi'): "Deh, se per avventura
> di ciascuna l'amante or qui venisse,
>   fuggiremo noi quinci per paura?".
> A cui le due risposer: "Chi fuggisse,
> poco savia saria, con tal ventura!" (I)

> [Beside a fountain in a little grove
> That fresh green fronds and pretty flowers did grace,
> Three maidens sat and talked methinks of love.
> Mid golden locks, o'ershadowing each sweet face,
> For coolness was entwined a leaf-green spray,
> And all the while a gentle zephyr played
> Through green and golden in a tender way,
> Weaving a web of sunshine and of shade.
> After a while, unto the other two
> One spoke, and I could hear her words: "Think you
> That if our lovers were to happen by
> We would all run away for very fright?"
> The others answered her: "From such delight
> She were a little fool who'd wish to fly!"][1]

---

[1] Giovanni Boccaccio: *Rime*. Edited by Vittore Branca. In: *Tutte le opere di G. Boccaccio*. Edited by Vittore Branca. 10 vols. Milan: Mondadori 1992, vol. V, 1, p. 33; trans. in: *An Anthology of Italian Poems. 13th–19th Century*. Selected and Translated by Lorna de' Lucchi. New York: Biblo and Tannen 1967, p. 93.

ə Open access. © 2018 Giorgio Ficara, published by De Gruyter. This work is licensed under the Creative Commons Attribution-NonCommercial-NoDerivatives 4.0 license.
https://doi.org/10.1515/9783110419306-015

It is impossible to approach these immature but charming verses of Boccaccio, this umpteenth *pastourelle*, without discovering within them not only his wit, but also the unripe and encouraging novelty of his thought: the 'angioletta' who, in interrupting her love list with that final exclamation, savors the immediate, voluptuous, desirous fulfillment of so many acute fantasies, and already accomplishes – tiny thing that she is – a small revolution. In speaking out, she leaves her lover speechless (we can imagine him nearby, hidden behind a shrub). Her legendary shyness is contradicted by a new impulse to speak and to live and to descend from that celestial throne which the Provençal poet constructed for her; her silence is shattered, and that silence is followed by a frenetic circulation of amorous words and actions, of snares set to capture lovers, of meticulous plans to cheat on husbands and wives, of profuse pleasures, dreamt of from one end of the world to the other. Abstraction crumbles majestically in the face of natural reality, as foreseen by William of Occam, whom Boccaccio glossed in two letters from his youth:[2] the universal understood as a 'natural sign' for things thus takes the place of the conventional universal; space and time do not exist in and of themselves, but only in relation to size and motion; the 'rational sciences' refute useless or complex entities outside of experience and logic. Thus the maiden who calls an embrace with her lover 'ventura' (fortune), rebellious heir of the sweetness and frigidity of the Dolce Stilnovo, is a sign not of corruption, but of a profound transformation of the concept of nature; she is also the prime mover of a universe in which men are meant to act amorously – poetically – together with women. If the "dama dei pensieri" [lady of thoughts] was poetically untouchable, here on the contrary poetry exists in the contact of woman and man, in the return to earth of that which has always been earthly, in the conflagration of bodies within the new flame of carnal love.

An "altro foco" [different fire] from that of the chaste, divine huntress ignites the women in the *Caccia di Diana*; that is, the fire of Venus, who, appearing in the form of an "ignuda giovinetta" [nude girl], grants handsome men to her faithful followers. The "venereo fuoco" [Venereal fire] suddenly ignites Florio and Biancifiore in the *Filocolo*, in such a way that "tardi la freddezza di Diana li avrebbe potuti rattiepidare" [it would have been too late for the coldness of Diana to be able to moderate them]: "Veramente," says Florio, "[...] tu sola sopra tutte le cose del mondo mi piaci." ["Indeed," says Florio, "(...) you alone please me above all the things of this world."] "Certo tu non piaci meno a me, che io a te" ["Certainly you please me no less than I do you"], Biancifiore responds

---

2 See Cesare Vasoli: *La dialettica e la retorica dell'Umanesimo*. Milan: Feltrinelli 1968, p. 12; Kurt Flasch: *Poesia dopo la peste. Saggio su Boccaccio*. Bari: Laterza 1995, p. 7 ff.

(II, 4, 3–8).[3] We should note that this reciprocal declaration overturns the rites of courtly love, and its simplicity, from the point of view of poetic invention, is quite novel with respect to the lover's traditional fear and trembling in the presence of the beloved. Here anything can be said as anything is possible, or better it is inherently and essentially disposed to amorous action. The beloved is transformed into lover, and her desire is equal to his; each one's desire is consecrated in a heretofore unthinkable reciprocity. Where is the troubadour's desire offered in sacrifice, his mad solitude, his sharp and obscure words? Here Florio, separated from Biancifiore, turns his eyes "tra 'l bianco vestimento e le colorite carni" [between the white garment and the colored flesh] of two other maidens; "con atto festevole" [reaching playfully] he tries out each part of their bodies, and Boccaccio observes objectively that "niuna gliene è negate" [none of them were denied him] (III, 11, 12–13). Standing before the Admiral's Tower, where Biancifiore, betrothed to the Sultan of Babylon, is locked away, Florio entertains a very realistic doubt: will Biancifiore still love him? "Tu t'inganni," he says to himself, "se tu pensi che colei ora di te si ricordi, essendo sanza vederti tanto tempo dimorata. Nulla femina è che sì lungamente in amare perseveri, se l'occhio o il tatto spesso in lei non raccende amore." ["You deceive yourself, if you think that she remembers you now, after having been without you for so long. There is no woman who perseveres so long in loving, if her love is not frequently rekindled by sight or touch."] (IV, 89, 7–8). (In this monologue we find hints of Nino's strident voice in *Purg.* VIII, 76–78: "Per lei assai di lieve si comprende / quanto in femmina foco d'amor dura, / se l'occhio o il tatto spesso non l'accende." [There is an easy lesson in her conduct: / how short a time the fire of love endures in woman / if frequent sight and touch do not rekindle it.])[4] A certain Ulyssean desire to prevail, a certain "essercizio" [experience] of the world, removes some of the heroic or spiritual or theoretical components from Florio's constancy, and from his thoughts about the beloved some of the contemplative and unbearable parts that were found in the Provençal poets; here instead it is preferable 'to look upon' rather than 'to think about,' and the sentimental pleasures of the *reverie* are shunned in favor of the innumerable, passionate, actual pleasures of "continuato vedere" [constant viewing]:

---

[3] Giovanni Boccaccio: *Filocolo*. Edited by Antonio Enzo Quaglio. In: *Tutte le opere di G. Boccaccio*. Edited by Vittore Branca. 10 vols. Milan: Mondadori 1967, I, p. 127–128. Translation in: Giovanni Boccaccio: *Il Filocolo*. Translated by Donald Cheney with the Collaboration of Thomas G. Bergin. New York and London: Garland 1985 (Garland Library of Medieval Literature, 43B), p. 49–50. All quotations and translations from the *Filocolo* are drawn from these editions, respectively.
[4] Translation in: Dante Alighieri: *Purgatorio*. A Verse Translation by Jean Hollander and Robert Hollander. Introduction and Notes by Robert Hollander. New York: Anchor Books 2003, p. 169.

Quella cosa ch'è amata [...] quanto più si vede più diletta; e però io credo che molto maggior diletto porga il riguardare che non fa il pensare, però che ogni bellezza prima per lo vederla piace, poi per lo continuato vedere nell'animo tale piacere si conferma, e generasene amore e quelli disii che da lui nascono. E niuna bellezza è tanto amata per alcuna altra cagione, quanto per piacere agli occhi, e contentare quelli; dunque vedendola si contentano, pensandone, loro di vederla s'accresce disio: e più diletto sente chi si contenta che chi di contentarsi disidera. (IV, 61, 1–2)

[The thing that is loved (...) delights more the more it is seen; and so I think that seeing brings much more delight than thinking does, since every beauty pleases first through being seen; and then through continuing to be seen, this pleasure is strengthened in one's spirit, and out of it love is generated, and those desires which are born from it. And no beauty is so much loved for any other reason than to please and satisfy the eyes; therefore, in seeing it they are satisfied, but in thinking of it the desire to see it is increased; and more delight is felt by the one who is satisfied than by the one who desires to be satisfied.]

With this astute reasoning, the *Filocolo* puts an end to the abstract and ritual *gentilezza* of the troubadours, and invents a *gentilezza* that is the producer of earthly grace, of pleasures offered like fruit from a basket. Boccaccio is quite clear on this point: the fervent sighs, the weeping, the flaming desires will never die, but will always be the just price and the sentimental frame for love; however, these aspects by themselves will no longer have a primary dignity, nor will they hold the unwavering attention of the lover, who instead will be eager to forget them or even to delight in them, like an aphrodisiac, in the arms of the beloved. So, just like the lover's "alto appetito" (large appetite), the woman's desire also acquires legitimacy: "Perfetta donna" – we read in the *Filostrato* – "ha più fermo disire / d'essere amata, e d'amar si diletta" [The perfect lady hath a stronger desire to be loved and taketh delight in loving] (VIII, 32, 1–2);[5] and it matters little if Boccaccio was thinking of some historical siren, such as Mariella Caracciola, Caterina Caradente, Lucrezia Barrile, or of some imaginary creature, or of women in general: she is on par with man in her desire ("Certo tu non piaci meno a me, che io a te"), and this electrical shock, this electrifying naturality is transmitted in every one of Boccaccio's amorous pages, even in the most formalistic and most heavily imbued with Alexandrian elegance. Even the *Ameto*, being, in Contini's terms, an example of "mannerism to the point of teratology,"[6] with its "gracious choir" of nymphs – Mopsa, Emilia, Adiona, Acrimonia, Agapes, Fiammetta – sings of

---

[5] Giovanni Boccaccio: *Filostrato*. Edited by Vittore Branca. In: *Tutte le opere di G. Boccaccio*. Edited by Vittore Branca. 10 vols. Milan: Mondadori 1964, II, p. 225. Trans. in: *The Filostrato of Giovanni Boccaccio. A Translation with Parallel Text* by Nathaniel E. Griffin and Arthur B. Myrick. Philadelphia: University of Pensylvenia Press 1929, p. 499.
[6] Gianfranco Contini: *Letteratura italiana delle origini*. Florence: Sansoni 1970, p. 716.

unanimous desire (the Virgilian "trahit sua quemque voluptas," *Ecl.* II, 65), of the happy and infinite embrace between women and men on this world's stage; and with the invocation to the "graziosa stella" [gracious star] Citerea projects on high (a height of tone and diction, obviously) the 'honest' ardor of men and women, so that it will be remembered and imitated in the future. Woman and man find themselves on the same plane. The principle of feminine spirituality, like that of fidelity – legislated by men – is absent from the discussion: Alatiel (*Decameron* II, 7), over the course of four years and in various locations, falls into the hands of gentle but greedy men, and her kissed mouth "non perde ventura, anzi rinnuova come fa la luna" (§ 122) [was never the worse: like as the moon reneweth her course]; in this new and exemplary character "desire is preserved and repentance eliminated," as Aleksander Veselovskij observed.[7] In even more obvious terms, Madonna Filippa (*Decameron* VI, 7), guilty of adultery, gives a speech against the very laws of man, which no woman was ever called upon to approve. In Boccaccio's world, love is first and foremost the expression of guiltless pleasure and of a constant search for pleasure without end: just as in the Golden Age, here women and men do not suffer mortal weariness of the flesh – a Christian benefit for generations of anxious folk – instead, they contrive to multiply their enjoyments and infinite surprises. However, in contrast to the Golden Age, these couples augment mere sensuality with art – that is, a type of bourgeois consecration of the primitive – while rejecting the invasiveness of the spirit itself as an extraneous and disruptive element. The "cura de' mortali" [cares of mortals] is not "insensata" [foolish], as Dante would want it, but is blessed by God as a principle of action; and man is not meant (only in his own nightmares) to exhaust himself "nel diletto della carne involto" [in the toils of flesh] (*Par.* XI, 8).[8] This 'exhaustion' is an invention of the mind: "e quel ben," we read in the *Ameto*, "che io prima avea gustato / puro, da quinci innanzi con disiri / di nuovo accesi venne mescolato [...]." [And that delight, that my heart had first tasted pure, from then on became mixed with newly lit desires] (XLIX, 28–30)[9] Culture and art (which allow for the mixing of that initial good ["quel bene"]) defeat the inventions of the spirit, sublime but useless in Boccaccio's bourgeois world. The inimitable grace of a gesture, a tone of voice, the silent appeal of a glance – along with a book standing open in the background – give concupiscence a sense of *honesty*, or as

---

7 Quotation in: Viktor Sklovskij: *L'energia dell'errore*. Rome: Editori Riuniti 1984, p. 76.
8 Translation in: Dante Alighieri: *Paradiso*. Translated by Robert Hollander and Jean Hollander. Introduction and Notes by Robert Hollander. New York: Anchor Books 2008, p. 255.
9 Giovanni Boccaccio: *Comedia delle ninfe fiorentine*. Edited by Antonio Enzo Quaglio. In: ibid., p. 832. Translation in: Giovanni Boccaccio: *L'Ameto*. Translated by Judith Serafini-Sauli. New York and London: Garland 1985 (The Garland Library of Medieval Literature, 33B), p. 143.

we would now say, the *form* it needs in order to be memorable. And there is memorable concupiscence in every page of Boccaccio. In the *Elegia di Madonna Fiammetta* ('elegy' meaning *stilus miserorum*, according to the *De Vulgari Eloquentia* II, 4, 5) the gestures, the voice, the glances all belong to Panfilo, and the open book in the background is Ovid's *Heroides*. Fiammetta, the first 'narrator' of Italian literature, "minutely analyzes her own state of mind" (Contini)[10] when confronted with her love for a man; and she describes this man, "negli atti piacevolissimo e onestissimo nell'abito suo" [he was hansome and very pleasing in his gestures and he was dressed most nobly] (I, 6, 3),[11] in the same way that a man typically describes a woman: with an intoxicated attention for physical details, with the misery and infinite melancholy that men often demonstrate at the sight of female beauty. Unlike her seventeenth-century descendent the Princess of Clèves – the very image of reticence – Fiammetta speaks for herself right from the first:

> Mentre che io in cotal guisa, poco alcuni rimirando, e molto da molti mirata, dimoro, credendo che la mia bellezza altrui pigliasse, avvenne che l'altrui me miseramente prese. E già essendo vicina al doloroso punto, il quale o di certissima morte o di vita più che altra angosciosa dovea essere cagione, non so da che spirito mossa, gli occhi, con debita gravità elevati, intra la moltitudine d'i circustanti giovini con aguto riguardamento distesi. E oltre a tutti, solo e appoggiato ad una colonna marmorea, a me dirittissimamente un giovine opposto vidi; e, quello che ancora fatto non avea d'alcuno altro, da incessabile fato mossa, meco lui e i suoi modi cominciai ad estimare. (I, 6, 1)
>
> [While I went on in this way, seldom looking at others but much admired by many and believing that my beauty captivated other people, it happened that someone else's beauty unfortunately captured me. And as I was already close to that fateful moment which was to be the cause of certain death or of a life more wretched than any other, I was moved by an unknown spirit, and with my eyes raised in due solemnity, I gazed piercingly through the crowd of surrounding youths, and apart from everyone else, alone and learning against a marble column, exactly opposite me, I saw a young man; moved by an inevitable fate, I did something I had never done before with anyone else: I began to take mental stock of him and his manner.]

A sequence of jealousy, fury, doubts, hopes, and desperations follows the initial flame, as is well known, but in the end nothing escapes from the spell of that "ricchissimo letto" [richest bed] – a sort of totem – in which Venus is "molto faticata"

---

10 Contini: *Letteratura*, p. 722.
11 Giovanni Boccaccio: *Elegia di Madonna Fiammetta*. Edited by Carlo Delcorno. In: *Tutte le opere di G. Boccaccio*. Edited by Vittore Branca. Vittore Branca.10 vols. Milan: Mondadori 1994, V, 2, p. 30. Translation in: Giovanni Boccaccio: *The Elegy of Lady Fiammetta*. Edited and Translated by Mariangela Causa-Steindler and Thomas Mauch. Chicago: Chicago University Press 1990, p. 7. See these two editions for text and translation of the other passages.

[completely worn out] by the two lovers. Even their separation (Panfilo to Florence, Fiammetta to Naples) and the subsequent rumors seem lusty; even distance becomes sensual:

> Egli mi pareva alcuna volta con lui tornato vagare in giardini bellissimi, di frondi, di fiori e di frutti varii adorni, con lui insieme quasi d'ogni temenza rimoti, come già facemmo; e quivi lui per la mano tenendo, e esso me, farmi ogni suo accidente contare. E molte volte, avanti che il suo dire avesse fornito, mi parea baciandolo romperli le parole, e quasi appena vero parendomi ciò ch'io vedea, dicea: "Deh, è egli vero che tu sii tornato? Certo sì è, io ti pur tengo!" E quindi di capo il baciava. (III, 12, 6–7)

> [Sometimes I had the impression that he had returned and that I was with him wandering about together, as we had done before, in magnificent gardens adorned with all sorts of trees, fruits, and flowers, and there, walking hand in hand, I made him tell me everything that had happened to him, and frequently I seemed to interrupt what he was saying with a kiss, but because what I was seeing seemed hardly true to me, I said: "Pray, is it true that you are back? Indeed it is, since I am holding you!" And then I kissed him again.]

Gentilezza is sensuality, and elegy is the mourning of sensuality. It is no coincidence that Boccaccio's models are the Oïlitan *Eneas*, or Chrétien de Troyes *Cligés*, or *Floire* (for the *Filocolo*), or Benoît de Sainte-Maure's *Roman de Troie* (for the *Filostrato*): all essentially narrative models dominated by a taste for adventure and plot twists, along with an Ovidian-like attention for the psychology of love. In this way Fiammetta (the lovestruck Boccaccio's Maria d'Aquino) becomes the heroine of a new mythology with respect to the Dolce Stilnovo, and of a tried and tested mythology with respect to the classical texts: She is Sappho who loves Phaon, Hypermnestra who loves Lynceus, Phyllis who loves Demophon, Dido who loves Aeneas. In her gestures are both grace and the nostalgia for carnal love; and in her thoughts the exalting image of The Embrace, the fidelity to this one and only symbol of happiness in life.

We must not underestimate Fiammetta; we must not believe that she is anything less, anything less splendid, than the abstract Occitan *dame*, nor that aloofness is any more seductive than passion. Indeed, for Boccaccio, passion itself emanates a new aura of *gentilezza*, in which the person in love acknowledges his or her own destiny. Florio's destiny, for example, is determined by his passion for Biancifiore, and his opposition to his father, in the name of passion, is full of pride:

> Se egli per forza la mi vorrà torre, e io con forza la difenderò. Io non sarò meno debole d'amici e di potenza di lui: e quando egli pur fosse più forte di me, puommi egli più che cacciar del suo regno? Se egli me ne caccia, io starò in un altro. Il mondo è grande assai: l'andare pellegrinando mi fia cagione d'essercizio. (III, 7, 10–12)

[If he wants to take her from me by force, I shall defend her by force. I shall be no less weak in friends and power than he; but even if he is the stronger, what can he do beyond exiling me from his realm? If he exiles me, I shall go to another. The world is very large, and wandering will give me the opportunity for experience.]

The destiny of Cimone (*Decameron* V, 1) – an illiterate man lacking "costume alcuno" (any manners), a man without a destiny – is born the moment he catches sight of Efigenia, on a day in May, in "un pratello d'altissimi alberi circuito" [a grove circled by tall trees]. Cimone is handsome and strong, but "quasi matto" [almost mad] and "di perduta speranza" [without hope]; he is the son of a Cypriot nobleman, but his ways are "più convenienti a bestia che ad uomo" [more similar to an animal than a man]; he is very wealthy, but lives a humble life in the country, among his father's farmers. In other words, he lacks one of the two conditions of Boccaccio's ideal man: a purpose in the world, and nobility and goodness of the soul. When Efigenia appears to be asleep "con un vestimento indosso tanto sottile, che quasi niente delle candide carni nascondea" [with garment worn so lightly that almost none of her fair flesh was hidden], Cimone is transfixed by her, enrapt in ecstasy at the sight of her mouth, her throat, her arms and her breast, "poco ancora rilevato" [as yet but in bud], Efigenia has her eyes closed and lies motionless:

> La quale come Cimon vide, non altramenti che se mai più forma di femina veduta non avesse, fermatosi sopra il suo bastone, senza dire alcuna cosa, con ammirazione grandissima la incominciò intentissimo a riguardare; e nel rozzo petto, nel quale per mille ammaestramenti non era alcuna impressione di cittadinesco piacere potuta entrare, sentì destrarsi un pensiero, il quale nella materiale grossa mente gli ragionava, costei essere la più bella cosa che giammai per alcuno vivente veduta fosse. (V, 1, 8)

> [No sooner did Cimon catch sight of her, than, as if he had never before seen form of woman, he stopped short, and leaning on his cudgel, regarded her intently, saying never a word, and lost in admiration. And in his rude soul, which, despite a thousand lessons, had hitherto remained impervious to every delight that belongs to urbane life, he felt the awakening of an idea, that bade his gross and coarse mind acknowledge, that this girl was the fairest creature that had ever been seen by mortal eye.][12]

In the case of Cimone the flesh redeems the spirit, the honest nudity of beauty restores an uncivilized man to civility, to the city, considered the opposite of the country throughout the Middle Ages. Cimone in fact learns "i modi, quali a' gentili

---

[12] Giovanni Boccaccio: *Decameron*. Edited by Vittore Branca. 2 vols. Turin: Einaudi 1992, p. 596. English translation in: *The Decameron of Giovanni Boccaccio Faithfully Translated by James M. Rigg*. 2 vols. London: The Navarre Society 1932, II, p. 3. All quotations and translations from the *Decameron* are drawn from these two editions, respectively.

uomini si convenieno e massimamente agl' innamorati" [the manners proper to gentlemen, and especially to lovers], he studies song and music, becomes "valorosissimo tra' filosofanti" [most eminent among the philosophic wits], and after four years is "il più leggiadro e meglio costumato e con più particulari virtú che altro giovane alcuno che nell'isola fosse di Cipri" [the most elegant and well-mannered of young men, of the young cavaliers that were in the island of Cyprus.] (§§ 18–20). His solitude – that is, his savageness – is overcome by desire, which creates destiny even in the deserts and on the mountaintops, and raises cities and traditions and languages even within the unimaginable void; this coarse and brutish man overcomes solitude by falling in love.

As to Boccaccio? How does this happy and sentimental man view solitude? Who, for him, is the lone artist standing before the world? Why would solitude, the enemy of plots, be represented as a sister and a lawgiver in the life of this writer? The apologue of Cimone reveals the divergence in views that Boccaccio eventually adopted in his fifties. Perhaps based on the exhortations of Petrarch, *gloriosus praeceptor* [the glorious teacher] who "amores meos [...] vertit in melius" [changed my loves for the better],[13] or perhaps from sacred scripture, or from the effects of melancholy, he drew the impression that women are not in fact the honest civilizing force he had once imagined. Indeed, in the *Corbaccio* – a brilliant little misogynistic book from 1365 – he applied himself to revealing their every baseness, stolidity and cupidity. And the intrusion of this quintessentially medieval antifeminist sentiment, amid so many pages in praise of feminine sweetness, is quite shocking. If the stupid, violent and vulgar women of the *Corbaccio* are perhaps the realistic extreme or the inevitable deformation of a pre-established harmony, they are most certainly the symptom of a spiritual crisis. Looking back on his world, on Gostanza who loves Martuccio, on Pietro Boccamazza who flees with Agnolella, on the Priest of Varlungo who lies with monna Belcolore, Boccaccio seeks distance and views all of it with a cold regard: the acts and loves of men, the beauty of women, all seem obstructed and faded as if on an old tapestry, or corruptible, or vain; pleasure itself seems worthy of his reproach, with all its intrigues and daring feats. Why should he go back down into the vast world? To visit castles, infamous alleys, ship dens? Why continue to love women, when instead he can choose the Muses?

> A te s'appartiene, e so che tu 'l conosci, più d'usare i solitari luoghi che le moltitudini ne' templi e negli altri pubblici luoghi raccolte, visitare; e quivi stando, operando, versificando, essercitare lo 'ngegno e sforzarti di divenir migliore e d'ampliare a tuo podere, più con cose

---

[13] Giovanni Boccaccio: *Epistole e lettere*. Edited by Ginetta Auzzas. In: *Tutte le opere di G. Boccaccio*. Edited by Vittore Branca. 10 vols. Milan: Mondadori 1994, V, 1, p. 720.

fatte che con parole, la fama tua; che, appresso quella salute ed etterno riposo il qual ciascuno che drittamente disidera dee volere, è il fine della tua lunga sollecitudine. Mentre che tu sarai ne' boschi e ne' rimoti luoghi, le Ninfe Castalide, alle quali queste malvage femmine si vogliono assomigliare, non t'abbandoneranno già mai; la bellezza delle quali, sì come io ho inteso, è celestiale. (§§ 196–197)

[Rather than visiting the moltitudes gathered in churches and other public places, it is fitting for you, and I know you are aware of it, to frequent solitary places, and there, by studying, working, and versifying, to exercise your intellect and to make an effort to better yourself, and, as best you can, to increase your fame more with deeds than words; for after that, salvation and eternal repose, which everyone who desires aright must want, are the goal of your long diligence.
While you are in the woods and remote places, the Castalian nymphs, with whom these wicked women would compare themselves, will never abandon you. Their beauty, as I have heard, is celestial.][14]

This classical, Heliconian solitude, suffused with Christian austerity, is the myth of the late Boccaccio; a great man who, at a certain point, comes to despise life's turmoil; a curious and happy man who, at a certain point, becomes melancholic: we can imagine him in the cold Certaldese nights, bundled up in the miniver cloak given to him by Petrarch, writing without pause, studying, researching, alone, tenaciously alone, he who invented Buffalmacco and the exhilarating celebration of life.

Petrarch, the master of solitude, continually describes this human state of excellence, and bequeaths it to his contemporaries as well as to posterity. Solitude is a treasure, a limitless hoard of which he studies and catalogues every gem: from Vaucluse, where he lives with two servants and a dog "blacker than pitch and faster than breeze" (*Fam.* XIII, 11, 1),[15] to his house among the fields of Sant'Ambrogio in Padua, where in one of his little gardens, "ornamented with fronds and flowers," he receives Boccaccio (*Ep.* X, 5),[16] to Arquà, in the Euganean hills, where he dies, all of his life is a succession of solitudes. "Wherever

---

14 Giovanni Boccaccio: *Corbaccio*. Edited by Giorgio Padoan. In: *Tutte le opere di G. Boccaccio*. Edited by Vittore Branca. 10 vols. Milan: Mondadori 1994, V, 2, p. 476. Trans. in: Giovanni Boccaccio: *The Corbaccio*. Translated and edited by Anthony K. Cassell. Urbana: University of Illinois Press 1975, p. 36.
15 "Canis tuus pice nigrior vento levrior [...]." See Francesco Petrarca: *Le familiari*. Edited by Vittorio Rossi (vols 1–3) and by Vittorio Rossi and Umberto Bosco (vol. 4). Firenze: Sansoni 1933–1942 (Edizione nazionale delle opere di Petrarca, 10–13), III, p. 91. English translation in: Francesco Petrarca: *Letters on Familiar Matters: Rerum familiarium libri*. Translated by Aldo S. Bernardo. 3 vols. Baltimore: Johns Hopkins University Press 1975–1985, II, p. 212.
16 "[...] et in ortulum ibamus tuum iam ob novum ver frondibus atque floribus ornatum." See Boccaccio's letter to Petrarch (1353). In: Boccaccio: *Epistole e lettere*, p. 574.

he went;" writes Ugo Foscolo, "he took up his abode in a sort of hermitage, and continued to compose whole volumes [...]."[17] Along with Augustine (the *Confessions*, the *Soliloquies*, *De vera religione*), his companions in solitude are the Roman writers (Virgil and his "dulcedo quedam et sonoritas" [sweetness and tunefulness of the words], Cicero and his *concinnitas*; *Sen*. XVI, 1),[18] and then the Davidian Psalms and Boethius and the Provençal poets; secret bosom friends, discrete and agreeable, who can join him from any part of the world and from any period of time; friends who settle themselves into a corner of the house and assist him attentively, who take leave at his merest signal, "redeantque vocati" (returning when called; *Epyst*. XVI, 187).[19] Petrarch does not squander a minute of his time; rather, he lives "today in the present day, content to live tomorrow if a morrow shall be granted." (*De vita sol*. I, 8).[20] His day is industrious and the hours follow one after another, each bringing new riches. Anxiety, which stalks the city dweller, is unknown to him, and among the books he has to read and those to write he knows nothing but happiness:

> Solitario, cui quid agere velit iam provisum est, cui non modo de partibus sed de tota etate semesl est constitutum, non dies aut nox longior, sepe vero brevior est quam vellet, dum honestis in rebus occupatum deserit et ante suscepti finem operis lux finitur.
>
> [But for the solitary man, who has regulated the entire course of his life and not merely some portions of it, there is no day or night that is too long, though it is often shorter than he would like when he is engaged in his innocent tasks and the light of day is gone before his labor is accomplished.] (ibid.).[21]

A collector of solitudes and occupant of hermit retreats, Petrarch is also, and exemplarily so, *homme accompli*: one cannot imagine a more perfect elegance

---

17 Ugo Foscolo: *An Essay on the Character of Petrarch* 16. In his: *Saggi e discorsi critici*. Edited by Cesare Foligno. Florence: Le Monnier 1953 (Edizione nazionale delle opere di U.F., 10), p. 104.
18 *Francisci Petrarchae Opera omnia*. Basle: Sebastianus Henricpetri 1581, p. 946. English translation in: Francesco Petrarca: *Letters of Old Age: Rerum Senilium Libri I–XVIII*. Translated by Aldo S. Bernardo, Saul Levin et al. 2 vols. Baltimore: Johns Hopkins University Press 1992, II, p. 600.
19 Francesco Petrarca: *Epistole metriche*. In his: *Rime, Trionfi e poesie latine*. Edited by Ferdinando Neri/ Guido Martellotti et al. Milan and Naples: Ricciardi 1951 (Letteratura italiana. Storia e testi, 6), p. 736.
20 "[...] hodiernum diem hodie vivit, crastinum, si dabitur, cras victurus." See Francesco Petrarca: *Prose*. Edited by Guido Martellotti / Pier Giorgio Ricci et al. Milan and Naples: Ricciardi 1955, p. 398. English translation in: *The Life of Solitude by Francis Petrarch*. Edited and translated by J. Zeitlin. Urbana: University of Illinois Press 1924, p. 180.
21 Ibid., p. 396–398. English trans., p. 180.

and cordiality than his, a more tempered eloquence, a gentler smile. Whether addressing himself to Robert of Anjou or to the sharecropper of Vaucluse, he expresses himself with the same measure and attention, with the same spirit he reserves for the great men of the past: "elegant, [...] inclined to melancholy, of a delicate and impressionable nature,"[22] as Francesco De Sanctis would say of him, with a hint of impatience. But in his self portrait within the *Posteritati* we find truth and modesty, intensity and charm, brilliance and temperance united so harmoniously as to repel even this impatience. To discover the true Petrarch, behind the veil of syntax, beyond the masterful and niggling unilingualism of his verses, was, to a certain extent, every scholar's dream, beginning in particular with De Sanctis ("Mai non puoi coglierlo in veste da camera; mai non ti viene innanzi che in guanti gialli e in cravatta bianca" [You can never surprise him in his nightrobes; he only ever comes to meet you in yellow gloves and a white tie]):[23] but the irreality with which the poet surrounds himself is not the enemy of truth; rather, it is his truth expressed freely in his works and in his own life. Solitude and irreality are the walls of the house in which Petrarch dwelled. All that is physical – material objects, his own body – was a great bore to him: "what do you find troublesome about it?" Augustine asks him in the *Secretum*. "Nothing other than the usual complaints: that it's mortal, that it involves me in its pains, that it weighs me down with its weight, that when my spirit wants to wake, it induces it to sleep [...]."[24] Everything that is present and historical alarms him: "I always disliked our own age," he confides in the *Posteritati*, "- so much so, that had it not been for the love of those dear to me, I would have preferred to have been born in any other time than our own."[25] Everything that is not of the spirit and that falls into the obtuseness of the senses terrifies him, and to Boccaccio, who urges him to rest, he responds almost sternly: "[...] so great is my hatred for sleep and lazy repose. [...]. whatever I may appear to you

---

22 "elegante [...] inchinevole alla malinconia, natura impressionabile e delicata." See Francesco De Sanctis: *Saggio critico sul Petrarca*. Edited by Niccolò Gallo. Turin: Einaudi 1964, p. 39.
23 Ibid., p. 106.
24 "Aug. [...] Quid in eo molestum experiris? Fr. Nichil equidem, nisi comunia quedam: quod mortale est, quod suis me doloribus implicat, mole pregravat, somnum suadet spiritu vigilante [...]." See Petrarca: *Prose*, p. 118. Trans. in: Francesco Petrarca: *My Secret Book*. Edited and Translated by Nicholas Mann. Cambridge, Mass.: Harvard University Press, 2016 (The I Tatti Renaissance Library, 72), p. 131.
25 "[...] michi semper etas ista displicuit; ut, nisi me amor carorum in diversum traheret, qualibet etate natus esse semper optaverim [...]." See Petrarca: *Prose*, p. 1–19, at p. 6. Trans. in: Petrarch: Letter to Posterity. In his: *Selections from the "Canzoniere" and Other Works*. Translated and Edited with an Introduction and Notes by Mark Musa. Oxford: Oxford University Press 1985, p. 1–10, at p. 3.

or to others, this is my view of myself." (*Senilis* XVII, 2, 9).[26] Reality is brutal and dull; human society – in every epoch – is *impious* (Avignon: "empia Babilonia," *RVF* CXIV, 1); life itself, among men, becomes incomprehensible, and so nature, which we never tire of admiring and praising, is transformed into a scene of frigid beauty ("Then indeed having seen enough of the mountain I turned my inner eyes within [...]," we read in the famous epistle to Dionigi di San Sepolcro).[27] But what do we find in solitude? Above all the sentiment of the vanity of the world and of time:

> [...] Sine tempore vivite; nam vos
> et magno partum delebunt tempora nomen,
> transibuntque cito que vos mansura putatis.
> Una manere potest occasus nescia virtus.
> Illa viam facit ad superos. Hac pergite fortes,
> nec defessa gravi succumbant terga labori.
> Quod si falsa vagam delectat gloria mentem,
> aspice quid cupias: transibunt tempora, corpus
> hoc cadet et cedent indigno membra sepulcro;
> mox ruet et bustum, titulusque in marmore sectus
> occidet: hinc mortem patieris, nate, secundam.
> Clara quidem libris felicibus insita vivet
> Fama diu, tamen ipsa suas passura tenebras. (*Africa* II, 423–435)
>
> [(...) Live beyond time,
> for Time devours both you and your renown,
> fruit of such arduous toil. For true it is:
> what seems most lasting does most swiftly fade.
> Virtue alone, that heeds not death, endures.
> Virtue alone prepares the way to Heaven.
> So hither, heroes, come! Let this last burden
> Be not too great for the weary backs to bear.
> But if your wayward heart still would find joy
> in empty glory, know what prize you seek:
> the years will pass, your mortal form decay;
> your limbs will lie in an unworthy tomb
> which in its turn will crumble, while your name
> fades from the sculptured marble. Thus you'll know
> a second death. Though honors registered
> on worthy scrolls have long and lustrous life,

---

[26] "[...] tantum somni et languide odium est quietis. [...] quicquid tibi, quicquid aliis videar, hoc de me iudicium meum est." See Petrarca: *Prose*, p. 1156. Trans., II, p. 654.
[27] "Tunc vero montem satis vidisse contentus, in me ipsum interiores oculos reflexi [...]." See Petrarca: *Le familiari*, I, p. 159. English translation in: Petrarca: *Letters on Familiar Matters*, I, p. 178.

yet they too in the end are likewise doomed
to fade away. (...)][28]

This biblical headlong rush of time and civilization toward ruin, this immense dust cloud to which the history of mankind is reduced, is a fixed point – the only fixed point – of the Petrarchan 'system.' If everything in his soul is uncertain and changeable ("Voluntates mee fluctuant, et desideria discordant et discordando me lacerant." [My wishes fluctuate and my desires are discordant and, being so, they tear me to pieces.], *Fam.* II, 9, 17),[29] if nearly every thought has its opposite and every passion has its own share of blame, Petrarch has not the least doubt about *vanitas*; indeed, this vanity, time's inability to endure, is the primary driving force of his poetry. In the verses of the *Africa*, Scipio weeps for history and for his times, which will leave no traces (not even ruins can be considered a trace, because even they become dust and nothing), and for fame, which is limited in time, and which stands in opposition to *virtus*. God, the immutable, is, for Christian Petrarch who, as E. H. Wilkins observed, "never questioned any article of the creed; he never explored the field of theology;"[30] the polar opposite of ruin, the ahistorical principle of every certainty, the heavenly *Festboden*. Just as the ruin of human actions is certain (and even, we should note, of poetry: "ipsa suas passura tenebras," *Afr.* II, 435), equally certain is God's perpetual splendor.

Between the two poles of human lability and divine consistency, time and eternity, Petrarch constructs his most perfect song: "Padre del ciel, dopo i perduti giorni, / dopo le notti vaneggiando spese [...]" [Father of Heaven, after the lost days, after the nights spent] (*RVF* LXII, 1–2).[31] This vertical rapture, this dream of absolute redemption ("reduci i pensier' vaghi a miglior luogo, " ibid., 13) is, in an inchoative sense, the religious consecration of solitude. In solitude, which will never result in absolute happiness, the word is above all a form of prayer, a question addressed to his "great friend" which would free the poet from the "binding" of his sins. Nevertheless, the poet knows himself to be weak and cannot find the spiritual energy to regain his health; he has grace in his sights, but something

---

28 Pétrarque: *L'Afrique*. Préface de Henri Lamarque. Introduction, traduction et notes de Rebecca Lenoir. Grenoble: Éditions Jérôme Millon 2002, p. 102. Trans. in: *Petrarch's Africa*. Translated and Annotated by Thomas G. Bergin and Alice S. Wilson. New Haven: Yale University Press 1977, p. 37.
29 Francesco Petrarca: *Le familiari*, I, p. 94. Trans., I, p. 101.
30 Ernst Hatch Wilkins: *Life of Petrarch*. Chicago: The University of Chicago Press 1961, p. 254.
31 All quotes from the *RVF* are taken from Francesco Petrarca: *Canzoniere*. Edited by Gianfranco Contini. Turin: Einaudi 1964; translations from *Petrarch's Lyric Poems. The "Rime sparse" and Other Lyrics*. Translated and Edited by Robert Durling. Cambridge, Mass.: Harvard University Press 1976.

within his own being impedes him from obtaining it. This friend of the Augustinians, Benedictines, Camaldoleses, Celestines, Cistercians, Dominicans, Franciscans, Vallumbrosans, this devotee of religious leisure, this ardent admirer of his own brother, a monk at Montrieux, this fanciful man so in love with decisive action remains beyond action himself: "all change occurs in his mind, while externally everything remains exactly the same" (De Sanctis).[32] In the Kierkegaardian stages of existence, Petrarch would be the "false aesthete," he who, having seen the ethical world, instead chooses the aesthetic world but does not live aesthetically because he sins and succumbs to ethical determinations; this weak man (*spiritus lenis*) is lacking the "baptism of the will," which gives an ethical character to reflection. Tormented by *aegritudo* and by sloth, "funesta quedam pestis animi" [dreadful sickness of the spirit],[33] Petrarch is like a warrior surrounded by cruel enemies and weapons of war, ladders and vines; alone and without a means of escape, he is left with nothing but the infinite pain of defeat, even if perhaps, in some part of heaven, victorious chariots do shine: "Who would not take fright and grieve at the sight of swords flashing everywhere and the threatening faces of the enemy, and at the thought of the approaching destruction, especially since, even in the absence of such threats the loss of freedom is itself unbearable for courageous men?" (*Secretum* II).[34] Compared with Augustine, who effected his own conversion, Petrarch is the man who does not know what he wants and whose life remains essentially static and filled with anguish. How many tears and how much anxiety in his solitude! True religious tears turn "Augustine into a different Augustine;" those of Petrarch, who sees the better and chooses the worse, take pathos and tenderness to the point of irremediable unhappiness.

As a guest of the poet's solitude, Laura is also its worst enemy. An immaterial creature like her ancestors in the Sicilian and Dolce Stilnovo traditions, with her mere appearance she creates a disturbance and an immediate ecstasy in the contemplator, whose solitude shifts from ascetic to amorous, from happy to unhappy. Laura, like glory, like the odious sexual act, like sloth, is a spiritual 'ball and chain'; her very appearance is an act of domination, and the enchained will never again break free from her grasp. Laura is evanescent: her golden tresses, her dark eyes, perfect hands, her veil, her glove, her (green) gown, her signal of greeting, whether denied or conceded, are nothing more than emblems; cruel or sweet, aloof or smiling, she herself is no more real than the abstract Provençal

---

[32] De Sanctis: *Saggio critico*, p. 119.
[33] Petrarca: *Prose*, p. 106. Trans. p. 113.
[34] "Undique fulgentes gladios, minantesque vultus hostium cernens vicinumque cogitans excidium, quidni paveat et lugeat, quando, his licet cessantibus, ipsa libertatis amissio viris fortibus mestissima est?" See Petrarca: *Prose*, p. 108. Trans., p. 117.

dames. But something escapes from the rule of evanescence: new elements, new ambiguities are found in that visage. Cesare De Lollis wrote that Laura is the type "of lady who has nothing to do with that angelic maiden, an artificial creation of the circle of Florentine youths, and little to do with that *châtelaine* of Provence, reigning from a distance."[35] Laura's secret is in her sweet and arcane proximity to Francesco, in her being a living presence – immaterial creature that she is – in his life. Despite its various attempts at allegorization – the encounter on the anniversary of the Passion of Christ ("Mille trecento ventisette, a punto / su l'ora prima, il dí sesto d'aprile" [One thousand three hundred twenty-seven, exactly at the first / hour of the sixth day of April], *RVF* CCXI, 12–13), the death of the lady on the twenty-first anniversary of their first meeting, 6 April 1348 – despite its general conception "as a counterpoint to the liturgical breviary" (Contini),[36] despite its ingeniousness, the *Canzoniere* is the story, or the daily journal, of a passion. Precisely because of its oscillation between salvation and perdition, occurrence and repetition, spiritual ascent and worldliness, Laura's appearance evokes surprise and creates quite an original psychological storyline. We can imagine Francesco who, one particular day, recognizes here on earth her who "era più degna d'immortale stato" [was more worthy of immortal state]: he sees "begli occhi lucenti" [beautiful shining eyes], he receives from her a "dolce saluto" [sweet greeting] (*RVF* CX, 8, 13, 14), and his reaction is similar to ecstasy: "I' mi riscossi; ed ella oltra, parlando, / passò, che la parola i' non soffersi, / né'l dolce sfavillar degli occhi suoi" [I trembled, and she, conversing, passed onward, for I could not / endure her speech or the sweet sparkling of her eyes] (*RVF* CXI, 9–11). His mind is entranced and taken prisoner by the image (Cassirer would speak of "mythical thought") and cannot distinguish or discern: "[…] avvezza / la mente a contemplar sola costei / ch'altro non vede […]" [accustomed / my mind to contemplate her alone that it sees nothing else] (*RVF* CXVI, 5–7); solitude is seemingly defeated by "tanta maiestade," and every goal of individual askesis is forever forgotten. Wouldn't a reciprocated love, an ecstatic love, a love between two souls, be happier than the solitary path of the Christian ascetic?

> Quel vago impallidir che 'l dolce riso
> d'un'amorosa nebbia ricoperse,
> con tanta maiestade al cor s'offerse
> che li si fece incontr'a mezzo 'l viso
>   Conobbi allor sí come in paradiso
> vede l'un l'altro, in tal guisa s'aperse

---

35 Cesare De Lollis: *Recensione al florilegio petrarchesco di N. Zingarelli*. In: *La Cultura* 6 (1927), p. 464–466.
36 Contini: *Letteratura*, p. 580.

quel pietoso penser, ch'altri non scerse;
ma vidil'io, ch'altrove non m'affiso.
   Ogni angelica vista, ogni atto umile
che già mai in donna ov'amor fosse apparve,
fora uno sdegno a lato a quel ch'i' dico.
   Chinava a terra il bel guardo gentile
e tacendo dicea come a me parve:
"Chi m'allontana il mio fedele amico?" (*RVF* CXXIII)

[The lovely pallor, which covered her sweet smile with a cloud
Of love, with so much majesty presented itself to my heart that
He went to meet it in the midst of my face.
I learned then how they see each other in Paradise; so clearly did
That merciful thought open itself, which no one else perceived,
But I saw it, for I fixed myself nowhere else.
Every angelic expression, every humble gesture that ever appeared in a lady who harbored love, would be scorn beside what
I speak of.
She bent to earth her lovely noble glance and in her silence said,
as it seemed to me: "Who sends away from me my faithful
friend?"]

Come in paradiso vede l'un l'altro: one can reach this state of exceptional communion only in a dream or, more precisely, in ecstasy; and Francesco completely abandons himself to his "pietoso penser," the private celebration of Love Absolute, which defies explanation and contracts, equivocations and words ("tacendo dicea"), and which annuls the fiction of time. But a similar love, so vertiginous and perfectly happy, cannot have a narration nor *fragmenta*. Laura's beauty is such that every other earthly beauty, in comparison, seems negligible; indeed, when Laura laughs or weeps or speaks, everything is *intent* and immobile, and the world itself is enchanted and suspended. But precisely this excellence, this being 'alone' at the summit of beauty itself, causes the lover – who, in the ecstasy of the meeting, loved Laura *sine tempore* – to fall headlong into time and into a solitude from which he once thought himself to be forever free. Laura is *ideal* ("In qual parte del Ciel, in quale Idea" [In what part of Heaven, in what Idea], *RVF* CLIX, 1), but also mysteriously alive and rich with earthly seductions: "non sa come Amor sana e come ancide, / chi non sa come dolce ella sospira / e come dolce parla e dolce ride" [he does not know how Love heals and how he kills, who does / not know how sweetly she sighs and how sweetly she speaks and / sweetly laughs] (ibid., 12–14). Francesco, enrapt by Laura's seductive ideality, is simultaneously repelled by it – Laura's greatness is not his greatness – and remains alone, still in love, a desperate celebrant of the rites of his little sacred story.

From this moment, in the fragmentary pages of the *Canzoniere*, Laura's portrait cedes a bit to Francesco's authority. Like Guidoriccio da Fogliano in Simone Martini's famous Sienese fresco, who rides through a lunar desert under the face of the sky, carrying with him his victories and his solitude, so Francesco, the solitary figure anointed by Love, the nobleman, wanders through the world, waving his exalted melancholy like a banner. He flees from Laura while carrying her in his own heart, flees "ma non sì ratto che 'l desio / meco non venga [...]" [but not so quickly that my desire / does not come with me] (*RVF* XVIII, 10–11), like a blind man, "che non sa ove si vada e pur si parte" [who does not / know where to go and still departs] (ibid., 4); his solitude is troubled because the 'ministers' – thoughts of love – visit it assiduously. His own ability to reason is disturbed: on the one hand he concludes that the amorous yoke and shackles are sweeter than "l'andare sciolto" [going free] (*RVF* LXXXIX, 11), and that he regrets this "nova libertà" [new liberty] (ibid., 4); on the other hand he sees his initial error quite clearly, when "[...] l'antica strada / di libertà mi fu precisa [...]" (*RVF* XCVI, 9–10). Francesco knows well that he cannot make head or tail of this contradiction:

> Pien d'un vago penser che me desvia
> da tutti gli altri, e fammi al mondo ir solo,
> ad or ad ora a me stesso m'involo,
> pur lei cercando che fuggir devria [...] (*RVF* CLXIX, 1–4)

[Full of a yearning thought that makes me stray away from all others and go alone in the world, from time to time I steal myself away from myself, still seeking only her whom I should flee]

Only Christ or death could free him, but Christ – whose cross broke apart the Stoic circle – can do nothing for a man entwined in an earthly love, and death seems a distant promise. Thus Francesco's love can neither be eliminated nor brought to fulfillment; love that renders the lover "tremante" [trembling] and "fioco" [feeble] seems to be a state of inexpressibility, a condition of obstruction which prevents one's words from being heard and understood by any other, and above all by the beloved:

> Più volte già dal bel sembiante humano
> ò preso ardir co' le mie fide scorte
> d'assalir con parole oneste accorte
> la mia nemica in atto humile e piano.
> Fanno poi gli occhi suoi mio penser vano,
> per ch'ogni mia fortuna, ogni mia sorte,
> mio ben, mio male, et mia vita et mia morte,
> quei che solo il pò far, l'à posto in mano.
> Ond'io non pote' mai formar parola

ch'altro che da me stesso fosse intesa;
così m'à fatto Amor tremante e fioco!
    E veggi' or ben che caritate accesa
lega la lingua altrui, gli spirti invola:
chi pò dir com'egli arde, è 'n picciol foco (*RVF* CLXX)

[Many times from her kind expression I have learned boldness,
with my faithful guides, to assail with virtuous skillful words my
enemy so humble and mild of bearing.
But her eyes then make my thought vain, for Love, who alone
can do so, has placed in her hands all my fortune, all my
destiny, my good, my ill, my life, and my death.
Wherefore I have never been able to form a word that was
understood by any but myself, Love has made me so trembling
and weak!
And I see well how burning Love binds one's tongue, steals away
one's breath: he who can say how he burns is in but a little fire.]

True love, like true desperation, has no words: "desperation that writes well is not really definitive," as Paul Valéry would say;[37] and Francesco, who fails to "formar" words that can be understood by anyone other than himself, now finds himself at the point of amorous aphasia. But, against all expectations, he continues to speak and write, demonstrating that the amorous word is a great deal stronger and larger than love itself. Thus, for once at least, we learn the truth from this fascinating liar.

Now let us proceed with our investigation. On his mythical boat, "sì lieve di saver, d'error sì carca" [so light of wisdom, so laden with error] (*RVF* CXXXII, 12), Francesco finds himself in a stormy sea, sailing against the wind; at times he feels that he no longer understands anything and he succumbs to anguish; perhaps Laura herself never existed at all, or is hiding in the fog ("Celansi i duo mei dolci usati segni" [My two usual sweet stars are hidden], *RVF* CLXXXIX, 12). Even God is absent, or has withdrawn or vanished among the enormous waves: "nuoto per mar che non à fondo o riva," Francesco says, "solco onde, e 'n rena fondo, e scrivo in vento" [I swim through a sea that has / no floor or shore, I plow the waves and found my house on sand / and write on wind] (*RVF* CCXII, 3–4). In this condition, Laura's presence, albeit ghostly and ambiguous, becomes necessary; if Laura were not there, "tanto et più fien le cose oscure e sole" [so dark and darker will / things be and deserted] (*RVF* CCXVIII, 13), as if the sun and moon were missing from the sky, the wind from the air, the plants and woods from the earth, and intellect and language from humankind. Thus she realizes and dramatizes Francesco's solitude, which is otherwise anguished, eternally mute and uninhabited: her absence

---

[37] Paul Valéry: *Variation sur une "Pensée" annotée par l'auteur*. Liége: Balancier 1930, p. 22.

is perhaps more inconceivable than the absence of God, at least on the level of fable, which in Petrarch becomes the pure transcription and repetition of the initial occurrence. God can conceal himself from the lover, reason can abandon him, 'art' can be forgotten, but Laura cannot die (her death, in the *Canzoniere*, is a mere formality). Indeed, her eternity, her eternal presence, competes with that of God: "Tal la mi trovo al petto ove ch'i' sia, / felice incarco; e con preghiere oneste / l'adoro e 'inchino come cosa santa." [Such do I find it in my breast, wherever I may be, a happy / burden, and with chaste prayers I adore it and bow to it as to a / holy thing.] (*RVF* CCXXVIII, 12–14). Already having moved beyond Guinizzelli and Dante, here the woman is not the mediator of divine grace, nor the contemplator of God; rather, she herself is the eternally reborn, the timeless phoenix, with her adorers, her churches and her heaven, just like God. Leopardi, in his masterful and laconic commentary on the *Canzoniere*, would ironize this phoenix ("Rumor has it that the Phoenix lives hidden in the mountains of Arabia, when in fact she lives in our own parts, and flies majestically through our skies. This means that Laura is the true phoenix, and the other is a fable!"),[38] but somewhat wrongfully, if we consider that Francesco, in his oscillation between Laura and God, is forced to accentuate Laura's majesty by any means possible. In the *canzone* CXXXV, for example, Laura is seen not as a phoenix but as a mythical African animal, the catoblepas, whose eyes destroy anyone coming under its gaze, and even as the Fountain of Epirus, icy cold, but which can ignite fires within itself. With these exaggerations Francesco portrays himself as prisoner of a curse, fatally deceived by love: "L'anima mia, ch'offesa / ancor non era d'amoroso foco, / appressandosi un poco / a quella fredda, ch'io sempre sospiro, / arse tutta [...]" [My soul, not yet harmed by any fire of love, ap- / proaching but a little that cold one for whom I ever sigh, / caught fire entirely] (ibid., 65–69) This indeed is the curse. But, "poi che 'nfiammata l'ebbe, / rispensela vertù gelata e bella" [and,/ after setting it on fire, frozen and lovely virtue put it out again.]: this is the deception, namely the discovery of the fallacy of amorous ecstasy and irreparable solitude of both lover and beloved (Lucretius in fact noted that lovers are denied fusion into a single being: "[...] nihil inde abradere possunt / nec penetrare et abire in corpus corpore toto." [they cannot rub nothing off, nor can they penetrate and be absorbed body in body], *De rer. nat.* IV, 1110–1111).[39] Therefore, Laura is the deception in which

---

[38] "La fama porta che la Fenice viva nascosta nelle montagne d'Arabia, quando ella in verità vive nelle nostre parti, e vola maestosamente per l'aria. Vuol dire che Laura è la vera fenice, e l'altra è una favola!" See Francesco Petrarca: *Canzoniere*. Introduction by Ugo Foscolo. Notes by Giacomo Leopardi. Edited by U. Dotti. Milan: Feltrinelli 2003⁶, p. 200.

[39] Lucretius: *De rerum natura*. With and English Translation by W. H. D. Rouse. Cambridge, Mass., Harvard University Press 1992, p. 362–363.

Francesco blindly persists, year after year; even when he runs "ver la stagion contraria" [nearing the season that is contrary] (*RVF* CLXVIII, 10), he feels his strength leave him, his words escape him, his life slip away little by little. To immortalize this deception for posterity, to render splendid, in his verses, the solitude of the lover and the "infinita bellezza" [infinite beauty] (CCIII, 5) of the beloved is, on the other hand, the thorn in Francesco's side:

> Quest'arder mio, di che vi cal sì poco,
> e i vostri onori in mie rime diffusi,
> ne porian infiammar fors'ancor mille;
>   ch'i' veggio nel penser, dolce mio foco,
> fredda una lingua e duo belli occhi chiusi
> rimaner, dopo noi, pien' di faville. (*RVF* CCIII, 9–14)

> [This ardor of mine, which matters so little to you, and your
> praises in my well-known rhymes, could perhaps yet inflame
> thousands;
> for in my thought I see, O my sweet fire, a tongue cold in death
> and two lovely eyes closed, which after us will remain full of
> embers.]

Francesco's love is handed down to posterity without ornament, nor pretense of beatitude, but rather in its naked and unhappy beauty; and the countless future readers of the *Canzoniere* will be gifted this absolute figure ("Tu sola mi piaci"), this monotonous succession of radiant instants and moments of solitude.

In one of the *Penitential Psalms*, Petrarch would say that love is the effect of a diversion and a desperation: "Non respexi ad orientem, nec unde debueram auxilium expectavi; nec sicut dignum fuerat, speravi." [Nor look I yet, Lord, to the east, / Nor hope for help, where I am will'd] (*Ps.* VI, 4);[40] and so I fell in love. Love, which in the poems is presented as the pivotal experience of human life, would be nothing more than a distraction, a force that draws the soul away from its purpose; and beauty is the supreme source of feeling (corruption) and lamenting elegy. After all, in one of the *Metrice* the poet regards his own love for Laura with severity, and in the *Posteritati* he dedicates only two lines to that *amor acerrimus sed unicus et honestus* [an overwhelming but pure love-affair.][41] But within these examples

---

40 Francesco Petrarca: *Salmi penitenziali*. In his: *Rime, Trionfi e poesie latine*. Edited by F. Neri, G. Martellotti, E. Bianchi, N. Sapegno. Milan: Ricciardi 1951 (Letteratura italiana. Storia e testi, 6), p. 842. Trans. in: *Petrarch's Penitential Psalms*. In: *The Works of George Chapman. Poems and Minor Translations*. With and Introduction by Algernon C. Swinburne. London: Chatto and Windus 1975, p. 133–142, at p. 140.

41 Petrarca: *Prose*, p. 4. Trans. p. 2.

we find reticence and silence. Is not the invocation of the eastern horizon, by this brilliant inventor of sunsets, spiritually unrealistic? And doesn't the human blaze of Laura's eyes have the quality of an eternal dawn? The late Jungian psychologist James Hillman, in his now classic work *Re-Visioning Psychology*, confirms that the Augustinian statement on interiority ("Noli foras ire, in te ipsum redi; in interiore homine habitat veritas [...]." [Do not go abroad. Return within yourself. In the inward man dwells truth.], *De vera relig.* XXXIX, 72)[42] acts 'poetically' on Petrarch's soul: if the external world – the mountains, the ocean waves, the flow of rivers, the stars – is refuted because of its vain beauty, then neither is interiority, to which Petrarch consecrates himself ("[...] in me ipsum interiores oculos reflexi" [I turned my inner eyes within], *Fam.* IV, 1),[43] lacking in beauty or form; just like the world outside, interiority has its own landscape, with trees, ocean waves, rivers and stars. In spite of what Augustine might teach, interiority is not pure spiritual intimacy or silent abyss or expectation, but the opening scene of a play, the locus of poetic action *par excellence*. It is in these scenographic terms that Francesco, solitary man and capable of marvelous feats, tells the story of his soul:

> Anzi tre dì creata era alma in parte
> da por sua cura in cose altere et nove,
> e dispregiar di quel ch'a molti è 'n pregio,
> quest'ancor dubbia del fatal suo corso,
> sola, pensando, pargoletta et sciolta,
> intrò di primavera in un bel bosco.
>   Era un tenero fior nato in quel bosco
> il giorno avanti; et la radice in parte
> ch'appressar nol potea anima sciolta;
> ché v'eran di lacciuo' forme sí nove,
> e tal piacer precipitava al corso
> che perder libertate ivi era in pregio.
>   Caro, dolce, alto, et faticoso pregio
> che ratto mi volgesti al verde bosco
> usato di sviarme a mezzo 'l corso!
>   Et ò cerco poi 'l mondo a parte a parte
> se versi o petre o suco d'erbe nove
> mi rendesser un dí la mente sciolta.
>   Ma, lasso, or veggio che la carne sciolta
> fia di quel nodo ond'è 'l suo maggior pregio
> prima che medicine antiche o nove
> saldin le piaghe ch'i' presi in quel bosco

---

[42] Translation in: Augustine: *Early Writings*. Selected and Translated with Introductions by John H. S. Burleigh. Philadelphia: The Westminster Press 1953, p. 262.
[43] Petrarca: *Le familiari*, I, p. 159. Trans. in: Petrarca: *Letters on Familiar Matters*, I, p. 178.

folto di spine: ond'i' ò ben tal parte,
che zoppo n'esco, e 'ntra'vi a sí gran corso.

    Pien di lacci et di stecchi un duro corso
aggio a fornire, ove leggera et sciolta
pianta avrebbe uopo e sana d'ogni parte.
Ma tu, Signor, ch'ài di pietate il pregio
porgimi la man destra in questo bosco;
vinca 'l tuo sol le mie tenebre nove.

    Guarda 'l mio stato, a le vaghezze nove
che 'nterrompendo di mia vita il corso
m'àn fatto habitador d'ombroso bosco;
rendimi, s'esser pò, libera, et sciolta
l'errante mia consorte, e fia Tuo 'l pregio
s'anchor teco la trovo in miglior parte.

    Or ecco in parte le question' mie nove:
s'alcun pregio in me vive, o 'n tutto è corso,
o l'alma sciolta, o ritenuta al bosco. (*RVF* CCXIV)

    [Three days before, a soul had been created in a place
where it might put its care in things high and new
and despise what the many prize.
She, still uncertain of her fated course,
alone, thoughful, young, and free,
in springtime entered a lovely wood.

    A tender flower had been born in that wood
the day before, with its root in a place
that could not be approached by a soul still free;
for there were snares there of form so new
and such pleasure hastened one's course
that to lose liberty was there a prize.

    Dear, sweet, high, laborious prize,
which quickly turned me to the green wood,
accustomed to making us stray in the midst of our course!
And I have later sought through the world from place to place
if verses or precious stones or juice of strange herbs
could one day make my mind free.

    But now, alas, I see that my flesh shall be free
from that knot for which it is most greatly prized,
before medicines old or new
can heal the wounds I received in that wood
thick with thorns; on account of them it is my lot
to come out lame, and I entered with so swift a course!

    Full of snares and thorns is the course
that I must complete, where a light, free
foot would be in need, one whole in every place.
But you, Lord, who have all pity's praise,
reach me your right hand in this wood:
let your sun vanquish this my strange shadow.

Guard my state from those new beauties
which, breaking off my life's course,
have made me a dweller in the shady wood:
Make again, if it can be, unbound and free
my wandering consort; and let yours be the praise
if I find her again with You in a better place.
 Now behold in part my strange doubts:
if any worth is alive in me or all run out,
if my soul is free or captive in the wood.]

This story of the soul, narrated in the six strophes and *commiato* of sestina CCXIV, is of an almost transparent, almost evanescent allegorism: there is a wood, a tender flower, thorns; nothing more. What a difference from Dante's *selva*! There the 'soul' was above all *forma corporis*, the primary creator of "natura riottosa" (unruly nature, according to Ungaretti), free to choose and pursue its aim among forms both real and spectral – the allegories, the three beasts – free to ascend "dall'imo del baratro all'empireo" (from the depths of the abyss up to the Empyrean). Here instead the soul, removed from conflict with the material world and placed in sweet captivity, completes imaginary voyages, raises muffled supplications and invocations to heaven, lives weakly, sings with a whisper of a voice. Having reached the third stage of life – adolescence – the soul hesitates in uncertainty; faced with a thousand possible directions, it still doesn't recognize its own destiny and has no idea which way to go; but it is young, and we catch a glimpse of the joy, the simple passion of *going*. The entrance to that shadowy wood is in fact enmeshed by a web of marvels, enticements and pleasures, whose point of diffusion is Laura – the tender flower – and whose primary seduction is the threshold, the choice, the distinction with respect to the rest of the world: the soul the soul would like to enter into this sort of place for all eternity, it must hand itself over as prisoner, it must exile itself in perpetuity. But this segregation in the delightful excellence of the wood coincides, in a certain sense, with oblivion and the abandoning of truth and the absence of means. The wood itself is an eminently ambiguous place which, on the one hand, reveals to the soul the "fatal suo corso" – that is, its perpetual captivity – and on the other *diverts* (distracts from) its ascetic intension as well as its disposition to "cose altere et nove": "perder libertate ivi era in pregio", says Francesco; and then: "Caro, dolce, alto et faticoso pregio / che ratto mi volgesti al verde bosco [...]." The wood therefore creates a form – a challenge, an acute vital principle, an agony – in his soul (*agony*, Rosenzweig reminds us, is the apex of solitude);[44] and the paradox of

---

44 See Franz Rosenzweig: *The Star of Redemption*. Translated by Barbara E. Galli. Madison: The University of Wisconsin Press 2005, p. 80.

this solitude is that, in this very place where it finally recognizes itself, the soul is dying, wounded by eternal thorns, mutilated, circumfused by stubborn shadows. Is it possible to escape from this paradoxical solitude? To look for the eastern horizon, from a place so sweetly cruel? "Ma tu, Signor, ch'ài di pietate il pregio, / porgimi la man destra in questo bosco; / vinca 'l tuo sol le mie tenebre nove." Like every Petrarchan invocation, this seems both 'absolute' and indefinitely replicable: extreme defender of his privilege of being in love, Francesco looks with glowing eyes toward eternity and hopes to find a new design for himself, an epilogue or a miraculous dissolution of love itself. But eternity is still far off, and his prayer becomes the elegy and grief of a lonely soul "ritenuta al bosco."

Bibliography

Primary Literature

Alighieri, Dante: *Purgatorio*. A Verse Translation by Jean Hollander and Robert Hollander. Introduction and Notes by Robert Hollander. New York: Anchor Books 2003.
Alighieri, Dante: *Paradiso*. Translated by Robert Hollander and Jean Hollander. Introduction and Notes by Robert Hollander. New York: Anchor Books 2008.
An Anthology of Italian Poems. 13th–19th Century. Selected and Translated by Lorna de' Lucchi. New York: Biblo and Tannen 1967.
Augustine: *Early Writings*. Selected and Translated with Introductions by John H. S. Burleigh. Philadelphia: The Westminster Press 1953.
The Filostrato of Giovanni Boccaccio. A Translation with Parallel Text by Nathaniel E. Griffin and Arthur B. Myrick. Philadelphia: University of Pennsylvenia Press 1929.
Boccaccio, Giovanni: *The Decameron of Giovanni Boccaccio Faithfully Translated by James M. Rigg*. 2 vols. London: The Navarre Society 1932.
Boccaccio, Giovanni: *Filostrato*. Edited by Vittore Branca. In: *Tutte le opere di G. Boccaccio*. Edited by Vittore Branca. 10 vols. Milan: Mondadori 1964, vol. II, p. 16–228.
Boccaccio, Giovanni: *Comedia delle ninfe fiorentine*. Edited by Antonio Enzo Quaglio. In: *Tutte le opere di G. Boccaccio*. Edited by Vittore Branca. 10 vols. Milan: Mondadori 1964, vol. II, p. 679–835.
Boccaccio, Giovanni: *Filocolo*. Edited by Antonio Enzo Quaglio. In: *Tutte le opere di G. Boccaccio*. Edited by Vittore Branca. 10 vols. Milan: Mondadori 1967, vol. I, p. 45–1024.
Boccaccio, Giovanni: *The Corbaccio*. Translated and edited by Anthony K. Cassell. Urbana: University of Illinois Press 1975.
Boccaccio, Giovanni: *Il Filocolo*. Translated by Donald Cheney with the Collaboration of Thomas G. Bergin. New York and London: Garland 1985 (Garland Library of Medieval Literature, 43B).
Boccaccio, Giovanni: *L'Ameto*. Translated by Judith Serafini-Sauli. New York and London: Garland 1985 (The Garland Library of Medieval Literature, 33B).

Boccaccio, Giovanni: *The Elegy of Lady Fiammetta*. Edited and Translated by Mariangela Causa-Steindler and Thomas Mauch. Chicago: Chicago University Press 1990.
Boccaccio, Giovanni: *Decameron*. Edited by Vittore Branca. 2 vols. Turin: Einaudi 1992.
Boccaccio, Giovanni: *Rime*. Edited by Vittore Branca. In: *Tutte le opere di G. Boccaccio*. Edited by Vittore Branca. 10 vols. Milan: Mondadori 1992, vol. V, 1, p. 1–374.
Boccaccio, Giovanni: *Epistole e lettere*. Edited by Ginetta Auzzas. In: *Tutte le opere di G. Boccaccio*. Edited by Vittore Branca. 10 vols. Milan: Mondadori 1994, V, 1, p. 493–856.
Boccaccio, Giovanni: *Elegia di Madonna Fiammetta*. Edited by Carlo Delcorno. In: *Tutte le opere di G. Boccaccio*. Edited by Vittore Branca.10 vols. Milan: Mondadori 1994, V, 2, p. 23–412.
Boccaccio, Giovanni: *Corbaccio*. Edited by Giorgio Padoan. In: *Tutte le opere di G. Boccaccio*. Edited by Vittore Branca.10 vols. Milan: Mondadori 1994, V, 2, p. 413–614.
De Sanctis, Francesco: *Saggio critico sul Petrarca*. Edited by Niccolò Gallo. Turin: Einaudi 1964² (Opere di Francesco de Sanctis, 6).
Lucretius: *De rerum natura*. With and English Translation by W. H. D. Rouse. Cambridge, Mass., Harvard University Press 1992.
Francisci Petrarchae Opera omnia. Basle: Sebastianus Henricpetri 1581.
Petrarch's Penitential Psalms. In: *The Works of George Chapman. Poems and Minor Translations*. With and Introduction by Algernon C. Swinburne. London: Chatto and Windus 1975, p. 133–142.
The Life of Solitude by Francis Petrarch. Ed. and trans. by J. Zeitlin. Urbana: University of Illinois Press 1924.
Petrarca, Francesco: *Le familiari*. Edited by Vittorio Rossi (vols 1–3) and by Vittorio Rossi and Umberto Bosco (vol. 4). Firenze: Sansoni 1933–1942 (Edizione nazionale delle opere di Petrarca, 10–13).
Petrarca, Francesco: *Epistole metriche*. In his: *Rime, Trionfi e poesie latine*. Edited by Ferdinando Neri/ Guido Martellotti et al. Milan and Naples: Ricciardi 1951 (Letteratura italiana. Storia e testi, 6).
Petrarca, Francesco: *Salmi penitenziali*. In his: *Rime, Trionfi e poesie latine*. Edited by F. Neri/ G. Martellotti et al. Milan and Naples: Ricciardi 1951 (Letteratura italiana. Storia e testi, 6).
Petrarca, Francesco: *Prose*. Edited by Guido Martellotti/ Pier Giorgio Ricci et al. Milan and Naples: Ricciardi 1955.
Petrarca, Francesco: *Canzoniere*. Edited by Gianfranco Contini. Turin: Einaudi 1964.
Petrarch's Lyric Poems. The "Rime sparse" and Other Lyrics. Translated and Edited by Robert Durling. Cambridge, Mass.: Harvard University Press 1976.
Petrarch's Africa. Translated and Annotated by Thomas G. Bergin and Alice S. Wilson. New Haven: Yale University Press 1977.
Petrarch: Letter to Posterity. In his: *Selections from the "Canzoniere" and Other Works*. Translated and Edited with an Introduction and Notes by Mark Musa. Oxford: Oxford University Press 1985, p. 1–10.
Petrarca, Francesco: *Letters on Familiar Matters: Rerum familiarium libri*. Translated by Aldo S. Bernardo. 3 vols. Baltimore: Johns Hopkins University Press 1975–1985.
Petrarca, Francesco: *Letters of Old Age: Rerum Senilium Libri I–XVIII*. Translated by Aldo S. Bernardo, Saul Levin et al. 2 vols. Baltimore: Johns Hopkins University Press 1992.
Pétrarque: *L'Afrique*. Préface de Henri Lamarque. Introduction, traduction et notes de Rebecca Lenoir. Grenoble: Éditions Jérôme Millon 2002.
Petrarca, Francesco: *Canzoniere*. Introduction by Ugo Foscolo. Notes by Giacomo Leopardi. Edited by U. Dotti. Milan: Feltrinelli 2003⁶.

Petrarca, Francesco: *My Secret Book*. Edited and Translated by Nicholas Mann. Cambridge, Mass.: Harvard University Press, 2016 (The I Tatti Renaissance Library, 72).

Secondary Literature

Monographs and Anthologies

Contini, Gianfranco: *Letteratura italiana delle origini*. Florence: Sansoni 1970.
Flasch, Kurt: *Poesia dopo la peste. Saggio su Boccaccio*. Bari: Laterza 1995.
Foscolo, Ugo: *Saggi e discorsi critici*. Edited by Cesare Foligno. Florence: Le Monnier 1953 (Edizione nazionale delle opere di U.F., 10).
Rosenzweig, Franz: *The Star of Redemption*. Translated by Barbara E. Galli. Madison: The University of Wisconsin Press 2005.
Sklovskij, Viktor: *L'energia dell'errore*. Rome: Editori Riuniti 1984.
Valéry, Paul: *Variation sur une "Pensée" annotée par l'auteur*. Liége: Balancier 1930.
Vasoli, Cesare: *La dialettica e la retorica dell'Umanesimo*. Milan: Feltrinelli 1968.
Wilkins, Ernest Hatch: *Life of Petrarch*. Chicago: The University of Chicago Press 1961.

Articles and Papers

De Lollis, Cesare: *Recensione al florilegio petrarchesco di N. Zingarelli*. In: *La Cultura* 6 (1927), p. 464–466.

Renzo Bragantini
Petrarch, Boccaccio, and the Space of Vernacular Literature

The subject matter entitling these pages has been broached innumerable times; therefore, one should not expect to gather from the present essay new findings of particular prominence. Rather, I will attempt to propose a more detailed reading – based wherever possible upon plausible motives and confirmed or well-established dates – of the instances in which Petrarch and Boccaccio discuss and confront the theme implied by the title above.

A preliminary caveat is necessary here: most recently, the occasional reading has surfaced that presents Boccaccio as completely "petrarchized" so to speak; that is, made subordinate to the personality of his friend and teacher, to the point of voluntarily disrobing him of his own individual traits. The goal of this exercise, at first glance seemingly laudable, is to free the relationship between these two individuals from an overly pacific reading; however, a careful inspection of their texts, above all but not exclusively epistolary, suggests the need for further scrutiny. Concerning this non-confrontational reading of the relationship between Petrarch and Boccaccio, Billanovich and Branca are traditionally identified as the primary representatives.[1] The necessity to revisit that position has been declared most recently by Rico, who interprets the fellowship between the two authors from a very different perspective. Rico in fact relegates Boccaccio to an exclusively auxiliary role with regard to Petrarch; however, he shores up his argument with a limited and tendentious selection of texts, resulting in an interpretation that entirely ignores any intellectual rapport between the two, the importance of which should be abundantly clear.[2] Given the authority of the critic and the prestige of the publisher, it is easy to see why this new and more casual path would attract proselytes, impatient with the tiresome work of fact-checking. In reality the dichotomy between an irenic and a conflictual reading, as indicated by Rico, cannot be presented in such absolute terms, if for no other reason than the

---

Note: I would like to thank Monica Berté for reading this article and giving me useful bibliographical suggestions.

1 See Giuseppe Billanovich: *Petrarca letterato. I. Lo scrittoio del Petrarca*. Rome: Edizioni di Storia e Letteratura 1947, p. 59–294; Vittore Branca: *G. Boccaccio. Profilo biografico*. Florence: Sansoni 1977, p. 82–91.
2 Francisco Rico: *Ritratti allo specchio (Boccaccio, Petrarca)*. Rome and Padua: Antenore 2012.

∂ Open access. © 2018 Renzo Bragantini, published by De Gruyter. [CC BY-NC-ND] This work is licensed under the Creative Commons Attribution-NonCommercial-NoDerivatives 4.0 license.
https://doi.org/10.1515/9783110419306-016

episodes that contradict this eternally rosy coexistence between the two personalities are well known to all and have been thoroughly investigated for quite some time.³ A prime example is the letter of 18 July 1353, in which Boccaccio accuses Petrarch of grave ethical and political inconsistency for having chosen to relocate to Milan among the enemy Visconti (whom Petrarch himself previously opposed quite vehemently)⁴ – testimony, it must be said immediately, of which Rico makes only the most passing mention.⁵ Naturally, the motives at play in the letter are primarily political, but not exclusively so, as often people would like us to believe. Also under discussion, and quite markedly, is Petrarch's moral consistency, as well as those very same principles constantly proclaimed in his intellectual activity. Boccaccio writes, addressing Petrarch both with "you" and with his bucolic denomination of Silvanus:

> Non se solum labe hac sua Silvanus infecit, sed te me reliquosque, qui vitam, qui mores, qui cantus et calamos eius toto ore, totis viribus, apud quascunque silvas, apud quoscunque pastores efferebamus, fedavit innocuos. Credisne quieturos hos ad quos venerit scelus hoc, quin in eum clamitent? imo iam clamitant et convitiis inhonestis veterem eius famam deturpant, falsam, fucatam, fictitio splendore coruscam dicentes [...]. Hic solitudinum commendator egregius atque cultor, quid multitudine circumseptus aget? quid tam sublimi preconio liberam vitam atque paupertatem honestam extollere consuetus, iugo alieno subditus et inhonestis ornatus divitiis faciet? quid virtutum exortator clarissimus, vitiorum sectator effectus, decantabit ulterius? Ego nil aliud nosco quam erubescere et opus summ dampnare, et virgilianum illud aut coram aut secus cantare carmen: "Quid non mortalia pectora cogis / auri sacra fames?"

> [Not only himself, but you, me and all the other innocents did Silvanus infect with his dishonorable act, whose life, traditions, whose song and pen we exalted with all our voice, with all our strength, in every wood, among all the shepherds. Do you truly believe that those who suffered this misdeed will endure it in silence instead of raising their voices? To the contrary: they already scream and sully his former reputation with dishonest insults, saying that it is false, constructed with a fictitious splendor [...]. What will this egregious praiser and lover of solitude do, now surrounded with a flock? What will he who usually extols a life of freedom and honest poverty do, now that he submits himself to the foreign

---

3 See Billanovich: *Petrarca letterato*, p. 178–86; and Branca, *G. Boccaccio. Profilo*, p. 93–95.
4 On the choice of Petrarch see the well-researched Enrico Fenzi: Petrarca a Milano: tempi e modi di una scelta meditata. In: Giuseppe Frasso/ Maurizio Vitale et al. (eds.): *Petrarca e la Lombardia. Atti del Convegno di Studi, Milano, 22–23 maggio 2003*. Rome and Padua: Antenore 2005, p. 221–263; Fenzi rightly remembers how Nelli (see here further on) distances himself from Boccaccio's position, but the claim that the latter's opinion is only a "harsh personal judgment of Petrarch" (p. 225) seems reductive.
5 One can find the letter in Giovanni Boccaccio: *Epistole e lettere*. Edited by Ginetta Auzzas/ Augusto Campana. In: Giovanni Boccaccio: *Tutte le opere di G. Boccaccio*. Edited by Vittore Branca. 10 vols. Milan: Mondadori 1992, vol. V, 1, p. 574–583. See also Rico: *Ritratti allo specchio*, p. 30.

yoke, adorned with dishonest riches? What will this renowned inspirer of virtues often repeat, now that he has become the follower of vices? I know that nothing remains to me if not to blush and to condemn his actions, and to sing, either openly or to myself, that passage from Virgil: "Quid non mortalia pectora cogis / auri sacra fames?"].[6]

Petrarch, at least to our knowledge, does not respond, and parries the blow with indirect justifications, offered to people he knew to be dear to Boccaccio, such as in the two *Fam.*, XVI 11 and 12, of 23 and 27 August 1353 to Francesco Nelli; and again in *Fam.*, XVII 10 of 1 January 1354 to Giovanni Aghinolfi. This patient mending of wounds would bear its own fruits in terms of Boccaccio's generosity of spirit, when very shortly he puts his contempt aside. Nevertheless, there is no doubt that however brief in duration, this crisis is the worst in their mutual relationship and represents a stance of exceptional intransigence on the part of Boccaccio, who underscores Petrarch's insufficient fidelity in real life to the behavior often ideally pursued in his works, and particularly in his letters. This rift between the two friends continues for some time, as demonstrated by *Sen.*, VI 2, this time addressed directly to Boccaccio – a letter that in its own turn integrates two others, the *Disp.*, 40 and 46, of 12 July 1357 and 18 August 1360, respectively.[7] The above-mentioned *Sen.* VI, 2 (traditionally dated to the first months of 1366), of a pointedly defensive tone, responds with a delayed outburst, reignited by the preoccupations of Boccaccio who learns that while Petrarch has by now transferred to Venice, he occasionally accepts the hospitality of Galeazzo II in Pavia.[8] An attentive reading of the two *Disperse* shows that while Boccaccio quickly abandoned his reproachful tone, the embers of his incomprehension still smolder beneath the ashes.

The *punctum dolens*, however, lies elsewhere, and I will treat it more directly. Rico's book presents a version of Petrarch and Boccaccio's relationship which is insufficiently discussed, and which, given the sketchiness of its treatment, can only be defined as aprioristic, if not truly hasty. He characterizes Petrarch as a man who conceals from one of his dearest friends both the pertinent facts of his own biography and above all the fruits of his own labor; he inhibits Boccaccio from using texts from his personal library; in other words, he treats his friend with an attitude that one could euphemistically define as condescending. These formulated accusations are easily dismantled by a heap of evidence, provided in

---

[6] The passage is in Giovanni Boccaccio: *Epistole e lettere*, p. 578, 580; English translations by Bridget Pupillo.
[7] The two letters are found in Francesco Petrarca: *Lettere disperse, varie e miscellanee*. Edited by Alessandro Pancheri. Milan-Parma: Fondaz. P. Bembo/U. Guanda 1994, p. 314–21, 338–59.
[8] See Francesco Petrarca: *Res seniles. Libri V–VIII*. Edited by Silvia Rizzo with the collaboration of Monica Berté. Florence: Le Lettere 2009, p. 118–121.

the first place by Boccaccio himself who, in the initial gestures of the very same indignant letter of 18 July 1353, makes reference to their Paduan meeting of 1351:

> Tu sacris vacabas studiis, ego compositionum tuarum avidus ex illis scribens summebam copiam.
>
> [You dedicated yourself to sacred studies; I, greedy for your compositions, made copies for myself].[9]

If these examples do not suffice, we might add the Milanese visit of March 1359, and the Venetian one of March 1363; occasions in which Boccaccio is Petrarch's guest for one month and for more than three, respectively. As Elsa Filosa plausibly hypothesizes, during those visits to his friend Boccaccio would likely have had access to the *Fam.*, XXI 8, which, together with the *De viris illustribus*, would act as the nucleus of the *De mulieribus claris*.[10] Filosa suggests, with good reason, that certain textual additions, recognizable in the lengthy editorial *iter* of the treatise, are precisely due to Boccaccio's reading of this Petrarchan letter.[11] Thus, just as Boccaccio was able to copy some of the *Familiares* and *Epistolae Metrice* during the earlier Paduan meeting of 1351, he returns from the Milanese visit of 1359 with copies of the *Bucolicum Carmen*, the *Itinerarium*, the beginning of the *Africa*, and probably some new *Familiares*.[12]

None of this evidence seems to carry any weight for Rico. In his reconstruction of the facts Boccaccio is nothing but a docile instrument in the hands of his friend, a humble servant of little intelligence, at most an avid observer, entirely ignorant of even the simplest philosophical and theological understanding.[13] In this case, then, Petrarch's tone in the famous (or rather infamous) *Sen.*, XVII 3 would assume the contours of a veritable rudeness with regard to Boccaccio, who had him receive a copy of the *Decameron*. I will discuss here only a few of the arguments that the scholar presents, but these should be sufficient to set up some firm lines of defense against these points. Regarding one of the decisive "facts" of this sort of reconstruction – the marginalization of Boccaccio from Petrarch's studio – one cannot but refer to the studies of Billanovich,

---

9 Giovanni Boccaccio: *Epistole e lettere*, p. 574.
10 On the importance of the Petrarchan letter in the project of the *De mulieribus* see Stephen Kolsky: La costituzione di una nuova figura letteraria. Intorno al 'De mulieribus claris' di G. Boccaccio. In: *Testo* 25 (1993), p. 36–52.
11 See Elsa Filosa: *Tre studi sul 'De mulieribus claris'*. Milan: LED 2012, p. 51–62.
12 See Vittore Branca: *G. Boccaccio. Profilo*, p. 88–89, 109–10 and n. 42.
13 For these judgments see Rico: *Ritratti allo specchio*, p. 11, 69, 75, 129. To counterbalance such a one-sided perspective, see Kurt Flasch: *Poesia dopo la peste: Saggio su Boccaccio*. Rome and Bari: Laterza 1995.

who resolutely refutes the very notion. Nevertheless, at least two passages from letters written to Boccaccio must be mentioned. In the *Fam.*, XXII 2, datable through internal evidence to the first ten days of October 1359, Petrarch at the opening of the text writes:

> Statim te digresso, etsi abitu tuo angerer [...], in opere tecum cepto amicum illum nostrum meo quodam iure detinui, *Bucolici carminis*, quod tecum abstuleras, exemplaribus revidendis. Que dum confero cum eodem illo utique viro bono priscique moris et lectore quidem tardo sed non segni amico, animadverti aliquot verbula crebrius repetita quam vellem, et nescio quid preterea nunc etiam lime indigum. Itaque ne transcribere festinares admonui neu Francisco nostro copiam dares, non ignarus ardoris vestri in omnibus et presertim meis literis, que, nisi amor iudicio obstaret, nec digitis certe nec oculis quidem vestris digne sunt.

> [Soon after your departure and despite my distress, (...) I detained as a personal favor our friend to have him help with the work that I had begun with you: revising the transcripts of the *Bucolicum carmen*, a copy of which you had taken with you. As I conferred with that good man with his old-fashioned ways, not a slow-witted friend but a really slow reader, I noticed several short words repeated more frequently than I wished as well as some other things in need of more polish. Thus, I urged you not to hasten your transcription or to give a copy to our Francesco, knowing your interest in all that I possess, especially my writings; indeed, were your love not interfering with your judgment, they would be unworthy of your fingers or your eyes.][14]

In another letter directed to Boccaccio, sent from Pavia on 28 October 1366 (*Fam.*, XXIII 19), after having described the uncommon abilities of his young copyist, traditionally identified as Giovanni Malpaghini, Petrarch admonishes the addressee for not having alerted him, as Malpaghini had done (albeit for different reasons), to the overtly obvious imitation of a Virgilian clause ("atque intonat ore"; *Aen.*, VI 607), found in the *Bucolicum carmen*, VI 193:[15]

> Obstupui; sensi enim, illo loquente, quod me scribente non senseram, finem esse virgiliani versus sexto divini operis; idque tibi nuntiare disposui, non quod ullus correctioni amplius locus sit, carmine illo late iam cognito ac vulgato, sed ut te ipsum arguas, qui michi errorem meum hunc indicari prius ab alio passus sis, vel si id forsan ignotum tibi hactenus fuit, notum esse incipiat [...].

> [I was astounded, for as he spoke I realized what I had not noticed while writing, that it is a verse ending in the sixth book of Virgil's divine poem. I decided to inform you of this, not because

---

14 *Fam.* XXII, 2. Latin texts are taken from Francesco Petrarca: *Familiarium rerum libri (XXI–XXIV)*. Edited by Vittorio Rossi, Ugo Dotti et al. Turin: Nino Aragno 2004–2009, p. 3106–3108. English translation in: Francesco Petrarca: *Letters on Familiar Matters: Rerum familiarium libri*. Translated by Aldo S. Bernardo. 3 vols. Baltimore: Johns Hopkins University Press 1975–1985, II, p. 211.
15 Monica Berté: Giovanni Malpaghini copista di Petrarca? In: *Cultura neolatina* 75 (2015), p. 205–216, has recently questioned this traditional identification.

of any possibility of correcting the passage since the poem is widely known and disseminated, but so that you might reprove yourself for allowing another to be first in pointing out this slip of mine, or that you might now take note of it, had it escaped your notice so far (...)].[16]

As examples of Petrarch's paltry faith in the abilities of Boccaccio and as signs of possessiveness toward his own texts with regard to his friend, these seem to provide more than ample evidence, given that we are not in fact dealing with isolated cases here! On the other hand, as to the more delicate personal rapport and friendship between the two men, one cannot but refer to an example among many, in the *Sen.*, I 5, of 28 May 1362, in the conclusion of which Petrarch accepts quite favorably the prospect of unifying their two libraries and expresses his hopes for a future cohabitation.[17]

Taking for granted that any reconsideration of the Petrarch-Boccaccio relationship – if based upon a reading drawn from new but solid premises – can bring to light a fundamental turning point for Italian literature and beyond, that which appears to lack quite clamorously in this kind of reconstruction is an adequate consideration of the intellectual figure of Boccaccio, who is denied the dignity of individual attention.[18] Not to mention that, in reweaving the threads of such a delicate and complex relationship, the pronouncement of definitive statements does not seem to be the best approach. The proclamation of Boccaccio's inherent intellectual inferiority leads us even farther from a real comprehension of this intense but elusive event. Rather, this interpretation does nothing but break down an already open door, and not even the correct one. Clearly, the ability to erect a monument stone by stone without a single loose join, such as that which Petrarch constructed during his lifetime, is entirely lacking to a reckless administrator of his own resources such as Boccaccio, who unlike his more prestigious correspondent never thinks to put together in a systematic way and circulate his own few letters.[19] It must be remembered above all that, even accounting for

---

16 *Fam.* XXIII, 19. Francesco Petrarca: *Familiarium rerum libri (XXI–XXIV)*. English translation from Francesco Petrarca: *Letters on Familiar Matters*, II, p. 302.
17 See Francesco Petrarca: *Res seniles. Libri I–IV*. Edited by Silvio Rizzo with the collaboration of Monica Berté. Florence: Le Lettere 2006, p. 56–85 (for the passage discussed here, see paragraphs 132–47, p. 82–85).
18 Marco Petoletti furnishes this reordering of ideas, giving each of the two authors his balanced and intelligent attention while providing an incomparable understanding of manuscript history, transmission, and of the intricately connected conveyances by hand. See Marco Petoletti: Boccaccio e i Classici. In: Marco Ballarini, Giuseppe Frasso et al. (eds.): *Verso il centenario del Boccaccio. Presenze classiche e tradizione biblica*. Milan-Rome: Biblioteca Ambrosiana-Bulzoni 2014, p. 179–191 (which I also recommend for its substantial final *Bibliographic Note*).
19 See, in addition to the classic studies of Billanovich, Karlheinz Stierle: *F. Petrarca. Ein Intellektueller im Europa des 14. Jahrhunderts*. Munich: C. Hanser 2003 (particularly Chapter 5). Huss

letters the two friends exchanged which have not come down to us (three from Petrarch and at least twelve from Boccaccio have not survived), the imbalance is still to Boccaccio's disadvantage.[20] We should also keep in mind that Boccaccio is so equitably generous toward all his friends as to include in the pages of the *Genealogies*, as well as in the *Expositions* to the *Commedia*, conspicuous lines of a letter sent to him by Pietro Piccolo of Monteforte, which Billanovich masterfully published and discussed.[21] A man of law, of proven and solid experience, but also skilled rather more than provisionally in the literary sphere, Monteforte cannot, however, compare to Boccaccio in this last sector. Still, Boccaccio, due to old age and the increasing discomfort of illness, decides to fortify his pages with Monteforte's contribution. In no way, however, can these late appropriations be considered, as far as their actual importance in the two last books of the *Genealogies*, at the same level as the structural and lasting effect that the *Fam.*, X 4 (sent to Gherardo on 2 December 1349) must have exercised, in which Petrarch not only offers the interpretative key to the first eclogue, but above all declares the compatibility of poetry and theology. It is truly a shame that a scholar such as Rico, to whom we all (first and foremost the current author) owe so much – particularly but not only in the field of Petrarch Studies – should pass over an intersection of such import to European culture at high speed and in the wrong direction. It is necessary at any rate to specify that Rico's position, which shies away from the actual, often contorted and ambiguous dynamics of the relationship between Petrarch and Boccaccio, is not in fact an isolated one, but quite the opposite!

For confirmation of this fact, one might read (citing one example among many) what Quondam writes in his introduction to the edition of the *Decameron* issued in conjunction with the seventh centenary of the birth of its author:

> Non può esserci concorrenza, e tanto meno contesa: Boccaccio si arrende a Petrarca e lo fa con gioioso entusiasmo. Arrendersi gli risolve problemi che forse neppure comprende fino in fondo e che soprattutto non riesce a gestire: è Petrarca il padre necessario, il patriarca di una discendenza annunciata.

---

and Regn justly define Petrarch as the "virtuoso of self-representation" in the Afterword of their bilingual edition of the *Secretum*: Francesco Petrarca, *Secretum meum: lateinisch-deutsch = Mein Geheimnis*. Edited and translated by Bernhard Huss/Gerhard Regn. Mainz: Dieterich 2004, p. 493.
20 Albanese offers a precise panorama of the epistolary exchanges between the two in Gabriella Albanese: La corrispondenza fra Petrarca e Boccaccio. In: Claudia Berra (ed.): *Motivi e forme delle 'Familiari' di F. Petrarca. Gargnano del Garda (2–5 ottobre 2002)*. Milan: Cisalpino 2003, p. 39–98 (with a final table of contents organized chronologically).
21 See Giuseppe Billanovich: Pietro Piccolo da Monteforte tra il Petrarca e il Boccaccio [1955]. In Giuseppe Billanovich: *Petrarca e il primo umanesimo*, Padua: Antenore 1996, p. 459–524. Monteforte's letter is from 2 February 1372 (see p. 469); Boccaccio responds on 5 April of the same year (see Giovanni Boccaccio: *Epistole e lettere* XX, p. 674–689).

[There cannot be a competition, and much less a dispute: Boccaccio yields to Petrarch and does so with joyous enthusiasm. To yield himself resolves problems that perhaps not even he himself understands deep down and with which, above all, he is not able to cope: Petrarch is the necessary father, the patriarch of a heralded lineage.][22]

I will overlook here all the other points that merit an in-depth discussion, about which exist arguments in favor and likewise of motivated and strong dissent. Among these last, the precocious leap forward – as viewed in terms of an anthropological ideal – of ten young narrators in the *Decameron*, forerunners, no less, of the "storia della nobiltà europea nei secoli di Antico regime, e in modo tutto particolare [del]la storia delle sue culture identitarie" [history of the European nobility in the centuries of the Old Regime, and in a very particular way of the history of its cultural identities]; not to mention the Boccaccio-Marino comparison that Quondam must have plucked out of the critical hyperuranium.[23] That which is most lacking in the pages under examination here is an historical analysis performed with a specifically medieval perspective on literature. Suffice it to say that, by the end of this long introduction, what emerges once again is the portrait of a Boccaccio subordinate to Petrarch, deprived of any and all intellectual autonomy, completely defeated by the latter's domineering personality, conscious that his vernacular works, which Quondam is too quick to define as being of a low level, would forever come second to the 'lofty' project of Petrarch. Evidently, the many studies published in recent years on the fine-tuned *mise en page* of the autograph and on the cunning intertextual strategy of the *Decameron* have not made much headway as far as Quondam is concerned. Needless to say, the scholar passes over in total silence the above-cited letter of Boccaccio to Petrarch regarding the decision of the latter to join the Visconti, as well as Petrarch's defensive position and justifications, both direct and indirect, to which I have previously referred. His interpretation of the relationship between Petrarch and Boccaccio is more of an axiom (moreover of hasty formulation and uncertain foundation, since we know that even concerning the definition of petrarchism, of which Quondam is an eminent scholar, there exists no univocal statement of the sort, not even among the practitioners of the Cinquecento), rather than a reasoned argument based upon the elucidation of individual facts and a necessary distinction between events.[24]

---

22 See Amedeo Quondam's introduction to Giovanni Boccaccio: *Decameron*. Edited by Amedeo Quondam, Maurizio Fiorilla et al. Milan: BUR 2013 (the passage is on p. 58).
23 Ibid., p. 25, 59–60.
24 Solid objections to the reconstructions of both Rico and Quondam, and to other points touched upon in those studies, are found in David Lummus: Review: Quondam, Amedeo, Maurizio Fiorilla, and Giancarlo Alfano. *Decameron*. Milan: Biblioteca Universale Rizzoli 2013. p. 1851. Francisco Rico: *Ritratti allo specchio (Boccaccio, Petrarca)*. Rome: Antenore, 2012, p. 160. In: *The Medieval Review* 14.02.01 (February 2014), online journal: <http://hdl.handle.net/2022/17342>.

Diagnoses such as those described here, which insist upon saturnine excerpts of a Petrarch poised to devour his disciple-sons (particularly in the case of his friend Boccaccio), not only ignore the actual ongoing literary dynamic, but fail to make clear the delicate games in which these two eminent characters engaged during those years, games that would have great effect in the realm of vernacular literature. Nor do such interpretations seem able – beyond the most beaten paths of criticism – to grasp those rifts that could indeed corroborate the idea of a less-than-idyllic rapport between Petrarch and Boccaccio. The very mention of such facts could put in jeopardy those same diagnoses, so the facts are at times put on the back burner by scholars who wish to continue defining Boccaccio's role as supportive. To mistake Boccaccio's undoubted malleability – often disguised as self deprecation – for intellectual dependence, could lead to error, above all because mildness can, if necessary, sting in a pungently allusive manner. We know that the *Fam.*, XXI 15 (which I will discuss a bit further on) suggests edits and reorganizations in the successive versions of the *Trattatello in laude di Dante* (*Treatise in Praise of Dante*);[25] and some scholars have already highlighted a passage of the Chigian revision which is worth citing here, because to say it contains an ambiguous but plausible antipetrarchan dig does not indeed seem to be a posthumous stretch:

> Che diranno qui coloro, a gli studii de' quali non bastando della lor casa, cercano le solitudini delle selve? che coloro, a' quali è riposo continuo, e a' quali l'ampie facultà senza alcun lor pensiero ogni cosa oportuna ministrano? che coloro che, soluti da moglie e da' figliuoli, liberi possono vacare a' lor piaceri? De' quali assai sono che, se ad agio non sedessero, o udissero un mormorio, non potrebbono, non che meditare, ma leggere, né scrivere, se non stesse il gomito riposato.
>
> [What will they say now, those for whom their own homes are not sufficient for quiet study, so that they must seek the solitude of the forest? Those who are at continuous repose, and whose ample faculties, free from worries, provide every opportunity? Those who, without wife or children, are free to idle about at their leisure? There are many of those who, if they were not seated comfortably, or if they were to hear a murmur, they could not but think, let alone read and write, if they did not have their elbow at rest.][26]

---

25 See most recently Giuseppe Ledda: Biografia, poesia e allegoria nel 'Trattatello in laude di Dante' di G. Boccaccio. In: Emilio Pasquini (ed.): *Fra biografia ed esegesi: crocevia danteschi in Boccaccio e dintorni*. Ravenna: Longo 2014 (*Letture Classensi*, 42), p. 41–77 (in particular p. 41–44, for the relationship between Petrarch and Boccaccio in relation to the *Trattatello*; I refer to that essay also for its dense bibliography of prior works).
26 Giovanni Boccaccio: *Trattatello in laude di Dante* (IIª red.). Edited by Pier Giorgio Ricci. In:Vittore Branca (ed.): *Tutte le opere di G. Boccaccio*. Milan: Mondadori 1974, volume III, 61, p. 510. English translation by Bridget Pupillo.

It is difficult to see how Boccaccio, whose revision was inspired by Petrarch's suggestions, would not have wanted to make himself perfectly clear here;[27] a comparison with the corresponding passage of the first redaction seems to confirm this notion, as the text, lacking in ironic stingers, simply states:

> E se, ostanti cotanti e così fatti avversarii, [...] egli [Dante] per forza d'ingegno e di perseveranza riuscì chiaro qual noi veggiamo, che si può sperare che esso fosse divenuto, avendo avuti altrettanti aiutatori, o almeno niuno contrario, o pochissimi, come hanno molti?
>
> [And if in the middle of the many taxing obstacles [...], by the strength of his genius and perseverance he [i. e. Dante] became as distinguished as we know him to be, what could we have hoped for him to become if, like many others, he had had many supporters, or at least no enemies, or very few enemies against him?][28]

However obvious the reference, we should not necessarily identify the intellectual type reproached in the second redaction only with the specific person of Petrarch. There is no doubt, however, that this portrait, which lambasts whoever manages to work only in conditions of extreme comfort, with the absence of any external disturbance, fits Petrarch perfectly.[29] But indeed, it is a defect of certain recent scholars to sift tendentiously through the primary bibliography, and to eliminate the secondary altogether, in order to get right to their point.

Better, therefore, to change one's perspective: rather than harping on their power struggles, from which, predictably, there emerges only one victor, it is

---

27 For this reading see Giuseppe Velli: Petrarca e Boccaccio: l'incontro milanese. In: Giuseppe Frasso/ Maurizio Vitale et al.: *Petrarca e la Lombardia*, p. 145–164 (in particular p. 148–149); it must be emphasized that Velli also insists on the independence of the execution (noted also in the timeline), and on the considerable difference of registers between the *Buccolicum carmen* of Boccaccio and of Petrarch (p. 152–164); Elsa Filosa: To Praise Dante, to Please Petrarch (Trattatello in laude di Dante). In: Victoria Kirkham, Michael Sherberg et al. (eds.): *Boccaccio. A Critical Guide to the Complete Works*. Chicago and London: The University of Chicago Press 2013, p. 213–220 (in particular p. 219–220); Jason Houston: Boccaccio at Play in Petrarch's Pastoral World. In: *MLN* 127 (January 2012, Italian Issue Supplement), p. 47–53.
28 Giovanni Boccaccio: *Trattatello in laude di Dante* (I^a red.). Edited by Pier Giorgio Ricci. In: *Tutte le opere di G. Boccaccio*. Edited by Vittore Branca. Milan: Mondadori 1974, III, 83, p. 457. English translation taken from Giovanni Boccaccio: *The Life of Dante (Trattatello in laude di Dante)*. Translated by Vincenzo Zin Bollettino. New York and London: Garland 1990 (Garland Library of Medieval Literature, 40), p. 23.
29 Carlo Paolazzi: Petrarca, Boccaccio e il 'Trattatello in laude di Dante' [1983]. Reprinted in Carlo Paolazzi: *Dante e la 'Comedia' nel Trecento. Dall'Epistola a Cangrande all'età di Petrarca*. Milan: Vita e Pensiero 1989, p. 131–221. This study reveals the influences of the *Fam.* XXI 15 on the Chigi edition of the *Trattatello*, but does not note the polemical tension that underlies the indicated passage (see p. 167–181).

opportune to shift one's attention toward the subject of their dialog, which is what truly counts. Try to imagine an isosceles triangle, the base of which is made up of Petrarch and Boccaccio, and the vertex of which we might identify with the convergence of their attentions. Only in that way can the peculiar intellectual physiognomy, both of Petrarch and Boccaccio, emerge with all its characterizing traits in relation to the problem under discussion.

The *Fam.*, XXI 15, of May or June 1359 – in response to a Boccaccian letter no longer available to us, in which Boccaccio sends Petrarch a second version of the Latin poem *Ytalie iam certus honos* (sent in its first redaction around 1353, accompanying the exemplar of the *Commedia*, now Vat. Lat. 3199) – has been overanalyzed so frequently that I cannot help but revisit it here, if only to reiterate that which is already known to all.[30] This being that, in spite of the constitutional ambiguity of a dictation that both denies and confirms, both praises and limits, the letter makes the presence of Dante in Petrarch's works – and not only those in the vernacular – an incontestable fact, and at the same time allows Petrarch to mark this presence as a literary and intellectual experience radically divergent from his own.[31] Certainly we can confirm from the unreachable reticence of this letter that Boccaccio must have dished out a bit of his own in the letter now lost, if Petrarch, at the opening of the text, can write:

> Primum ergo te michi excusas, idque non otiose, quod in conterranei nostri -popularis quidem quod ad stilum attinet, quod ad rem hauddubie nobilis poete- laudibus multus fuisse videare; atque ita te purgas quasi ego vel illius vel cuiusquam laudes mee laudis detrimentum putem.

---

[30] For the *carmen* of Boccaccio see Giovanni Boccaccio: *Carmina*. Edited by Giuseppe Velli. In: *Tutte le opere di G. Boccaccio*. Edited by Vittore Branca. Milan: Mondadori 1974, V 1, p. 375–492. The cited text is on p. 430, 432; Velli's excellent commentary is on p. 476–480, which goes alongside the no less important *Introduction*, p. 377–402 (particularly p. 386–91 for the text in question). See also Giancarlo Breschi: Il ms. Vaticano Latino 3199 tra Boccaccio e Petrarca. In: *Studi di Filologia Italiana* 72 (2014), p. 95–117. The double drafting of the Latin poem has been recently questioned. See Paolo Trovato /Elisabetta Tonello et al.: La tradizione e il testo del carme "Ytalie iam certus honos" di Giovanni Boccaccio. In: *Studi sul Boccaccio* 41 (2013), p. 1–111. Restating the idea of the two versions of the poem is Angelo Piacentini: Il carme "Ytalie iam certus honos" di Giovanni Boccaccio. In: Luca Azzetta/ Andrea Mazzucchi (eds.): *Boccaccio editore e interprete di Dante. Atti del Convegno internazionale di Roma, 28–30 ottobre 2013*. Rome: Salerno Editrice 2014, p. 185–221.
[31] I limit my references to Michele Feo: Petrarca. In: *Enciclopedia dantesca*. 6 vols. Rome: Istituto della Enciclopedia Italiana 1984, IV, p. 450–58 (in particular p. 451–52 for the well-known epistle); more recently see Emilio Pasquini: Dantismo petrarchesco. Ancora su 'Fam.' XXI, 15 e dintorni. In: Claudia Berra (ed.): *Motivi e forme delle 'Familiari'*, p. 21–38.

[In the first place, you ask pardon, somewhat heatedly, for seeming to praise unduly a fellow countryman of ours who is popular for his poetic style but doubtless noble for his theme; and you beg pardon for this as though I believe that praises for him or for anyone else would detract from my personal glory.][32]

Here, without doubt, Petrarch has a much more candid and clearer regard than his more generous but less clear-headed friend, to whom we owe gratitude for the memorable result of that impossible conciliation, the ms. Vat. Chigiano L V 176 – definitive book form for the culture of the Trecento and beyond, as well as the foundation on which the great triad of that century was constructed.[33] However, it is more fruitful, as far as our interests are concerned, to return to the *Sen.*, V 2, dated to 28 August. The year is almost certainly 1364, no later,[34] as demonstrated by Boccaccio's letter to Donato Albanzani, which Augusto Campana rediscovered in the ms. Vat lat. 3134 (f. 334 *r–v*) and subsequently published. The Boccaccian epistle is dated 4 April, while Campana establishes the year as 1365.[35] In it appear undoubted references to the *Sen.*, V 2.[36] Boccaccio writes:

> Ceterum hortaris ut epistolam longissimam, quam dicis Silvanum in severitatem meam scripsisse, deposcam. Quod ego te, per amicitiam nostram, tua voce meis precibus facias horo. Nil michi carius hodie quam suas videre epistolas, et potissime quibus mordeor. Ridebis? Sed dicam tamen. Numquam michi iuveni adeo fuere dulcia suavia mulierum uti seni sunt morsus mei venerandissimi preceptoris. Eos quidem omnes in argumentum sincere atque certissime dilectionis deduco. Quam sepe hanc ob causam legam credis quam etiam longissimam in bestialitatem meam scripsit, dum primo apud Ravennam

---

32 *Fam.*, XXI 15. See Francesco Petrarca: *Familiarium rerum libri (XXI–XXIV)*, volume V, p. 3068–87 (cited passage on p. 3070–71). English translation from Francesco Petrarca: *Letters on Familiar Matters*, II, p. 202.

33 Given the accumulated bibliography on the importance of this manuscript, I will limit my references, beyond the fundamental Domenico De Robertis: *Il codice Chigiano L. V. 176 autografo di G. Boccaccio*. Rome and Florence: Archivi edizioni-Alinari 1974 (including the detailed *Introduction*), to the recent Martin Eisner: *Boccaccio and the Invention of Italian Literature: Dante, Petrarch, Cavalcanti, and the Authority of the Vernacular*. Cambridge: Cambridge University Press 2013 (with bibliography of prior works). As far as more generally concerns Boccaccio's activity as a Dantista, I refer to the various collected studies in Luca Azzetta and Andrea Mazzucchi (eds.): *Boccaccio editore e interprete di Dante*.

34 See Francesco Petrarca: *Senile V 2: introduzione, testo e traduzione con quattro tavole fuori testo*. Edited by Monica Berté. Florence: Le Lettere 1998 (from which I cite, also adopting the paragraph numbering; see also Francesco Petrarca: *Res seniles: Libri V–VIII*. Edited by Silvia Rizzo, with the collaboration of Monica Berté. Florence: Le Lettere 2009, p. 30–51); Francesco Petrarca: *Rerum senilium libri (I–VI) – Le senili (Libri I–VI)*. Edited by Ugo Dotti, Elvira Nota et al. 3 vols. Turin: Nino Aragno 2004–2010, I, p. 567–593.

35 See Giovanni Boccaccio: *Epistole e lettere*, p. 738–743 (for its dating, see p. 742).

36 This identification is established in a private letter of Guido Martellotti to Augusto Campana; see Francesco Petrarca, *Senile V 2*, p. 14 and note 34.

amicus tuus effectus sum? Profecto sepissime, iam fere purgato stomaco dulces sentiens quos alias arbitrabar amaros.[37]

[As for the rest, you urge me to ask for the lengthy letter in which, according to you, Silvano wrote to challenge my severity. In the name of our friendship, I beg you to voice my supplications to him. Nothing is more precious to me now than reading his letters, especially those in which he admonishes me. I know it will make you laugh, but I wanted to tell you all the same. Never, even in my youth, did feminine beauty please me half as much as do the reproofs of my most highly esteemed preceptor now that I've reached old age. I consider them all to be a mark of sincere and most resolute affection. How often do you believe that, precisely for this reason, I read what he wrote in that interminable letter against my foolishness, when you and I first became friends at Ravenna? Truly I read it many times, having already cleansed my stomach, so that I could enjoy like sweets those foods that in other circumstances would have seemed bitter to me.][38]

There is no doubt as to Boccaccio's references here: his *severitas*, which Petrarch reproaches, is due to the rumor, at first anonymous and then confirmed by Donato, of the fire to which Boccaccio had purportedly condemned his early vernacular compositions (*Sen.*, V 2 13, 16–18). The *bestialitas* certainly alludes to an attitude of flaunted humility which Petrarch, in the same letter, judges in fact to be ill-concealed arrogance: according to him, Boccaccio refuses to accept his position in the hierarchy of vernacular poets, given that the first place goes without question to the unnamed Dante (*Sen.*, V 2, 21–49).[39] In the letter at least two points

---

[37] In the last passage Boccaccio seems to be reminiscent of Boethius: *De consolatione Philosophiae* III prose 1: "Talia sunt quippe quae restant, ut degustata quidem mordeant, interius autem recepta dulcescant" [What now remains is of such sort that to the taste indeed it is biting, but when received within it turns to sweetness]. English translation from Boethius: *The Consolation of Philosophy of Boethius*. Translated by H. A. James. London: Eliot Stock 1897, p. 93. See also Dante Alighieri: *Paradiso*. Edited by Giorgio Inglese. Rome: Carocci 2016, p. 235.
[38] Giovanni Boccaccio: *Epistole e lettere*, Appendix, p. 739–40.
[39] Auzzas misunderstands the significance of this portion of the letter to Donato, reading it as a reference to the polemic triggered by the Boccaccian letter to Petrarch, regarding the latter's preference for the Visconti (see Giovanni Boccaccio, Epistole e lettere, p. 792–93, n. 35). Rico succumbs to yet another and no less errant misconception, which identifies in the term *bestialitas* a Petrarchan rebuke against Boccaccio's sins of the flesh, in Rico: *Ritratti allo specchio*, p. 125–28 (n. 62 manages to garble what the letter seems to confirm with clarity). Apart from the specificity of the texts, I wish to note that *bestialità* in the *Decameron* always signifies 'foolishness', 'stupidity' (I *Intr.*, 64; II 9 54 and 10 3; VIII 10 40; X 10 3, in the last case associated with cruelty); only in one passage (III 3 45) does it mean 'improper, unacceptable behavior', never implying deeds connected explicitly to the sexual sphere. The same can be said of the adjective 'bestiale', and of the unique occurrence of the adverb 'bestialmente'. It should be added that *bestialità* is an Aristotelian category (*Nicomachean Ethics* VII, 1145a), which has nothing to do with sexual incontinence, but rather with behavior contrary to reason, and as such is glossed by Thomas Aquinas, whose commentary was well-known to Boccaccio, since he copied it in the autograph

remain controversial: 1) the rumor of the fire to which Boccaccio, discouraged by Petrarch's superiority in vernacular lyric, had fed his youthful verses – an event that has never been verified, but is attributed above all to the Petrarchan epistle and to a passage of the Boccaccian letter to Pietro Piccolo da Monteforte that evokes the episode and the position assumed by Petrarch ("[...] ut percipere potes ex litera, cum in primum locum pervenire non possem non sufficientibus ingenii viribus, ardens mea vulgaria et profecto iuvenilia nimis poemata, dedignari visus sum in secundo utinam meo convenienti ingenio consistere"; [(...) as you will see from the letter (...) unable to achieve first place due to an insufficient strength of intellect, it seemed, with the burning of my vernacular works and especially those I considered too juvenile, that I refused to remain in second place, if only my intellect were worthy of it]);[40] 2) Petrarch's allusion to the juvenile "magnum [...] opus" (53) left to fall by the wayside (on which many different hypotheses have been made).

Apart from the final polemic on the corruption of the times (that channels Petrarch's disdain toward rulers, kings, those contemptuous of the classics, new theologians who take inspiration from Averroes instead of Paul and Augustine), the true nuclei of the letter are different and end up intertwining. These are identifiable as the following: 1) the hierarchy of vernacular poetry, that a "senex [...] Ravenn*as*" (identified as the Dantista and poet Menghino Mezzani) establishes in the order Dante – Petrarch – Boccaccio (a hierarchy to which Petrarch ironically demonstrates his assent when he declares himself disposed to cede the second place to Boccaccio: "Si is sordet sique a primo obstare tibi videor, qui non obsto, ecce volens cedo, locus tibi linquitur secundus" [If [third place] is too lowly, if I

MS Milan, Biblioteca Ambrosiana, A 204 inf., around 1340, a decade before the composition of the *Decameron*. On this manuscript, see Marco Cursi/Maurizio Fiorilla: G. Boccaccio. In: Giuseppina Brunetti et al. (eds.): *Autografi dei letterati italiani. Le Origini e il Trecento*, to. I. Rome: Salerno Editrice 2016, p. 43–103 (particularly p. 52–53, n. 20; p. 74, plate 2b); Marco Petoletti. In: Teresa De Robertis et al. (eds.): *Boccaccio autore e copista*. Florence: Mandragora 2013, item n. 64 (MS Milan, Biblioteca Ambrosiana, A 204 inf.), p. 348–350. On *bestialità* see Lucia Battaglia Ricci: Decameron X, 10: due 'verità' e due modelli etici a confronto. In: *Italianistica* 42 (2013), p. 79–90.
40 In Giovanni Boccaccio: *Epistole e lettere*, XX 44, p. 686–687. On the truth of Boccaccio's book-burning (which Branca believes and Billanovich treats with suspicion) see most recently Roberto Fedi: Pathways through the Lyric Forest (Rime). In: Victoria Kirkham, Michael Sherberg et al. (eds.): *Boccaccio. A Critical Guide*, p. 283–293 (with bibliography). Fedi (p. 284) maintains that the burning is not credible. The most recent editor of Boccaccio's lyric does not enter into this discussion, as he aims rather to make the text as reliable as possible (given the extremely complex textual situation and delicate questions of attribution). See Giovanni Boccaccio: *Rime*. Edited by Roberto Leporatti. Florence: SISMEL-Edizioni del Galluzzo 2013. At any rate, substantial evidence is lacking, in one sense or another.

appear to block your way to first place, which I do not, look, I gladly yield and leave second place to you]);[41] 2) the mockery made of his own vernacular works, which had fallen victim to an uncontrolled dissemination (52–55; here return the polemical sparks of the *Fam.*, XXI 15 17–18).[42] The remark is significant if one reads it in light of the fact that two administrators so aware of their own textual traditions as Petrarch and Boccaccio had secured with a robust unifying structure (at least for the *Canzoniere* and the *Decameron*; but the discussion can be broadened to include other works as well) the conglomeration of pieces that, lacking adequate protection, had until then been tossed into the melting pot along with other scattered components of dubious paternity, both within the lyric and the novelistic traditions (from the first *Novellino* to the same Dantean *Rime disperse*). If this behavior in Petrarch has been noted for quite some time, much more recent is the awareness, acquired as a result of the research of Marco Cursi, that the control Boccaccio exercised upon the very first circulated edition of the *Decameron* seems to have been quite strict. Concluding his examination of Decameronian manuscript witnesses of the proto-circulation (during the years 1360–1375), Cursi writes:

> Il dato più significativo [...], fino ad oggi non valutato in tutta la sua importanza, è offerto da un comune denominatore che contraddistingue tutti i testimoni costituenti la proto-tradizione del *Centonovelle*, sia quelli che sono effettivamente giunti fino a noi (oltre all'autografo berlinese, il *frammento magliabechiano*, il codice Parigino Italiano 482 e le carte piacentine Vitali 26), sia quelli dei quali abbiamo sicure attestazioni [...]: i testimoni citati, senza eccezioni, sono riconducibili a copisti e lettori-possessori che ebbero rapporti di conoscenza diretta con l'autore stesso o con persone che [...] furono vicine al Boccaccio [...]. [...] L'immagine che si sta gradualmente mettendo a fuoco [...] è quella di una circolazione in qualche modo catalizzata intorno alla figura dell'autore e [...] inevitabilmente soggetta alla sua sorveglianza, diretta o indiretta.
>
> [The most significant fact (...), its full importance not appreciated until now, is offered by a common denominator that marks all the witnesses constituting the proto-tradition of the *Centonovelle*, both those that have actually reached us (beyond the Berlin autograph, the *Magliabechian fragment*, the codex Parigino Italiano 482 and the Piacentine papers Vitali 26), and those of which we have assured evidence (...): the cited witnesses, without exception, are attributable to copyists and reader-owners who had direct personal relationships

---

41 *Sen.*, V 2 33. English translation taken from Francesco Petrarca: *Letters of Old Age: Rerum Senilium Libri I–XVIII*. Translated by Aldo S. Bernardo, Saul Levin et al. Baltimore: Johns Hopkins University Press 1992, volume 1, p. 160.
42 On the decisive importance of the authorial control Petrarch exercises upon his own writings, see the excellent synthesis (relative to a chronological arch from the eighth to the fourteenth century) by Armando Petrucci: Scrivere il testo. In: *La critica del testo. Problemi di metodo ed esperienze di lavoro. Atti del Convegno di Lecce, 22–26 ottobre 1984*. Rome: Salerno Editrice 1985, p. 209–227 (in particular p. 224–227).

with the author himself or with individuals who (...) were close to Boccaccio (...). (...) The image that is gradually coming into focus (...) is that of a circulation catalyzed in some way by the figure of the author and (...) inevitably under his supervision, directly or indirectly].[43]

These observations are of extreme importance, and lead us directly to the urgency and anxieties demonstrated by Petrarch in the *Sen.*, V 2, with regard to the uncontrolled spread of his vernacular texts.

It is also worthwhile to read – I would say above all in light of these proven facts – the second letter sent by Boccaccio to Mainardo Cavalcanti, very close in its date to 13 September 1372 (if not on that exact day).[44] I will only select the passage that is most within our interests, certainly relative to the *Decameron*, but perhaps to other works as well (as the accusative plural at the beginning of the line might imply):[45]

> Te libellos meos non legisse, quod quasi magnum fateris crimen, cum rideam, non miror; non enim tanti sunt ut, aliis pretermissis, magna cum solertia legi debeant. Dato estivus calor, noctes breves et sponsa nova, ut domestice rei curam omiserim, nedum novum et iuvenem militem, sed etate provectum, canum et scolasticum hominem a sacris etiam studiis et amovisse potuissent et excusatum redderent. Quod autem te hieme futura facturum scribis, laudo ni melior adsit cura. Sane, quod inclitas mulieres tuas domesticas nugas meas legere permiseris non laudo, quin imo queso per fidem tuam ne feceris. Nosti quot ibi sint minus decentia et adversantia honestati, quot veneris infauste aculei, quot in scelus impellentia etiam si sint ferrea pectora, a quibus etsi non ad incestuosum actum illustres impellantur femine, ei potissime quibus sacer pudor frontibus insidet, subeunt tamen passu tacito estus illecebres et impudicas animas obscena concupiscentie tabe nonnunquam inficiunt irritantque, quod omnino ne contingat agendum est. Nam tibi, non illis, si quid minus decens cogitaretur, imputandum esset. Cave igitur iterum meo monitu precibusque ne feceris. Sine illas iuvenibus passionum sectatoribus, quibus loco magni muneris est vulgo arbitrari quod multas infecerint petulantia sua pudicitias matronarum. Et si decori dominarum tuarum parcere non vis, parce saltem honori meo [...]. Existimabunt enim legentes me spurcidum lenonem, incestuosum senem, impurum hominem, turpiloquum maledicum et alienorum scelerum avidum relatorem. Non enim ubique est qui in excusationem meam consurgens dicat: «Iuvenis scripsit et maioris coactus imperio». Hec autem quantum etati mee conveniant, sino studiis, tu nosti; et quanquam minus honestus sim et longe minus iamdudum fuerim, non facile vellem iudicio talium mulierum mea fedaretur fama vel nomen.

---

[43] Marco Cursi: *Il 'Decameron': scritture, scriventi, lettori. Storia di un testo*. Rome: Viella 2007, p. 43.

[44] Here I restate briefly and specifically that which I wrote in Renzo Bragantini: *Il governo del comico. Nuovi studî sulla narrativa italiana dal Tre al Cinquecento*. Manziana (Rome): Vecchiarelli 2014, p. 45–54.

[45] Daniels maintains quite plausibly that Boccaccio refers not only to the *Decameron* here. See Rhiannon Daniels: Rethinking the Critical History of the 'Decameron': Boccaccio's Epistle XXII to Mainardo Cavalcanti. In: *Modern Language Review* 106 (2011), p. 423–447.

[I am not at all surprised that you have not read my little books, which you confess almost as a great offense, while I simply laugh; they are not, in fact, of such worth that they must be read with great quickness, leaving everything else aside. Given the summer heat, the brief nights and your new bride, not to mention all your domestic affairs, not only a young fresh soldier, but a white-haired and lettered old man, would be enough to remove him from his sacred studies and excuse him. You write then that you plan to read them next winter: I encourage you to do so only if you have nothing better to do. But I certainly do not advise that you permit your honorable housemaids to read my trifles, in fact I beg your promise that you will not do so. You know how much of the subject matter is indecent and false, how the stories stimulate unhealthy appetites, how they push even the most steadfast souls to wicked actions. And even if the tales do not urge illustrious women, and above all those whose minds are possessed of sacred modesty, to commit deplorable acts, at any rate they insinuate imperceptibly titillating passions and sometimes make the mind indecent and infect and irritate it with the obscene decay of lust, so that one must act to prevent this from happening. Thus it would be considered your fault, not theirs, if ever they should think of something so indecent. Therefore make sure you don't do it, I ask and beg you once again. Leave the stories to the young men who go in search of passions, to whom it is a big deal if they say they have, with their petulance, spoiled the modesty of many matrons. And if you don't wish to respect the decorum of your women, respect at least my own honor [...]. Having read me, they will consider me, in fact, a filthy panderer, a dirty old man, an immodest, vulgar and greedy peddler of others' evils. Indeed not everywhere does someone rise to my defense, saying: "As a young man he wrote this under the command of a greater force." As far as these things are befitting to my age, not to mention my studies, you already know; and although I am not very honest and was much less so before, I would not wish that due to the judgment of such women my name and reputation become tarnished].[46]

Two contrasting interpretations of the passage are given: the first (made in fact by Branca and others in his wake) retains that Boccaccio's words are a rhetorical exercise, aiming to reiterate his complete faith in the endurance of the *Decameron*;[47] the second reads beneath these same words a distancing on the part of Boccaccio from his own masterpiece, triggered by moral scruples fostered through Petrarchan tutelage (it goes without saying that this second interpretation is manna for the supporters of a Boccaccio fearfully prone to the mastery of his dearest friend). Neither of the two readings, in my view, hits the target, which I believe to be something else entirely, linked to reading methods that Boccaccio fears could be exercised upon the text. Referring to Cavalcanti, the author knows well that his youngest and most generous friend, who had helped him

---

[46] See Giovanni Boccaccio: *Epistole e lettere*, XXII 17–24, p. 704–707.
[47] See Vittore Branca: *Tradizione delle opere di G. Boccaccio*. II. *Un secondo elenco di manoscritti e studi sul testo del 'Decameron', con due appendici*. Rome: Edizioni di Storia e Letteratura 1991, p. 176; Giovanni Boccaccio: *Epistole e lettere*, n. 9 p. 836–37; Maurizio Vitale: La riscrittura del 'Decameron'. I mutamenti linguistici. In: Maurizio Vitale and Vittore Branca: *Il capolavoro del Boccaccio e due diverse redazioni*. 2 vols. Venice: Istituto Veneto di Scienze, Lettere ed Arti 2002, I, n. 1 e p. 545.

quite liberally in a moment of grave difficulty, is not a culturally adept person, and dreads that the reading would not take place in an integral form, but rather privileging the narrations that most obviously contain erotic themes, thus contributing on the one hand to the sullying of his reputation, and on the other to the crippling of the ambitious design of his work. Important evidence in this vein would have come to us from the witness read by Cavalcanti and the women of his household, which may very well have been a manuscript lacking the text in its entirety;[48] unfortunately, we know nothing of it. The fact remains that Boccaccio's letter, more than an expression of self defense (in the form of a playful palinode) or self accusation, displays the doubt that the stratified, complex textual strategy of the *Decameron*, visible at its highest level in the Berlin autograph, would not be understood to its very depths. Boccaccio's fear, in other words, betrays his underlying diffidence toward an uncontrolled circulation of his greatest vernacular work, and in this respect can be compared to the same disdainful refusal expressed by Petrarch in the *Sen.*, V 2. I say compared to, not derived from, because we find recognizable signs that Boccaccio has arrived at an awareness of the issue already in the ms. Parigino Italiano 482, transcribed by Giovanni d'Agnolo Capponi in the seventh decade of the XIVth century, but reflecting a draft (a term that seems preferable to 'redaction') made during the years 1349–1351,[49] therefore – keeping in mind Cursi's observations in regard to the author's supervision, direct or indirect, of the proto-circulation – well prior in date to the *Sen.*, V 2.[50] In any case, we must maintain as plausible that Boccaccio and Petrarch focused their attentions independently upon a problem both felt to be pressing.

Given the aims of this investigation, we cannot escape a discussion of the *Seniles*, in particular of Book XVII, composed of four letters, all addressed to Boccaccio. More specifically, we must look at the last two: *Librum tuum* (from the spring of 1373), in which Petrarch sends to Boccaccio his Latin version of the story of Griselda; and *Ursit amor tui* (of 8 June 1374), with considerations on the

---

48 See also Cursi's writings on the subject in Marco Cursi: *Il 'Decameron'*, p. 44.

49 I refer, using the term 'redaction' with caution, to the thesis put forth by Vitale and Branca in Maurizio Vitale and Vittore Branca: *Il capolavoro del Boccaccio*.

50 This supervision, not precisely definable, cannot at any rate extend, as has long been maintained, to the possibility that Boccaccio is the author of the drawings in the Parisian manuscript. I limit my references to Lucia Battaglia Ricci: Edizioni d'autore, copie di lavoro, interventi di autoesegesi: testimonianze trecentesche. In: Guido Baldassarri/ Matteo Motolese et al. (eds.): *"Di mano propria". Gli autografi dei letterati italiani. Atti del Convegno internazionale di Forlì, 24–27 novembre 2008*. Rome: Salerno Editrice 2010, p. 123–157 (in particular p. 145–157 and bibliographic information). The author provides new in-depth analyses in Lucia Battaglia Ricci: *Scrivere un libro di novelle. G. Boccaccio autore, lettore, editore*. Ravenna: Longo 2013, p. 60–96.

narrative rhetoric and his final farewell to his friends and to epistolary writing.[51] First of all, I must confess a doubt on my part: can we truly believe that Petrarch read Boccaccio's masterpiece so late? I think we cannot.[52] I have to add that I find rather exaggerated the emphasis often placed on the initial tone of hurried impatience exhibited by Petrarch in the first of the two letters. More than ever vexed by his obsession with the passage of time, Petrarch feels the end approaching, and, at least officially, has abandoned vernacular poetry some time ago. In reality, he is still working on a draft of the *Triumphus Eternitatis* in the first two months of the year of his death, and will return to it later, just as, in that same final spring, he reworks probably for the last time the order of texts in the *Rerum vulgarium fragmenta*, sharing with Boccaccio once again a tendency to work simultaneously on Latin and vernacular texts. Certainly, Petrarch claims to have rapidly glimpsed the *Decameron*, and to have lingered above all on the initial description of the plague and on the final *novella*. We must not forget, however, that he also claims to have read the *Introduction* to the fourth day:

> Excuccurri eum [*scil.*: 'librum'], et festini viatoris in morem, hinc atque hinc circumspiciens, nec subsistens, animadverti alicubi librum ipsum canum dentibus lacessitum, tuo tamen baculo egregie tuaque voce defensum.
>
> [I leafed through it (i. e.: the book), and, like a hurried traveler who looks around from side to side without halting, I noticed somewhere that the book itself had been attacked by dogs' teeth, but admirably defended by your walking-stick and your yells].[53]

The passage is relevant for one of two reasons: either Petrarch did hastily skim the *Introduction* to the fourth day (which we must find to be rather improbable, given the conspicuous care with which that section was written and the incredible intelligence of the reader);[54] or, he passed over without mention one of its more significant passages – the reference to the Cavalcanti-Dante-Cino triad and (of great importance for Petrarch) to the "istorie [...] tutte piene [...] d'antichi uomini e valorosi" [stories of noble men of old time][55] who did not dismiss love as

---

51 In front of an interminable list of studies, I refer only to the recent study by Kenneth Clarke: On Copying and not Copying 'Griselda': Petrarch and Boccaccio. In: Emilia Di Rocco/Piero Boitani (eds.): *Boccaccio and the European Literary Tradition*. Rome: Edizioni di Storia e Letteratura 2014, p. 57–71 (from which one can glean most of the preceding bibliography).
52 The same doubt is expressed by Monica Berté/ Silvia Rizzo: "Valete amici, valete epistolae": l'ultimo libro delle 'Senili'. In: *Studi medievali e umanistici* 12 (2014), p. 83–90.
53 English translation from Petrarca: *Letters of Old Age*, II, p. 655.
54 Clarke shares the same opinion. See Kenneth Clarke: On Copying and not Copying, p. 68–69.
55 *Dec.* IV Introduction 33–34. English translation is taken from Giovanni Boccaccio: *The Decameron of Giovanni Boccaccio Faithfully Translated by James M. Rigg*. 2 vols. London: The Navarre Society 1903.

an instrument of intellectual development in advanced years. Moreover, to this very concept Petrarch alludes, with some sense of distance, in *RVF*, CCCIV – the sonnet that concludes the second part of the *Canzoniere* in the form found in the Chigi autograph of Boccaccio.[56] The Chigi form is datable, based on both internal and external evidence, to the time span between 1359 and 1363, but the draft of the sonnet dates to 1350, or a little after, its timing being substantially synchronous with the *Decameron*. However, the *canzone* 'of quotations' (*RVF*, LXX), would already have been sufficient for Boccaccio, because the succession of authors (pseudo-Arnaut, Cavalcanti, Dante, Cino) quoted before the conclusion, in which the poet refers to his first *canzone* (*RVF*, XXIII), leaves no doubts about Petrarch's movement away from his previously practiced ideas on love (and from the poetic activity connected to it). There exist a considerable number of hypotheses concerning its date of composition, spanning from the peak years (1337–1340) to the lowest (after 1350–1351); but once again we are looking at a time period certainly not incompatible with Boccaccio's masterpiece.[57] Arguments *ex silentio* must be employed with caution and, as always, taken with a grain of salt; nevertheless, it seems clear that in the *Introduction* to the fourth day one finds indications of a distancing from the thorny problem – not precisely from Petrarch's positions, but certainly from those he appropriated as his own. Even if, after clarifying the chronology, the influence should turn out to be reversed, the argument stands unchanged. The distance between Petrarch and Boccaccio, in this realm, remains massive.[58]

As to the Latin version of the *novella* of Griselda – a veritable rewriting that would bring European fame to this last story of the *Decameron* – it pushes sharply in the direction of *exemplum* a text that for so long was considered among the

---

[56] The same observation appears previously in Francesco Petrarca: *Le rime del Petrarca brevemente esposte*. Edited by Lodovico Castelvetro. Venice: Zatta 1756 [1582], volume II, p. 79, regarding verse 11 ("[as already seen in other cases] well into old age"): "In which the activity of composing lasted well into old age, just as the already aged Dante, and ancient Sir Cino, thus writes Boccaccio". See most recently Francesco Petrarca: *Canzoniere. Rerum vulgarium fragmenta*. 2 vols. Edited by Rosanna Bettarini. Turin: Einaudi 2005 (Nuova raccolta di classici italiani annotati, 20), II, p. 1338, the note on verses 10–11; and Martin Eisner: *Boccaccio and the Invention of Italian Literature*, p. 88–90.

[57] For the two proposed dates see, respectively, Francesco Petrarca: *Canzoniere*. Edited by Rosanna Bettarini, volume 1, p. 345–346; and Francesco Petrarca: *Canzoniere*. Edited by Marco Santagata. Milan: Mondadori 2004, p. 349. Frasso demonstrates how much more must be unearthed in the way of Petrarch's continued revisions (and of their possible circulations beyond the author's writing table) in Giuseppe Frasso: Pallide sinopie: ricerche e proposte sulle forme pre-Chigi e Chigi del 'Canzoniere'. In: *Studi di Filologia italiana*, 55 (1997), p. 23–64.

[58] See also Marco Veglia: *La strada più impervia. Boccaccio fra Dante e Petrarca*. Rome and Padua: Antenore 2014, p. 100–110.

most elusive of the collection, at least until the studies of Igor Candido clarified, with a plethora of evidence and comparisons, that the *Metamorphoses* of Apuleius, already influencing Boccaccio in his early years, also holds sway over this story through a subtle recall of the fable of Cupid and Psyche.[59] This retelling of the *novella*, which naturally cuts off the biting extremes of Dioneo's comments, is also a result of Petrarch's own uncertainty whether to define the work as 'fable' or 'history.' Within the vulgate text a famous passage from the beginning of *Seniles* XVII, 4 has often been read in this manner: "Et dicam tibi quid de hac historia, quam fabulam dixisse malim, michi contigerit" [And I shall tell you what happened to me in connection with this story, which I would rather call a tale]. However, Berté and Rizzo, who have carefully inspected the manuscript tradition, read the same passage as follows: "Et dicam tibi quid de hac -historiam ego quam fabulam dixisse malim- michi contigerit" [And I shall tell you what happened to me about this narration, which I would call history rather than fable].[60]

Significant in this regard is Leonardo Bruni's letter of accompaniment on 15 January 1437 to Bindaccio Ricasoli, with which he sends to the addressee his Latin version of the *novella* of Tancredi and Ghismunda, as well as his own vernacular *novella* of Seleuco, Antioco and Stratonica; here he claims that the Latin work stems from the earlier Petrarchan *novella* of Griselda. For both of his narrations Bruni uses the designation of *fable*; however, in the initial lines of this last *novella*, the narrator, described as a "huomo di grande studio in greco e in latino e molto curioso de l'antiche storie" [man of great knowledge in Greek and Latin and very curious about ancient histories], possibly Bruni himself, defines his narration as "novella overo historia" [*novella* or rather history], implying that the conjunction, given the lattice of sources underlying the story, has a paraphrastic rather than a distinctive worth ['to say it better'].[61] In so doing, Bruni seems to be very close to Petrarch's definition in the above-mentioned passage from *Seniles* XVII, 4, as it is conveyed by the manuscript tradition. I would like to stress the importance

---

59 See Igor Candido: *Boccaccio umanista. Studi su Boccaccio e Apuleio*. Ravenna: Longo 2014, in particular p. 141–158 (with bibliography; Candido's studies on the question date back to 2007; see p. 98 and n. 36).
60 See Monica Berté/ Silvia Rizzo: "Valete amici, valete epistolae", p. 102–104.
61 The two passages from the *novella* of Seleuco in the edition – already published in *Interpres* 22 (2003) – now published in Nicoletta Marcelli: *Eros, politica e religione nel Quattrocento fiorentino. Cinque studi tra poesia e novellistica*. Manziana (Rome): Vecchiarelli 2010, paragraphs 6 and 8, p. 116–117. Bruni's letter to Ricasoli is on p. 102. On the *novella* of Seleuco and its influence on sixteenth-century writing, but also on other themes touched upon here, see Elisabetta Menetti: *Enormi e disoneste: le novelle di Matteo Bandello*. Rome: Carocci 2005, p. 71–84; Elisabetta Menetti: *La realtà come invenzione. Forme e storia della novella italiana*. Milan: Franco Angeli 2015, p. 124–129 and 147–50.

of such a definition. In calling the Griselda tale a history, Petrarch (and Bruni after him) not only emphasizes the exemplary side of the story offered by his translation, but also pays tribute to the final tale of Boccaccio's collection; at the same time he presents a retort against those who claim that the literary genre of the novella has no roots in history, thus echoing Boccaccio's sharp rebuke to his critics (*Decameron* IV, *Intr.* 39).

To understand the sense of the Petrarchan exercise and its intricate bonds, I turn again to the pages of Candido, in which he adds another stone to the more-than-necessary restoration of a classical Boccaccio, a subject to which Velli had already dedicated fundamental but often overlooked pages (suffice it to say that Velli's name never appears in the very ample bibliography of the edition directed by Quondam, an edition in which the results of Boccaccio's rewriting of the Latin classics are often passed over in silence).[62] The extreme example of the *novella* of Griselda and of its Latin rewriting confirms that the indubitable mastery of Petrarch over Boccaccio is sometimes exaggerated, for a twofold and connected order of reasons: first, the more ample stylistic democracy of Boccaccio in respect to the noted intransigence of Petrarch; and second, the more acutely 'modernistic' availability of the former in respect to the latter.[63] It is more correct therefore to maintain that both share and, in their own way, nurture a culture and an approach to writing that aims toward a commingling of classical exemplars and the contributions of more recent and contemporary medieval literature.

Naturally then it is a fact that, in the long term, and specifically regarding the realm of vernacular literature, the influential model of Petrarch has prevailed in Italian tradition in respect to that of Boccaccio (and before him, obviously, of Dante). In time this preference will be deemed the result, as has already occurred (in terms of the author of the *Canzoniere*, not of the most eminent intellectual of his European contemporaries, the master of a perfect Latin), of the prestige of an unparalleled formal refinement together with the asphyxiating restriction of the canon. A similar outcome cannot however truly be ascribed to the historical person of Petrarch, but rather to his overly zealous and partial modern commentators.[64]

---

[62] See Giuseppe Velli: Memoria. In: Renzo Bragantini/Pier Massimo Forni (eds.): *Lessico critico decameroniano*. Turin: Bollati Boringhieri 1995, p. 222–248 (and bibliography); as well as Marco Petoletti: Boccaccio e i Classici.
[63] See Martin Eisner: Boccaccio's Renaissance. In: Emilia Di Rocco/Piero Boitani (eds.): *Boccaccio and the European Literary Tradition*, p. 45–55.
[64] Only after submitting the text of the present study was I able to examine (on the recommendation of Johnny L. Bertolio, whom I thank) two essays, both of which appear in the very recent publication: Guyda Armstrong, Rhiannon Daniels et al. (eds.): *The Cambridge Companion to Boccaccio*. Cambridge: Cambridge University Press 2015: Gur Zak: Boccaccio and Petrarch,

Bibliography

Primary Literature

Alighieri, Dante: *Commedia. Paradiso*. Edited by Giorgio Inglese. Rome: Carocci 2016.
Boccaccio, Giovanni: *Carmina*. Edited by Giuseppe Velli. In: *Tutte le opere di Giovanni Boccaccio*. Edited by Vittore Branca. 10 vols. Milan: Mondadori 1974, V, 1, p. 375–492.
Boccaccio, Giovanni: *Trattatello in laude di Dante* (Iª red.). Edited by Pier Giorgio Ricci. In: *Tutte le opere di Giovanni Boccaccio*. Edited by Vittore Branca. 10 vols. Milan: Mondadori 1974, III, p. 437–496.
Boccaccio, Giovanni: *Trattatello in laude di Dante* (IIª red.). Edited by Pier Giorgio Ricci. In: *Tutte le opere di Giovanni Boccaccio*. Edited by Vittore Branca. 10 vols. Milan: Mondadori 1974, III, p. 497–538.
Boccaccio, Giovanni: *Epistole e lettere*. Edited by Ginetta Auzzas / Augusto Campana. In: Giovanni Boccaccio: *Tutte le opere di G. Boccaccio*. Edited by Vittore Branca. 10 vols. Milan: Mondadori 1992, V, 1, p. 506–856.
Boccaccio, Giovanni: *Decameron*. Edited by Amedeo Quondam/ Maurizio Fiorilla et al. Milan: BUR 2013.
Boccaccio, Giovanni: *Rime*. Edited by Roberto Leporatti. Florence: SISMEL – Edizioni del Galluzzo 2013.
Boethius: *The Consolation of Philosophy of Boethius*. Translated by H. A. James. London: Eliot Stock 1897.
Petrarca, Francesco: *Le rime del Petrarca brevemente esposte*. Edited by Lodovico Castelvetro. 2 vols. Venice: Zatta 1756 [1582].
Petrarca, Francesco: *Letters on Familiar Matters: Rerum familiarium libri*. Translated by Aldo S. Bernardo. 3 vols. Baltimore: Johns Hopkins University Press 1975–1985.
Petrarca, Francesco: *Letters of Old Age: Rerum Senilium Libri I–XVIII*. Translated by Aldo S. Bernardo, Saul Levin et al. 2 vols. Baltimore: Johns Hopkins University Press 1992.
Petrarca, Francesco: *Lettere disperse, varie e miscellanee*. Edited by Alessandro Pancheri. Milan and Parma: Fondaz. P. Bembo/U. Guanda 1994.
Petrarca, Francesco: *Senile V 2: introduzione, testo e traduzione con quattro tavole fuori testo*. Edited by Monica Berté. Florence: Le Lettere 1998.
Petrarca, Francesco: *Rerum senilium libri (I–VI) – Le senili (Libri I–VI)*. 3 vols. Edited by Ugo Dotti/ Elvira Nota et al. Turin: Nino Aragno 2000–2010, I, p. 567–593.
Petrarca, Francesco: *Secretum meum: lateinisch-deutsch = Mein Geheimnis*. Edited and translated by Bernhard Huss/Gerhard Regn. Mainz: Dieterich 2004.
Petrarca, Francesco: *Canzoniere*. Edited by Marco Santagata. Milan: Mondadori 2004.

---

p. 139–154; Tobias Foster Gittes: Boccaccio and Humanism, p. 155–170. While aiming at somewhat diverse goals, both agree on the urgent need to confer upon Boccaccio the specific cultural and intellectual profile that must be objectively applied to him. I must also agree: to misunderstand Petrarch's influence would certainly be foolish; to insist on Boccaccio's prone subalternity is to risk falling inadmissibly behind the times. Interesting remarks also in Edoardo Fumagalli: Giovanni Boccaccio tra Leonzio Pilato e Francesco Petrarca: appunti a proposito della "prima translatio" dell''Iliade'. In: *Italia medioevale e umanistica* 54 (2013), p. 213–283.

Petrarca, Francesco: *Canzoniere. Rerum vulgarium fragmenta*. Edited by Rosanna Bettarini. 2 vols. Turin: Einaudi 2005.
Petrarca, Francesco: *Res seniles. Libri I–IV*. Edited by Silvia Rizzo with the collaboration of Monica Berté. Florence: Le Lettere 2006.
Petrarca, Francesco: *Familiarium rerum libri (XXI–XXIV)*. Edited by Vittorio Rossi/Ugo Dotti et al. Turin: Nino Aragno 2004–2009.
Petrarca, Francesco: *Res seniles: Libri V–VIII*. Edited by Silvia Rizzo, with the collaboration of Monica Berté. Florence: Le Lettere 2009.

Secondary Literature

Monographs and Anthologies

Armstrong, Guyda/Rhiannon Daniels et al. (eds.): *The Cambridge Companion to Boccaccio*. Cambridge: Cambridge University Press 2015.
Azzetta, Luca/Andrea Mazzucchi (eds.): *Boccaccio editore e interprete di Dante. Atti del Convegno internazionale di Roma, 28–30 ottobre 2013*. Rome: Salerno Editrice 2014.
Baldassarri, Guido/Matteo Motolese et al. (eds.): *"Di mano propria". Gli autografi dei letterati italiani, Atti del Convegno internazionale di Forlì, 24–27 novembre 2008*. Rome: Salerno Editrice 2010.
Ballarini, Marco/Giuseppe Frasso et al. (eds.): *Verso il centenario del Boccaccio. Presenze classiche e tradizione biblica*. Milan and Rome: Biblioteca Ambrosiana-Bulzoni 2014.
Battaglia Ricci, Lucia: *Scrivere un libro di novelle. G. Boccaccio autore, lettore, editore*. Ravenna: Longo 2013.
Berra, Claudia (ed.): *Motivi e forme delle 'Familiari' di F. Petrarca. Gargnano del Garda (2–5 ottobre 2002)*. Milan: Cisalpino 2003.
Billanovich, Giuseppe: *Petrarca letterato. I. Lo scrittoio del Petrarca*. Rome: Edizioni di Storia e Letteratura 1947.
Bragantini, Renzo/Pier Massimo Forni (eds.): *Lessico critico decameroniano*. Turin: Bollati Boringhieri 1995.
Bragantini, Renzo: *Il governo del comico. Nuovi studî sulla narrativa italiana dal Tre al Cinquecento*. Manziana (Rome): Vecchiarelli 2014.
Branca, Vittore: *G. Boccaccio. Profilo biografico*. Florence: Sansoni 1977.
Branca, Vittore: *Tradizione delle opere di G. Boccaccio. II. Un secondo elenco di manoscritti e studi sul testo del 'Decameron', con due appendici*. Rome: Edizioni di Storia e Letteratura 1991.
Brunetti, Giuseppina et al. (eds.): *Autografi dei letterati italiani. Le Origini e il Trecento*, to. I. Rome: Salerno Editrice 2013.
Candido, Igor: *Boccaccio umanista. Studi su Boccaccio e Apuleio*. Ravenna: Longo 2014.
Cursi, Marco: *Il 'Decameron': scritture, scriventi, lettori. Storia di un testo*. Rome: Viella 2007.
De Robertis, Domenico: *Il codice Chigiano L. V. 176 autografo di G. Boccaccio*. Rome and Florence: Archivi edizioni-Alinari 1974.
De Robertis, Teresa et al. (eds.): *Boccaccio autore e copista*. Florence: Mandragora 2013.
Di Rocco, Emilia/Piero Boitani (eds.): *Boccaccio and the European Literary Tradition*. Rome: Edizioni di Storia e Letteratura 2014.

Eisner, Martin: *Boccaccio and the Invention of Italian Literature: Dante, Petrarch, Cavalcanti, and the Authority of the Vernacular*. Cambridge: Cambridge University Press 2013.
Filosa, Elsa: *Tre studi sul 'De mulieribus claris'*. Milan: LED 2012.
Flasch, Kurt: *Poesia dopo la peste. Saggio su Boccaccio*. Rome and Bari: Laterza 1995.
Frasso, Giuseppe/Maurizio Vitale et al. (eds.): *Petrarca e la Lombardia. Atti del Convegno di Studi, Milano, 22–23 maggio 2003*. Rome and Padua: Antenore 2005.
Kirkham, Victoria/Michael Sherberg et al. (eds.): *Boccaccio. A Critical Guide to the Complete Works*. Chicago and London: The University of Chicago Press 2013.
Marcelli, Nicoletta: *Eros, politica e religione nel Quattrocento fiorentino. Cinque studi tra poesia e novellistica*. Manziana (Rome): Vecchiarelli 2010.
Menetti, Elisabetta: *Enormi e disoneste: le novelle di Matteo Bandello*. Rome: Carocci 2005.
Menetti, Elisabetta: *La realtà come invenzione. Forme e storia della novella italiana*. Milan: Franco Angeli 2015.
Pasquini, Emilio (ed.): *Fra biografia ed esegesi: crocevia danteschi in Boccaccio e dintorni*. Ravenna: Longo 2014 (*Letture Classensi*, 42).
Rico, Francisco: *Ritratti allo specchio (Boccaccio, Petrarca)*. Rome and Padua: Antenore 2012.
Stierle, Karlheinz: *F. Petrarca. Ein Intellektueller im Europa des 14. Jahrhunderts*. Munich: C. Hanser 2003.
Veglia, Marco: *La strada più impervia. Boccaccio fra Dante e Petrarca*. Rome and Padua: Antenore 2014.
Vitale, Maurizio: La riscrittura del 'Decameron'. I mutamenti linguistici. In: Maurizio Vitale/Vittore Branca: *Il capolavoro del Boccaccio e due diverse redazioni*. 2 vols. Venice: Istituto Veneto di Scienze, Lettere ed Arti 2002.

Articles and Papers

Albanese, Gabriella: La corrispondenza fra Petrarca e Boccaccio. In: Claudia Berra (ed.): *Motivi e forme delle 'Familiari'*, p. 39–98.
Battaglia Ricci, Lucia: Edizioni d'autore, copie di lavoro, interventi di autoesegesi: testimonianze trecentesche. In: Guido Baldassarri/Matteo Motolese et al. (eds.): *"Di mano propria". Gli autografi dei letterati italiani, Atti del Convegno internazionale di Forlì, 24–27 novembre 2008*. Rome: Salerno Editrice 2010, p. 123–157.
Battaglia Ricci, Lucia: Decameron X, 10: due 'verità' e due modelli etici a confronto. In: *Italianistica* 42 (2013), p. 79–90.
Berté, Monica: Giovanni Malpaghini copista di Petrarca?. In: *Cultura neolatina* 75 (2015), p. 205–216.
Berté, Monica/ Silvia Rizzo: "Valete amici, valete epistolae": l'ultimo libro delle 'Senili'. In: *Studi medievali e umanistici* 12 (2014), pp. 71–108.
Billanovich, Giuseppe: Pietro Piccolo da Monteforte tra il Petrarca e il Boccaccio [1955]. In: Giuseppe Billanovich: *Petrarca e il primo umanesimo*. Padua: Antenore 1996, p. 459–524.
Breschi, Giancarlo, Il ms. Vaticano Latino 3199 tra Boccaccio e Petrarca. In: *Studi di Filologia Italiana* 72 (2014), p. 95–117.
Clarke, Kenneth: On Copying and not Copying 'Griselda': Petrarch and Boccaccio. In: Emilia Di Rocco/Piero Boitani (eds.): *Boccaccio and the European Literary Tradition*. Rome: Edizioni di Storia e Letteratura 2014, p. 57–71.

Cursi, Marco/Maurizio Fiorilla: *G. Boccaccio*. In: Giuseppina Brunetti et al. (eds.): *Autografi dei letterati italiani*, p. 43–103.
Daniels, Rhiannon: Rethinking the Critical History of the 'Decameron': Boccaccio's Epistle XXII to Mainardo Cavalcanti. In: *Modern Language Review* 106 (2011), p. 423–447.
Eisner, Martin: Boccaccio's Renaissance. In: Emilia Di Rocco/Piero Boitani (eds.): *Boccaccio and the European Literary Tradition*. Rome: Edizioni di Storia e Letteratura 2014, p. 45–55.
Fedi, Roberto: Pathways through the Lyric Forest (Rime). In: Victoria Kirkham/Michael Sherberg et al. (eds.): *Boccaccio. A Critical Guide*, p. 283–293.
Fenzi, Enrico: Petrarca a Milano: tempi e modi di una scelta meditata. In: Giuseppe Frasso/ Maurizio Vitale et al. (eds): *Petrarca e la Lombardia*, p. 221–263.
Feo, Michele: Petrarca. In: *Enciclopedia dantesca*. 6 vols. Rome: Istituto della Enciclopedia Italiana 1970–1978, IV, p. 450–458.
Filosa, Elsa: To Praise Dante, to Please Petrarch (Trattatello in laude di Dante). In: Victoria Kirkham/Michael Sherberg et al. (eds.): *Boccaccio. A Critical Guide*, p. 283–293.
Frasso, Giuseppe: Pallide sinopie: ricerche e proposte sulle forme pre-Chigi e Chigi del 'Canzoniere'. In: *Studi di Filologia italiana* 55 (1997), p. 23–64.
Fumagalli, Edoardo: Giovanni Boccaccio tra Leonzio Pilato e Francesco Petrarca: appunti a proposito della «prima translatio» dell' 'Iliade'. In: *Italia medioevale e umanistica* 54 (2013), p. 213–283.
Gittes, Tobias Foster: Boccaccio and Humanism. In: Guyda Armstrong/Rhiannon Daniels et al. (eds.): *The Cambridge Companion to Boccaccio*, p. 155–170.
Houston, Jason: Boccaccio at Play in Petrarch's Pastoral World. In: *MLN 127* (January 2012, Italian Issue Supplement), p. 47–53.
Kolsky, Stephen: La costituzione di una nuova figura letteraria. Intorno al 'De mulieribus claris' di G. Boccaccio. In: *Testo* 25 (1993), p. 36–52.
Ledda, Giuseppe: Biografia, poesia e allegoria nel 'Trattatello in laude di Dante' di G. Boccaccio. In: Emilio Pasquini (ed.): *Fra biografia ed esegesi: crocevia danteschi in Boccaccio e dintorni*. Ravenna: Longo 2014 (*Letture Classensi* 42), p. 41–77.
Lummus, David: Review: Amedeo Quondam/ Maurizio Fiorilla et al. *Decameron*. Milan: Biblioteca Universale Rizzoli 2013, p. 1851. Francisco Rico. *Ritratti allo specchio (Boccaccio, Petrarca)*. Rome and Padua: Antenore 2012, p. 160. In: *The Medieval Review* 14.02.01 (February 2014), online journal: <http://hdl.handle.net/2022/17342>.
Paolazzi, Carlo: Petrarca, Boccaccio e il 'Trattatello in laude di Dante' [1983]. Reprinted in Carlo Paolazzi: *Dante e la 'Comedia' nel Trecento. Dall'Epistola a Cangrande all'età di Petrarca*. Milan: Vita e Pensiero 1989, p. 131–221.
Pasquini, Emilio: Dantismo petrarchesco. Ancora su 'Fam.' XXI 15 e dintorni. In: Claudia Berra (ed.): *Motivi e forme delle 'Familiari'*, p. 21–38.
Petoletti, Marco. In: Teresa de Robertis et al. (eds.): *Boccaccio autore e copista*. Florence: Mandragora 2013, item n. 64 (MS Milan, Biblioteca Ambrosiana, A 204 inf.), p. 348–350.
Petoletti, Marco: Boccaccio e i Classici. In: Marco Ballarini/Giuseppe Frasso et al. (eds.): *Verso il centenario del Boccaccio. Presenze classiche e tradizione biblica*. Milan and Rome: Biblioteca Ambrosiana-Bulzoni 2014, p. 179–191.
Petrucci, Armando: Scrivere il testo. In: *La critica del testo. Problemi di metodo ed esperienze di lavoro. Atti del Convegno di Lecce, 22–26 ottobre 1984*. Rome: Salerno Editrice 1985, p. 209–227.

Piacentini, Angelo: Il carme 'Ytalie iam certus honos' di Giovanni Boccaccio. In: Luca Azzetta/Andrea Mazzucchi (eds.): *Boccaccio editore e interprete di Dante*, p. 185–221.

Trovato, Paolo/Elisabetta Tonello, Sandro Bertelli, Leonardo Fiorentini: La tradizione e il testo del carme 'Ytalie iam certus honos'. In: *Studi sul Boccaccio* 41 (2013), p. 1–111.

Velli, Giuseppe: Memoria. In: Renzo Bragantini/Pier Massimo Forni (eds.): *Lessico critico decameroniano*, p. 222–248.

Velli, Giuseppe: Petrarca e Boccaccio: l'incontro milanese. In: Giuseppe Frasso/Maurizio Vitale et al. (eds.): *Petrarca e la Lombardia*, p. 145–164.

Zak, Gur: Boccaccio and Petrarch. In: Guyda Armstrong/Rhiannon Daniels et al. (eds.): *The Cambridge Companion to Boccaccio*, p. 139–154.

Giulio Ferroni
Between Petrarch and Boccaccio: Strategies of the End

It is often the case that great literary masterpieces contain within themselves the mark of epochal events. Quite unique, however, is the fact that two works such as the *Canzoniere* and the *Decameron* (created by two authors linked by many personal connections) – works that, even in their diversity, assume a fundamental significance for an entire culture – would give such a decisive significance to a single event and to its date, inscribed in different ways within their own literary fabric, attributing to it the sense of the experience that forms it. The date of 1348, of the terrible plague that devastated Europe, is variously inscribed in the great vernacular works of Petrarch and Boccaccio, which were destined to become major canonical models for the contemporary literature of Italy and all of Europe. Perhaps a parallel could be found in the manner in which three great masterpieces of the early 1900s – *Le temps retrouvé* by Marcel Proust, *La coscienza di Zeno* by Italo Svevo, and *Der Zauerberg* by Thomas Mann (none of which could be said to take on a canonical role comparable to those fourteenth-century works) – describe the event of the first world war. It must be mentioned, however, that the description of the events of 1348 in the *Decameron* and in the *Canzoniere* are often perceived quite differently from one work to the other. As the *Introduction* to the *Decameron* demands, with the explicit affirmation of importance that the author attributes to the 'horrid beginning,' universal and insistent is the attention that readers and critics have given to the plague of Florence, to Boccaccio's narration and description of the event, and to the way in which, from its destructive horizon, arises in the youthful *brigata* the flight toward the Edenic countryside and the decision to narrate the *novelle*. Regarding the *Rerum vulgarium fragmenta* on the other hand, apart from the attention given to the symbolic significance of the date Petrarch falls in love and the date of Laura's death, and to the nexus that links them, in general little attention has been given to the specific historical substance of the year 1348 or to the singular implicit parallelism that Francesco, by inserting this date into the *Canzoniere*, manages to establish with the very different work of his friend Giovanni.

Immediately after the *Proem*, having justified with his readers the "grave e noioso principio" [heavy and distressful prelude] from which his work stems, Boccaccio quickly names the "pestifera mortalità trapassata" [late mortal pestilence], which the work itself "porta nella sua fronte" [bears upon its very front]. Likewise, having amply justified the initial significance of the "orrido cominciamento" [horrid beginning], he begins the narration, establishing in precise terms its time and place:

> Dico adunque che già erano gli anni della fruttifera incarnazione del Figliuolo di Dio al numero pervenuti di milletrecentoquarantotto, quando nella egregia città di Fiorenza, oltre a ogn'altra italica bellissima, pervenne la mortifera pestilenza [...].
>
> [I say, then, that the years of the beatific incarnation of the Son of God had reached the tale of one thousand three hundred and forty-eight, when in the illustrious city of Florence, the fairest of all the cities of Italy, there made its appearance that deadly pestilence (...).][1]

By contrast, the date 1348 appears much later in the *Canzoniere*, just at the threshold of its ending, in the last tercet of the sonnet *Tornami a mente (anzi v'è dentro quella)* [*She comes to mind (no, she is always there)*] (CCCXXXVI), likely composed toward the end of the 1360s:

> Sai che 'n mille trecento quarantotto,
> il dí sesto d'aprile, in l'ora prima,
> del corpo uscío quell'anima beata.
>
> [You do know that in thirteen forty-eight,
> At hour one of the sixth day of April
> That soul now blest departed from its body.][2]

In the codex Vaticano latino 3195 this text is the first of a series in which Petrarch inscribed in Arabic characters the definitive numeration (correcting the order in which the poems had been transcribed previously), as well as the only one of the series, together with the final *canzone* of the Virgin, whose placement was not changed. It remains fixed in position 336, and the number 1 placed above it indicates that we are dealing with the first of that final series, to which the poet felt the need to make those late changes in position, propelled by an anxiety and a dissatisfaction we cannot consider thoroughly resolved by the numeration suggested at the end. It is well known, moreover, that the date appeared explicitly in the famous note of the Ambrosiano Virgil, in correspondence with that attributed

---

[1] I cite the text of the *Decameron* from that given by Vittore Branca in his classic edition: Giovanni Boccaccio: *Decameron*. Edited by Vittore Branca. In: *Tutte le opere di Giovanni Boccaccio*. Edited by Vittore Branca. Milano: Mondadori 1976, indicating the relevant paragraph (here I, *Introduzione*, 8). English translations are drawn from Giovanni Boccaccio: *The Decameron of Giovanni Boccaccio Faithfully Translated by James M. Rigg*. 2 vols. London: The Navarre Society 1903.
[2] For the *Canzoniere* I cite from Francesco Petrarca: *Canzoniere: Rerum vulgarium fragmenta*. Edited by Rosanna Bettarini. Torino: Einaudi 2005 (Nuova raccolta di classici italiani annotate, 20). English translations are drawn from Francesco Petrarca: *The Canzoniere or Rerum vulgarium fragmenta*. Translated with commentary by Mark Musa. Bloomington, Ind.: Indiana University Press 1996.

to Petrarch's falling in love: "et in eadem civitate, eodem mense Aprili, eodem die VI°, eadem hora prima, anno autem M° III^c XLVIII°, ab hac luce lux illa subtracta est."[3] Evident is the link between the insertion of the date 1348 into CCCXXXVI and of 1327 into the last tercet of CCXI, previously lacking a specific year, according to the version documented in the 'codice degli abbozzi':

> Nel laberinto intrai, né veggio ond'esca,
> su l'ora prima, il dí sesto d'aprile,
> lasso me, inseme presi l'amo e l'ésca!
>
> [I entered the labyrinth, and I see no way to escape,
> at the first hour, the sixth day of April,
> alas, I took both bait and hook together!][4]

As the marginalia of Vaticano latino 3196 indicates, this sonnet *Voglia mi sprona, Amor mi guida e scorge,* [*Desire spurs me, Love sees and guides my way,*] was at first put aside and then later recovered in June of 1369 as part of the final revision, in evident and intentional correspondence with the final tercet of CCCXXXVI:

> Mille trecento ventisette, a punto
> su l'ora prima, il dí sesto d'aprile,
> nel laberinto intrai, né veggio ond'esca.
>
> [In thirteen twenty-seven, and precisely
> at the first hour of the sixth of April
> I entered the labyrinth, and I see no way out.]

Overlooking the disagreement between the actual and symbolic dates – defined by the identification of April 6 with Good Friday (indicated in III and in LXII) and by the relative incongruence with the actual date of 1327 – and the undulating numerological horizon that, *a posteriori*, as viewed after the fact, imposes itself upon the global structure of the *Canzoniere*,[5] it remains evident that the insertion of the date 1327 into the sonnet CCXI formed an intentional correspondence

---

[3] See Pierre de Nolhac: *Pétrarque et l'humanisme*. 2 vols. Paris: H. Champion 1907, II, p. 286. The same correspondence between April 6, the date of falling in love, and that of the death of Laura, occurs in *Triumphus Mortis*, I, 133–134: "L'ora prima era, il dì sesto d'aprile,/ che già mi strinse, ed or, lasso, mi sciolse." [April the sixth, it was, and the first hour, / When I was bound-and now, alas, set free!] I cite from the following editions: Francesco Petrarca: *Triumphi*. Edited by Marco Ariani. Milano: Mursia 1988; *The Triumphs of Petrarch*. Trans. by Ernest H. Wilkins. Chicago: University of Chicago Press 1962.

[4] English translation by Bridget Pupillo.

[5] Above all see Marco Santagata: *I frammenti dell'anima. Storia e racconto nel Canzoniere di Petrarca*. Bologna: il Mulino 1992, p. 321–330, and the textual notes cited in his edition of the *Canzoniere*: Francesco Petrarca: *Canzoniere*. Edited by Marco Santagata. Milano: Mondadori 2004.

with that of 1348 in CCCXXXVI. This date was imbued with a significance both final and absolute, which entails a radical intrusion of the external reality of that *annus horribilis* (while 1327, the date of Petrarch's falling in love, remains historically neutral, referring instead to a personal experience, set within the *topos* of love in a church, albeit projected into the symbolic nexus of April 6/Good Friday).

The date 1348 is inscribed at the very opening of the great collection of the *Familiares*: the proemial letter *Ad Socratem suum* (*To his Socrates*) starts with the disastrous consequences of that year, with the ruinous flow of a time that saw no peace but rather the collapse of all hopes, with the death of so many friends, the pain of which can be only partially assuaged in knowing that one's own death is nigh:

> Quid vero nunc agimus, frater? Ecce, iam fere omnia tentavimus et nusquam requies. Quando illam expectamus? Ubi eam querimus? Tempora, ut aiunt, inter digitos effluxerunt; spes nostre veteres cum amicis sepulte sunt. Mille trecentesimus quadragesimus octavus annus est, qui nos solos atque inopes fecit; neque enim ea nobis abstulit, que Indo aut Caspio Carpathio ve mari restaurari queant: irreparabiles sunt ultime iacture; et quodcumque mors intulit, immedicabile vulnus est. Unum est solamen: sequemur et ipsi quos premisimus. Que quidem expectatio quam brevis futura sit, nescio; hoc scio, quod longa esse non potest. Quantulacunque sane est, non potest esse non molesta. (I, 1, 1–2)
>
> [What are we to do now, dear brother? Alas, we have already tried almost everything and no rest is in sight. When can we expect it? Where shall we seek it? Time, as they say, has slipped through our fingers; our former hopes are buried with our friends. The year 1348 left us alone and helpless; it did not deprive us of things that can be restored by the Indian or Caspian or Carpathian Sea. It subjected us to irreparable losses. Whatever death wrought is now an incurable wound. There is only one consolation in all this: we too shall follow those who preceded us. How long our wait will be I do not know; but this I do know, that it cannot be long. And however short the wait may be, it cannot avoid being burdersome.][6]

The impossibility of the much desired *requies*, the anxiety of *expectatio*, the inexorable passage of time, the death of hopes and of friends: it is as though from this year springs forth a confirmation in extreme terms of the irreparable loss of existence. And one notes the significance imbued in those negative adjectives that have an essential presence in Petrarch's Latin: *irreparabiles* and *immedicabile*, referring to the effects of temporality and to the actions of time on desire. In this same initial epistle Petrarch turns his gaze toward the hope of his work reaching its conclusion, once again entrusting to his friend this final image of his soul:

---

6 I cite the *Familiares* from the following edition: Francesco Petrarca: *Le Familiari*. Edited and translated by Ugo Dotti and Felicita Audisio. 5 vols. Torino: Nino Aragno 2004–2009. English translations drawn from Francesco Petrarca: *Letters on Familiar Matters: Rerum familiarium libri*. Translated by Aldo S. Bernardo. 3 vols. Baltimore: Johns Hopkins University Press 1975–1985, I, p. 3.

> Illam vero non Phidie Minervam, ut ait Cicero, sed qualemcunque animi mei effigiem atque ingenii simulacrum multo michi studio dedolatum, si unquam supremam illi manum imposuero, cum ad te venerit, secure qualibet in arce constituito. (I, 1, 37)
>
> [The other work I have been polishing with great care, though not a Phidian Minerva, as Cicero asserts, but a true portrait and likeness such as it is of my talent if ever I shall be able to give it the last touches, that work, I say, when it reaches you, you may set up without concern at the summit of whatever stronghold you please.]

Indeed, due to this deep bond Petrarch shares with his friends, the intertwining of the subject matter of the *Familiares* with the life of the author allows him to identify the act of finishing these epistles with the end of his own life ("[…] scribendi enim michi vivendique unus, ut auguror, finis erit." [(…) for me writing and living are the same and I hope will be so to the very end.] I, 1, 44). The scope of this work is delineated solely by Petrarch's love for his friends, to whom he bestows the gift of his words; and this love may be dissolved only by death:

> Tum demum et michi immunitatem huius muneris quesitam et huic operi positum finem scito, cum me defunctum et cuntis vite laboribus absolutum noveris. Interea iter inceptum sequar, non prius vie quam lucis exitum operiens; et quietis michi loco fuerit dulcis labor. (I, 1, 45)
>
> [Only then will I no longer feel this obligation and will have to consider this work ended when you hear that I am dead and that I am freed from all the labors of life. In the meantime I shall continue along the path I have been following, and shall avoid any exits so long as there is light. And the sweet labor will serve for me almost as a place of rest.]

This equation of the span of life and the span of writing, an idea that governs both the letters already written and those yet to be penned, seems to be submerged within the conclusion of this proemial epistle, which fixes its composition within the time span of the (unspecified) day presently coming to an end. The day ends, the letter ends; just as the letters collected in the book will end with the ending of life:

> Dulce michi colloquium tecum fuit, cupideque et quasi de industria protractum; vultum enim tuum retulit per tot terras et maria teque mihi presentem fecit usque ad vesperam, cum matutino calamum cepissem. Diei iam et epystole finis adest. (I, 1, 47)
>
> [This discourse with you has been most pleasant for me and I have drawn it out eagerly and as though by design. It has kept your face constantly before me throughout a great number of lands and seas, as if my presence until dusk, though it was with the early morning light that I had taken up my pen.]

Amidst the various signs of apprehension concerning the passage of time and the confrontation with the end which disturb the fabric of the *Familiares*, the date of 1348 irrupts with more immediate urgency in Book VIII, with the famous Letter

7, also addressed *Ad Socratem suum*, which Petrarch, in the footsteps of Cicero, begins with the desperate triple invocation to his dear friend:

> Mi frater, mi frater, mi frater – novum epystole principium, imo antiquum, et ante mille fere quadringentos annos a Marco Tullio usurpatum –; heu michi, frater amantissime, quid dicam? unde ordiar? quonam vertar? undique dolor, terror undique. (VIII, 7, 1)

> [Oh brother, brother, brother (a new kind of beginning for a letter, indeed an ancient one used by Marcus Tullius almost fourteen hundred years ago); alas dearest brother, what shall I say? Where shall I begin? Where shall I turn? Everywhere we see sorrow, on all sides we see terror.]

The flood of pain and the sense of death, coupled with the inability to respond to these sensations in a language worthy of the task, have given rise to a desperate outburst; the force of these feelings has pushed the author's soul as well as his literary style outside the control of reason. More than a year passed before the author, struggling against the ravages of fortune, managed to create something of worth; without equal, however, is the exceptionality of that year, which comes to be associated with its numerical figure and with its dangerous extension into the present:

> Qua in re benigno sub iudice forsan excuser, si ad examen venerit illud quoque, non leve aliud, sed millesimum trecentesimum quadragesimum octavum sexte etatis annum esse quem lugeo, qui non solum nos amicis, sed mundum omnem gentibus spoliavit; cui siquid defuit, sequens ecce annus illius reliquias demetit, et quicquid illi procelle superfuerat, mortifera falce persequitur. (VIII, 7, 11)

> [Because of this I may perhaps be executed by a benign judge if he were also to consider that I am bewailing not something inconsequential, but the 1348th year of the sixth age, which not only deprived us of our friends but the entire world of actual nations. If anyone escaped, the coming year is gathering its harvest so that whatever survived that storm is being pursued by death's sickle.]

Indeed, something unprecedented occurred in that year, with a devastation and an emptying of the world the likes of which had never been seen before, and to which later generations cannot truly give credence (after all, the historians are silent, the philosophers shrug their shoulders, wrinkle their brows and with a finger ask for silence):

> Credes ista, posteritas, cum ipsi qui vidimus, vix credamus, somnia credituri nisi experrecti apertis hec oculis cerneremus, et lustrata urbe funeribus suis plena, domum reversi, exoptatis pignoribus vacuam illam reperientes, sciremus utique vera esse que gemimus? (VIII, 7, 13)

> [Will you believe such things, oh posterity, when we ourselves who see them can scarcely believe them and would consider them dreams except that we perceive them awake and with our eyes open and that after viewing a city full of funerals we return to our homes only to find them empty of our loved ones.]

After posing heartfelt questions to God on the incomprehensible reason for all of this, Petrarch introduces once again his grief over the personal emptiness that this year has left in its wake, over the necessity and impossibility of finding new friends, now that the human race is nearly extinct and the end of the world is near:

> Stipati eramus, prope iam soli sumus. Nove amicitie contrahende sunt. Unde autem sive ad quid, humano genere pene extincto, et proximo, ut auguror, rerum finem? (VIII, 7, 21)
>
> [We used to be a crowd, now we are almost alone. We must seek new friendships. But where or for what reason when the human species is almost extinct and the end, as I hope, is near?]

The perception of this solitude does not elicit much trust in the stability of the common stage of the world. Rather, it provokes the sensation that each life is disappearing, in this world's shadowy consistency and in the reciprocal anticipation of the news of death:

> E tanta sodalium turba ad quem redacti numerum sumus, vides; et ecce, dum loquimur, ipsi etiam fugimus atque umbre in morem evanescimus, momentoque temporis abiisse alter alterum accipiet, et ipse mox previum secuturus. (VIII, 7, 23)[7]

---

[7] It will not be necessary to reference the widespread presence in the *Canzoniere* of metaphors of life and of reality such as "ombra/sogno/sonno" and of various possible references to classical Latin works (in primis Orazio, *Carmina*, IV, 7, 16) as well as to the Psalms. The emblematic final verse of the proemial sonnet ("che quanto piace al mondo è breve sogno" ["that worldly joy is just a fleeting dream"]) will certainly take on an archetypal importance for the tradition that proceeds it; other notable examples occur in CLVI, 4 ("ché quant'io miro par sogni, ombre et fumi" ["for all I see seems shadow, smoke, and dreams"]), CCXCIV, 12 ("Veramente siam noi polvere et ombra" ["In truth we are nothing but dust and shadow"]), CCCXXXI, 22 ("Nebbia o polvere al vento" ["A mist or dust caught in the wind [...]"]), CCCL, 1–2 ("Questo nostro caduco et fragil bene,/ ch'è vento et ombra, et à nome beltate" ["This frail and perishable good of ours / which is a wind and shadow known as beauty"]), beyond other similar occurrences in the Latin works and within the *Familiares* itself (in XI, 3, 10 in concurrence with the formidable image of the *fabula inexpleta*: "video eam ipsam que vita dicitur, fugacis umbram nebule vel fumum ventis impulsum denique vel confusum somnium esse vel fabulam inexpletam vel siquid inanius dici potest" ["I see that even what is called life is but a shadow of a fleeting cloud, or smoke wafted by the winds, or finally troubled sleep or an unfinished tale or anything else conceivably more empty."]). A remark on this theme can be attributed to the ample reflection of the epistle to Boccaccio on the prophetic threats of Pietro Petroni, where one finds among others this sequence: "Profecto fumus, umbra, somnium, prestigium, nichil denique nisi luctus et laboris archa vita est que hic agitur; quod unum bonum habet: ad aliam vitam via est" ("Indeed the life we live here is only smoke, a shadow, a dream, an illusion, in short, nothing but a threshing floor for grief and toil. Its one good is that it leads to another life [...]," *Seniles*, I, 5, 16). On the theme of the plague and its many sorrows, one must remember as well the *Epystule metrice*, I, 14 and *Bucolicum carmen*, IX e X.

[See to what a small number we have been reduced from so large a group of comrades: and note that while we are speaking we ourselves are also fleeing and are vanishing in the fashion of shades, and in the moment of time one of us receives the news of the departure of the other and the survivor will in turn be following upon the footsteps of the other.]

At the end of the following letter to the same Socrates (which reports the death of Paganino of Bizzozzero), the author places the well-known image of life as "sonno/sogno," from which only death arises:

> Somnus est vita quam degimus, et quicquid in ea geritur somnio simillimum. Sola mors somnum et somnia discutit. (VIII, 8, 5)[8]
>
> [The life we live is but a sleep, and in whatever occurs in it is very similar to a dream. Death alone breaks up the sleep and disperses the dreams.]

Approaching the completion of his *Familiares* after many long years, Petrarch places, at the opening of the final book almost entirely addressed to the writers of antiquity, a letter to Philippe de Cabassoles, dedicated to the insistent theme of the passage of time (*Ad Philippum Cavallicensem Epyscopum, de inestimabili fuga temporis*). The letter begins with a true and proper measure of the time that has passed from the start of the collection, the thirty years during which he arranged his life into this mise-en-scène: it refers back to I, 3, in which the then youthful author addresses the elderly Raimondo Subirani, discussing *de flore etatis instabili*. With the passage of those years, that which was once a simple moral consideration becomes directly verified through experience: the end connects back to the beginning, with the realization, in old age, of a truth already understood in youth:

> [...] familiariter ut solebam scribens, in epystola quadam, que pro ratione temporis in prima acie stans procul hanc preit, ingenue professus sum cepisse me iam tunc orientis vite fugam cursumque cognoscere. Nunc autem miror quisem sed, fateor, verum scripsi. Quodsi illa etate verum fuit, quid nunc putas, quando quod presagiebam accidit? (XXIV, 1, 3)
>
> [I wrote a friendly letter, as was my wont, to this elder who had begun to feel such affection for my extreme youth and my budding mind as to cultivate and favor it with example,

---

8 In the same Book VIII the letter to Luca Cristiani (Olimpio) concerning the author's intention to leave Vaucluse, in addition to indicating the necessity to look toward the end ("Nobis sane, si sapimus, non in longum modo, sed in finem quoque prospiciendum est" [Without doubt we must look ahead not only at the long run but to the very end] (VIII, 3, 8)), records the recent death of Laura: "quodque sine suspirio dici nequit, virentissima olim laurus mea vi repentine tempestatis exaruit, que una michi non Sorgiam modo sed Ruentiam Ticino fecerat cariorem; velumque, quo oculi mei tegebantur, ablatum est [...]." [Furthermore, I can hardly add this without deep sighs, that laurel of mine which was once so green as been withered by the power of an unexpected storm, that laurel which made not only the Sorgue but the Durance dearer than the rushing Ticino. And the veil which covered my eyes has been lifted (...).] (VIII, 3, 16–17).

counsel, and words. In that letter, which stands because of its date at the beginning of this collection quite a distance from this one, I even then confessed to a dawning recognition about the flight and swiftness of my young life. I now find this astonishing, but what I wrote was true. And if my words were true then, how do you think they now apply when what I had foreseen has come to pass?]

Thereafter follows a veritable catalog of Latin quotes on the *topos* of the transience of youth and the passage of time (for instance with the famous Virgilian formula "fugit irreparabile tempus," *Georgics*, III, 284, which occurs often in the writings of Petrarch), and again an ample series of considerations, in which this *topos* is married with points of particular intensity, with a fervent insistence, with a dogged syntax, producing a result quite different from the most noted and famous developments of the theme in the *Canzoniere*. Thus Petrarch records his notations on a theme that he continually worked into his books, beginning in his youth:

> Notabam certa fide non verborum faleras sed res ipsas, misere scilicet vite huius angustias, brevitatem velocitatem festinationem, lapsum cursum volatum occultasque fallacias, tempus irreparabile, caducum et mutabile vite florem, rosei oris fluxum decus, irrediture iuventutis effrenem fugam et tacite obrepentis insidias senectutis; ad extremum rugas et morbos et tristitiam et laborem et indomite mortis inclementiam implacabilemque duritiem. (XXIV, 1, 10)

> [Diligently I would note not the verbal facility but the substance of the thought – the distresses and brevity of this life, its haste, tumbling course and hidden deceits, time's irrecoverability, the perishable and changing flower of life, the fugitive beauty of a rosy face, the frantic flight of unreturning youth, the deceits of a silently stealthy old age, and finally, the wrinkles, illnesses, sadness, toils, and implacable cruelty and harshness of indomitable death.]

Now, however, he feels each of the days, hours, moments "ad ultimam urgere" [propels me toward the end]; every day he is dying and is at the point of seeing his entire life as a thing of the past. In and around him everything has changed. This changing and passage of time weighs upon his perception of the present, on the very act of writing and reading:

> Nunc eo, et sicut hic calamus movetur sic ego moveor, sed multo velocius; hic enim pigre dictanti animo obsequitur, ego dum nature legem sequor, propero curro rapio ad extrema iamque oculis metam cerno.
> [...]
> Ecce ad hunc locum epystole perveneram deliberansque quid dicerem amplius seu quid non dicerem, hec inter, ut assolet, papirum vacuum inverso calamo feriebam. Res ipsa materiam obtulit cogitanti inter dimensionis morulas tempus labi, meque interim collabi abire deficere et, ut proprie dicam, mori. Continue morimur; ego dum hec scribo, tu dum leges, alii dum audient dumque non audient; ego quoque dum hec leges moriar, tu moreris

dum hec scribo, ambo morimur, omnes morimur, semper morimur, nunquan vivimus dum hic sumus [...] (XXIV, 1, 24, 26–27)

[Now I proceed, and just as this pen moves, so do I, but much more rapidly, for my pen obeys the mind's sluggish dictation whereas I follow nature's law, and thus hasten, run, gallop to my end, already beholding my goal.
(...)
Having reached this point in the letter, I was wondering what more to say or not to say, and meanwhile, as is my custom, I was tapping the blank paper with my pen. This action provided me with a subject, for I considered how, during the briefest of intervals, time rushes onward, and I along with it, slipping away, failing, and, to speak honestly, dying. We all are constantly dying, I while writing these words, you while reading them, others while hearing or not hearing them; I too shall be dying while you read this, you are dying while I write this, we both are dying, we all are dying, we are always dying; we never live here (...)]

If, in pointing toward the end, this first letter of Book XXIV measures thus the thirty years passed since that third letter of Book I, in which the young Petrarch displayed to an old sage his awareness of the impermanence of his own youth, the last letter of this final book reconnects more directly to the first of the entire collection, closing the circle with the very same addressee, to whom the *Familiares* is dedicated (*Ad Socratem suum, conclusio huius libri*). This direct reference to the collection's first letter reminds us just how much was said there on the continuity of this familial writing, on its direct correspondence with life, in such a way that, even if it is now at a close, in reality it is not concluding, because the conversation with friends may be ended only by death:

Et hoc quidem opus adelescens cepi, senex perago; imo vero ceptum prosequor; unum est enim hoc ex omnibus, cui supremam sola mors imponet manum. Quomodo ego alium amici colloquii quam vite funem sperem? aut quenam dies me spirantem inter eos tacitum efficiet, cum quibus ore gelido sepultusque loqui cogito? (XXIV, 13,3)

[I began this work as a young man; I am completing it in my old age, or rather I am continuing it since it is the only one that death alone can end. What other end can I expect for my conversations with friends but the end of life? Or how could I possibly remain silent with them while still alive if I plan to speak to them with my cold lips from the grave?]

If indeed the *Familiares* are at an end, the *Seniles*, in the proem to Francesco Nelli (*Ad Simonidem suum*) spring forth from the memory of that former work's dedication (*Ad Socratem suum*) and of the death of its own Ludwig van Kempen, in an intertwining of dates and tragic events which connects the two collections quite closely. Immediately within the text appears the 1348 from the incipit of the *Familiares*, tying that date to the present year of 1361, a new pestilential year:

Olim, Socrati meo scribens, questus eram quod etatis huius annus ille, post millesimum trecentesimum, quadragesimus octavus, omnibus me prope solatiis vite amicorum mortibus spoliasset; quo dolore, nam memini, questibus et lacrimis cunta compleveram. Quid nunc primo et sexagesimo faciam anno qui, cum cetera ornamenta ferme omnia, tum id quod carissimum unicumque habui, ipsum michi Socratem eripuit? (*Seniles*, I, 1,1)

[Writing some time ago to my Socrates (Ludwig van Kempen), I had complained that the year 1348 of our era had deprived me of nearly every consolation in life because of my friends' deaths. For I remember with what grief I gave vent to uncontrollable laments and tears. Now what shall I do in the sixty-first year of this century, which has snatched away, together with nearly every other treasure, even my dearest and most precious one, Socrates himself?][9]

In referring to the *Familiares*, Petrarch reiterates once again the correspondence between the end of life and the end of the composition:

Est ad Socratem Librum Familiarium Rerum noster, corpore quidem ingens et, si sineretur, ingentior futurus. Proinde quod illic presagiebam video: nullus michi alius epystolaris stili quam vite finis ostenditur. (*Seniles*, I, 1, 4).[10]

[My book, *Letters on Familiar Matters*, is dedicated to Socrates; vast in its bulk, it would become still more so if I were to allow it. Now I see just what I then guessed: nothing but the end of my life will bring an end to my letter writing.]

Essential, but certainly very different, is the connection between life and writing in the *Canzoniere*: there we find a growing tension concerning the end which finds order in the final redaction of Vaticano latino 3195, but which also animates the better part of the book and demonstrates itself through diverse strategies that influence both the conclusive tension of the individual components and the systemization of the whole during the process of its formation and organization. This arrangement certainly tends toward a 'closure'; nevertheless, it inevitably remains marked by an irreparable conflict, caused by the furtive persistence of that *inexpletum* which inevitably and continually steers the collection of the *sparsa anime fragmenta* toward correction, toward displacement, toward a definitive

---

9 I cite the *Seniles* from the following edition: Francesco Petrarca: *Le senili*. Edited by Ugo Dotti and Felicita Audisio. 3 vols. Torino: Nino Aragno 2004–2010. English translations are drawn from Francesco Petrarca: *Letters of Old Age: Rerum Senilium Libri I–XVIII*. Translated by Aldo S. Bernardo, Saul Levin et al. 2 vols. Baltimore: Johns Hopkins University Press 1992.
10 Petrarch returns to this motif again in the *Seniles*, I, 3, 22 and III, 1, 22: in this last letter, to Boccaccio, dated Venice, September 7 (1363), he justifies the fact that the new collection will be dedicated to Nelli, despite the man's death, and once again he makes reference to the terrible dates of 1348 and 1361, together with the misfortunes of the following year. This letter was not immediately sent: he mailed it together with the next much briefer letter, dated September 20, in which Petrarch displays an anguished apprehension concerning the fate of his friend, about whom he has heard no news. Having expressed his fear that Boccaccio is no longer alive, he concludes with this striking salutation: "Vale si vivis; si defunctus, eternum" ("Farewell, if you live, and if you are no more, farewell forever," *Seniles*, III, 2, 4).

impossibility of systemization, on which only the peace of death can place limits. On the other hand, this continual contradictory movement is balanced by an urge to define every single text as absolute: as if each of the fragments (or at least those with the most intense accents) presents itself as definitive, as a sort of 'last word' ("dolenti mie parole extreme"; [these my mournful, my last words] of CXXVI, 13, for example), which arches toward and eventually congeals within its final pen stroke, within the authoritativeness of its own existence, and within the impression of revelation it lends to its own closure (in the *canzoni* this effect often occurs even at the end of single stanzas).

Apart from the critical work of Santagata, the attention given in recent years to the book-like structure of the *Canzoniere* has given rise to a new perception of broader coherence within the work as a whole, as well as of the complexity and aim of its constructive process. It seems to me, however, that equating the *Rerum vulgarium fragmenta* with a novel – that is, identifying within the work an actual storyline moving toward the penitential resolution already present in the proemial sonnet – can in fact lead us astray. Among other things, this comparison negates the long historical life of this masterpiece, giving the illusion that our modern – or postmodern – interpretation finally liberates us from age-old misunderstandings and incomprehension. Petrarch's poetry continues to assert its grandness and appeal precisely through its contradictory measure, through the jagged movement that led to its final draft, allowing for various perceptions of the end and for diverse outcomes of that anxiety for the dissolution of life and beauty which, as the above-mentioned reference of *Familiares* XXIV, 1 to *Familiares* I, 3 demonstrates, stirred Petrarch from a young age.

It should be quite evident once again that the date of 1348 is crucial to the very organization of the *Canzoniere* as a book, with all misfortunes culminating in the death of the beloved, and with the renewed and more radical sense of the end that this date implies. Following above all the reconstruction of Santagata, it is the so-called Coreggio edition that traces a path toward disillusion and repentance, found in the proemial sonnet (which appears there for the first time). This path, in which one does not distinguish between a first and second part of the collection (despite the presence of the *canzone* CCLXIV, which would eventually come to introduce the second part), culminates in what would become sonnet CCXCII, *Gli occhi di ch'io parlai sì caldamente* (*Those eyes of which I spoke with such emotion*), based on a neat bipartition of the quatrains, which emphasize Laura's death and her beauty turning 'to dust', and the tercets, which treat the condition of the poet who, without Laura's light, falls prey to an incurable sorrow that annuls any possibility of poetic production. The second tercet marks with its own conclusion the end of all love poetry, which would be replaced instead by tears:

> Or sia qui fine al mio amoroso canto:
> secca è la vena de l'usato ingegno,
> et la cetera mia rivolta in pianto. (CCXCII, 12–14)
>
> [Let my love song finish right here and now;
> dry is the vein of my habitual art,
> my lyre now has turned to playing tears.]

Already present in this edition is the group of *canzoni* CXXV–CXXIX, in which we can verify, in a different manner, the anxiety to define the text in absolute terms, to bring the language to a sort of closure of experience, imbuing it with a hint of the definitive, as if to redeem the ephemeral substance of life. It seems that the poetic word wants to impose a definitive persistence on the visible, on beauty, on the amorous tension of the self; it justifies and recognizes the loss of the self within the other; to it is entrusted the revelation of a value that loses itself, and through this word it presents itself as definitive, radical and absolute, truly 'final'! Absolute and final is the revelation of Laura in the landscape of Vaucluse in CXXV and CXXVI; absolute and final is her appearance and constant presence in the unreachable, intrusive distance as described in CXXVII and CXXIX. In the substance and conclusions of the individual stanzas, as in the *congedi*, each of which is adressed to the same *canzone*, one finds various configurations of this absoluteness, the manifestation of an insurmountable anxiety to give a definitive sense to the word and to reality as it is experienced and remembered, in which one exhausts and exalts the entire space of the experience. Without being able to conduct here an expansive reading of these *canzoni*, I will limit myself to noting how in the first *canzone*, *Se 'l pensier che mi strugge* (*If this thought paining me*), the very terrain of the Vaucluse (even the vegetation that sprouts from it) produces the effect of being watched and lightly touched by Laura, so that the last trace of her is not completely lost:

> Ovunque gli occhi volgo
> trovo un dolce sereno
> pensando: Qui percosse il vago lume.
> Qualunque herba o fior colgo
> credo che nel terreno
> aggia radice, ov'ella ebbe in costume
> gir fra le piagge e'l fiume,
> et talor farsi un seggio
> fresco, fiorito et verde.
> Cosí nulla se'n perde,
> et piú certezza averne fôra il peggio. (CXXV, 66–76)
>
> [Wherever my eyes turn
> I find sweet brightness there
> and think: "That lovely light once struck right here."

All grass or blooms I pick
I think have had their roots
in that same ground where she was wont to walk
between the banks and river
and sometimes made a seat,
fresh, flowering, and green.
This way no part is lost,
and knowing more exactly would be worse.]

In *Chiare, fresche e dolci acque* (*Clear, cool, sweet, running waters*), this definitive horizon establishes itself beyond the death of the subject, in the posthumous fantasy of a woman weeping over his bodily remains, interred in that same place and now identified with the earth and rocks, with the specific geological makeup of the Vaucluse:

Tempo verrà anchor forse
ch'a l'usato soggiorno
torni la fera bella et mansüeta,
et là 'v'ella mi scorse
nel benedetto giorno,
volga la vista disïosa et lieta,
cercandomi; et, o pieta!,
già terra in fra le pietre
vedendo, Amor l'inspiri
in guisa che sospiri
sí dolcemente che mercé m'impetre,
et faccia forza al cielo,
asciugandosi gli occhi col bel velo. (CXXVI, 27–39)

[And there will come a time, perhaps,
that to the well-known place
the lovely animal returns, and tamed,
and there where she first saw me
that day which now is blessed,
she turns her eyes with hope and happiness
in search of me, and – ah, the pity –
to see me there as dust
among the stones, Love will
inspire her and she will sigh
so sweetly she will win for me some mercy
and force open the heavens
drying her eyes there with her lovely veil.]

While *In quella parte dove Amor mi sprona* ends with a symbolic postponement of death, separated from the persistence – even in its absence – of the thought of love, *Di pensiero in pensier, di monte in monte* (*From thought to thought, mountain to mountain top*) epitomizes within the mountainous landscape the images of absent Laura and of the poet himself ("me freddo, pietra morta in pietra viva" [down cold as dead stone set on living rock], CXXIX, 51), who in the *congedo* splits his actual bodily substance between Vaucluse and the present location (below is his *cor*, here is merely his *imagine*):

> Canzone, oltra quell'alpe
> là dove il ciel è piú sereno et lieto
> mi rivedrai sovr'un ruscel corrente,
> ove l'aura si sente
> d'un fresco et odorifero laureto.
> Ivi è'l mio cor, et quella che'l m'invola;
> qui veder pôi l'imagine mia sola. (CXXIX, 66 I–72)

> [My song, beyond those Alps
> where skies are more serene and happier,
> you'll see me by a running brook once more
> where you can sense the aura
> distilling from the fresh and fragrant laurel:
> there is my heart and there is one who steals it;
> what you see here is but the ghost of me.]

Perhaps the most extreme symbol – one that shapes the very grass on which Laura appears into an ultimate locus of peace, one that excludes from itself every other experience, every other vital element, one that establishes within itself the entire significance of language and of life – occurs at the end of the last stanza of *Chiare, fresche e dolci acque*, just before the very brief *congedo*:

> Quante volte diss'io
> allor pien di spavento:
> Costei per fermo nacque in paradiso.
> Cosí carco d'oblio
> il divin portamento
> e'l volto e le parole e'l dolce riso
> m'aveano, et sí diviso
> da l'imagine vera,
> ch'i' dicea sospirando:
> Qui come venn'io, o quando?;
> credendo d'esser in ciel, non là dov'era.
> Da indi in qua mi piace
> questa herba sí, ch'altrove non ò pace. (CXXVI, 53–65)

> [How often I would say
> at that time, full of awe:
> "For certain she was born up there in Heaven!"
> And her divine behavior,
> her face and words and her sweet smile
> so filled me with forgetfulness

and so divided me
from the true image
that I would sigh and say:
"Just how and when did I come here?"
thinking I was in Heaven, not where I was;
and since then I have loved
this bank of grass and find peace nowhere else.]

Within this theme of peace one might also consider the cycle that includes the *canzone* dedicated to Italy: quite different from that ultimate peace of *eros* and its paradisiacal setting, but nevertheless longed for within the concrete political and civil arena, as it is invoked in the heartfelt final clause of the *canzone* (an authoritative ending, much like that of the very famous penultimate stanza, which Machiavelli would employ as the closing words of his *Principe*):

> Canzone, io t'ammonisco
> che tua ragion cortesemente dica,
> perché tra gente altera ir ti convene,
> et le voglie son piene
> già de l'usanza pessima et antica,
> del ver sempre nemica.
> Proverai tua ventura
> fra' magnanimi pochi a chi'l ben piace.
> Di' lor: – Chi m'assicura?
> I' vo gridando: Pace, pace, pace. (CXXVIII, 112–122)

> [My song, I bid that you
> express your sentiments with courtesy,
> for you must go among a haughty people
> whose wills are still so full
> of that ancient, most vicious of all habits,
> always truth's enemy.
> But you must try your fortune
> among the valiant few who love the good;
> tell them: "Who will protect me?
> I go my way beseeching: Peace, peace, peace."]

It is evident that 'peace' is a word of essential importance in the *Canzoniere*, with thirty-seven occurrences, in which it functions both implicitly and explicitly in an oxymoronic relationship with 'war,' as demonstrated symbolically in the famous incipit of CXXXIV, *Pace non trovo, et non ò da far Guerra* (*I find no peace, and I am not at war*).[11]

---

[11] Similar to the term 'peace,' but with less intensity, Petrarch utilizes the adjectives *queto/queta* and the verb *acquetare*, in its various forms.

The thought of Laura functions as a continual disturbance, while simultaneously seeming to offer the only possible peace for the subject's incurable angst. In the second part, and particularly in the final portion of the *Canzoniere*, 'peace' acquires a religious significance; however, the work never resolves itself in the affirmation of a peace definitively attained; rather, 'peace' will be identified above all with a final homecoming, with the tranquility of a death under the aegis of God's grace, in the assured realization of that hope for the afterlife. The word 'peace' returns thus in the last two 'penitential' sonnets, CCLXIV, 11, and CCCLXV, 10, and closes the *canzone* to the Virgin, the last of the entire *Canzoniere*:

> Il dí s'appressa, et non pòte esser lunge,
> sí corre il tempo et vola,
> Vergine unica et sola,
> e'l cor or cosc̈ientia or morte punge.
> Raccomandami al tuo figliuol, verace
> homo et verace Dio,
> ch'accolga'l mïo spirto ultimo in pace. (CCCLXVI, 131–137)

> [The day draws near, it cannot be far off;
> time runs and flies so fast,
> Virgin, the one and only one,
> and death and conscience now stab at my heart;
> commend me to your Son who is the true
> man and the truth of God,
> that He accept my final breath in peace.]

This final 'peace,' disturbed as it is by the eternal return of the theme of time's passage, certainly cannot hope to resolve within itself the entire significance of the *Canzoniere*, in which the term has assumed diverse meanings, often aiming at an absolute identification of the self and of the revelation of beauty, in a contradictory arrangement of experience, in a lacerating perception of fragility and of the elusiveness of life. This laceration, this contradictory tension, remains at play right up to the conclusion of the *Canzoniere*: it informs the choice of the last texts of the first part, from the Chigi form through to the final version, as well as the arrangement of the key texts of the second part, such as the inaugural CCLXIV, *I' vo pensando, et nel penser m'assale* (*I go on thinking, and I'm seized in thought*), and the two *canzoni* CCCLIX, *Quando il soave mio fido conforto* (*When that kind, faithful comforter of mine*) and CCCLX, *Quel'antiquo mio dolce empio signore* (*That old and sweet yet cruel master of mine*), which simultaneously seem to recapitulate and to project into the otherworldly future – all while continuing to justify – the event of Petrarch's love for Laura.

Onto this ending, with all the additions and rearrangements enacted by the poet in his last days, is imposed the significance of that date of 1348, inserted, as we have seen, into sonnet CCCXXXVI, that which is likely the first sonnet of the series which Petrarch indicates as final (number one of the new Arabic numeration that gives rise to a reorganization of the book's end). In the very last section, however, the above-mentioned sonnet CCCLXV, *Tennemi Amor anni ventuno ardendo* (*Twenty-one years Love kept me burning gladly*), defines within its first verse the number of years of his love, those twenty-one years that span from 1327 to 1348, to which the fourth verse adds ten years spent successively in sorrow – years and events which the poet now views through the lens of repentance, of a confident trust in God concerning the impending liberation from the prison of life. These symbolic numbers extend likewise into the *canzone* to the Virgin where, within the poet's repentance and anticipation of peace – almost within the name of Mary herself – Laura still remains inscribed (for what other meaning could we ascribe to the fact that 'Virgin' is repeated twenty-one times, just like those burning years recorded by the preceding sonnet? Or to the fact that the stanzas of the *canzone* number ten, the same as those years spent weeping?).[12]

Through a less problematic process occurs a pacifying perception of the death of Laura in the *Triumphus Mortis*, in the famous clause of canto I ("Morte bella parea nel suo bel viso" [And even death seemed fair in her fair face.]); however, canto II instead concludes with the indication, through Laura's own voice, of a "gran tempo" in which the poet would remain "in terra" without her:

> Però saper vorrei, madonna, s'io
> Son per tardi seguirvi, o se per tempo. –
> Ella, già mossa, disse: – al creder mio,
>
> tu starai in terra senza me gran tempo. (*Triumphus Mortis*, II, 188–191)

> [Therefore, Madonna, this I fain would know:
> Shall it be soon or late that I follow you?
> And she, departing, said: "'Tis my belief
> Thou wilt be long without me on the earth."]

Direct projection toward an 'after' that does not negate, but rather renews the 'before', determined by a view toward the 'present' (from the "felice sasso" of

---

12 It may be significant that the sonnet CCLXV was previously inserted a bit further from the final *canzone*, in position 360, then relocated in that definitive version by the abovementioned Arabic numeration. On the movement that leads the *Canzoniere* toward its final systemization, see Paolo Cherchi: *Verso la chiusura: Saggio sul 'Canzoniere' di Petrarca*. Bologna: Il Mulino 2008 (Saggi, 686). A separate study would lead to the conclusion that Petrarch was preparing for the unfinished *Africa*, a conclusion in which was inscribed the death of Robert of Anjou, to whom the work was dedicated, and which addressed the work, entrusting its own fame to it, bidding it a long life in better times than the present and a new birth in an age more favorable to poets.

Laura's tomb emerges the image of the future "rivederla in cielo" clothed in the "bel velo," the source of an eternal beatitude that will renew and perfect her former appearance "in terra") is the idea that seals the *Triumphus Eternitatis*, 142–145:

> felice sasso che'l bel viso serra!
> ché, poi ch'avrà ripreso il suo bel velo,
> se fu beato chi la vide in terra
>
> or che fia dunque rivederla in cielo?
>
> [Happy the stone that covers her fair face!
> And now that she her beauty hath resumed,
> If he was blest who saw her here on earth,
> What then will it be to see her again in heaven!]

The fact that the *Decameron* carries "nella sua fronte" [upon its very front] the date 1348, with "la dolorosa ricordazione della pestifera mortalità trapassata" [the sorrowful memory of the late mortal pestilence], assumes a significance paradoxically opposed to the ways in which Petrarch evokes that same year. It deals instead with an "orrido cominciamento" [horrid beginning], with a tragic – albeit already overcome – suspension of every civil bond, with an invasion of death which lay the threat of the end over the horizon of society as a whole. Boccaccio's intention provokes a polemical rebirth, the construction of an ideal and entirely literary society, capable of achieving "quella festa, quella allegrezza, quello piacere [...] senza trapassare in alcuno atto il segno della ragione" [(...) all cheer of festal gathering and other delights, so long as in no particular we overstep the bounds of reason, I, *Introduzione*, 65], in a more open and 'honest' practice of existence. At play is the relationship between death and narration, the idea of narration as a banishment of death, as critics and readers have insistently observed, referring repeatedly to the example of Shahrazād, whose own storytelling suspends death. Boccaccio's narrative, however, is not an attempt to impede the homicidal intentions of a king or human authority; it functions instead as a response to the ruinous, destructive force of nature, incomprehensible within human parameters (as Petrarch also noted in his abovementioned letter on the plague, *Familiares*, VIII, 7).

From death and destruction arises a surge of vitality, not casual and disordered, but elegantly constructed and organized, well defined in its order and in the accurate rules governing life in the country villas as well as the narration of the *novelle*. All of this storytelling – the pleasure it elicits – is marked by the close presence of destruction; and after all, these festive settings – this Eden on which the critics insist – are very near to Florence. There is no lack of examples in which the narrators refer to the "presenti avversità" [time of adversity, I, I, 91], the "pistolenzia presente" [present pestilence, VI, 3, 8], the "soprastante pistolenzia" [time of pestilence, IX, *Introduzione*, 2]. Asking his readers' pardon before undertaking the narration of the events of the plague, for the *noia* that they will suffer from this sort of beginning, the author underscores that, without these events, the narration never would have come about:

> A questa brieve noia (dico brieve in quanto in poche lettere si contiene) seguita prestamente la dolcezza e il piacere il quale io v'ho davanti promesso e che forse non sarebbe da così fatto inizio, se non si dicesse, aspettato. E nel vero, se io potuto avessi onestamente per altra parte menarvi a quello che io desidero che per così aspro sentiero come fia questo, io l'avrei volentier fatto: ma per ciò che, qual fosse la cagione per che le cose che appresso si leggeranno avvenissero, non si poteva senza questa ramemorazion dimostrare, quasi da necessità constretto a scriverle mi conduco. (I, *Introduzione*, 6–7)

> [To this brief exordium of woe – brief, I say, inasmuch as it can be put within the compass of a few letters – succeed forthwith the sweets and delights which I have promised you, and which, perhaps, had I not done so, were not to have been expected from it. In truth, had it been honestly possible to guide you whither I would bring you by a road less rough than this will be, I would gladly have so done. But, because without this review of the past, it would not be in my power to shew how the matters, of which you will hereafter read, came to pass, I am almost bound of necessity to enter upon it, if I would write of them at all.]

Another sign of the end – though certainly less radical and disastrous – was already present before the narrative's beginning in the *Proemio* to women, where Boccaccio, in accounting for his disposition to console the afflicted, attributes it to his own gratitude toward those from whom he in his own turn received consolation during a period of painful love now ended. Right from its very beginning the book sets forth in the name of an autobiographical experience of the end of love; this emotion's progressive diminution, to the point of reducing itself to a pleasing echo of memory, is attributed to the divine law that brings all things to an end:

> Ma sì come a Colui piacque il quale, essendo Egli infinito, diede per legge incommutabile a tutte le cose mondane aver fine, il mio amore, oltre a ogn'altro fervente e il quale niuna forza di proponimento o di consiglio o di vergogna evidente, o pericolo che seguir ne potesse, aveva potuto né rompere né piegare, per se medesimo in processo di tempo si diminuì in guisa, che sol di sé nella mente m'ha al presente lasciato quel piacere che egli è usato di porgere a chi troppo non si mette ne' suoi più cupi pelaghi navigando; per che, dove faticoso esser solea, ogni affanno togliendo via, dilettevole il sento esser rimaso. (*Proemio*, 5)

> [But, as it pleased Him, who, being infinite, has assigned by immutable law an end to all things mundane, my love, beyond all other fervent, and neither to be broken nor bent by any force of determination, or counsel of prudence, or fear of manifest shame or ensuing danger, did nevertheless in course of time abate of its own accord, in such wise that it has

now left nought of itself in my mind but that pleasure which it is wont to afford to him who does not adventure too far out in navigating its deep seas; so that, whereas it was used to be grievous, now, all discomfort being done away, I find that which remains to be delightful.]

At any rate the narration of the *Decameron* rests upon a suspension and distortion of the view of experience; and one can indeed imagine that the actual experience of 1348, the fact of having survived that terrible year, has produced a sort of knee-jerk reaction in the author, causing him to introduce into the new and unimagined horizon of this book his own passion for 'pleasurable' literature, for the romance tradition, for those same outcomes for Florentine culture and civilization. Apart from the plague functioning to give rise to the fiction of the *brigata* of storytellers, one can assert that, had Boccaccio not suffered through that anguished experience of death and chaos, the *Decameron* would not have come into being; it would not have come to be his life's most formidable creation, his perspective on threatened Florentine civilization as depicted through the model of contemporary European narration. Within this frame he imposes, with even more decisive significance, a critical detachment from the penitential consequences with which the *Decameron* covertly vies;[13] and the subtitling of the book as the *cognominato prencipe Galeotto* creates an even more ambiguous and complex density.

Thus in the development of the frame, if the central roles are played on the one hand by Pampinea, creator of the 'buen retiro' and first queen of the *brigata*, and on the other hand by Panfilo, victorious alter ego of the author and inaugural narrator (with the *novella* of ser Ciappelletto), another crucial role is that of Dioneo, whom Giancarlo Mazzacurati accurately defines as "spirito dell'ebrezza, dell'ilarità terrestre, degli umori improvvisi, [...] lo scarto e l'antidoto che impedisce la morte del testo, il passaggio dalla festa alla noia" [the spirit of euphoria, of earthly mirth, of sudden mood swings, (...) the deviation and the antidote that impedes the death of the text, the passage from celebration to boredom], inviting his reimagining as "archetipo della moderna soggettività romanzesca" [the archetype of modern romance subjectivity], comparing him "ad altri eroi della scrittura fuorilegge, ai *fools*, ai portatori di *tics*, agli sghembi, ai maniacali" [to other heroes of renegade writing, to fools, to persons with a tic, to the physically deformed, to the mentally insane].[14] In his crooked position, Dioneo is the antidote to death, and not only to that of the text, but to the outside threat of death which that

---

[13] Essential to this argument, obviously, is the monograph of Lucia Battaglia Ricci: *Ragionare nel giardino: Boccaccio e i cicli pittorici del "Trionfo della morte."* Roma: Salerno editrice 1987 (particularly chapter 2, *La peste e la "cultura della penitenza,"* p. 45–96).

[14] Giancarlo Mazzacurati: *La regina e il buffone: ordo e varietas nella costruzione del* Decameron. In: Matteo Palumbo (ed.): *All'ombra di Dioneo: Tipologie e percorsi della novella da Boccaccio a Bandello*. Scandicci: La Nuova Italia 1996, p. 37–43: p. 42.

'horrid beginning' reveals most fully. His role is a necessary one, because from it emerges that surge of life, that dream of a happy society devoted to honest pleasure; it enables the author to express at the highest level the characters of Florentine society and to explore the contradictory plurality of the world, the diverse forms and occurrences of human life in the present and in the past. Panfilo, the first narrator, is charged with ruling the last day, the *novelle* of which express the highest courtly values of liberality and magnificence, and the passage with which he inaugurates that last morning immediately professes a concern for the future:

> [...] Panfilo, levatosi, le donne e' suoi compagni fece chiamare. E venuti tutti, con loro insieme diliberato del dove andar potessero al lor diletto, con lento passo si mise innanzi accompagnato da Filomena e da Fiammetta, tutti gli altri appresso seguendogli; e molte cose della loro futura vita insieme parlando e dicendo e rispondendo, per lungo spazio s'andaron diportando [...] (X, *Introduzione*, 2–3)
>
> [(...) when uprose Pamfilo, and roused the ladies and his comrades. And all the company being assembled, and choice made of the place whither they should betake them for their diversion, he, accompanied by Filomena and Fiammetta, led the way at a slow pace, followed by all the rest. So fared they no little space, beguiling the time with talk of their future way of life, whereof there was much to tell and much to answer (...)]

This concern for the future, appearing just before the work's end, connects back to quips Pampinea made in her first speech:

> [...] e tanto dimorare in tal guisa, che noi veggiamo, se prima da morte non siam sopragiunte, che fine il cielo riserbi a queste cose. (I, *Introduzione*, 71)
>
> [(...) and in such way of life continue, until we see – if death should not first overtake us – the end which Heaven reserves for these events.]

The last *novella*, that of Griselda and the marquis of Saluzzo, variously "Petrarchized" and moralized, allows for the famous resolution of the *Decameron* in an upward-moving rhythm, a trajectory that leads from the depraved Ciappelletto to the virtuous Griselda (perhaps seen directly as *figura Mariae*, with an implicit convergence of the finale of the *Decameron* and that of the *Canzoniere*, as well as the Dantean *Commedia*).[15] However, aside from the fact that this *novella* comes from the mouth of the 'crooked' Dioneo, one should give more attention to its paradoxical opening: the narrator begins "laughing," directly evoking the first

---

15 Among the well-justified denials of Griselda's final exemplarity, see Francesco Bruni: *Boccaccio: L'invenzione della letteratura mezzana*. Bologna: Il Mulino 1990, p. 271–273, where he rightly insists on the fact that "l'opera rimane esposta alla controversia, alla discussione" ("the work continues to arouse controversy and discussion") (p. 273).

novella of the seventh day, with the ambiguous metaphor of the "coda ritta della fantasima" [erect tail of the phantasm] (nor should it be overlooked that the *novella* in question ends with the proposal of diverse hypotheses on what actually occurred and on the true name of the protagonist, Gianni Lotteringhi or Gianni di Nello). Dioneo now addresses the female portion of his audience, ironically calling them 'gentle' and declaring that he wishes his storytelling to bring him nearer to the world of women, yet presenting a protagonist characterized by a "mad folly":

> [...] e per ciò, acciò che io troppo da voi non mi scosti, vo' ragionar d'un marchese, non cosa magnifica ma una matta bestialità, come che ben ne gli seguisse alla fine; la quale io non consiglio alcun che segua, per ciò che gran peccato fu che a costui ben n'avenisse. (X, 10, 3)
>
> [(...) wherefore, that I stray not too far from you, I am minded to tell you somewhat of a Marquis; certes, nought magnificent, but a piece of mad folly, albeit there came good thereof to him in the end. The which I counsel none to copy, for that great pity'twas that it turned out well with him.]

Before the actual story begins, the happy ending is introduced as an incongruous outcome, a sort of perversion, a true shame. Dioneo affirms and reinforces this idea of reversal within the long *novella* through words with which he concludes it, with the erotic metaphor of 'dusting the pelisse,' which mirrors perfectly that initial metaphor of the 'tail of the phantasm':

> Chi avrebbe, altri che Griselda, potuto col viso non solamente asciutto ma lieto sofferir le rigide e mai più non udite pruove da Gualtier fatte? Al quale non sarebbe forse stato male investito d'essersi abbattuto a una che quando, fuori di casa, l'avesse fuori in camiscia cacciata, s'avesse sì a un altro fatto scuotere il pilliccione che riuscito ne fosse una bella roba. (X, 10, 68–69)
>
> [Who but Griselda had been able, with a countenance not only tearless, but cheerful, to endure the hard and unheard-of trials to which Gualtieri subjected her? Who perhaps might have deemed himself to have made no bad investment, had he chanced upon one, who, having been turned out of his house in her shift, had found means so to dust the pelisse of another as to get herself thereby a fine robe.]

Panfilo, however, gives the concluding speech, which, after having vindicated the "continua onestà, continua concordia, continua fraternal dimestichezza" [seemliness and the sweet intimacy of brothers and sisters] of this time spent together, affirms the necessity of departure, to avoid any fastidious or malevolent criticisms against them as well as the risk of being joined by importunate folk. Having given instructions for departure the next morning, they pass their final evening in dining, dance and song: jealous Fiammetta sings the appropriately themed ballad *S'amor venisse senza gelosia* (*So came but Love, and brought no jealousy*), ending with a warning to every possible rival. Then, after implying that the final celebration lasted nearly to midnight, the text hastily records the morning's departure and return to Florence, with an arrival back at the starting point of Santa Maria Novella, and notes the farewells between the young men who "a' lor altri piaceri attesero" [departed to find other diversions elsewhere], and the young ladies who "quando tempo lor parve, se ne tornarono alle lor case" [in due time repaired to their homes, X, *Conclusione*, 16]. A most rapid closure, if compared with the long course of the *Introduzione* to the first day, and of the plague that is so precisely described there, of which we find no more mention, nor of the situation in which Florence must still find itself, considering only two weeks have since passed. In this very rapid disappearance of the *brigata* we might perhaps catch a trace of that final melancholy that often accompanies great narrations, the events of worlds teeming with life, the characters and the situations lovingly followed by the author who seems able to disconnect himself from them only in this brusque manner, almost with a jerk.

At any rate, Boccaccio, to avoid misunderstandings with the 'most gracious ladies' to whom the work is addressed, seals the work with the *Author's Conclusion*, where he affirms above all his satisfaction with having reached the goal that he had indicated at the beginning:

> Nobilissime giovani, a consolazion delle quali io a così lunga fatica messo mi sono, io mi credo, aiutantemi la divina grazia, sì come io avviso, per li vostri pietosi prieghi non già per li miei meriti, quello compiutamente aver fornito che io nel principio della presente opera promisi di dover fare [...] (*Conclusione dell'autore*, 1)
>
> [Most noble damsels, for whose solace I addressed me to this long and toilsome task, meseems that, aided by the Divine grace, the bestowal whereof I impute to the efficacy of your pious prayers, and in no wise to merits of mine, I have now brought this work to the full and perfect consummation which in the outset thereof I promised you.]

In putting forth here the various justifications for the defense of his book with regard to the 'trifling objections' that some female reader "o altri potrebbe dire" [or other might advance], the author continually inserts internal folds, ironic and self-parodic outbursts, which highlight internal contradictions, like digressive reservations toward the persuasive gravity of the assertions on the honesty of the substance and style. Here we move from the list of erotic metaphors (after all, it is not unbecoming for men and women "di dir tutto dì 'foro' e 'caviglia' e 'mortaio' e 'pestello' e 'salsiccia' e 'mortadelle,' e tutto pien di simiglianti cose," [to make use of such terms as hole, and pin, and mortar, and pestle, and sausage, and polony, and plenty more besides of a like sort, 5] to the characterization of the time of the plague as that in which "andar con le brache in capo per iscampo di sé era alli più onesti non disdicevole" [the most sedate might without disgrace walk abroad with his breeches for headgear, 7], to the nicknames of Cinciglione and Scolaio (9), to the allusive quips concerning the sanctimonious and the fanatical who, among other things, "dicono e anche fanno delle cosette otta per vicenda," [there are little matters that even the beguines tell, ay, and do, now and again, 15], to the self-parodying hint at his own 'weight' and his own levity ("parlando a quelle che pesato non m'hanno, affermo che io non son grave, anzi son io sì lieve, che io sto a galla nell'acqua" [in answer to the fair that have not weighed me, I affirm that I am not of gravity; on the contrary I am so light that I float on the surface of the water, 23],[16] to an apparent denial of any satire against the friars, which in reality turns out to be an augmented version ("per ciò che i frati son buone persone e fuggono il disagio per l'amor di Dio e macinano a raccolta e nol ridicono; e se non che di tutti un poco vien del caprino, troppo sarebbe più piacevole il piato loro" [seeing that the friars are good folk, and eschew hardship for the love of God, and grind intermittently, and never blab; and, were they not all a trifle malodorous, intercourse with them would be much more agreeable, 26].

Through this ironic filigree he insists once again on the legitimacy of an unbiased view of reality and of the uncontrollable multiplicity of the world, beyond all false modesty. In the foreground is the responsibility of the reading, the disposition of the book to follow different paths and to allow for a free selection among the *novelle*: the author, wishing to encourage this type of reading, claims to have prepared the rubrics with summaries of the *novelle* in order to support their individual selection (the *novelle* "nella fronte portan segnato quello che esse dentro dal loro seno nascoso tengono," [each bears on its brow the epitome of that which it hides within its bosom, § 19].

The compactness of the book can be counteracted through the ever-changing variety of the world and of language itself. Into the tableau of this changeability the author inscribes his opinions on his own language, responding to the accusations of those who say he has an "evil tongue and venomous"; to this purpose he adds the statements of a female neighbor of his who, when he had but a few *novelle* left to write in order to complete the book, had noted the sweetness of his language:

> Confesso nondimeno le cose di questo mondo non avere stabilità alcuna ma sempre essere in mutamento, e così potrebbe della mia lingua essere intervenuto; la quale, non credendo io al mio giudizio, il quale a mio potere io fuggo nelle mie cose, non ha guari mi disse una mia vicina che io l'aveva la migliore e la più dolce del mondo: e in verità, quando questo fu, egli erano poche a scrivere delle soprascritte novelle. (§ 27)

---

16 Following this statement are other ironic outbursts, referring to the banter that friars insert into their sermons and the pious lamentations appropriate to those who fear laughing too much (among these, with comic misrepresentation, "the Complaint of the Magdalen").

> [Nevertheless, I acknowledge that the things of this world have no stability, but are ever undergoing change; and this may have befallen my tongue, albeit, no great while ago, one of my fair neighbours – for in what pertains to myself I trust not my own judgment, but forgo it to the best of my power – told me 'twas the goodliest and sweetest tongue in the world; and in sooth, when this occurred, few of the said stories were yet to write (...)]

Beneath this reference to the neighbor's testimony one can perhaps glimpse a veiled erotic allusion (a turn of phrase such as "'twas the goodliest and sweetest tongue in the world" in this context does not seem to limit itself to a literal interpretation; it seems, rather, to convey a possible double meaning). The book closes under the influence of these ironic diversions: it centers the defense of 'honesty' within this game of lighthearted deviations which, just before the conventional thanks to God (who conducted the 'so long travail' to its 'desired goal') and salute to the benevolent memory of its female readers, leaves open – with apparent indifference – the path to an uncontrollable multiplicity of opinions and points of view:

> E lasciando omai a ciascheduna e dire e credere come le pare, tempo è da por fine alle parole, Colui umilmente ringraziando che dopo sì lunga fatica col suo aiuto n'ha al desiderato fine condotto. E voi, piacevoli donne, con la sua grazia in pace vi rimanete, di me ricordandovi, se a alcuna forse alcuna cosa giova l'averle lette. (§ 29)
>
> [So, then, be every lady at liberty to say and believe whatever she may think fit: but 'tis now time for me to bring these remarks to a close, with humble thanks to Him, by whose help and guidance I, after so long travail, have been brought to the desired goal. And may you, sweet my ladies, rest ever in His grace and peace; and be not unmindful of me, if, peradventure, any of you may, in any measure, have been profited by reading these stories.]

The text seals this notion of the freedom and responsibility of its readership (primarily female) within the rubric that marks its end, with the title of the work and with the return of the 'surname' of 'prince Galeotto,' already displayed in the initial title. This mild evaporation of the work's end seems to wipe away every trace of its 'horrid beginning.'

Bibliography

Primary Literature

Boccaccio, Giovanni: *The Decameron of Giovanni Boccaccio Faithfully Translated by James M. Rigg*. 2 vols. London: The Navarre Society 1903.

Boccaccio, Giovanni: *Decameron*. Edited by Vittore Branca. In: Tutte le opere di Giovanni Boccaccio. Edited by Vittore Branca. Milano: Mondadori 1976.

Petrarca, Francesco: *Letters on Familiar Matters: Rerum familiarium libri*. Translated by Aldo S. Bernardo. 3 vols. Baltimore: Johns Hopkins University Press 1975–1985.
Petrarca, Francesco: *Triumphi*. Edited by Marco Ariani. Milano: Mursia 1988.
Petrarca, Francesco: *Letters of Old Age: Rerum Senilium Libri I–XVIII*. Translated by Aldo S. Bernardo, Saul Levin et al. 2 vols. Baltimore: Johns Hopkins University Press 1992.
Petrarca, Francesco: *The Canzoniere or Rerum vulgarium fragmenta*. Translated with commentary by Mark Musa. Bloomington, Ind.: Indiana University Press 1996.
Petrarca, Francesco: *Canzoniere*. Edited by Marco Santagata. Milano: Mondadori 2004.
Petrarca, Francesco: *Le Familiari*. Edited and translated by Ugo Dotti and Felicita Audisio. 5 vols. Torino: Nino Aragno 2004–2009.
Petrarca, Francesco: *Le senili*. Edited by Ugo Dotti and Felicita Audisio. 3 vols. Torino: Nino Aragno 2004–2010.
Petrarca, Francesco: *Canzoniere: Rerum vulgarium fragmenta*. Edited by Rosanna Bettarini. Torino: Einaudi 2005 (Nuova raccolta di classici italiani annotati, 20).

Secondary Literature

Monographs and Anthologies

Battaglia Ricci, Lucia: *Ragionare nel giardino: Boccaccio e i cicli pittorici del "Trionfo della morte."* Roma: Salerno editrice 1987.
Bruni, Francesco: *Boccaccio: L'invenzione della letteratura mezzana*. Bologna: Il Mulino 1990.
Cherchi, Paolo: *Verso la chiusura: Saggio sul "Canzoniere" di Petrarca*. Bologna: Il Mulino 2008 (Saggi, 686).
Mazzacurati, Giancarlo: *La regina e il buffone:* ordo e varietas *nella costruzione del 'Decameron'*. In Matteo Palumbo (ed.): *All'ombra di Dioneo: Tipologie e percorsi della novella da Boccaccio a Bandello*. Scandicci: La Nuova Italia 1996, p. 37–43.
de Nolhac, Pierre: *Pétrarque et l'humanisme*. 2 vols. Paris: H. Champion 1907.
Santagata, Marco: *I frammenti dell'anima: Storia e racconto nel Canzoniere di Petrarca*. Bologna: il Mulino 1992.

Contributors

Renzo Bragantini was born in Venice (Italy) in 1945 and lives in Rome. Full professor of Italian literature, now emeritus, he taught Italian Literature at the University of Rome ("La Sapienza"). He has been visiting professor at Yale University, UCLA, Johns Hopkins University, the University of Toronto, and the Universidade de São Paulo. His interests mainly focus on Medieval and Renaissance literature (Dante, Petrarch, Boccaccio, Renaissance *novella*, Tasso, etc.), but he has also extensively written on Manzoni, Pascoli, Literature and Music, Literature and the Visual Arts. He is Co-editor of *Filologia e Critica* and of the *Archivio Novellistico Italiano*. A book on the Italian Trecento (*Ingressi laterali al Trecento maggiore. Dante, Petrarca, Boccaccio*) appeared in Italy (Naples, Liguori 2012). Most recently he has published *Il governo del comico. Nuovi studî sulla narrativa italiana dal Tre al Cinquecento* (Manziana, Rome, Vecchiarelli 2014). He's currently working a book on Boccaccio's *Decameron*, which will be published by Carocci, Rome.

Igor Candido is Assistant Professor/ Lecturer at Trinity College Dublin. He holds two doctoral degrees in Italian literature (Johns Hopkins University 2011 and University of Turin 2009). In 2013–2014 he was the recipient of the Alexander von Humboldt Research Fellowship. He has lectured and taught in Italy, the US, and Germany, and written on Dante, Petrarch, Boccaccio, Poliziano, Emerson, and Longfellow. He has provided the critical edition of Ralph Waldo Emerson's translation of Dante's *Vita nuova* (Turin: Aragno editore 2012) as well as a monograph on Boccaccio as reader and imitator of Apuleius of Madauros (*Boccaccio umanista. Studi su Boccaccio e Apuleio*. Ravenna: Longo 2014). He is currently working on a new commented edition of Petrarch's *The Life of Solitude* (Toronto University Press). He is one of the editor of *Lettere italiane* and of the *Archivio Novellistico Italiano*. He collaborates with Italian and American journals such as *L'Indice dei libri del mese*, *Modern Language Notes*.

Christopher S. Celenza is Dean of Georgetown College at Georgetown University, where he is also a professor of History and Classics. He is the author or editor of ten books and over forty scholarly articles in the fields of Italian Renaissance history, post-classical Latin literature and philosophy, and the history of classical scholarship. His book, *Machiavelli: A Portrait* was published by Harvard University Press in 2015. His most recent book is *Petrarch: Everywhere a Wanderer* (London: Reaktion 2017). He has held Fellowships from the Guggenheim Foundation, the ACLS, Villa I Tatti, the American Academy in Rome, and the Fulbright Foundation.

Paolo Cherchi is a professor Emeritus of Romance Languages and Literatures at the University of Chicago. His work deals mostly with Medieval and Renaissance literarures. His latest books are: *La rosa dei venti. Una mappa delle teorie letterarie* (Rome: Carocci 2011), a collection of essays, *Erudizione e leggerezza* (Rome, Viella, 2013), a translation of the Catalan novel, *Tirante il Bianco* (Turin: Einaudi, "I Millenni", 2013), and *Il tramonto dell'onestade* (Rome: Edizioni di Storia e Letteratura 2016).

Francesco Ciabattoni received his Ph.D. from Johns Hopkins University. He is Associate Professor in the Italian Department at Georgetown University. He has published on international journals on Dante, Petrarch, Boccaccio, Berto, Pasolini and Primo Levi. His monograph *Dante's Journey to Polyphony* (Toronto: University of Toronto Press 2010) is a comprehensive study of the role of music in Dante's *Commedia*. With Pier Massimo Forni he has edited *The Decameron Third Day in Perspective: Volume Three of Lectura Boccaccii* (University of Toronto Press 2014). Professor Ciabattoni's main research focus is the interplay of music and literature. His book *La citazione è sintomo d'amore* (Rome: Carocci 2016) is a study of the intertextual practice of literary in Italian songwriters. He is currently working on a book-length project about music and liturgical drama in Dante's *Commedia*.

Karl Enenkel is Professor of Medieval Latin and Neo-Latin at the University of Münster. Previously he was Professor of Neo-Latin at Leiden University (Netherlands). He has published widely on international Humanism, early modern culture, paratexts, literary genres 1300–1600, Neo-Latin emblems, word and image relationships, and the history of scholarship and science. Among his major book publications are Francesco Petrarca: *De vita solitaria* (1991), *Die Erfindung des Menschen. Die Autobiographik des frühneuzeitlichen Humanismus von Petrarca bis Lipsius* (2008), *Die Stiftung von Autorschaft in der neulateinischen Literatur (ca. 1350–ca. 1650)*. (2015), and *Oudheid als ambitie* (2017). He has co-edited and co-authored some 30 volumes on a great variety of topics, among others, *Modelling the Individual. Biography and Portrait in the Renaissance* (1998), *Recreating Ancient History* (2001), *Cognition and the Book* (2004), *Petrarch and his Readers* (2006), *The Neo-Latin Epigram* (2009), *Portuguese Humanism* (2011), *The Authority of the Word* (2011), *The Reception of Erasmus* (2013), *Transformation of the Classics* (2013), *Die* Vita *als Vermittlerin von Wissenschaft und Werk* (2013), *Neo-Latin Commentaries and the Management of Knowledge* (2013), *Iohannes de Certaldo. Beiträge zu Boccaccios lateinischen Werken und ihrer Wirkung* (2015), and *Jesuit Image Theory* (2016). He has founded the international series *Intersections* (Brill); *Proteus. Studies in Early Modern Identity Formation*; and *Scientia universalis. Studien und Texteditionen zur Wissensgeschichte der Vormoderne*. He is member of the board of, among others, *Humanistica Lovaniensia*, the *Conseil international pour l'edition des oeuvres complètes d'Erasme*, and of the *Royal Netherlands Academy of Arts and Sciences*.

Giulio Ferroni (Rome, 1943), professor of Italian Literature at the University of Calabria from 1975 to 1982 and at the University of Rome, La Sapienza, from 1982 to 2012. He has written numerous literary essays on Machiavelli, Ariosto, Aretino, Leopardi, the eighteenth and twentieth century Italian literature, and on many contemporary writers. He is staunchly "militant" in the cultural debate, with a focus on contemporary literature and the school system. Among his books: *Mutazione e riscontro nel teatro di Machiavelli* (Bulzoni 1972); *Il comico nelle teorie contemporanee* (Bulzoni 1974); *Le voci dell'istrione: Pietro Aretino e la dissoluzione del teatro* (Liguori 1977); *Dopo la fine: Sulla condizione postuma della letteratura* (Einaudi 1996, new edition Donzelli 2010); *Machiavelli, o dell'incertezza* (Donzelli 2003); *Ariosto* (Salerno 2008); *Prima lezione di letteratura italiana* (Laterza 2009); *La passion predominate* (Liguori 2009); *Gli ultimi poeti: Giovanni Giudici* *e Andrea Zanzotto* (Il Saggiatore 2013); *La fedeltà della ragione* (Liguori 2014); *La scuola impossibile* (Salerno 2015). He has also authored *Storia della letteratura italiana* (in four volumes) published by Einaudi Scuola in 1991, new edition Mondadori Università 2012–2013, and *Letteratura italiana contemporanea* 1900–2014 (in two volumes), Mondadori Università 2015.

Giorgio Ficara is Professor of Italian Literature at the University of Turin and has been a Visiting Professor at Columbia University, Stanford University, UCLA, and the University of Chicago. He has taught at the Sorbonne and the Collège de France, Paris. Among his books: *Solitudini. Studi sulla letteratura italiana dal Duecento al Novecento* (Garzanti, 1993 – Premio Lerici 1994), *Il punto di vista della Natura. Saggio su Leopardi* (Il Melangolo, 1996 – runner-up Premio Viareggio 1997); *Casanova e la malinconia* (Einaudi, 1999); *Stile Novecento* (Marsilio, 2007); *Montale sentimentale* (Marsilio, 2012); *Lettere non italiane* (Bompiani, 2016). In 1984 he won the Borgia Prize, Accademia Nazionale dei Lincei. He is co-Editor of *Lettere italiane* and is a regular contributor to *Il Domenicale del Sole 24 ore*.

Manuele Gragnolati is Full Professor of Italian Literature at the University of Paris-Sorbonne and Associate Director of the ICI Berlin Institute for Cultural Inquiry, as well as Senior Research Fellow at Somerville College, Oxford. A major part of his research, including his first monograph *Experiencing the Afterlife: Soul and Body in Dante and Medieval Culture* (2005), focuses on the significance of corporeality in thirteenth- and fourteenth-century eschatology. He is also interested in the concept of linguistic subjectivity from Dante's *Vita Nova* to the present, in modern appropriations of medieval texts, and in feminist and queer theory. His latest monograph, *Amor che move. Linguaggio del corpo e forma del desiderio in Dante, Pasolini e Morante* (2013), offers a 'diffractive' exploration of body, language, and desire in Dante and authors who have engaged with Dante's oeuvre in the late twentieth century from a 'feminine'/feminist and queer position. He has run several interdisciplinary projects on Dante, Elsa Morante, and Pier Paolo Pasolini, which have resulted in a dozen collective volumes.

Andreas Kablitz, born in 1957, studied Romance Languages at the University of Cologne. In 1981 he began to work as an Assistant at the University of (West-)Berlin, where he earned his Ph.D. with a thesis on Lamartine in 1983. Within three years, he finished his 'Habilitation', qualifying him to lecture in Romance Languages and Literatures. In 1989 he started to lecture in Tübingen, and in 1990 he received and accepted a call to the University of Munich as a full professor and head of the department of Italian Literature. In 1994 he returned to Cologne, where – in addition to his professorial lecturing activities – he is now also the director of the Petrarca-Institute, head of the editorial board of *Poetica* and member of the editorial board of the Dante Society of America as well as a member of the academic comittee of the Fritz-Thyssen-Stiftung. In 1997 he was awarded the Leibniz-Preis of the Deutsche Forschungsgemeinschaft. In 2006 Andreas Kablitz became a member of the Bavarian Academy of Sciences and of the North Rhine-Westphalian Academy of Sciences. In 2007 he became a member of the German National Academy of Sciences (Leopoldina), where he was nominated senator and president of the section for cultural sciences in 2016. In 2010 he was appointed *Commendatore of the Ordine della Stella della Solidarietà Italiana* by the President of the Italian Republic. Although his special research interests center on Dante, his essays cover a wide range of topics from French, Italian, German and English Literature, featuring Petrarch, Tasso and other authors from the Italian and French Renaissance as well as Shakespeare, Thomas Mann or Oscar Wilde. He has also been working on philosophers as Aristotle, Kant and Wittgenstein.

Joachim Küpper is Professor of Comparative Literature and of Romance Literatures at Freie Universität Berlin, Germany. He has published on literary, historiographical and philosophical texts from Homer to the 20th century. He was awarded the Heinz Maier-Leibnitz prize as well as the Leibniz prize of the Deutsche Forschungsgemeinschaft. He is currently working on a network theory of cultural dynamics (ERC Advanced Grant). He is a corresponding member of the Göttingen Academy of Sciences, and a member of the German National Academy of Sciences/ Leopoldina as well as the American Academy of Arts and Sciences.

Giuseppe Mazzotta is the Sterling Professor of Humanities for Italian at Yale University. He specializes in medieval literature but his publications address all periods of Italian literature. His books include: *Dante, Poet of the Desert: History and Allegory in the Divine Comedy* (Princeton, 1979); *The World at Play in Boccaccio's Decameron* (Princeton, 1986); *Dante's Vision and the Circle of Knowledge* (Princeton, 1993); *The Worlds of Petrarch* (Duke UP, 193); *The New Map of the World: the Poetic Philosophy of Giambattista Vico* (Princeton, 1998) (Italian translation, Turin: Einaudi, 2001); *Cosmopoiesis: The Renaissance Experiment* (Toronto UP, 2001) (Italian translation, Palermo: Sellerio 2008). He has also edited or co-edited several boooks, such as *Critical Essays on Dante* (Hall, 1991) and *Master Regis* (Fordham UP, 1985). In 2008, he published the Norton edition of Dante's *Inferno* (translated by M. Palma).

Marco Petoletti is a Professor of Medieval Latin Literature at the Catholic University of Milan. He is currently pursuing a range of research projects concerning the transmission of Latin texts in the Middle Ages, the medieval epigraphy and the Latin production of Dante, Petrarch and Boccaccio, with particular reference to the libraries of Petrarch and Boccaccio, of whom he discovered new autographs. He is co-editor of *Italia medioevale e umanistica*. He is also a member of the Academic Board of *Corpus Christianorum* and the Scientific Committee of the Edizione Nazionale delle opere di Francesco Petrarca. He has edited or authored: Petrarca: *Rerum memorandarum libri* (Florence: Le lettere 2014); Dante: *Egloge* (Rome: Salerno 2016, Nuova Edizione Commentata delle Opere di Dante); *Un poeta alla corte dei papi. Bonaiuto da Casentino e Bonifacio VIII* (Rome: Viella 2016). He is the editor of *Autografi dei letterati italiani. Le Origini e il Trecento* (Rome: Salerno 2013); *Boccaccio autore e copista* (Florence: Mandragora 2013); *Dante e la sua eredità a Ravenna nel Trecento* (Ravenna: Longo 2015).

Gerhard Regn is Professor Emeritus of Italian Philology at the University of Munich and Honorary Professor at the University of Cologne. His research focuses on Italian medieval and pre-modern literature, and on nineteenth- and twentieth-century literature in Italy and France. He is a full member of the Bavarian Academy of Siences and Humanities. In 2007 he was nominated Commendatore dell'Ordine della Solidarietà italiana of the Italian Republic. Regn has published numerous books and articles, including *Letture petrarchesche* (2007, co-editor); *Lyriktheorie(n) der italienischen Renaissance* (2012 co-author); Francesco Petrarca: *Secretum meum*. Lateinisch-Deutsch (second newly revised edition, 2013, co-editor and translator).

Francesca Southerden is Associate Professor of Medieval Italian at the University of Oxford and Fellow of Somerville College. She has published several articles on the relationship between language and desire in Dante and Petrarch and is author of *Landscapes of Desire in the Poetry of Vittorio Sereni* (Oxford: Oxford University Press, 2012). She is co-editor, with Manuele Gragnolati, Tristan Kay, and Elena Lombardi, of *Desire in Dante and the Middle Ages* (Oxford: Legenda, 2012). She is currently working on completing her second book entitled, *Dante and Petrarch in the Garden of Language*.

Wayne Storey is Professor of Italian at Indiana University–Bloomington and the former Editor-in-chief of *Textual Cultures*, the journal of the Society for Textual Scholarship. He is one of the principal proponents of material philology ("Method, History, and Theory in Material Philology", *Neo-Latin Philology, Old Tradition, New Approaches*, 2014, and "La prassi nordamericana della filologia materiale", *Zeitschrift für romanische Philologie* 132.4 [2016]). He is author or co-author of seven volumes, including *Transcription and Visual Poetics in the Early Italian Lyric* (1993), *Petrarch and the Textual Origins of Interpretation* (2007), and the two-volume facsimile edition/commentary on Petrarch's partial autograph of the *Rerum vulgarium fragmenta*: Vat. Lat. 3195 (2003–2004). His new digital edition of Petrarch's *Fragmenta* can be consulted at: http://petrarchive.org, and will eventually contain his complete commentary, critical apparatus, a library of manuscripts and related studies.

Ronald G. Witt held the William B. Hamilton Professorship of History at Duke University. His most recent book, *The Two Latin Cultures and the Foundation of the Renaissance in the Middle Ages* (Cambridge University Press 2012; Ital. trans., Viella 2017) was awarded the Haskins Medal by the Medieval Academy of America and the Otto Gründler Prize by the International Congress on Medieval Studies in 2014. His previous volume *"In the Footsteps of the Ancients"*: *The Origins of Humanism from Lovato to Bruni* (Brill 2000; Ital. trans. 2005) received the Phyliss Gordan Book Prize of the Renaissance Society of America, the Marraro Prize of the American Historical Society, and the Jacques Barzun Prize of the American Philosophical Society.

Index of Manuscripts

Berlin
- Staatsbibliothek Preussischer Kulturbesitz, Hamilton 90: 178n, 327, 330

Bloomington
- Lilly Library, Poole 26: 16n, 17n, 32

Cesena
- Biblioteca Malatestiana, s.IV.2: 16

Città del Vaticano
- Biblioteca Apostolica Vaticana, Vaticano Chigiano L v 176: 39n, 40n, 324
- Biblioteca Apostolica Vaticana, Vaticano latino 1406: 14n
- Biblioteca Apostolica Vaticana, Vaticano latino 1411: 16
- Biblioteca Apostolica Vaticana, Vaticano latino 2193: 25
- Biblioteca Apostolica Vaticana, Vaticano latino 3134: 324
- Biblioteca Apostolica Vaticana, Vaticano latino 3195: 5, 17n, 39, 40, 43–46, 341, 350
- Biblioteca Apostolica Vaticana, Vaticano latino 3196: 32, 44, 45, 164n, 342
- Biblioteca Apostolica Vaticana, Vaticano latino 3199: 323n
- Biblioteca Apostolica Vaticana, Vaticano latino 3793: 16, 20
- Biblioteca Apostolica Vaticana, Vaticano Reginense latino 1110: 39
- Biblioteca Apostolica Vaticana, Vaticano Urbinate latino 161: 16

Cologny
- Bibliotheca Bodmeriana, 146: 5, 28–31, 46

Cortona
- Biblioteca Comunale e dell'Accademia Etrusca, 88: 15n

El Escorial
- Real Biblioteca de San Lorenzo de El Escorial, e.III.23: 16

Florence
- Biblioteca Medicea Laurenziana, Fondo Ashburnham, App. 1856: 231n
- Biblioteca Medicea Laurenziana, Plut. 29.2: 213
- Biblioteca Medicea Laurenziana, Plut. 29.8 (Zibaldone Laurenziano): 9, 227, 228, 230, 231
- Biblioteca Medicea Laurenziana, Plut. 33.31: 9, 228, 230
- Biblioteca Medicea Laurenziana, Plut. 34.1: 5, 32–40, 46
- Biblioteca Medicea Laurenziana, Plut. 34.39: 212
- Biblioteca Medicea Laurenziana, Plut. 37.19: 230
- Biblioteca Medicea Laurenziana, Plut. 41.42: 21
- Biblioteca Medicea Laurenziana, Plut. 51.10: 229
- Biblioteca Medicea Laurenziana, Plut. 54.32: 213
- Biblioteca Medicea Laurenziana, Plut. 68.2: 213
- Biblioteca Medicea Laurenziana, Martelli 12: 21
- Biblioteca Nazionale Centrale, II.III.47: 16
- Biblioteca Nazionale Centrale, Banco rari 37 (olim II.I.23): 16n
- Biblioteca Nazionale Centrale, Banco rari 50 (Zibaldone Magliabechiano): 9, 232, 237
- Biblioteca Nazionale Centrale, Fondo Magliabechiano, Classe VI 143: 21
- Biblioteca Nazionale Centrale, II.II. 8 (Frammento Magliabechiano): 180n, 191, 327
- Biblioteca Riccardiana, Ricc. 2533: 16n
- Biblioteca Riccardiana, Ricc. 2795: 232n
- Biblioteca Riccardiana, Ricc. 627: 232

London 27, 28
- British Library, Harley 5383: 232n
- British Museum, Harley 2493: 27, 28

Milan
- Biblioteca Ambrosiana, A 79 inf. Sala Prefetto 10/27: 5, 22, 25n, 26, 46
- Biblioteca Ambrosiana, A 204 inf.: 326n
- Biblioteca Ambrosiana, Ambr. C 67 sup.: 239

New Haven
- Yale University, Beinecke Library, M 706: 39

Padova
- Biblioteca universitaria, 1490: 28

Paris
- Bibliothèque Nationale de France, lat. 1994: 30
- Bibliothèque Nationale de France, lat. 2201: 21n
- Bibliothèque Nationale de France, lat. 2923: 72
- Bibliothèque Nationale de France, lat. 4939: 234
- Bibliothèque Nationale de France, lat. 6802: 233
- Bibliothèque Nationale de France, fr. 12584: 212n
- Bibliothèque Nationale de France, Parigino Italiano 482: 179, 180, 188, 327, 330

Toledo 236
- Archivo y Biblioteca Capitulares, Zelada 104 6: 9, 236

Index Nominum

Abelard 72, 273
Accursio, Mainardo 70
Aghinolfi, Giovanni 315
Alain de Lille 280, 281
Albanese, Gabriella 319n
Albanzani, Donato 24, 324
Alberti, Leon Battista 265
Alexander the Great 252, 273
Alighieri, Dante 3, 4, 6–9, 11, 12, 16, 91,
    129, 130, 132–139, 141–144, 146–150,
    153, 155, 156, 158–173, 180, 187,
    189–191, 206, 209, 213, 220–223, 229,
    236, 238, 239, 270–273, 276–278, 282,
    290, 305, 309, 321–323, 325–327, 331,
    332, 334
– Commedia, or Comedy 7, 8, 16, 131, 133,
    135–137, 142–144, 148, 149, 153, 158,
    159, 161, 167, 171, 172, 180, 187–189,
    238, 319, 323, 361
– Convivio 16, 130, 138, 139, 155
– De vulgari eloquentia 291
– Rime disperse 327
– Vita nova 6, 21, 91, 136, 146n, 150n, 161,
    236
Ambrose 66, 181, 275
Anaximander 279
Antonius Abbas 59
Apuleius 9, 25, 26, 30, 209, 213, 214, 216,
    218, 333
Aquinas, Thomas 8, 198–201, 205, 207,
    231, 325n
d'Aquino, Maria 292
Ariani, Marco 148n, 164
Aringheri, Beltramo 231
Aristotle 6, 67, 68, 84–88, 93, 94n, 95n, 96,
    98, 123, 275
– Nicomachean Ethics 88, 325n
Arnaud de Villeneuve 104n
(pseudo-) Arnaut Daniel 332
Arnulf of Orléans 230
Augustine, Saint 1, 17n, 28, 30, 65–67,
    70, 78, 88, 154, 155, 157, 158, 166,
    167, 198, 201, 236n, 245, 255, 270,
    271, 274, 275, 279, 296, 297, 300,
    307, 326
– Confessions 17n, 65, 78, 154, 155, 167, 296
– De civitate Dei 28
– De vera religione 296
– Enarrationes in Psalmos 30
– Soliloquia, or Soliloquies 296
Augustus 275
Auzzas, Ginetta 325n
Averroè 1, 92, 95, 125, 274, 326
Avicenna 92, 98, 99n

Baglio, Marco 24
Baldwin of Exeter, Archbishop of
    Canterbury 231n
Barlaam Calabro 279
Barolini, Teodolinda 130, 135, 142, 172, 173n
Baron, Hans 1, 2, 71, 73
Barrile, Lucrezia 289
Bartholomew Anglicus 273
Battaglia Ricci, Lucia 179
Baudelaire, Charles 91n
Bede, Saint 273
Benedict XII, Saint 137
Benoît de Saint-Maure 292
Benvenuto da Imola 275
Bernard of Clairvaux, Saint 132, 134n, 166,
    167, 274
Bernard Silvestre or Silvester 230, 280–282
Bernardo, Aldo 24
de Bernardo di Venezia, Paolo 25
Bernardus Gordonius 98
Bersani, Leo 149
Bersuire, Pierre, or Bercorius 251, 262,
    263, 265n
Berté, Monica 313n, 333
Bertelli, Sandro 238
Berthold of Hohenburg 230
Bertolani, Maria Cecilia 137
Berzoli da Gubbio, Pietro 21
Betussi, Giuseppe 265

Note: Modern authors are indexed only when they contribute to the discussion.

Billanovich, Giuseppe 3, 21n, 71, 74, 213n, 313, 316, 319, 326n
de Blois, Guillaume 230
de Blois, Vital 230
Boccaccio, Giovanni passim
– Allegoria mitologica 229
– Buccolicum carmen 27n, 281
– Comedia delle ninfe fiorentine 289
– Corbaccio 294
– Decameron 2, 8–12, 16, 17n, 168, 176–183, 185–191, 194–196, 202, 204–207, 209, 213, 215, 216, 222, 223, 230, 239, 249, 252, 271, 275, 279, 280, 282, 283, 290, 293, 316, 319, 320, 325n, 326n, 327–332, 334, 340, 341n, 358, 360–362
– De casibus virorum illustrium 172, 217, 221–223, 235, 273
– De mulieribus claris 217, 218, 235, 264, 316
– De vita et moribus domini Francisci Petracchi 73n
– Elegia di Madonna Fiammetta, or Elegy of Madonna Fiammetta 12, 280, 291, 292
– Elegia di Costanza, or Elegy to Constance 227n, 229
– Esposizioni sopra la Commedia, or Expositions 319
– Filocolo 2, 287, 289, 292
– Filostrato 2, 222, 280, 289, 292
– Genealogia deorum gentilium, or Genealogie 2, 9–11, 233, 235, 239, 244, 245, 247–257, 259–266, 272, 275–279, 281–284, 319
– Teseida 2
– Trattatello in laude di Dante 236, 239, 321, 322n
– Ytalie iam certus honos 323
– Zibaldone Laurenziano See Index of Mss, Biblioteca Medicea Laurenziana, Plut. 29.8
– Zibaldone Magliabechiano See Index of Mss, Biblioteca Nazionale Centrale, Banco rari 50
Boethius 274, 275, 281, 296, 325n
Bona Fortuna 97n
Bonaventure, Saint 274
Botterill, Steven 132

Bragantini, Renzo 10, 11
Branca, Vittore 2, 3, 11, 171, 172, 177n, 178–180, 181n, 194n, 206, 212n, 215, 313, 326n, 329, 330n
Brucker, Jacob 78
Bruni, Leonardo 333, 334
Burckhardt, Jacob 4
Burley, Walter 16n
Bynum, Caroline Walker 136, 137n

de Cabassoles, Philippe 17, 53, 56, 80, 347
Caesar, Julius 137n, 232
Campana, Augusto 324
Candido, Igor 88n, 209, 213, 333
Caracciola, Mariella 289
Caradente, Caterina 289
Carena, Carlo
Cartari, Vincenzo 265
Casamassima, Emanuele 213n
Cassirer, Ernst 1
Castelvetro, Lodovico 164
Castiglionchio, Lapo da 19, 20
Cato the Censor 247
Cavalcanti, Guido 159, 331, 332
Cavalcanti, Mainardo 328–332
Celenza, Christopher 6
Cervantes, Miguel de 109, 124
Chalcydius 279, 280
Chance, Jeane 246n
Checco di Meletto of Romagna 229
Cherchi, Paolo 10
Chiavacci Leonardi, Anna Maria 171
Chiecchi, Giuseppe 216
Chrétien de Troyes 189n, 292
Christ 26, 60, 67, 72, 85, 94n, 142, 146, 166, 183n, 263, 301, 303
Ciabattoni, Francesco 9
Ciampi, Sebastiano 232
Ciardi Duprè dal Poggetto, Maria Grazia 179
Ciavolella, Massimo 95n, 98n
Cicero 1, 19, 20, 28, 30, 66, 67, 68n, 70, 74, 82, 226, 229, 270, 275, 296, 344, 345
Cino da Pistoia 331, 332
Clement V, Pope 236n
Clement VI, Pope 81, 95n, 276
Cola di Rienzo 271

Colonna, Giovanni 56
Condren, Conal 79
Conti, Natale 265, 266
Contini, Gianfranco 289, 291, 301
Costantinus Africanus 97n, 98, 99
Cristiani, Luca 70, 347n
Cursi, Marco 179, 209, 213n, 238, 327, 330

d'Agnolo Capponi, Giovanni 179, 180, 330
Dante, see: Alighieri, Dante
Dares Phrygius 231n
da Strada, Zanobi 213, 226, 228, 229, 233
David 66, 296
degli Albizzi, Franceschino 233
Delcorno Branca, Daniela 187n
della Scala, Cangrande 169, 170, 276
De Lollis, Cesare 301
de Nolhac, Pierre 72
De Robertis, Teresa 232n
De Sanctis, Francesco 153, 167, 168, 194n, 297, 300
Descartes, René 1, 13, 168
Dictys of Crete 273
Di Negro, Andalò 228
Dino del Garbo 97n
Dionigi da Borgo San Sepolcro 73, 74, 79, 165, 298
Donati, Forese 233
Donnino da Parma 276, 277
Dotti, Ugo 165n
Duby, Georges 123n
Durand of St. Pourçain 137n

Enenkel, Karl 5
Epicurus 247
Erasmus, Desiderius 2
Euhemerus 245, 248
Euripides 216n
Eusebius 252
Ezzelino da Romano 234

Falconi, Nicolaus 236n
Fedi, Roberto 326n
Feo, Michele 23n
Ferguson, Wallace K. 2n
Ferroni, Giulio 12

Ficara, Giorgio 11
Ficino, Marsilio 265n
Filosa, Elsa 216n, 218, 316
Fiorilla, Maurizio 209, 213n
Folena, Gianfranco 16n
Foresti, Arnaldo 19n
Fortunatianus 30
Foscolo, Ugo 2, 296
Foucault, Michel 93n
Frasso, Giuseppe 332n
Freccero, John 7
Frederick, King of Sicily 276
Friedrich, Hugo 107n
Fulgentius 246

Galen 7, 92, 98
Gaukroger, Stephen 79
Genette, Gérard 176n
Gerard de Berry 97n, 98, 99, 102
Giles 98
Gilissen, Leon 15, 34
Gilson, Étienne 159, 167n
Giovanni da Lodi 236
Giraldi, Lelio Gregorio 265
Gorgias the Sophist 247
Gorni, Guglielmo 159
Gragnolati, Manuele 7, 129, 130n
Greenblatt, Stephen 176n
Gregory the Great 66
Guglielmo da Pastrengo 61, 247
Guido, Guinizzelli 305
Guidoriccio da Fogliano 303
Guillaume de Conches 280
Guittone d'Arezzo 16

Hayton of Corycus 234–237
Hegel, Georg Wilhelm F. 91, 122n, 124
Heraclides of Pontus 82
Herodotus 245
Hollander, Robert 159n, 163n
Homer 9, 66, 238, 239, 278
Honorius of Autun 273
Horace 5, 6, 23, 30, 32–34, 38–40, 46, 54, 59, 67
 – Ars poetica 33, 34, 38
 – Carmen Saeculare 33

– Epistles 33, 34
– Epodes 33, 34, 38
– Odes 23, 33, 34
– Satires 32–34, 54
Hugh of Saint Victor 246, 274
Hugh IV, King of Jerusalem and Cyprus 249, 275, 277
Hunter, Ian 79
Huss, Bernhard 319n
Husserl, Edmund 168
Hyginus 279

Innocent VI, Pope 276
Isidore of Seville, Saint 246, 273

Jean de Meung 282
Jerome 66, 70
John XXII, Pope 234
John, King of France 276
John Scotus Erigena 282
Joseph of Exeter 231n
Josephus Flavius 246, 259
Juvenal 211, 212

Kablitz, Andreas 8, 190n, 194
van Kempen, Ludwig 349, 350
Kierkegaard, Søren 300
Kirkpatrick, Robert 132
Konig, Bernhard 105n
Kristeller, Paul Oskar 1, 95
Kristeva, Julia 135n
Küpper, Joachim 6, 166

Lactantius 245, 255, 270, 277
Laín Entralgo, Pedro 284
Latini, Brunetto 4, 273, 280–282
Livy 28, 79
Lombardi, Elena 149
Louis IX of France 232
dei Lovati, Lovato 2, 65, 153
Lucretius 245, 305
Lummus, David 248n, 253, 279n, 320n

Machiavelli, Niccolò 284, 355
Macrobius 246, 257, 259
Malaspina, Currado 221

Malpaghini, Giovanni 17n, 40n, 317
Manfred, King of Sicily 170–172, 220
Mann, Thomas 340
Marino, Giovan Battista 320
Marsh, David 158
Martellotti, Guido 324
Martial 209, 239
Martinelli Tempesta, Stefano 238
Martini, Simone 303
fra Martino da Signa 228
Mary, the Virgin 148
Mazza, Antonia 212
Mazzacurati, Giancarlo 360
Mazzoni, Francesco 49n
Mazzotta, Giuseppe 10
Mercati, Giovanni 22
Mezzani, Menghino 326
Moevs, Christian 132, 142, 143, 150n, 161
Molière 95
de Montaigne, Michel 167
Monte Andrea 21n
Morante, Elsa 369
Moses 1, 85, 246
Muhammad 234
Mussato, Albertino 2, 65, 153, 229n
Mythographi vaticani 246, 255

Neckham, Alexander 273
Nelli, Francesco 66, 67, 314n, 315, 349, 350n
Neuschäfer, Hans-Jörg 185, 194n

Orosius, Paulus 232
Ossola, Carlo 4
Ovid 9, 23, 103, 180n, 209, 213, 214, 216–219, 221, 222, 230, 232, 251, 262, 263, 279, 292
– Heroides 291
– Remedia amoris 23, 24, 103

Paganino of Bizzozzero 347
Pani, Laura 209
Paolino Veneto 234
Paolo da Perugia 233, 251
Pascal, Blaise 167, 168
Pasolini, Pier Paolo 369

Paul, Saint 66, 86, 165, 190n, 196, 209, 326
Paul the Deacon 209, 232n
Persius 230
Pertile, Lino 132
Peter Comestor 273
Peter Damian, Saint 236
Petoletti, Marco 9, 22n, 23n, 209, 318n
Petrarca, Francesco passim
- Africa 71, 75, 156, 298, 299, 316, 357n
- Bucolicum carmen 60, 276, 281, 316, 317, 346n
- De otio religioso, or On Religious Leisure 80, 154
- De remediis utriusque fortune 276
- De sui ipsius et multorum ignorantia, or On his Own Ignorance and That of Many Others 6, 66, 83, 273, 274, 277, 279
- De viris illustribus 79, 156, 316
- De vita solitaria, or On the Solitary Life 5, 6, 17, 52–54, 56–58, 60, 68, 72, 75, 80
- Epistole metrice 54, 61
- Epistole sine nomine 55
- Familiares, or Letters on Familiar Matters 12, 17, 19n, 20, 66, 71, 74, 75, 78, 81, 165, 229, 233, 295, 299, 307, 315–319, 321, 322n, 323, 324, 327, 343, 344, 346n, 347, 349–351, 358
- Invective, or Invectives 1, 6, 81–84, 95, 274, 277
- Itinerarium ad sepulcrum Domini 316
- Psalmi penitentiales, or Penitential Psalms 306
- Posteritati, or Letter on Posterity 2, 56, 71–72, 75, 297, 306
- Rerum memorandarum libri 53, 273
- Rerum vulgarium fragmenta (Canzoniere) 2, 5, 6, 12, 17n, 36, 39, 136, 137, 146–149, 331, 340, 351
- Secretum 2, 7, 73, 74, 138, 139n, 142, 153–156, 158–161, 163–165, 167, 297, 300
- Seniles, or Letters of Old Age 16n, 17, 18n, 32, 72, 249n, 270, 271, 275, 296, 315, 316, 318, 324, 325, 327, 328, 330, 333, 346n, 349, 350
- Triumphi, or Trionfi 7, 136–138, 148–150, 165n, 166, 167, 283

Petrarca, Gherardo 17n, 319
Petrarch, see: Petrarca, Francesco
Petrocchi, Giorgio 15n
Petroni, Pietro 346
Petrucci, Armando 17, 18n, 28, 30
Petrus Hispanus 97–99, 101
Picone, Michelangelo 9, 223
Pier della Vigna 231
Pietro di Parenzo di Garzo (ser Petracco) 22, 23n
Pietro Piccolo of Monteforte 319, 326
Pilatus, Leontius 216n, 239
Plato 6, 66–68, 78, 82, 91–93, 96, 105, 123, 124, 164, 244, 281, 282
Plautus 270
Pliny the Elder 233
Poliziano, Angelo, or Politianus 78, 265
Polonus, Martinus 232, 233
Pomaro, Gabriella 15n
Ponciroli, Guido 266
Proust, Marcel 340
Pythagoras 82, 258, 259

de Quevedo, Francisco 95
Quintilian 57, 275
Quondam, Amedeo 319, 320, 334

Rabanus, Maurus 257, 258, 273
Randall, John H., Jr. 1
Regn, Gerhard 8, 319n
Ricasoli, Bindaccio 333
Riccobaldo of Ferrara 232
Richard of Saint Victor 274
Rico, Francisco 73, 74, 154n, 313–316, 319, 320n, 325n
Ripa, Cesare 265
Rizzo, Silvia 333
Robert of Anjou, King of Naples 137n, 276, 297, 357n
Robinson, Pamela 20n
Romano, Marco 231
Romano, Pasquale 232n, 234
Rossi, Luciano 185n, 215
Rousseau, Jean-Jacques 91, 122n

Sabellico, Marcantonio 266
Sallust 233

Salutati, Coluccio 76, 264, 266
Santagata, Marco 149n, 154, 351
Savino, Giancarlo 16n
Schiller, Friedrich 204
Scipio the African 252, 273, 299
Seneca 67, 209, 210, 234, 275
Servius 22, 23, 25, 46
Severianus 30
Singleton, Charles 156–158, 167, 168, 172
Socrates 83, 343, 347
Solomon 133
Southerden, Francesca 7
Statius 22, 23, 26, 46
– Achilleid 23, 26
Stierle, Karlheinz 105n
Storey, Wayne H. 5, 9
Subirani, Raimondo 347
Svevo, Italo 340

Tacitus 213, 226
Tempier, Étienne 125
Thales 279
Theodontius 257–259, 278
Thierry of Chartres 280
Tortelli, Giovanni 266
Tristano, Caterina 25

Ungaretti, Giuseppe 309
Usher, Jonathan 215

Valéry, Paul 304
Varro 229, 245, 261, 279
Velli, Giuseppe 3, 9, 209, 211, 218, 323n, 334
Veselovskij, Alexander 290
Vico, Giambattista 266, 284
de Victoria, Baltasar 265
Vincent of Beauvais 234, 273, 274
Virgil 22, 24–26, 28, 30, 32, 40n, 46, 60, 66, 123, 129, 156, 160, 172, 216, 228, 257, 258, 270, 276, 278, 281, 290, 296, 314, 315, 317, 341, 348
– Aeneid 23–26, 281, 283
– Eclogues 60, 229, 281
– Georgics 23, 24, 281, 348
pseudo-Virgil 230
del Virgilio, Giovanni 229
Virgilius, Polydorus 221, 266

Wack, Mary F. 97, 98, 104n, 122n, 123n, 126n
Wilkins, Ernst H. 299
William of Occam 287
Witt, Ronald 2, 6, 80, 153

Xenophon of Ephesus 212

Zamponi, Stefano 41
Zatti, Sergio 222, 223

www.ingramcontent.com/pod-product-compliance
Lightning Source LLC
Chambersburg PA
CBHW021336300426
44114CB00012B/972